Supply Chain Analytics

Wiley Analytics Series for Management

Supply Chain Analytics

T. A. S. Vijayaraghavan
Professor
Production, Operations and Decision Sciences & Information Systems Area
XLRI – Xavier School of Management, India

WILEY

Supply Chain Analytics

Author: T. A. S. Vijayaraghavan

Published by Wiley India Pvt. Ltd.,
4436/7, Ansari Road, Daryaganj, New Delhi-110002.

Printed at: SDR Printers

First Edition: 2021

Reprint: 2026

ISBN: 978-93-5424-343-1

ISBN: 978-93-5424-351-6 (ebk)

Other Wiley Editorial Offices:
John Wiley & Sons, Inc. 111 River Street, Hoboken, NJ 07030, USA
Wiley-VCH Verlag GmbH, Pappellaee 3, D-69469 Weinheim, Germany
John Wiley & Sons Australia Ltd, 42 McDougall Street, Milton, Queensland 4064, Australia
John Wiley & Sons (Asia) Pte Ltd, 1 Fusionpolis Walk #07-01 Solaris, South Tower Singapore 138628
John Wiley & Sons Canada Ltd, 22 Worcester Road, Etobicoke, Ontario, Canada, M9W ILI

www.wileyindia.com

To

my Acharya

Thirumalai Ananthaazhvaan

and
my dear parents

Late T.A. Srinivasan and T.A. Srivaramangai

Foreword

Managing supply chains efficiently in firms is vital to succeed in the present context of fierce competition. Business managers have to be equipped with an array of tools and techniques to deal with decisions in warehousing operations, location of facilities, layout decisions, inventory decisions, network planning and optimization, transportation decisions, etc., and this book on Supply Chain Analytics provides an in-depth knowledge about all these topics.

I am indeed privileged to write the Foreword to this book. I had the pleasure of working with the author, Dr. T. A. S. Vijayaraghavan, for the last 2 years while I was the Director of XLRI – Xavier School of Management, Jamshedpur. This book is the outcome of the author's long experience in teaching, research, and consultancy in the area of supply chain management. He has taken serious efforts to explain the important Supply Chain Analytical tools and techniques in a lucid style with relevant and interesting examples and Excel screenshots. He has tried to explain even the complicated mathematical tools and techniques in a simple style so that anyone can understand and implement them in his/her workplace.

The book is an excellent addition to the Supply Chain literature that takes a contemporary approach and comprehensive coverage. The chapters are well organized and structured building the concepts and tools with some initial overview on supply chain management and optimization techniques. The coverage of topics ranges from simple situations to complex situations in supply chain areas where he has shown how mathematical tools are useful and how they are used. Even a non-mathematics student or a professional would be able to read and understand the contents. I recommend this book to every supply chain professional, teacher, and student of Management, particularly those specializing in Operations and Supply Chain management areas.

Fr. P. Christie S.J.
Former Director and Professor of Decision Sciences,
XLRI Jamshedpur
Secretary – Higher Education for the Society of Jesus, Rome

Preface

Ever since the phrase "Supply Chain Management" was coined by **Keith Oliver**, a British logistician and consultant working with the then Booz Allen Hamilton consulting company, who first used the phrase in public in an interview with Arnold Kransdorff of the *Financial Times* on 4 June 1982, it has gained increasing prominence over the past three decades. There are many reasons for the popularity of the phrase and the concept. Customers demand quality products, better innovations, variety and expect them to be consistently delivered, faster, on time, and with no damage. Each of these necessitates closer coordination with suppliers and distributors. This has increased performance-based competition, combined with changing technology and economic conditions contributing to marketplace uncertainty. This necessitates greater flexibility in the way the individual companies and supply chains perform, and demands more flexibility in supply chain relationships. Despite the popularity of the term Supply Chain Management (SCM), both in academia and in practice, there remains considerable confusion as to its meaning. In practice, there is also some conceptual mix up between the phrases "logistics management" and "supply chain management". In spite of this, the need for supply chain management has gained importance.

WHY STUDY SUPPLY CHAIN ANALYTICS?

When supply chains generate Big Data, supply chain analytics turns that data into real insights. The explosive impact of e-commerce is just one notable example of the data-driven revolution. Very few companies, however, have been able to apply the same degree of "big analytics" techniques that could transform the way they define and manage their supply chains.

The full impact of Big Data in supply chain is restrained by two major challenges. First, there is a lack of capabilities. Supply chain managers – even those with a high degree of technical skills – have little or no experience with the data analysis techniques used by data scientists. As a result, they often lack the vision to see what might be possible with Big Data analytics. Second (and perhaps more significant), most companies lack a structured process to explore, evaluate, and capture Big Data opportunities in their supply chains. Supply chain analytics uses data and quantitative methods to improve decision making for all activities across the supply chain. In particular, it does two new things. First, it expands the dataset for analysis beyond the traditional internal data held in Enterprise Resource Planning (ERP) and supply chain management (SCM) systems. Second, it applies powerful and advanced statistical and quantitative methods to both new and existing data sources. This creates new insights that help improve supply chain decision making, all the way from the improvement of front-line operations to strategic choices. Analytics historically played a significant role in supply chain management, starting with military operations during and after World War II – particularly with the development of the Simplex Method for solving linear programming by George Dantzig in the 1940s. Supply chain analytics became more ingrained in decision making with the advent of ERP systems in the 1990s and more recently with "Big Data" applications, particularly in descriptive and predictive analytics.

ORGANIZATION OF THE BOOK

This book presents popular analytical tools and techniques that are quite useful in supply chain management areas and are found to be effective in getting results. With the use of simple tools like Excel, many techniques can be applied with the available data. The exercises included at the end of the chapters give a variety of decision situations faced and give additional insight into the application of tools.

Section I contains Chapter 1 that is the building block for the rest of the chapters in this book.

- **Chapter 1** gives an overview of the concepts of Logistics Management and Supply Chain Management and offers various perspectives on them in practice. In this chapter, different views of Supply Chain Management have been presented and the process view of Supply Chain Management has been explained in detail. Towards the end of the chapter, the need for supply chain analytics has been emphasized, setting the background for the book. This chapter is an overview only, and readers are expected to have gone through a course on Supply Chain Management to completely appreciate the context in which the book is pitched. The Bibliography listed at the end of the chapters will provide more insight on the concepts discussed.

Section II contains Chapter 2 which provides an overview of optimization techniques and the use of Excel Solver which will be very useful for the rest of the chapters which uses them more.

- **Chapter 2** presents an overview of optimization techniques, such as Linear Programming, Transportation Problems, and Assignment Problems as a prerequisite for the other chapters that are specific to the supply chain domain. Although readers are expected to have gone through courses on Statistics and Operations Research for better understanding, this chapter provides a quick recap of the optimization techniques as a building block for the remaining chapters with simple examples and Excel Solver screenshots.

Section III covers analytical tools that address different types of decisions, from strategic to tactical to operational levels concerning warehousing aspects in a supply chain. This section consists of three chapters: Chapters 3 to 5.

- **Chapter 3** deals with the understanding of why locational considerations are important in warehousing decisions and the basic types of location problems in locating facilities in a supply chain network, how to locate a single facility using the Centre of Gravity (COG) method and how to locate multiple facilities using the Multi-COG method. Detailed descriptions of how to formulate different types of discrete location problems using mathematical programming approaches, such as Set Covering, Maximal Covering, P-Median, P-Centre, P-Dispersion, and Fixed Charge Facility and their practical uses are presented using Excel Solver. Exercises at the end of the chapter provide more understanding and insight.
- **Chapter 4** presents a few heuristic approaches such as greedy drop and how they help in the location of facilities in a supply chain network. Then, we discuss with examples how mixed integer programming approaches using the transportation problems approach (viz., Guided LP and Baumol & Wolfe Method, etc.) can lead to decisions on warehouse choices. Towards the end of the chapter, we cover how the Gravity model can be used to decide locational considerations along with how Huff's model can be used to decide retail locations. The methods discussed in this chapter are also explained using Excel Solver for easy understanding along with applications. Exercises at the end of the chapter provide some practice problems to understand the concepts better.
- **Chapter 5** outlines the tactical and operational considerations in warehouse design and operations. It provides a good understanding of how to determine space requirements for a warehouse and evaluate options of private and third-party alternatives and different types of warehouses (viz., consolidation break bulk, mixing, etc.) for storing and trade-off decisions relating to them. Basic concepts of handling decisions are explained and how layout decisions are based on them is described with illustrations in this chapter. A mathematical investigation into tactical decisions about allocation of products to storage locations using mathematical programming is presented with the use of Excel Solver. Towards the end of the chapter,

decisions covering layout configurations with respect to size, height, floor storage length, width, etc., for various choices of layouts are analysed. Some insights about unit load area layouts regarding lane width, floor storage, aisle configurations, and fast pick area concepts are also provided with examples. Exercises at the end of the chapter present some interesting problems for the readers to attempt and gather more insights.

Section IV focuses on the important aspects of inventory decisions in supply chains and presents various inventory models that are popular and practically applied. This section consists of three chapters: Chapters 6 to 8.

- **Chapter 6** describes why inventory management is important in the supply chain of a firm and the reasons for and against keeping inventory. It identifies different types of inventory and various costs of inventory that are relevant for any inventory decision. Then, the importance and application of ABC analysis and Pareto Principle for determining inventory policies is explained with examples. Towards the end of the chapter, very popular types of Single period and Repetitive period types of Inventory models (e.g., Newsvendor model, EOQ Models, their assumptions, and their applications in determining inventory levels) are explained. Exercises at the end of the chapter provide many practice problems that are useful in thinking about inventory complications and applications.
- **Chapter 7** provides an understanding of how inventory policies are formulated when faced with demand and lead-time uncertainties in practice and how to formulate the Re-order levels and Safety Stock policies when faced with demand uncertainty that is discrete or continuous. Detailed explanations of the types of service levels (viz., Order Service Level and Unit Service Level) are provided, and mathematical expressions for them are derived to explain the inventory policies in depth. Then, how safety stock is determined when both demand and lead time uncertainties are faced is explained with various what-if scenarios in inventory situations. Further, how the expressions derived in this chapter can help in resolving the uncertainties is demonstrated. A deeper understanding of stock-outs under the back order and lost sales situations is provided with appropriate expressions for them while formulating inventory policies. Exercises are provided at the end of the chapter for practice.
- **Chapter 8** underscores the importance and appreciation for inventory policies when dealing with multiple items and with inventory investment limits. Inventory decisions, when total setup times are constrained to a maximum limit, are explained with examples. Detailed discussions on how to deal with various optimization scenarios in inventory situations where setup times or inventory costs or other parameters are constraints, using Lagrangian multipliers, have been provided in this chapter. Various joint replenishment strategies for inventory policies (viz., complete and tailored aggregation scenarios) using algorithms are presented. Towards the end of the chapter, numerous techniques of dynamic lot sizing under time-varying demand and implications of multi-echelon inventory decisions are given. Exercises at the end of the chapter present additional practice and insights on inventory scenarios.

Section V deals with transportation decisions in supply chain and with tools and techniques concerning trade-off decisions and network evaluations. This section consists of three chapters: Chapters 9 to 11.

- **Chapter 9** starts with describing the basic trade-offs in transportation decisions and the types of trade-offs (viz., horizontal and vertical trade-offs). Varieties of trade-off situations in selecting transport modes and services, trade-offs in centralized inventories and transportation, trade-offs in transportation consolidation are explained with examples. Factors affecting transportation modes and various design options in transportation networks are presented for understanding options in transportation choices. The basic notions of network models are presented and various network models are explained. Types of problems like minimal spanning tree algorithms (viz., Prim's and Kruskal's), shortest path algorithms (viz., Labelling algorithm, Dijkstra's algorithm, Bellman-Ford's, Floyd-Warhsall's), and maximum flow models are explained with illustrations in this chapter.
- **Chapter 10** presents the key issues in operational planning in transportation decisions in a supply chain and the important characteristics of Routing and Scheduling including the basic ideas of tours, such as the Travelling Salesman Problem (TSP), Multiple Travelling Salesman

Problem, and Vehicle Routing Problems. Detailed descriptions of the concept of the travelling salesman problem and its nature using the Euler graphs and Hamiltonian paths and circuits have been presented in this chapter. A general formulation of a TSP and solution using Excel Solver is shown and various approaches using Dynamic Programming, branch and bound methods and popular heuristics are presented.

- **Chapter 11** outlines the complexities and types of Vehicle Routing Problems (VRPs) and solution approaches initially, and then presents integer programming formulations using Solver to solve VRPs. Various branch and bound approaches to solve a VRP and heuristics like Clarke and Wright Savings Method and Sweeping Methods are discussed with examples. Towards the end, the nature of scheduling problems is discussed along with a few simple approaches to solve them. A few scientific approaches to solve vehicle scheduling problems using the deficit function approach and linking algorithms are also presented. Exercises at the end of the chapter give varieties of problems to practice and understand the methods.

Section VI comprises Chapter 12 describing multi-criteria decision-making methods with examples.

- **Chapter 12** first describes what multi-criteria decision making (MCDM) and multi-attribute decision making (MADM) are, and expounds on their uses and popularity. Then, the basics of multi-attribute utility theory (MAUT) and its simple applications are presented. Very detailed explanations of the Analytic Hierarchy Process (AHP), TOPSIS, the basic notions of fuzzy numbers, and logic, and how fuzzy logic is used in AHP and TOPSIS are provided. A few exercises are given at the end of the chapter for more understanding and practice.

WHO SHOULD USE THE BOOK

This book is written with a practical perspective to help readers appreciate analytical approaches and address supply chain issues. Students in the postgraduate levels of business schools, executive students, and doctoral level students who wish to specialize in Supply Chain Management as their career choice are encouraged to use this book and apply the recommended tools and techniques at their workplaces. Through a mix of concepts, tools, techniques, applications, and exercises, this book has made every attempt to provide the readers with the best understanding on the subject.

FEATURES OF THE BOOK

Several features are incorporated in the book to make learning effective.

Learning Objectives

Learning objectives provide key takeaways and a summary of key concepts that would be discussed in the chapter.

LEARNING OBJECTIVES

After reading this chapter, you would be able to:

- Describe why inventory management is important in the supply chain of a firm and the reasons for and against keeping inventory.
- Understand different types of inventory and the various costs of inventory.
- Comprehend the importance and application of the ABC analysis and the Pareto principle for determining inventory policies.
- Learn various types of single period and repetitive period types of inventory models, their assumptions, and applications of their use in determining inventory levels.

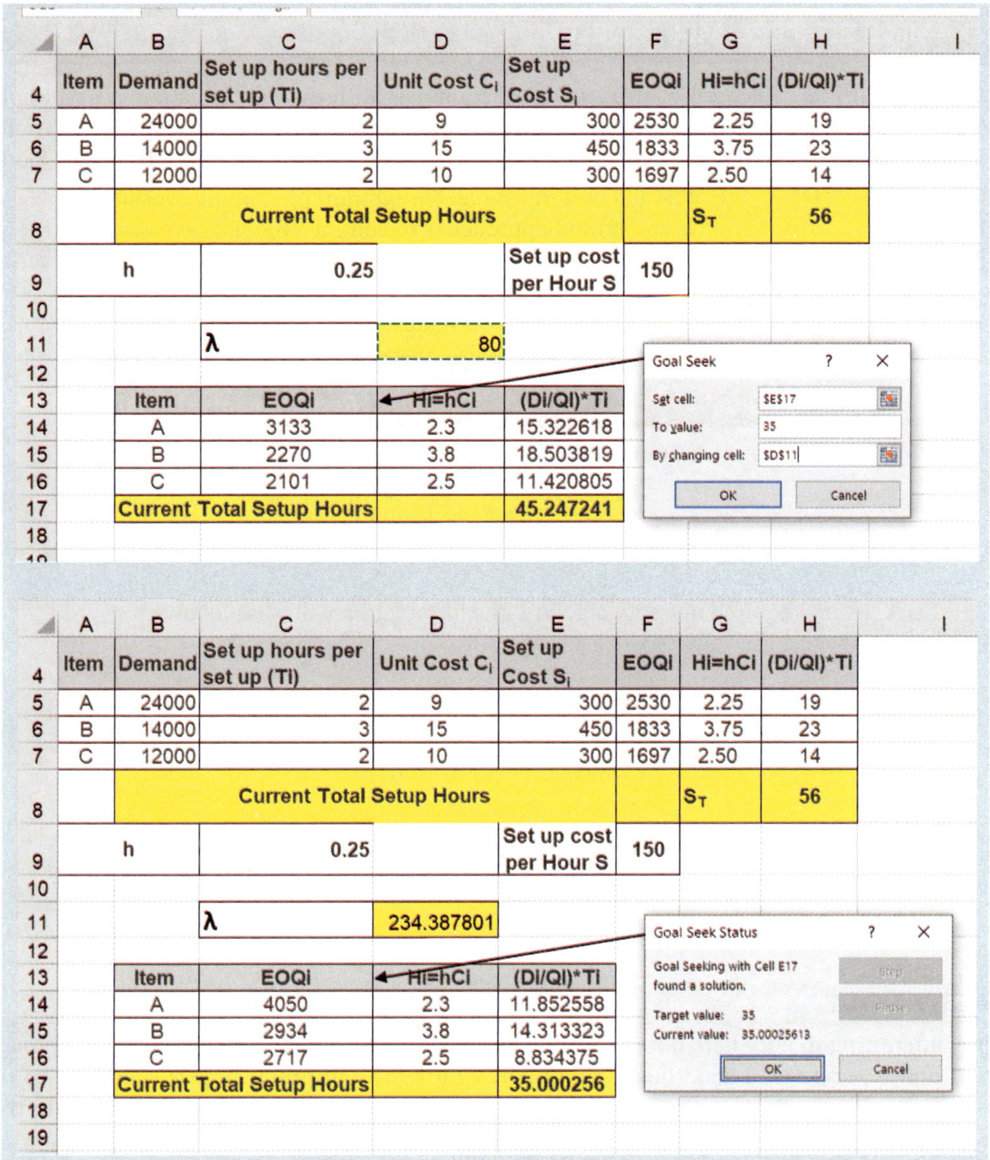

	A	B	C	D	E	F	G	H
4	Item	Demand	Set up hours per set up (Ti)	Unit Cost C_i	Set up Cost S_i	EOQi	Hi=hCi	(Di/QI)*Ti
5	A	24000	2	9	300	2530	2.25	19
6	B	14000	3	15	450	1833	3.75	23
7	C	12000	2	10	300	1697	2.50	14
8		Current Total Setup Hours					S_T	56
9		h	0.25		Set up cost per Hour S	150		
11			λ	80				
13		Item	EOQi	Hi=hCi	(Di/QI)*Ti			
14		A	3133	2.3	15.322618			
15		B	2270	3.8	18.503819			
16		C	2101	2.5	11.420805			
17		Current Total Setup Hours			45.247241			

	A	B	C	D	E	F	G	H
4	Item	Demand	Set up hours per set up (Ti)	Unit Cost C_i	Set up Cost S_i	EOQi	Hi=hCi	(Di/QI)*Ti
5	A	24000	2	9	300	2530	2.25	19
6	B	14000	3	15	450	1833	3.75	23
7	C	12000	2	10	300	1697	2.50	14
8		Current Total Setup Hours					S_T	56
9		h	0.25		Set up cost per Hour S	150		
11			λ	234.387801				
13		Item	EOQi	Hi=hCi	(Di/QI)*Ti			
14		A	4050	2.3	11.852558			
15		B	2934	3.8	14.313323			
16		C	2717	2.5	8.834375			
17		Current Total Setup Hours			35.000256			

FIGURE 8.8 Using Goal Seek to perform the Lagrangian and obtaining the adjusted quantities.

Excel Solver for Solving Problems in Supply Chain Analytics

Excel Solver is an optional Excel add-in designed to do more complex "what-if" calculations using different solving methods. It educates on how to formulate various problems and solve them through Excel Solver. Solver is one of the most powerful tools in Excel to solve optimization problems – both linear and nonlinear. You will see many applications of Solver in solving many such problems in the supply chain area in various chapters in this book.

Center of gravity is one of the easiest methods in determining a single facility using the simple concept of weighted average of the forces on a given set of points and determining the center of gravity of them as the best location. With less data and less mathematical complications, this method is useful for many practical applications.

Important Concepts

This feature points out additional insights for better understanding and other important truths for readers to take note of. It also provides a clear understanding of the concept that is discussed to make readers think about it.

Solved Example

With the objective of strengthening the conceptual understanding, this feature aims to help the readers to infer general idea of the concepts described in the chapter.

EXAMPLE 2.2 (FEED MIX PROBLEM)

A poultry farm is considering farm feed for the animals with two nutrients and six types of foods where the nutrients are available. How many units of nutrients are available from each type of food for a nutrient? How much is the minimum daily requirement with the cost of food per kilogram as given in Table 2.1.

Solution
Formulate this as an LPP to minimize the total cost of food.

TABLE 2.1 Number of units of nutrients per kilogram of food

Nutrients	1	2	3	4	5	6	Minimum Daily Requirements (Units)
Vitamin A	1	0	2	2	1	2	9
Vitamin C	0	1	3	1	3	2	19
Cost of food ($/kg)	35	30	60	50	27	22	

Let X_j be the required quantity of food j. The formulation will be as follows:

Minimize

$$35X_1 + 30X_2 + 60X_3 + 50X_4 + 27X_5 + 22X_6$$

subject to

$$X_1 + 2X_2 + 2X_3 + X_5 + 2X_6 \geq 9$$

$$X_2 + 3X_3 + X_4 + 3X_5 + 2X_6 \geq 19$$

$$X_j \geq 0$$

Activity

This feature presents some extra effort that a reader can put in to carry out an exercise for better understanding.

ACTIVITY 4.1

It is interesting to note here how the drop heuristic is quite similar to the P-median approach and how it serves as a good heuristic for solving a P-median problem. It is suggested to try out the problems given in the exercises at the end on this topic for getting insights into this observation.

Important Equations and Formulae

This feature is enriched with important equations and formulae for quick recap with ease.

Important Equations and Formulae

1. $Q^* = \sqrt{\dfrac{2D[S + g\pi]}{H}}$
   where S is the ordering cost, H is the carrying cost (i.e., $h \times C$), e is the excess inventory, g is the shortage (units stock-out), and π is the shortage cost (stock-out cost per unit).
2. Reorder level (ROP) when it is assumed that the demand during the lead time follows a normal distribution.

   $$\text{ROP} = d \times LT + z \times s_d \times \sqrt{LT}$$

   where d is the average demand per period (say a week), s_d is the standard deviation of the demand per period (say a week), and LT is the lead time in time periods (say weeks).
3. Safety stock (SS) is

   $$\text{Safety stock (SS)} = z \times s_d \times \sqrt{LT}$$

Appendix 7.1

If the lead time is LT and the demand is normally distributed with a mean of d and standard deviation of s_d in each period, then we can determine the mean and the standard deviation of the total lead time LT as follows:

Let the average demand during the L periods be d' and the standard deviation of the demand during this lead time LT periods be s'_d. Let lead time $LT = n$.

Let the total demand in these n periods be $X = X_1 + X_2 + X_3 + \cdots + X_n$.

Then $E(X) = d' = E(X_1 + X_2 + X_3 + \cdots + X_n) = E(X_1) + E(X_2) + E(X_3) + \cdots + E(X_n)$.

That is, $d' = d + d + d + \cdots + d$ (n times) $= d \times n = d \times LT$. So

$$d' = d \times LT$$

$\text{Var}(X) = \text{Var}(X_1 + X_2 + X_3 + \cdots + X_n) = \text{Var}(X_1) + \text{Var}(X_2) + \text{Var}(X_3) + \cdots + \text{Var}(X_n)$ assuming independence of demands between periods.

That is, $s'^2_d = s^2_d + s^2_d + s^2_d + \cdots + s^2_d$ (n times) $= s^2_d \times n = s^2_d \times LT$. Therefore,

$$s'_d = s_d \times \sqrt{LT}$$

Appendix

Appendices, wherever required, have been provided in various chapters that include supplementary information and derivations on the concepts discussed.

Case Study

It is suggested to take up the following cases for discussions that are described in this chapter:

1. **Paper and More (A)** by Noel Watson 9-606-023 Rev: January 7, 2009 of the Harvard Business Publishing of Harvard Business School for explaining the concepts of Service Levels (both Order Service Level and Unit Service Level and use of Newsvendor Model for determining inventory policies (https://hbsp.harvard.edu/product/606023-PDF-ENG).
2. **Scientific Glass Incorporated: Inventory Management (Brief Case)** by Steven C. Wheelwright, William Schmidt, 4208 Rev: January 7, 2009 of the Harvard Business Publishing of Harvard Business School No. 4208 for explaining the concept of reorder levels, safety stocks, average inventory levels and evaluating a few strategies using these concepts in an organizational context (https://hbsp.harvard.edu/product/4208-PDF-ENG).

Case Study

Case studies suggested in the chapters intend to provide frameworks for evaluation and analysis of complex issues. By going through these case studies, readers would be able to have in-depth analysis of the topics presented in the chapters.

SUPPLEMENTAL MATERIALS

Instructor Resources

The following resources are available for instructors on request. To register, please log onto https://www.wileyindia.com/Instructor_Manuals/Register/login.php

- Instructor Solution Manuals
- PowerPoint Lecture Slides
- PDF Lecture Slides
- Excel Templates
- R codes

Student Resources

Students can access the following resources via https://www.wileyindia.com/student-resources

- Student solution manuals
- Excel templates
- R codes

About the Author

T. A. S. Vijayaraghavan is currently a Professor in the Production, Operations Management and Decision Sciences (PODS) and Information Systems Area at XLRI (Xavier School of Management), Jamshedpur. He is also a Member of the Board of Governors of XLRI Jamshedpur and the Chairperson of the Centre for Logistics and Supply Chain Management. Prior to joining XLRI, he taught at the Central Institute of Road Transport (CIRT), Pune and the Xavier Institute of Management (XIM), Bhubaneswar. He did his B.Sc. in Mathematics from the Vivekananda College in Chennai, M. Stat and PGD SQC & OR from the Indian Statistical Institute, and Doctorate from the Indian Institute of Management (IIM), Bangalore. He has been teaching for the past 34 years and has published several papers in international and national journals. He is on the editorial board of various international journals and serves on many professional bodies, such as the Association of Supply Chain Professionals and the Indian Institute of Materials Management. He has also served on many national committees such as AICTE and BIS.

Acknowledgments

I wish to thank my father, Late Sri T.A. Srinivasan, who always encouraged me to pursue my dreams and contribute meaningfully to society. He inspired me immensely and it was his dream for me to be an academician. With his blessings, I have had over 30 glorious years as a professor at a leading business school in India. My mother, T.A. Srivaramangai, who turns 95 next year, has been my emotional pillar of support and continues to shower me with her affection to this day. I remain ever grateful to my wife, Vijayasudha, who has supported and motivated me throughout this journey, especially during the rough patches I faced in the writing of this book. I wish to thank my daughter Sruthi for her untiring efforts with the editing, and my son Shravan for helping me with drawing out the figures in the book. They were my primary motivators to initiate this project, without whom this book would not have seen the light of day. I am also thankful to my extended family for their love, affection and blessings throughout my career.

I am grateful to Fr. P. Christie, S.J., Former Director, XLRI Jamshedpur, for his unwavering support and for kindly agreeing to write the Foreword for this book. I thank Fr.Paul Fernandes S.J., the present Director of XLRI for supporting me in the completion of this book. I am thankful to my colleagues in the institute and my secretaries for all their help in bringing this book to its present shape. My heartfelt thanks to my students across all programmes at XLRI for supporting and motivating me by subscribing to the course and helping me fine-tune the content over the years. They made writing this book possible.

My sincere thanks to Mr. Syed Haroon, Ms. Yoofisaca Nongpluh, and Mr. Rupnarayan Das of Wiley India for their extraordinary support in the development of this book and for their patience.

My salutations and obeisance to my Acharya and the Almighty for their grace and blessings for writing a book, that would hopefully, be useful to Supply Chain Management students and professionals alike.

T. A. S. Vijayaraghavan

Contents

SECTION IV Inventory Decisions 203

SECTION

I

Overview of Logistics and Supply Chain Management

CHAPTER 1

Overview of Logistics and Supply Chain Management

LEARNING OBJECTIVES

After reading this chapter, you would be able to:

- Understand the phrases "logistics" and "supply chain management".
- Understand the basic driving forces in business.
- Get insights into the definitions of logistics management, the different approaches and its interface with other functional areas.
- Understand various views of supply chain management and derive few brief insights.
- Understand the popular process view of supply chain management.
- Learn about the drivers of supply chain performance.
- Understand the need for supply chain analytics.

1.1 | INTRODUCTION

The phrase "supply chain management" (SCM) has gained prominence over the past three decades. Keith Oliver, a British logistician and consultant working with the consulting company Booz Allen Hamilton, is believed to have coined the term by first using it in an interview with Arnold Kransdorff of the *Financial Times* on 4 June 1982. There are reasons for the popularity of the phrase and concept. Customers keep demanding quality products, better innovations, and variety and expect them to be consistently delivered on time and with no damage. This necessitates closer coordination with suppliers and distributors, which has increased performance-based competition, combined with changing technology and economic conditions contributing to marketplace uncertainty. This also necessitates greater flexibility in the way individual companies and supply chains perform and demands more flexibility in supply chain relationships.

Despite the popularity of the term "supply chain management," both in academia and practice, there remains considerable confusion about its meaning. In practice, there is also some conceptual mix-up between the phrases "logistics management" and "supply chain management." Some authors define SCM in operational terms involving the flow of materials and products, while others view it as a management philosophy and in terms of a management process. Some views mention that SCM is also integrated logistics management in the interorganizational contexts. Such ambiguity suggests a need to examine the phenomena of logistics management and supply chain management more closely to clearly define the terms and concepts, identify factors that contribute to effective SCM, and suggest how the adoption of an SCM approach can affect corporate strategy and performance.

1.2 | SCM AND COMPETITIVE ADVANTAGE

SCM is now part of the business vocabulary in the wake of the global marketplace drastically changing the landscape of business. Most of the changes observed in the performance of companies were rapid and continuous in the 1990s. There is a realization among many firms that doing business in one's comfort zone is no longer synonymous with success. Strategic management literature suggests that success in the marketplace is based on the triangular linkage of the company, its customers, and its competitors—the "three C's" as shown in Figure 1.1.

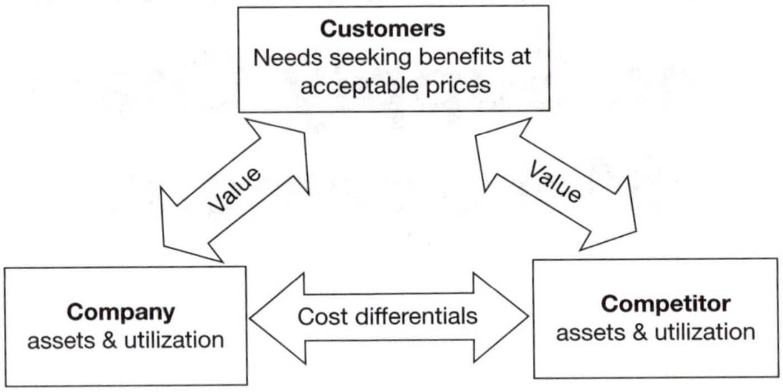

FIGURE 1.1 Interlink of three C's.

Companies in the marketplace compete using value proposition or cost differentials or both. We have seen that successful companies either have a productivity advantage using cost efficiency or they have a "value" advantage through responsiveness or a combination of the two. Productivity advantage gives a lower cost profile, and the value advantage gives the product or offering a differential "plus" over competitive offerings. Supply chain and logistics management can provide a multitude of ways to increase efficiency and productivity and, hence, contribute significantly to reduced unit costs. Companies have focused upon service as a means of competitive advantage, as seen in Figure 1.2.

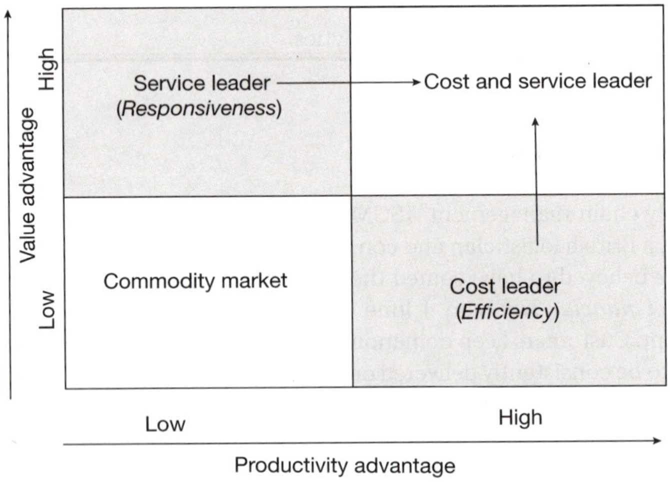

FIGURE 1.2 Supply chain management and competitive advantage.

As seen in Figure 1.2, the matrix suggests that the cost leadership quadrant makes sense to derive cost advantage in terms of productivity where firms that adopt such strategies focus on cost efficiency in their supply chains. For example, companies such as Tata Steel believe in producing high-quality steel but, to remain as the least cost producer of steel, focus on various strategies that reduce cost through interventions such as Six Sigma, total quality management, theory of constraints, etc. The Service Leader quadrant in Figure 1.2 suggests that value advantage through value creation makes sense to implement strategies achieving responsiveness in the supply chain through innovations, reduced lead time, quick response to orders, speed delivery flexibility, etc. For example, companies dealing with fashion garments focus more on responsiveness as the target customers are not that price sensitive but look for fashion, flexibility, and quick response. So the framework suggests that firms adopt either efficiency or responsiveness options in the supply chain design to eventually reach the top quadrant where both cost and service leadership could be achieved.

1.3 | DRIVING FORCES IN BUSINESS AND SCM

When we try to explore the conceptual understanding of what a supply chain is all about, we need to understand the three flows that take place in a supply chain: material flow, funds (or money) flow, and information flow. How to manage these three flows will be a quick way to define an SCM. But to understand them, we need to recognize that businesses are faced with constant driving forces that always make them dynamic, and a good understanding of them is essential for understanding a supply chain. That is, these driving forces always influence any business, and any supply chain design should recognize these forces and reckon with them. They are as follows:

1. The empowered consumer
2. Power shift in the supply chain
3. Liberalization
4. Globalization
5. Technology

Strategic management framework gives the basic insight into two important dimensions of value and cost, which are the building blocks of strategy formulation for a firm. How SCM is linked to this completive advantage is seen from the Boston Consulting Group (BCG) matrix given here.

Understanding the five forces listed here will be fundamental in understanding supply chain concepts, as very often these forces are not per se the supply chain issues. Supply chains should take them as constraints and look for designs to incorporate them and tackle them or using them.

1.3.1 The Empowered Consumer

The consumer is always a major driving force in any business. Most businesses emphasize the need for consumer-centric business activities and focus on consumers or customer service. Logistics plays an important role here where it becomes a key customer-contact activity and enables the time and place utilities. The impact on logistics is more direct in serving consumers. Moreover, over the years we have noticed that informed consumers have low tolerance for poor quality in products and services, and changing demographics commands a 24/7 service. Increased customer service also increases the importance of logistics and supply chains. Demand management is an important process that businesses have to appreciate, and so effectiveness and efficiency in supply chains become imperative to achieve customer delight.

1.3.2 Power Shift in the Supply Chain

Over the years, the power has shifted from manufacturers to retailers and end customers and this power shift has made supply chains realize the need for more responsive behavior to face this shift (as shown in Figure 1.3). Large retailers are more demanding and commanding, and there is an increasing focus on distribution costs. Shifts in the balance of such power have changed logistics and supply chain strategies for many companies.

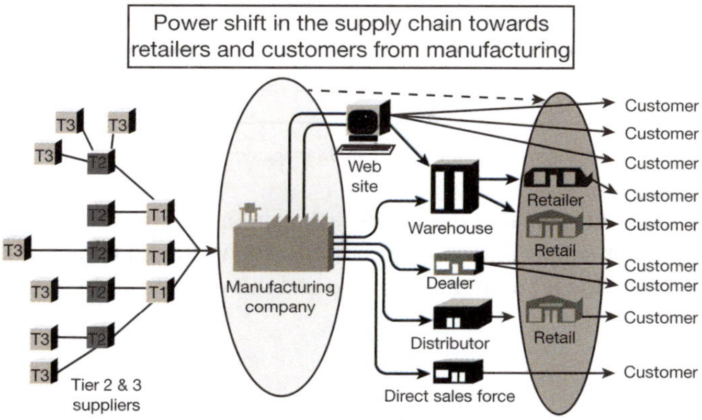

FIGURE 1.3 Power shift in supply chains.

This power shift has made companies realize that manufacturing is part of the supply chain and has resulted in many paradigm shifts in manufacturing strategies—quick response manufacturing, flexible manufacturing, modular manufacturing, lean and agile manufacturing—to manage such power shifts to quickly respond to the needs of retailers and customers. Although this can discipline the supply chain to be more responsive, it can also cause some other developments in the supply chain: the bullwhip effect. This is because the supply chains have to respond to demand signals from the lower echelons or points of sale, which are likely to get amplified at the top echelons of the supply chains and may result in an imbalance of demand and supply. This is illustrated in Figures 1.4 and 1.5.

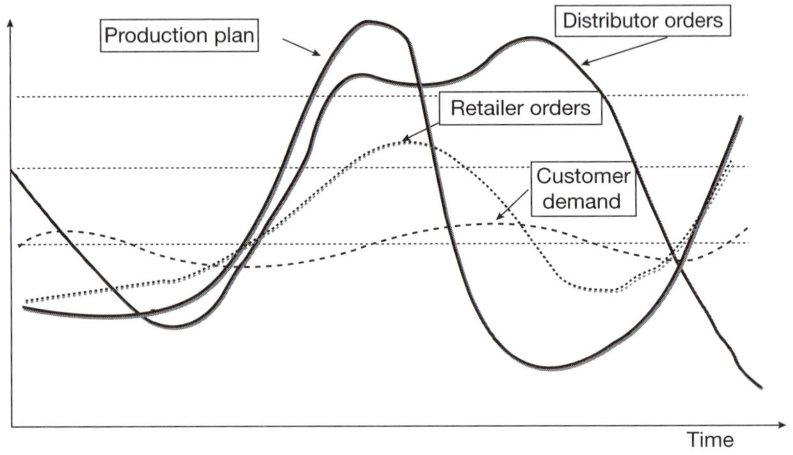

FIGURE 1.4 Order variability in supply chains.

Source: Tom McGuffry, Electronic Commerce and Value Chain Management, 1998.

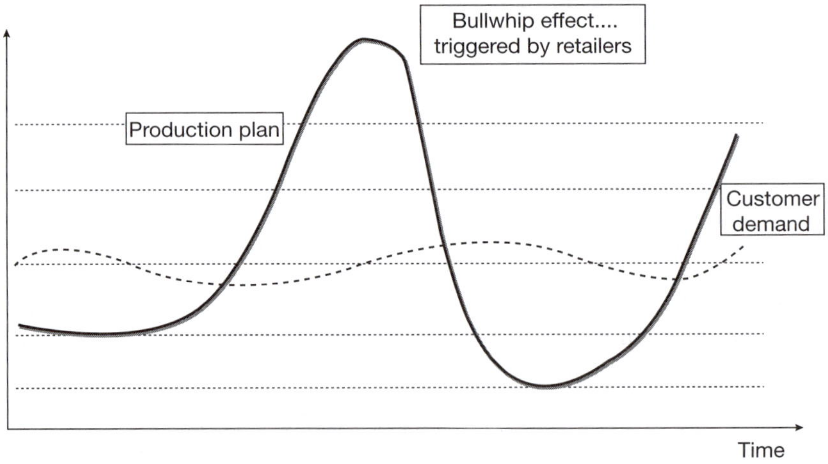

FIGURE 1.5 Bullwhip effect in supply chains.

Source: Tom McGuffry, Electronic Commerce and Value Chain Management, 1998.

However, this amplification is created due to the lack of information about the Point of Sale (POS) demand and the need for supply chains to respond to such inflated demand. But ideally, supply chains need POS information for demand planning and this amplification has to be minimized (as shown in Figure 1.6).

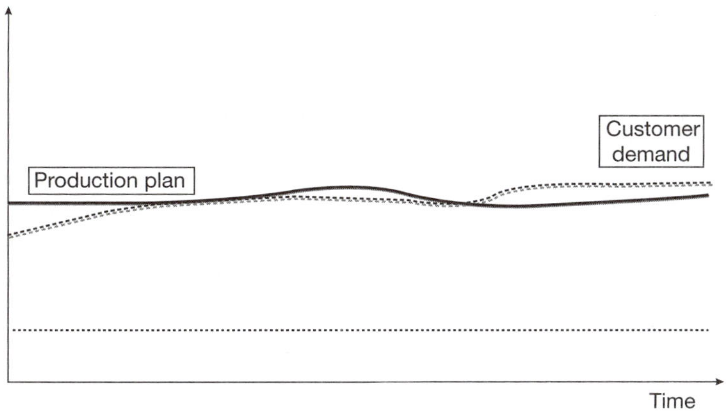

FIGURE 1.6 Ideal amplification in supply chains.

Source: Tom McGuffry, Electronic Commerce and Value Chain Management, 1998.

1.3.3 Liberalization

Liberalization is one of the major driving forces that keep influencing any business as this is caused by economic policies of governments and political changes. Such policy changes have been witnessed in India since 1995 when economic liberalization of the Indian Economy started with many decontrol measures. The economy was opened up for many changes, and opportunities such as changing economic controls empowered creativity and competition among companies and industries. Many policy changes in taxes and licensing resulted in changes in transportation with fewer or no economic controls over rates and services. This has made many third-party logistics operators and service providers enter the logistics field in India and has strengthened supply chain operations. International cargo movements were simplified, and more trade took place. Changes in policies governing financial institutions removed traditional differences and increased competition. Many policy changes in telecommunications and information technology resulted in more opportunities and competition and opened new areas in ecommerce. In addition, many changes in the utility industry allowed more competition. Recent policy changes in the Goods and Services Tax (GST), introduction of electronic waybill, Fast-tags for toll collections, etc. will keep influencing the way goods are produced and moved in supply chains. These policy changes will keep happening and will make supply chains anticipate such changes.

The bullwhip effect is ubiquitous in all businesses and supply chains. Although the degree may vary, the supply chains suffer from this effect. All the coordination and technology efforts are basically to minimize this effect and make the supply chains more efficient.

1.3.4 Globalization

Globalization trends include a growing interdependence of the world's economies, cultures, and populations, brought about by cross-border trade in goods and services, technology, and flows of investment, people, and information. This has made countries build economic partnerships to facilitate movements across the globe, and such cooperative arrangements have shaped modern life. In the supply chain context, it has resulted in a global marketplace concept with global network sourcing, manufacturing, marketing, and distribution. Since economies have opened up the world over, this has also given many global alternatives for new supply and strategic sources. Companies can exercise options for alternatives, but along with that supply chains have also faced many challenges as competition came from nowhere and forced them to be more competitive. Strategic sourcing became a new opportunity in supply chains due to globalization trends.

1.3.5 Technology

Increased globalization, product complexity, and customer demands have made companies scale up advanced technologies to transform their supply chains from pure operations into focusing on business innovation. With the speed of Internet connectivity, many firms collect data at every checkpoint in the supply chain from acquisition points until final consumption ranging from the status of raw materials flow to the condition and location of finished goods. Hence, looking into the future, it is about resiliency and an ability to adapt to changes in the marketplace and new business models. Advanced technologies, hence, enable such resilience and adaptation for business models. A quick review of the literature presents a few important technologies such as machine learning, artificial intelligence (AI), and advanced analytics, which help achieve such efficiencies. Development in 3D printing has allowed firms to localize production of goods closer to customers, allowing for faster turnaround, reduced transportation costs, and greater personalization. We see that many top technologies are expected to change and overhaul supply chain operations. The Internet of Things (IoT), Block Chain Technology, AI, machine learning, analytics, robots, automation, and 3D printing are those primary technological changes that will drive supply chains in the future. Technology will be one of the driving forces that keep enabling supply chains, and there will be even more and more challenges in adapting such technologies in the future.

The preceding driving forces constantly make any business challenging and make them reckon with themselves for survival. While supply chains have to take them in their design, they also make them volatile and dynamic. In the following section, we will briefly introduce the concept of logistics management and understand the key issues in it.

1.4 | OVERVIEW OF LOGISTICS MANAGEMENT

Logistics management is historically a branch of military science and operations dealing with the procurement, supply, and maintenance of equipment, with the movement, evacuation, and hospitalization of personnel, with the provision of facilities and services, and with related matters. It is an offshoot of the tools and techniques that were employed during World War II, and like other branches (operations research, project management), it also was gaining popularity after the World War. The word logistics is derived from the French word *logistiques*, which is equivalent to *loger* (to lodge) or to a quarter of troops. One of the common-sense and practical definitions of logistics that some individuals refer to is the layperson's description of logistics as the seven R's, which means ensuring the availability of the following:

1. Right product, in the
2. Right quantity and the
3. Right condition, at the
4. Right place, at the
5. Right time, for the
6. Right customer, at the
7. Right cost

1.4.1 Definitions

We look at logistics as a function that addresses the planning, organization, and controlling of all move–store activities that facilitate product flow from the point of raw material acquisition to the point of final consumption, as illustrated in Figure 1.7.

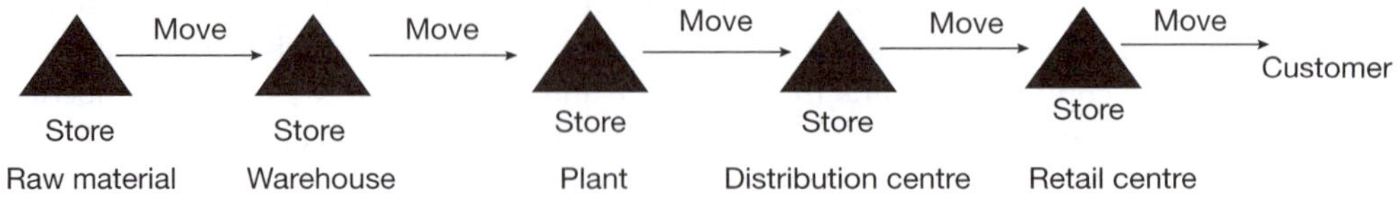

FIGURE 1.7 Move–store activities from raw material acquisition to final consumption.

But merely organizing the flow of move–store activities is not enough to justify it as a management function. Let us consider a situation of two competing companies X and Y on a similar product in the market. It is known that company X maintains a policy of keeping 10 days inventory for the product, while company Y maintains 15 days inventory for its product. If we ask who is managing well, the response would be that the policy of keeping inventory depends on the corporate goal of the company of whether it is a cost leader or a service leader. Cost leadership would justify an inventory of 10 days as the cost efficiency would force it to have least inventory, while service leadership would justify an inventory of 15 days to maintain high service levels and avoid stock out as service is more important than cost for such companies. Therefore, logistics addresses precisely the concern that the move and store activities have to be carried out in order to align itself with the corporate objectives of a company. Therefore, a more appropriate understanding of logistics management will be as follows:

> *"Logistics is the physical movement of goods from supply points to final sale to customers and the associated transfer and holding of such goods at various intermediate storage points, accomplished in such manner as to contribute to the explicit goals of the organization."*

A formal definition of logistics management is given by the Council of Supply Chain Management Professionals (CSCMP), which was formerly knowns as the Council of Logistics Management:

> *"Logistics Management is that part of Supply Chain Management that plans, implements, and controls the efficient, effective forward and reverse flow and storage of goods, services and related information between the point of origin and the point of consumption in order to meet customers' requirements."*

The definition of CSCMP is more comprehensive and addresses all the facets of logistics that are:

1. It is part of SCM as one of the processes,
2. It is a management function,
3. It addresses the efficiency and effectiveness of the forward and reverse flow and storage of goods,
4. It addresses the intangible side of logistics as a service,
5. It covers the entire flow from raw material point till final consumption,
6. It should be served from a customer's point of view and not internally but externally.

This definition covers goods that are predominately consumer goods and not all types of goods. Another definition by the Society of Logistics Engineers (SOLE), USA, which was referred to later as the International Society of Logistics, presents a different perspective of logistics that are mostly industrial goods:

> *"The area of support management used throughout the life of the product or system to efficiently utilize resources assuring the adequate consideration of logistics elements during all phases of the life cycle so that timely influence on the system assures an effective approach to resource expenditures."*

This definition addresses types of goods that have implications of life cycle, such as machinery, defense equipment, etc., which need logistical support throughout the life cycle of such products. Hence, logistical elements are different for different types of products. We can classify products under two broad categories as follows:

1. **Consumer goods**, which are directed to ultimate consumers where usually the buyer seeks goods and marketing is important.
2. **Industrial goods**, which are used to produce other goods and services with mostly raw materials, components, equipment, and where usually vendors seek buyers.

We can classify consumer goods further into three subcategories (Figure 1.8) with a few examples:

FIGURE 1.8 Categories of consumer goods and services.

Their characteristics are shown in Figure 1.9.

Consumer Goods & Logistics

	Convenience goods	Shopping goods	Specialty goods
Substitutability	HIGH	MEDIUM	LOW
Availability	HIGH	MEDIUM	LOW
Value	LOW	MEDIUM	HIGH

FIGURE 1.9 Characteristics of consumer goods.

As evident from Figures 1.8 and 1.9, the logistics elements depend on the type of product that is under consideration and the characteristics should be understood while designing a logistics system for a product.

1.4.2 Activities in Logistics

The logistics function of a company focuses on the following activities, and a good understanding of these activities is required to analyze the complexities and trade-offs among them while designing logistics.

1. Customer service
2. Demand forecasting/planning
3. Inventory management
4. Logistics communications
5. Material handling
6. Order processing
7. Packaging
8. Parts and service support
9. Plant and warehouse site selection
10. Procurement
11. Return goods handling
12. Reverse logistics
13. Traffic and transportation
14. Warehousing and storage

Some of them are core to the logistics function, and some of them are interface areas with marketing and production functions. For example, customer service and demand forecasting are interface activities with marketing, and procurement, warehousing, etc. are interface activities with production, while inventory, transportation, packaging, etc. are core to the logistics function.

1.4.3 Approaches in Logistics

While designing logistics systems, the following approaches and perspectives separately or in combination can help in understanding the complexities and help planning strategies in logistics:

Logistics often is mixed up with supply chain concepts in practice. While logistics is more concerned with move–store activities, supply chain goes beyond this. The interface activities of logistics have always been mixed up, and of late there is some understanding in the industry about such interface roles that they need to be coordinated and cooperated with well and not to get confused with them.

1.4.3.1 Materials Management versus Physical Distribution

Frequently, the movement and storage of raw materials is far different from the movement and storage of finished goods. Four different classifications of logistics systems that depend on the nature of products are as follows:

1. Balanced system, such as consumer products
2. Heavy inbound, such as aircraft, construction
3. Heavy outbound, such as chemicals, fertilizers
4. Reverse systems, such as returnable products (e.g., gas cylinders, empty bottles)

Figure 1.10 presents the nature of flow of materials and shows the demarcation of physical supply, often referred to as materials management, and physical distribution, often referred to as marketing logistics.

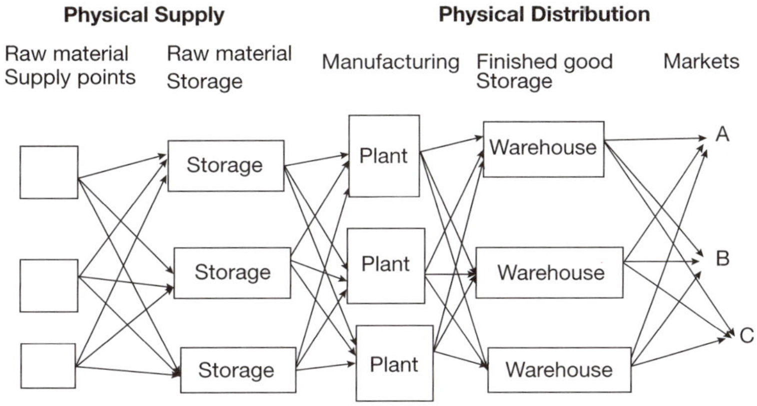

FIGURE 1.10 Physical supply versus physical distribution.

In the past, all move and store activities that were carried out before production were handled by the production function and the move and store activities that were carried out post-production were handled by the marketing function. Now wherever move and store activities take place, one logistics function takes up the entire responsibility. The division into physical supply and physical distribution is an extremely useful managerial or control perspective of the logistics activities. Cost differences that may exist between physical supply and physical distribution in terms of logistics requirements may have implications for the design of the logistics system. Although different management approaches may result in viewing these two, close coordination between them is necessary. This approach or perspective brings out the fact that a big picture should be seen by a single logistics function instead of breaking them into pieces where each is handled by different functions. That is, losing forest for the trees should be avoided and the logistics function should be given the responsibility for such managerial control.

1.4.3.2 Cost Centers

In this approach, logistics is analyzed based on activity centers or cost centers since the possibility for reducing total logistics costs and/or improving service will occur by trading off one of these activity centers against another. This is one of the most powerful approaches, and in most of the decision areas, this approach gives better alternatives when options are evaluated based on trade-offs. The following two examples shown in Tables 1.1 and 1.2 illustrate the trade-off situations in comparing transport modes and evaluating warehouses, respectively.

TABLE 1.1 Analysis of total logistics cost with a change to mode of transport

Cost Centers	Rail Cost ($) per Unit	Road Cost ($) per Unit
Transportation	3.00	4.20
Inventory	5.00	3.75
Packaging	4.50	3.20
Warehousing	1.50	0.75
Cost of lost sales	2.00	1.00
Total cost	**16.00**	**12.90**

TABLE 1.2 Analysis of total logistics cost with a change to more warehouses

Cost Centers	System 1	System 2
	Three Warehouses (Cost in $)	Five Warehouses (Cost in $)
Transportation	850,000	500,000
Inventory	1,500,000	2,000,000
Warehousing	600,000	1,000,000
Cost of lost sales	350,000	100,000
Total cost	**3,300,000**	**3,600,000**

As can be seen that the trade-offs are evaluated based on the components, and the total cost is considered to choose the option or the system. These trade-offs can be seen comparing cost with cost or cost with service. We will present a few trade-off situations in Figures 1.11 to 1.13.

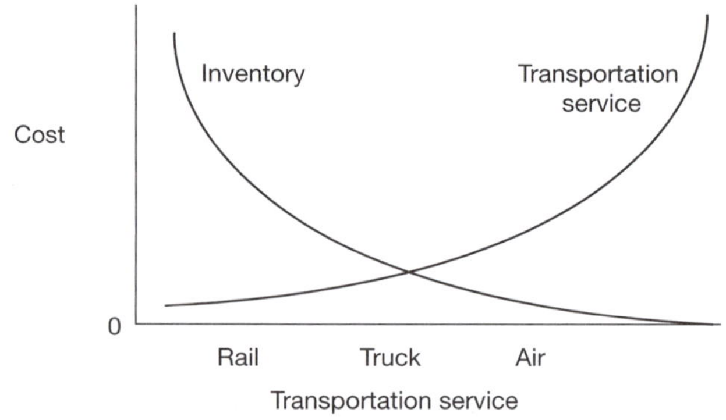

FIGURE 1.11 Transportation versus inventory.

Here the trade-off exists between modes of transport and the cost of inventory and transportation depending on the transit time the mode takes and the cost of service.

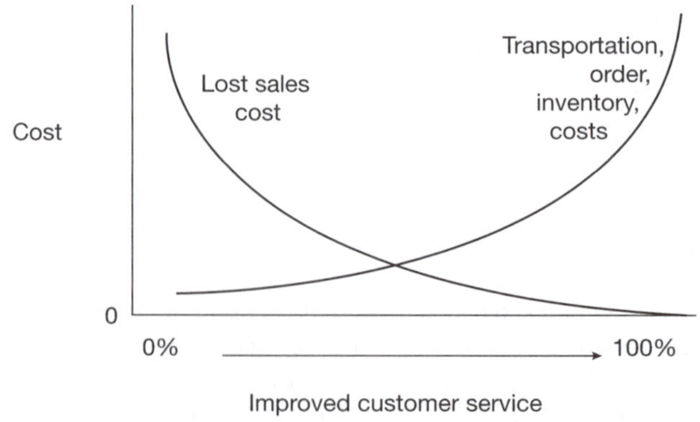

FIGURE 1.12 Customer service versus cost.

Here the trade-off exists between service level and inventory or transport. For example, the service level can be determined by the stock availability for customer service. The higher the inventory level, the higher will be the service level, but the cost also will be higher with stock-outs being lesser. Therefore, the total cost will trade off with respect to the customer service a company wants to achieve.

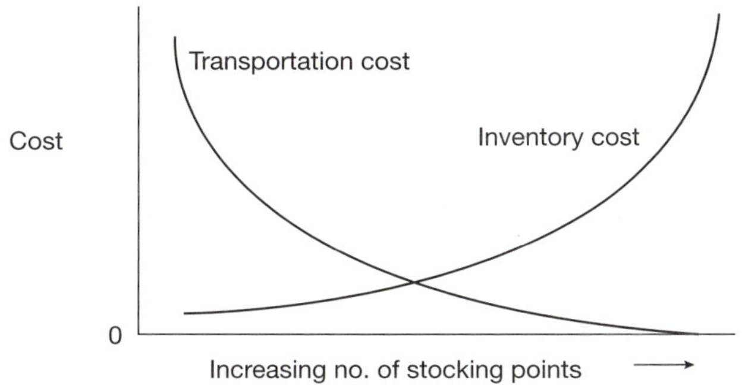

FIGURE 1.13 Number of warehouses.

Here the trade-off exists between the number of warehouses in the network and the resulting inventory position and transport cost. The higher the number of warehouses, the higher the cost of warehousing, the higher the cost of inventory, and the lower the cost of transportation.

There are many more situations where such trade-offs exist and some of them are listed here:

1. Faster transportation versus reduction in pipeline (transit) inventories
2. Make versus buy decisions regarding finished products and/or components
3. Centralized versus decentralized warehousing
4. Adding or reducing private fleet equipment versus outsourcing transportation
5. Increasing frequency of shipments versus carrying larger inventories
6. Public versus private warehousing
7. Higher service levels versus lower inventory levels
8. Locations/types/number of manufacturing facilities and/or warehouses
9. Holding orders for consolidation (transportation) versus immediate shipping to reduce inventories
10. Inventory-carrying costs versus order-set-up costs
11. Trucking or quantity discount savings with larger lots versus cost of extra inventory

1.4.3.3 Nodes versus Links (Network Perspective)

In this perspective or approach, we look at the network of facilities such as plants, warehouses, and markets and understand the concept of flows in a network and other aspects. The nodes are the established spatial points where the movement of goods is stopped for storage or processing. The links represent the transportation network connecting the nodes. This has paved the way for **operations research/management science** techniques and models to play a significant role in logistics. An illustrative depiction of the network is shown in Figure 1.14.

For example, suppose we have a situation where we have a network of 5 plants producing 10 products distributed through 100 warehouses having 5000 distributors and 100,000 retailers with millions of customers. If the network handles a volume of say 10 million tons of units as business and if a market projection is made to have an increase of another 20% in demand, the typical what-if scenario will be whether the current network can handle the surge in the demand. For any review of the network, the key points of interest will be the additional number of warehouses and distributors required, the size of the warehouses, the locations of the warehouses and distributors, etc. This perspective can be quite useful to analyze such what-if scenarios using network models and graph theory. Most of the companies review their logistics network once in every 4 or 5 years, and for such reviews, this perspective is of great use.

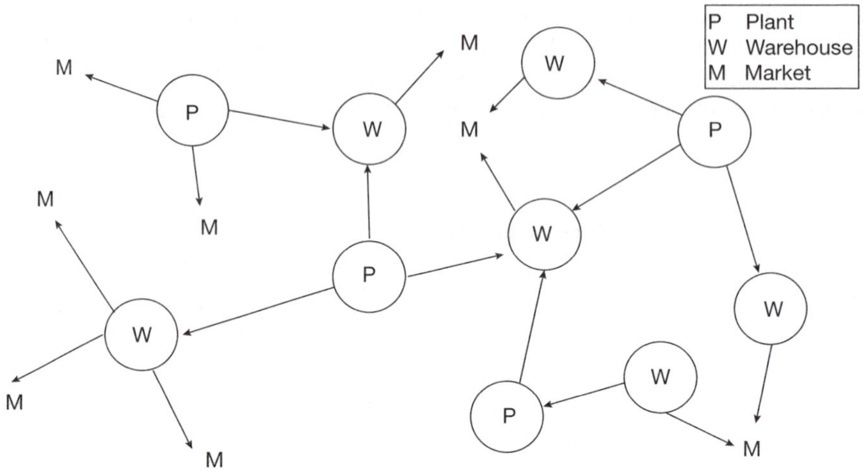

FIGURE 1.14 Network of plants, warehouses, and markets.

1.4.3.4 Logistics Channel (Channel Perspective)

This approach considers the strong interface of marketing and logistics and emphasizes the need to coordinate between the possible overlaps that may come in the decision areas of both functions. . This represents the network of intermediaries engaged in various functions such as transfer, storage, handling, and communication that contribute to the efficient flow of goods, as illustrated in Figure 1.15.

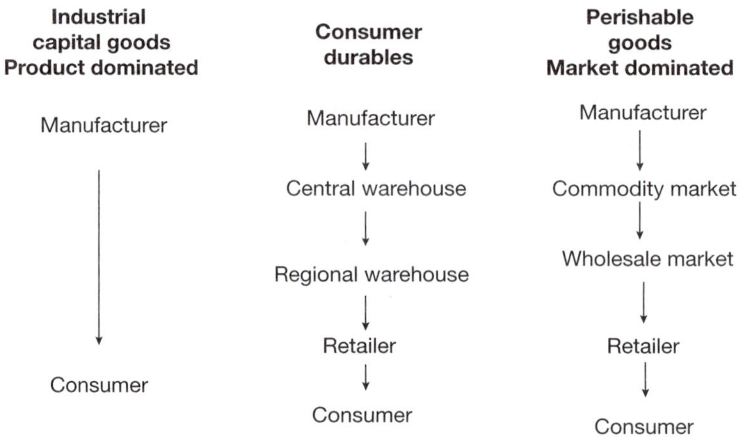

FIGURE 1.15 Channel perspective of logistics.

The approach is very important to understand the role of channel members such as distributors and retailers in a supply chain. The complexities are evident in the absence of such intermediaries and how coordination and cooperation among them is essential to manage the move–store activities between manufacturers and consumers when dealing with different types of products.

The preceding four approaches or perspectives either individually or in combination can be useful in developing logistics strategies and evaluating them.

1.4.4 Cost Considerations in Logistics

While implementing a logistics plan, it is important to understand the major factors that affect the cost of logistics and its importance. They are categorized as follows:

The four perspectives or approaches discussed here are very useful in developing logistics plans. The trade-off concept and the total cost approach outlined here are the most popular approaches, which are found useful in evaluating alternatives for many situations. In decision-making situations, many strategies are formulated and evaluated with trading one or few cost components with the other components to arrive at the best. Many practices like cross-docking, break-bulk, consolidation, etc. are trade-off concepts only when cost drivers such as inventory and transportation are traded off.

1. **Competitive relationships:** These costs are incurred due to the nature of competitive relationships of the firm in the market. For example, inventory cost is incurred as the firm needs to keep a higher service level in order not to lose its customers to its competitors. These are
   - Inventory versus order cycle length,
   - Inventory versus lost sales effect,
   - Transportation versus lost sales effect.
2. **Product relationships:** These costs are incurred due to the nature of the product itself irrespective of its competition or marketplace. Weight density, volume, packaging cost, etc. are the reasons for such costs being incurred. These are
   - Product dollar value versus logistics costs,
   - Weight density versus logistics costs,
   - Susceptibility to loss and damage versus logistics costs.
3. **Spatial relationships:** These costs are incurred due to spatial distance and cost differences in different geographical regions and tax structures.

1.4.5 Interfaces of Logistics with Other Functions

As discussed earlier, logistics as a function has emerged with its own core activities and with some interface with other functions such as marketing and production. Some of the interfaces are as follows:

1.4.5.1 Logistics with the Manufacturing and Production Function

1. Length of production runs balances economies of long production runs against increased costs of high inventories.
2. Seasonal demand accepts a seasonal inventory to balance lead production times.
3. Supply-side interfaces maintain stocks and adequate supplies to ensure uninterrupted production.
4. Protective packaging is done to protect the product from damage.
5. Foreign and third-party alternatives are evaluated for outsourcing.

1.4.5.2 Logistics with the Marketing Function

Logistics is often referred to as the other half of marketing as it has very strong interfaces with sales and marketing functions. The major customer-contact activities in an organization are sales and logistics. The major interface with marketing is with the four P's of marketing: price, product, place, and promotion. In this marketing mix, the logistics interface is quite evident. They are briefly explained as follows:

1. **Carrier pricing:** Generally, the larger the shipment, the cheaper the transportation rate. So shipment sizes should be tailored to the carrier's vehicle capacity where possible.
2. **Matching schedules:** Quantity discounts should be tied to carrier quantity discounts.
3. **Volume relationships:** Volumes sold will affect inventory requirements.
4. Generally, since the size, shape, weight, and other physical characteristics of the product impact its storage, transportation, and handling, logistics managers should be included in any decisions regarding these product traits. A minor correction in any of these traits could conceivably cost (or save) millions of dollars in logistics costs. Logistics costs are not necessarily paramount, but they need to be considered in the decision-making process.
5. **Push versus pull:** The most important factor is that the logistics division is aware of any changes in demand patterns so that it can plan for any consequences. Pull strategies tend to be more erratic. Push strategies tend to be more predictable.
6. **Channel competition:** The more popular a product, the easier it is to persuade channel members to promote your product.

7. **Wholesalers:** Generally, since wholesalers combine purchases for multiple retailers, the shipment sizes tend to be larger and the number of transactions that have to be processed is small, with the result that logistics costs are smaller.
8. **Retailers:** With the exception of very large retailers who act more like wholesalers, smaller sales are the norm. These generally cost more in terms of transportation and order processing.
9. Logistics can have a major impact on return on assets and return on investment. Inventory turnover ratio is one of the powerful financial ratios that indicates the inventory management of a firm and combines sales and inventory to a large extent.

1.4.6 Key Actors in Logistics

While the production function addresses the form utility of what to produce and the marketing function addresses the possession utility of why to consume, it is the logistics function that creates the place and time utility and addresses where and when a product will be consumed. This is how an economy grows with the efficient use of logistics at the macro and micro level. Following are the key actors that create the place and time utility of products and foster the economic growth of a country:

1. The shipper (user of logistics)
2. The carrier (rail, road, air, water, pipeline, etc.)
3. Warehousing corporations
4. Freight forwarders
5. Terminal operators (ports, stevedores, etc.)
6. Government (regulator of logistics)

The role of the government in all these is very crucial for the effective use of infrastructure to support the logistics movement of goods and services through various policies governing movement and storage, such as goods and services tax, excise duties, packaging material, cold storage facilities, public warehousing facilities, strong transport infrastructural support like roads, railways, ports, etc., and subsidies.

1.5 | OVERVIEW OF SUPPLY CHAIN MANAGEMENT

The term SCM started appearing in 1982 and still has many semantic definitions that have since appeared in many research journals. The term logistics also has many interpretations. From some statements of SCM, it appeared that SCM is logistics across interorganizational boundaries. In 1990, academics first described SCM from a theoretical standpoint to clarify the difference from more traditional approaches to managing the flow of materials and associated information. The initial usage of the term SCM emphasized a reduction in inventory both within and across firms, but that initial perspective has been broadening. There is a need for the integration of business operations in supply chain that goes beyond logistics. For example, let us look at a context where a company is engaged in new product development. The list of possible activities can include all aspects of business such as internal marketing of the concept, R&D for the formulation, manufacturing, logistics for their respective capabilities, finance for funding external organizations for product development to reduce the time to market, early supplier involvement, even second-tier suppliers if necessary. We are, in fact, looking at the integration of business processes across the supply chain, and that is what we seem to be calling SCM. We will develop this concept in the following sections. Before we define SCM, let us look at a few views of the concept: integrated logistics management, cycle view, push/pull view, and process view.

1.5.1 Integrated Logistics Management View

This view looks at logistics processes in the inter-firm levels and the integration of the same. In Section 1.3, we discussed the key concerns and activities of the same. But we also noticed that the activities in a firm go beyond this, and this view can be a good start to understanding the concept of SCM but it is not a complete view. This is shown in Figure 1.16.

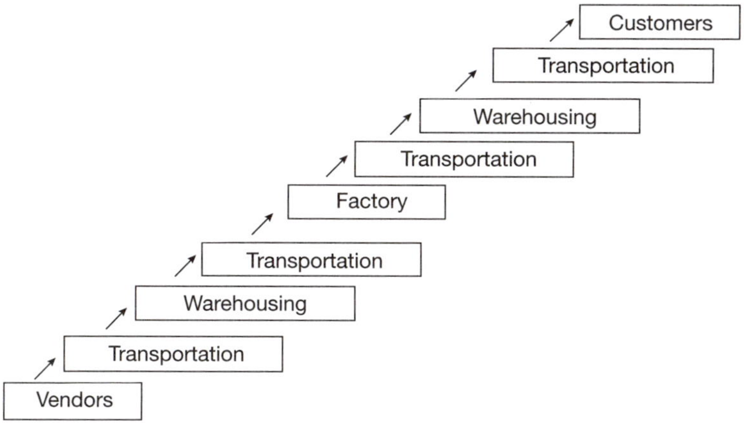

FIGURE 1.16 Integrated logistics management view.

1.5.2 Cycle View

In this view, each cycle occurs at the interface between two stages. For example, the customer order cycle happens between customer and retailer, the replenishment cycle happens between retailer and distributor, the manufacturing cycle happens between distributor and manufacturer, and the procurement cycle occurs between the manufacturer and supplier. This is shown in Figure 1.17.

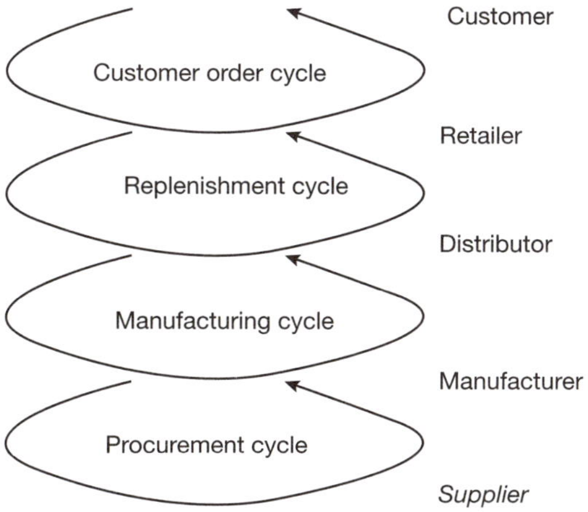

FIGURE 1.17 Cycle view of supply chain.

The cycle view defines the processes involved along with the owners of each process and specifies the roles and responsibilities of each member and the desired outcome of each process. As the saying goes, the strength of a chain lies in the weakest link, this view emphasizes that all links must be strengthened and any weak link in these cycles will impact the supply chain performance. In a way, the Theory of Constraints (TOC) adopts this view in SCM. For example, if we look at the typical sequence of activities in the customer order cycle, it involves all processes directly involved in receiving and filling the customer's order as follows:

1. Customer arrival
2. Customer order entry
3. Customer order fulfillment
4. Customer order receiving

If we move one level up and look at the replenishment cycle, it involves all processes in replenishing retailer inventories (retailer is now the customer) and will have the following sequence of activities:

1. Retail order trigger
2. Retail order entry
3. Retail order fulfillment
4. Retail order receiving

The manufacturing cycle involves all processes involved in replenishing the distributor (or retailer) inventory with the following sequence of activities:

1. Order arrival from the distributor, retailer, or customer
2. Production scheduling
3. Manufacturing and shipping
4. Receiving at the distributor, retailer, or customer

The procurement process covers all processes necessary to ensure that materials are available according to schedule with the following activities:

1. The manufacturer orders components from suppliers to replenish component inventories
2. However, component orders can be determined precisely from production schedules (different from retailer/distributor orders that are based on uncertain customer demand)
3. Important that suppliers be linked to the manufacturer's production schedule

Therefore, as seen here, the cycle view emphasizes a series of activities to be carried out at every stage and for the respective process owner to make the supply chain function seamlessly and efficiently. The roles and responsibilities are clearly defined.

1.5.3 Push and Pull View

This view is an important view and looks at SCM from the manufacturing point of view. The view identifies the push/pull boundaries that take place in a supply chain and looks at the manufacturing strategy to handle the boundaries. This is briefly shown in Figure 1.18.

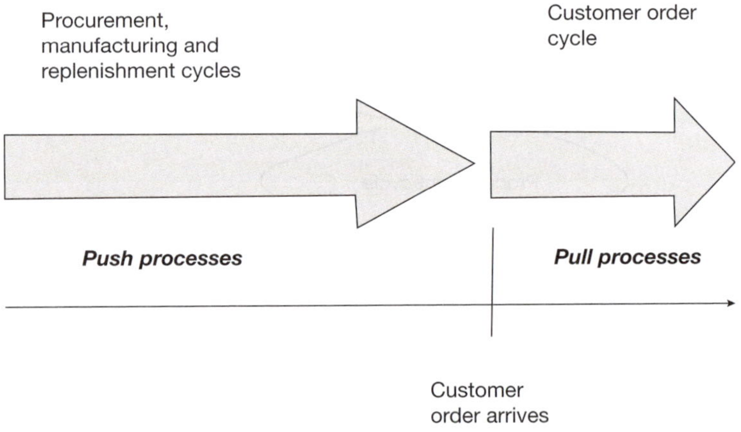

FIGURE 1.18 Push/pull boundaries in a supply chain.

Supply chain processes fall into push or pull depending on the times of execution and customer demand. In the pull situation, execution is initiated in response to a customer order. It is reactive and usually happens for "made or assembled to order" type of products. In the push situation, execution is initiated in anticipation of customer orders. It is more speculative and usually happens for "made or assemble to stock" type of products. The push/pull boundary separates push processes from pull processes. This is schematically explained in Figure 1.19.

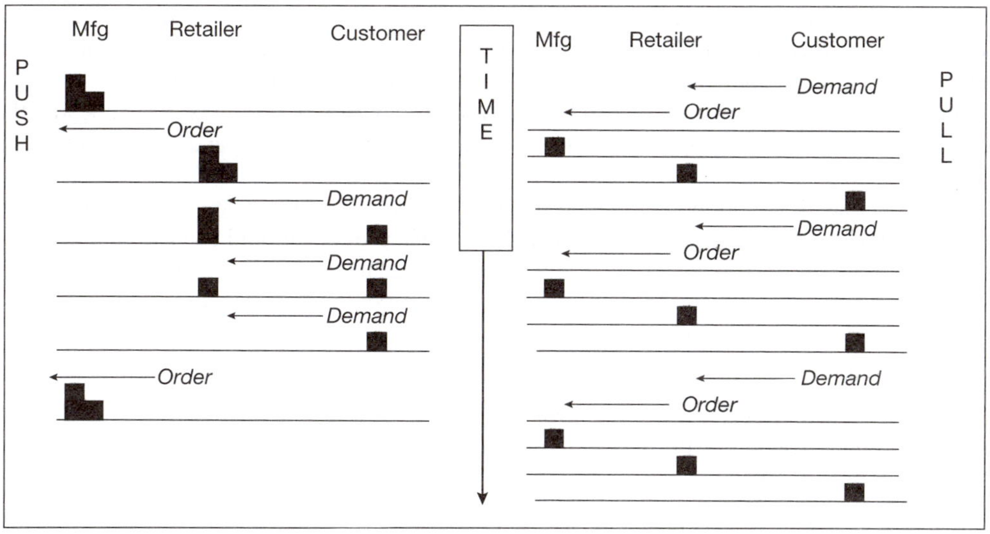

FIGURE 1.19 Push and pull in supply chain.

The supply chain identifies the order decoupling point that makes such push/pull boundaries occur, which may be different for different types of products, as shown in Figure 1.20.

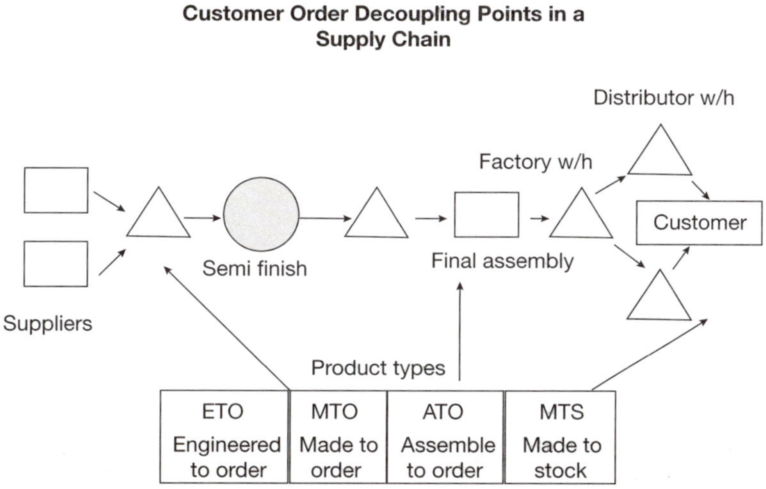

FIGURE 1.20 Decoupling points in a supply chain.

In the manufacturing context, supply chains also look at the point where product differentiation can be done for customers. There is always a tendency for these points to be in opposite directions, as manufacturers prefer decoupling points closer to the points of manufacturing to minimize the uncertainty while customers would prefer differentiation points closer to them, as shown in Figure 1.21.

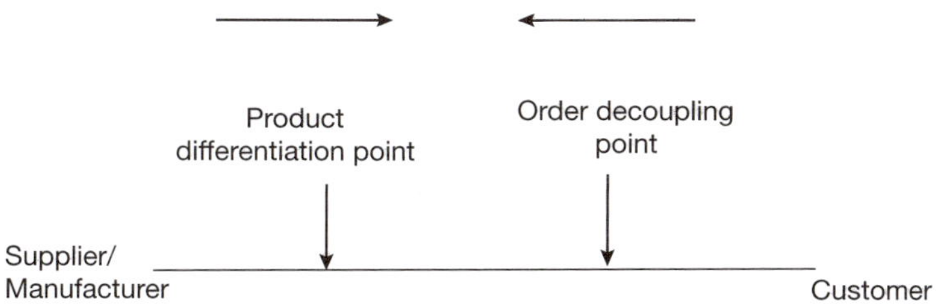

FIGURE 1.21 Order decoupling point versus product differentiation point.

This leads to conflicts in these points, and hence manufacturers adopt postponement strategies to handle and resolve such conflicts. The strategy suggests postponement of the task of final differentiation of the product until the latest possible point in the supply chain. The concept of postponement lies in organizing the production and distribution of products in such a way that the customization of these products is made as close to the point where the demand is known as possible.

The principle of postponement can be stated as follows: The time of shipment and the location of the final product processing in the distribution of a product should be delayed until a customer order is received. The idea is to avoid shipping goods in anticipation of when demand will occur (time postponement) and to avoid creating the form of the final product in anticipation of that form (form postponement).

Postponement is favored when the following characteristics appear to be present:

1. Technology and process characteristics
    - Feasible to decouple primary and postponed operations
    - Limited complexity of customizing
    - Modular product design
    - Sourcing from multiple locations
2. Product characteristics
    - High commonality of modules
    - Specific formulation of products
    - Specific peripherals
    - High value density of products
    - Product cube and/or weight increases through customization
3. Market characteristics
    - Short product life cycles
    - High sales fluctuations
    - Short and reliable lead times
    - Price competition
    - Varied markets and customers

Table 1.3 presents the types of postponement strategies and potential firms that can benefit from such strategies.

TABLE 1.3 Types of postponement and potential firms

Postponement Type	Potentially Interested Firms
Labeling	• Firms selling a product under several brand names • Firms with high unit value products • Firms with high product value fluctuations (Example: Nike, Bata, ice creams, soap powders under different packs)
Packaging	• Firms selling a product under several package sizes • Firms with high unit value products • Firms with high product sales fluctuations (Example: consumer groceries, combo trade promotions)
Assembly	• Firms selling products with several versions • Firms selling a product whose cube is greatly reduced if shipped unassembled • Firms with high unit value products • Firms with high product sales fluctuations (Example: Dell, Subway)

(Continued)

TABLE 1.3 (Continued)

Postponement Type	Potentially Interested Firms
Manufacturing	• Firms selling products with a high proportion of ubiquitous materials • Firms with high unit value products • Firms with high product sales fluctuations (Example: Asian Paints, Benetton t-shirts, HP-Printers with different power supply, on-street dosa vendors)
Time	• Firms with high unit value products • Firms with a large number of distribution warehouses • Firms with high product sales fluctuations (Example: Seasonal products like crackers, season greetings, idols for various Indian festivals)

The push/pull view thus enables strategic decisions of supply chain design and is a global view of how supply chain processes relate to customer orders. It is also beneficial sometimes to combine the push/pull and cycle views for designing supply chains. The relative proportion of push and pull processes often impacts supply chain performance.

1.5.4 Process View of Supply Chain

The discussion so far has led us to think that to implement SCM, some level of coordination across organizational boundaries is needed. Many leading-edge companies have realized that the real competition is not company against company, but rather supply chain against supply chain. Therefore, "How do we integrate our supply chain?" is the major concern that is often raised as an important issue in understanding and implementing SCM. The major question asked is how an integrated supply chain of partners without common ownership must be managed as compared to managing a single monolithic bureaucracy. For example, if a basic managerial question is asked, say, how is Tata Motors, a leading automobile manufacturer in India is managed, we can describe various management components that are required to manage it as a company, such as, span of control, unity of authority and different structures. But if we ask the question "how should the supply chain of Tata Motors be managed," it is not as simple as managing Tata Motors. This is because the partners of Tata Motors consist of companies that are as big as Tata Motors and each one of them is managed well as individual entities. Therefore, a supply chain of partners has to be managed in a different way, and it is not easy to define ownership in such SCM. Here, different forms of relationships are appropriate and not all links in the supply chain need to be partnerships. The process view of SCM is useful in this context. We will briefly present this view in the following sections.

The postponement concept is one of the popular offshoots of the push/pull view of supply chain, which finds an important application. It is very commonsensical and practiced even at home. Imagine a set of guests coming to your home and you want to make, say, Upma, a South Indian dish, with and without onion for them! You make the Upma without onion first, keep it aside, and postpone adding onion at the end to make onion Upma for the remaining! This concept is used in manufacturing to postpone the final form of the product only when the order is confirmed. This has given tremendous scope for the scale of economy in the procurement side, manufacturing side, and dispatching side for a few primary forms and differentiate many at a later stage for generating many stock keeping units.

Companies can achieve supply chain integration only if there is a common understanding of the key business processes. In order to build links between supply chain members, it is imperative that partner companies implement a standard set of supply chain processes. Hence, to implement supply chain integration, we need a common definition of supply chain management, and a shared understanding of the processes. The following definition of SCM developed and used by The Global Supply Chain Forum in 1998 (and the International Center for Competitive Excellence, 1994) is recommended and is popularly adopted by many professionals:

> "*Supply Chain Management is the integration of key business processes from end user through original suppliers that provides products, services, and information that add value for customers and other stakeholders.*"

The conceptual framework of this approach is based on the following three elements that are major and closely related:

1. **Business processes**, which are activities that produce a specific output of value to the customer.
2. **Management components** by which business processes are structured and managed.

3. **Supply chain network structure**, which is the configuration of companies within a supply chain. Figure 1.22 is used to define the process view of supply chain management.

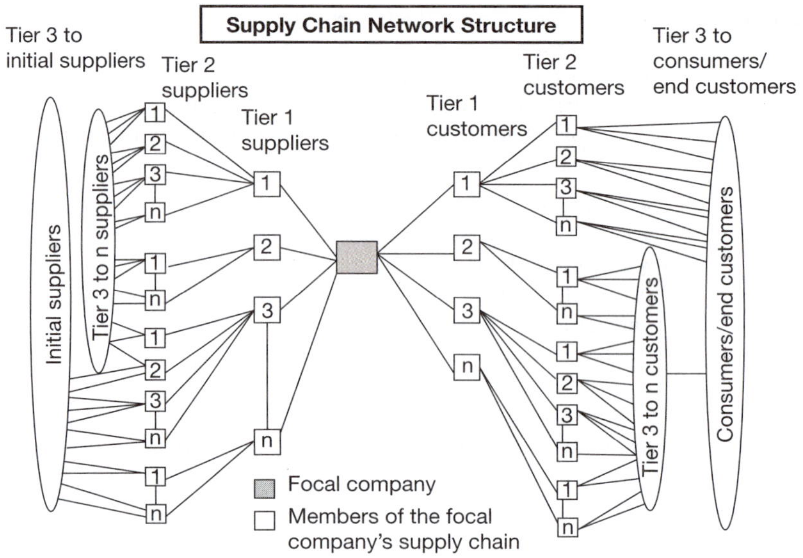

FIGURE 1.22 Framework for the process view of supply chain.

The Global Supply Chain Forum identified the eight key processes that make up the core of SCM, which need to be implemented within and across firms in the supply chain. Here, process is defined as "a structured and measured set of activities designed to produce a specific output for a particular customer or market".

1. Customer relationship management
2. Supplier relationship management
3. Customer service management
4. Demand management
5. Order fulfillment
6. Manufacturing flow management
7. Product development and commercialization
8. Returns management

These are briefly mentioned here:

1.5.4.1 Customer Relationship Management

The customer relationship management process provides the structure for developing and maintaining relationships with customers. It identifies and targets key customers and customer groups for a firm's business. Customer teams develop Product and Service Agreements (PSAs) to meet the needs of key accounts and segments of customers. They also work with key accounts to improve processes and eliminate demand variability and non-value-added activities. Performance reports are designed to measure the profitability of individual customers as well as the firm's financial impact on those customers.

1.5.4.2 Customer Service Management

The customer service management process provides the firm's face to the customers. It provides the single source and window of customer information, such as product availability, shipping dates, and order status. Real-time information is provided to customers through interfaces with the firm's functions, such as manufacturing and logistics. Customer service management is responsible for administering the PSA.

1.5.4.3 Demand Management

The demand management process attempts to balance the customer requirements (known as demand) with the firm's supply capabilities. This includes forecasting demand and synchronizing it with production, procurement, and distribution. The process is also concerned with developing and executing contingency plans when operations are interrupted.

1.5.4.4 Order Fulfillment

This process is key to SCM and attempts to meet customer requirements in terms of order fulfillment. An effective order fulfillment process requires integration of the firm's manufacturing, logistics, and marketing plans in a coordinated manner. In this process, the firm develops partnerships with key members of the supply chain to meet customer requirements and reduce total delivered cost to customers.

1.5.4.5 Manufacturing Flow Management

The manufacturing flow process enables the firm to make the products that a customer or customer target market wants and establish the manufacturing flexibility needed to serve them. The process includes all activities necessary for managing the product flow through the manufacturing facilities and for obtaining, implementing, and managing flexibility.

1.5.4.6 Supplier Relationship Management

Supplier relationship management is the process that defines how a company interacts with its suppliers. This is a mirror image of customer relationship management. While it is important that a company needs to develop relationships with its customers, it is equally important that it develops deeper relationships with its suppliers. It is realized that companies now pay attention to this process, something that did not get much attention in the past. Companies focus on two important developments: first, to reduce the supplier base, and second, to have close and long-term relationships with suppliers. There is an increased awareness to move from the traditional transactional reactive relationship to more long-term and proactive relationships with suppliers. Each supplier agrees to a PSA that defines the terms of the relationship. Supplier relationship management is about defining and managing these PSAs.

1.5.4.7 Product Development and Commercialization

Product development is critical to the continuing success of the firm. Developing new products quickly and getting them to the marketplace are important business processes for success in the marketplace. Time to market is very critical for this objective. For this, the SCM should integrate customers and suppliers into the product development process. As product life cycles shorten, the right products must be developed and successfully launched in ever-shorter timeframes to remain competitive.

1.5.4.8 Returns Management

Effective returns management is one of the critical parts of SCM. The cost of returns is often very expensive as compared to the forward movement of products in the supply chain. While this process is ignored, it should be noted that this process can assist the firms to achieve a sustainable competitive advantage. Effective management of the returns process enables the firm to identify productivity improvement opportunities and breakthrough projects.

The eight key business processes run the length of the supply chain and cut across firms and functional silos within each firm (see Figure 1.23). Functional silos include marketing, research and development, finance, production, purchasing, and logistics. Although activities in these processes will be in a functional silo, the entire process will not be contained within one function.

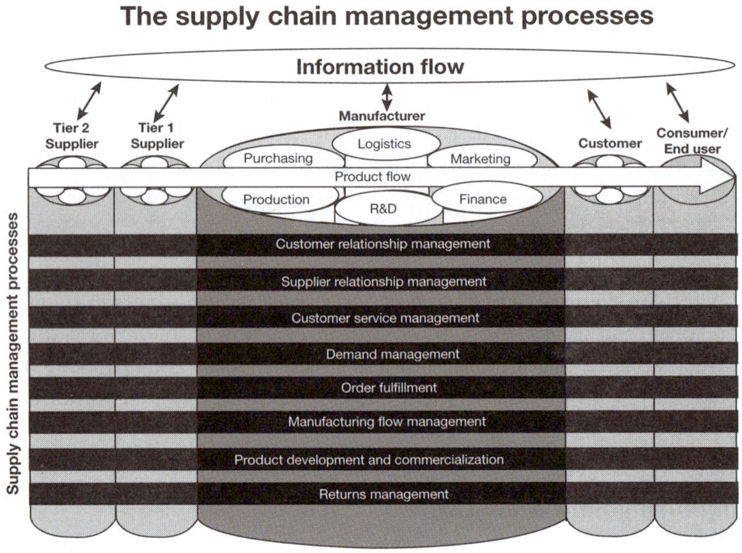

FIGURE 1.23 Supply chain management processes.

Source: Supply Chain Management: Processes, Partnerships, Performance, p. 3. Supply Chain Management Institute.

The process view is the most popular view of supply chain as it views supply chains from the process point of view. Most of the businesses need their processes to be always integrated and managed well, and so this view is more amenable to look at supply chain integration from such process point view. Business process engineering and reengineering are fundamentally look at this integration for seamless flows in supply chains.

The key implementation issues in SCM will be identifying the supply chain members who it is critical to link, the processes to be linked with each of these key members, and the type/level of integration that applies to each process link. Successful SCM involves the coordination of activities within the firm and between members of the supply chain. Although the focus does not reduce the importance of functional expertise, SCM requires transition from a functional organization to one focused on business processes first inside the firm and then across firms in the supply chain. Figure 1.24 illustrates how each function within the organization can be mapped with the eight supply chain processes. This figure provides examples of activities that might exist at each junction of a functional area and process.

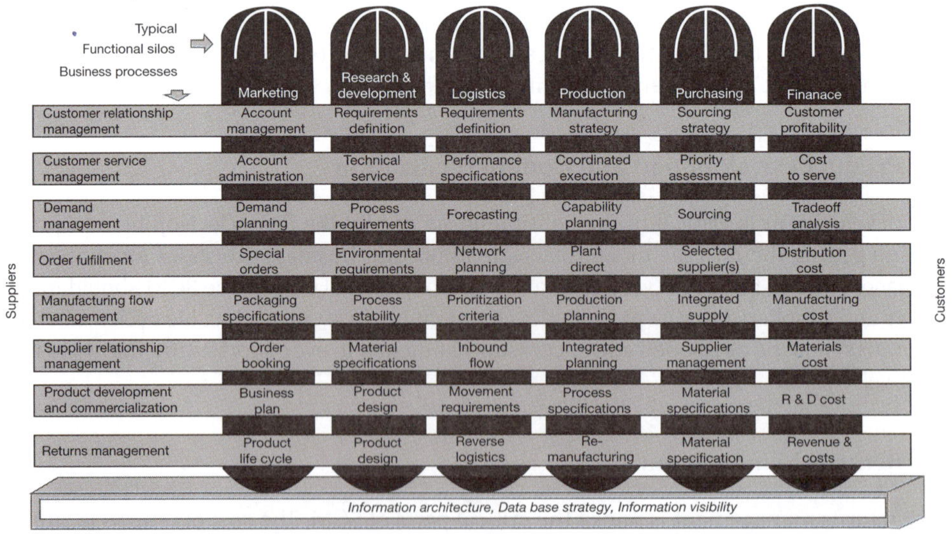

FIGURE 1.24 Implementing processes in the supply chain.

Note: Process sponsorship and ownership must be established to drive the attainment of the supply chain vision and eliminate the functional barriers that artificially separate the process flows.

Source: Supply Chain Management: Processes, Partnerships, Performance, p. 15. Supply Chain Management Institute.

1.5.4.9 Management Components

The processes explained earlier have to be managed within each company with their management components that include physical and technical components: planning and control methods, workflow structure, organizational structure, communication and information flow, facility structures such as product flow facility structure, and managerial and behavioral management components such as management methods, power and leadership structure and styles, risk and reward structure, culture and attitude, etc.

1.5.4.10 Supply Chain Network Structure

In this dimension of the framework, we determine the following:

1. How much of the supply chain needs to be managed and the factors it depends on, such as complexity of the product, number of suppliers, availability of raw materials, etc.
2. Dimensions to consider, which include length of the supply chain and the number of suppliers and customers at each level.
3. The knowledge on configuring the network structure to manage the supply chain.

Three primary structural aspects to study are as follows:

1. Members of the supply chain
2. Structural dimensions of the network
3. Different types of process links

1.5.4.11 Members

The members of the supply chain include the primary members and the supporting members. The primary members are those autonomous companies or strategic business units that perform operational and/or managerial activities in the business processes designed to produce a specific output for a particular customer or market, and the supporting members are companies that simply provide resources, knowledge, utilities, or assets for the primary members of the supply chain.

1.5.4.12 Structural Dimensions

While configuring the network, we analyze the structural dimensions covering the horizontal and vertical structures and the horizontal position with respect to proximity to the end customer.

1.5.4.13 Types of Business Links

We also need to determine the types of business links to establish with the members of the supply chain, which may be categorized as managed process links, monitored process links, not-managed process links, and non-member process links.

In summary, Figure 1.25 presents the three elements of the framework of the SCM.
Supply chain mapping helps to understand the different types of links and the configuration. Firms need to start with relationship-based maps to get a visual representation of the complexities of their supply chain. It is important to remember that supply chain maps will look different depending on a company's position in the supply chain. A sample mapping is shown in Figure 1.26 to illustrate the types of links that can be established in the inter-firm contexts.

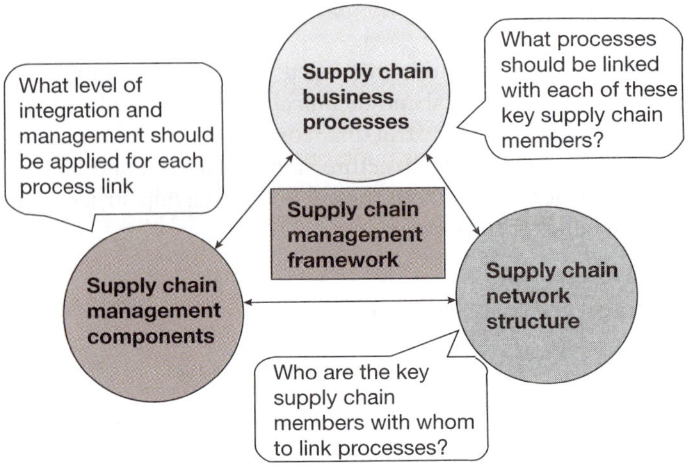

FIGURE 1.25 Framework of elements of supply chain management.

Source: Supply Chain Management: Processes, Partnerships, Performance, p. 23, Supply Chain Management Institute

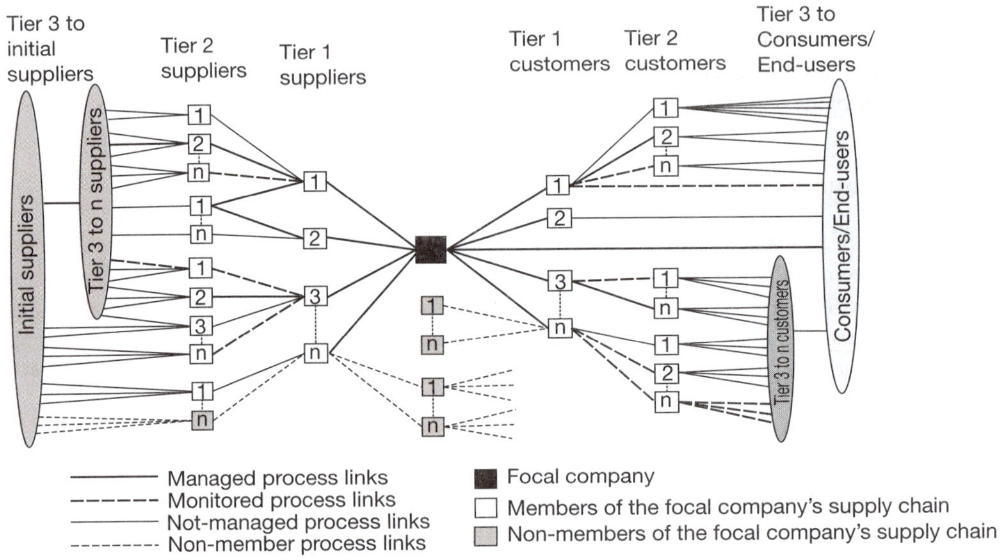

FIGURE 1.26 Types of inter-company business process links.

Source: Supply Chain Management: Processes, Partnerships, Performance, p. 207, Supply Chain Management Institute.

1.5.4.14 Other Definitions

Many more definitions are also available to define SCM. Two popular definitions are as follows:

1. Mentzer et al. defined SCM as follows:
   "*Systematic, strategic coordination of the traditional business functions and the tactics across the business functions within a particular company and across businesses within the supply chain, for the purposes of improving the long-term performance of the individual companies and the supply chain as a whole.*"
2. The Council of Supply Chain Management Professionals (CSCMP) defines SCM as follows:
   "*Supply Chain Management encompasses the planning and management of all activities involved in sourcing and procurement, conversion, and all Logistics Management activities. Importantly, it also includes coordination and collaboration with channel partners, which can be suppliers, intermediaries, third-party service providers, and customers. In essence,*

Supply Chain Management integrates supply and demand management within and across companies."

In other words, SCM is an integrating function with primary responsibility for linking major business functions and business processes within and across companies into a cohesive and high-performing business model. It includes all the logistics management activities noted earlier, as well as manufacturing operations, and it drives coordination of processes and activities with and across marketing, sales, product design, finance, and information technology.

More details of various frameworks, definitions, and literature on SCM are given in the bibliography for an in-depth reading.

1.5.5 Drivers of Supply Chain Performance

The important drivers of supply chain performance are as follows:

1. **Facilities**, places where inventory is stored, assembled, or fabricated production sites and storage sites.
2. **Inventory**, covering raw materials, WIP, finished goods within supply chain inventory policies.
3. **Transportation**, moving inventory from point to point in a supply chain and combinations of transportation modes and routes.
4. **Information**, data and analysis regarding inventory, transportation, facilities throughout the supply chain and potentially the biggest driver of supply chain performance.

1.6 | SUPPLY CHAIN ANALYTICS

When supply chains generate Big Data, supply chain analytics turns that data into real insights. The explosive impact of ecommerce is just one notable example of the data-driven revolution. Very few companies, however, have been able to apply to the same degree the "big analytics" techniques that could transform the way they define and manage their supply chains.

The full impact of Big Data in supply chain is restrained by two major challenges. First, there is a lack of capabilities. Supply chain managers—even those with a high degree of technical skills—have little or no experience with the data analysis techniques used by data scientists. As a result, they often lack the vision to see what might be possible with Big Data analytics. Second (and perhaps more significantly), most companies lack a structured process to explore, evaluate, and capture Big Data opportunities in their supply chains.

Supply chain analytics uses data and quantitative methods to improve decision making for all activities across the supply chain. Particularly, it does two new things. First, it expands the dataset for analysis beyond the traditional internal data held on Enterprise Resource Planning (ERP) and SCM systems. Second, it applies powerful and advanced statistical and quantitative methods to both new and existing data sources. This creates new insights that help improve supply chain decision making, all the way from improvement in frontline operations to strategic choices.

Analytics historically played a significant role in SCM, starting with military operations during and after World War II—particularly with the development of the simplex method for solving linear programming by George Dantzig in the 1940s. Supply chain analytics became more ingrained in decision making with the advent of ERP systems in the 1990s and more recently with Big Data applications, particularly in descriptive and predictive analytics.

The Supply Chain Operations Reference (SCOR) model developed by the Supply Chain Council (www.supply-chain.org) provides a good framework for classifying the analytics applications in SCM. The SCOR model outlines four domains of supply chain activities: source, make, deliver, and return. A fifth domain of the SCOR model—plan—is behind all four activity domains. Furthermore, a key input of the supply chain planning process is demand forecasting at all timeframes: long, mid, and short term with planning horizons of years, months, and days, respectively. Figure 1.27 illustrates different decisions in each of the four SCOR domains that can be aided by analytics. These decisions are further classified into strategic, tactical, and operational according to their timeframe.

SCOR model and examples of decisions at the three levels				
SCOR domain	Source	Make	Deliver	Return
Activities	Order and receive materials and products	Schedule and manufacture, repair, remanufacture, or recycle materials and products	Receive, schedule, pick, pack, and ship orders	Request, approve, and determine disposal of products and assets
Strategic (time frame: years)	• Strategic sourcing • Supply chain mapping	• Location of plants • Product line mix at plants	• Location of distribution centers • Fleet planning	• Location of return centers
Tactical (time frame: months)	• Tactical sourcing • Supply chain contracts	• Product line rationalization • Sales and operations planning	• Transportation and distribution planning • Inventory policies at locations	• Reverse distribution plan
Operational (time frame: days)	• Materials requirement planning and inventory replenishment orders	• Workforce scheduling • Manufacturing, order tracking, and scheduling	• Vehicle routing (for deliveries)	• Vehicle routing (for returns collection)
Plan	Demand forecasting (long term, mid term, and short term)			

FIGURE 1.27 SCOR model and decisions at different levels.

Analytics techniques can be categorized into four types: descriptive, predictive, prescriptive, and cognitive.

1.6.1 Descriptive Analytics

Descriptive analytics answers the question of what is happening. Real-time information about the location and quantities of goods in the supply chain provides managers with tools to make adjustments to delivery schedules, place replenishment and emergency orders, change transportation modes, and so forth. Traditional data sources include Global Positioning System (GPS) data on the location of trucks and ships that contain inventories, Radio Frequency Identification (RFID) data originating from passive tags embedded in pallets (even at the product level), and transactions involving barcodes.

1.6.2 Predictive Analytics

In supply chain planning, predictive analytics derives demand forecasts from past data and answers the question of what will be happening. It actually tells us what will happen in the future, and it gets pretty close to that. This process unveils all the patterns and motifs from the existing data to present a set of trends that are likely to occur in the future.

1.6.3 Prescriptive Analytics

Prescriptive analytics derives decision recommendations based on descriptive and predictive analytics models and mathematical optimization models. It answers questions of a what-if nature and what should be happening. Prescriptive analytics helps businesses take decisions based on analytical findings. Since it is based on data, it is scalable and can provide businesses with direction. The bulk of academic research, software, and practitioner activities in supply chain analytics focuses on prescriptive analytics.

1.6.4 Cognitive Analytics

Cognitive analytics tries to mimic the human brain by studying data and understanding patterns and interpreting them to draw conclusions. This knowledge, thus gained, is further used for future reference.

In this book, some of the popular analytics methods that are useful in supply chain planning and management are presented in various modules covering the major drivers of supply chain performance: facilities, inventory, and transportation and some additional tools that are useful in decision making.

SUMMARY

This chapter gives an overview of the concepts of logistics management and supply chain management as a building block for the rest of the chapters in this book. Since this is not a textbook on logistics and supply chain management, the chapter only provides the concepts briefly and states the basic decision issues in each of them. Initially, it starts with how driving forces affect business and become imperative for any supply chain to reckon with such forces. Then, logistics management was introduced with a few definitions, and different perspectives and approaches were presented to analyze logistics systems with interface areas of logistics such as the manufacturing and marketing functions. Then the context for supply chain management was introduced, and four different views of supply chain management were presented. The process view was presented with more details as it is the popular view of supply chain management.

Case Study

Besides the cases that are given in the introductory chapters in bibliography 1, 4 and 6, the following cases from Harvard Publishing are good for classroom discussion:

1. Walmart: Supply Chain Management by P. Fraser Johnson, Ken Mark (https://hbsp.harvard.edu/product/W19317-PDF-ENG?Ntt=Walmart%3A%20Supply%20Chain%20Management).
2. Amazon.com: Supply Chain Management by P. Fraser Johnson, Ken Mark (https://hbsp.harvard.edu/product/W18451-PDF-ENG?Ntt=Amazon.com%3A%20Supply%20Chain%20Management).
3. Nokia's Supply Chain Management by Russell Walker, Joanna Wilson (https://hbsp.harvard.edu/product/KEL673-PDF-ENG?Ntt=Nokia%E2%80%99s%20Supply%20Chain%20Management).
4. Seven-Eleven Japan Co., Sunil Chopra (https://hbsp.harvard.edu/product/KEL026-PDF-ENG?Ntt=Seven-Eleven%20Japan%20Co).

Exercises

1. Consider a retail chain like Big Bazaar. Describe the supply chain processes of such retail stores giving details on their supply chain drivers, supply integration issues and challenges.
2. Imagine that you are buying a TV from a dealer show room. Identify the different cycles in the supply chain proceses and describe them from the Cycle View of Supply Chain Management.
3. List few items you buy in your household. For these items, identify the Push/Pull boundaries and describe the complications that are involved in the supply chain of them from the Push/Pull view of supply chain management.

4. Identify various business processes that have to be managed for a car manufacturing company and explain them briefly.
5. Suppose you are a food caterer supplying different types of food items for working people and households in and around your location. Describe how you will increase your responsiveness.
6. A furniture manufacturer wants to improve his supply chain efficiency. Identify the components of his supply chain and use various supply chain frameworks to formulate strategies for improving the supply chain efficiency.
7. Select two organizations from a particular industry (viz., automobile, mobile, steel, etc.) and compare their supply chain strategies using the frameworks discussed in this chapter.
8. Illustrate few situations how postponement and standardization strategies are practiced in various organizations.
9. Describe situations in supply chains of few products where supply chain analytics will be required and will give better solutions.
10. Analyze the logistics challenges of e-commerce organizations like Amazon, Flipkart etc. and present few approaches for solving them.
11. What are the improvements that are required in transportation strategy of e-commerce organizations like Amazon?
12. What are the supply chain challenges during pandemic like Covid-19? Describe few approaches that can help mitigate supply issues of essential commodities to public during such pandemics.

Bibliography

1. Ballou, R. H. and S. K. Srivastava (2007). ***Business Logistics/Supply Chain Management.*** Delhi: Pearson India.
2. Bardi, E. J., C. John Langley, and J. J. Coyle (1976). ***The Management of Business Logistics: A Supply Chain Perspective.*** South-Western.
3. Bowersox, D., D. Closs, and M. Bixby Cooper (2018). ***Supply Chain Logistics Management.*** McGraw-Hill Education.
4. Chopra, S., P. Meindl, and D. V. Kalra (2016). ***Supply Chain Management: Strategy, Planning and Operation.*** Delhi: Pearson India.
5. Croxton, K. L., S. J. García-Dastugue, D. M. Lambert, and D. S. Rogers. (2001). The supply chain management processes. ***The International Journal of Logistics Management,*** **12**(2), 13–36.
6. David Simchi Levi, Edith Simchi Levi, Ravi Shankar, Philip Kaminsky (2019). Designing And Managing the Supply Chain : Concepts, Strategies and Case studies, 3rd Edition, McGraw Hill.
7. Fisher, M. L. (1997). What is the right supply chain for your product? ***Harvard Business Review,*** March–April.
8. Lambert, D. M. (2008). ***Supply Chain Management: Processes, Partnerships, Performance.*** Florida: Supply Chain Management Institute.
9. Lambert, D. M., M. A. Emmelhainz, and J. T. Gardner. (1996) Developing and implementing supply chain partnerships. ***The International Journal of Logistics Management,*** **7**(2), 1–18.
10. Lambert, D. M., M. C. Cooper, and J. D. Pagh. (1998) Supply chain management: Implementation issues and research opportunities. ***The International Journal of Logistics Management,*** **9**(2), 1–20.
11. Lee, H. L., V. Padmanabhan, and S. Whang. (1997) The bullwhip effect in supply chains. ***Sloan Management Review,*** 93–102.
12. Mentzer, J. T. (2001). ***Supply Chain Management.*** Sage.
13. Mentzer, J. T., W. DeWitt, J. S. Keebler, S. Min, N. W. Nix, C. D. Smith, and Z. G. Zachari (2001). Defining supply chain management. ***Journal of Business Logistics,*** **22**(2), 1–25.

SECTION

II

Overview of Optimization Methods

CHAPTER 2

Overview of Optimization Methods

LEARNING OBJECTIVES

After reading this chapter, you would be able to:

- Get an overview of important optimization techniques such as linear programming, transportation problems, and assignment problems.
- Learn the basic formulation approaches to a linear optimization structure known as linear programming.
- Understand how the solution is obtained using a graphical method and suggestions for the simplex method.
- Use Excel Solver for solving a linear programming problem.
- Understand how to formulate a transportation problem and solve it using Excel Solver.
- Formulate an assignment problem and solve it using Excel Solver.
- Recognize a few situations in different applications where such optimization techniques are useful to make decisions.

2.1 | INTRODUCTION AND HISTORICAL PERSPECTIVE

Mathematical techniques date back to the turn of the century or even before. The momentum started when military operations research groups were formed during World War II in Great Britain in 1939. Teams consisting of individuals from different fields of science were formed to conduct research on military operations. One of the famous teams was the "Blackett's Circus" named after its leader Nobel Laureate P. M. S. Blackett of the University of Manchester and a former Naval Officer. This and a few more teams were responsible for the famous victory in the Battle of Britain. Then success stories then went to the United States, and more teams were formed in the MIT, such as Project RAND and Project SCOOP. Techniques that were secrets were released after the war for business applications.

Mathematical models are used in decision-making areas in management and engineering, and advances in research in such areas and computer technology have tremendous impact on their applications. A model represents the essential features of an object, system, or problem without unimportant details. The models use variables, parameters, and functions. Analyzing and manipulating the model gives insights into how the real-world system behaves under various conditions and helps decision makers visualize problems with all their what-if scenarios. This helps them to arrive at the best solutions and systems and actions to take.

Mathematical models are easier, faster, and safer as compared to building, constructing, and manipulating real systems. Mathematical modeling is quicker and less expensive than using the trial-and-error approach. Facility location, vehicle routing and scheduling, personnel, machine and job scheduling, product mixes, and inventory management problems are formulated as constrained optimization models. The constrained optimization models are mathematical models that find the best solution with respect to some evaluation criterion from a set of alternative solutions. These solutions are defined by a set of mathematical constraints: mathematical inequalities or equalities.

Programming problems are concerned with the efficient use of or allocation of limited resources to meet the desired objectives. A subclass is known as Linear Programming Problem (LPP) where the relationship among the variables of the problem is linear. The celebrated work of George B. Dantzig on "Programming in a Linear Structure," which appeared in *Econometrica*, Vol. 17, in 1949, started the application of linear programming models in business applications. T. C. Koopmans suggested the name "Linear Programming" for this subclass, and according to Dantzig, the name "Simplex Method" was suggested by T. S. Motzkin. Linear programming was first developed by Dantzig along with Marshall Wood and Associates in 1947 while he was head of the Air Force Statistical Control's Combat Analysis Branch at the Pentagon, US Department of Air Force. He formed a group called Project SCOOP (**S**cientific **C**omputation **Of O**ptimum **P**rograms), an American research program that resulted from the intensive scientific activity during World War II, in the USA, aimed at rationalizing the logistics in the war effort. The military referred to its plans for training, supplying, and deploying combat unit as "programs." When Dantzig analyzed the Air Force Planning problems, he realized they could be formulated as a system of linear inequalities. Hence, his original name for the technique, "Programming in a Linear Structure," was later shortened to linear programming. Dantzig proposed that "Inter-relations between activities of a large organisation can be viewed as a linear programming problem type of model and the optimizing program determined by minimizing a linear objective function."

In the Soviet Union, Kantorovitch had already proposed a similar method for the analysis of economic plans, but his contribution remained unknown to the general scientific community (http://www.mathsoc.spb.ru/pantheon/Kantorovich.html). It also seems that the 19th century mathematicians, particularly Fourier (1823), had also thought about similar methods (http://www-history.mcs.st-and.ac.uk/history/Mathematicians/Fourier.html).

The parallel development of the paradigm of inter-industry exchange table, also known as the input/output matrix, was proposed by W. A. Leontief, which showed that the whole economy could be represented in a sort of linear programming structure. What made the contribution of Dantzig so important is the concomitance with the considerable development of the digital computer that permitted the implementation of the algorithm to solve full-size, real-life problems. Therefore, the method of linear programming was providing both an efficient instrument to compute solutions of large-scale linear optimization problems and a general paradigm of economic equilibrium between different sectors exchanging resources and services.

2.2 | CONSTRAINED OPTIMIZATION MODELS

Constrained optimization models have three major components: decision variables, objective functions, and constraints.

1. **Decision variables** are fundamental output variables of any mathematical model and physical quantities the decision maker will be interested in and are represented by mathematical symbols. For example, the decision variable xj can represent the number of units of a product j a manufacturer wishes to produce during a period that depends on the resource availability and the consumption rate of the products using such resources. Decision variables take on any of a set of possible values.
2. **An objective function** is the criterion for evaluating the solution which the decision maker wishes to optimize. It is a mathematical function of the decision variables that can be evaluated based on the solution. For example, the objective function may be to measure the total profit or cost that results as a function of the levels of various products that will be produced. The objective function also specifies a direction of optimization, to either maximize or minimize. An optimal solution for the given mathematical model is the best solution as measured by that criterion.
3. **Constraints** are a set of functional equalities or inequalities that represent physical, economic, technological, legal, ethical, or other restrictions on what numerical values can be assigned to the decision variables. For example, constraints may be that the total resources

available to make products are limited and not more than available. Constraints can be definitional, recursive depending on the problem definition. In constrained optimization models, we find values for the decision variables that maximize or minimize the objective function and satisfy all constraints.

Example 2.1 is adopted from the example used by Saul I. Gass (the first PhD student of Dr. Dantzig) and shows how an operational problem can be represented and analyzed using a constrained optimization model.

A model is very fundamental to understand a business situation. Construction of a mathematical model is to represent a reality into abstraction, use it for mathematical manipulation, and analyze the reality with such construction. So careful understanding and formulations are required to derive the best benefit of any mathematical models.

EXAMPLE 2.1 (FURNITURE PROBLEM)

A furniture manufacturer wants to produce two products: chairs and tables. Available resources are wood and man hours of labor with the following levels:

Resource level of wood	400 cubic feet
Resource level of man hours	450 hours

Input/Output Coefficients (Technological Coefficients)

To produce 1 unit of chair, he requires 5 cft wood and 10 man hours.

To produce 1 unit of table, he requires 20 cft of wood and 15 man hours.

Profit Levels

Profit/Chair	\$450
Profit/Table	\$800

The objective of the manufacturer is to maximize the Total Profit.

What should be the Optimal Product Mix of Chairs and Tables which would maximize the Total Profit?

Solution

The problem can be formulated as follows:

Let X_1 be the number of Chairs to be produced
X_2 be the number of Tables to be produced.

We call these *Decision Variables* in the problem. Let us see how these variables relate to the given problem.

To produce 1 chair if he requires 5 cft, then to produce X_1 chairs he would require $5 \times X_1$ cft. Similarly, to produce 1 table if he requires 20 cft, then to produce X_2 tables he requires $20 \times X_2$ cft. So, the total requirement of wood to produce X_1 chairs and X_2 tables is $5X_1 + 20X_2$ cft. But this cannot be more than what is available as the wood resource, that is, 400 cft. Therefore, this can be expressed as a resource constraint for the wood availability:

$$5X_1 + 20X_2 \leq 400$$

Similarly, the resource constraint for the man hours can be expressed as

$$10X_1 + 15X_2 \leq 450$$

The objective function can be expressed similarly as

$$450X_1 + 800X_2$$

which he wants to maximize.

Therefore, the entire problem can be expressed mathematically as follows:

$$\text{Maximize } 450X_1 + 800X_2$$

Subject to

$$5X_1 + 20X_2 \leq 400$$
$$10X_1 + 15X_2 \leq 450$$
$$X_1, X_2 \geq 0$$

We observe that the constraints expressed are linear constraints (linear inequalities) and the objective function is also a linear equation. Hence the label "Linear Programming Problem" (LPP) for these kinds of problems.

2.3 | ASSUMPTIONS OF AN LPP

The assumptions of these linear programming models are as follows:

1. **Linearity:** Proportionality and additivity are assumed in the objective and constraint inequalities or equations.
2. **Certainty:** The parameters objective function coefficients, resource levels, and input/output coefficients are known and certain, that is, deterministic. They are not variables or stochastic.
3. **Continuity (or Divisibility):** The decisions variables can assume continuous real values and need not be integer values.

2.4 | GENERAL FORM OF LPP

The linear programs are written in the following general form:

Let us define the variables and parameters as follows in the matrix form:

$$X=\begin{bmatrix} X_1 \\ X_2 \\ .. \\ .. \\ .. \\ X_n \end{bmatrix} \quad c=\begin{bmatrix} c_1 \\ c_2 \\ .. \\ .. \\ .. \\ .. \\ c_n \end{bmatrix} \quad A=\begin{bmatrix} a_{11} & a_{12} & .. & .. & .. & a_{1n} \\ a_{21} & a_{22} & .. & .. & .. & a_{2n} \\ .. & .. & .. & .. & .. & .. \\ .. & .. & .. & .. & .. & .. \\ .. & .. & .. & .. & .. & .. \\ a_{m1} & a_{m2} & .. & .. & .. & a_{mn} \end{bmatrix} \quad b=\begin{bmatrix} b_1 \\ b_2 \\ .. \\ .. \\ .. \\ b_m \end{bmatrix}$$

where the *xj* values are decision variables and *cj*, *aij*, and *bi* values are constants, called **parameters** or **coefficients**, corresponding to the objective function, input/output, and Right-Hand Side (RHS) resource level, respectively, which are given or specified by the problem assumptions. Most linear programs require that all decision variables be non-negative. Then the LPP can be expressed as follows:

$$\text{Max } Z = c^{T}X$$

$$\text{subject to}$$

$$AX \le b$$

$$X \ge 0$$

The characteristic that makes linear programs easy to solve is their simple geometric structure. Let us define some terminology. A solution to a linear program is any set of numerical values for the variables. These values need not be the best values and do not even have to satisfy the constraints or make sense. For example, in the furniture problem, $X_1 = 10$ and $X_2 = 10$ is a solution but need not be the best solution. We define a **feasible solution** as a solution that satisfies all the constraints. The **feasible set** or **feasible region** is the set of all feasible solutions. Finally, an **optimal solution** is the feasible solution that produces the best objective function value possible. We will show how to solve a two-variable problem graphically. We will revisit the furniture problem for this.

2.5 | GRAPHICAL SOLUTION TO FURNITURE PROBLEM

The constraint equations are drawn to identify the feasible region, which is shown in Figure 2.1. The four corner points are (0, 0), (45, 0), (24, 14), and (0, 20). The objective function is evaluated at all these four corner points, and the optimum solution is found at (24, 14) with the objective function value of $22,000, as indicated in Figure 2.2.

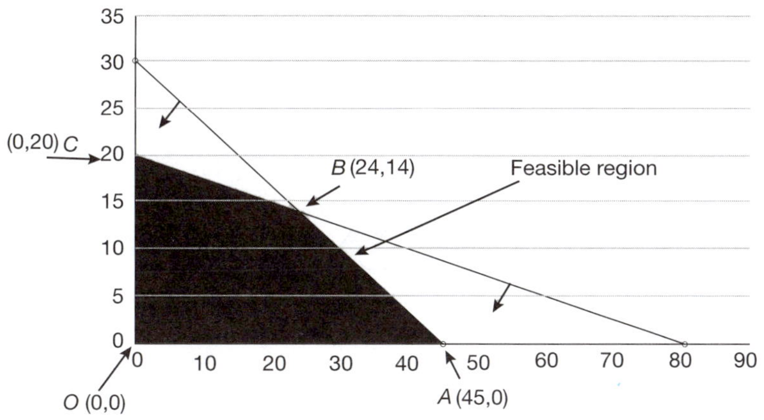

FIGURE 2.1 Feasible region for the furniture problem.

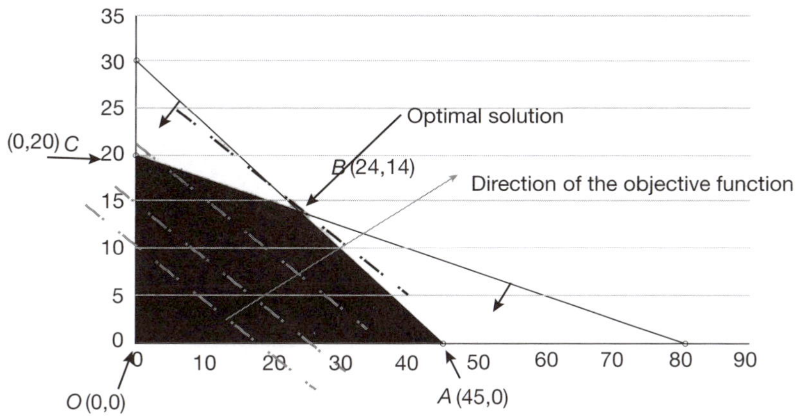

FIGURE 2.2 Optimal solution for the furniture problem.

2.6 | SIMPLEX METHOD

In 1949, George B. Dantzig developed an efficient procedure for solving linear programs called the **simplex method** or **simplex algorithm**. This is the most widely used method in instructional and commercial computer packages. A method developed by Narendra Karmarkar in 1984 is also gaining popularity, but it requires more sophisticated mathematics.

The fundamental approach of the simplex method reduces the number of feasible solutions to a finite number that has to be evaluated. One obvious way is identifying the coordinates of every extreme point and then evaluating the objective function at each. The coordinate that produces the best objective function value can be chosen as the optimum. However, in practice, this approach is not difficult when we wish to solve a large-scale problem with even moderate numbers of variables and constraints. The simplex algorithm begins by identifying an initial extreme point of the feasible set. The algorithm then looks along each edge intersecting at the extreme point and computes the net effect on the objective function if we were to move along the edge. If the objective function value does not improve by moving along at least one of these edges, it can be proved that the extreme point is optimal. If movement along one or more of the edges improves the objective function value, we move along one of these edges until we reach a new extreme point. We repeat the previous steps, checking along each edge intersecting at the extreme point, and then either stopping or sliding along another edge that improves the objective function value.

The graphical method is the best way to illustrate an optimization problem with its objective direction and constraints. In addition, it gives an insight into understanding the basic logic of the most famous simplex algorithm of George B. Dantzig.

The simplex algorithm can be described geometrically as follows: The optimal solution that is searched is an "extreme point" of a polytope as shown in Figure 2.3 for a three-dimensional space.

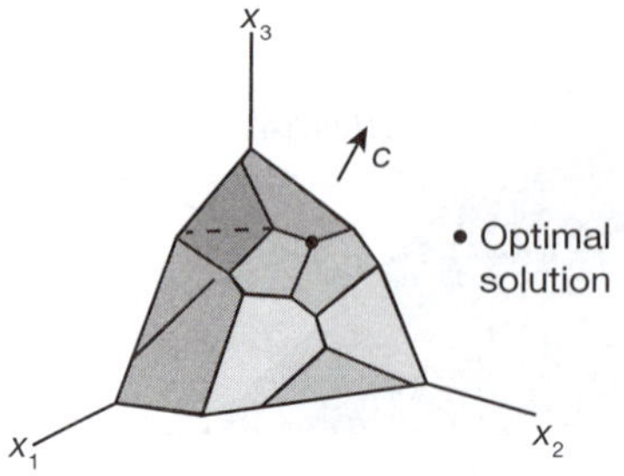

FIGURE 2.3 The polytope of feasible points and the "optimal one."

*Source: **Mysteries in Linear Programming**,* K. Fukuda.

The arrow c represents the profit vector. One looks for the point x in the polytope, which maximizes the scalar product $c'x$. In the simplex method, one moves from one feasible extreme point to another one improving the performance criterion, as indicated in the figure. The initial extreme point, in this illustration, is the origin of the axes. The path of the algorithm is represented by the arrows. One can easily check that, at each step, one passes from an extreme point to a neighboring one where the objective function increases (one progresses in the direction c). See Figure 2.4.

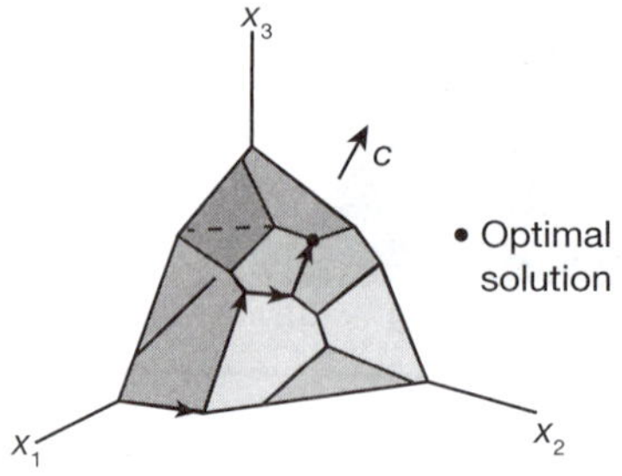

FIGURE 2.4 The simplex algorithm path.

Indeed, the principle of the method is to enumerate only a small fraction of the very large number of extreme points of the polytope before reaching the optimal solution.

The exact simplex algorithm can be seen in the references given in the bibliography. The mathematical explanation and the steps of the algorithm are skipped here. However, we will present the Solver method to solve an LPP in the following section.

The simplex algorithm is one of the revolutions in the optimization literature. Although many improved algorithms have been developed later like Karmarkar's algorithm, the simplex method remains one of the applied and most amenable for economic interpretation compared to other algorithms. Paul Samuelson gave an interesting economic interpretation of the simplex algorithm using shadow prices and unit worth of resources that made simplex used more widely in industrial applications.

2.6.1 Excel Solver for Solving LPP

We will revisit the furniture problem and explain how to create an Excel worksheet for solving it. Screenshots of the sequence of steps are shown in Figures 2.5–2.9.

Solving the problem with Solver:

1. First take some time to see how the problem has been set up in the table format. The colored cells are the answers you are after—the optimal product mix and the total profit.
2. To "play" with the problem, try changing the number of chairs and tables by entering some numbers. What happens to the column E31:E32? Does your "play mix" satisfy the constraints?

3. Note that the objective is to maximize profit, the expression for which is in cell F37. Go to that cell and see how the formula is entered. Also go to other cells with data and see how they are entered.

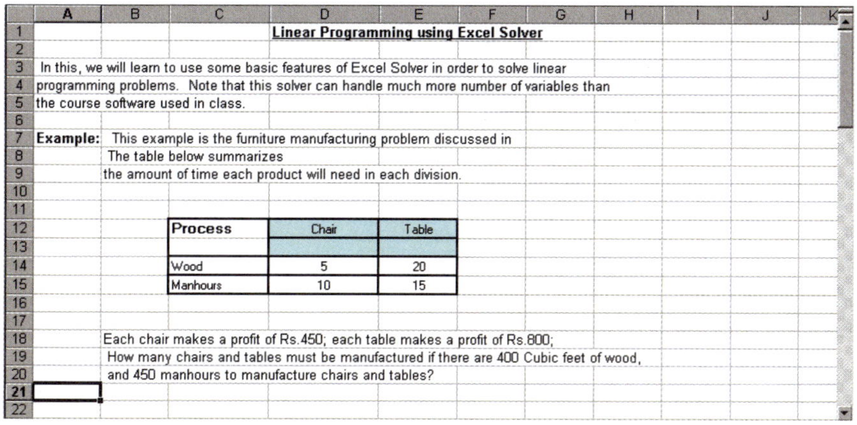

FIGURE 2.5 Problem description and setting up the columns in Excel.

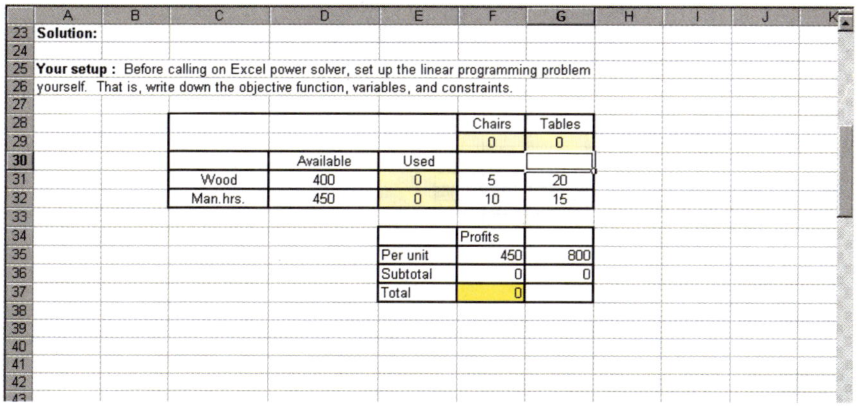

FIGURE 2.6 Setting up constraints and objective functions.

Note: Sometimes you will see $F$29 for a cell reference instead of F29. $F$29 is called an absolute reference. No matter where you copy a formula using $F$29, F29 will always be its location. See the Online Help topic on Formulas for more information.

4. To see the Excel solution for this problem, click on Tools in the menu bar. Pick the Solver option. It will give you a dialog box. Pause; look at the constraints and the objective.
5. The Excel Solver accepts the constraints in a way that is compact and follows the structure of the spreadsheet. This is summarized as follows:

Problem Specifications

Target Cell	F37	Goal is to maximize profit
Variables	F29:G29	Units of each product to build
Constraints	E31:E32 <= D31:D32	Number of hours used must be less

6. How do these constraints follow from the setup you did earlier?
7. Click on the Solve button in the dialog box.

The steps are as follows:

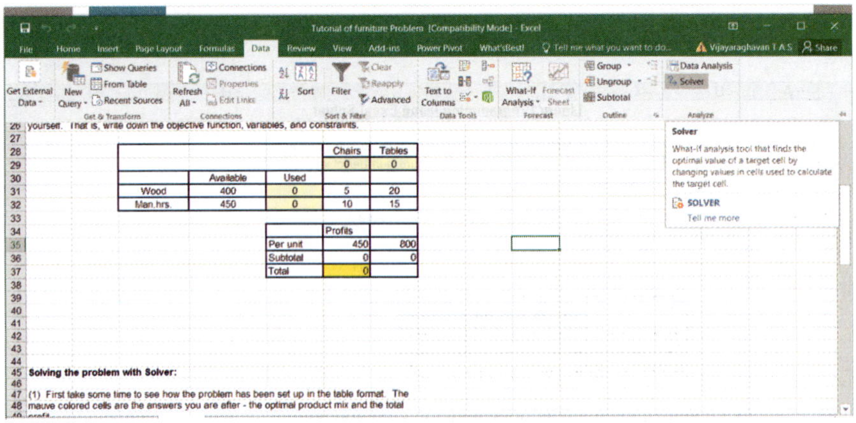

FIGURE 2.7 Using Solver menu under Tools option to set up the formulation.

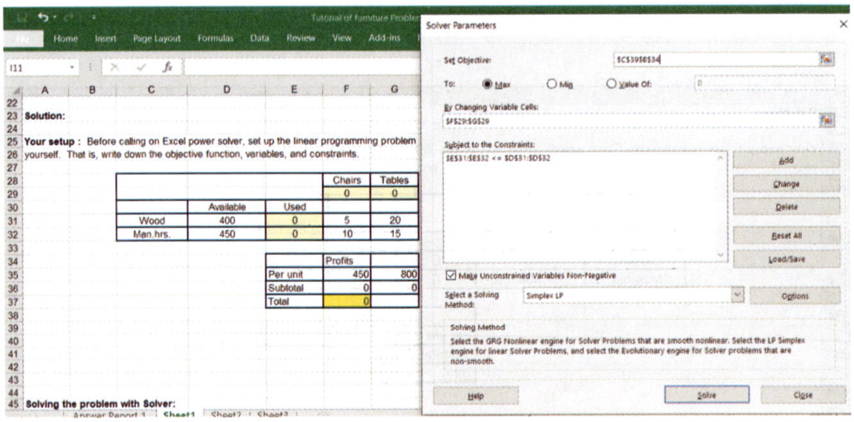

FIGURE 2.8 Entering the model description in the Solver menu.

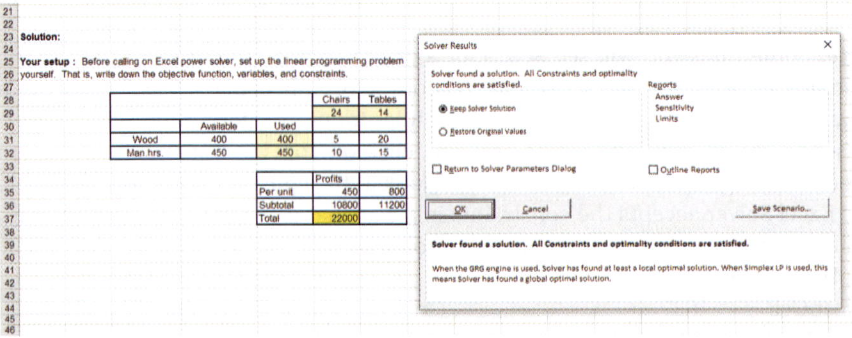

FIGURE 2.9 Solver output.

After using Solver, the setup table looks like this where the optimal solutions are seen in F29:G29 and the target cell F37 as having the objective function value.

2.7 | A FEW EXAMPLES OF FORMULATION OF LPP

We will present a few popular examples of formulations of LPP in this section to familiarize ourselves with how a situation can be formulated as an LPP. They are shown as Examples 2.2, 2.3, 2.4, 2.5, and 2.6 in the following boxes.

Solver is one of the powerful tools in Excel to solve optimization problems—both linear and nonlinear. Solver is used for many applications when we formulate a problem as an optimization problem. You will see many applications of Solver in solving many such problems in the supply chain area in various chapters in this book.

EXAMPLE 2.2 (FEED MIX PROBLEM)

A poultry farm is considering farm feed for the animals with two nutrients and six types of foods where the nutrients are available. How many units of nutrients are available from each type of food for a nutrient? How much is the minimum daily requirement with the cost of food per kilogram as given in Table 2.1.

Solution

Formulate this as an LPP to minimize the total cost of food.

TABLE 2.1 Number of units of nutrients per kilogram of food

Nutrients	1	2	3	4	5	6	Minimum Daily Requirements (Units)
Vitamin A	1	0	2	2	1	2	9
Vitamin C	0	1	3	1	3	2	19
Cost of food ($/kg)	35	30	60	50	27	22	

Let X_j be the required quantity of food j. The formulation will be as follows:

Minimize

$$35X_1 + 30X_2 + 60X_3 + 50X_4 + 27X_5 + 22X_6$$

subject to

$$X_1 + 2X_2 + 2X_3 + X_5 + 2X_6 \geq 9$$

$$X_2 + 3X_3 + X_4 + 3X_5 + 2X_6 \geq 19$$

$$X_j \geq 0$$

EXAMPLE 2.3 (INVESTMENT PROBLEM)

We will consider the following investment problem where an investor has $100,000 to invest. The options for investing in Portfolios A, B, C, D, and E and in money markets are available for him to invest. The time to invest and the returns per dollar are summarized in Table 2.2.

TABLE 2.2 Cash flow at time (for every dollar)

		0	1	2	3
From	Inv. A	−1	0.5	1	0
	Inv. B	0	−1	0.5	1
	Inv. C	−1	1.2	0	0
	Inv. D	−1	0	0	1.9
	Inv. E	0	0	−1	1.5

We have the following considerations:

1. −1 means outflow
2. At most $75,000 in any portfolio
3. Can earn interest @ 8% per annum for uninvested cash in money market funds
4. Returns from investments may be immediately reinvested
5. Cannot borrow funds

The objective is to maximize the cash on hand at the end of time 3.

Solution

The formulation is done by looking at the recursive equations based on the logic of money in hand at the time it is invested, time *t*. Let A, B, C, D, and E be the amounts to be invested in portfolios A, B, C, D, and E, respectively, and let S_0, S_1, and S_2 be the amounts to be invested in the money market at time 0, 1, and 2, respectively.

$t=0$

$$100{,}000 = \mathrm{A} + \mathrm{C} + \mathrm{D} + S_0 \tag{2.1}$$

$t=1$

$$0.5\mathrm{A} + 1.2\mathrm{C} + 1.08\, S_0 = \mathrm{B} + S_1 \tag{2.2}$$

$t=2$

$$\mathrm{A} + 0.5\mathrm{B} + 1.08\, S_1 = \mathrm{E} + S_2 \tag{2.3}$$

$t=3$

$$\text{Maximize } \mathrm{B} + 1.9\mathrm{D} + 1.5\mathrm{E} + 1.08\, S_2$$

It has to be the maximized subject to the preceding equations and

$$\mathrm{A} \le 75{,}000,\ \mathrm{B} \le 75{,}000,\ \mathrm{C} \le 75{,}000,\ \mathrm{D} \le 75{,}000,\ \mathrm{E} \le 75{,}000$$

EXAMPLE 2.4 (FLEET ASSIGNMENT PROBLEM)

We will consider a fleet assignment problem. We have three types of vehicles A, B, and C, and they are expected to operate on four routes 1, 2, 3, and 4. The capacity of vehicles, number of each type of vehicles, number of daily trips that a vehicle can make on a route, daily demand on each route, the operating cost of a type of vehicle on a route, and the penalty cost of each vehicle if passengers are not carried are given in Table 2.3.

TABLE 2.3 Data details of fleet assignment problem

Vehicle Type	Capacity (Passengers)	Number of Vehicles	Number of Daily Trips on Route			
			1	2	3	4
A	50	5	3	2	2	1
B	30	8	4	3	3	2
C	20	10	5	5	4	2
Daily Number of Customers			100	200	90	120

Associated Costs

Vehicle Type	Operating Cost per Trip on Given Route (₹)			
	1	2	3	4
A	1000	1100	1200	1500
B	800	900	1000	1000
C	600	800	800	900
Penalty Cost per Lost Customer	40	50	45	70

Solution

This can be formulated as follows: Let X_{ij} be the number of trips of ith type of vehicle on jth route. The maximum number of trips of ith type on jth route can be calculated as the number of trips of each type on a route and the number of available vehicles. For example, type A vehicle on route 1 can make a maximum of $5 \times 3 = 15$ trips as there are five vehicles available and each one can make three trips on route 1. So, this would translate into a constraint of $X_{A1} \leq 15$. The lower bound is, of course, the non-negativity, that is, $X_{A1} \geq 0$. So this would mean $0 \leq X_{A1} \leq 15$. Similar constraints can be listed for all types of vehicles on all routes. So, the constraints will be

$$
\begin{array}{lll}
0 \leq X_{A1} \leq 15 & 0 \leq X_{B1} \leq 32 & 0 \leq X_{C1} \leq 50 \\
0 \leq X_{A2} \leq 10 & 0 \leq X_{B2} \leq 24 & 0 \leq X_{C2} \leq 50 \\
0 \leq X_{A3} \leq 10 & 0 \leq X_{B3} \leq 24 & 0 \leq X_{C3} \leq 40 \\
0 \leq X_{A4} \leq 5 & 0 \leq X_{B4} \leq 16 & 0 \leq X_{C4} \leq 20
\end{array}
$$

Next, we will establish the capacity versus demand constraints for each route 1, 2, 3, and 4.

$50X_{A1} + 30X_{B1} + 20X_{C1} \leq 100$ (Since penalty is imposed for lost customers, the number of passengers lost will be $100 - 50X_{A1} - 30X_{B1} - 20X_{C1}$.)

$50X_{A2} + 30X_{B2} + 20X_{C2} \leq 200$ (The number of passengers lost will be $200 - 50X_{A2} - 30X_{B2} - 20X_{C2}$.)

$50X_{A3} + 30X_{B3} + 20X_{C3} \leq 90$ (The number of passengers lost will be $90 - 50X_{A3} - 30X_{B3} - 20X_{C3}$.)

$50X_{A4} + 30X_{B4} + 20X_{C4} \leq 120$ (The number of passengers lost will be $120 - 50X_{A4} - 30X_{B4} - 20X_{C4}$.)

The objective function will be to minimize the total operating cost plus the penalty cost.

Minimize $[\{1000X_{A1} + 1100X_{A2} + 1200X_{A3} + \cdots + 900X_{C4}\} + 40\{(100 - 50X_{A1} - 30X_{B1} - 20X_{C1})\} + 50\{(200 - 50X_{A2} - 30X_{B2} - 20X_{C2})\} + 45\{(90 - 50X_{A3} - 30X_{B3} - 20X_{C3})\} + 70\{(120 - 50X_{A4} - 30X_{B4} - 20X_{C4})\}]$

(This can be simplified to have an expression in terms of the decision variables.)

EXAMPLE 2.5 (TRIM LOSS PROBLEM)

A paper company produces paper rolls with a standard width of 20 feet each. Customer orders with different widths are produced by cutting or slitting the standard rolls. Typical orders that may be different for different days are as follows:

Typical Orders	Desired Width (feet)	Number of Rolls
1	5	150
2	7	200
3	9	300

The objective is to meet the orders with the least trim loss.

Solution

The formulation can be as follows: We have to basically determine the knife-setting combinations (variables in this context) that will fill the required orders (constraints in this context) with least trim loss area (objective for the context). The variables are the number of standard rolls that can be cut or slit according to a given knife setting. The possible setting and the requirements are presented in Table 2.4.

TABLE 2.4 Possible knife settings for formulation

Required Width	Knife Settings						Required Rolls
	1	2	3	4	5	6	
5	0	0	1	2	2	4	150
7	1	0	2	1	0	0	200
9	1	2	0	0	1	0	300
Trim Loss Length	4	2	1	3	1	0	

Let X_j be the number of rolls to be sent according to the setting j.

$$\text{Minimize } X_1 + X_2 + X_3 + X_4 + X_5 + X_6$$

subject to

$$X_3 + 2X_4 + 2X_5 + 4X_6 \geq 150$$
$$X_1 + 2X_3 + X_4 \geq 200$$
$$X_1 + 2X_2 + X_5 \geq 300$$
$$x_j \geq 0 \text{ for all } j$$

EXAMPLE 2.6 (STAFF SCHEDULING PROBLEM)

For a 24-hour cafeteria, the requirement of waiters/waitresses is as follows:

Time of Day	Minimum Number of Waitresses Required
2–6	4
6–10	8
10–14	10
14–18	7
18–22	12
22–2	4

Each waitress works for eight consecutive hours per day. The objective is to find the smallest number of waiters/waitresses required to comply with the preceding requirement.

Solution

The formulation can be as follows: Let

X_1 be the number of waiters/waitresses reporting for duty at 2 hours.
X_2 be the number of waiters/waitresses reporting for duty at 6 hours.
X_3 be the number of waiters/waitresses reporting for duty at 10 hours.
X_4 be the number of waiters/waitresses reporting for duty at 14 hours.
X_5 be the number of waiters/waitresses reporting for duty at 18 hours.
X_6 be the number of waiters/waitresses reporting for duty at 22 hours.

When each waiters/waitresses joins duty for a particular slot, they work for eight consecutive hours. This is illustrated in Figure 2.10.

So during the 6–10 slot, there will be $X_1 + X_2$ number of waiters/waitresses available (see Figure 2.10). This must be at least 8 as per the requirement. Thus, the formulation will become

$$\text{Minimize } X_1 + X_2 + X_3 + X_4 + X_5 + X_6$$

Subject to

$$X_1 + X_2 \geq 8$$
$$X_2 + X_3 \geq 10$$
$$X_3 + X_4 \geq 7$$

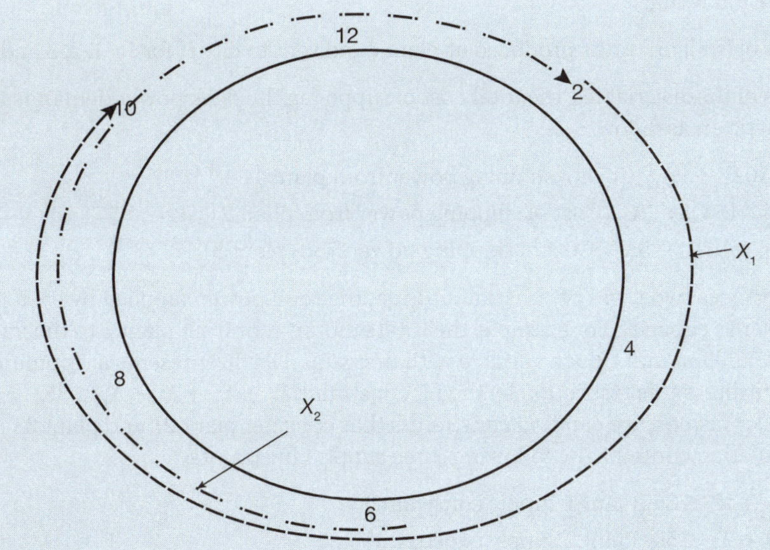

FIGURE 2.10 Illustration of duties of waiters/waitresses.

$$X_4 + X_5 \geq 12$$
$$X_5 + X_6 \geq 4$$
$$X_6 + X_1 \geq 4$$
$$X_j \geq 0$$

These preceding examples give some insights into defining decision variables in a problem environment and the formation of constraints and objective functions. Many such formulation examples are available in the books that are given in the bibliography section.

2.8 | TRANSPORTATION PROBLEM

Let us consider the following situation: (*This example is adopted with modification from Aarvik and Randolph, 1975.*)

A company has three plants that supply the needs of four cities. Each plant can supply the following numbers of units: plant 1—35 million; plant 2—50 million; plant 3—40 million (see Table 2.5). The demands in these cities are as follows: city 1—45 million; city 2—20 million; city 3—30 million; and city 4—30 million. The costs of sending 1 unit from the plant to the city depend on the distance that must be travelled and is given in Table 2.5. Formulate an LPP to minimize the cost of meeting each city's demand with the plants' available capacities.

TABLE 2.5 Shipping unit costs ($), supply, and demand

	1	2	3	4	Supply (million tons)
1	8	6	10	9	35
2	9	12	13	7	50
3	14	9	16	5	40
Demand (million tons)	45	20	30	30	

We define the following:

X_{ij} = number of (million) units produced at plant i and sent to city j (for $i = 1, 2, 3$ and $j = 1, 2, 3, 4$)

In terms of these variables, the total cost of supplying the peak power demands to cities 1–4 may be written as follows:

$8X_{11} + 6X_{12} + 10X_{13} + 9X_{14}$ (Cost of shipping power from plant 1)
$+ 9X_{21} + 12X_{22} + 13X_{23} + 7X_{24}$ (Cost of shipping power from plant 2)
$+ 14X_{31} + 9X_{32} + 16X_{33} + 5X_{34}$ (Cost of shipping power from plant 3)

The company faces two types of constraints. First, the total power supplied by each plant cannot exceed the plant's capacity. For example, the total amount sent from plant 1 to the four cities cannot exceed 35 million units. Each variable with first subscript 1 represents a shipment from plant 1, so we may express this restriction by the LP constraint $X_{11} + X_{12} + X_{13} + X_{14} \leq 35$.

In a similar fashion, we can find constraints that consider plant 2's and plant 3's capacities. The LP formulation contains the following three supply constraints:

$X_{11} + X_{12} + X_{13} + X_{14} \leq 35$ (Plant 1 supply constraint)
$X_{21} + X_{22} + X_{23} + X_{24} \leq 50$ (Plant 2 supply constraint)
$X_{31} + X_{32} + X_{33} + X_{34} \leq 40$ (Plant 3 supply constraint)

Second, we need constraints that ensure that each city will receive sufficient supply to meet its demand. For example, city 1 must receive at least 45 million units. Each variable with second subscript 1 represents a shipment of units to city 1, so we obtain the following constraint: $X_{11} + X_{21} + X_{31} \geq 45$.

Similarly, we obtain a constraint for each of the cities 2, 3, and 4. The company must satisfy the following four demand constraints:

$X_{11} + X_{21} + X_{31} \geq 45$ (City 1 demand constraint)
$X_{12} + X_{22} + X_{32} \geq 20$ (City 2 demand constraint)
$X_{13} + X_{23} + X_{33} \geq 30$ (City 3 demand constraint)
$X_{14} + X_{24} + X_{34} \geq 30$ (City 4 demand constraint)

Because all the X_{ij}'s must be non-negative, we add the non-negativity restrictions $X_{ij} \geq 0$ ($i = 1, 2, 3$; $j = 1, 2, 3, 4$).

Now combining the supply and demand constraints along with the objective function, the formulation becomes

Minimize $8X_{11} + 6X_{12} + 10X_{13} + 9X_{14} + 9X_{21} + 12X_{22} + 13X_{23} + 7X_{24} + 14X_{31} + 9X_{32} + 16X_{33} + 5X_{34}$
(Total cost of shipment)

Subject to

$$\left.\begin{aligned} X_{11} + X_{12} + X_{13} + X_{14} &\leq 35 \\ X_{21} + X_{22} + X_{23} + X_{24} &\leq 50 \end{aligned}\right\} \text{Supply constraints}$$
$$X_{31} + X_{32} + X_{33} + X_{34} \leq 40$$

$$\left.\begin{aligned} X_{11} + X_{21} + X_{31} &\geq 45 \\ X_{12} + X_{22} + X_{32} &\geq 20 \\ X_{13} + X_{23} + X_{33} &\geq 30 \end{aligned}\right\} \text{Demand constraints}$$
$$X_{14} + X_{24} + X_{34} \geq 30$$

$X_{ij} \geq 0$ ($i = 1, 2, 3$; $j = 1, 2, 3, 4$)

This is presented pictorially in Figure 2.11.

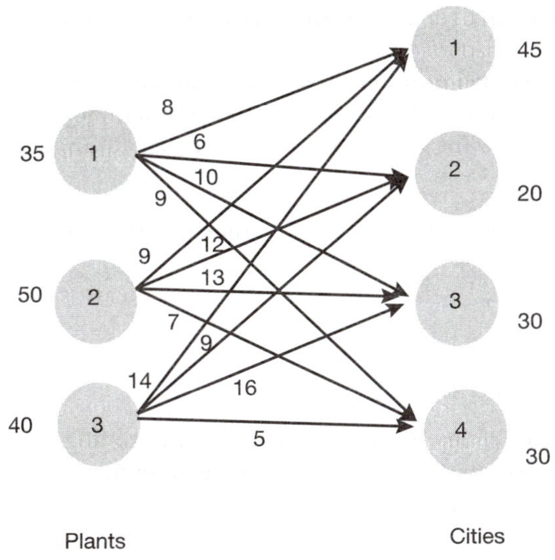

FIGURE 2.11 Graphical representation of example in Section 2.8.

2.8.1 General Description of a Transportation Problem

In general, a transportation problem is described as follows:

1. Let there be a set of m supply points (or sources or plants) from which a good is shipped. Let a_i be the total supply of units that supply point i can supply. That is, the capacity of the ith point is a_i. In the example, $m = 3$, $a_1 = 35$, $a_2 = 50$, and $a_3 = 40$.
2. Let there be a set of n demand points (or markets or cities) to which the good is shipped. Let b_j be the demand of the jth point in units. That is, the demand point j must receive at least b_j units of the shipped good. In the example, $n = 4$, $b_1 = 45$, $b_2 = 20$, $b_3 = 30$, and $b_4 = 30$.
3. Each unit produced at supply point i and shipped to demand point j incurs a variable unit cost of c_{ij}. In the example, $c_{12} = 6$.

Let X_{ij} be the number of units shipped from supply point i to demand point j. Then the general formulation of a transportation problem is as follows:

$$\text{Minimize} \sum_{i=1}^{m}\sum_{j=1}^{n} C_{ij}X_{ij}$$

Subject to

$$\sum_{j=1}^{n} X_{ij} \leq a_i \text{ for all } i = 1 \text{ to } m$$

$$\sum_{i=1}^{m} X_{ij} \geq b_j \text{ for all } j = 1 \text{ to } n$$

$$X_{ij} \geq 0 \text{ for all } i, j$$

When $\sum_i a_i = \sum_j b_j$, it is known as a balanced transportation problem. Given an unbalanced problem, it is always possible to bring it to a balanced problem by adding dummy sources or dummy destinations with appropriate costs defined as the case may be. When the problem is balanced, then all the inequalities become equations.

2.8.2 Finding Solutions to Transportation Problems

Approaches to find the optimal solutions to a transportation problem involve two stages. Initially a basic feasible solution is obtained by various methods, and then an optimal solution is obtained through an iterative method. The following methods are usually used to obtain the starting basic feasible solution.

1. North West Corner Rule
2. Row Minima
3. Column Minima
4. Matrix Minima
5. Vogel's Approximation Method (VAM)
6. Russel's Approximation Method (RAM).

Among these methods, VAM and RAM are very efficient in getting to the optimal solution faster than with the basic feasible solution obtained from the other methods.

Using the initial basic feasible solution from these methods, the simplified simplex method obtains the optimal solution through an iterative methods using the optimality and termination criteria. The method is referred to by many names: Modified Distribution Method or Stepping Stone Method or U-V Method. The exact mathematical algorithm is skipped here, and they can be seen in the textbooks mentioned in the bibliography at the end of the chapter. We will present the Excel Solver method to obtain the optimal solution in the following section.

2.8.3 Excel Solver Method

We will revisit the example in Section 2.8 and set up the Excel worksheet shown in Figure 2.12.

	C	D	E	F	G	H	I	J
3					Cities			
4		C_{ij}	1	2	3	4		Supply
5		1	8	6	10	9		35
6	Plants	2	9	12	13	7		50
7		3	14	9	16	5		40
8								
9		Demand	45	20	30	30		

	C	D	E	F	G	H	I	J
13		Decision Variable			Cities			
14		X_{ij}	1	2	3	4	LHS	Supply
15		1					=SUM(E15:H15)	35
16	Plants	2					=SUM(E16:H16)	50
17		3					=SUM(E17:H17)	40
18		LHS	=SUM(E15:E17)	=SUM(F15:F17)	=SUM(G15:G17)	=SUM(H15:H17)		
19		Demand	45	20	30	30		
21	Total Cost		=SUMPRODUCT(E5:H7,E15:H17)					

FIGURE 2.12 Excel sheet for solving the transportation problem in Section 2.8.

We use the Data option in the Menu to use Solver after setting up the worksheet, as shown in Figure 2.12. In the Solver menu, we set cell E21 as the objective cell, which is the total cost and choose Min as the direction of solving as we have to minimize the total cost. Then we add two sets of constraints: first for the supply constraints that are shown in the rows 15 to 17 for columns I and J, and second for the demand constraints that are shown in columns E to H for rows 18 to 19. Then we choose the method as the simplex method for solving. This is shown in Figures 2.13 and 2.14.

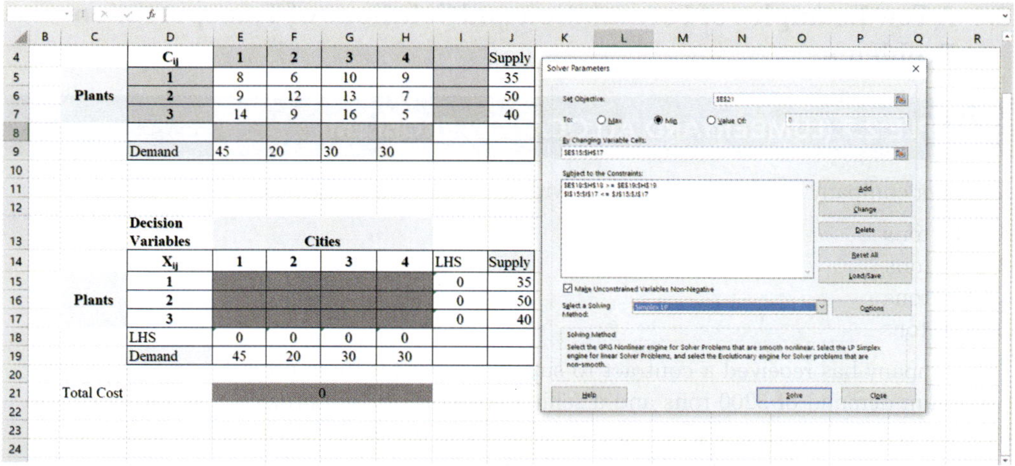

	C_{ij}	1	2	3	4		Supply
Plants	1	8	6	10	9		35
	2	9	12	13	7		50
	3	14	9	16	5		40
	Demand	45	20	30	30		

Decision Variables	X_{ij}	1	2	3	4	LHS	Supply
Plants	1					0	35
	2					0	50
	3					0	40
	LHS	0	0	0	0		
	Demand	45	20	30	30		

Total Cost: 0

FIGURE 2.13 Setting up Solver Parameters for the example.

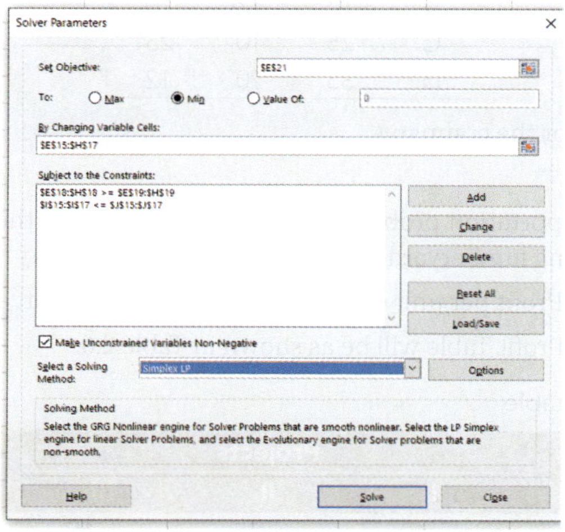

FIGURE 2.14 Solver Parameters.

After solving, the output is shown in the decision variable cells E15 to H17 and the total cost in cell E21, as shown in Figure 2.15.

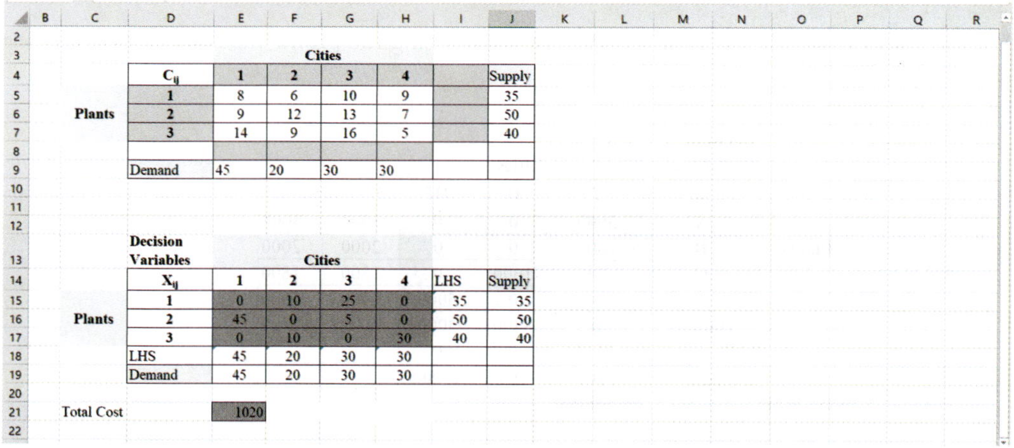

	C_{ij}	1	2	3	4		Supply
Plants	1	8	6	10	9		35
	2	9	12	13	7		50
	3	14	9	16	5		40
	Demand	45	20	30	30		

Decision Variables	X_{ij}	1	2	3	4	LHS	Supply
Plants	1	0	10	25	0	35	35
	2	45	0	5	0	50	50
	3	0	10	0	30	40	40
	LHS	45	20	30	30		
	Demand	45	20	30	30		

Total Cost: 1020

FIGURE 2.15 Solver output.

2.8.4 A Few Examples of Formulation and Solutions of Transportation Problems

EXAMPLE 2.7 (LUMBERYARD ALLOCATION PROBLEM)

A lumber company has four lumberyards with the following capacities:

A: 3000 tons
B: 2000 tons
C: 1800 tons
D: 6000 tons

The company has received a contract to supply lumber for three projects: project 1 with a maximum demand of 5200 tons and a selling price of $70/ton; project 2 with a maximum demand of $10,000 tons and a selling price of $50/ton; project 3 with a maximum demand of 10,000 tons with a selling price of $45/ton. Transportation costs per ton are as follows:

	Projects		
	I	II	III
A	10	25	30
B	18	12	20
C	25	10	25
D	35	20	12

Find the best schedule for the company.

Solution

We can set up the transportation problem as follows: We calculate the profit for each of the projects and the supplying lumberyards as

Profit per unit – Transportation cost per unit

Therefore, the Unit Profit Table will be as shown in Table 2.6.

TABLE 2.6 Unit profit table

		Projects			
	Profits	**I**	**II**	**III**	**Supply**
	A	60	25	15	3000
Plants	**B**	52	38	25	2000
	C	45	40	20	1800
	D	35	30	33	6000
	Dummy	0	0	0	12400
	Demand	5200	10000	10000	

We use Solver to obtain the best schedule by maximizing the profit. The solution will be as shown in Figure 2.16.

Decision Variables

		Cities				
	X_{ij}	I	II	III	LHS	Supply
	A	3000	0	0	3000	3000
Plants	B	2000	0	0	2000	2000
	C	200	1600	0	1800	1800
	D	0	0	6000	6000	6000
	Dummy	0	8400	4000	12400	12400
	LHS	5200	10000	10000		
	Demand	5200	10000	10000		
Total Profit		555000				

FIGURE 2.16 Optimum schedule for Example 2.7.

EXAMPLE 2.8 (WAREHOUSE-RETAIL SUPPLY PROBLEM)

A supply company has to supply to its four retail outlets from its four distribution warehouses. Shipping costs per shipment from each warehouse to each retail outlet, supply from the warehouses, and demand of the retail outlets are given in Table 2.7.

TABLE 2.7 Data table

		Retail Outlets				
	C_{ij} ($)	1	2	3	4	Supply
Warehouses	1	500	800	500	300	10
	2	200	900	700	500	20
	3	300	400	600	200	20
	4	200	500	200	400	10
	Demand	20	10	10	20	

Find the optimal allocation to minimize the total shipment cost.

Solution

We will use Solver with parameters entered as shown in Figure 2.17 and the Solver output in Figure 2.18.

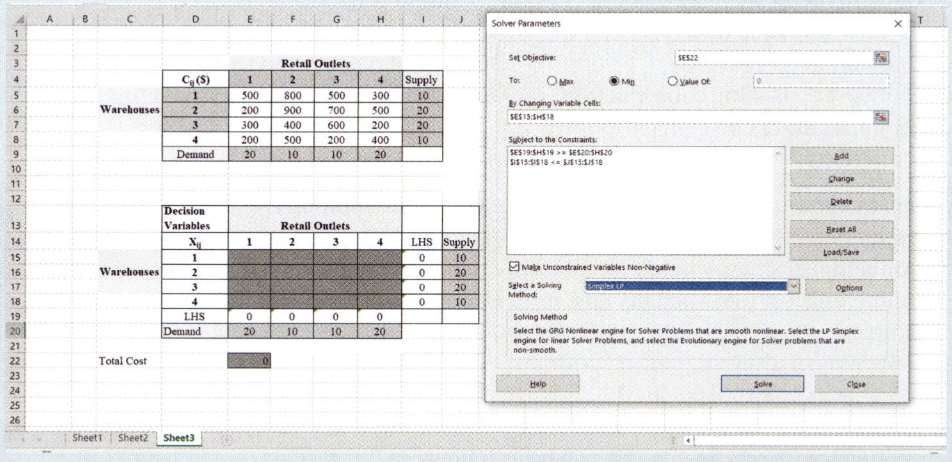

FIGURE 2.17 Solver Parameters for Example 2.8.

	Decision Variables	Retail Outlets					
	X_{ij}	1	2	3	4	LHS	Supply
	1	0	0	0	10	10	10
Warehouses	2	20	0	0	0	20	20
	3	0	10	0	10	20	20
	4	0	0	10	0	10	10
	LHS	20	10	10	20		
	Demand	20	10	10	20		
Total Cost		15000					

FIGURE 2.18 Solver output for Example 2.8.

EXAMPLE 2.9 (PRODUCTION–INVENTORY PROBLEM)

A company manufactures gear system motor bikes. The demand for its product usually occurs during July to October each year. It estimates the demand for these 4 months to be 150, 250, 200, and 350 units, respectively. The company uses part-time labor in manufacturing, and its production capacity also varies monthly. It is estimated that it can produce 100, 300, 350, and 200 units for July to October, respectively. Because the production capacity and demand for the different months do not match, a current month's demand may be satisfied in one of three ways:

1. Current month's production
2. Surplus production in an earlier month
3. Surplus production in a later month

In the first case, the production cost per unit is $45.00. In the second case, it incurs an additional holding cost of $0.60 per unit per month. In the third case, an additional penalty cost of $3.00 per unit is incurred for each month's delay. The company wishes to determine the optimal production schedule for the 4 months.

Solution

The situation can be modeled as a transportation model by recognizing the following parallels between the elements of the production–inventory problem and the transportation model.

Production–Inventory	**Transportation**
1. Production Periods i	Sources i
2. Demand Periods j	Destinations j
3. Production Capacity of period i	Supply amount of source i
4. Demand for period j	Demand at destination j
5. Unit cost consisting of production, Inventory and penalty in period i for period j	Unit cost of transportation from i to j

The unit "transportation cost" from period i to period j is computed as follows:

C_{ij} = Production cost in i, $i = j$

Production cost in i + holding cost from i to j if $i < j$

Production cost in i + penalty cost from i to j if $i > j$

For example,

$C_{11} = \$45$

$C_{24} = \$45 + (\$0.60 + \$0.60) = \$46.20$

$C_{41} = \$45 + (\$3 + \$3 + \$3) = \$54$

The resulting transportation matrix will be as follows:

C_{ij} (\$)	July	August	September	October	Capacity
July	45	45.6	46.2	46.8	100
August	48	45	45.6	46.2	300
September	51	48	45	45.6	350
October	54	51	45	45.6	200
Demand	150	250	200	350	

The optimum production schedule can be solved through Solver and the Solver output is given in Figure 2.19.

X_{ij}	July	August	Septemeber	October	LHS	Supply
July	100	0	0	0	100	100
August	50	250	0	0	300	300
Septemeber	0	0	200	150	350	350
October	0	0	0	200	200	200
LHS	150	250	200	350		
Demand	150	250	200	350		
Total Cost		43110				

FIGURE 2.19 Solver output for Example 2.9.

2.9 | ASSIGNMENT PROBLEM

The assignment problem is a special type of LPP and more specifically a transportation problem. It is an optimization problem of a one-to-one matching of two sets. For example, assigning people to jobs, raw materials to production areas, retailers to warehouses, people to jobs or machines, etc. The goal of the assignment problem is to carry out this matching at a minimum cost. We will consider the following example to explain the problem context and the formulation.

A shop floor in a firm has four machines, and four jobs have to be completed. Each machine must be assigned to complete one job. The time required to complete each job is shown in Table 2.8. If the firm wants to minimize the total completion time of all the four jobs, what will be the best assignment of each machine to each job. We will use linear programming to solve this problem.

TABLE 2.8 Machines to jobs assignment problem

		Jobs			
		1	**2**	**3**	**4**
Machines	**1**	12	6	9	6
	2	3	15	8	7
	3	8	9	4	10
	4	3	5	7	11

We define for

$X_{ij} = 1$ if machine i is assigned to job j
0 if machine i is not assigned to job j, for $i, j = 1, 2, 3, 4$

We can formulate the problems as follows:

$$\text{Minimize } 12X_{11} + 6X_{12} + 9X_{13} + 6X_{14} + 3X_{21} + 15X_{22} + 8X_{23} + 7X_{24} + 8X_{31}$$
$$+9X3_{32} + 4X_{33} + 10X_{34} + 3X_{41} + 5X_{42} + 7X_{43} + 11X_{44}$$

Subject to

$$X_{11} + X_{12} + X_{13} + X_{14} = 1$$
$$X_{21} + X_{22} + X_{23} + X_{24} = 1$$
$$X_{31} + X_{32} + X_{33} + X_{34} = 1$$
$$X_{41} + X_{42} + X_{43} + X_{44} = 1$$

(These are machine constraints that a machine is assigned to one job only.)

$$X_{11} + X_{21} + X_{31} + X_{41} = 1$$
$$X_{12} + X_{22} + X_{32} + X_{42} = 1$$
$$X_{13} + X_{23} + X_{33} + X_{43} = 1$$
$$X_{14} + X_{24} + X_{34} + X_{44} = 1$$

(These are job constraints that a job is assigned to one machine only.)

We see that this is a balanced transportation problem in which each supply point has a supply of 1 and each demand point has a demand of 1. In general, an assignment problem is a balanced transportation problem in which all supplies and demands are equal to 1. Thus, an assignment problem is characterized by the knowledge of the cost of assigning each supply point to each demand point. The assignment problem's matrix of costs is its **cost matrix**. Since there will be a high degree of degeneracy in an assignment problem when the transportation simplex method is used, it results in an inefficient way of solving assignment problems. For this reason, a simple approach—the Hungarian method (named after the Hungarian mathematician T. Konig)—is usually used to solve assignment (min) problems. The exact algorithm and the steps are skipped here, and they can be found in the textbooks listed in the bibliography at the end of the chapter. We will present the use of Solver to solve assignment problems in the following section.

2.9.1 Solver Solution to Assignment Problem

We will revisit the example in Section 2.9 and set up the Excel worksheet for Solver as shown in Figures 2.20 and 2.21.

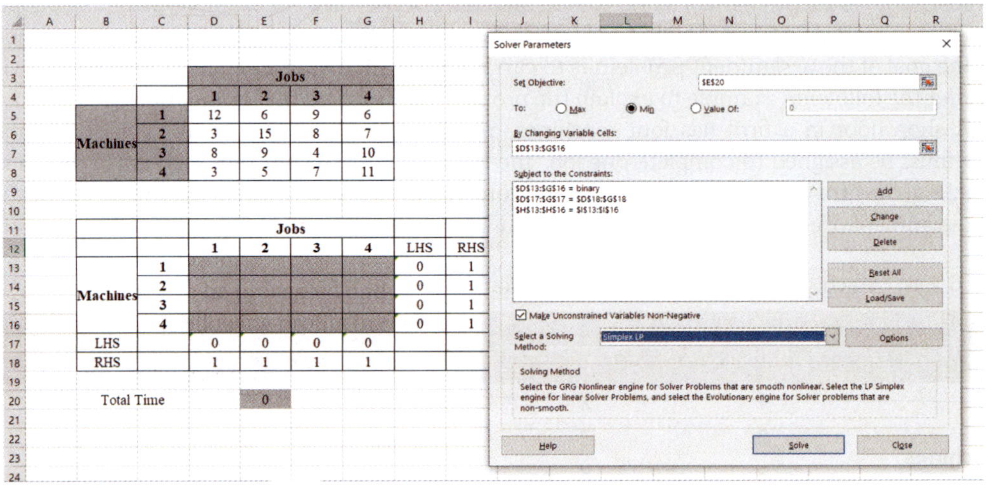

FIGURE 2.20 Solver Parameters for the example in Section 2.9.

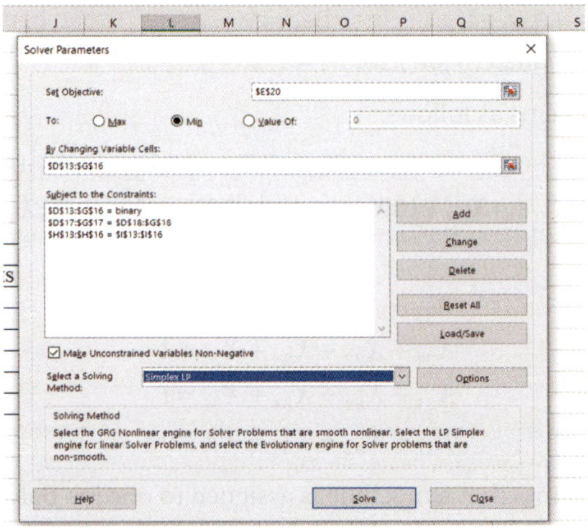

FIGURE 2.21 Solver screen for the example in Section 2.9.

The problem is solved using Solver, and the Solver output is shown in Figure 2.22. As can be seen, machine 1 is assigned to job 4, machine 2 to job 1, machine 3 to job 3, and machine 4 to job 2 with a total time of 18.

		Jobs					
		1	2	3	4	LHS	RHS
Machines	1	0	0	0	1	1	1
	2	1	0	0	0	1	1
	3	0	0	1	0	1	1
	4	0	1	0	0	1	1
LHS		1	1	1	1		
RHS		1	1	1	1		
Total Time			18				

FIGURE 2.22 Solver output for the example in Section 2.9.

2.9.2 A Few Examples of Balanced Assignment Problems

EXAMPLE 2.10 (ATHELETIC ASSIGNMENT PROBLEM)

The coach of a local athletic club in Jamshedpur needs to assign sprinters to an 800-meter relay team to send them for a district-level championship. Since most of them are very fast in all the four laps of the relay race, it is not clear which one should be assigned to which lap. The best four sprinters and their best times (in seconds) in each of the laps (of 200 meter) are given in Table 2.9.

TABLE 2.9 Data on running times

Lap	Adhi	Bhaskar	Chandra	Dhanush
1	21.37	30.2	24.5	27.4
2	32.4	26.8	28.8	29.4
3	31.3	23.7	26.8	31.2
4	22.8	27.5	29.5	24.6

The coach wishes to find out how to assign the sprinters to these four laps to minimize the total time taken to complete the laps.

Solution

We solve it by using Solver, as shown in Figure 2.23 and the Solver solution is shown in Figure 2.24.

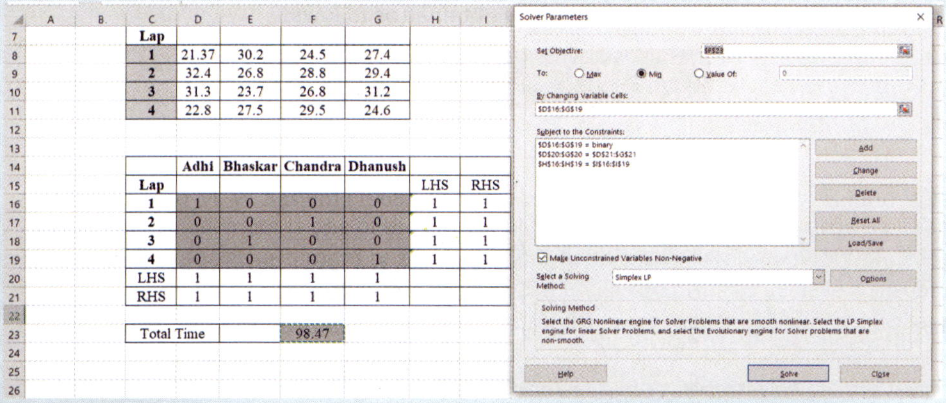

FIGURE 2.23 Solver Parameters for Example 2.10.

	Adhi	Bhaskar	Chandra	Dhanush		
Lap					LHS	RHS
1	1	0	0	0	1	1
2	0	0	1	0	1	1
3	0	1	0	0	1	1
4	0	0	0	1	1	1
LHS	1	1	1	1		
RHS	1	1	1	1		

Total Time		98.47

FIGURE 2.24 Solver output for Example 2.10.

As can be observed from Figure 2.24, sprinter Adhi is assigned to lap 1, Bhaskar to lap 3, Chandra to lap 2, and Dhanush to lap 4 with a total time of 98.47 seconds for the relay race.

EXAMPLE 2.11 (SALESFORCE ASSIGNMENT PROBLEM)

A company has four territories open and four salespersons available for the assignments. The territories are not equally rich in their sales potential. It is estimated that a typical salesperson operating in each territory would bring in the following annual sales:

Territory	Annual Sales ($)
I	60,000
II	50,000
III	40,000
IV	30,000

The four salespersons are considered to differ in ability. It is estimated that working under the same conditions, their yearly sales will be proportionately as follows:

Salesperson	Proportion
A	7
B	5
C	5
D	4

The criterion is maximum expected total sales. Find the best assignment.

Solution

If the criterion is maximum expected total sales, then the answer is to assign the best salesperson to the richest territory, the next best salesperson to the second richest, and so on. We will solve this by the assignment method using Solver.

We can construct the effectiveness matrix by taking $10,000 as one unit, and the sales proportion and the maximum sales matrix is obtained as follows:

		Sales in $10,000			
		6	5	4	3
Sales in Proportion		I	II	III	IV
7	A	42	35	28	21
5	B	30	25	20	15
5	C	30	25	20	15
4	D	24	20	16	12

We find C_{11} = Sales proportion × Sales of territory = 7 × 6 = 42. It is continued for the remaining cells in the same way.

We will use Solver to maximize the sales. The Solver Parameters and the Solver output are shown in Figures 2.25 and 2.26.

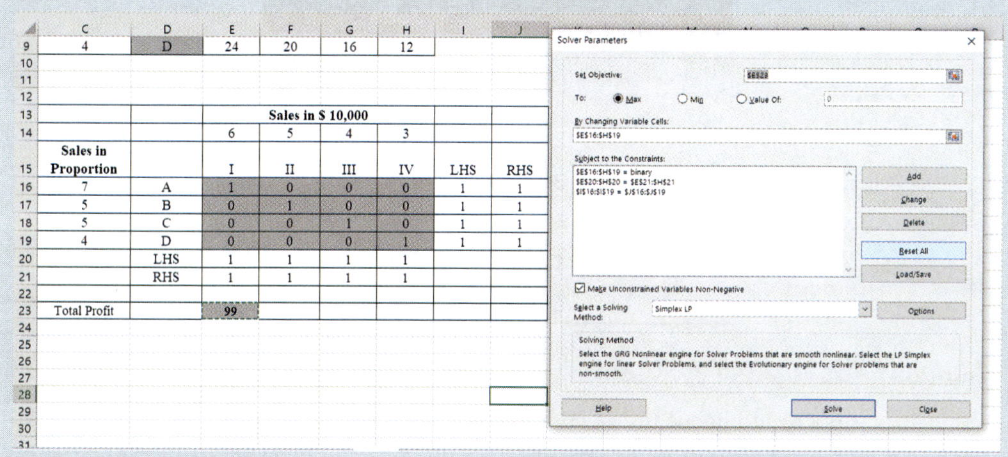

FIGURE 2.25 Solver Parameters for Example 2.11.

			Sales in $ 10,000				
		6	5	4	3		
Sales in Proportion		I	II	III	IV	LHS	RHS
7	A	1	0	0	0	1	1
5	B	0	1	0	0	1	1
5	C	0	0	1	0	1	1
4	D	0	0	0	1	1	1
	LHS	1	1	1	1		
	RHS	1	1	1	1		
Total Profit		99					

FIGURE 2.26 Solver output for Example 2.11.

As can be seen, salesperson A is assigned to territory I, B to territory II, C to territory III, and D to territory IV in order to maximize the total sales.

2.9.3 Unbalanced Assignment Problem

If the cost matrix of an assignment problem is not a square matrix (number of sources is not equal to the number of destinations), the assignment problem is called an unbalanced assignment problem. In such cases, dummy rows and columns are added in the matrix with appropriate costs or the utility in question to form a square matrix. Then the usual assignment algorithm can be applied to this resulting balanced problem.

EXAMPLE 2.12 (UNBALANCED MACHINE TO JOB ASSIGNMENT PROBLEM)

A company is faced with the problem of assigning six different machines to five different jobs. The costs are estimated as follows (in hundreds of $):

		Jobs				
		1	**2**	**3**	**4**	**5**
Machines	**1**	3	6	2	7	2
	2	3	6	3	8	5
	3	5	7	4	9	5
	4	4	7	3	8	8
	5	4	7	3	9	6
	6	7	10	5	11	7

Solution

The matrix is 6 × 5, and hence the given problem is an unbalanced assignment problem. We introduce a dummy job, Job 6, in the cost matrix in order to get the balanced assignment problem. The costs corresponding to such columns are taken as zero. The modified cost matrix is as follows:

		Jobs					
		1	**2**	**3**	**4**	**5**	**Dummy**
Machines	**1**	3	6	2	7	2	0
	2	3	6	3	8	5	0
	3	5	7	4	9	5	0
	4	4	7	3	8	8	0
	5	4	7	3	9	6	0
	6	7	10	5	11	7	0

The problem is then solved by the usual way of solving an assignment problem. We will use Solver as before to get the solution. The Solver Parameters and the Solver Output are shown in Figures 2.27 and 2.28.

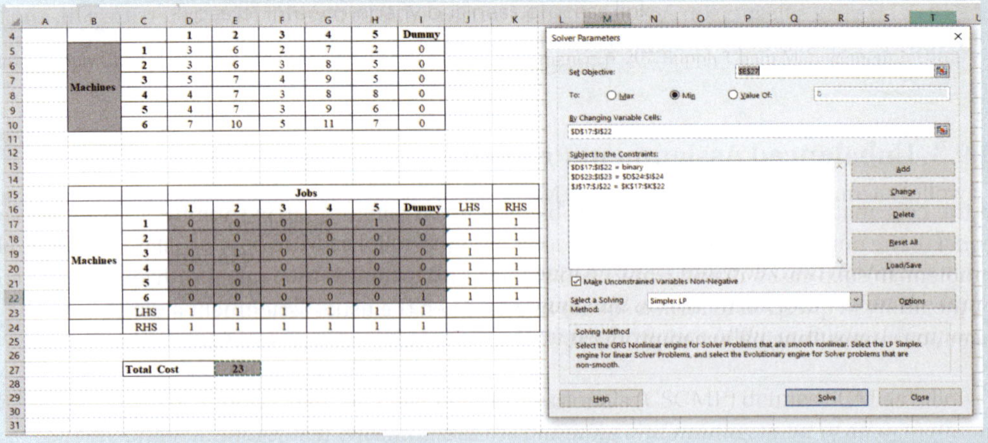

FIGURE 2.27 Solver Parameters for Example 2.12.

		Jobs							
		1	2	3	4	5	Dummy	LHS	RHS
Machines	1	0	0	0	0	1	0	1	1
	2	1	0	0	0	0	0	1	1
	3	0	1	0	0	0	0	1	1
	4	0	0	0	1	0	0	1	1
	5	0	0	1	0	0	0	1	1
	6	0	0	0	0	0	1	1	1
	LHS	1	1	1	1	1	1		
	RHS	1	1	1	1	1	1		

Total Cost	23

FIGURE 2.28 Solver output for Example 2.12.

As can be seen, machine 1 is assigned to job 5, machine 2 to job 1, machine 3 to job 2, machine 4 to job 4, machine 5 to job 3, and machine 6 is not assigned any job so as to minimize the total cost to 23.

There are many examples and exercises that are available in the textbooks listed in the bibliography at the end of the chapter.

SUMMARY

This chapter gives an overview of optimization techniques that are usually used in supply chain analytics. Methods like linear programming, transportation models, and assignment models are popularly applied in various situations in supply chain management areas. The chapter introduces briefly the historical perspectives of operations research techniques and the concept of linear programming using a simple furniture manufacturing problem. Then a graphical method is introduced to illustrate the way to depict the constraints and the feasible regions and how a problem of such nature is solved. This also gave an idea of how the simplex method works as an algorithm. Then the Excel Solver is introduced to show how Solver is a powerful tool to solve such optimization problems. Many examples from different areas of management are presented to illustrate the formulation exercise required for such problems. Later, two important special topics of linear programming, transportation problem and assignment problems, are introduced with their respective formulations and how they can be solved through Excel Solver. Many examples are given to show a variety of problems that can be solved by such approaches. This chapter is one of the building blocks for the later chapters on specific analytics that are introduced in supply chain areas. Good practice and understanding are necessary to understand the other chapters in this book.

Case Study

The following case studies are popular for discussing the Linear Programming and Transportation Problems:

1. Mertron Truck Company by Anirudh Debbar, Harvard Business Publishing (https://hbsp.harvard.edu/product/189163-PDF-ENG).
2. Kamadhenu Dairy by Desai, D. K., Mote, V. L., IIM Ahmedabad (https://cases.iima.ac.in/index.php/kamdhenu-dairy-a.html).
3. Global Oil Company Michael Trick's Page on Operations Research Material (http://www.math.clemson.edu/~mjs/courses/mthsc.810/case1-bak).
4. SinoFert Holdings Limited: Urea distribution Planning by Duan Shangshan et al., Ivey Publishing (https://hbsp.harvard.edu/product/W13398-PDF-ENG).
5. Southern Brewery, Ronald H. Ballou, *Business Logistics Management*, Chapter 13, Fourth Edition.

Exercises

1. Ruchi Company purchases Lemons and makes two kinds of pickles: Sweet and Hot. Ruchi has made it a policy that at least 30% but no more than 60% of the pickles it produces be sweet. Ruchi wants to produce up to, but not more than, the demand for each product. The marketing manager estimates that the demand for sweet pickles is 5000 bottles plus an additional 3 bottles for each 1 dollar spent on advertising and the demand for hot pickles is 4000 bottles plus an additional 5 bottles for every 1 dollar spent on advertising.

   Sweet pickles sell for $16.50 per bottle, while hot pickles sell for $18.50 per bottle. It costs $7.00 to produce a bottle of sweet pickles and $ 9.50 to produce a bottle of hot pickles. Ruchi has $200,000 to spend on producing and advertising for pickles. It wants to know how many units of each product to produce and how much to spend on advertising separately for each product to maximize profit. Formulate this as a LPP and solve it using Excel Solver.
2. A refinery takes four raw gasolines, blends them to produce three types of fuel. Here are the data. (*Source*: Murthy Katta, "Linear Programming", John Wiley & Sons)

Raw Gas Type	Octane Rating (OcR)	Available Daily (Barrels)	Price per Barrel (in $)
1	68	4000	31.02
2	86	5050	33.15
3	91	7100	36.35
4	99	4300	38.75

Fuel Type	Minimum OcR	Selling Price($)	Demand
1	95	45.15	at most 10,000 barrels/day
2	90	42.95	No limit
3	85	40.99	At least 15,000 barrels/day

The company sells raw gasoline not used in making fuels at $ 38.95/barrel if its OcR is > 90, and at $ 36.85/barrel if its OcR is ≤ 90. The problem is to determine the compositions of the three fuels to maximize total daily profit. Assume that the linearity assumptions hold good. This implies that the value for a characteristic of a mixture is the weighted average of the values that characteristic for the constituents in the mixture. Formulate this as a LP Problem and solve it using Excel Solver.

3. A certain farming organisation operates three farms of comparable productivity. The output of each farm is limited both by the usable acreage and by the amount of water available for irrigation. Following are the data for the upcoming season:

Farm	Usable Acreage	Water Available in Acre Feet
1	500	2500
2	800	3000
3	450	1200

The organisation is considering three crops for planting, which differ, primarily in their expected profit per acre and in their consumption of water. Furthermore, the total acreage that can be devoted to each of the crops is limited by the amount of appropriate harvesting equipment available.

Crop	Maximum Acreage	Water Consumption in Acre Feet per Acre	Expected Profit per Acre
A	700	5	$400
B	900	4	$300
C	500	3	$100

In order to maintain a uniform workload among the farms, it is the policy of the organisation that the percentage of the usable acreage planted must be the same at each farm. However, any combination of the crops may be grown at any of the farms. The organisation wishes to know how much of each crop should be planted at the respective farms in order to maximize expected profit. Formulate this as an LP Problem. Use Excel Solver to obtain the solution.

4. A caterer is to organise garden parties for a week. He needs a total of 160, 120,60,90,110 and 120 fresh napkins during the seven days of the week. Each new napkin costs $3. He can use soiled napkins after getting them washed from a laundry. Ordinarily, washing charges are $0.60 per napkin and they are returned after four days. However, the laundry also provides express service at a cost of $1 per napkin, in which case they are returned after two days. Determine the planning schedule the caterer should adopt to buy or send napkins to the laundry so as to minimize the cost in the mixture. Formulate this as a LP Problem. Obtain the Solution using Excel Solver.
5. The following table reflect unit profits(Rs.). You are required to determine the **profit maximization** solution.

		Destination			Supply
		1	2	3	
	1	10	15	40	400
Origin	2	5	20	35	600
	3	15	10	30	500
Demand		800	600	400	

6. Solve the following Selection problem using Transportation Method. We are given the available graduates from management institutes and the demands of various regions of a Consulting Company with unit cost of selection and recruitment in dollars.

	Region-A	Region-B	Region-C	Availability
IIM-A	75	60	69	50
IIM-B	79	73	68	100
XLRI	85	76	70	50
Requirements	80	90	100	

Obtain the optimal solution.

7. ABC manufacturing company wishes to develop a monthly production schedule for the next few months. Depending upon the sales commitments, the company can either keep the production constant, allowing fluctuations in inventory or inventories can be maintained at a constant level with a fluctuating production. Fluctuating production necessitates in working overtime, the cost of which is estimated to be double the normal production cost of $12 per unit. Fluctuating inventories result in inventory carrying cost of $.2 per unit per month. If the company fails to fulfill its sales commitment, it incurs a shortage cost of $4 per unit per month. The production capacities for the next 3 months are shown as follows:

	Production Capacity		Sales
Month	Regular	Overtime	
1	50	30	60
2	50	0	120
3	60	50	40

Determine the optimal production schedule.

8. A company has three factories at A, B and C which supply to warehouses 1,2,3 and 4. The factory capacities are 230, 280 and 180, respectively, for regular production. If overtime production is utilised, the capacities can be **increased to** 300, 360 and 190, respectively. The current warehouse requirements are 165, 175, 205 and 165, respectively. Unit transportation costs in dollars between factories and the warehouses are as follows:

	1	2	3	4
A	7	8	9	11
B	5	11	8	7
C	4	23	3	12

Determine the optimum distribution for the company to minimize costs if the incremental unit overtime costs are \$5, \$4, and \$6, respectively, for the three factories. Obtain the Optimum solution.

9. Five jobs are to be processed and five machines are available. Any machine can process any job, with the following profits in rupees:

		Machines				
		1	2	3	4	5
Job	1	40	37	36	21	40
	2	35	24	28	28	37
	3	27	25	33	30	36
	4	34	33	40	36	40
	5	43	38	42	37	38

What is the maximum profit that may expected if an optimum assignment is made and what is the optimal assignment?

10. There are five employees available to perform four jobs. The time it takes each person to perform each job is given in the following table. Determine the assignment of employees to jobs that minimizes the total time required to perform the four jobs.

	Time (Hours)			
	Job 1	Job 2	Job 3	Job 4
Amar	22	18	30	18
Akbar	18	-	27	22
Anthony	26	20	28	28
Tom	16	22	-	14
Dick	21	-	25	28

Note: Dashes indicate person cannot do that particular job.

11. An airfreight company picks up and delivers freight where customers require. The company has two types of aircrafts X and Y with equal loading capacities but different operating costs. These are shown as follows:

Type of Aircraft	Operating Costs ($/km)	
	Empty	Loaded
X	1.00	2.00
Y	1.50	3.00

The present four locations of the air crafts which the company has are: J-X; K-Y; L-Y; and M-X. Four customers of the company located at A, B, C and D want to transport nearly the same load to their final destinations. The final destinations are at a distance of 600, 300, 1000 and 500 kms. from the loading points A, B, C and D, respectively.

Distance (in kilometers) between the aircraft and the loading points are as follows:

Aircraft Location	Loading Points			
	A	B	C	D
J	200	200	400	100
K	300	100	300	300
L	400	100	100	500
M	200	200	400	200

Determine the **allocations,** which will minimize the total cost of transportation. Problem can be considered only up to loading points only and not about returning.

12. A Company has one surplus truck in each of the cities A, B, C, D, and E and one deficit truck in each of the cities 1, 2, 3, 4, 5, and 6. The distance between the cities in km is as shown below.

	1	2	3	4	5	6
A	12	10	15	22	18	8
B	10	18	25	15	16	12
C	11	10	3	8	5	9
D	6	14	10	13	13	12
E	8	12	11	7	13	10

Find the assignment of trucks from cities in surplus to cities in deficit so that the total distance covered by vehicles **is minimum.**

Bibliography

1. Ackoff, R. F. and M. W. Sasieni (1968). ***Fundamentals of Operations Research.*** John Wiley & Sons.
2. Ackoff, R. L. and P. Rivett (1967). ***A Manager's Guide to Operations Research.*** John Wiley & Sons.
3. Churchman, C. W., R. E. Ackoff, and E. L. Arnoff (1957). ***Introduction to Operations Research.*** John Wiley.
4. Dantzig, G. B. (1963). ***Linear Programming and Extensions.*** Princeton University Press.
5. Enrick, N. L. (1964). ***Management Operations Research.*** Hotel Rinehart and Winston.

6. Gass, S. I. (1975). *Linear Programming: Methods and Applications,* 5th ed. Tata-McGraw Hill, International Student Edition. Dover Publications Inc.
7. Hadley, G. (1962). *Linear Programming.* Addison Wesley.
8. Hillier, F. S. and G. J. Lieberman (1967). *Introduction to Operations Research.* McGraw Hill.
9. Lawrence, L. (1981). *Quantitative Methods for Business Decision.* Harcourt Brace Jovanovich.
10. Levin, R. I. and C. A. Kirkpatrick (1979). *Quantitative Approaches to Management.* McGraw Hill.
11. Loomba, N. P. (1964). *Linear Programming: An Introductory Analysis.* Tata-McGraw Hill.
12. Moore, P. G. (1968). *Basic Operational Research.* Sir Isaac Pitman & Sons.
13. Murty, K. G. (1983). *Linear Programming.* Wiley.
14. Sasieni, M., A. Yaspan, and L. Friedman (2013). *Operations Research: Methods and Problems.* John Wiley.
15. Taha, H. A. (1967). *Operations Research: An Introduction.* Macmillan Inc.
16. Vanderbei, R. J. (2014). *Linear Programming: Foundations and Extensions*, 4th ed. Springer.
17. Vatter, A. P., S. P. Bradley, S. C. Frey Jr., and B. B. Jackson (1978). *Quantitative Methods in Management: Text and Cases.* Richard D. Irwin.
18. Vazsonyi, A. (1963). *Scientific Programming in Business and Industry.* John Wiley & Sons.
19. Wagner, H. M. (1975). *Principles of Operations Research.* Prentice-Hall.
20. Wayne L. Winston (1994). *Operations Research: Applications and Algorithms*, Duxbury Resource Center.
21. Wicks, C. T. and G. A. Yeddall (1971). *Operational Research.* Pan Books Ltd.

SECTION

III

Facilities Location and Warehousing Decisions

III

CHAPTER 3

Facility Locations and Discrete Location Models

LEARNING OBJECTIVES

After reading this chapter, you would be able to:

- Understand why locational considerations are important in warehousing decisions and the basic types of problems in locating facilities in a supply chain network.
- Locate single facility using the Center of Gravity (COG) method.
- Locate multiple facilities using the multi-COG method.
- Formulate different types of discrete location problems using mathematical programming approaches and use of them in practice.
- Use Excel Solver to solve such formulations.

3.1 | INTRODUCTION

The efficient and effective movement of goods from raw material sources to conversion and processing facilities, manufacturing plants, assembly plants, distribution centers and warehouses, retailers, and customers is critical in today's competitive environment. Such facilities in the supply chain network are key to a supply chain's success. The role of warehousing in a supply chain is a valued-added function due to varied activities in a warehouse. Supply chain management deals with not only the movement of goods but also strategic decisions about where to locate plants, warehouses, and distribution centers besides decisions about production and inventory.

For a supply chain to be more effective and efficient, location decisions are the most critical and difficult decisions. The other supply chain performance drivers like transportation and inventory decisions can often be changed on relatively short notice in response to changes in the operating environment such as the availability of raw materials, labor, component prices, transportation costs, inventory holding costs, exchange rates, and tax norms. Information-sharing decisions are also relatively flexible and can be altered in response to changes in corporate strategies and alliances. But facility location decisions are often fixed and difficult to change even in the intermediate term. For example, the location of a multibillion-dollar automobile manufacturing and assembly plant cannot be changed because of the situations mentioned earlier. Even facilities like modern distribution centers or warehouses with huge investments on construction with semi-automated or automated material-handling equipment are also difficult to relocate. Inefficient location decisions of such facilities will result in excess costs being incurred throughout the lifetime of the facilities, no matter how well the other decisions are made that respond to the changing needs of the markets. More on this can be seen in (2) and (7) for in-depth understanding. Here we focus more on the analytical side of such decisions and present various analytical tools and approaches to locate facilities in a supply chain network.

Facility location problems have been the focus of many researchers in the operations research domain for modeling, algorithm development, and complexity theory. Applications of these models are found in locating public utilities like fire stations, police stations, medical centers and hospitals, warehouses, service centers, and retail outlets to mention a few. Location theory and modeling has its roots in the pioneering work of Weber in 1909 and later by Hotelling in 1929. Location models are broadly classified into four major groups: analytical models, continuous models, network models, and discrete models.

Analytic models are simple location models that assume that the demand is distributed in some way (e.g., uniformly) over a given service area and that facilities can be located anywhere within the area. They are usually solved using calculus or other simple techniques.

Continuous models assume that demands occur only at discrete points. The Weber problem is a classic example of this type. The location of demand point i is given by (x_i, y_i) for $i = 1, 2, ..., n$, and the intensity of demand at this location is given by h_i. The Weber problem seeks the location (X, Y) of a single facility to minimize the demand-weighted total distance between the facility and the demand points.

Network models assume that demands exist and facilities can be located only in a network composed of nodes and links. Usually demands occur only on the nodes, while facilities can be located anywhere in the network.

Discrete models assume that there may or may not be an underlying distance metric and distances or costs between any pair of nodes may be assumed under some rule like the Euclidean, Manhattan, network, or great circle distances. Demands generally exist on the nodes, and the facilities are restricted to a finite set of candidate locations. We will discuss about some of the popular models in this chapter.

3.2 | SINGLE FACILITY LOCATION PROBLEMS

Most of the single facility problems are approached and solved conceptually by using simple applied mathematical tools and computers. These are usually locating a single plant, terminal, warehouse, or retail/service point. It is referred to as the exact Center of Gravity (COG) approach, the grid method, or the centroid method. We will describe the method briefly in the following section.

Location of facilities in a supply chain network is a strategic decision, and a scientific approach will help in determining them more efficiently. Factors affecting the choice of locations may include economic, social, and political considerations. A good understanding of them is essential before embarking on a scientific approach, as those factors will be the basic inputs on which such scientific approaches are built on.

3.2.1 Center of Gravity Method

Given a set of supply (or source) and demand (or destination) points with their respective volumes that are to be moved to and from a facility of unknown location and their associated transportation rates, the problem is to find the location of that facility. We seek to minimize the total transportation cost. The approach is simple since the transportation rate and the point volume are the only location factors. This model is classified mathematically as a static continuous location model. These methods use the grid approach where the source and destination points are shown in a (X, Y) grid and with coordinates as shown in Figure 3.1.

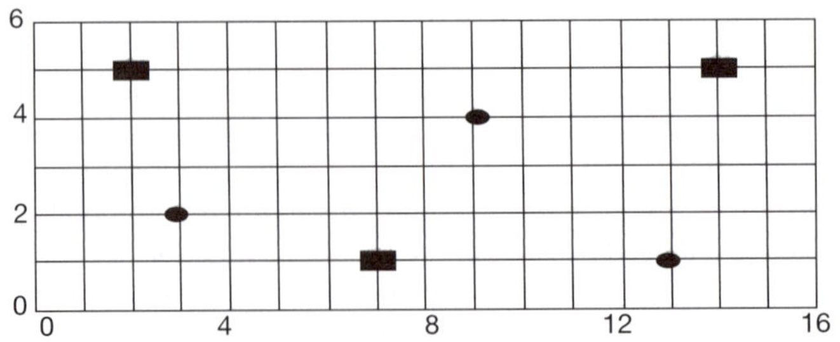

FIGURE 3.1 Example representation of locations in (X, Y) grid.

Let us assume that the sources and the markets are located at (X_i, Y_i) and that the location of the unknown facility be denoted by $(\bar{X}, \bar{Y})$. We will use the following notations:

1. TC: total transportation cost
2. V_i: volume at point i
3. R_i: transportation rate at point i
4. d_i: distance to point i from the facility to be located $(\bar{X}, \bar{Y})$
5. K: scaling factor

where

$$d_i = K\sqrt{(X_i - \bar{X})^2 + (Y_i - \bar{Y})^2} \tag{3.1}$$

The problem becomes finding the optimal location $(\bar{X}, \bar{Y})$ by minimizing

$$TC = \sum V_i d_i R_i \tag{3.2}$$

With the help of calculus, we can find the optimal locations as follows:

Equation *X*

$$\bar{X} = \frac{\sum_i (V_i R_i X_i)/d_i}{\sum_i (V_i R_i)/d_i}$$

Equation *Y*

$$\bar{Y} = \frac{\sum_i (V_i R_i Y_i)/d_i}{\sum_i (V_i R_i)/d_i}$$

Although the optimal coordinates are obtained, it is not straightforward that we get the coordinates by plucking in the values of V_i, R_i, X_i, Y_i, and d_i. There is a circular problem where the expressions for $\bar{X}, \bar{Y}$ require d_i's, and the respective d_i's require $\bar{X}, \bar{Y}$. Hence, we have to break this and have an iterative process as follows:

Step 1: Determine the (X, Y) coordinates of each source and demand points, the volumes, and transportation rates.

Step 2: Approximate the initial location from the COG by omitting the d_i terms as follows:

$$\bar{X} = \frac{\sum_i (V_i R_i X_i)}{\sum_i (V_i R_i)}, \bar{Y} = \frac{\sum_i (V_i R_i Y_i)}{\sum_i (V_i R_i)}$$

Step 3: Using the coordinates from Step 2, calculate d_i by Eq. (3.1).

Step 4: Substitute the values from Step 3 into Eqs. (X) and (Y) above and compute the coordinates $\bar{X}, \bar{Y}$.

Step 5: Recalculate d_i based on the new $\bar{X}, \bar{Y}$.

Step 6: Repeat Steps 4 and 5 until the changes in successive iterations are very little.

Step 7: Finally, calculate the total cost for the best location, if desired, by using Eq. (3.2).

EXAMPLE 3.1

Let us consider the example given in Table 3.1.

TABLE 3.1 Example of a single facility problem

Point (i)	Products	Total Volume Moving V_i	Transportation Rate per Weighted Distance	Coordinates X_i	Y_i
1-P1	A	5000	0.08	4	8
2-P2	B	8000	0.08	9	12
3-P3	C	2000	0.08	2	4
4-M1	ABC	4000	0.10	7	5
5-M2	ABC	5000	0.10	9	9
6-M3	ABC	6000	0.10	10	12

The Step 1 and Step 2 computations are shown in Tables 3.2 and 3.3.

Step 1

TABLE 3.2 Computations of initial coordinates of COG

	X_i	Y_i	V_i	R_i	V_iR_i	$V_iR_iX_i$	$V_iR_iY_i$
P1	4	8	5000	0.08	400.0	1600	3200
P2	9	12	8000	0.08	640.0	5760	7680
P3	2	4	2000	0.08	160.0	320	640
M1	7	5	4000	0.1	400.0	2800	2000
M2	9	9	5000	0.1	500.0	4500	4500
M3	10	12	6000	0.1	600.0	6000	7200
				SUM	**2700.0**	**20980**	**25220**

X-BAR **7.77037** Y-BAR **9.340741**

Step 2

TABLE 3.3 Computations of using initial coordinates to obtain the next set of coordinates

	X_i	Y_i	V_i	R_i	d_i	V_iR_i	V_iR_i/d_i	$V_iR_iX_i/d_i$	$V_iR_iY_i/d_i$
P1	4	8	5000	0.08	80.03	400.00	4.998	19.992	39.983
P2	9	12	8000	0.08	58.60	640.00	10.922	98.301	131.068
P3	2	4	2000	0.08	157.25	160.00	1.017	2.035	4.070
M1	7	5	4000	0.1	88.17	400.00	4.537	31.756	22.683
M2	9	9	5000	0.1	25.52	500.00	19.593	176.337	176.337
M3	10	12	6000	0.1	69.41	600.00	8.645	86.448	103.738
						SUM	**49.712**	**414.869**	**477.878**

X-BAR **8.345** Y-BAR **9.613**

Note: $d_1 = 20\sqrt{(4-7.77)^2 + (8-9.341)^2} = 80.03$

The subsequent iterations will be as follows:

Iteration	X Coordinate	Y Coordinate	Cost
0	7.770	9.341	184,346.62←COG
1	8.345	9.613	178,134.44
2	8.568	9.728	177,104.55
3	8.626	9.791	176,964.62
4	8.638	9.838	176,911.33
5	8.641	9.877	176,878.13
6	8.642	9.908	176,856.33
7	8.643	9.933	176,841.89
8	8.645	9.954	176,832.28
9	8.646	9.971	176,825.85
10	8.647	9.985	176,821.52
11	8.648	9.996	176,818.61
12	8.649	10.006	176,816.64
13	8.650	10.014	176,815.30
14	8.651	10.020	176,814.39
15	8.651	10.025	176,813.77
16	8.652	10.030	176,813.35
17	8.652	10.033	176,813.06
18	8.652	10.036	176,812.87
32	8.654	10.049	176,812.44

The final facility location will be at 8.65 and 10.05 with a total cost of 176,812.44.

However, this can be easily computed using Excel Solver as follows: We set up Table 3.2 in an Excel sheet along with two more columns for *d* and cost. We use the formula for computing distance from the initial $(\bar{X}, \bar{Y})$ and compute the cost as Volume × Distance × Rate (V*d*R). The screenshot is shown in Figure 3.2.

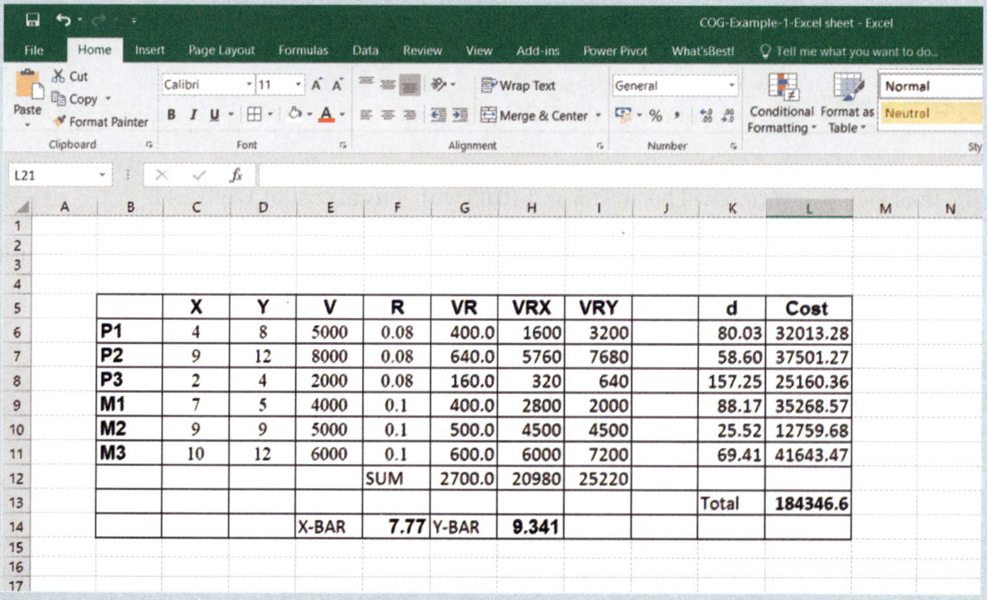

	X	Y	V	R	VR	VRX	VRY		d	Cost
P1	4	8	5000	0.08	400.0	1600	3200		80.03	32013.28
P2	9	12	8000	0.08	640.0	5760	7680		58.60	37501.27
P3	2	4	2000	0.08	160.0	320	640		157.25	25160.36
M1	7	5	4000	0.1	400.0	2800	2000		88.17	35268.57
M2	9	9	5000	0.1	500.0	4500	4500		25.52	12759.68
M3	10	12	6000	0.1	600.0	6000	7200		69.41	41643.47
				SUM	2700.0	20980	25220			
									Total	184346.6
			X-BAR	7.77	Y-BAR	9.341				

FIGURE 3.2 COG solving through Excel.

We use the Solver option in Data and choose the Total Cost Cell L13 as the Objective Cell and choose to Minimize it by taking Cell F14 and H14 as variables. Then we choose the Nonlinear option for solving, as shown in Figure 3.3.

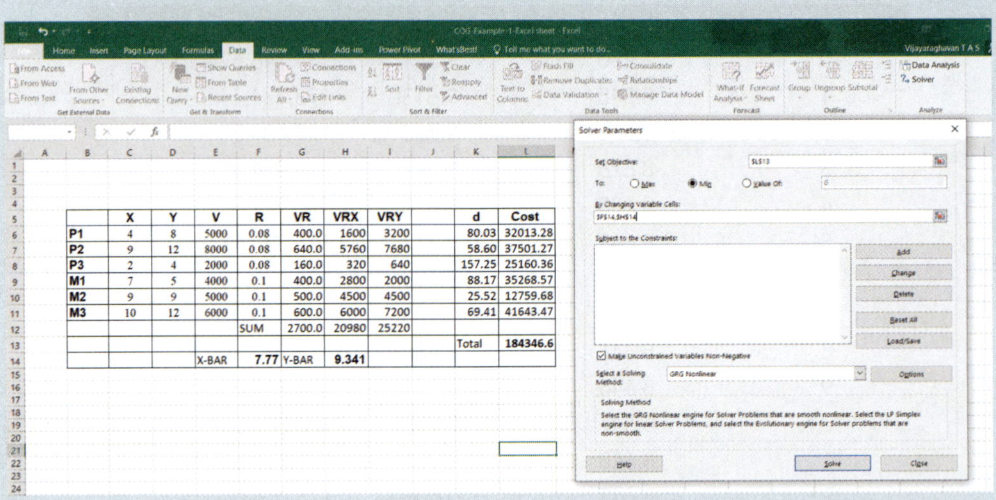

FIGURE 3.3 Solver steps for the COG example.

The Solve option gives the optimal solution as shown earlier and as given in Figure 3.4.

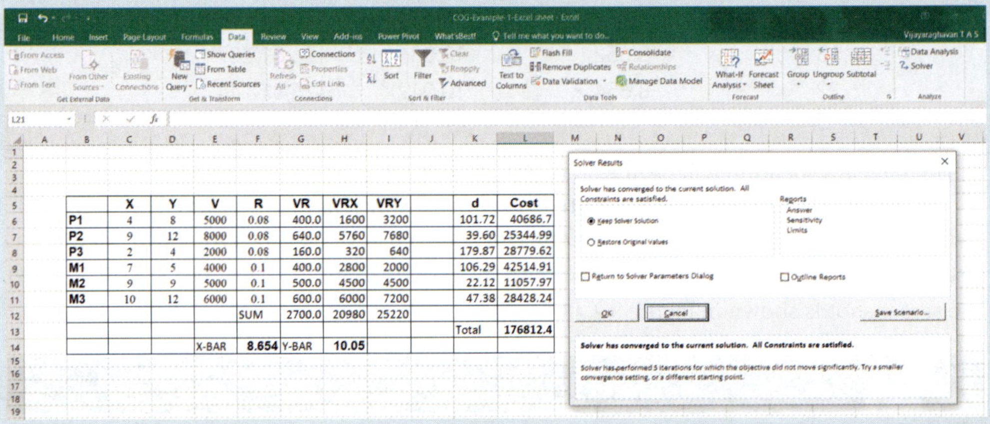

FIGURE 3.4 Solver solution for the COG problem.

The final facility location will be at 8.65 and 10.05 with a total cost of 176812.44.

Center of gravity is one of the easiest methods in determining a single facility using the simple concept of weighted average of the forces on a given set of points and determining the center of gravity of them as the best location. With less data and less mathematical complications, this method is useful for many practical applications.

The COG approach of locating a single facility is a good search method for the "best" solution with enough reality. It is also simplified due to the following reasons:

1. Demand concentrated at points
2. Choice based on variable costs
3. Transportation cost proportional to distance
4. Straight line distance or simple distance metrics used
5. Choice not dynamic

Although single facility location problems are simple to discuss, in practice we come across more complex problems. The primary difference being that many a time, we need multiple facilities and not a single facility. Some of the basic decision issues in such general warehouse location problems are as follows:

1. How many warehouses should there be in the logistics network?
2. How large should they be?

3. Where should they be located?
4. Which customers should be assigned to a warehouse?
5. Which warehouses should be assigned to which plant, vendor, or port?
6. Which products should be stocked in which warehouse?
7. Which products should be shipped directly from plant(s) to customers?

3.3 | MULTIPLE FACILITY LOCATION PROBLEMS

Multiple facility location problems are more complex and are those that most firms face in their supply chain network design decisions. These involve a trade-off between several costs, which include the following:

1. Inbound and outbound transportation costs
2. Storage and handling costs
3. Inventory carrying costs
4. Production/purchase costs
5. Facility fixed costs

A few constraints are important to consider while deciding the number of locations and the locations themselves:

1. Customer service constraints
2. Facility capacity restrictions
3. Throughput policy constraints
4. Production capacity constraints
5. Facility, plant, and customer assignment constraints
6. Many more constraints specific to organizations

Mathematical programming approaches are usually popular for these types of problems, which attempt to search for the best combinations of facilities to minimize costs within a reasonable computational time and which do not require enormous amounts of data for analysis. The trade-offs can be understood by Figure 3.5.

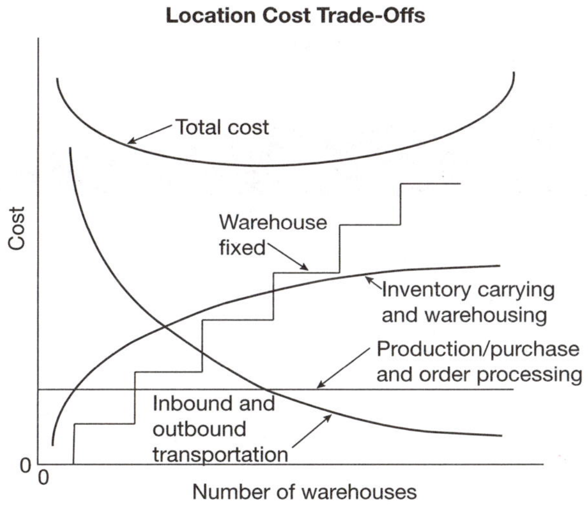

FIGURE 3.5 Cost trades-offs in locating facilities.

We have seen the application of COG for locating a single facility in the previous section. A similar approach can also be applied for locating multiple facilities using the multi-COG approach.

3.3.1 Multiple Centers of Gravity

Multiple COG is usually formulated as a basic COG model and can search for the best locations for a selected number of sites. The other cost drivers such as fixed costs, handling costs, and inventory costs are usually handled outside the model. The search procedure for a multi-COG is as follows:

1. Rank demand points from the highest to the lowest volume.
2. Use the largest *P* as the initial facility locations and assign the remaining demand centers to these locations.
3. Compute the COG of the *P* locations.
4. Reassign all demand centers to the *P* COGs based on proximity.
5. Re-compute the COGs and repeat the demand center assignments, stopping this iterative process when there is no further change in the assignments or COGs.

Although the logic of multi-COG is straightforward from the concept of simple COG, it may involve many iterations and may end up with solutions that may not be as simple as the one we obtained in COG. But it has its own practical use to avoid mathematical rigor in solving locational problems.

EXAMPLE 3.2

Table 3.4 gives the details of an example with 10 markets, and we decide to choose three locations for the facilities.

TABLE 3.4 Example for using multi-COG method

Markets	X Coordinate	Y Coordinate	Volume	Rate
M1	2	1	3,000,000	0.02
M2	5	2	5,000,000	0.015
M3	9	1	17,000,000	0.002
M4	7	4	12,000,000	0.0013
M5	10	5	10,000,000	0.0012
M6	2	5	9,000,000	0.0015
M7	2	7	24,000,000	0.002
M8	4	7	14,000,000	0.0014
M9	5	8	23,000,000	0.0024
M10	8	8	30,000,000	0.0011

A few iterations are shown in Tables 3.5, 3.6, and 3.7.

TABLE 3.5 Iteration 1

Location	X	Y	V	R	M10	M7	M9
M10	8	8	30,000,000	0.0011			
M7	2	7	24,000,000	0.002			
M9	5	8	23,000,000	0.0024			
M3	9	1	17,000,000	0.002	353.5534	460.9772	403.1129
M8	4	7	14,000,000	0.0014	206.1553	100	70.71068
M4	7	4	12,000,000	0.0013	206.1553	291.5476	223.6068
M5	10	5	10,000,000	0.0012	180.2776	412.3106	291.5476
M6	2	5	9,000,000	0.0015	335.4102	100	212.132
M2	5	2	5,000,000	0.015	335.4102	291.5476	300
M1	2	1	3,000,000	0.02	460.9772	300	380.7887

	COG Location		
M10, M3, M4, M5,	8	8	M10
M7, M6, M1	2	5	M6
M9, M8, M2	5	2	M2

TABLE 3.6 Iteration 2

			M10	M6	M2
M10	8	8			
M6	2	5			
M2	5	2			
M3	9	1	353.5534	403.1129	206.1553
M8	4	7	206.1553	141.4214	254.951
M4	7	4	206.1553	254.951	141.4214
M5	10	5	180.2776	400	291.5476
M7	2	7	304.1381	100	291.5476
M9	5	8	150	212.132	300
M1	2	1	460.9772	200	158.1139

	COG Location		
M10, M5, M9	10	5	M5
M6, M8, M7, M1	2	5	M6
M2, M3, M4	5	2	M2

TABLE 3.7 Iteration 3

			M5	M6	M2
M5	10	5			
M6	2	5			
M2	5	2			
M3	9	1	206.1553	403.1129	206.1553
M8	4	7	316.2278	141.4214	254.951
M4	7	4	158.1139	254.951	141.4214
M10	8	8	180.2776	335.4102	335.4102
M7	2	7	412.3106	100	291.5476
M9	5	8	291.5476	212.132	300
M1	2	1	447.2136	200	158.1139

M5, M3, M10
M6, M8, M7, M9, M1
M2, M4

Finally, the iterations will converge with M7, M3, and M9 as the facilities. The markets 1, 6, and 7 will be attached to M7, markets 2, 3, 4, and 5 will be attached to M3, and markets 8, 9, and 10 will be attached to M9 as the final solution with a total cost of 16,586,090.

The multi-COG model can be of great use when it comes to the location of truck maintenance terminals, public facilities such as offices, police and fire stations, medical facilities, facilities where transportation cost (rather than inventory carrying cost and facility fixed cost) is the driving factor in location decisions, and as a suggested set of sites for further evaluation.

3.4 MATHEMATICAL FORMULATIONS OF POPULAR LOCATION PROBLEMS

In this section, we will discuss six popular basic facility location models: (1) set covering, (2) maximal covering, (3) P-median, (4) fixed charge (with variants), (5) P-center, and (6) P-dispersion.

In all these models, the underlying network is given with details on the locations of the demands to be served by the facilities and the locations of existing facilities in a few cases. The general problem is to locate new facilities to optimize some objective function. Distance or some measure that is functionally related to distance (e.g., travel time or cost, demand satisfaction) is fundamental to such problems. Consequently, we have classified them according to their consideration of distance. The first two are based on maximum distance, and the second four are based on the total (or average) distance or demand-weighted distances. The general classification of them is shown in Figure 3.6.

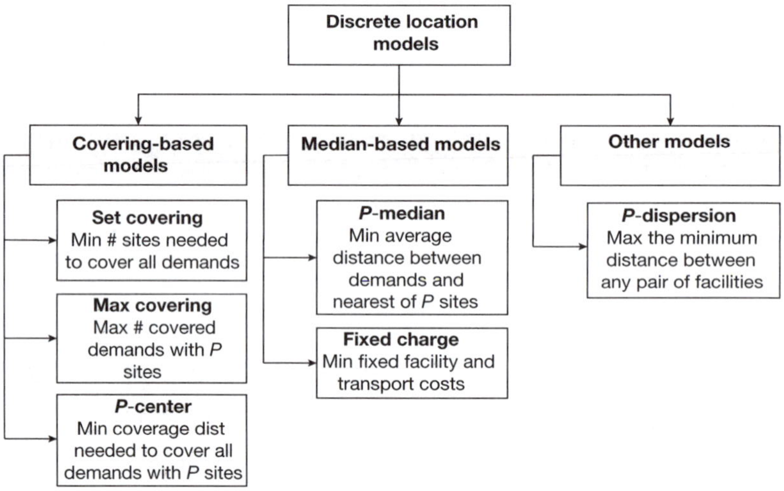

FIGURE 3.6 Classification of discrete location models.

3.4.1 Set Covering Problems

One of the popular location models is the set covering model. For example, in locating emergency service facilities such as fire stations or ambulances and public utility services like schools, primary health centers, and license bureaus, the critical nature of demands for such services will require a maximum "acceptable" travel distance or time as a criterion for the facility. Such locations will require a different measure of efficiency where the covering of all demand nodes necessarily with a minimum number of facilities and with the acceptable maximum travel distance or time will be the primary motive. In a nutshell, a set covering problem is to find the minimum cost set of facilities from among a finite set of candidate facilities so that every demand node is covered by at least one facility. The formulation of these set covering models can be described as follows:

Let I be the set of demand nodes, J be the set of candidates for facility locations, d_{ij} be the distance between demand node $i \in I$ and candidate facility site $j \in J$, and D_c be the coverage distance (a policy input to be given for the facility to cover the demand node). (It can be seen that the demand node i is covered by candidate facility site j if $d_{ij} \le D_c$.)

Define $N_i = \{j \in J : d_{ij} \le D_c\}$. In other words, N_i is the set of all candidate sites that can cover demand node i. Also

$X_j = 1$, if we locate a facility at candidate site j
$= 0$, otherwise.

The location set covering model can be formulated as follows:

$$\text{Min} \sum_j X_j$$

Subject to

$$\sum_{j \in N_i} X_j \ge 1 \forall i \in I$$

$$X_j \in \{0,1\} \forall j \in J$$

Alternatively, we can also formulate this as follows: Let

$a_{ij} = 1$, if the demand node i is covered by a facility node j (i.e., distance $d_{ij} \le D_c$)
$= 0$, if not

Then the formulation becomes

$$\text{Min} \sum_j X_j$$

Subject to

$$\sum_j a_{ij} X_j \ge 1 \forall i \in I$$

$$X_j \in \{0,1\} \forall j \in J$$

If f_j is the fixed cost of the candidate facility j, then the formulation of the set covering problem becomes

$$\text{Min} \sum_j f_j X_j \qquad \text{(cost of covering all nodes)}$$

Subject to

$$\sum_j a_{ij} X_j \ge 1 \quad \forall i \in I \qquad \text{(each node covered)}$$

$$X_j \in \{0,1\} \forall j \in J \qquad \text{(integrality)}$$

Set covering is the simplest of all the formulations without considering many data inputs and with just few inputs. It is very useful for many applications in locating public utilities like fire stations, police stations, license bureaus, schools, etc.

EXAMPLE 3.3

Consider the following example network as shown in Fig. 3.7 with the details of link distances, demand at nodes, and fixed costs for each node as a facility. The data is shown in Table 3.8.

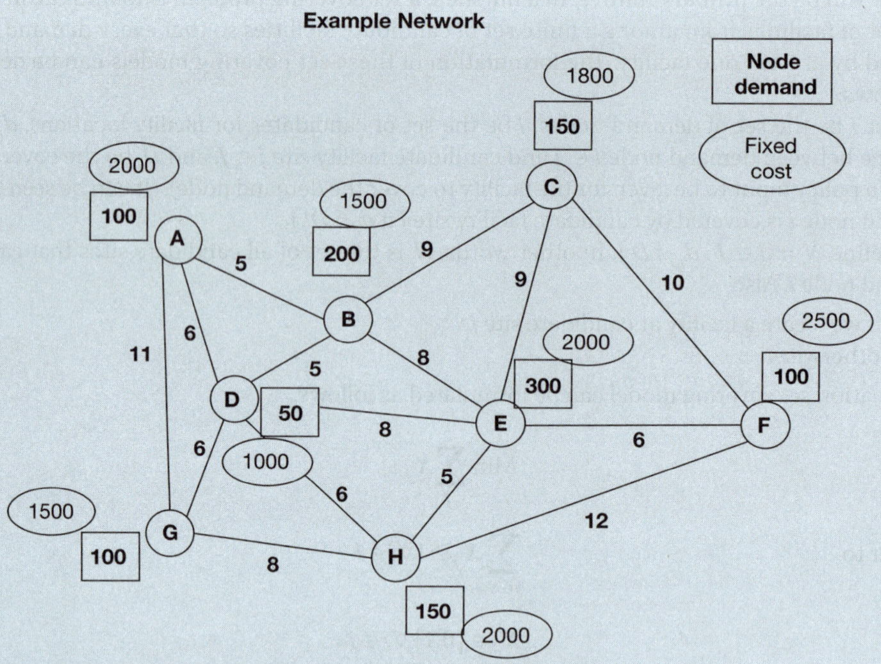

FIGURE 3.7 Example network for discrete location models.

TABLE 3.8 Data inputs for the example on location models

Inputs											
Distances									**Demands and Fixed Costs**		
	A	**B**	**C**	**D**	**E**	**F**	**G**	**H**	**Node**	**Demand**	**Fixed Costs**
A	0	5	14	6	13	19	11	12	A	100	2000
B	5	0	9	5	8	14	11	11	B	200	1500
C	14	9	0	14	9	10	20	14	C	150	1800
D	6	5	14	0	8	14	6	6	D	50	1000
E	13	8	9	8	0	6	13	5	E	300	2000
F	19	14	10	14	6	0	19	12	F	100	2500
G	11	11	20	6	13	19	0	8	G	100	1500
H	12	11	14	6	5	12	8	0	H	150	2000
Coverage Distance	12										

For example, the coverage matrix can be constructed (as given in Table 3.9) for a policy of coverage distance of 12 km, with an IF condition as IF(dist[[i,j]<=Coverage_Distance,1,0). This is shown in Table 3.9.

TABLE 3.9 Coverage matrix for a coverage distance of 12 km

Coverage Matrix								
	A	B	C	D	E	F	G	H
A	1	1	0	1	0	0	1	1
B	1	1	1	1	1	0	1	1
C	0	1	1	0	1	1	0	0
D	1	1	0	1	1	0	1	1
E	0	1	1	1	1	1	0	1
F	0	0	1	0	1	1	0	1
G	1	1	0	1	0	0	1	1
H	1	1	0	1	1	1	1	1

The formulation for this case would be as follows:

$$\text{Minimize } 2000\,X_A + 1500X_B + 1800X_C + 1000X_D + 2000X_E + 2500X_F + 1500X_G + 2000X_H$$

$$X_A + X_B + X_D + X_G + X_H \geq 1$$
$$X_A + X_B + X_C + X_D + X_E + X_G + X_H \geq 1$$
$$X_B + X_C + X_E + X_F \geq 1$$
$$X_A + X_B + X_D + X_E + X_G + X_H \geq 1$$
$$X_B + X_C + X_D + X_E + X_F + X_H \geq 1$$
$$X_C + X_E + X_F + X_H \geq 1$$
$$X_A + X_B + X_D + X_G + X_H \geq 1$$
$$X_A + X_B + X_D + X_E + X_F + X_G + X_H \geq 1$$
$$X_A, X_B, X_C, X_D, X_E, X_F, X_G, X_H \in 0,1$$

The model is explained step by step using screenshots from Excel and is shown in Figures 3.8, 3.9, 3.10, and 3.11.

Step 1

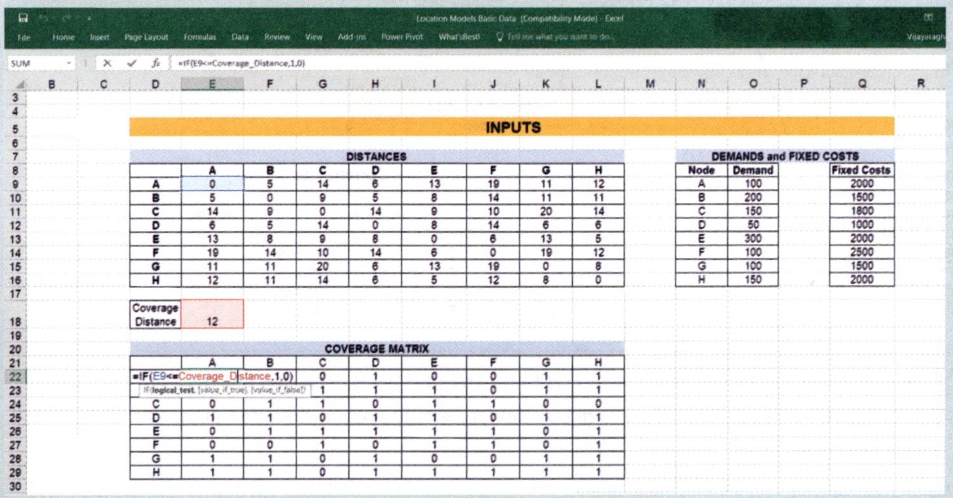

FIGURE 3.8 Basic inputs and coverage matrix.

Step 2

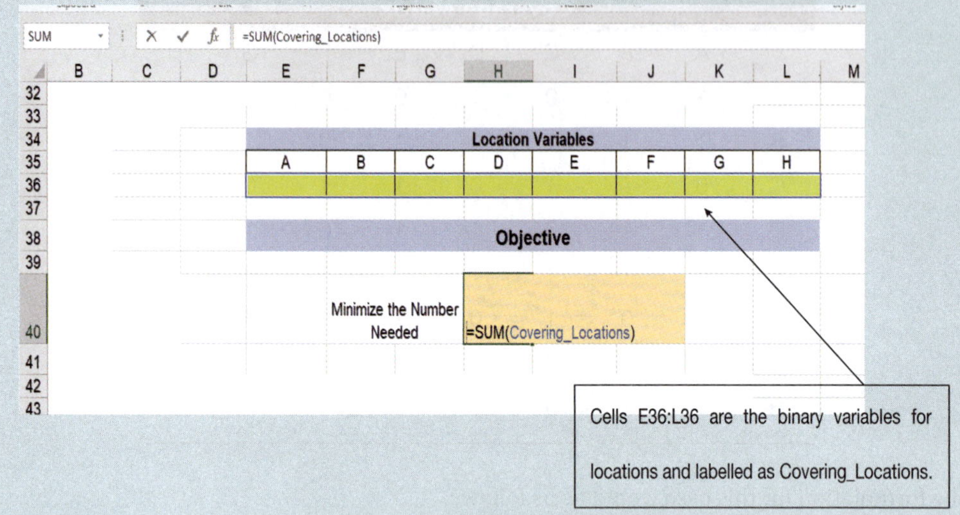

FIGURE 3.9 Decision variables and the objective function.

Step 3

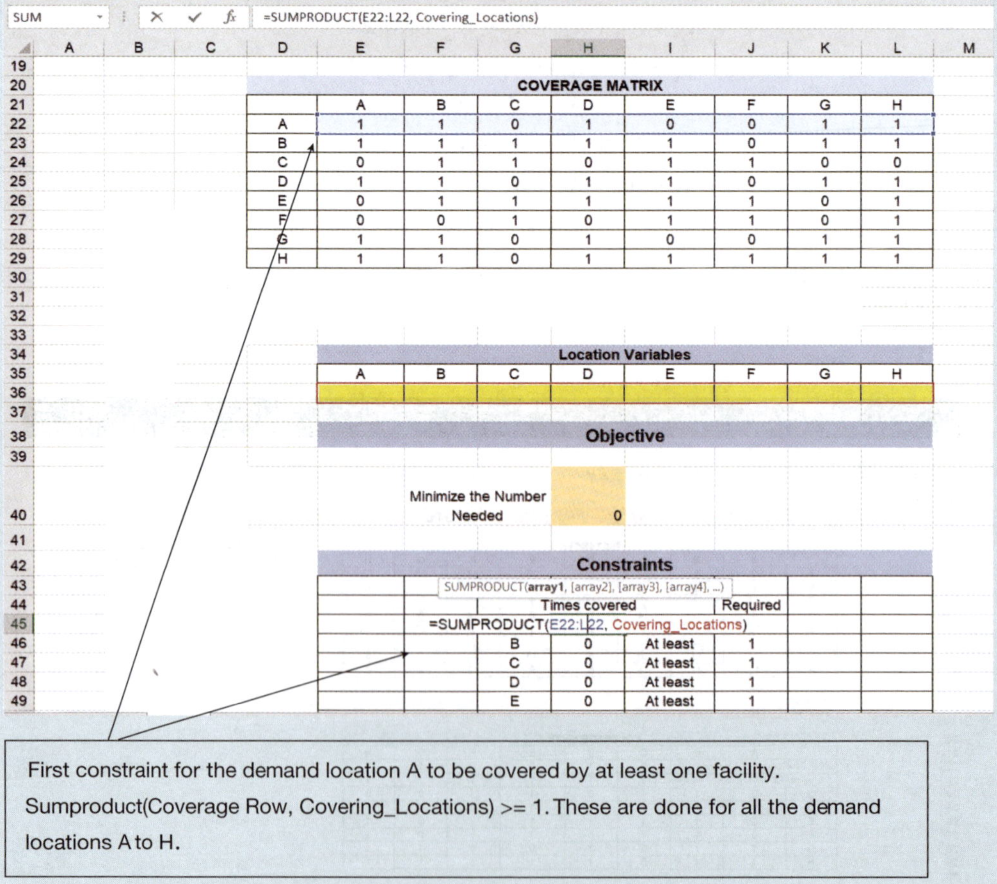

FIGURE 3.10 Formation of constraints using decision variables and the coverage matrix.

Step 4: Use Solver to enter the details and solve it.

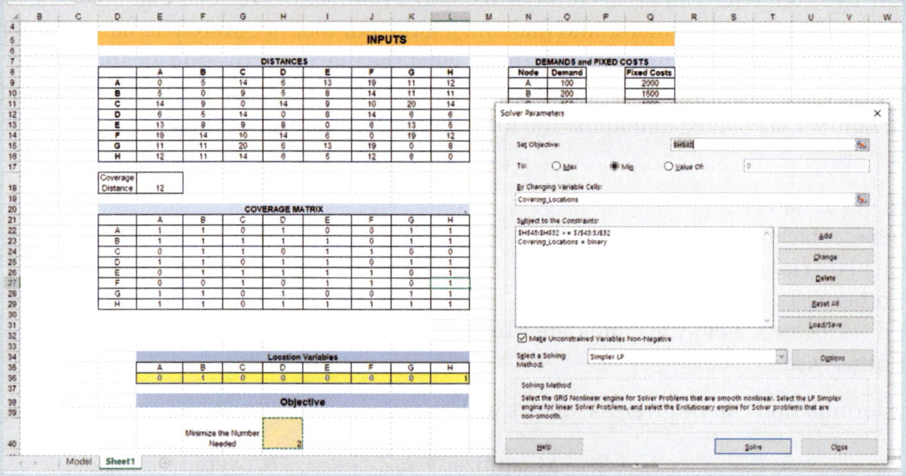

FIGURE 3.11 Using Solver to solve the problem.

Locations B and H are selected to serve as facility locations as shown in Figure 3.12.

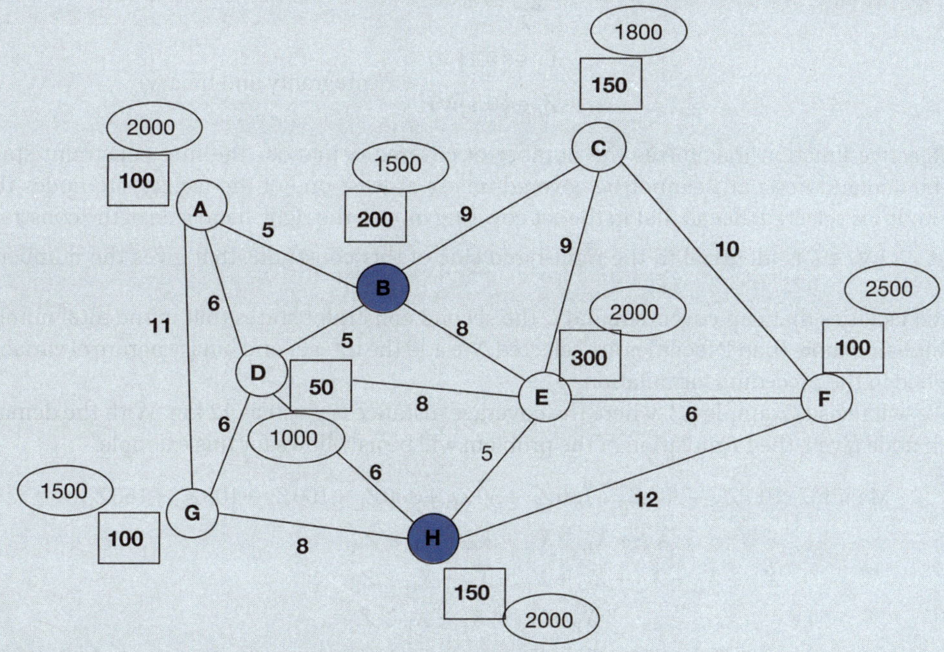

FIGURE 3.12 Selected location for facilities shown in blue circles.

There can be multiple optimum solutions as well.

3.4.2 Maximal Covering Problems

The set covering model has an inherent problem; the number of facilities that are needed to cover all demand nodes is likely to exceed the number that can actually be built (for budgetary and other administrative reasons). Furthermore, the set covering model does not take into account the demand at each node and treats all demand nodes with equal importance irrespective of the quantum of demand. It is equally important in this model to cover a demand node that generates 10 tons of products per year as it is to cover a node that generates 10,000 tons of demand per year!

These two concerns lead us to consider fixing the number of facilities that are to be located a priori as a given input parameter and maximizing the number of covered demands as opposed to the number of covered demand nodes. This is what the maximal covering location model does. So the formulation of the maximal covering problem is to find the locations of *P* facilities to maximize the number of covered demands. The formulation steps are as follows:

Let

h_i = Demand at node *i*

P = Number of facilities to locate

$$Z_i = \begin{cases} 1, \text{ if node } i \text{ is covered} \\ 0, \text{ otherwise} \end{cases}$$

$$X_j = \begin{cases} 1, \text{ if we locate a facility at candidate site } j \\ 0, \text{ otherwise} \end{cases}$$

The formulation can be given as follows with these notations:

$$\text{Maximize} \sum_j h_i Z_i \qquad \text{(Covered Demands)}$$

Subject to

$$Z_i \le \sum_j a_{ij} X_j \; \forall i \in I \qquad \text{(node } i \text{ not covered unless we locate at a node covering it)}$$

$$\sum_j X_j = P \qquad \text{(locate } P \text{ sites)}$$

$$\left.\begin{aligned} X_j &\in \{0,1\} \forall j \\ Z_i &\in \{0,1\} \forall i \end{aligned}\right\} \text{(integrality and binary)}$$

The objective function maximizes the number of covered demands. The first constraint states that the demand node at *i* cannot be covered unless at least one of the facility site nodes that cover node *i* is selected. Recall that in the set covering model, the right-hand side of the constraint $\sum_j a_{ij} X_j \ge 1 \forall i \in I$ is identical to the right-hand side of this constraint that gives the number of selected facilities that can cover demand *i*. The second constraint states that in the total number of facilities, no more than P facilities are selected. We add the integer and binary nature of variables at the end in the preceding formulation.

We will revisit Example 3.3, where the coverage distance is given as 12 km. With the demand of each node given, the formulation of the problem will be as follows for this example.

Maximal covering formulation addresses the practical constraints like policies of a given number of facilities only and coverage distances. It is very useful for experimenting various policies to study the cost benefit of facilities varying these policy inputs.

$$\text{Maximize } 100 Z_A + 200 Z_B + 150 Z_C + 50 Z_D + 300 Z_E + 100 Z_F + 100 Z_G + 150 Z_H$$

$$X_A + X_B + X_D + X_G + X_H \ge Z_A$$

$$X_A + X_B + X_C + X_D + X_E + X_G + X_H \ge Z_B$$

$$X_B + X_C + X_E + X_F \ge Z_C$$

$$X_A + X_B + X_D + X_E + X_G + X_H \ge Z_D$$

$$X_B + X_C + X_D + X_E + X_F + X_H \ge Z_E$$

$$X_C + X_E + X_F + X_H \ge Z_F$$

$$X_A + X_B + X_D + X_G + X_H \ge Z_G$$

$$X_A + X_B + X_D + X_E + X_F + X_G + X_H \ge Z_H$$

$$X_A, X_B, X_C, X_D, X_E, X_F, X_G, X_H \in 0,1$$

$$Z_A, Z_B, Z_C, Z_D, Z_E, Z_F, Z_G, Z_H \in 0,1$$

The model is explained step by step using screenshots from Excel and is shown in Figures 3.13, 3.14, 3.15, and 3.16.

Step 1

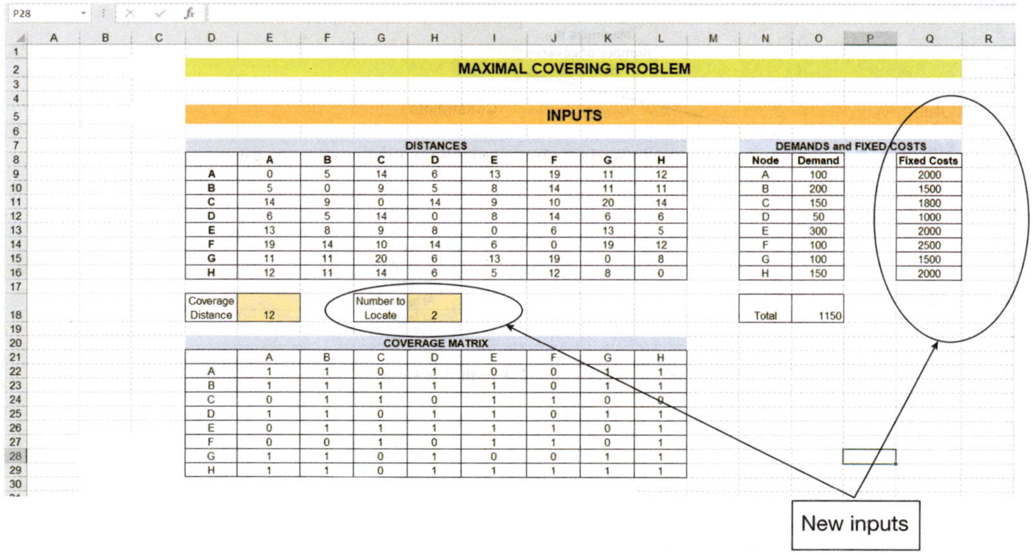

MAXIMAL COVERING PROBLEM

INPUTS

DISTANCES

	A	B	C	D	E	F	G	H
A	0	5	14	6	13	19	11	12
B	5	0	9	5	8	14	11	11
C	14	9	0	14	9	10	20	14
D	6	5	14	0	8	14	6	6
E	13	8	9	8	0	6	13	5
F	19	14	10	14	6	0	19	12
G	11	11	20	6	13	19	0	8
H	12	11	14	6	5	12	8	0

Coverage Distance	12	Number to Locate	2

COVERAGE MATRIX

	A	B	C	D	E	F	G	H
A	1	1	0	1	0	0	1	1
B	1	1	1	1	1	0	1	1
C	0	1	1	0	1	1	0	0
D	1	1	0	1	1	0	1	1
E	0	1	1	1	1	1	0	1
F	0	0	1	0	1	1	0	1
G	1	1	0	1	0	0	1	1
H	1	1	0	1	1	1	1	1

DEMANDS and FIXED COSTS

Node	Demand	Fixed Costs
A	100	2000
B	200	1500
C	150	1800
D	50	1000
E	300	2000
F	100	2500
G	100	1500
H	150	2000
Total	1150	

FIGURE 3.13 Basic inputs with number of facilities to locate, coverage distance, and the coverage matrix.

Step 2

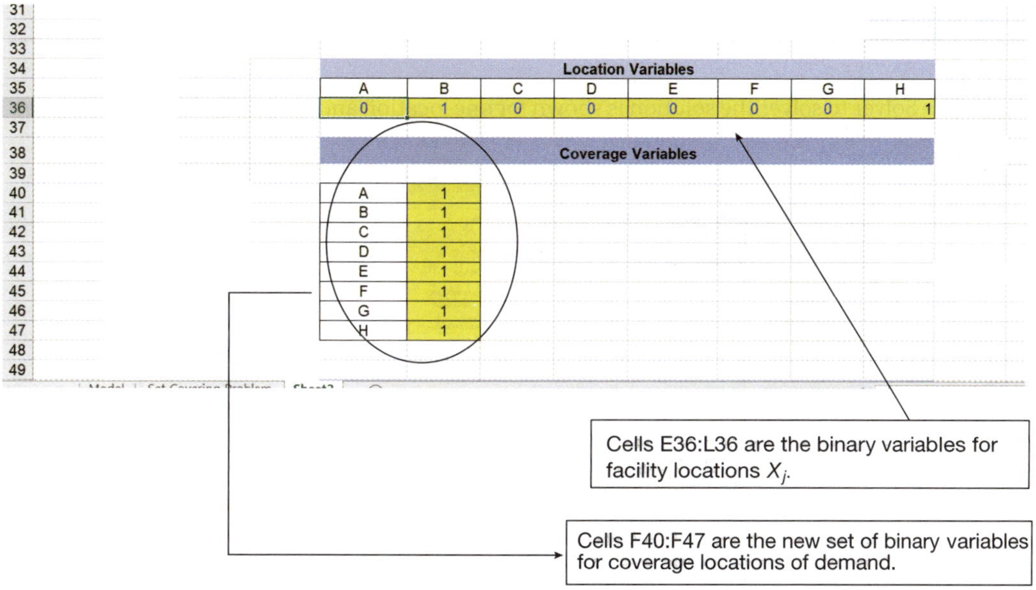

Location Variables

A	B	C	D	E	F	G	H
0	1	0	0	0	0	0	1

Coverage Variables

A	1
B	1
C	1
D	1
E	1
F	1
G	1
H	1

FIGURE 3.14 Defining location variables and coverage variables.

Step 3

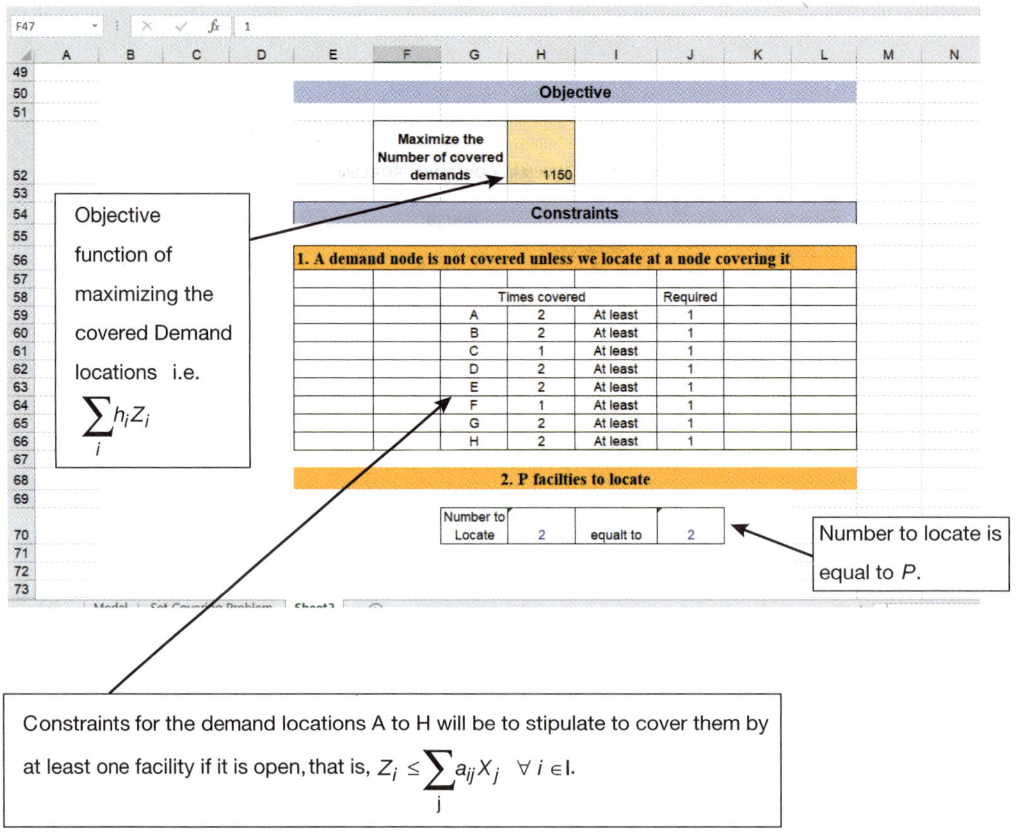

FIGURE 3.15 Defining objective function and constraints set.

Step 4: Use Solver to solve. The solution is shown for one location and a coverage distance of 12 km.

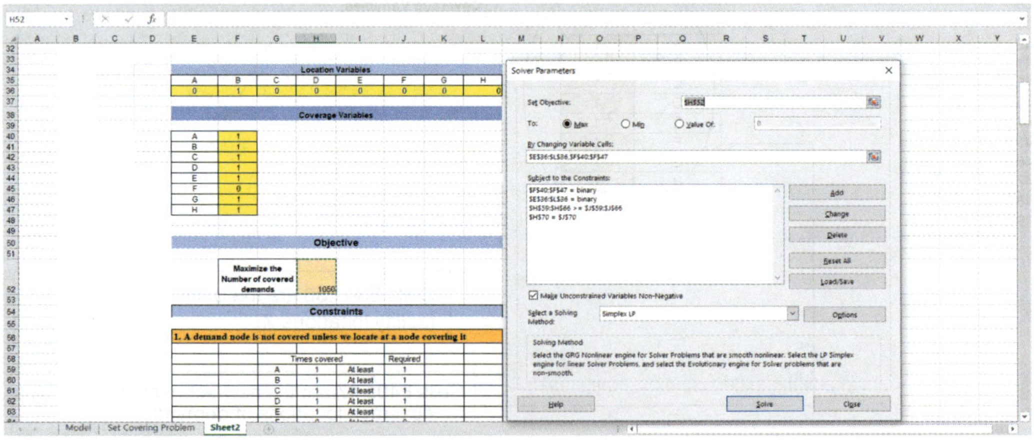

FIGURE 3.16 Using Solver to solve the problem.

Location B is chosen to cover demands at A, B, C, D, E, G, and H covering a demand 1050 and not covering demand location F as shown in Figure 3.17.

By systematically varying P from 1 to k, where k is the minimum number of facilities required to cover the entire demand, one can use the preceding formulation to determine the marginal benefits associated with additional facilities.

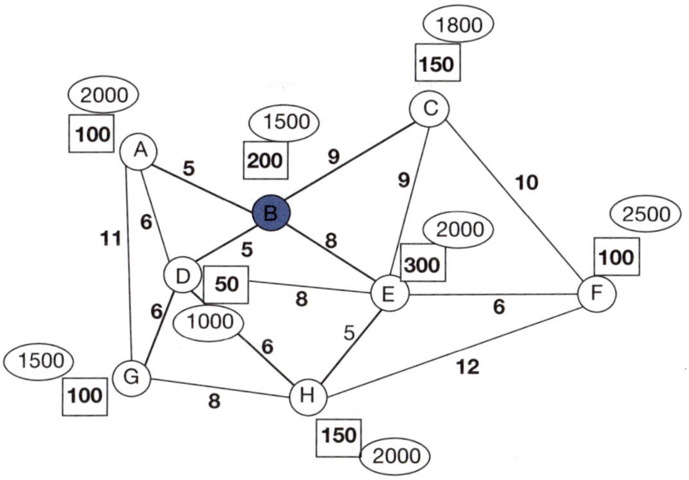

FIGURE 3.17 Selected location shown in blue circle and the covered nodes shown by thick black lines. Note that the node C is not covered.

3.4.3 P-Center Problem

Given that we are locating facilities in a predetermined P number of facilities, the P-center problem addresses the problem of minimizing the maximum distance that demand is from its closest facility. There can be a few possible variations of this basic model. The "vertex" P-center problem considers the set of candidate facility locations to the nodes of the network, while the "absolute" P-center problem considers them to be anywhere along the links or arcs. Both versions can be either weighted or unweighted. In the unweighted problem, all demand nodes are assumed to be equally important. Whereas in the weighted model, the distances between demand nodes and facilities are multiplied by a weight associated with the demand node. For example, this weight might include a node's importance or, more commonly, the level of its demand.

It is a minimax problem where given P facilities, we find the minimum coverage distance such that all demands are covered. In effect, we are minimizing the maximum demand from any customer to the nearest facility, no matter how insignificant. The most "remote" demand node drives the solution.

The P-center problem tries to minimize the maximum demand from any customer to the nearest facility, no matter how insignificant. The most "remote" demand node drives the solution. Hence in practice, it is very good for taking care of market coverages in physical distribution and to address the last-mile deliveries using this approach.

Given our previous definitions and the following decision variables,

W = the maximum distance between a demand node and the facility location to which it is assigned

y_{ij} = 1, if demand node i is assigned to a facility at node j

0, if not

the P-center problem can be formulated as follows:

Minimize W

Subject to

$$\sum_j X_j = P$$

$$\sum_{j \in J} Y_{ij} = 1 \forall i \in I$$

Ensure coverage, limit number of facilities

$$Y_{ij} - X_j \leq 0 \forall i \in I, j \in J$$

Linkage constraint. Cannot claim credit for non-existent

$$W - \sum_{j \in J} d_{ij} Y_{ij} \geq 0 \; i \in I, \forall j \in J$$

Force W equal to max distance

$$X_j \in \{0,1\} \forall j$$

$$Y_{ij} \in \{0,1\} \forall i \quad \forall j$$

Integrality and binary

We will revisit Example 3.3 where we will take the number to locate as 2 and the value of W, the maximum covering distance as 12 km. The model is explained step by step using screenshots from Excel and is shown in Figures 3.18, 3.19, and 3.20.

Step 1

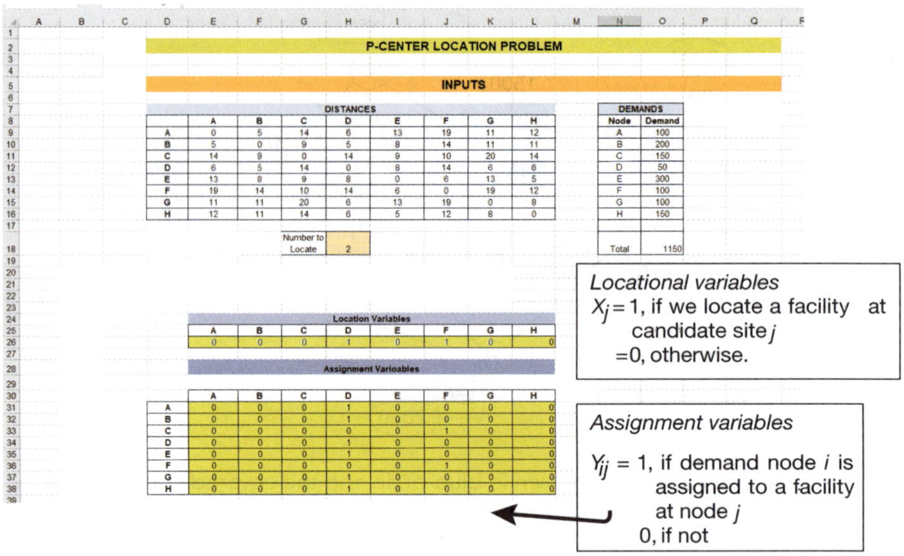

FIGURE 3.18 Basic inputs with location and assignment variables defined.

Step 2

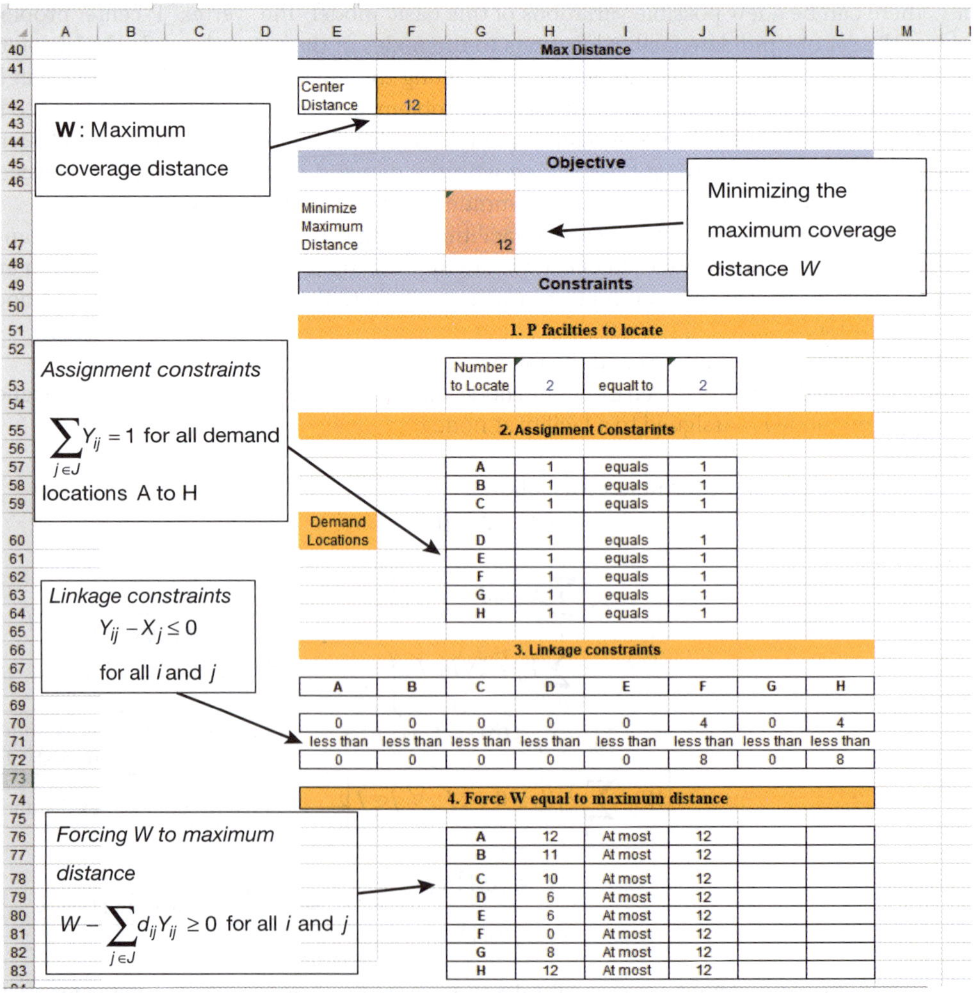

FIGURE 3.19 Defining max distance, objective function, and constraints.

Step 3: Use Solver to solve the problem.

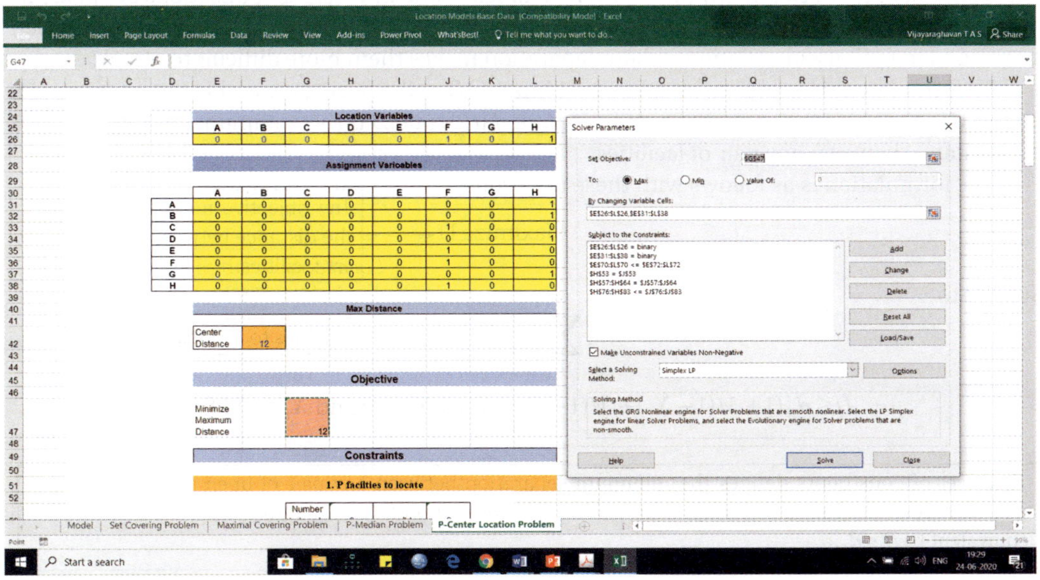

FIGURE 3.20 Using Solver to solve the problem.

Locations F and H are chosen, and the coverage is shown in Figure 3.21.

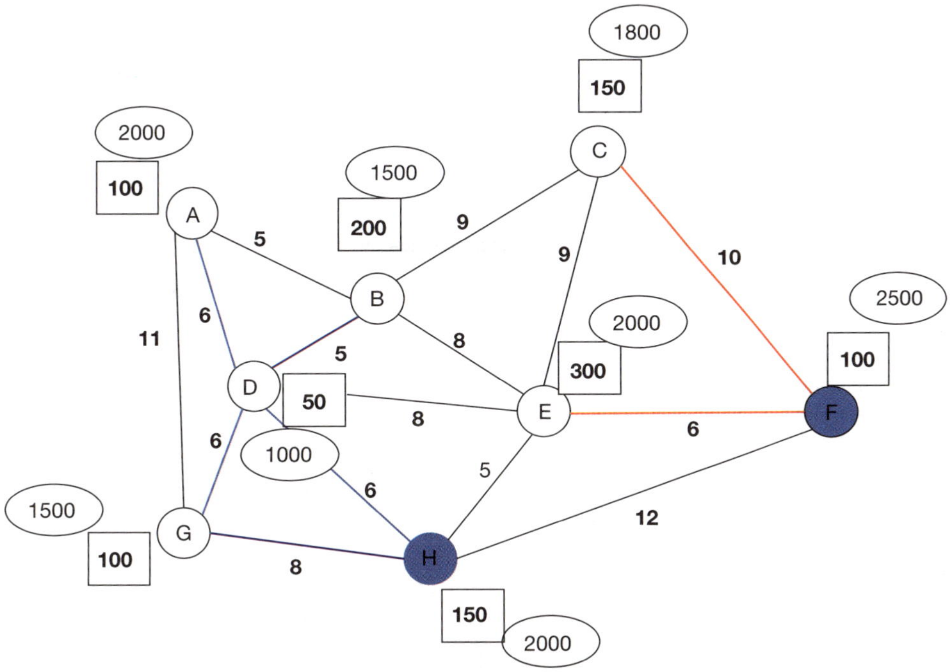

FIGURE 3.21 Selected nodes shown in blue circles and the covered nodes shown by thick red and blue lines.

3.4.4 P-Dispersion Problem

The models discussed so far focus more on the distance between a demand location and new facilities and on covered distances. They also implicitly focus on the fact that being close to a facility is desirable. The P-dispersion problem is slightly different from these models and is concerned with (1) only the distance between new facility locations and (ii) the objective to maximize the minimum distance between any pair of such facilities. Some interesting applications are in locating franchise locations for retail outlets where separation reduces the cannibalization between stores, and in military installations where separation makes them more difficult to attack.

To formulate this problem, an additional input (M) and a decision variable (D) are required, where M is a very large constant (e.g., max $i \in I, j \in J\{d_{ij}\}$) and D is the minimum desirable separation distance between any pair of facilities.

The formulation is as follows with these notations:

$$\text{Maximize } D$$

← The objective function maximizes the distance between the two closest facilities.

Subject to

$$\sum_j X_j = P$$

← P facilities to be located

$$D \le d_{ij}(1 + M(1 - X_i) + M(1 - X_j) \forall i, j \text{ and } i < j \text{ and } X_i \in (0,1))$$

These set of constraints defines the minimum separation between any pair of open facilities. If either X_i or X_j is zero, the constraint will not be binding. However, if both are equal to 1, then the constraint is equivalent to $D \le d_{ij}$.

Or simplified as

$$D + (M - d_{ij})X_i + (M - d_{ij})X_j \le 2M - d_{ij} \quad \forall i, j \text{ and } i < j$$

$$X_j \in \{0, 1\} \; \forall j \in J$$

← Integrality and binary

Therefore, maximizing the objective of D will result in forcing the smallest interfacility location distance to be as large as possible.

We will revisit Example 3.3 for this. The model is explained step by step using screenshots using Excel and is shown in Figures 3.22, 3.23, 3.24, and 3.25.

While P-center is a minimax problem, P-dispersion is more of a maximin problem in locating facilities. Here the objective is to maximize the minimum distance between any pair of such facilities. This is very useful in locating retail centers, shopping centers, or convenience stores where the cannibalization effect of facilities can be avoided.

Step 1

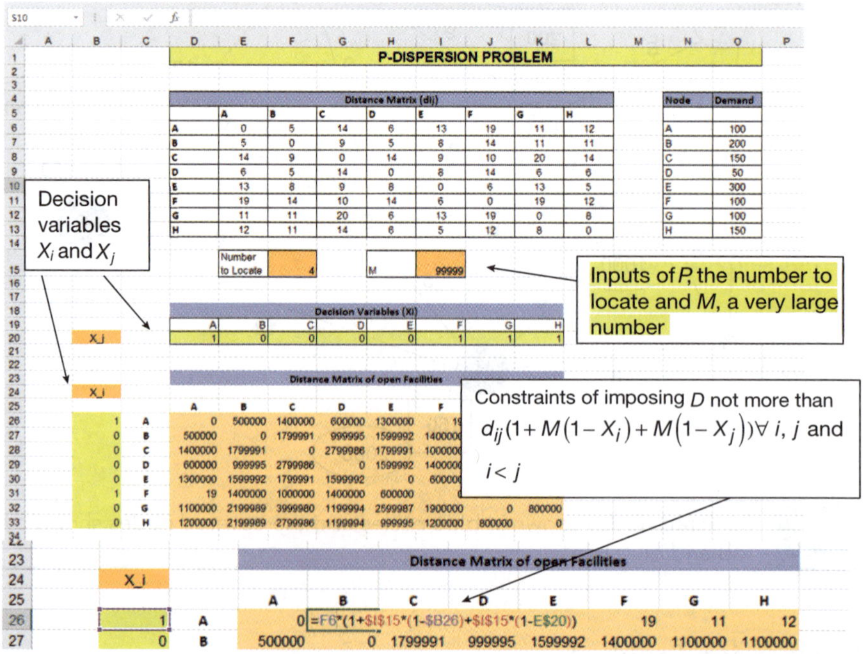

FIGURE 3.22 Basic inputs and variables.

Step 2

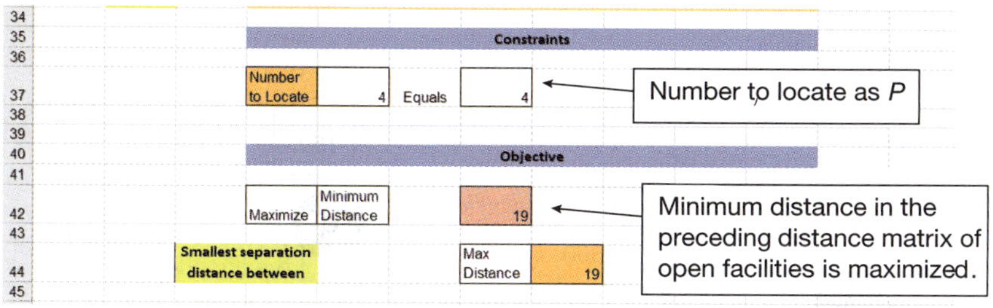

FIGURE 3.23 Constraints and the objective function.

The explanation of Figure 3.23 is shown in Figure 3.24.

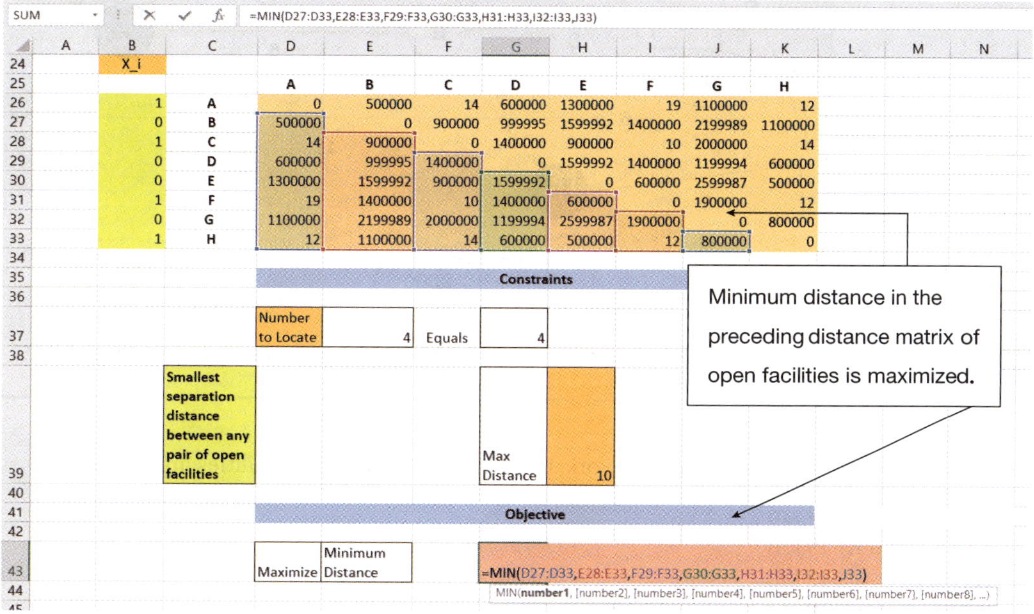

FIGURE 3.24 Explanation of Figure 3.23.

Use Solver using the GRG nonlinear engine.

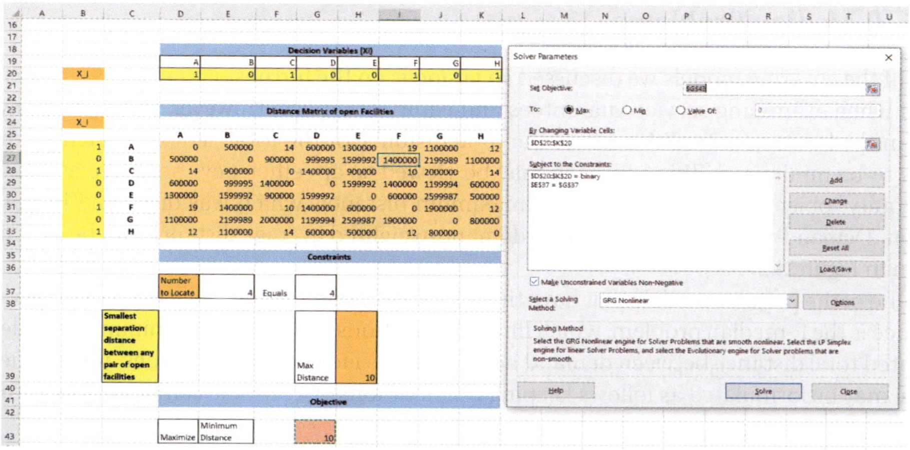

FIGURE 3.25 Using Solver to solve the problem.

The output will show results to locate at A, C, F, H for $P = 4$ and the maximized minimum distance is 10 km (Figure 3.26).

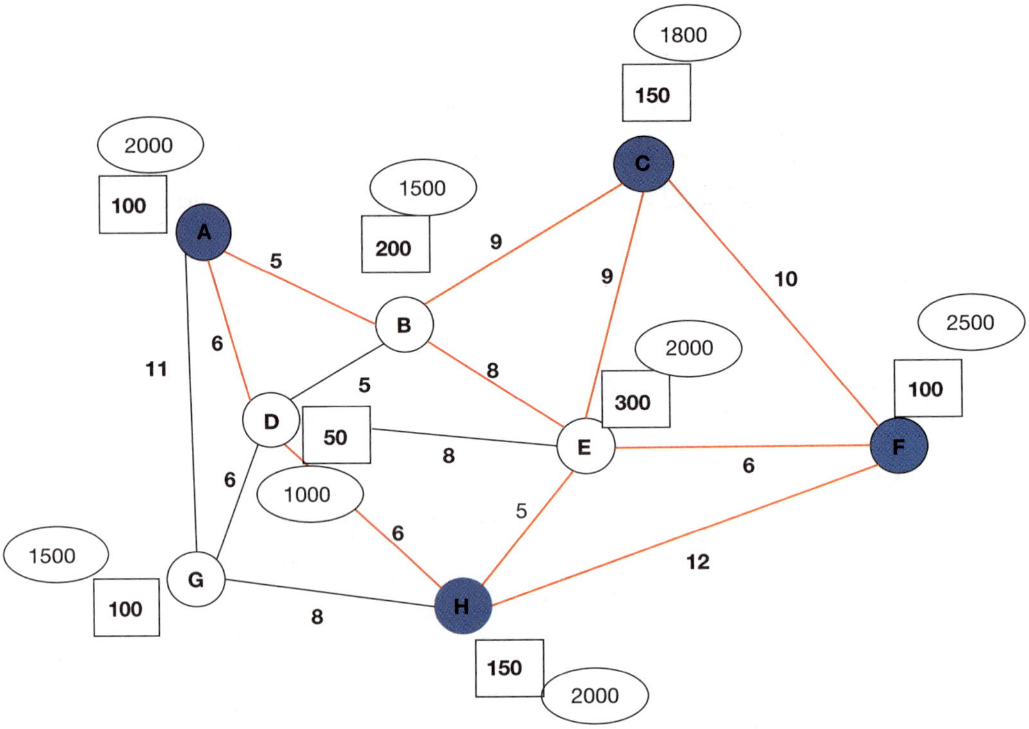

FIGURE 3.26 Selected nodes shown in blue circles and the connected nodes are shown in thick red lines.

As can be seen from the preceding network, the distances among the facilities are as follows:

A–C (via B)	14 km
A–F (via B and E)	19 km
A–H (via D)	12 km
C–F	10 km
C–H (via E)	14 km
F–H	12 km

with a minimum of 10 km. There may be a possibility of multiple solutions for a given value of *P*.

3.4.5 P-Median Problems

Most of the covering models we discussed so far focus on the furthest node from a facility and are useful when examining service guarantees and equity of service. However, there are many situations in the location of facilities where the total distance or the total demand-weighted distance needs to be minimized. This approach may be viewed as an "efficiency" objective as opposed to the "equity" objective of minimizing the maximum distance, which was discussed in the earlier section. Demand-weighted distance and demand-weighted average distance can be explained as shown in Figure 3.27.

One of the popular models that have the objective of minimizing using the demand-weighted distance is the P-median problem, which finds the locations of *P* facilities to minimize the demand-weighted total distance between demand nodes and the facilities to which they are assigned. This model may be formulated as follows keeping the notations given in the earlier location problems.

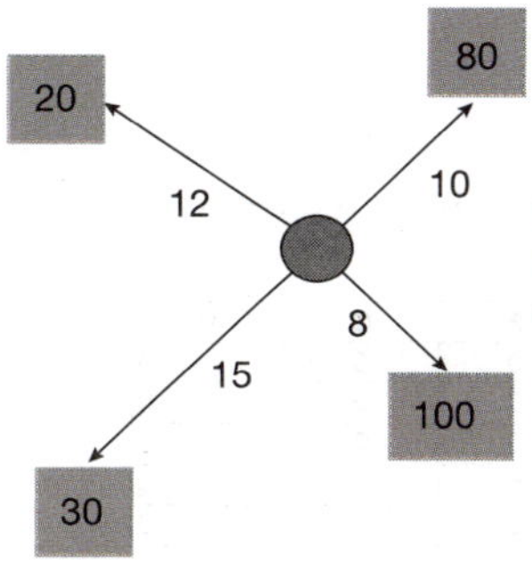

Demand-weighted total distance = (80)10 + (100)8 + (30)15 + (20)12 = 2290
Demand-weighted average distance = 2290/(80 + 100 + 30 + 20) = 9.95
and is not equal to the "average distance" of (10 + 8 + 12 + 15)/4 = 11.25

FIGURE 3.27 Demand-weighted distance and demand-weighted average distance.

$$\text{Minimize} \sum_{i}\sum_{j} h_i d_{ij} Y_{ij}$$

← Minimizing the total demand-weighted distance

Subject to

$$\sum_{j} X_j = P$$

$$\sum_{j \in J} Y_{ij} = 1 \quad \forall i \in I$$

← Ensure number of facilities is P and coverage of each demand node is assigned only once to a facility node

$$Y_{ij} - X_j \le 0 \quad \forall i \in I, j \in J$$

← Linkage constraint. Cannot assign demands to an unopened facility

$$X_j \in \{0,1\} \forall j$$

$$Y_{ij} \in \{0,1\} \forall i \quad \forall j$$

← Integrality and binary for the decision variables

It is interesting to note that this formulation also **minimizes the average travel distance between the facility location nodes and the demand location nodes.**

We will revisit Example 3.3 for locating $P = 2$ facilities. The model is explained step by step using screenshots from Excel and is shown in Figures 3.28, 3.29, 3.30, and 3.31.

P-median formulation addresses the very important practical considerations of locating facilities by taking into account the total weighted distance rather than weights or distances only to be minimized. It also considers the number of given facilities to ensure covering all demand locations but at the same time minimizing the total incurred weighted distance to achieve the same.

Step 1

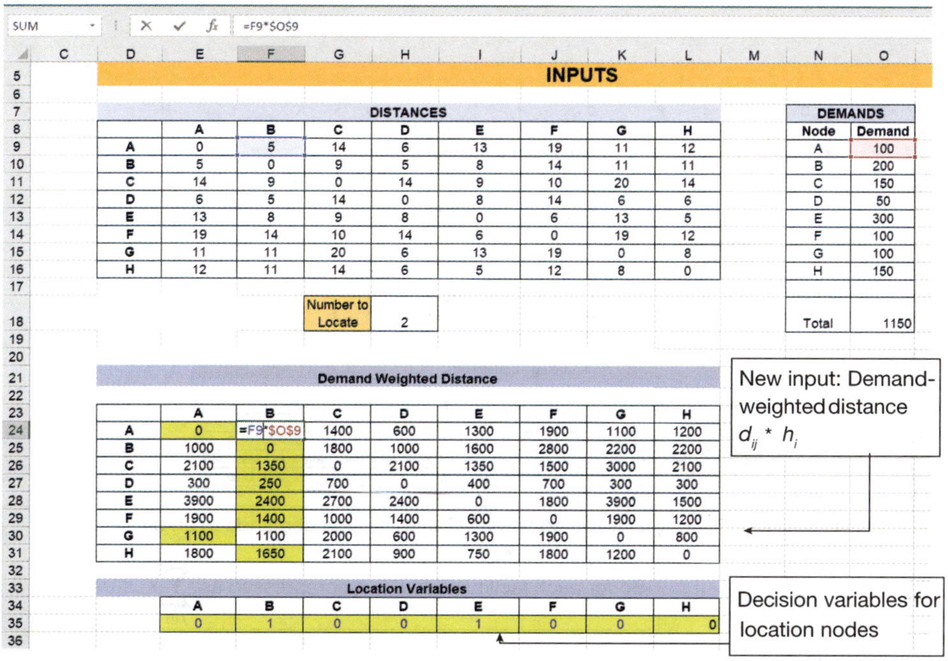

DISTANCES

	A	B	C	D	E	F	G	H
A	0	5	14	6	13	19	11	12
B	5	0	9	5	8	14	11	11
C	14	9	0	14	9	10	20	14
D	6	5	14	0	8	14	6	6
E	13	8	9	8	0	6	13	5
F	19	14	10	14	6	0	19	12
G	11	11	20	6	13	19	0	8
H	12	11	14	6	5	12	8	0

Number to Locate	2

DEMANDS

Node	Demand
A	100
B	200
C	150
D	50
E	300
F	100
G	100
H	150
Total	1150

Demand Weighted Distance

	A	B	C	D	E	F	G	H
A	0	=F9*$O$9	1400	600	1300	1900	1100	1200
B	1000	0	1800	1000	1600	2800	2200	2200
C	2100	1350	0	2100	1350	1500	3000	2100
D	300	250	700	0	400	700	300	300
E	3900	2400	2700	2400	0	1800	3900	1500
F	1900	1400	1000	1400	600	0	1900	1200
G	1100	1100	2000	600	1300	1900	0	800
H	1800	1650	2100	900	750	1800	1200	0

Location Variables

A	B	C	D	E	F	G	H
0	1	0	0	1	0	0	0

FIGURE 3.28 Basic inputs with demand-weighted distance.

Step 2

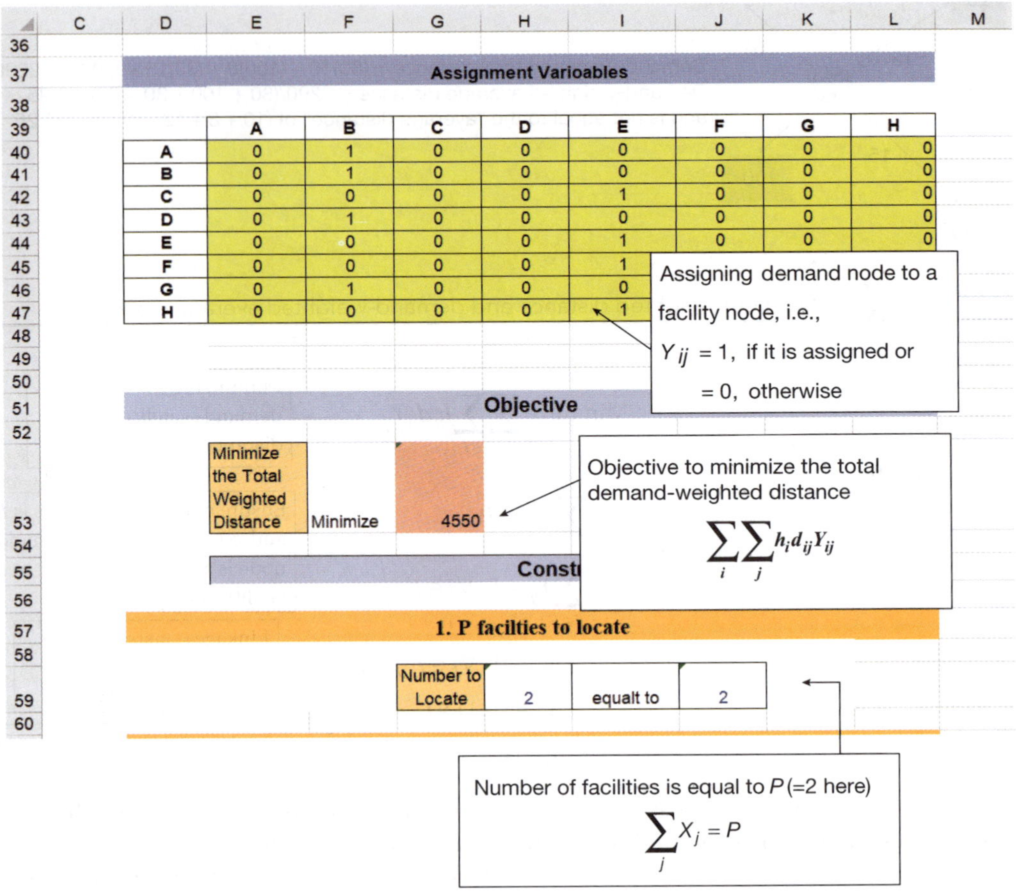

FIGURE 3.29 Defining assignment variables, objective function, and constraints.

Step 3

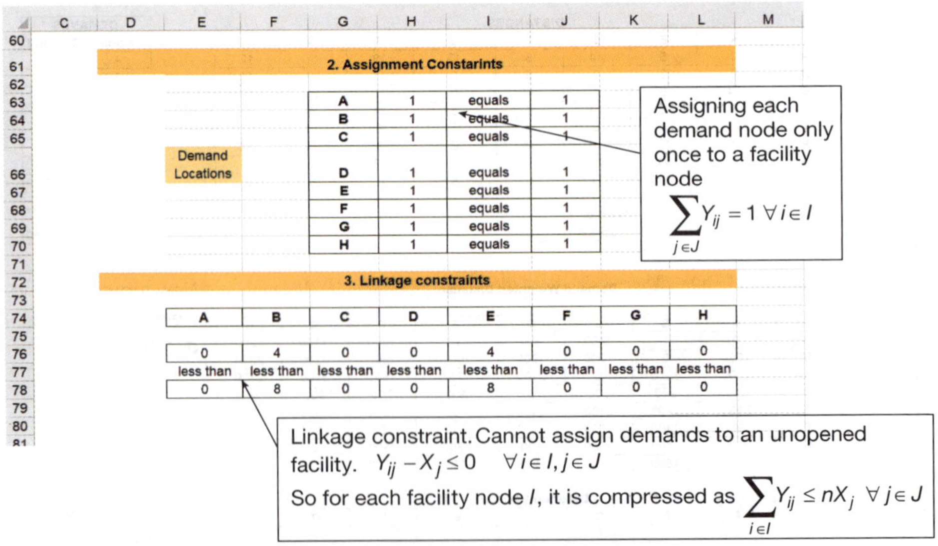

FIGURE 3.30 Defining constraints.

Step 4: Use Solver to obtain the solution as follows:

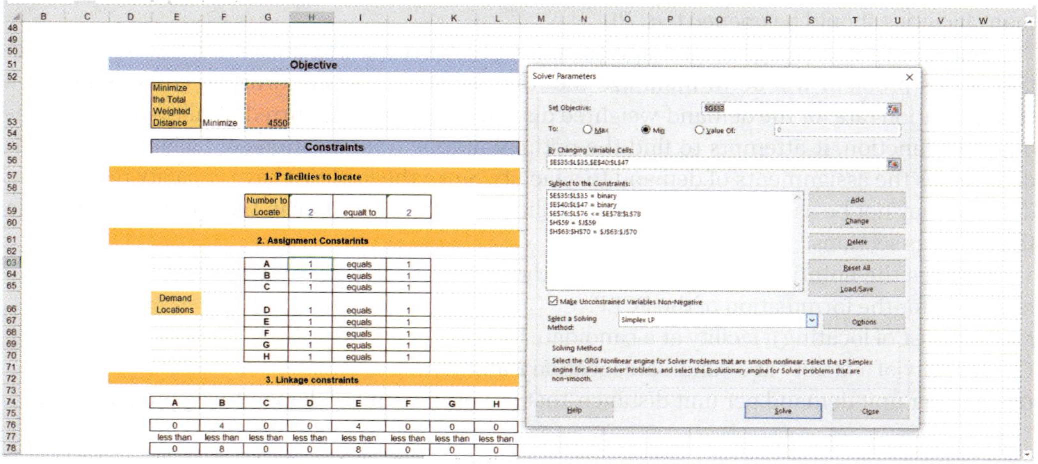

FIGURE 3.31 Using Solver to solve the problem.

The solution locates the facilities at locations B and E with a total demand-weighted distance of 4550. Node B will serve A, B, D, and G, while node E will serve C, E, F, and H. The same is shown in Figure 3.32.

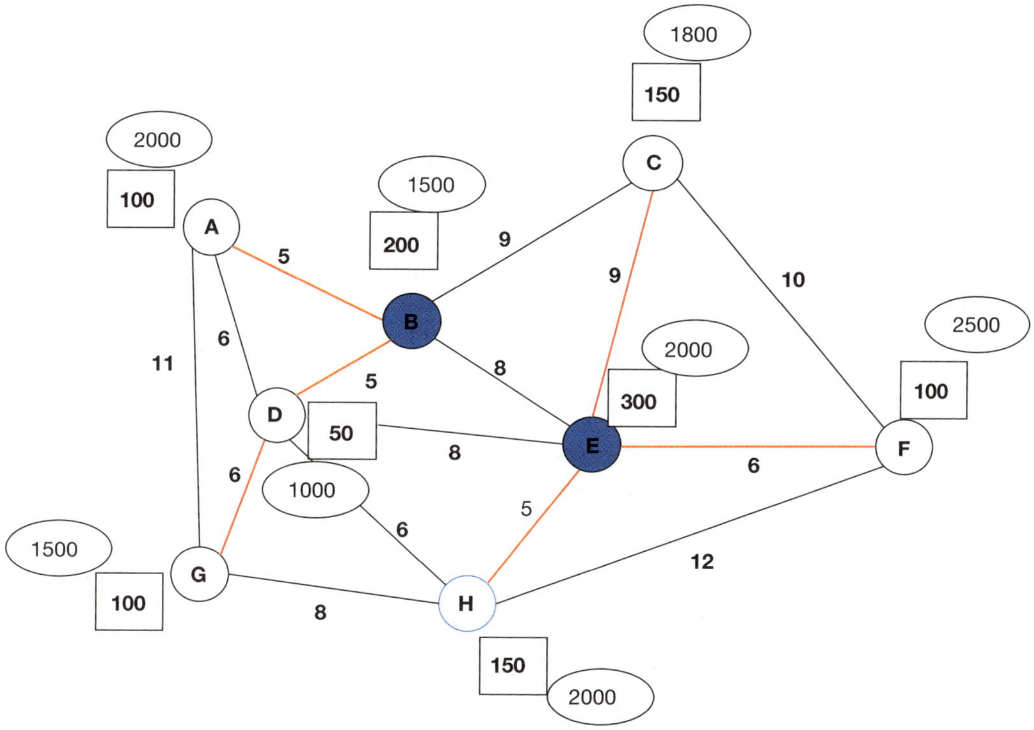

FIGURE 3.32 Selected nodes with the covered nodes by them shown in thick red lines.

3.4.6 Capacitated Fixed Charge Location Problem

The P-median problem discussed in the previous section assumes three important considerations for locating the facilities. First, it assumes that each potential location site has the same fixed costs for locating a facility at it. Second, it assumes that the facilities being located do not have capacity restrictions, that is, uncapacitated problem. Finally, it also assumes that we are given, a priori, how many facilities should be opened (i.e., P).

But in the fixed charge location problem (FCLP), these assumptions are relaxed. The objective of this problem will be to minimize the total facility and transportation costs assuming a transportation rate for the demand-weighted distance that will be incurred. While optimizing this objective function, it attempts to find the optimal number and locations of facilities, as well as determines the assignments of demand to a facility. Since the facilities have capacity restrictions, demand may not be assigned to its closest facility, which was the case in the models discussed in the previous sections.

Besides the notations that were used in the previous sections, we will use a few additional notations for the formulation of the FCLP:

f_j = fixed cost of locating a facility at a candidate location j,
C_j = capacity of a facility at a candidate location j, and
α = cost per unit demand per unit distance, that is, cost per unit of demand-weighted distance.

$$\text{Minimize } \sum_j f_j X_j + \alpha \sum_i \sum_j h_i d_{ij} Y_{ij}$$

To minimize the total cost of fixed cost plus the demand-weighted transportation cost

Subject to

$$\sum_{j \in J} Y_{ij} = 1 \quad \forall i \in I$$

Coverage constraint, i.e., each demand node is assigned only once to a facility node

$$Y_{ij} - X_j \le 0 \quad \forall i \in I, j \in J$$

Linkage constraint. Cannot assign demands to an unopened facility

$$\sum_j h_i Y_{ij} \le C_j X_j \forall i \in I$$

Imposing the capacity of the jth node is not more than the total demand covered

$$\left.\begin{aligned} X_j &\in \{0,1\} \forall j \\ Y_{ij} &\in \{0,1\} \forall i \forall j \end{aligned}\right\}$$

Integrality and binary for the decision variables

We will revisit Example 3.3 for this problem where we assume a constant capacity of 400 for each of the facility nodes. However, this can always be changed to varying capacities. The model is explained step by step using screenshots from Excel and is shown in Figures 3.33, 3.34, 3.35, and 3.36.

Step 1

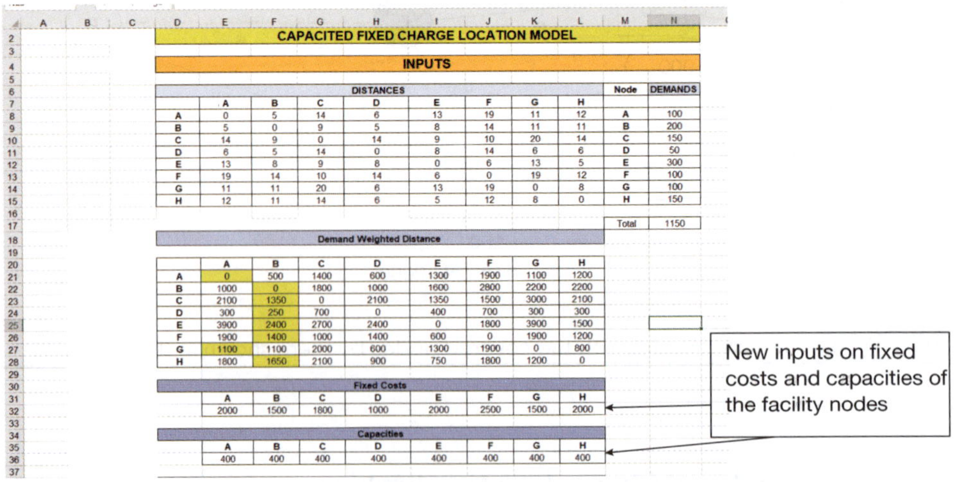

CAPACITED FIXED CHARGE LOCATION MODEL

INPUTS

DISTANCES

	A	B	C	D	E	F	G	H	Node	DEMANDS
A	0	5	14	6	13	19	11	12	A	100
B	5	0	9	5	8	14	11	11	B	200
C	14	9	0	14	9	10	20	14	C	150
D	6	5	14	0	8	14	6	6	D	50
E	13	8	9	8	0	6	13	5	E	300
F	19	14	10	14	6	0	19	12	F	100
G	11	11	20	6	13	19	0	8	G	100
H	12	11	14	6	5	12	8	0	H	150
									Total	1150

Demand Weighted Distance

	A	B	C	D	E	F	G	H
A	0	500	1400	600	1300	1900	1100	1200
B	1000	0	1800	1000	1600	2800	2200	2200
C	2100	1350	0	2100	1350	1500	3000	2100
D	300	250	700	0	400	700	300	300
E	3900	2400	2700	2400	0	1800	3900	1500
F	1900	1400	1000	1400	600	0	1900	1200
G	1100	1100	2000	600	1300	1900	0	800
H	1800	1650	2100	900	750	1800	1200	0

Fixed Costs

A	B	C	D	E	F	G	H
2000	1500	1800	1000	2000	2500	1500	2000

Capacities

A	B	C	D	E	F	G	H
400	400	400	400	400	400	400	400

FIGURE 3.33 Basic inputs with demand-weighted distance, fixed costs, and capacities.

Step 2

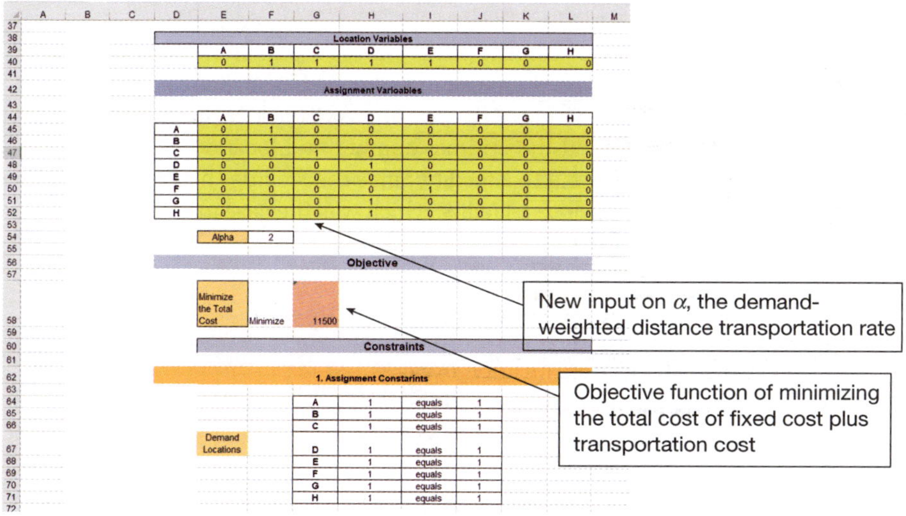

FIGURE 3.34 Defining location and assignment variables with objective function and constraints.

Step 3

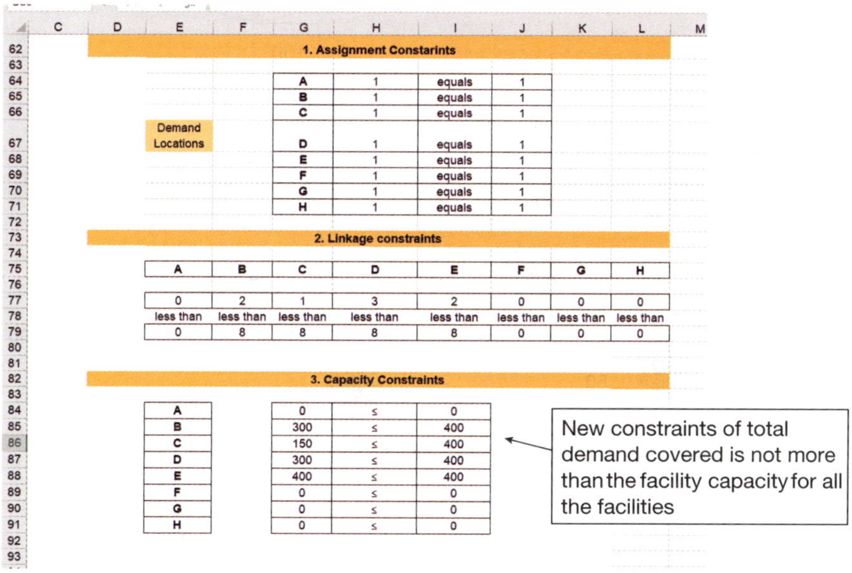

FIGURE 3.35 Defining constraints.

Step 4: Use Solver using Simplex LP to obtain the optimal number of facilities that will minimize the total cost.

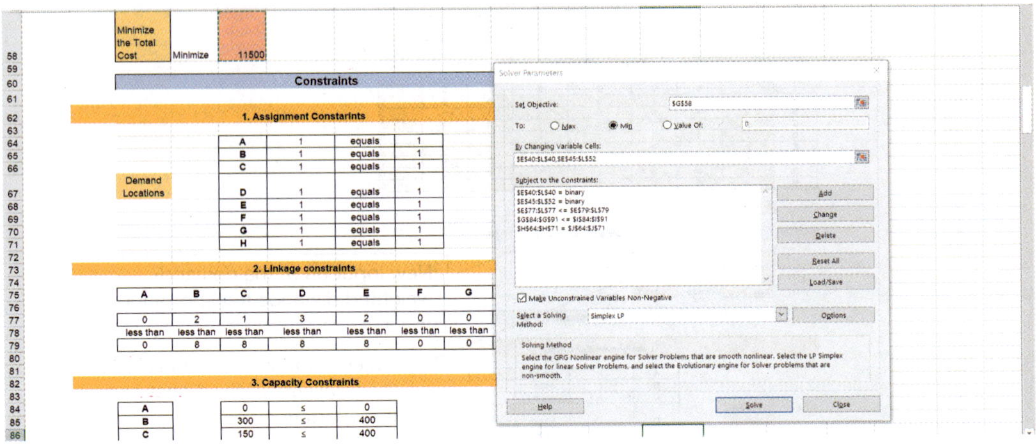

FIGURE 3.36 Using Solver to solve the problem.

For this case, Solver gives locations B, C, D, and E as the optimal number of allocations with a total cost of 11,500. The facility at B serves A and B, the facility at C serves C, the facility at D serves D, G, and H, and the facility at E serves E and F. They are shown in Figure 3.37.

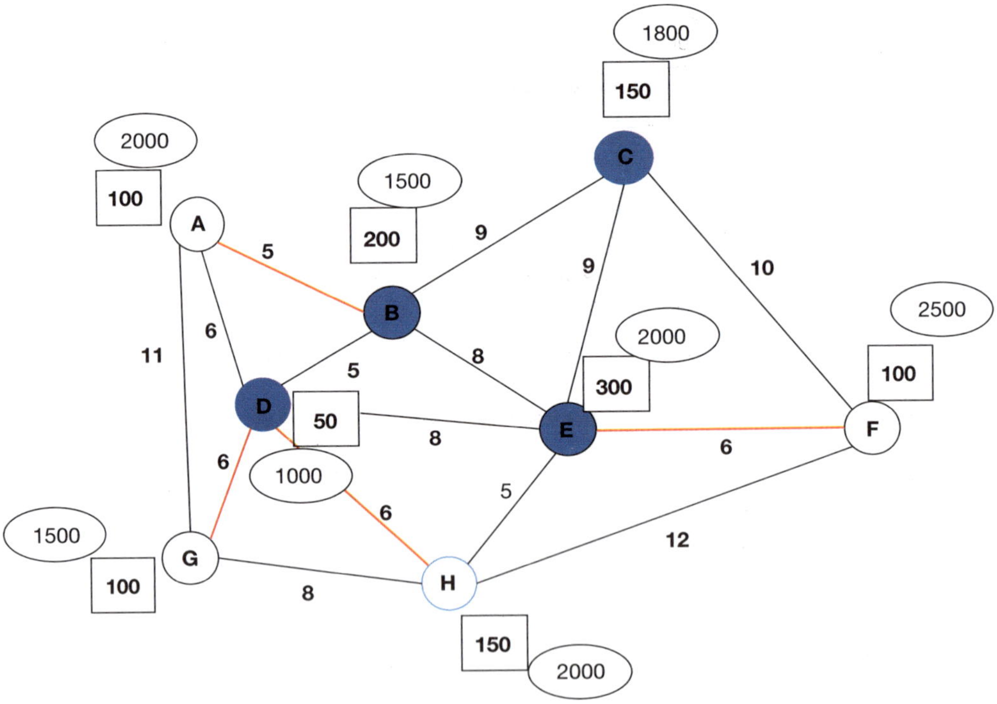

FIGURE 3.37 Selected nodes shown in blue circles and the connected nodes in thick red lines.

Another variation of this capacitated fixed charge model is to impose the number of facilities as P and remove the capacity constraints. In effect, keep the set of constraints as that of P-median problems and change the objective function to the objective function of the capacity fixed charge model. So the formulation becomes

$$\text{Minimize} \sum_j f_j X_j + \alpha \sum_i \sum_j h_i d_{ij} Y_{ij} \leftarrow$$

To minimize the total cost of fixed cost plus the demand-weighted transportation cost

Subject to

$$\left.\begin{array}{l}\sum_{j} X_j = P \\ \sum_{j \in J} Y_{ij} = 1 \ \forall i \in I\end{array}\right\} \longleftarrow \text{Ensure number of facilities is } P \text{ and coverage of each demand node is assigned only once to a facility node}$$

$$Y_{ij} - X_j \leq 0 \ \forall i \in I, j \in J \longleftarrow \text{Linkage constraint. Cannot assign demands to an unopened facility}$$

$$\left.\begin{array}{l}X_j \in \{0,1\} \forall j \\ Y_{ij} \in \{0,1\} \forall i \ \forall j\end{array}\right\} \longleftarrow \text{Integrality and binary for the decision variables}$$

Since the earlier sections have already shown them, Figures 3.38, 3.39, and 3.40 show the steps and the Solver window for this problem.

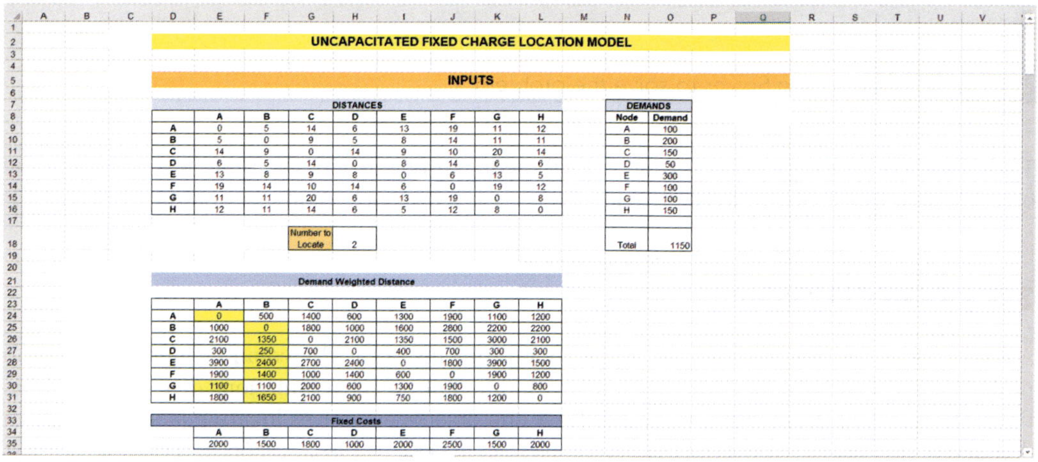

UNCAPACITATED FIXED CHARGE LOCATION MODEL

INPUTS

DISTANCES

	A	B	C	D	E	F	G	H
A	0	5	14	6	13	19	11	12
B	5	0	9	5	8	14	11	11
C	14	9	0	14	9	10	20	14
D	6	5	14	0	8	14	6	6
E	13	8	9	8	0	6	13	5
F	19	14	10	14	6	0	19	12
G	11	11	20	6	13	19	0	8
H	12	11	14	6	5	12	8	0

DEMANDS

Node	Demand
A	100
B	200
C	150
D	50
E	300
F	100
G	100
H	150
Total	1150

Number to Locate	2

Demand Weighted Distance

	A	B	C	D	E	F	G	H
A	0	500	1400	600	1300	1900	1100	1200
B	1000	0	1800	1000	1600	2800	2200	2200
C	2100	1350	0	2100	1350	1500	3000	2100
D	300	250	700	0	400	700	300	300
E	3900	2400	2700	2400	0	1800	3900	1500
F	1900	1400	1000	1400	600	0	1900	1200
G	1100	1100	2000	600	1300	1900	0	800
H	1800	1650	2100	900	750	1800	1200	0

Fixed Costs

A	B	C	D	E	F	G	H
2000	1500	1800	1000	2000	2500	1500	2000

FIGURE 3.38 Basic inputs.

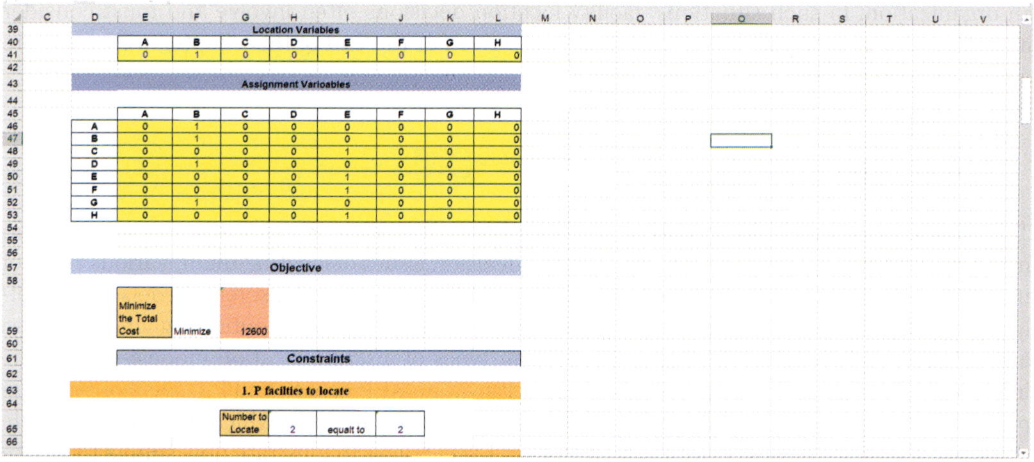

Location Variables

A	B	C	D	E	F	G	H
0	1	0	0	1	0	0	0

Assignment Varioables

	A	B	C	D	E	F	G	H
A	0	1	0	0	0	0	0	0
B	0	1	0	0	0	0	0	0
C	0	0	0	0	1	0	0	0
D	0	1	0	0	0	0	0	0
E	0	0	0	0	1	0	0	0
F	0	0	0	0	1	0	0	0
G	0	1	0	0	0	0	0	0
H	0	0	0	0	1	0	0	0

Objective

Minimize the Total Cost	Minimize	12600

Constraints

1. P facilties to locate

Number to Locate	2	equalt to	2

FIGURE 3.39 Variables, objective function, and constraints.

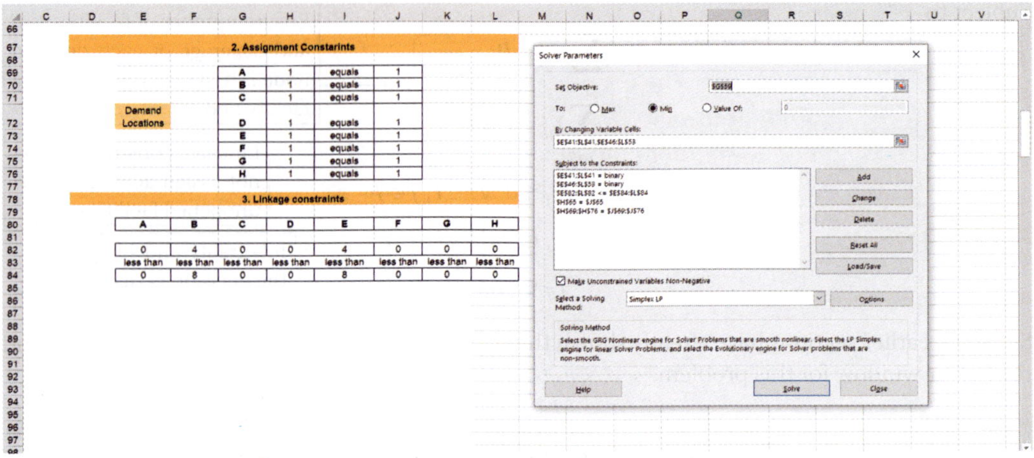

FIGURE 3.40 Using Solver to solve the problem.

The solution remains the same as that of the P-median problem with locations at B and E, but the objective function is quantified as 12,600 with the given transportation rate and the fixed cost.

3.5 | CONCLUSION

Capacitated or uncapacitated fixed charge formulations are variations of P-median problems where the facilities may or may not have capacity issues and have the fixed cost of operating them. This helps to address the formulation to minimize the total cost in locating the facilities.

A few more interesting formulations of location problems of the P-median include hub location problems and maxisum location problems with different objective functions dealing with situations like hub and spoke systems, and at least one objective involves locating facilities far from demand nodes, respectively. (The details can be seen in O'Kelly, 1986a, 1986b; and Campbell, 1990, 1994). A good amount of literature review is given by Mark Daskin in [7] and [8].

Facility location decisions are often strategic in nature as they involve very large capital outlays and long-term planning horizons and remain inflexible and not static in nature. Such decisions also have an impact on all the stakeholders of the supply chain and various functions within an organization. In such situations, facility location decisions often involve and must consider multiple, often conflicting, objectives. References given at the end of this chapter will give more details on such models.

| SUMMARY

This chapter starts with the importance of locating facilities like warehouses in a supply chain network and types of approaches to address the decision issues of locating them. Various types of models—analytical models, continuous models, network models, and discrete models—are briefly explained. Detailed discussions on analytical and discrete models are outlined giving examples and using Excel Solver to solve them. Six popular types of discrete location models—set covering, maximal covering, P-median, fixed charge (with variants), P-center, and P-dispersion—are explained with the basic mathematical formulations and the contexts in which they are applicable and used. Examples are given with screenshots of Excel Solver to illustrate how simple tools like Solver can help in solving such problems.

Case Study

It is suggested to take up the **Karnataka Engineering Company Limited** Case (http://hdl.handle.net/11718/6682) by G. Raghuram and D. Mathew, Indian Institute of Management, Ahmedabad, to explain all the methods and formulations on the data exhibits of the case and analyze the solutions from various formulations.

Important Equations and Formulae

1. Center of Gravity

Equation *X* **Equation *Y***

$$\bar{X} = \frac{\sum_i (V_i R_i X_i)/d_i}{\sum_i (V_i R_i)/d_i}, \qquad \bar{Y} = \frac{\sum_i (V_i R_i Y_i)/d_i}{\sum_i (V_i R_i)/d_i}$$

2. Set Covering Problem

$$\text{Min} \sum_j X_j$$

Subject to

$$\sum_j a_{ij} X_j \geq 1 \ \forall i \in I$$

$$X_j \in \{0,1\} \forall j \in J$$

3. Maximal Covering Problem

Maximize $\sum_j h_i Z_i$ (cost of covering all nodes)

Subject to $Z_i \leq \sum_j a_{ij} X_j \forall i \in I$ (node i not covered unless we locate at a node covering it)

$\sum_j X_j = P$ (locate P sites)

$X_j \in \{0,1\} \forall j$
$Z_i \in \{0,1\} \forall i$ } Integrality and binary

4. P-Center Problem

Minimize W

Subject to

$\sum_j X_j = P$
$\sum_{j \in J} Y_{ij} = 1 \forall i \in I$ } ← Ensure coverage, limit number of facilities

$Y_{ij} - X_j \leq 0 \forall i \in I, j \in J$ ← Linkage constraint. Cannot claim credit for non-existent

$W - \sum_{j \in J} d_{ij} Y_{ij} \geq 0 \ i \in I, \forall j \in J$ ← Force W equal to max distance

$X_j \in \{0,1\} \forall j$
$Y_{ij} \in \{0,1\} \forall i \forall j$ } ← Integrality and binary

5. P-Dispersion Problem

Maximize D ← The objective function (3.17) maximizes the distance between the two closest facilities.

Subject to

$\sum_j X_j = P$ ← P facilities to be located

$$D \leq d_{ij}(1 + M(1 - X_i) + M(1 - X_j)) \forall i, j \text{ and } i < j \text{ and } X_i \in (0,1)$$

These set of constraints defines the minimum separation between any pair of open facilities. If either X_i or X_j is zero, the constraint will not be binding. However, if both are equal to 1, then the constraint is equivalent to $D \leq d_{ij}$.

Or simplified as

$$D+(M-d_{ij})X_i+(M-d_{ij})X_j \le 2M-d_{ij}\,\forall i, j \text{ and } i<j$$

$$X_j \in \{0, 1\}\ \forall j \in J$$ ← Integrality and binary

6. P-Median Problem

Minimize $\sum_i \sum_j h_i d_{ij} Y_{ij}$

Subject to

$$\sum_j X_j = P$$

$$\sum_{j \in J} Y_{ij} = 1\ \forall i \in I$$

← Ensure number of facilities is P and coverage of each demand node is assigned only once to a facility node

$$Y_{ij} - X_j \le 0\ \forall i \in I, j \in J$$ ← Linkage constraint. Cannot assign demands to an unopened facility

$$X_j \in \{0,1\}\ \forall j$$

$$Y_{ij} \in \{0,1\}\ \forall i\ \forall j$$

← Integrality and binary for the decision variables

7. Capacitated Fixed Charge Location Problem

$$\text{Minimize} \sum_j f_j X_j + \alpha \sum_i \sum_j h_i d_{ij} Y_{ij}$$ ← To minimize the total cost of fixed cost plus the demand-weighted transportation cost

Subject to

$$\sum_{j \in J} Y_{ij} = 1 \forall i \in I$$ ← Coverage constraint, i.e., each demand node is assigned only once to a facility node

$$Y_{ij} - X_j \le 0\ \forall i \in I, j \in J$$ ← Linkage constraint. Cannot assign demands to an unopened facility

$$\sum_j h_i Y_{ij} \le C_j X_j \forall i \in I$$ ← Imposing the capacity of the jth node is not more than the total demand covered

$$X_j \in \{0,1\}\ \forall j$$

$$Y_{ij} \in \{0,1\}\ \forall i\ \forall j$$

← Integrality and binary for the decision variables

Exercises

1. Two plants in Mumbai and Chennai are to serve three market points—Hyderabad, Bangalore, and Delhi—through one or two warehouses. The volume flowing either to or from each point and the associated transportation rates are given as follows.

Point Number	Place	Approximate (X, Y) Coordinates	Volume V_i (tons)	Transportation Rate R_i (/$/ton)
1	Mumbai	(50, 65)	8000	0.15
2	Chennai	(60, 45)	9000	0.18
3	Hyderabad	(45, 60)	5000	0.20
4	Bangalore	(45, 45)	7000	0.16
5	Delhi	(45, 120)	5000	0.18

a. Using the center of gravity method, find the approximate location for a single warehouse.
b. Using the exact center of gravity method, find the optimum single warehouse location.

c. Compare the solutions in (a) and (b). What additional factor should be considered in this model and why?

d. If we need two locations for two warehouses to serve these markets, how will you assign the markets to the warehouses? Assume that each plant serves each warehouse in proportion to the market volume assigned to the warehouse.

2. Apollo Hospitals wishes to locate a clinic or clinics in an urban township. The project appraisal suggests that one or two such clinics should be sufficient for the township. The best locations are determined based on weighted distance (number of patients multiplied by the distance from the facility). The following figure shows the annual demand of patients who are likely to visit the clinic(s) and their coordinate locations in a grid. It is estimated that it costs an average of $0.80 per kilometer for a patient to travel or be transported to the clinic(s).

a. What is the best location for a single clinic?

b. If two clinics are to be located, what are the best locations for them?

c. A clinic costs $800,000 per year to equip and staff. Does it make economic sense to build the second clinic?

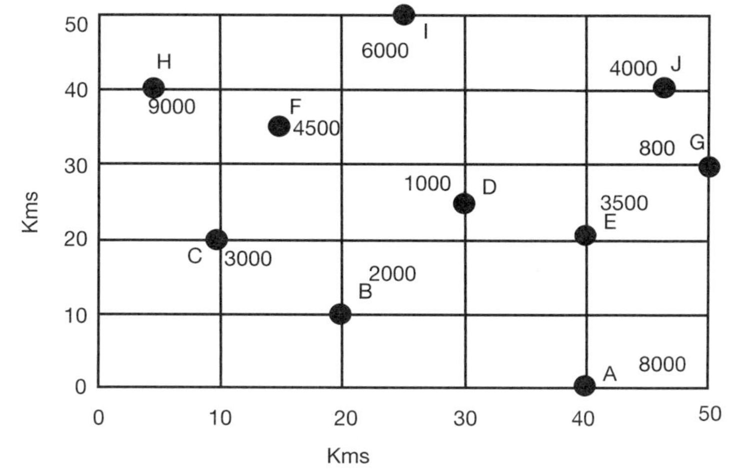

3. Consider the following network:

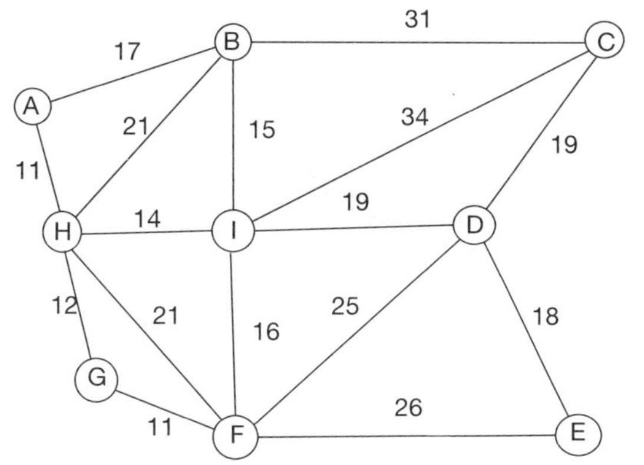

a. Solve the set covering problem with a policy of covering distance $D_c = 18$ and compare the solution with a policy of covering distance $D_c = 20$.

b. If we use the same network for solving a maximal covering problem with both the covering distance policies of $D_c = 18$ and $D_c = 20$ and locating at $P = 2$ facilities only, how do the solutions change from the set covering problem?

4. Consider the following network:

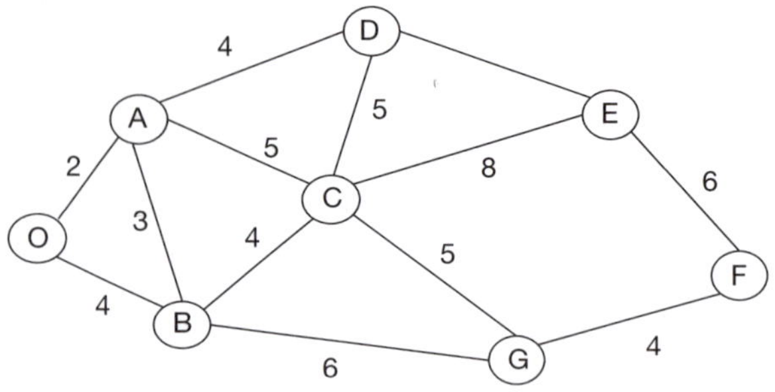

Solve the three-center problem for this network and indicate the location of facilities. What is the objective function values for this?

5. For the following network, obtain the four-center solution with the objective function value.

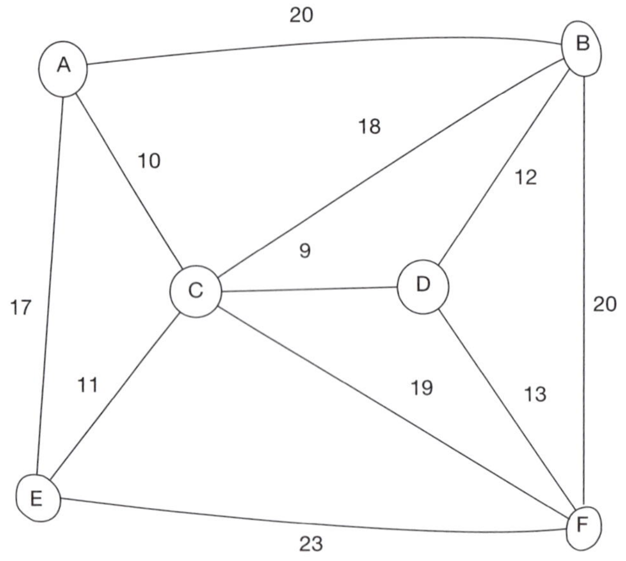

6. Mars Medical equipment company produces medical equipment that are sold in various medium and large hospitals located in various cities. Their locations and annual demand projections are given in the following table.

Cities	Latitude	Longitude	Sales (Number of Equipment)
Ahmedabad	23.03	72.58	6000
Bangalore	12.93	77.57	30000
Bhopal	23.26	77.41	7000
Bhubaneswar	20.29	85.82	14000
Chandigarh	30.74	76.77	12000
Chennai	13.07	80.24	45000
Delhi	28.61	77.23	42000
Gandhinagar	23.24	72.65	13000
Guwahati	16.15	91.73	15000
Hyderabad	17.39	78.49	24000
Jaipur	26.92	75.78	18000

Cities	Latitude	Longitude	Sales (Number of Equipment)
Kolkata	22.5	88.36	38000
Lucknow	26.85	80.94	26000
Mumbai	19.07	72.88	48000
Patna	25.61	85.16	27000
Pondicherry	11.91	79.81	30000
Raipur	21.25	81.63	18000
Ranchi	23.34	85.29	16000
Shimla	31.1	77.17	14000
Trivandrum	8.52	76.94	25000

Products are shipped using GATI Express at the transport rate of \$0.08/kg/km. The operating cost of maintaining the equipment at the hospitals is estimated as \$100,000/sqrt(N) where N is the number of locations that are chosen to serve as laboratories. Every city is a potential location for locating a laboratory. Determine the number and locations of laboratories that can serve these hospitals that will minimize the total cost. (Determine the distances of this network of cities and use the P-median approach to solve the problem.)

7. For problem 6, the fixed costs of laboratories in these cities are given in the following table.

Cities	Fixed Cost of Laboratory ($,000)
Ahmedabad	50
Bangalore	100
Bhopal	30
Bhubaneswar	40
Chandigarh	45
Chennai	120
Delhi	100
Gandhinagar	45
Guwahati	30
Hyderabad	110
Jaipur	60
Kolkata	120
Lucknow	80
Mumbai	140
Patna	70
Pondicherry	80
Raipur	60
Ranchi	50
Shimla	60
Trivandrum	70

Will the solution change from what is obtained in problem 6? Explain.

8. Consider the following network where the distances and demands are shown in the network. If we have to locate three facilities in the network using the P-median method, what would be the locations?

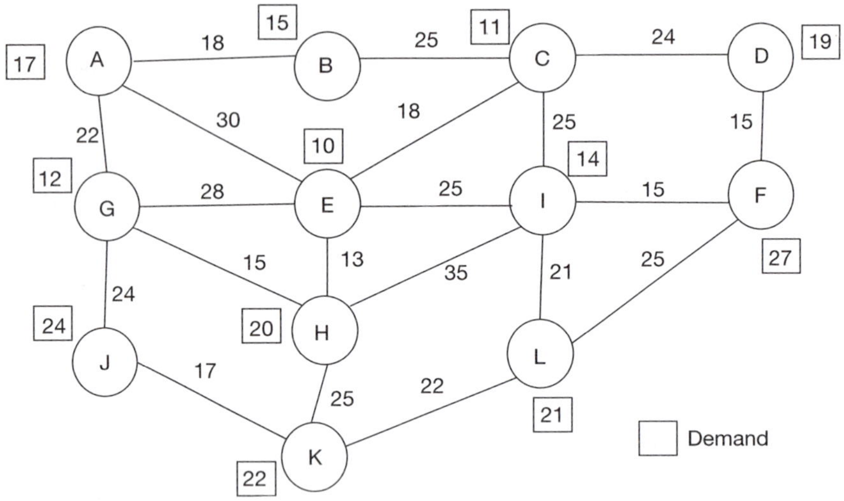

9. For the network in problem 8, if the P-dispersion method is used, where will be the locations if we need three facilities?

Bibliography

1. Balinski, M. L. (1965). Integer programming: Methods, uses, computation. *Management Science*, **12**, 253–313.
2. Ballou, R. H. and S. K. Srivastava (2007). *Business Logistics/Supply Chain Management*. Delhi: Pearson India.
3. Campbell, J. F. (1990). Locating transportation terminals to serve an expanding demand. *Transportation Research*, **24B**, 173–192.
4. Campbell, J. F. (1994). Integer programming formulations of discrete hub location problems. *European Journal of Operational Research*, **72**, 387–405.
5. Church, R. L. and C. ReVelle (1974). The maximal covering location problem. *Papers of the Regional Science Association*, **32**, 101–118.
6. Current, J., M. Daskin, and D. Schilling (2001). *Discrete Network Location Models, Facility Location: Applications and Theory*, Z. Drezner and H. W. Hamacher (Eds.). Springer-Verlag.
7. Daskin, M. S. (1995). *Network and Discrete Location: Models, Algorithms and Applications*. John Wiley Science Publications.
8. Daskin, M. S. (2008). What you should know about location modeling. *Naval Research Logistics*, **55**, 283–294.
9. Daskin, M. S., L. V. Snyder, and R. T. Berger. Facility location in supply chain design, Working Paper No. 03-010, Department of Industrial Engineering and Management Sciences. Northwestern University, Evanston, Illinois 60208-3119, U.S.A.
10. Goldman, A. J. (1971). Optimal center location on simple networks. *Transport Science*, **5**, 212–221.
11. Hakimi, S. (1965). Optimum location of switching centers in a communications network and some related graph theoretic problems. *Operations Research*, **13**, 462–475.
12. Hakimi, S. L. (1964). Optimum locations of switching centers and the absolute centers and medians of a graph. *Operations Research*, **12**, 450–459.
13. Hale, T. S. and C. R. Moberg (2003). Location science research: A review. Annals of Operations Research, **123**, 21–35.
14. Kuby, M. (1987). The p-dispersion and maximum dispersion problems. *Geographical Analysis*, **19**, 315–329.

15. O'Kelly, M. E. (1986a). Activity levels at hub facilities in interacting networks. *Geographical Analysis*, **18**, 343–356.

16. O'Kelly, M. E. (1986b). The location of interacting hub facilities. *Transportation Science*, **20**, 92–106.

17. Toregas, C. and C. ReVelle (1972). Optimal location under time or distance constraints. *Papers of the Regional Science Association*, **28**, 133–143.

18. Toregas, C., R. Swain, C. ReVelle, and L. Bergman (1971). The location of emergency service facilities. *Operations Research*, **19**, 1363–1373.

CHAPTER 4

Facility Locations through Heuristic and Other Approaches

LEARNING OBJECTIVES

After reading this chapter, you would be able to:

- Understand how a few heuristic approaches such as greedy drop help in the location of facilities in a supply chain network.
- Learn how mixed integer programming approaches using the transportation problem approach, such as guided LP and Baumol and Wolfe method, can lead to decisions on warehouse choices.
- Comprehend how the gravity model can be used to decide locational considerations.
- Understand how Huff's model can be used to decide retail locations.
- Learn to use Excel Solver to solve such problems.

4.1 | INTRODUCTION

In the previous chapter, we discussed some of the popular discrete location models. In this chapter, we will see more approaches to locate facilities using a few heuristic methods and approaches using mathematical programming models.

4.2 | HEURISTIC METHODS

Heuristic algorithms are simple and use a logical gut feeling approach, which systematically reach optimal solutions that are near optimal but not always optimal solutions.

4.2.1 Greedy Drop Heuristic

The basic approach of the drop heuristic is as follows:

Step 1: Initially, all the given m potential sites are selected, and each customer is assigned to the most cost-effective facility. Let $K = m$. This is taken as the baseline.

Step 2: Pick a selected site such that if this site is dropped and the customers are reassigned, the increase in total cost will be minimum comparing with the baseline.
Let $K = K - 1$.

Heuristics are very useful in the location of facilities as they use a simple and logical approaches but give very effective solutions. Drop heuristic is one which gives the number of facilities by dropping choices that are expensive and systematically arrives at the solution that is largely near optimal.

Step 3: Repeat Step 1 until $K = P$ (the number of facilities required).

EXAMPLE 4.1

We will illustrate these steps in this example where we have identified $m = 4$ depot locations at A, B, C, and D and want to choose $P = 2$ locations from these four locations to serve the given eight customers, as shown in Figure 4.1. While the demands for the eight customers and the unit costs of transportation to these eight customers from these four identified depots are given, it is assumed that the capacities of the four depots are not imposed and they can handle any quantity. We will see later how capacity considerations can be handled in the same situation.

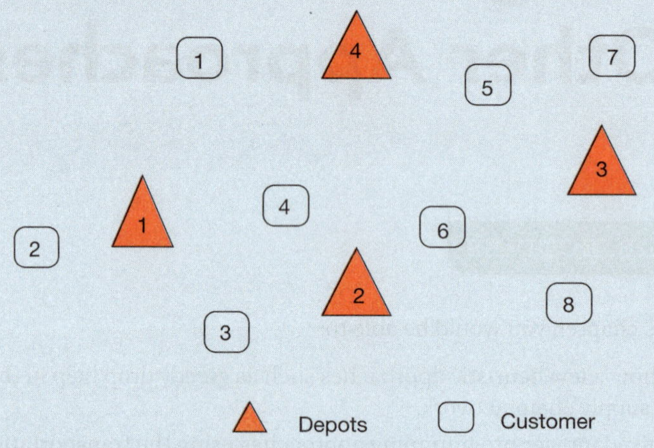

FIGURE 4.1 Depots and customers.

The data is given in Table 4.1.

TABLE 4.1 Data on four depots and eight customers

Data					
Customer	Depot Location				Demand (in Thousand Truck Loads)
	1	2	3	4	
1	4	12	20	6	100
2	2	10	25	10	50
3	3	4	16	14	120
4	6	5	9	2	80
5	18	12	7	3	200
6	14	2	4	9	70
7	20	30	2	11	60
8	24	12	6	22	100
		Number of depots to locate (*P*)		2	

Per truck load shipment costs

The steps of establishing the baseline are shown in Table 4.2 and Figure 4.2.

Round 1

Step 1: Establishing the baseline considering all the $m = 4$ depots.

Row minimum for each customer 1 to 8 is taken as the efficient allocation

TABLE 4.2 Baseline total cost

		Depot				Min Cost	Demand (in Thousand Truck Loads)	Cost in $ ('000)
		1	2	3	4			
Customer	**1**	4	12	20	6	4	100	400
	2	2	10	25	10	2	50	100
	3	3	4	16	14	3	120	360
	4	6	5	9	2	2	80	160
	5	18	12	7	3	3	200	600
	6	14	2	4	9	2	70	140
	7	20	30	2	11	2	60	120
	8	24	12	6	22	6	100	600
							Total Cost	**2480**

Baseline total Cost

The allocation is as follows:

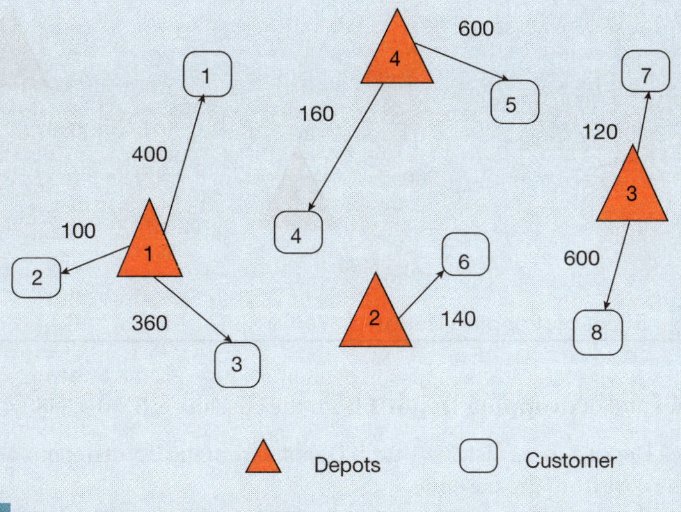

FIGURE 4.2 Baseline allocation of depots to customers.

Hence the baseline is taken as $2480.

Step 2: We will drop Depot 1 from the list of depots and evaluate the increment in the cost from the baseline.

The effect of dropping Depot 1 is shown in Table 4.3 and Figure 4.3. (Depot 1 is highlighted in red color to indicate that it is dropped, and the row minimum is taken for Depots 2, 3, and 4 for all customers).

TABLE 4.3 Effect of dropping Depot 1 from the list of depots

		Depot				Min Cost	Demand (in Thousand Truck Loads)	Cost in $ ('000)
		1	2	3	4			
Customer	1	4	12	20	6	6	100	600
	2	2	10	25	10	10	50	500
	3	3	4	16	14	4	120	480
	4	6	5	9	2	2	80	160
	5	18	12	7	3	3	200	600
	6	14	2	4	9	2	70	140
	7	20	30	2	11	2	60	120
	8	24	12	6	22	6	100	600
							Total Cost	**3200**

Total cost has increased from 2480 to 3200 by dropping Depot 1

The allocation is as follows:

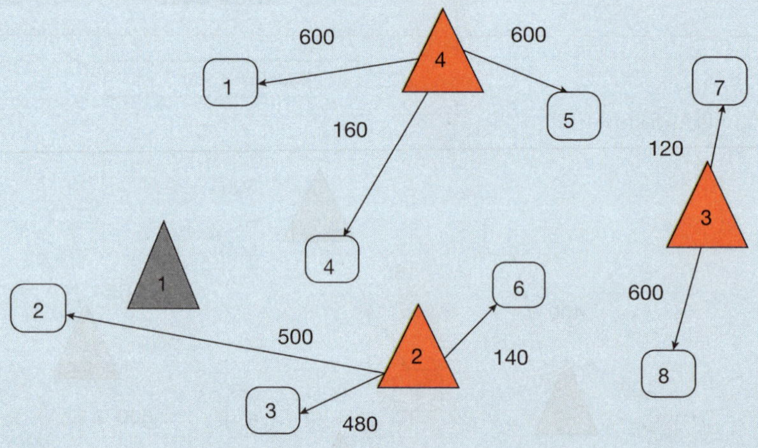

FIGURE 4.3 Effect of dropping Depot 1.

The logic is based on establishing a baseline and comparing the results of dropping facilities one by one and evaluating the cost differences with the baseline. The logic is to then drop the one facility that is expensive and the dropping of which makes the cost incremental minimum.

The cost incremental of **dropping Depot 1** from the baseline is 3200 – 2480 = **720.**

Step 3: Put back Depot 1 in the list. Now drop Depot 2 from the list of depots, and evaluate the increment in the cost from the baseline.

The effect of dropping Depot 2 is shown in Table 4.4 and Figure 4.4. (Depot 2 is highlighted in red color to indicate that it is dropped, and the row minimum is taken for Depots 1, 3, and 4 for all customers.)

TABLE 4.4 Effect of dropping Depot 2 from the list of depots

		Depot				Min Cost	Demand (in Thousand Truck Loads)	Cost in $ ('000)
		1	2	3	4			
Customer	1	4	12	20	6	4	100	400
	2	2	10	25	10	2	50	100
	3	3	4	16	14	3	120	360
	4	6	5	9	2	2	80	160
	5	18	12	7	3	3	200	600
	6	14	2	4	9	4	70	280
	7	20	30	2	11	2	60	120
	8	24	12	6	22	6	100	600
							Total Cost	**2620**

Total cost has increased from 2480 to 2620 by dropping Depot 2

The allocation is as follows:

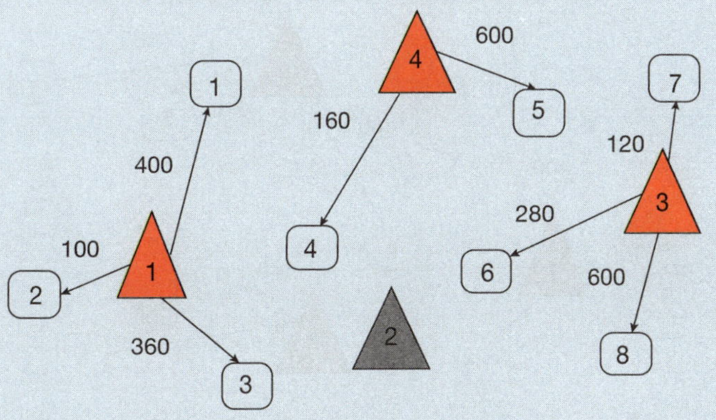

FIGURE 4.4 Effect of dropping Depot 2.

The cost incremental of **dropping Depot 2** from the baseline is 2620 – 2480 = **140**.

Step 4: Put back Depot 2 in the list. Now drop Depot 3 from the list of depots, and evaluate the increment in the cost from the baseline.

The effect of dropping Depot 3 is shown in Table 4.5 and Figure 4.5. (Depot 3 is highlighted in red color to indicate that it is dropped, and the row minimum is taken for Depots 1, 2, and 4 for all the customers.)

TABLE 4.5 Effect of dropping Depot 3 from the list of depots

		Depot				Min Cost	Demand (in Thousand Truck Loads)	Cost in $ ('000)
		1	2	3	4			
Customer	1	4	12	20	6	4	100	400
	2	2	10	25	10	2	50	100
	3	3	4	16	14	3	120	360
	4	6	5	9	2	2	80	160
	5	18	12	7	3	3	200	600
	6	14	2	4	9	2	70	140
	7	20	30	2	11	11	60	660
	8	24	12	6	22	12	100	1200
							Total Cost	**3620**

Total cost has increased from 2480 to 3620 by dropping Depot 3

The allocation is as follows:

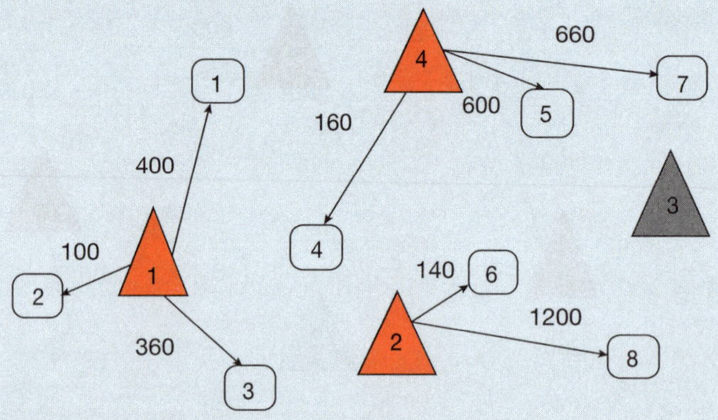

FIGURE 4.5 Effect of dropping Depot 3.

The cost incremental of **dropping Depot 3** from the baseline is 3620 – 2480 = **1140**.

Step 4: Put back Depot 3 in the list. Now drop Depot 4 from the list of depots, and evaluate the increment in the cost from the baseline.

The effect of dropping Depot 4 is shown in Table 4.6 and Figure 4.6. (Depot 4 is highlighted in red color to indicate that it is dropped, and the row minimum is taken for Depots 1, 2, and 3 for all the customers.)

TABLE 4.6 Effect of dropping Depot 3 from the list of depots.

		Depot				Min Cost	Demand (in Thousand Truck Loads)	Cost in $ ('000)
		1	2	3	4			
Customer	1	4	12	20	6	4	100	400
	2	2	10	25	10	2	50	100
	3	3	4	16	14	3	120	360
	4	6	5	9	2	5	80	400
	5	18	12	7	3	7	200	1400
	6	14	2	4	9	2	70	140
	7	20	30	2	11	2	60	120
	8	24	12	6	22	6	100	600
							Total Cost	**3520**

Total cost has increased from 2480 to 3520 by dropping Depot 4

The allocation is as follows:

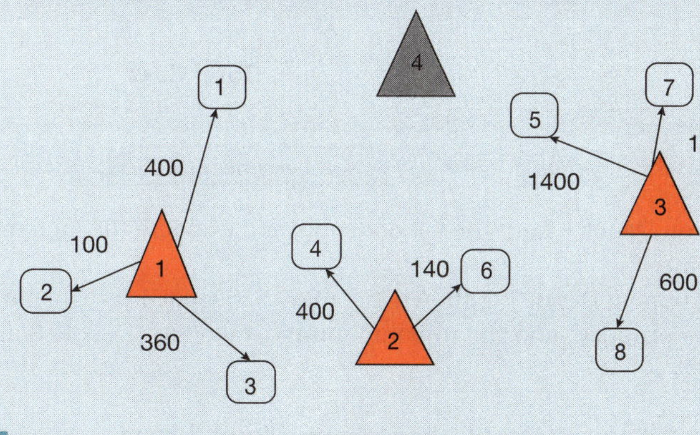

FIGURE 4.6 Effect of dropping Depot 4.

The cost incremental of **dropping Depot 4** from the baseline is 3520 – 2480 = **1040**.

The summary of the dropping of depots and its effect on the baseline in the first round is summarized in Table 4.7.

TABLE 4.7 Summary of drop procedure (first round)

Depots Considered	Depot Dropped	Total Cost	Incremental from the Baseline Total Cost
1, 2, 3, 4	—	**2480 (baseline)**	
2, 3, and 4	1	3200	720
1, 3, and 4	**2**	**2620**	**140**
1, 2, and 4	3	3620	1140
1, 2, and 3	4	3520	1040

Best to drop Depot 2 from the list as the total cost is the least by dropping the depot

So it is better to drop Depot 2 from the list as the total cost is the least if we drop Depot 2 and the incremental cost is also the least by dropping it.

Round 2

This makes us start Round 2 with Depots 1, 3, and 4 with the new baseline 2620, as shown in Table 4.8.

Step 1: Establishing the new baseline with the total cost of 2620 with Depots 1, 3, and 4 and dropping Depot 2.

TABLE 4.8 New baseline with Depots 1, 3, and 4

		Depot			Min Cost	Demand (in Thousand Truck Loads)	Cost in $ ('000)
		1	3	4			
Customer	1	4	20	6	4	100	400
	2	2	25	10	2	50	100
	3	3	16	14	3	120	360
	4	6	9	2	2	80	160
	5	18	7	3	3	200	600
	6	14	4	9	4	70	280
	7	20	2	11	2	60	120
	8	24	6	22	6	100	600
						Total Cost	**2620**

New baseline total cost

Step 2: We will drop Depot 1 from the list of depots and evaluate the increment in the cost from the new baseline.

The effect of dropping Depot 1 is shown in Table 4.9. (Depot 1 is highlighted in red color to indicate that it is dropped, and the row minimum is taken for Depots 3 and 4 for all the customers.)

TABLE 4.9 Effect of dropping Depot 1 from the new list of depots

		Depot			Min Cost	Demand (in Thousand Truck Loads)	Cost in $ ('000)
		1	3	4			
Customer	1	4	20	6	6	100	600
	2	2	25	10	10	50	500
	3	3	16	14	14	120	1680
	4	6	9	2	2	80	160
	5	18	7	3	3	200	600
	6	14	4	9	4	70	280
	7	20	2	11	2	60	120
	8	24	6	22	6	100	600
						Total Cost	**4540**

Total cost has increased from 2620 to 4540 by dropping Depot 1

The cost incremental of **dropping Depot 1** from the new baseline is 4540 – 2620 = **1920**.

Step 3: We will put back Depot 1 and drop Depot 3 from the list of depots and evaluate the increment in the total cost from the new baseline.

The effect of dropping Depot 3 is shown in Table 4.10. (Depot 3 is highlighted in red color to indicate that it is dropped, and the row minimum is taken for Depots 1 and 4 for all the customers.)

Here, the steps are repeated until we reach the number that we wish to locate. The procedure is basically dropping sites one by one and getting the number we wish to get. This process can be easily automated with the help of a computer routine or on Excel.

TABLE 4.10 Effect of dropping Depot 3 from the new list of depots

		Depot			Min Cost	Demand (in Thousand Truck Loads)	Cost in $ ('000)
		1	3	4			
Customer	1	4	20	6	4	100	400
	2	2	25	10	2	50	100
	3	3	16	14	3	120	360
	4	6	9	2	2	80	160
	5	18	7	3	3	200	600
	6	14	4	9	9	70	630
	7	20	2	11	11	60	660
	8	24	6	22	22	100	2200
						Total Cost	**5110**

Total cost has increased from 2620 to 5110 by dropping Depot 3

The cost incremental of **dropping Depot 3** from the new baseline is 5110 – 2620 = **2490**.

Step 4: We will put back Depot 3 and drop Depot 4 from the list of depots and evaluate the increment in the total cost from the new baseline.

The effect of dropping Depot 4 is shown in Table 4.11. (Depot 4 is highlighted in red color to indicate that it is dropped, and the row minimum is taken for Depots 1 and 3 for all the customers.)

TABLE 4.11 Effect of dropping Depot 4 from the new list of depots

		Depot			Min Cost	Demand (in Thousand Truck Loads)	Cost in $ ('000)
		1	3	4			
Customer	1	4	20	6	4	100	400
	2	2	25	10	2	50	100
	3	3	16	14	3	120	360
	4	6	9	2	6	80	480
	5	18	7	3	7	200	1400
	6	14	4	9	4	70	280
	7	20	2	11	2	60	120
	8	24	6	22	6	100	600
						Total Cost	**3740**

Total cost has increased from 2620 to 3740 by dropping Depot 4

The cost incremental of **dropping Depot 4** from the new baseline is 3740 – 2620 = **1120**.

The summary of dropping of depots and its effect on the new baseline in the second round is summarized in Table 4.12.

TABLE 4.12 Summary of drop procedure (second round)

Depots Considered	Depot Dropped	Total Cost	Incremental from the Baseline Total Cost
1, 3, 4	—	**2620 (baseline)**	
3 and 4	1	4540	1920
1 and 4	3	5110	2490
1 and 3	**4**	**3740**	**1120**

Best to drop Depot 4 from the list as the total cost is the least by dropping that depot

So, it is better to drop Depot 4 from the list as the total cost is the least if we drop Depot 4 and the incremental cost is also the least by dropping it.

Since we wanted to reach $P = 2$ depots, we have reached that at the end of the second round with the selection of **Depots 1 and 3** with a total cost of 3740, which is "supposed" to be good and we have dropped Depots 2 and 4 from the list as not required.

We see that we are selecting Depots 1 and 3 and assigning customers 1, 2, 3, and 4 to Depot 1 and customers 5, 6, 7, and 8 to Depot 3 with a total cost of 3740. The same is shown in Figure 4.7.

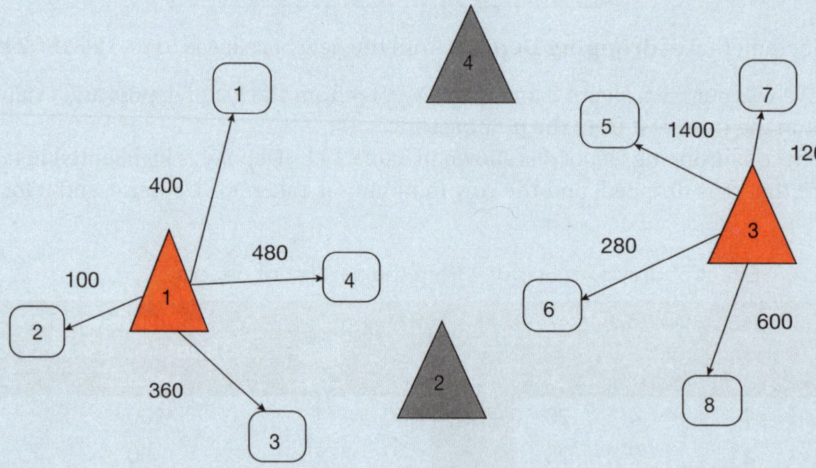

FIGURE 4.7 Final allocation depots and customers.

4.3 | P-MEDIAN SOLUTION FOR EXAMPLE 4.1

We discussed the P-median problem in the last chapter. A solution obtained by using the P-median approach for Example 4.1 leads to the same result of selecting Depots 1 and 3 with a total cost of 3540 and dropping Depots 2 and 4. The same is shown in Figure 4.8 (screenshots of the Excel sheet).

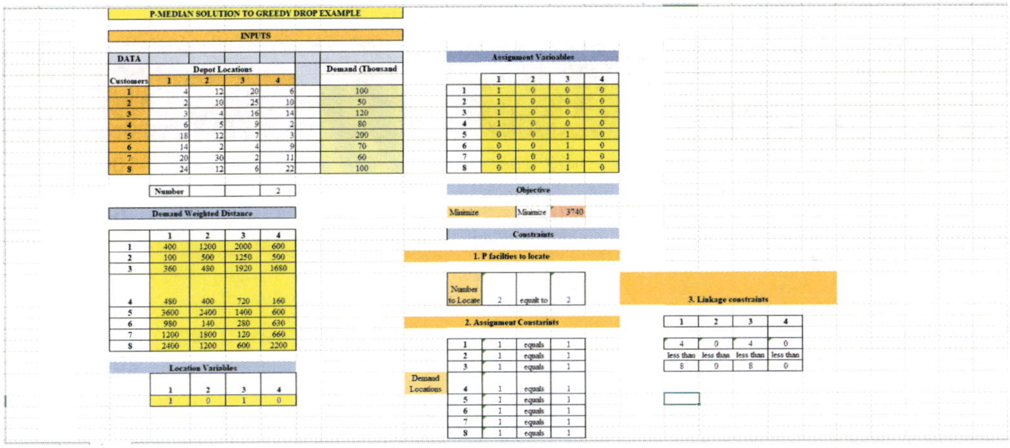

FIGURE 4.8 P-median solution to Example 4.1.

The Solver screen is given in Figure 4.9.

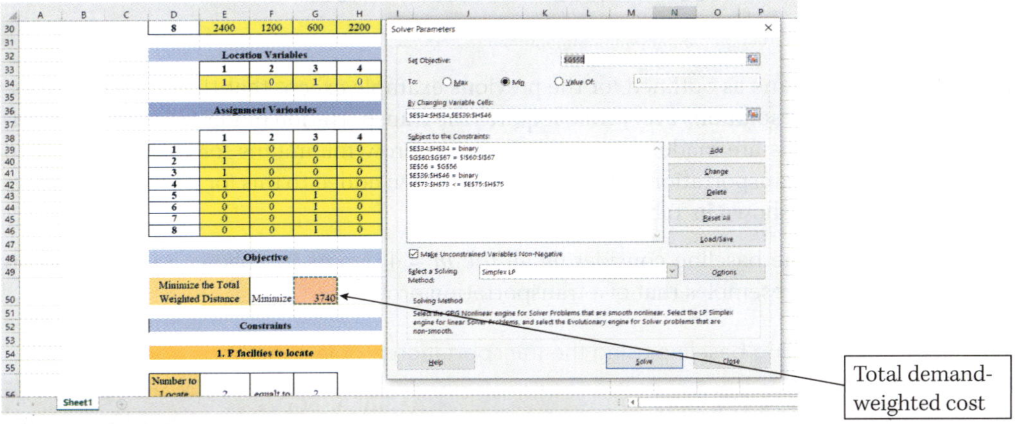

FIGURE 4.9 Solver solution to the P-median formulation of Example 4.1.

We see that the Solver solution select Depots 1 and 3 and assign customers 1, 2, 3, and 4 to Depot 1 and customers 5, 6, 7, and 8 to Depot 3 with a total cost of 3740, which is the same as what we obtained by applying the greedy drop heuristic on this example.

So, in a way, the greedy drop heuristic is a good heuristic for solving P-median problems!

ACTIVITY 4.1

It is interesting to note here how the drop heuristic is quite similar to the P-median approach and how it serves as a good heuristic for solving a P-median problem. It is suggested to try out the problems given in the exercises at the end on this topic for getting insights into this observation.

4.4 GREEDY DROP HEURISTIC FOR CAPACITATED DEPOTS WITH FIXED COSTS

In this section, we will take Example 4.1 with the capacity constraints (assumed equal) and the fixed cost of the depots as additional information (as given in Table 4.13).

TABLE 4.13 Data with capacities of depots and fixed costs

		Depot				Demand (in Thousand Truck Loads)
		1	2	3	4	
Customer	1	4	12	20	6	100
	2	2	10	25	10	50
	3	3	4	16	14	120
	4	6	5	9	2	80
	5	18	12	7	3	200
	6	14	2	4	9	70
	7	20	30	2	11	60
	8	24	12	6	22	100
Capacity		400	400	400	400	
Fixed cost		1500	1800	1400	1600	

The procedure is the same as outlined for the previous example except that the procedure to establish the baseline and solutions every time requires the transportation model (allocation model) to be solved. Allocations are made accordingly instead of row minimums for each customer to determine the cost of transportation. The fixed costs are then added to this for the opened depots to get the total cost, as shown in Table 4.14.

Step 1: Establishing the baseline considering all the $m = 4$ depots by solving a transportation problem as the format resembles that of a transportation problem.

TABLE 4.14 Establishing baseline using the transportation problem method

		Depot				Demand (in Thousand Truck Loads)
		1	2	3	4	
Customer	1	4	12	20	6	100
	2	2	10	25	10	50
	3	3	4	16	14	120
	4	6	5	9	2	80
	5	18	12	7	3	200
	6	14	2	4	9	70
	7	20	30	2	11	60
	8	24	12	6	22	100
Capacity		400	400	400	400	
Fixed cost		1500	1800	1400	1600	

(Continued)

TABLE 4.14 (Continued)

		Decision Variable Depot						
		1	2	3	4	LHS		Demand (in Thousand Truck Loads)
Customer	1	100	0	0	0	100	equals	**100**
	2	50	0	0	0	50	equals	**50**
	3	120	0	0	0	120	equals	**120**
	4	0	0	0	80	80	equals	**80**
	5	0	0	0	200	200	equals	**200**
	6	0	70	0	0	70	equals	**70**
	7	0	0	60	0	60	equals	**60**
	8	0	0	100	0	100	equals	**100**
LHS		150	70	160	280			
		equals	equals	equals	equals			
Capacity		**400**	**400**	**400**	**400**			
	Total Transportation Cost				**2480**			
	Total Cost				**8780**			

Hence the baseline is taken as 8780 with the following allocation.

Step 2: We will drop Depot 1 from the list of depots and evaluate the change in the cost from the baseline.

The effect of dropping Depot 1 is shown in Table 4.15. (Depot 1 is highlighted in light green color to indicate that it is dropped by assigning a high cost of 999 to all the customers for Depot 1 and the problem is solved as a transportation problem keeping Depots 2, 3, and 4 for all the customers.)

The capacitated problem is quite similar to the discussion earlier on drop heuristic except that in the process of arriving at the baseline and later for evaluations of the drop process, we solve a transportation problem every time instead of taking a row minimum as done earlier.

TABLE 4.15 Effect of dropping Depot 1 from the list of depots

		Depot				
		1	2	3	4	Demand (in Thousand Truck Loads)
Customer	1	999	12	20	6	**100**
	2	999	10	25	10	**50**
	3	999	4	16	14	**120**
	4	999	5	9	2	**80**
	5	999	12	7	3	**200**
	6	999	2	4	9	**70**
	7	999	30	2	11	**60**
	8	999	12	6	22	**100**
Capacity		**400**	**400**	**400**	**400**	
Fixed cost		**1500**	**1800**	**1400**	**1600**	

(Continued)

TABLE 4.15 (Continued)

		Decision Variable Depot 1	2	3	4	LHS		Demand (in Thousand Truck Loads)
Customer	**1**	0	0	0	100	100	equals	**100**
	2	0	50	0	0	50	equals	**50**
	3	0	120	0	0	120	equals	**120**
	4	0	0	0	80	80	equals	**80**
	5	0	0	0	200	200	equals	**200**
	6	0	70	0	0	70	equals	**70**
	7	0	0	60	0	60	equals	**60**
	8	0	0	100	0	100	equals	**100**
LHS		0	240	160	380			
		equals	equals	equals	equals			
Capacity		**400**	**400**	**400**	**400**			
	Total Transportation Cost				**3200**			
	Total Cost				**8000**			

The cost decremental of **dropping Depot 1** from the baseline is 8000 – 8780 = **780**.

Step 3: We will put back Depot 1 in the list and drop Depot 2 from the list of depots and evaluate the change in the total cost from the baseline.

The effect of dropping Depot 2 is shown in Table 4.16. (Depot 2 is highlighted in light green color to indicate that it is dropped by assigning a high cost of 999 to all the customers for Depot 2, and the problem is solved as a transportation problem keeping Depots 1, 3, and 4 for all the customers.)

TABLE 4.16 Effect of dropping Depot 2 from the list of depots

		Depot 1	2	3	4	Demand (in Thousand Truck Loads)
Customer	**1**	4	999	20	6	**100**
	2	2	999	25	10	**50**
	3	3	999	16	14	**120**
	4	6	999	9	2	**80**
	5	18	999	7	3	**200**
	6	14	999	4	9	**70**
	7	20	999	2	11	**60**
	8	24	999	6	22	**100**
Capacity		**400**	**400**	**400**	**400**	
Fixed cost		**1500**	**1800**	**1400**	**1600**	

(*Continued*)

TABLE 4.16 (Continued)

		Decision Variable Depot 1	2	3	4	LHS		Demand (in Thousand Truck Loads)
Customer	1	100	0	0	0	100	equals	**100**
	2	50	0	0	0	50	equals	**50**
	3	120	0	0	0	120	equals	**120**
	4	0	0	0	80	80	equals	**80**
	5	0	0	0	200	200	equals	**200**
	6	0	0	70	0	70	equals	**70**
	7	0	0	60	0	60	equals	**60**
	8	0	0	100	0	100	equals	**100**
LHS		270	0	230	280			
		equals	equals	equals	equals			
Capacity		**400**	**400**	**400**	**400**			
	Total Transportation Cost				**2620**			
	Total Cost				**7120**			

The cost decremental of **dropping Depot 2** from the baseline is 7120 – 8780 = **1660**.

Step 4: We will put back Depot 2 in the list and drop Depot 3 from the list of depots and evaluate the change in the total cost from the baseline.

The effect of dropping Depot 3 is shown in Table 4.17. (Depot 3 is highlighted in light green color to indicate that it is dropped by assigning a high cost of 999 to all the customers for Depot 3, and the problem is solved as a transportation problem keeping Depots 1, 2, and 4 for all the customers.)

TABLE 4.17 Effect of dropping Depot 3 from the list of depots

		Depot 1	2	3	4	Demand (in Thousand Truck Loads)
Customer	1	4	12	999	6	**100**
	2	2	10	999	10	**50**
	3	3	4	999	14	**120**
	4	6	5	999	2	**80**
	5	18	12	999	3	**200**
	6	14	2	999	9	**70**
	7	20	30	999	11	**60**
	8	24	12	999	22	**100**
Capacity		**400**	**400**	**400**	**400**	
Fixed cost		**1500**	**1800**	**1400**	**1600**	

(Continued)

TABLE 4.17 (Continued)

		Decision Variable Depot 1	2	3	4	LHS		Demand (in Thousand Truck Loads)
Customer	**1**	100	0	0	0	100	equals	**100**
	2	50	0	0	0	50	equals	**50**
	3	120	0	0	0	120	equals	**120**
	4	0	40	0	40	80	equals	**80**
	5	0	0	0	200	200	equals	**200**
	6	0	70	0	0	70	equals	**70**
	7	0	0	0	60	60	equals	**60**
	8	0	100	0	0	100	equals	**100**
LHS		150	210	0	300			
		equals	equals	equals	equals			
Capacity		**400**	**400**	**400**	**400**			
	Total Transportation Cost				**3740**			
	Total Cost				**8640**			

The cost decremental of **dropping Depot 3** from the baseline is 8640 – 8780 = **140.**

Step 5: We will put back Depot 3 in the list and drop Depot 4 from the list of depots and evaluate the change in the total cost from the baseline.

The effect of dropping Depot 4 is shown in Table 4.18. (Depot 4 is highlighted in light green color to indicate that it is dropped by assigning a high cost of 999 to all the customers for Depot 4, and the problem is solved as a transportation problem keeping Depots 1, 2, and 3 for all the customers.)

TABLE 4.18 Effect of dropping Depot 4 from the list of depots

		Depot 1	2	3	4	Demand (in Thousand Truck Loads)
Customer	**1**	4	12	20	999	**100**
	2	2	10	25	999	**50**
	3	3	4	16	999	**120**
	4	6	5	9	999	**80**
	5	18	12	7	999	**200**
	6	14	2	4	999	**70**
	7	20	30	2	999	**60**
	8	24	12	6	999	**100**
Capacity		**400**	**400**	**400**	**400**	
Fixed cost		**1500**	**1800**	**1400**	**1600**	

(Continued)

TABLE 4.18 (Continued)

		Decision Variable Depot 1	2	3	4	LHS		Demand (in Thousand Truck Loads)
Customer	**1**	100	0	0	0	100	equals	**100**
	2	50	0	0	0	50	equals	**50**
	3	120	0	0	0	120	equals	**120**
	4	0	80	0	0	80	equals	**80**
	5	0	0	200	0	200	equals	**200**
	6	0	70	0	0	70	equals	**70**
	7	0	0	60	0	60	equals	**60**
	8	0	0	100	0	100	equals	**100**
LHS		270	150	300	0			
		equals	equals	equals	equals			
Capacity		**400**	**400**	**400**	**400**			
	Total Transportation Cost				**3520**			
	Total Cost				**8220**			

The cost decremental of **dropping Depot 4** from the baseline is 8220 – 8780 = **560**.

The summary of the dropping of depots and its effect on the baseline in the first round is summarized in Table 4.19.

TABLE 4.19 Summary of drop procedure (first round)

Depots Considered	Depot Dropped	Total Cost	Cost Decrement from the Baseline Total Cost
1, 2, 3, 4	—	**8780 (baseline)**	
2, 3, and 4	1	8000	780
1, 3, and 4	**2**	**7120**	**1660**
1, 2, and 4	3	8640	140
1, 2, and 3	4	8220	560

Best to drop Depot 2 from the list as the total cost is the least by dropping the depot

So it is better to drop Depot 2 from the list as the total cost is the least if we drop Depot 2 and the decremental cost is also the maximum by dropping it.

Round 2

This makes us start Round 2 with Depots 1, 3, and 4 with the new baseline 7120 as shown in Table 4.20.

TABLE 4.20 Baseline with Depots 1, 3, and 4

		Depot			Demand (in Thousand Truck Loads)
		1	3	4	
Customer	**1**	4	20	6	**100**
	2	2	25	10	**50**
	3	3	16	14	**120**
	4	6	9	2	**80**
	5	18	7	3	**200**
	6	14	4	9	**70**
	7	20	2	11	**60**
	8	24	6	22	**100**
Capacity		**400**	**400**	**400**	
Fixed Cost		**1500**	**1400**	**1600**	

		Decision Variable					
		Depot					Demand (in Thousand Truck Loads)
		1	3	4	LHS		
Customer	**1**	100	0	0	100	equals	**100**
	2	50	0	0	50	equals	**50**
	3	120	0	0	120	equals	**120**
	4	0	0	80	80	equals	**80**
	5	0	0	200	200	equals	**200**
	6	0	70	0	70	equals	**70**
	7	0	60	0	60	equals	**60**
	8	0	100	0	100	equals	**100**
LHS		270	230	280			
		equals	equals	equals			
Capacity		**400**	**400**	**400**			

Total Transportation Cost	**2620**
Total Cost	**7120**

We repeat this process by dropping Depots 1, 3, and 4 one by one and drop one more from this to reach the number $P = 2$. The steps are the same as earlier, and they are thus skipped here.

The summary of the dropping of depots and its effect on the new baseline in the second round is summarized in Table 4.21.

TABLE 4.21 Summary of drop procedure (second round)

Depots Considered	Depot Dropped	Total Cost	Incremental from the Baseline Total Cost
1, 3, 4	—	**7120 (baseline)**	
3 and 4	1	7900	780
1 and 4	3	8450	1330
1 and 3	**4**	**6940**	**180**

Best to drop Depot 4 from the list as the total cost is the least by dropping that depot

So it is better to drop Depot 4 from the list as the total cost is the least if we drop Depot 4 and the incremental cost is also the least by dropping it.

Since we wanted to reach $P = 2$ depots, at the end of round 2 we have reached that with the selection of **Depots 1 and 3** with the total cost of 3740, which is "supposed" to be good and we have dropped Depots 2 and 4 from the list as not required.

We see that we are selecting Depots 1 and 3 and assigning customers 1, 2, 3, 4, and 6 (partially) to Depot 1 and customers 5, 6, 7, and 8 to Depot 3 with a total cost of 6940 as shown in Table 4.22.

TABLE 4.22 Final allocation of depots and customers

		Depot		Demand (in Thousand Truck Loads)
		1	3	
Customer	**1**	4	20	**100**
	2	2	25	**50**
	3	3	16	**120**
	4	6	9	**80**
	5	18	7	**200**
	6	14	4	**70**
	7	20	2	**60**
	8	24	6	**100**
	Capacity	**400**	**400**	
	Fixed Cost	**1500**	**1400**	

(Continued)

TABLE 4.22 (Continued)

		Decision Variable				
		Depot				
		1	3	LHS		Demand (in Thousand Truck Loads)
Customer	**1**	100	0	100	equals	**100**
	2	50	0	50	equals	**50**
	3	120	0	120	equals	**120**
	4	80	0	80	equals	**80**
	5	0	200	200	equals	**200**
	6	30	40	70	equals	**70**
	7	0	60	60	equals	**60**
	8	0	100	100	equals	**100**
LHS		380	400			
		equals	equals			
		400	**400**			

Total Transportation Cost	**4040**
Total Cost	**6940**

As can be seen in both the situations without and with capacity constraints, the choice is made for Depots 1 and 3 by dropping Depots 2 and 4.

4.5 CAPACITATED FIXED CHARGE MODEL SOLUTION FOR EXAMPLE 4.1

We discussed the capacitated fixed charge location models in the previous chapter. A solution obtained by using this approach for this example leads to the same solution of selecting Depots 1 and 3 with the total cost of 6640 and dropping Depots 2 and 4, which is shown in Table 4.23.

TABLE 4.23 Solution using capacitated fixed charge location model

Capacitated Fixed Charge Location Model for Greedy Drop Example					
			Input		
	Distance				
	1	2	3	4	Demand
1	4	12	20	6	**100**
2	2	10	25	10	**50**

(Continued)

TABLE 4.23 (Continued)

3	3	4	16	14	**120**
4	6	5	9	2	**80**
5	18	12	7	3	**200**
6	14	2	4	9	**70**
7	20	30	2	11	**60**
8	24	12	6	22	**100**
				Total	**780**

Demand-Weighted Distance

	1	**2**	**3**	**4**
1	400	1200	2000	600
2	100	500	1250	500
3	360	480	1920	1680
4	480	400	720	160
5	3600	2400	1400	600
6	980	140	280	630
7	1200	1800	120	660
8	2400	1200	600	2200

Fixed Cost

1	**2**	**3**	**4**
1500	**1800**	**1400**	**1600**

Capacity

1	**2**	**3**	**4**
400	400	400	400

Location Variable

A	**B**	**C**	**D**
1	0	1	0

Assignment Variable

	A	**B**	**C**	**D**
1	1	0	0	0
2	1	0	0	0

(*Continued*)

TABLE 4.23 (Continued)

3	1	0	0	0
4	1	0	0	0
5	0	0	1	0
6	0	0	1	0
7	0	0	1	0
8	0	0	1	0

Alpha	1

Objective

Minimize the Total Cost	Minimize	6640

Constraint

1. Assignment Constraint

Demand Location	**1**	1	equals	1
	2	1	equals	1
	3	1	equals	1
	4	1	equals	1
	5	1	equals	1
	6	1	equals	1
	7	1	equals	1
	8	1	equals	1

1	**2**	**3**	**4**
4	0	4	0
8	0	8	0

(Continued)

TABLE 4.23 (Continued)

2. Capacity Constraint

1	350	≤	4000
2	0	≤	0
3	430	≤	4000
4	0	≤	0

3. Number to Locate

Number to Locate	2	equals to	2

Solver solution is provided in Figure 4.10.

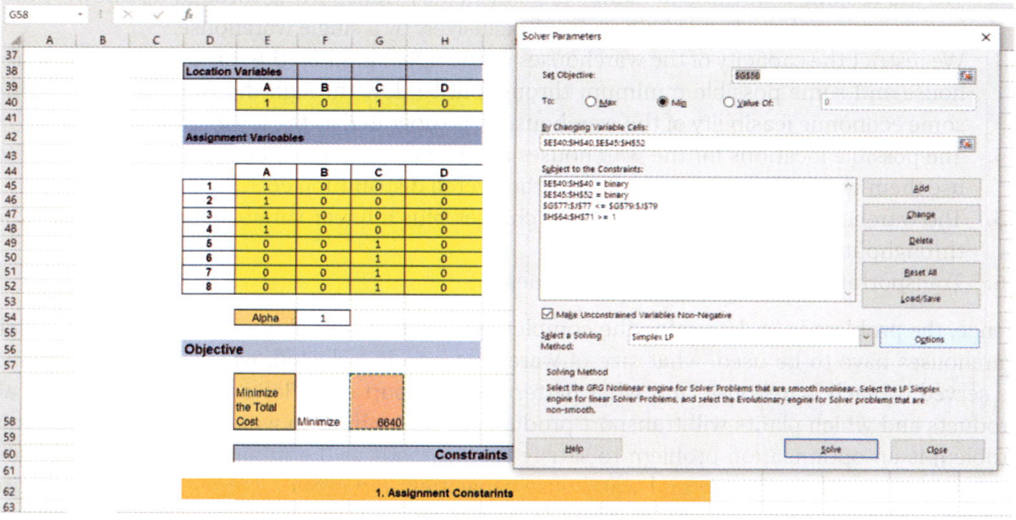

FIGURE 4.10 Solver solution to the capacitated fixed charge problem for the example.

There is a small difference in the allocation because in the fixed charge model, the allocation is not split across depots, while in the greedy drop heuristic, it splits the allocation. In this example, in the greedy drop heuristic, customer 6 is served from both Depots 1 and 3 with the allocation of 30 and 40, while in the capacitated fixed charge model, customer 6 is served only by Depot 1 for the entire demand of 70. So, there is a small difference of 300 in the transportation cost.

ACTIVITY 4.2

The greedy drop heuristic is a good heuristic for solving P-median and fixed charge location problems. It is suggested to try out the problems given in the exercises at the end to get insights into this observation.

4.6 MATHEMATICAL PROGRAMMING APPROACH TO FACILITIES LOCATION PROBLEMS

In this section, we will discuss a few approaches using mathematical programming through mixed integer programming and multilevel transportation problems. Here we assume that the location coordinates or locating facilities, per se, are not the focus of the problems but to choose or decide when to open a facility, etc. will be the focus of the problems.

4.6.1 Mixed Integer Programming Approach

Mixed integer linear programming approach is the most popular methodology used in commercial location models. One of the main benefits of using the mixed integer linear programming approach is its ability to handle fixed costs in an appropriately optimal way. Considerable research has been done in this area of applying the integer programming approach. The following example uses one of the popular applications. The situation is explained as follows:

1. Consider a situation wherein several products can be produced at several plants of an organization with their known production capacities and also with the known demand for each product for each of the known customers.
2. We will assume that these demands are satisfied by transporting through its known warehouses with each customer being served exclusively by a single warehouse.
3. We restrict the capacity of the warehouses as the upper limit on the throughput of the warehouse and some possible minimum throughput to flow through the warehouse satisfying some economic feasibility of the warehouse to be operated as the lower limit.
4. The possible locations for the warehouses are given as mentioned earlier, but the choice to use them will be important to optimize the overall distribution cost.
5. The warehouse costs are given as fixed charges plus a linear variable cost per unit for the throughput as handling cost.
6. Transportation costs are also taken as linear.

Hence, the problem is to determine the complete production–distribution plan to decide which warehouses have to be used, what size of warehouses to be selected, which customers should be served by each warehouse, and what pattern of transportation flows there should be for all products and which plants will transport products as throughput to which warehouse, etc. This problem is an optimization problem to satisfy the demands at the minimum total distribution cost, subject to plant capacity and warehouse capacities, and economic feasibility of the entire distribution with the following descriptions.

Find the number, size, and locations of warehouses in a network that will minimize the fixed and linear variable costs of moving all products through the selected network subject to the following:

1. The available supply of the plants cannot exceed the capacities for each product.
2. The demand for all products must be met.
3. The throughput of each warehouse cannot exceed its capacity.
4. A minimum throughput of a warehouse must be achieved before it can be opened for its economic feasibility.
5. All products for the same customer must be served from a single warehouse.

EXAMPLE 4.2

Figures 4.11 and 4.12 pictorially present the situation with data on production costs of two products at two plants, primary transportation unit cost from these two plants to the two warehouses, capacities for the throughputs, handling costs, fixed costs of the two warehouses and the secondary unit costs of transportation to three customers, and demands of each product of the three customers.

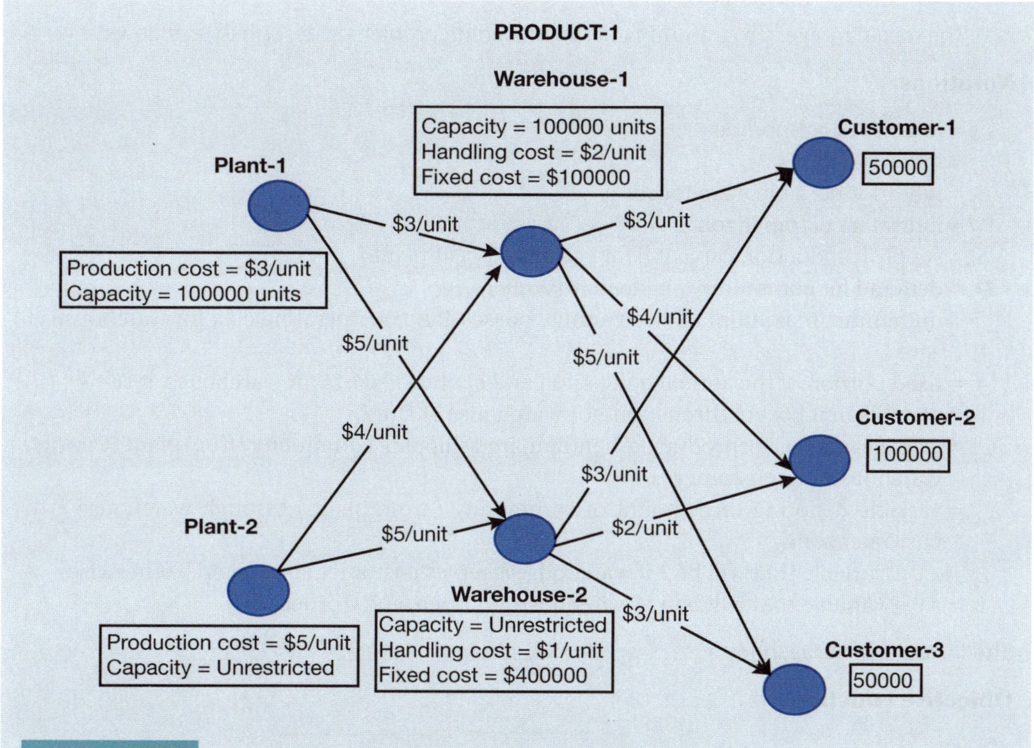

FIGURE 4.11 Multiproduct multi-warehouse example: Product 1.

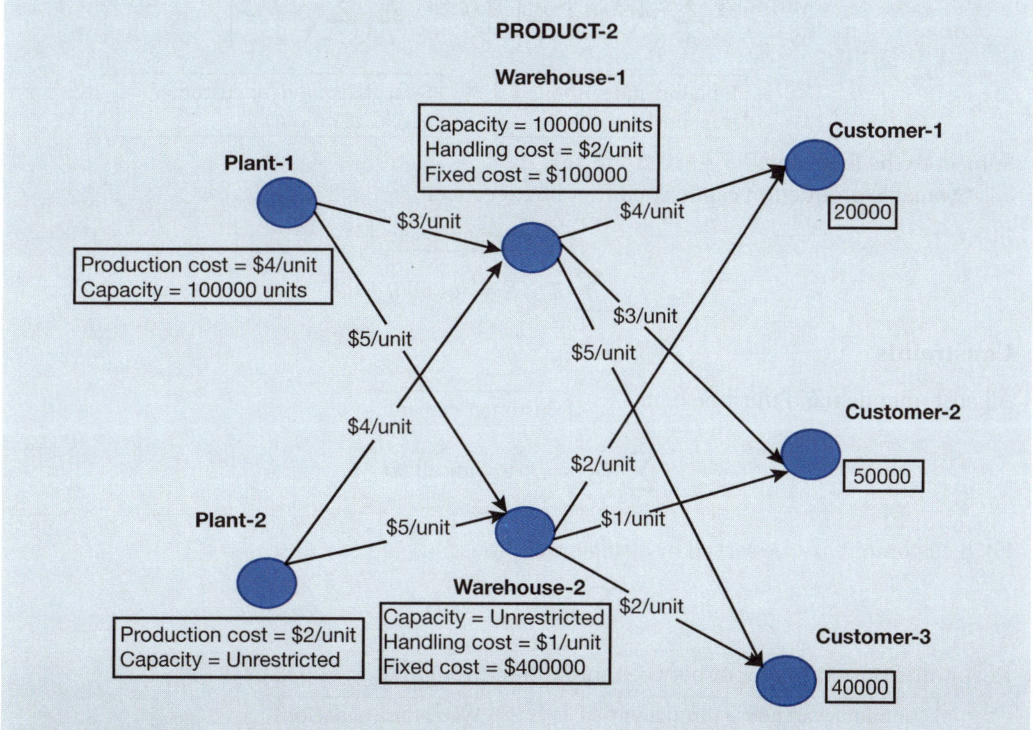

FIGURE 4.12 Multiproduct multi-warehouse example: Product 2.

The mixed integer programming of the preceding problem is described as follows:

Notations

i = index for commodities
j = index for plants
k = index for possible warehouses
l = index for customer zones
S_{ij} = supply (production capacity) for commodity i at plant j
D_{ij} = demand for commodity i in demand zone j
$V_k, \overline{V}_k$ = minimum, maximum allowed annual possession and operating cost for warehouse at site k
f_k = fixed portion of the annual possession and operating costs for warehouse at site k
v_k = variable unit cost of throughput for warehouse at site k
C_{ijkl} = average unit cost of producing, handling, and shipping commodity i from plant j through warehouse k to customer zone l
X_{ijkl} = variable denoting the amount of commodity i from plant j through warehouse k to customer zone l
y_{kl} = a 0-1 variable that will be 1 if warehouse k serves customer zone l, and 0 otherwise
z_k = a 0-1 variable that will be 1 if warehouse k is open, and 0 otherwise

The formulation is as follows:

Objective Function

Fixed costs; Handling rate

$$\text{Minimize} \sum_{ijkl} C_{ijkl} X_{ijkl} + \sum_{k} \left[f_k z_k + v_k \sum_{l} \left(\sum_{i} D_{il} \right) y_{kl} \right]$$

Inbound and outbound transport rates; Sum of demand for customer l across all products

Subject to the following:

Available production capacity cannot be exceeded:

Plant capacity

$$\sum_{kl} X_{ijkl} \le S_{ij} \text{ for all } ij$$

Constraints

All customer demand must be met:

Customer demand

$$\sum_{j} X_{ijkl} = D_{il} y_{kl} \text{ for all } ikl$$

Each customer must be served by a single warehouse:

$$\sum_{k} y_{kl} = 1 \text{ for all } l$$

Keep warehouse throughput between minimum throughput V_k and capacity $\overline{V}_k$:

Minimum warehouse throughput; Warehouse capacity

$$V_k \le \sum_{l} \left(\sum_{i} D_{il} \right) y_{kl} \le \overline{V}_k$$

And

All $X \ge 0$

All $y = 0$ or 1

All $z = 0$ or 1

The data can be entered in the Excel sheet and solved using Excel Solver. The screenshot is shown in Figure 4.13.

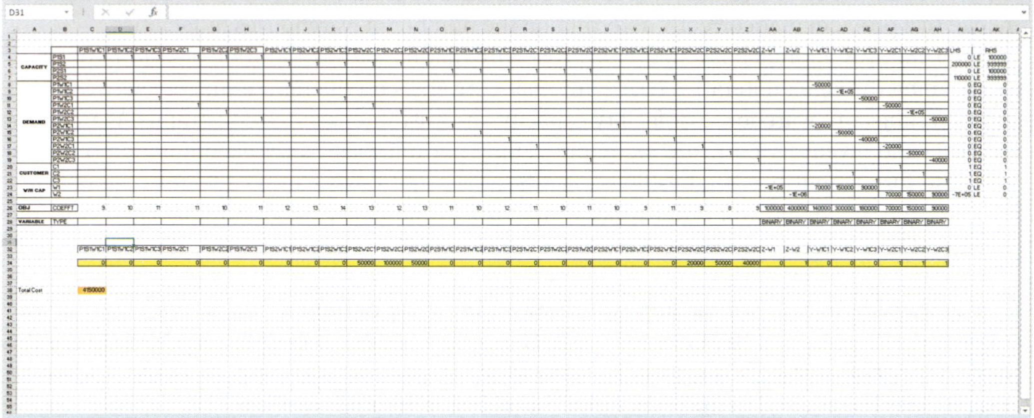

FIGURE 4.13 Screenshot of the solution to Example 4.2.

The solution recommends operating only Warehouse 2 and all products 1 and 2 be produced in Plant 2 and distributed through Warehouse 2 to all the three customers. The total cost comes to $4,150,000. The break-up of the total cost is as follows:

Warehouse fixed cost	400,000
Handling cost	310,000
Production and transportation cost	3,440,000
Total	**4,150,000**

The mixed integer programming is immensely helpful in solving such multi-commodity multi-plant distribution problems. It is also quite flexible in performing sensitivity analyses in terms of adding or deleting a few constraints and performing a few what-if scenarios as the situations may warrant. It has also a few limitation such as in handling large-scale problems and considering a few more cost drivers like inventory cost and other costs like warehousing costs, handling rates, etc., which may be nonlinear in nature.

Use of mathematical programming in facilities location problems has been discussed in detail in many research papers. Many variations based on various situations and assumptions have been formulated as mathematical programming problems and solved. However, only a few popular versions have been presented here in this chapter. Researchers can always do a literature review on this topic for more details.

Simulation and heuristics can be used when dealing with nonlinear cost functions. We will describe a procedure developed by Ronald H. Ballou in solving such problems using nonlinear inventory costs in the following section.

4.6.2 DISPLAN or Guided Linear Programming Approach Tackling Nonlinear Inventory Costs (Ronald H. Ballou)

Ronald H. Ballou developed a model in 1984 known as DISPLAN, which is a large-scale computer-based model used in the planning of physical supply and distribution networks. Many mathematical models have been developed for various contexts and situations, and the literature is very rich in this area. However, this procedure has a unique way of handling nonlinear inventory costs.

We have seen that most of the solution approaches in solving supply chain decision problems in various areas require the relevant cost drivers for the contexts and the optimizing approaches mostly look at the cost trade-offs among the cost drivers to achieve the best solution in optimizing an objective function. Some of the important costs are warehouse or facility inbound and outbound transportation costs, warehouse or facility storage and handling costs, order-processing costs, warehouse or facility fixed costs, and inventory-carrying costs at these facilities among the various other costs. As discussed in the earlier sections, it is very important to describe the inventory-carrying costs appropriately as it is an important cost driver for many supply chain decisions and also an important factor to determine the strategic decision of the number of facilities in a network. It is often seen that such inventory costs are neglected or approximated by some linear function in many solution approaches. However, in most cases, the relationship between the number of facilities and the total inventory in the network is nonlinear, commonly referred to as the inventory consolidation effect. The "square root rule" is one of the popular thumb rules for such consolidation or centralization. Hence, inaccurate approximation through linear functions can lead to a problem of incorrectly determining the number of warehouses or facilities.

The DISPLAN approach is a heuristic procedure that uses transportation algorithm of linear programming through an iterative procedure that converges on the minimum cost network configuration subject to warehouse or facility capacity and customer service constraints. Warehouse fixed costs and inventory costs are recomputed on a per-unit basis after each iteration once the warehouse throughput has been established. These per-unit costs can be added to the per-unit transportation, handling, and order-processing costs of the linear programming algorithm. The revised problem is resolved. The process is repeated until the best number, location, and size of warehouses are determined.

It is possible that the procedure will result in the local optimum due to the nature of the nonlinear cost function of the inventory cost. Hence, the termination criterion should trace the change if the total cost between successive iterations is less than a given percentage. Additional iterations may be required to make sure that the global optimum is realized.

4.6.3 Model Description

The mathematical description of the models is described here. More details of the model scope and other relevant details can be seen in Ronald H. Ballou (*Journal of Operations Management*,1984).

Objective

$$z_{\min} = \sum_{i}^{M}\sum_{j}^{L}\sum_{k}^{N}\sum_{l}^{P} C_{ijkl}X_{ijkl}$$

$$+\sum_{l}^{P}\sum_{J}^{L} k_{jl}\left(w_l + m_l D_{jl} + a_l D_{jl}^{\ bl}\right)$$

$$+\sum_{j}^{L} F_j Y_j$$

where $D_{ji} = \sum_{i}^{M}\sum_{k}^{N} X_{ijkl}$ for each j and l

and $Y_j = \begin{cases} 1 & \text{if warehouse } j \text{ is open} \\ 0 & \text{if closed} \end{cases}$

subject to:

plant capacity $\quad \sum_{j}^{L}\sum_{k}^{N} X_{ijkl} \le S_{il}$ for each i and l

warehouse capacity $\quad \sum_{i}^{M}\sum_{k}^{N} X_{ijkl} \le R_{jl}$ for each j and l

demand requirements $\quad \sum_{i}^{M}\sum_{j}^{L} X_{ijkl} \le B_{kl}$ for each k and l

all $Xs \ge 0$

where:

X_{ijkl} = Amount of product group l flowing between plant i to warehouse j to customer k.

D_{jl} = Amount of product l flowing through warehouse j.

C_{ijkl} = Per unit costs of production, stock order processing, customer order processing, inbound transportation, outbound transportation, and warehouse handling from plant i through warehouse j to customer k for product group l based on warehouse throughput (X_{ijkl}).

k_{jl} = Per-unit costs based on average inventory level of product group l in warehouse j of capital, warehouse storage, insurance, and personal property taxes.
w_l = Start up inventory level in a warehouse for product group l.
m_l = Constant of proportionality between average warehouse inventory level and warehouse throughput for product group l.
a_l, b_l = Power function coefficient and exponent relating average inventory level in a warehouse to warehouse throughput in a nonlinear fashion for product group l.
F_j = Fixed costs of warehouse j.
S_{il} = Plant i capacity for product group l.
R_{jl} = Throughput capacity of warehouse j for product group l.
B_{kl} = Period demand of customer k for product group l.
Y_j = 0, 1 variable depending on whether warehouse is open (1) or closed (0).

The preceding formulation is for a multiproduct transshipment problem additionally considering the fixed costs for the transshipment points and the nonlinearity of carrying inventories at the transshipment points. The total cost objective function is minimized subject to constraints on plant capacity, warehouse capacity, and demand requirements. It is also flexible in adding a few additional constraints such as customer distances from stocking points or forcing demand to warehouses, and warehouses to source points, etc., by manipulating the cell costs in the transportation algorithm of linear programming.

4.6.4 Computational Procedure

The computational procedure begins with a high cost but feasible solution and eventually tries to converge on the optimum, or approximately optimum, solutions through the iterative methods of solving a transportation problem in linear programming. We have seen earlier that there are cost trade-offs in a decision environment with many cost drivers. This approach forces a computational start with the maximum number of warehouses or stocking points with high fixed costs and inventory costs. Based on the warehouse throughput that are basically allocations based on the transportation algorithm through successive iterations, per-unit costs are revised in such a way that solving the linear transportation problem takes us to the solution toward fewer warehouses and lower total costs. The computations are terminated when the change in total costs from one iteration to the next is less than a preset percentage, usually between 0.1 and 0.001%. The steps are as follows:

DISPLAN is another example to illustrate how multistage transportation problems are brought as single-stage transportation problems and the existing methods are used to solve them. This has tremendous practical applications since supply chain planners always face these problems, and this approach will help in resolving locational choices in a supply chain network.

1. Initialize the solution procedure.
   a. Estimate inventory levels and related charges based on the total demand equally apportioned through all warehouses. In the absence of the exact figure of throughput of each warehouse, usually the total demand of the customers is equally apportioned among each of the warehouses as the initial throughput for starting the solution procedure. This creates the highest inventory level and associated costs that can occur given the starting number of warehouses.
   b. Estimate the throughput on each available warehouse so that warehouse fixed costs may be computed on a per-unit basis. Usually, the total demand is taken as the throughput for each of the warehouses and the fixed cost is apportioned by this throughput to obtain the per-unit cost as an effective way to start the procedure. This not only allows per-unit fixed cost differences between warehouses to be considered along with variable costs, but it also encourages the maximum number of warehouses to appear in the initial iteration, which is consistent with the drop heuristic approach we discussed earlier.

      It can be observed that these two costs, namely, fixed cost allocation and inventory costs, are affected by the throughput and hence the procedure starts with these estimates to obtain the throughputs after solving using the transportation algorithm.
2. By means of the transportation (or transshipment) linear programming algorithm, solve the starting problem. We notice that the cell costs of this initial table for the transportation algorithm are all variable costs (like handling costs, transportation costs on a per-unit basis) and the per-unit allocations of inventory and fixed costs. Source and stocking point capacities are also included. This initial table is then solved by the transportation algorithm.

3. The iteration will result in a table of optimal allocations, which are actually the flows or throughputs from the sources through the transshipment points to the customers. With this output of throughput and the total cost information gained in this iteration, per-unit inventory and fixed cell costs are revised and added to variable cell costs in the previous table that was used for the transportation algorithm. Re-allocations are determined for this revised table of costs, and the total costs are computed and compared with the previous total cost level. If the change in total costs between successive iterations exceeds the desired percentage and demand assignments differ, another iteration is called for. All warehouses having no throughput are locked out from further consideration.
4. Step 3 is repeated until no further cost improvement is realized or the change in the total cost from successive iterations is within the specified percentage.

4.6.5 Determining the Nonlinear Inventory Costs

We observed that the inventory costs are nonlinear and the DISPLAN procedures take into account this aspect while computing. In the model description, the nonlinear form of this cost assumes the following nature:

$$I = \alpha D^{\beta}$$

where α and β are power function coefficient and exponent relating average inventory level (I) in a warehouse-to-warehouse throughput (D) in a nonlinear fashion for the product group. Hence estimating the values of α and β becomes essential while applying this procedure. This relationship, in a way, captures the inventory practices linking it to the throughput of warehouses in an organization and if we have sufficient data on them across the current operating warehouses, it is possible to establish the relationship using statistical tools like regression analysis.

We will illustrate this through an example where the sales data of the current depots and their average inventory positions are available. Although sales is not exactly the demand or throughput, it is taken as a surrogate. The following data is taken from a case study: Karnataka Engineering Company by G. Raghuram et al., Indian Institute of Management, Ahmedabad, and Exhibits 4 and 7 from the case study are used here to establish the relationship. Exhibits 4 and 7 are given in Tables 4.24 and 4.25.

TABLE 4.24 Sales details–illustration

S. No.	State/UT	Branch Location		Mopeds	Scooters	Sales Value (₹'000)
1	Andhra Pradesh	1	Adoni	465	78	3571.5
		2	M'Nagar	1460	210	10760
2	Bihar	3	Ranchi	360	125	3605
3	Daman	4	Daman	15	300	3982.5
4	Delhi	5	Delhi	65	30	747.5
5	Goa			55	50	952.5
6	Gujarat	6	Vadodara	80	70	1350
7	Haryana	7	Faridabad	60	20	590
8	Himachal Pradesh			10	10	185
9	Jammu and Kashmir	8	Jammu	5	25	352.5
10	Karnataka	9	Raichur	2400	150	15150
11	Kerala	10	Cochin	80	60	1220
12	Madhya Pradesh	11	Bhopal	290	80	2635

(Continued)

TABLE 4.24 (Continued)

S. No.	State/UT		Branch Location	Mopeds	Scooters	Sales Value (₹'000)
		12	Raipur	300	60	2430
13	Maharashtra	13	Mumbai	180	360	5670
14	North East			30	35	620
15	Orissa			60	20	590
16	Pondicherry			65	25	682.5
17	Punjab and Chandigarh	14	Chandigarh	300	180	3990
18	Rajasthan	15	Jaipur	210	120	2715
19	Tamil Nadu	16	Vellore	1100	120	7610
20	Uttar Pradesh	17	Lucknow	750	170	6335
		18	Varanasi	300	70	2560
21	West Bengal	19	Medinipur	100	40	1070
			Total	**8740**	**2408**	**79374**

TABLE 4.25 Inventory position—illustration

S. No.	Branches	Mopeds	Scooters
1	Adoni	63	24
2	M'Nagar	58	30
3	Ranchi	30	14
4	Daman	39	91
5	Delhi	20	32
6	Vadodara	96	112
7	Faridabad	0	0
8	Jammu	29	25
9	Cochin	0	0
10	Bhopal	143	132
11	Raipur	55	59
12	Mumbai	63	109
13	Chandigarh	75	119
14	Jaipur	115	53
15	Vellore	53	32
16	Lucknow	165	146
17	Varanasi	86	146
18	Medinipur	50	32
Average Inventory at Branches		**63.33**	**64.22**
19	Raichur	1122	768

We will use the Table 4.24 values as the throughput D and the average inventory values after converting them into monetary values (by multiplying the scooters by ₹13,000 and mopeds by ₹5500, respectively), as I.

Since $I = \alpha D^{\beta}$ is in nonlinear form, we can use the following conversion to perform the regression analysis:

$$I = \alpha D^{\beta}$$

Taking logarithms on both sides gives

$$\log I = \log \alpha + \beta \log D$$

This is of the form $Y = A + BX$. So, taking the values of $\log I$ and $\log D$ as Y and X, we can use the regression option in Excel and get the estimates of A and B. Then taking the antilog of A and keeping B as it is, the values of α and β can be estimated. These are shown in Table 4.26 for the preceding example.

TABLE 4.26 Estimation of parameters for the illustration

S. No.	Depot	*I* (Inventory)	*D* (Demand Throughput)	log(*I*) = *Y*	log(*D*) = *X*
1	Adoni	658500	3571500	13.39772	15.0885
2	M'Nagar	709000	10760000	13.47161	16.19135
3	Ranchi	347000	3605000	12.75708	15.09783
4	Daman	1397500	3982500	14.1502	15.19742
5	Delhi	526000	747500	13.17306	13.52449
6	Vadodara	1984000	1350000	14.50063	14.11562
7	Jammu	484500	352500	13.09087	12.77281
8	Bhopal	2502500	2635000	14.7328	14.78439
9	Raipur	1069500	2430000	13.8827	14.7034
10	Mumbai	1763500	5670000	14.38281	15.5507
11	Chandigarh	1959500	3990000	14.4882	15.1993
12	Jaipur	1321500	2715000	14.09428	14.8143
13	Vellore	707500	7610000	13.46949	15.84497
14	Lucknow	2805500	6335000	14.84709	15.6616
15	Varanasi	2371000	2560000	14.67882	14.75552
16	Medinipur	691000	1070000	13.4459	13.88317

Regression Analysis Output

	Coefficient	
A	Intercept	10.77929
B	X Variable 1	0.211204
α	**48016**	← Antilog of 10.77929
β	**0.21**	

Hence, for this example, the following can be an approximate expression of the inventory cost as a function of the demand:

$$I = 48016D^{0.21}$$

EXAMPLE 4.3

We will adopt the same example from the original paper of R. H. Ballou (1984) for Product 1 and consider a single product case as an illustration. The problem is depicted with information in Figure 4.14.

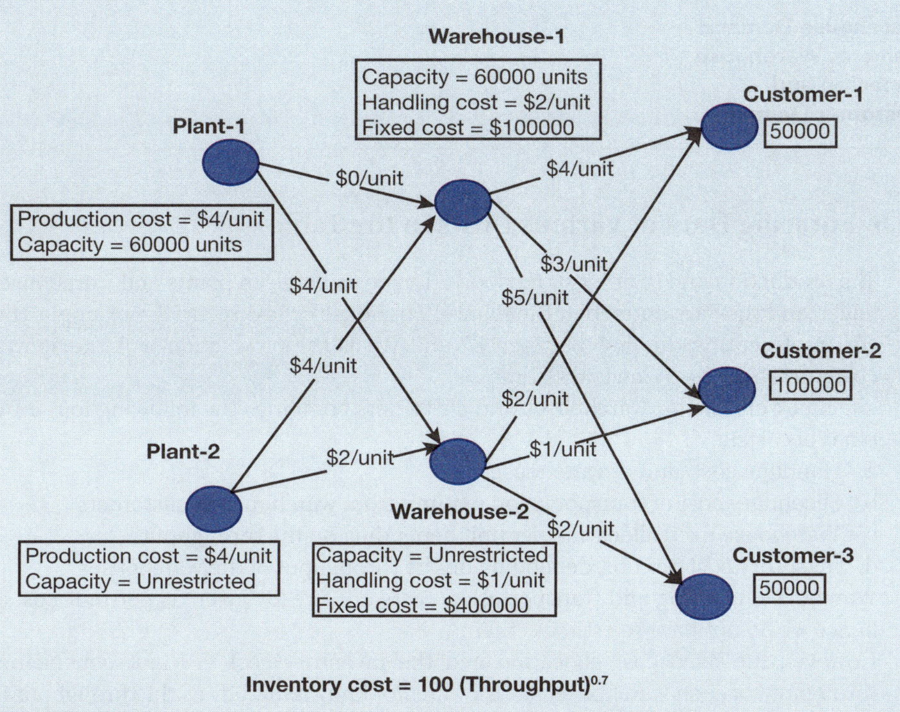

FIGURE 4.14 Details of DISPLAN example.

As explained earlier, the basic approach of DISPLAN is to bring a multistage transportation or transshipment problem to a single-stage problem with an appropriate estimation of costs for the various cost drivers that have to be considered in the problem.

The initial step is constructing a matrix of costs that is similar to the format of a transportation problem in linear programming. The typical format is given in Table 4.27. The heuristic process explained earlier is guided by entering the cell costs in the matrix. Here it is assumed that there are no direct flows between warehouses and from plants to customers, and hence a cost of ∞ is assigned to these cells. However, a scenario other than this can also be considered where such flows are allowed. The shaded block of cells—Plant–Warehouse block and Warehouse–Customer block—are the ones that need to be estimated and put in the matrix with the information of the plant, warehouse capacities, and the customer demands.

TABLE 4.27 Typical format for DISPLAN example

		Warehouse		Customer			Plant–Warehouse Capacity
		WH 1	WH 2	Cust 1	Cust 2	Cust 3	
Plant	**Plant 1**			∞	∞	∞	
	Plant 2			∞	∞	∞	
Warehouse	**WH 1**		∞				
	WH 2	∞					
Warehouse Demand (same as Warehouse Capacity) and Customer Demand							

4.6.6 Entering Data of Various Costs in the Table

1. The production and (primary) transportation costs between plants and warehouses are linear, and they are entered in the Plant–Warehouse cells directly. For example, the cell cost representing the flow between P2 and W1 is the production plus transportation costs, or \$4/cwt. + \$4/cwt. = \$8/unit.
2. The block of cells for warehouses and customers combines the following four different types of costs:
   a. Handling cost/unit at warehouses
   b. Secondary cost of transportation per unit from warehouse to customers
   c. Warehouse fixed allocation per unit depending on the throughput
   d. Inventory cost per unit depending on the throughput of the warehouses
3. Warehouse handling and transportation costs are already given as per-unit costs, and hence we do not have to estimate them.
4. However, the fixed cost allocation and the inventory cost per unit depend on the throughput of each warehouse. But they are not known initially as the throughput is not known. Hence, we must assume starting throughputs to initiate the process of iteration. As outlined in the steps for the heuristic, for fixed costs, each warehouse is initially given the most favorable status by assuming that all demand flows through it. Thus, for Warehouse 1, the rate associated with fixed costs would be the annual warehouse fixed cost divided by the total customer demand, or \$100,000/200,000 = \$0.50/unit. For Warehouse 2, it is \$400,000/200,000 = \$2.00/unit.
5. For inventory costs, the per-unit cost depends on the number of warehouses and the demand assigned to them. Again, as explained in the steps for the heuristic, we give each warehouse the greatest opportunity to be selected and the assumed throughput for each warehouse is equal. That is, the total customer demand (which is 200,000 units) divided by the number of warehouses (which is 2) being evaluated. And so, the assumed throughput for this example will be 200,000/2 = 100,000 units. Each warehouse is assigned a throughput of 100,000 units for estimating the initial inventory costs.

The inventory cost is defined as the inventory cost in a warehouse divided by the warehouse throughput, that is,

$$IC_i = \alpha(\text{Throughput}_i)^{\beta}/\text{Throughput}_i$$

Initially for each warehouse, the per-unit inventory cost is

$$100(100000)^{0.7}/100000 = 3.16$$

The estimated per-unit fixed and inventory-carrying rates are now entered in the warehouse–customer cells of the matrix. The initial matrix, thus, with all these cost estimates is given in Table 4.28.

TABLE 4.28 Initial table for the DISPLAN example

		Warehouse		Customer			Plant–Warehouse Capacity
		WH 1	WH 2	Cust 1	Cust 2	Cust 3	
Plant	**Plant 1**	4[a]	9	99[b]	99	99	60000
	Plant 2	8	6	99	99	99	999999[c]
Warehouse	**WH 1**	0	99	9.66[d]	8.66	6	60000
	WH 2	99	0	8.16	7.16	8.16	999999
Warehouse Demand (same as Warehouse capacity) and Customer Demand		60000	999999	50000	100000	50000	

[a] Unit production cost of Plant 1 plus the unit cost of transportation from Plant 1 to WH 1: 4 + 0 = 4.
[b] Represents a high cost to indicate that there is no direct link between plants and customers.
[c] Represents a high capacity indicating unrestricted capacity.
[d] Handling cost per unit plus the transportation cost from WH 1 to Cust 1 plus unit inventory cost plus fixed cost allocation per unit: 2 + 4 + 3.16 + 0.5 = 9.66. For all the cells in the block warehouse to customers, the costs are estimated similarly and entered.

This is solved using the transportation algorithm that is used in linear programming. We will use Solver on Excel and obtain the initial solution for this matrix, as shown in Figure 4.15.

		Warehouses		Customers			Plant-Warehouse Capacities
		WH-1	WH-2	Cust-1	Cust-2	Cust-3	
Plants	Plant-1	4	9	99	99	99	60000
	Plant-2	8	6	99	99	99	999999
Warehouses	WH-1	0	99	9.66	8.66	10.66	60000
	WH-2	99	0	8.16	7.16	8.16	999999
Warehouse Demand and Customer Demand		60000	999999	50000	100000	50000	

	Warehouses		Customers			LHS		RHS
	WH-1	WH-2	Cust-1	Cust-2	Cust-3			
Plant-1	60000	0	0	0	0	60000	LT	60000
Plant-2	0	140000	0	0	0	140000	LT	999999
WH-1	0	0	50000	10000	0	60000	LT	60000
WH-2	0	859999	0	90000	50000	999999	LT	999999
LHS	60000	999999	50000	100000	50000			
	GE	GE	GE	GE	GE			
RHS	60000	999999	50000	100000	50000			

Total Cost	2702000

FIGURE 4.15 Initial solution for the example using Excel Solver.

Now, incorporating them in Table 4.27, we get Table 4.29, which shows the flows from plants to warehouses and warehouses to customers.

TABLE 4.29 Flows from plants to warehouses to customers

		Warehouse		Customer			Plant–Warehouse Capacity
		WH 1	WH 2	Cust 1	Cust 2	Cust 3	
Plant	**Plant 1**	4 **60000**	9	99	99	99	60000
	Plant 2	8	6 **140000**	99	99	99	999999
Warehouse	**WH 1**	0	99	9.66 **50000**	8.66 **10000**	10.66	60000
	WH 2	99	0	8.16	7.16 **90000**	8.16 **50000**	999999
Warehouse Demand and Customer Demand		100000	999999	50000	100000	50000	

It can be observed that Warehouse 1 gets a throughput of 60,000 units and Warehouse 2 gets a throughput of 140,000 units from Plants 1 and 2, respectively.

This completes the first round of computations. Subsequent iterations will use the throughputs from their previous round to improve upon the estimate of the per-unit inventory costs and fixed costs for a warehouse.

For our second round, we note that the throughput for Warehouse 1 is 60,000 units and for Warehouse 2 is 140,000 units (see Table 4.29 and Figure 4.15). Thus, the estimated unit costs of the fixed cost allocation will be as follows:

Warehouse	Per-Unit Fixed Cost	Per-Unit Inventory Cost
WH 1	100000/60000 = 1.67	$100(60000)^{0.7}/60000 = 3.69$
WH 2	400000/140000 = 2.86	$100(140000)^{0.7}/140000 = 2.86$

Hence, for the second round of calculations, the warehouse–customer cells will have to be modified as follows:

	Cust 1	Cust 2	Cust 3
WH 1	11.36[a]	10.36	12.36
WH 2	8.72[b]	7.72	8.72

[a] 2 + 4 + 3.69 + 1.67 = 11.36
[b] 1 + 2 + 2.86 + 2.86 = 8.72

The values are updated in Table 4.29, and again using Solver, we get the following allocations (shown in Figure 4.16):

		Warehouses		Customers			Plant-Warehouse Capacities
		WH-1	WH-2	Cust-1	Cust-2	Cust-3	
Plants	Plant-1	4	9	99	99	99	60000
	Plant-2	8	6	99	99	99	999999
Warehouses	WH-1	0	99	11.36	10.36	12.36	60000
	WH-2	99	0	8.72	7.72	8.72	999999
Warehouse Capacity and Customer Demand		60000	999999	50000	100000	50000	

	Warehouses		Customers			LHS		RHS
	WH-1	WH-2	Cust-1	Cust-2	Cust-3			
Plant-1	0	0	0	0	0	0	LT	60000
Plant-2	0	200000	0	0	0	200000	LT	999999
WH-1	60000	0	0	0	0	60000	LT	60000
WH-2	0	799999	50000	100000	50000	999999	LT	999999
LHS	60000	999999	50000	100000	50000			
	GE	GE	GE	GE	GE			
RHS	60000	999999	50000	100000	50000			

Total Cost	2844000

FIGURE 4.16 Solutions for the second round.

Incorporating them in Table 4.29, we get Table 4.30, which shows the flows from plants to warehouses and warehouses to customers.

TABLE 4.30 Flows from the plants to customers for the second round

		Warehouse		Customer			Plant–Warehouse Capacity
		WH 1	WH 2	Cust 1	Cust 2	Cust 3	
Plant	**Plant 1**	4 **0**	9	99	99	99	60000
	Plant 2	8	6 **200000**	99	99	99	999999
Warehouse	**WH 1**	0	99	11.36	10.36	12.36	60000
	WH 2	99	0	8.72 **50000**	7.72 **100000**	8.72 **50000**	999999
Warehouse Capacity and Customer Demand		100000	999999	50000	100000	50000	

It can be observed that the entire demand of 200,000 units is shipped from Plant 2 through Warehouse 2 to all the customers.

With this modified throughput, if we perform further iterations, the solution does not change and hence a stopping point has been reached. We use the costs from the original data given in Figure 4.14 and calculate the costs and not from the cell costs from the preceding table as they are estimates of warehouse and inventory costs for iteration purposes. The final Table 4.31 is shown here with the original costs.

TABLE 4.31 Cost calculations for the final solution

Cost Type	Warehouse 1	Warehouse 2	
Production	0	200000 × 4	**800000**
Transportation cost from plant to warehouse	0	200000 × 2	**400000**
Transportation cost from warehouse to customers	0	50000 × 2	**100000**
	0	100000 × 1	**100000**
	0	50000 × 2	**100000**
Fixed cost	0		**400000**
Inventory cost	0	$100(200000)^{0.7}$	**513714**
Handling cost	0	200000 × 1	**20000**
Total	**0**		**2433714**
		2433714	

Although the heuristic procedure illustrates the steps for a single product, it can be applied to multiproduct cases too. With some slight modification where fixed costs for a warehouse are shared among the products according to their warehouse throughput, this DISPLAN or the guided linear programming procedure explained earlier can be extended to handle the multiproduct case.

As can be observed, this heuristic is quite good in arriving at a decision because in practice, a manager would like to see an implementable and better solution than the current practice rather than an accurate mathematical solution. However, the heuristic may have some limitations and requires strong assumptions to perform the iterations. They are as follows:

1. The costs are always taken as average costs per unit rather than marginal costs. If an additional unit is added in a warehouse, the practice is to consider its marginal cost rather than its average cost. Thus, the extra cost of adding an additional unit is more sensible than just costing it on an average basis.
2. The inventory cost is added to the outbound cost and levied on the warehouse–customer block, while the throughput in the warehouse flows from the plants only to warehouses. Hence, it is more sensible to add the marginal cost of inventory to the costs from the plant to the warehouse rather than adding it to the warehouse to the customer cost.

We will discuss a heuristic procedure developed by Baumol and Wolfe in handling such situations where the costs are considered on a marginal basis and the flow costs in different echelons are considered appropriately in the following section.

4.7 | BAUMOL AND WOLFE METHOD

In their approach, Baumol and Wolfe (INFORMS, 1958) suggested a method for determining more profitable geographic locations of warehouses by a firm for delivering known quantities of finished products to customers, where the number of warehouses can vary. This means that the firm can decide which warehouses to operate or not operate when conditions are known in terms of their demand and capacity and other costs relevant to the problem. This problem can be normally expected to be a concave minimization problem. Since it is difficult to determine the values of the variables that correspond to the absolute minimum of a concave cost function practically, a local optimum can be determined by a method described by these authors. The method involves a sequence of transportation computations that are shown to converge to the solution. The actual formulation of the problem is as follows:

Let

X_{ijk} be the quantity shipped from factory i ($i = 1, 2, \ldots, m$) via warehouse j ($j = 1, \ldots, n$), to retailer location k ($k = 1, \ldots, q$),

$C_{ijk}(X_{ijk})$ be the cost of this shipment including the relevant inventory cost,
Q_i be the quantity shipped from plant i,
R_j be the capacity of warehouse j,
S_k be the quantity required at destination k
The problem is to minimize the total delivery cost, i.e., to minimize

$$\sum_{ijk} C_{ijk}(X_{ijk}), \tag{4.1}$$

subject to

$$\sum_{jk} X_{ijk} = Q_i \tag{4.2}$$

(all goods must be shipped out of the factory),

$$\sum_{i,k} A_{ijk}\left(X_{ijk}\right) \le R_j \tag{4.3}$$

(no warehouse capacity can be exceeded), and

$$\sum_{i,j} X_{ijk} = S_k \tag{4.4}$$

(all customer demands must be met), where all $X_{ijk} \ge 0$. The expression $A_{ijk}(X_{ijk})$ in (4.3) represents the amount of inventory that will be held as a result of the flow X_{ijk}.

We notice that the formulation resembles that of a standard transportation problem in linear programming. However, there are some differences such as those listed below:

1. The possibility of the objective function, which is a cost function, being nonlinear,
2. The addition of warehouse constraints,
3. The need for three-dimensional subscripts for the variables arising out of the necessity of moving the goods from a factory to a customer through a warehouse.

However, the original paper explains the procedure, assumptions, and logic behind them. We will refer the reader to see the original paper mentioned in the references for details. Here we will explain the method with a modified example from the original paper of Baumol and Wolfe involving three factories (referred to as F1, F2, and F3), five warehouses (referred to as WH 1 to WH 5) and eight retailers (referred to as R1 to R8), as shown in Figure 4.17.

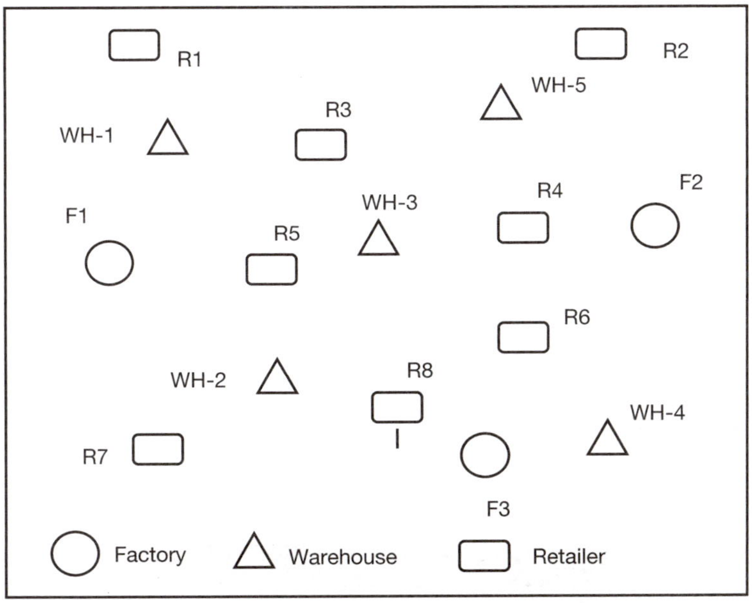

FIGURE 4.17 Example of warehouse locations using Baumol and Wolfe method.

The basic inputs for the problem are as follows:

Capacities of Factories

F1	100
F2	150
F3	150

Retailer Demands

R1	R2	R3	R4	R5	R6	R7	R8
40	50	60	70	60	50	30	40

Transportation costs from factory to warehouses

	WH 1	WH 2	WH 3	WH 4	WH 5
F1	8	6	9	13	14
F2	14	16	11	8	9
F3	10	13	13	10	8

Transportation costs from warehouses to retailers

	R1	R2	R3	R4	R5	R6	R7	R8
WH 1	8	14	6	11	8	13	14	14
WH 2	17	19	11	12	7	10	7	7
WH 3	13	14	6	8	5	8	12	8
WH 4	18	16	12	9	10	5	13	5
WH 5	12	10	6	5	9	8	15	11

The warehousing costs for warehouses WH 1 to WH 5, respectively, are assumed to be

$$75\sqrt{Z_1}, 80\sqrt{Z_2}, 75\sqrt{Z_3}, 80\sqrt{Z_4}, 70\sqrt{Z_5}$$

where Z_i is the throughput of the ith warehouse. They are in the form of $\alpha Z_i^{0.5}$.

The marginal cost of the ith warehouse is computed as $0.5\alpha Z_i^{-0.5}$ or $\frac{\alpha}{2}/\sqrt{Z_i}$ (which is obtained by differentiating the original function $\alpha Z_i^{0.5}$ with respect to Z_i). Hence, the marginal costs will be calculated using the following for all the warehouses, respectively:

$$\frac{37.5}{\sqrt{Z_1}}, \frac{40}{\sqrt{Z_2}}, \frac{37.5}{\sqrt{Z_3}}, \frac{40}{\sqrt{Z_4}}, \frac{35}{\sqrt{Z_5}}$$

where Z_i is the throughput of the ith warehouse. This is calculated for every iteration after we obtain the throughput Z_i for that iteration.

This method is more scientific as it includes the procedure that treats the cost components appropriately, as they should be. Very often, the marginal cost is more appropriate when considering any incremental load on a warehouse compared to the average cost, and also, the costs should be allocated as they flow into the warehouse as throughput. As a result, this method should give more logical and appropriate solutions for locational problems.

Cycle 0

TABLE 4.32 Minimum transportation costs

	R1	R2	R3	R4	R5	R6	R7	R8
F1	16	22	14	17	13	16	13	13
F2	21	19	15	14	16	13	21	13
F3	18	18	14	13	17	15	20	15

TABLE 4.33 Warehouse for minimal route*

	R1	R2	R3	R4	R5	R6	R7	R8
F1	1	1	1	3	2	2	2	2
F2	5	5	5	5	3	4	4	4
F3	1	5	5	5	5	4	2	3

*The minimal route for F1 to R1 (cost of 16) is explained in Figure 4.18.

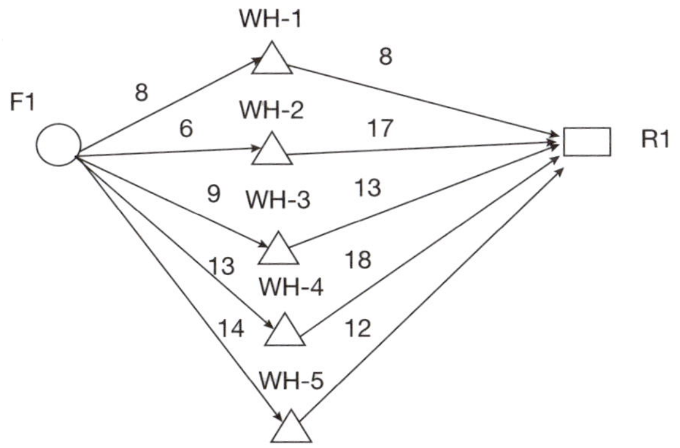

F1 → WH-1 → R1 8 + 8 = 16 ← minimum cost through WH-1
F1 → WH-2 → R1 6 + 17 = 23
F1 → WH-3 → R1 9 + 13 = 22
F1 → WH-4 → R1 13 + 18 = 31
F1 → WH-5 → R1 14 + 12 = 26

FIGURE 4.18 Illustration of calculating the minimum transportation cost.

The minimum route is calculated using the rule shown in Figure 4.18 for all the routes from F1 and F2 to R1 to R8. Tables 4.31 and 4.32 are constructed using the preceding rule giving the minimum transportation costs and an index table indicating which warehouse to go through to each customer as the warehouse for the minimum route table. Solution is obtained using Excel Solver to arrive at the cost of transportation and the allocations as shown in Table 4.33. Allocations in Table 4.33 are used together with Table 4.32 to determine the throughput of the warehouses as shown in Table 4.34.

TABLE 4.34 Allocations using Excel Solver

Solution to the initial transportation table

Warehouse load or the throughputs can be calculated from this solution table and the warehouse route table.

	R1	R2	R3	R4	R5	R6	R7	R8
F1	10	0	0	0	60	0	30	0
F2	0	0	0	60	0	50	0	40
F3	30	50	60	10	0	0	0	0

Transportation Cost	5750

TABLE 4.35 Throughput of the warehouses

Load Z^0

Throughput of Warehouses				
WH 1	WH 2	WH 3	WH 4	WH 5
40	90	0	90	180

Warehousing Cost					Total WH Costs
WH 1	WH 2	WH 3	WH 4	WH 5	
474	759	0	759	939	2931

Total cost = Transportation cost + Warehousing cost

Total Cost	**8681**

Cycle 1

Marginal costs of warehouses are obtained as follows for the throughput obtained in Table 4.35.

WH 1	5.93
WH 2	4.22
WH 3	9999
WH 4	4.22
WH 5	2.61

37.5/sqrt(40) =5.93

Adding this to the cost of the transportation from factory to warehouses. Revised transportation costs from factory to warehouses are as follows:

	WH 1	WH 2	WH 3	WH 4	WH 5
F1	13.93	10.22	9999	17.22	16.61
F2	19.93	20.22	9999	12.22	11.61
F3	15.93	17.22	9999	14.22	10.61

Minimum transportation cost table is as follows:

	R1	R2	R3	R4	R5	R6	R7	R8
F1	21.93	26.61	19.93	21.61	17.22	20.22	17.22	18.93
F2	27.93	26.61	22.61	21.22	22.22	17.22	25.22	17.22
F3	22.61	20.61	16.61	15.61	19.61	18.61	24.22	19.22

Warehouse minimum route becomes as follows:

	R1	R2	R3	R4	R5	R6	R7	R8
F1	1	5	1	5	2	2	2	2
F2	1	5	4	4	4	4	4	4
F3	5	5	5	5	5	5	2	4

Solution to the revised transportation table becomes as follows:

	R1	R2	R3	R4	R5	R6	R7	R8
F1	40	0	0	0	30	0	30	0
F2	0	0	0	30	30	50	0	40
F3	0	50	60	40	0	0	0	0

Transportation Cost	7414

Load Z^1

Throughput of Warehouses				
WH 1	WH 2	WH 3	WH 4	WH 5
40	60	0	150	150

Warehouse cost becomes

Warehousing Cost					Total WH Costs
WH 1	WH 2	WH 3	WH 4	WH 5	
474	620	0	980	857	2931

Total cost = Transportation cost + Warehousing cost

Total Cost	10345

Cycle 2 will start with these warehouse loads Z^1, and marginal costs are computed for the same as discussed in the previous cycle. Steps are repeated until we get the modified load and the costs. The summary results of Cycles 2, 3, and 4 are presented in Table 4.36.

TABLE 4.36 Summary results of the iterations

Cycle Number (j)	Transportation Cost	Throughput or Loads of Warehouses (Z_j)					Warehousing Cost	Total Cost
		WH 1 (Z_1)	WH 2 (Z_2)	WH 3 (Z_3)	WH 4 (Z_4)	WH 5 (Z_5)		
2	7228	10	90	0	90	220	2769	9997
3	7150	**0**	**100**	**0**	**80**	**220**	2554	9704
4	7137	**0**	**100**	**0**	**80**	**220**	2554	9691

Table 4.36 shows that the throughputs of warehouses in Cycle 3 and Cycle 4 remain the same and do not change with a small reduction in the total cost. We terminate the iterations here and conclude that Warehouses 1 and 3 are not required and the entire distribution from the two factories to the eight retailers can be sent through Warehouses 2, 4, and 5.

4.8 | SPATIAL INTERACTION MODELS

Spatial interaction models are used in transportation planning to develop land use/transportation plans for regional development, and it is one of the four-step processes in such exercises. The purpose of these models is to estimate the spatial generation and distribution of trips. These models assume that flows are a function of the attributes of the locations of origin, the attributes of the locations of destination, and the friction of distance between the origins and the destinations. The general formulation of a spatial interaction model is as follows:

$$T_{ij} = f(V_i, W_j, S_{ij})$$

where

- T_{ij} is the interaction between location i (origin) and location j (destination). Its units of measurement are varied and can involve the number of passengers, tons of freight, traffic volume, etc. It also relates to a time period such as interactions by the hour, day, month, or year.
- V_i is the attribute of the location of origin i. Variables often used to express these attributes are socioeconomic in nature, such as population, number of jobs available, industrial output or any proxy of the level of economic activity such as gross domestic product.
- W_j is the attribute of the location of destination j. It uses similar socioeconomic variables like the previous attribute to underline the reciprocity of the locations.
- S_{ij} is the attribute of separation between the location of origin i and the location of destination j, also known as **transport friction, friction of distance**, or **impedance**. Variables often used to express these attributes are distance, transport costs, or travel time.

From the general nature of spatial interaction models, the following three basic types of interaction models can be constructed:

1. **Gravity model:** Measures interactions between all the possible location pairs.
2. **Potential model:** Measures interactions between one location and every other location.
3. **Retail model:** Measures the boundary of the market areas between two locations competing over the same market based upon the intensity of their respective interactions.

The general nature of these models is shown in Figure 4.19.

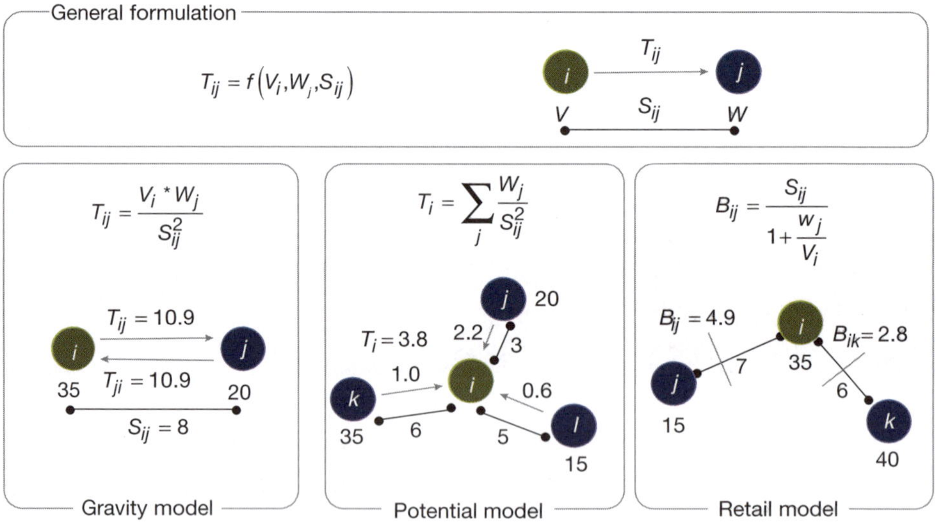

FIGURE 4.19 General nature of spatial interaction models.

4.8.1 Gravity Model

The Gravity model is one of the fundamental and most popular spatial interaction models. It is named based on a similar formulation of Newton's law of gravity. These types of re-orientations can be seen in many applications like migration movements, commodity flows in a logistics network, traffic flows, commuting, and evaluating boundaries between market areas. This translated into capturing a simple principle of the attraction between two objects as being **proportional to their mass and inversely proportional to their respective distance**. So the general formulation of spatial interactions can be developed reflecting this basic principle. The basic formulation of the gravity model is given as

$$T_{ij} = k\frac{P_i P_j}{d_{ij}}$$

where

- P_i and P_j are importance of the location of origin and the location of destination.
- d_{ij} is the distance between the location of origin and the location of destination.
- k is a proportionality constant related to the rate of the event. For instance, if the same system of spatial interactions is considered, the value of k will be higher if interactions were considered for a year compared to the value of k for one week.

Thus, spatial interactions between locations i and j are proportional to their respective importance divided by their distance. The gravity model can be extended to include several calibration parameters:

$$T_{ij} = k\frac{P_i^{\lambda} P_j^{\alpha}}{d_{ij}^{\beta}}$$

where

- P, d, and k refer to the variables previously discussed.
- β (beta) is the parameter of transport friction related to the efficiency of the transport system between two locations. The further the movement, the greater the friction of distance. For instance, two locations serviced by a highway will have a lower beta index as compared to two locations serviced by a normal and regular road.
- λ (lambda) is the parameter to represent the potential to generate movements. It is logical to infer that for retailing flows, a location having higher income levels will generate more movements (customers).
- α (alpha) is the parameter to represent the potential to attract movements. It is related to the nature of economic activities at the destination. For instance, a center having important commercial activities will attract more movements.

A consistent **calibration** process can be more rigorous and can be practically implementable in real-life contexts.

4.8.2 Huff Model of Retail Locations

The Huff model was introduced by David Huff in 1963 (Huff 1963). It is quite popular due to its conceptual appeal, simplicity, and ease of use. The probability (P_{ij}) that a consumer located at i will choose to shop at store j is calculated according to the following formula (Huff 2003):

$$P_{ij} = \frac{A_j^{\alpha} D_{ij}^{-\beta}}{\sum_{j=1}^{n} A_j^{\alpha} D_{ij}^{-\beta}}$$

where

- A_j is the measure of attractiveness of store j, such as square footage or size of the location j.
- D_{ij} is the distance from i to j or travel time between customer location i and retail location j.
- α is an attractiveness parameter estimated from empirical observations.
- β is the distance decay parameter estimated from empirical observations.
- n is the total number of stores including store j.

The quotient that is obtained by dividing A_j^{α} by D_{ij}^{β} is often referred to as the "perceived utility of store j by a consumer located at i." The parameter α is an exponent by which a store j's

As a special type of spatial interaction model, the gravity models are very popular in transportation planning exercises when we plan for comprehensive transport plans for a region. Trip generation, trip attraction, and trip assignment steps in a transport planning exercise use these models for estimating trips across traffic zones and are able to identify traffic corridors for planning transport infrastructure. Some references at the end of the chapter give more details on them.

attractiveness value is raised. The parameter β captures the rate of decay in the attracting power of the store as potential customers are located further away from the store. And so, increasing the exponent would decrease the relative influence of a store on more distant customers. Thus the modified model can be expressed as

$$E_{ij} = P_{ij}C_i = \frac{A_j^{\alpha} / D_{ij}^{\beta}}{\sum_j A_j^{\alpha} / D_{ij}^{\beta}} C_i$$

where

- E_{ij} is the expected demand from population center i that will be attracted to retail location j.
- P_{ij}, A_j, α, β, and n are as defined earlier.
- C_i is customer demand at the ith retail location.

EXAMPLE 4.4

Consider building a new shopping center at C. Suppose this center will compete directly with two other major shopping centers at A and B. They are expected to serve four demand locations at Northern Town (NT), Central Town (CT), Western Town (WT), and Southern Town (ST). We will assume $\alpha = 1$ and $\beta = 2$ for this example.

Size (A_j):	A	650,000 square feet
	B	850,000 square feet
	C	750,000 square feet
Revenues (C_i):	NT	\$7.5 million/year
	CT	\$10 million/year
	WT	\$12.5 million/year
	ST	\$5 million/year

The total is \$35 million/year. Instead of distance, we will use travel time as given in Table 4.37.

TABLE 4.37 Travel time in minutes

D_{ij}		To		
		A	B	C
From	NT	40	25	30
	CT	15	25	30
	WT	40	50	45
	ST	40	30	20

The steps will be as follows:

1. Calculate A_j/D_{ij}^2.
2. Sum for each town location or city (to get denominator of P_{ij}).
3. Calculate P_{ij}.
4. Calculate E_{ij}.

The values are shown in Table 4.38.

TABLE 4.38 Calculation of E_{ij}

		A	B	C	Sum
A_j/D_{ij}^2	NT	406	1360	833	2600
	CT	2889	1360	833	5082
	WT	406	340	370	1117
	ST	406	944	1875	3226
		A	B	C	Sum
P_{ij}	NT	0.16	0.52	0.32	1
	CT	0.57	0.27	0.16	1
	WT	0.36	0.30	0.33	1
	ST	0.13	0.29	0.58	1
		A	B	C	Sum
Revenue	NT	1.17	3.92	**2.40**	7.50
	CT	5.68	2.68	**1.64**	10.00
	WT	4.55	3.81	**4.15**	12.50
	ST	0.63	1.46	**2.91**	5.00
		12.03	11.87	**11.10**	35.00

The total estimated revenue for the **new shopping center C is $11.1** million/year.

SUMMARY

In this chapter, we focused on methods that are based on some simple heuristics and rules with minimum data requirements. These methods are quite useful in practice when decisions relating to locating facilities like warehouses, stores, service centers, etc. are made. These methods do not require too much of data and have little rigor in getting practical solutions. For more complicated situations, mathematical programming approaches are useful, and the chapter discussed a few such approaches with examples. DISPLAN and the Baumol and Wolfe methods are quite useful when we are faced with multistage situations, and such methods use a simple transportation problem solution approach to solve the problem. Toward the end, a special type of spatial interaction model known as the gravity model is presented with a specific description of the Huff model for retail locations. Dynamic locations are also possible in locating warehouses when relocations of the facilities are required to change profits and for other economic considerations. Such models are also discussed in the literature.

Case Study

1. It is suggested to take up the **Karnataka Engineering Company Limited** Case by G. Raghuram and D. Mathew, Indian Institute of Management, Ahmedabad (http://hdl.handle.net/11718/6682), to explain all the methods on the data exhibits of the case and analyze the solutions.
2. Case on "Ohio Auto and Driver's Licence Bureaus" by Ronald H. Ballou, Business Logistics Management, Pearson, Chapter 13.
3. Case on "Usemore Soap Company" by Ronald H. Ballou, Business Logistics Management, Pearson, Chapter 14.

Exercises

1. Consider the following problem where five locations are shortlisted to serve 10 customers. The details of the distances and the demands are shown in the following table. It is desired to locate
   a. two facilities
   b. three facilities
   from the shortlist. Determine them using the drop heuristic.

Location → Retailer↓	1	2	3	4	5	Demand (in Thousands)
1	7	9	12	24	15	100
2	8	12	21	16	25	120
3	16	14	23	12	34	80
4	15	16	17	20	13	150
5	8	9	13	15	16	160
6	9	14	7	13	19	180
7	16	23	13	17	16	240
8	6	4	15	14	12	190
9	24	23	16	10	9	80
10	12	15	17	16	7	100

2. Solve the preceding problem using the P-median approach and check if the solutions are the same.
3. For problem 1, if the capacities and the fixed costs are as follows, how do the solutions change for the same decision of locating two and three facilities from the shortlist? Assume the transport rate is $1.20 per ton/km.

	1	2	3	4	5
Capacity	750	750	800	800	900
Fixed cost ($)	10,00,000	10,00,000	12,00,000	12,00,000	15,00,000

4. If the capacitated fixed charge problem is used for problem 3, will the decisions change for the same decisions of locating two and three facilities? Explain.
5. Triveni Motors is the sole distributor in Tamil Nadu for a popular car manufacturer and is contemplating locating field warehouses for storing cars for its 32 retailers in different cities and towns in Tamil Nadu. Triveni Motors has shortlisted seven potential cities from its initial evaluation on various considerations for this purpose, and from this shortlist, it wants to decide on a few warehouses. The details of the distances and the annual demand of cars are given in the following table.

S. No.	Potential Location→ Retailer↓	Chennai	Coimbatore	Erode	Madurai	Salem	Tiruchirappalli	Tirunelveli	Demand in Units
1	Ambur	190	341	228	414	184	350	558	2000
2	Chennai	0	507	406	505	342	330	640	15000
3	Coimbatore	507	0	102	227	168	210	372	10000
4	Cuddalore	190	360	256	203	194	183	516	4000
5	Dindigul	434	165	141	63	170	106	208	3500

S. No.	Potential Location→ Retailer↓	Chennai	Coimbatore	Erode	Madurai	Salem	Tiruchirappalli	Tirunelveli	Demand in Units
6	Erode	406	102	0	195	64	138	347	8000
7	Gudiyatham	170	390	275	463	232	341	608	1500
8	Hosur	311	315	200	388	157	293	533	3500
9	Kancheepuram	76	481	377	482	315	302	662	4000
10	Karaikkudi	423	271	236	106	237	97	286	2500
11	Karur	401	130	67	142	95	80	287	5000
12	Krishnagiri	258	275	160	348	117	253	492	3500
13	Kumbakonam	282	320	273	219	210	118	410	4000
14	Madurai	505	227	203	0	233	180	160	9000
15	Nagapattinam	317	374	336	271	273	140	451	3500
16	Nagercoil	721	453	429	242	458	394	83	5000
17	Neyveli	56	317	425	530	363	349	709	3500
18	Pollachi	447	43	137	188	203	211	333	3000
19	Pudukkottai	381	264	194	126	195	54	306	2500
20	Rajapalayam	528	322	298	110	327	263	88	1500
21	Ranipet	113	445	341	513	279	332	692	2000
22	Salem	342	168	64	233	0	138	377	6500
23	Sivakasi	561	293	268	81	298	233	104	3500
24	Thanjavur	319	288	211	190	192	86	370	4500
25	Thoothukkudi	637	367	343	143	385	309	56	5500
26	Tiruchirappalli	330	210	138	180	138	0	312	8000
27	Tirunelveli	640	372	347	160	377	312	0	7000
28	Tiruppur	468	52	62	178	128	175	323	4500
29	Tiruvannamalai	194	329	225	366	163	186	546	3000
30	Udhagamandalam	558	101	152	282	218	279	427	2500
31	Vaniyambadi	209	302	198	369	136	292	514	1500
32	Vellore	138	420	316	487	253	307	667	3500
								Total	**146500**

a. Use the drop heuristic to determine two, three, and four possible locations from the shortlist of seven cities for locating the warehouses.

b. If the P-median approach is used for this problem, would the solutions change? Explain.

6. Consider problem 5. If the capacities and the fixed costs are as follows, how do the solutions change for the same decision of locating two, three, and four facilities from the shortlist? Assume the transport rate is $1.30 per ton/km.

Location	Chennai	Coimbatore	Erode	Madurai	Salem	Tiruchirappalli	Tirunelveli
Capacity	80000	70000	70000	80000	70000	80000	70000
Fixed Charge ($)	30,00,000	25,00,000	25,00,000	30,00,000	25,00,000	30,00,000	25,00,000

7. If the capacitated fixed charge problem is used for problem 6, will the decisions change for the same decisions of locating two, three, and four facilities? Explain.
8. Consider the examples given in Figures 4.11 and 4.12 in the chapter for a multiproduct multi-warehouse situation. Suppose the data is changed to the following: Capacity of Warehouse 1 (combined) to 150,000 and Warehouse 2 (combined) to 300,000. How does this change the solution?
9. From the output of problem 8, perform a sensitivity analysis on model parameters and determine within which ranges the model is stable and a manager can be sure about his or her solutions. Prepare a report on the what-if analysis that will be useful for a managerial decision-making process and can be presented by a supply chain manager to his or her higher authorities.
10. Consider the example in Figure 4.17 for the Baumol and Wolfe method. Suppose the data has the following changes:
    a. Capacities of F1, F2, and F3 are increased by 50%.
    b. Demands of R1 to R3 are increased by 60% and R4 to R8 by 50%.
    c. Transport costs are increased by 50% for the F-W leg and 60% for the W-R leg.
    d. Warehousing costs remain the same.

    Obtain the decision with these changes. Can we get any meaningful ranges within which these solutions remain the same?

Bibliography

1. Ballou, R. H. (1968). Dynamic warehouse location analysis. *Journal of Marketing Research*, **5**(3), 271–276.
2. Ballou, R. H. (1984). DISPLAN: A multiproduct plant/warehouse location model with nonlinear inventory costs. *Journal of Operations Management*, **5**(1), 75–90.
3. Ballou, R. H. and S. K. Srivastava (2007). *Business Logistics/Supply Chain Management*. Delhi: Pearson India.
4. Baumol, W. J. and P. Wolfe (1958). A warehouse location problem. *Operations Research*, **6**(2), 252–263.
5. Grifith, D. A. (1982). A generalized Huff model. *Geographical Analysis*, **14**(2), 135–144.

CHAPTER 5

Tactical and Operational Decisions in Warehousing

LEARNING OBJECTIVES

After reading this chapter, you would be able to:

- Understand the tactical and operational decisions in warehouse design and operations.
- Determine space requirements for a warehouse and evaluate options of private and third-party alternatives.
- Understand different types of warehouses—consolidation break bulk, mixing, etc.—for storing and trade-off decisions related to them.
- Make handling decisions and make layout decisions based on them.
- Understand mathematical investigations into tactical decisions about allocation of products to storage locations.
- Layout configuration decisions with respect to size, height, floor storage length, width, etc. for various choices of layouts.
- Get some insights into unit-load area layouts regarding lane width, floor storage, aisle configurations, and fast pick area concepts.

5.1 INTRODUCTION AND SPACE DETERMINATION IN WAREHOUSE PLANNING

In this chapter, we will discuss a few tools that are useful in making tactical and operational decisions that are key to warehouse operations.

An important decision to be made after locating warehouses in a supply chain network is determining how much space would be needed to execute plans in the warehouse to support supply chain activities and sales growth. The next decision to be made is how this space will be used best.

Important factors to be considered for such decisions are as follows:

1. Stock-keeping unit (SKU) and sales growth
2. Inventory turnover
3. Think "cubic feet of the space" rather than just the building's footprint
4. Warehouse shape matters
5. Number and position of dock doors
6. Material-handling solutions and automation
7. Warehouse layout and processes

8. Expansion of the building for growth
9. Some key metrics you will need for warehouse planning
10. Consider professional warehouse planning assistance

For more details of these factors, readers can go through the link https://www.fcbco.com/blog/warehouse-planning-space-in-distribution-center by Brian Barry.

We will illustrate the calculation of space for a single SKU with the following example.

One of the key decisions in warehouse operations is about space determination. Since it involves capital expenditures and outsourcing decisions, a scientific approach is required to anticipate growth and determine such space. Very often, lack of vision about the future leads to space constraints for storing products and escalates costs in the supply chain.

EXAMPLE 5.1

XYZ Manufacturing Company is planning for its warehouse needs and has to determine its warehouse requirements. Its main business is spare parts for heavy and commercial vehicles. Due to volatile market demands and production policies, space requirements vary considerably. But space requirements can be estimated due to the nature of business being replacement markets. Monthly sales as throughput for a typical year are as shown in Table 5.1.

TABLE 5.1 Monthly throughput

Month	Sales (Throughput in kg)
January	1200000
February	900000
March	800000
April	500000
May	300000
June	100000
July	250000
August	550000
September	700000
October	600000
November	900000
December	750000

An inventory turnover ratio of 3 to 1 has to be maintained in the warehouse. Each item of merchandise occupies 0.7 cu ft of the warehouse space and can be stacked at 12 ft height. Administrative spaces, aisles, and other operations require 50% of the warehouse space to be utilized and only 70% is to be utilized to anticipate variability in space requirements. This means that only 35% of the total warehouse space is actually used for storage. The company has three options:

1. Constructing a private warehouse equipped with all material-handling facilities for $40 per sq ft, which can be amortized over 20 years. The cost of operations in the warehouse is $0.025 per kg of throughput (kg). Annual fixed costs amount to $6 per sq ft of total space.
2. Availing the services of a third-party vendor on a rental basis who will charge $0.05 per kg per month as storage charge on inventory and a handling charge of $0.08 per kg of throughput.
3. A mixed strategy of using both private and third-party vendor services.

What should be the best strategy in terms of (1) the size of private warehouse to be constructed, to the nearest 10,000 sq ft, or (2) the amount of public warehouse space to be rented? (3) To what extent and when should each type of space be used?

We will evaluate all the alternatives using Excel. We will incorporate all the inputs and the calculations in different cells as shown in the Excel sheet for a space of 40,000 sq ft of a private warehouse as an illustration.

The conversion factor to determine the space is obtained by the following steps:

1. The inventory turnover ratio is 3 per month, that is, for every 3 kg of the item (i.e., spare parts through the warehouse), 1 kg is maintained in the inventory.
2. For each kg stored, 0.7/12 sq ft space is required. Due to the aisles, this space requirement needs to be doubled (1/0.5) and then increased for the rate of space utilization (1/0.70). Therefore, to convert demand to space requirements in square feet, we have
3. Square feet = Monthly demand (lb) × (1/3)(0.5/16)(1/0.5)(1/0.7)
   = monthly demand (kg) × 0.055556

For the selected size of 40,000 sq ft, let us work out the fixed cost per month.

Cost $40 ft × 40,000 = $1,600,000 to construct. Amortizing over 20 years would give an annual fixed cost of $80,000.

The annual fixed cost @ $6 per sq ft for 40,000 sq ft is 240,000.

So, the total fixed cost is $80,000 + $240,000 = $320,000. Hence, the monthly fixed cost will be $320,000/12 = $26,667. This is reflected in the Excel sheet shown in Figure 5.1.

Space Determination Worksheet

Month	Throughput(kg)	Space Requirement	Allocated	Monthly Fixed Cost	Monthly Variable cost	Rented	Monthly storage Costs	Monthly Handling costs	Total Cost
January	1200000	66667	0.60	26667	18000	0.40	8000	38400	91067
February	900000	50000	0.80	26667	18000	0.20	3000	14400	62067
March	800000	44444	0.90	26667	18000	0.10	1333	6399	52399
April	500000	27778	1.00	26667	12500	0.00	0	0	39167
May	300000	16667	1.00	26667	7500	0.00	0	0	34167
June	100000	5556	1.00	26667	2500	0.00	0	0	29167
July	250000	13889	1.00	26667	6250	0.00	0	0	32917
August	550000	30556	1.00	26667	13750	0.00	0	0	40417
September	700000	38889	1.00	26667	17500	0.00	0	0	44167
October	600000	33333	1.00	26667	15000	0.00	0	0	41667
November	900000	50000	0.80	26667	18000	0.20	3000	14400	62067
December	750000	41667	0.96	26667	18000	0.04	500	2400	47567
Total	**6800000**	**419446**		**320000**	**165000**		**15833**	**76000**	**576833**

Inputs for the workings

Monthly Inventory Turnover	3	Cost of construction per sq.ft for private warehouse	40
Aisle Space	0.5	Number of years for Amortization	20
Variability Provison	0.7	Variable cost per kg in private warehouse	0.025
Space Occupied per kg	0.7	Annual Fixed cost per sq.ft	6
Stack Height in ft	12	Rented charges per sq.ft for storage	0.05
		Rented Handling charges per sq.ft	0.08
Conversion Factor	0.055556	Space Option in sq.ft	40000

FIGURE 5.1 Space determination sheet.

We will explain each of the columns in Figure 5.1.

Column D: Space Requirement

As shown earlier, the space will be monthly throughput (kg) × 0.055556.

Column E: Allocated, to be Seen with Column H; Rented

This means how much portion of the throughput is taken care of by the chosen size of 40,000 sq ft. For example, for the month of January, we require 66677 sq ft and hence the chosen 40,000 sq ft can only take care of 40,000/66,667, that is, 60% (Column D). Hence, the remaining (1 – 0.60), that is, 40% (Column H) of the throughput has to be given to a third party. The third party will charge for this 40% of the throughput for both storage and handling.

Column F: Monthly Fixed Cost

As shown earlier, the monthly fixed cost is worked out for the chosen space and shown for this choice of 40,000 sq ft as $26,667.

Column G: Monthly Variable Cost, to be Seen along with Column I (Rented Charges for Storage) and Column J (Rented Charges for Handling)

It will be the monthly throughput × Allocated proportion $0.025. For example, for January, it will be 1,200,000 × 0.6 × $0.025 = $18,000 (Column D). The reason is that only 60% of the throughput will be handled at the private warehouse. The remaining 40% of the throughput will be rented from the third party who will charge for storage and handling. For storage, the calculation will be Monthly throughput × Rented proportion × Inventory turnover × Storage charges (Column I). For January, it will be 1,200,000 × 0.4 × (1/3) × $0.05 = $8000 (Column I). For handling charges, the calculation will be Monthly throughput × Rented proportion × Handling charges (Column J). For January, for example, it will be 1,200,000 × 0.4 × $0.08 = $38,400 (Column J).

The total cost for this option of constructing a 40,000 sq ft warehouse is **$576,833**. We will show later how for different options of the space choice, we can work out the best strategy.

Case 1: Completely Private Warehouse (i.e., Fully Constructed)

Since the maximum space required for the throughput shown in Table 5.1 is 66,667, we will construct a warehouse of 70,000 sq ft as we are required to construct in multiples of 10,000 sq ft. The scenario is shown as a screenshot of the Excel sheet in Figure 5.2.

Space Determination Worksheet

Month	Throughput(kg)	Space Requirement	Allocated	Monthly Fixed Cost	Monthly Variable cost	Rented	Monthly storage Costs	Monthly Handling costs	Total Cost
January	1200000	66667	1.00	46667	30000	0.00	0	0	76667
February	900000	50000	1.00	46667	22500	0.00	0	0	69167
March	800000	44444	1.00	46667	20000	0.00	0	0	66667
April	500000	27778	1.00	46667	12500	0.00	0	0	59167
May	300000	16667	1.00	46667	7500	0.00	0	0	54167
June	100000	5556	1.00	46667	2500	0.00	0	0	49167
July	250000	13889	1.00	46667	6250	0.00	0	0	52917
August	550000	30556	1.00	46667	13750	0.00	0	0	60417
September	700000	38889	1.00	46667	17500	0.00	0	0	64167
October	600000	33333	1.00	46667	15000	0.00	0	0	61667
November	900000	50000	1.00	46667	22500	0.00	0	0	69167
December	750000	41667	1.00	46667	18750	0.00	0	0	65417
Total	**6800000**	**419446**		**560000**	**188750**		**0**	**0**	**748750**

Inputs for the workings

Monthly Inventory Turnover	**3**	Cost of construction per sq.ft for private warehouse	**40**
Aisle Space	**0.5**	Number of years for Amortization	**20**
Variability Provison	**0.7**	Variable cost per kg in private warehouse	**0.025**
Space Occupied per kg	**0.7**	Annual Fixed cost per sq.ft	**6**
Stack Height in ft	**12**	Rented charges per sq.ft for storage	**0.05**
		Rented Handling charges per sq.ft	**0.08**
Conversion Factor	**0.055556**	Space Option in sq.ft	**70000**

FIGURE 5.2 Completely private warehouse scenario.

As can be seen, the total cost for this case will be **$748,750.**

Case 2: Completely Outsourced to Third Party as a Rented Option

Since it is going to be completely rented, the space option cell DE 27 is marked 0. The scenario is shown as a screenshot of the Excel sheet in Figure 5.3.

Space Determination Worksheet

Month	Throughput(kg)	Space Requirement	Allocated	Monthly Fixed Cost	Monthly Variable cost	Rented	Monthly storage Costs	Monthly Handling costs	Total Cost
January	1200000	66667	0.00	0	0	1.00	20000	96000	116000
February	900000	50000	0.00	0	0	1.00	15000	72000	87000
March	800000	44444	0.00	0	0	1.00	13333	64000	77333
April	500000	27778	0.00	0	0	1.00	8333	40000	48333
May	300000	16667	0.00	0	0	1.00	5000	24000	29000
June	100000	5556	0.00	0	0	1.00	1667	8000	9667
July	250000	13889	0.00	0	0	1.00	4167	20000	24167
August	550000	30556	0.00	0	0	1.00	9167	44000	53167
September	700000	38889	0.00	0	0	1.00	11667	56000	67667
October	600000	33333	0.00	0	0	1.00	10000	48000	58000
November	900000	50000	0.00	0	0	1.00	15000	72000	87000
December	750000	41667	0.00	0	0	1.00	12500	60000	72500
Total	6800000	419446		0	0		125833	604000	729833

Inputs for the workings

Monthly Inventory Turnover	3	Cost of construction per sq.ft for private warehouse	40
Aisle Space	0.5	Number of years for Amortization	20
Variability Provison	0.7	Variable cost per kg in private warehouse	0.025
Space Occupied per kg	0.7	Annual Fixed cost per sq.ft	6
Stack Height in ft	12	Rented charges per sq.ft for storage	0.05
		Rented Handling charges per sq.ft	0.08
Conversion Factor	0.055556	Space Option in sq.ft	0

FIGURE 5.3 Completely outsourced to third party.

As can be seen, the total cost for this case will be **$729,833**.

Case 3: Mixed Strategy of Private and Rented

We have already seen one scenario in this case for 40,000 sq ft privately constructed and the remaining rented, and the total cost was **$576,833**. We will see another case of 30,000 sq ft privately constructed and the remaining rented. The scenario is shown in Figure 5.4.

Space Determination Worksheet

Month	Throughput(kg)	Space Requirement	Allocated	Monthly Fixed Cost	Monthly Variable cost	Rented	Monthly storage Costs	Monthly Handling costs	Total Cost
January	1200000	66667	0.45	20000	13500	0.55	11000	52800	97300
February	900000	50000	0.60	20000	13500	0.40	6000	28800	68300
March	800000	44444	0.68	20000	13500	0.32	4333	20800	58633
April	500000	27778	1.00	20000	12500	0.00	0	0	32500
May	300000	16667	1.00	20000	7500	0.00	0	0	27500
June	100000	5556	1.00	20000	2500	0.00	0	0	22500
July	250000	13889	1.00	20000	6250	0.00	0	0	26250
August	550000	30556	0.98	20000	13500	0.02	167	801	34467
September	700000	38889	0.77	20000	13500	0.23	2667	12800	48967
October	600000	33333	0.90	20000	13500	0.10	1000	4800	39300
November	900000	50000	0.60	20000	13500	0.40	6000	28800	68300
December	750000	41667	0.72	20000	13500	0.28	3500	16800	53800
Total	6800000	419446		240000	136750		34667	166400	577817

Inputs for the workings

Monthly Inventory Turnover	3	Cost of construction per sq.ft for private warehouse	40
Aisle Space	0.5	Number of years for Amortization	20
Variability Provison	0.7	Variable cost per kg in private warehouse	0.025
Space Occupied per kg	0.7	Annual Fixed cost per sq.ft	6
Stack Height in ft	12	Rented charges per sq.ft for storage	0.05
		Rented Handling charges per sq.ft	0.08
Conversion Factor	0.055556	Space Option in sq.ft	30000

FIGURE 5.4 Mixed strategy of private and outsourced.

As can be seen, the total cost for this case will be **$577,817**.

A thorough understanding of all variables and parameters that affect the determination of space is important to estimate warehousing choices and sophisticated tools using computers can be useful to generate what-if scenarios while making such strategic decisions.

Table 5.2 gives a summary of scenarios from options 0 sq ft to 70,000 sq ft.

TABLE 5.2 Summary of scenarios

Scenario	Warehouse Space	Total Cost ($)
1	0	729833
2	10000	660767
3	20000	611050
4	**30000**	**577817**
5	**35000**	**574100**
6	**40000**	**576833**
7	50000	610250
8	60000	677350
9	70000	748750

The total cost is shown in the graph in Figure 5.5 for all these scenarios.

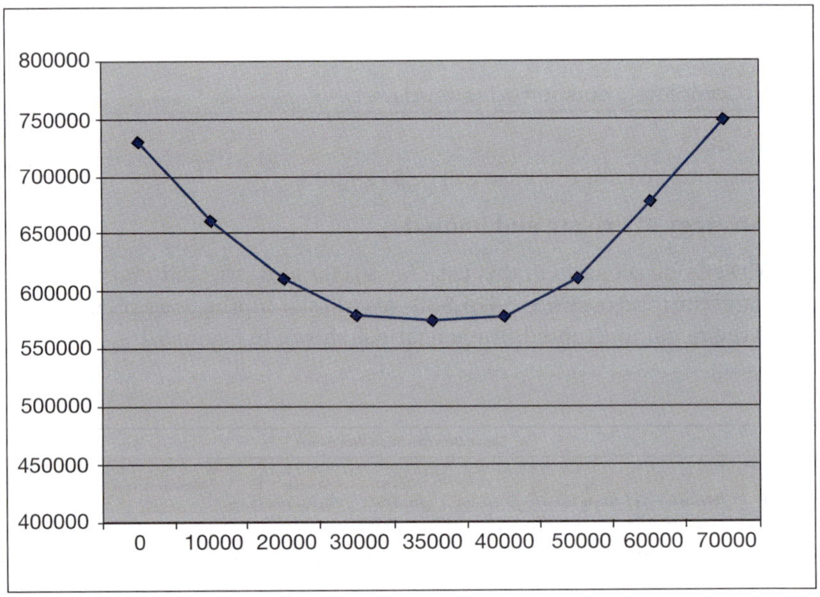

FIGURE 5.5 Graph showing the total cost of scenarios.

As can be seen, if we consider the option of 40,000 sq ft as a private warehouse option and the remaining as rented, the total cost is the least if we consider increments of 10,000 sq ft. However, if we consider increments of 5000 sq ft, we can see that the total cost is the least at 35,000 sq ft.

A mixed strategy and avoiding extreme choices of warehousing can give good results when the throughputs are varying.

The method we have described here is only a decision support tool to determine the space requirements and is shown as an illustration of the computations required and how the scenario can be varied to evaluate alternatives. However, in practice, we may have to deal with more variants of this and more complexities.

5.2 | WAREHOUSE OPERATIONS AND LAYOUT DECISIONS

Historically, warehouses were established to hold safety stock and support plant production. Eventually, customers began asking, "If you're supporting plant production, what else can you do?" Warehousing services grew from that to encompass complete solutions for consolidation (of inbound material and receiving of finished goods). Other services such as packaging and other product preparation were also added to help customers reduce costs. While the theory of product postponement is still valid, it does not mean that the warehouse function is disappearing. It just means that what is going on inside is being transformed. In recent years, many companies have been pushed to adopt the concept of lean supply reducing inventory and overheads to trim costs and operate more efficiently and flexibly. Warehouses, like every other component in the supply chain, came under scrutiny. Some even wondered whether warehouses, at least how they were currently operating, were relevant at all. But the warehouse is still at the heart of the supply chain.

Storage is an economic convenience, not a necessity, except where customer service is a concern.

5.2.1 Reasons for Storage

The main reasons for storage in a supply chain are as follows:

1. Transportation and production costs can be reduced
2. Better coordination of supply and demand
3. Storage can be an integral part of the production process
4. Storage may enhance sales

The storage functions include the following:

1. Holding
2. Consolidation
3. Break bulk
4. Mixing (merge-in-transit)

5.2.2 Holding

The holding function basically provides protection and the orderly holding of inventories. The length of time for holding goods and the requirements for storage dictate the facility's configuration and layout. Facilities vary from long-term, specialized storage to general-purpose merchandise to temporary holding of goods.

5.2.3 Consolidation

Consolidation is useful when transportation rate structures, especially rate breaks, influence the use of storage facilities. It is economical to consolidate small shipments to larger ones to reduce overall transportation costs, the logic being that the freight differential may offset the field warehousing charges. The consolidation situation is explained with the following example and is depicted in Figure 5.6.

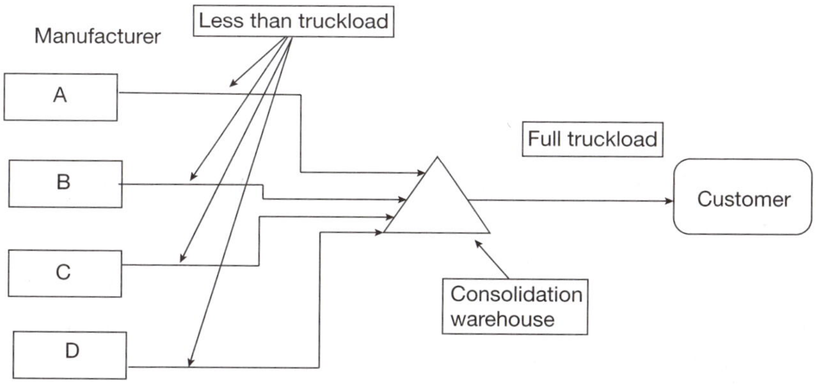

FIGURE 5.6 Consolidation warehouse.

Suppose the details of direct shipping to customer are given in Table 5.3.

TABLE 5.3 Direct shipments to customers

Manufacturer	Shipping Weight (kg)	Less than Truck Rate to Customer ($)	Cost in $
A	100,000	0.02/kg	200
B	8000	0.018 /kg	133
C	15,000	0.34 /kg	510
D	7000	0.16/kg	112
Total			**$966**

If the shipments are through a consolidation warehouse, Tables 5.4 and 5.5 give the cost implications.

TABLE 5.4 Shipment costs through consolidation warehouse

Manufacturer	Shipping Weight (kg)	Less than Truck Rate to Consolidation Warehouse	Total LTL
A	100000	0.075/kg	75
B	8000	0.06 /kg	48
C	15000	0.12 /kg	180
D	7000	0.05/kg	35
Total			**$338**

TABLE 5.5 Warehousing and full truck costs from consolidation warehouse

Consolidation Warehouse Charges ($) @ 0.001/kg	Full Truck Rate from Consolidation Warehouse to Customer @ 0.10/kg	Truck Cost	Total Cost
$10	$.10/kg	$100	$185
8	1.00	80	136
15	1.00	150	345
7	1.00	70	112
$40		**$400**	**$778**

From Tables 5.3, 5.4, and 5.5, it can be seen that a saving of $966 – $778 = $188 can be possible if shipments are made though the consolidation warehouse.

5.2.4 Differences between a Holding Warehouse and a Distribution Warehouse

The main differences between a Holding Warehouse and a Distribution Warehouse are as follows:

1. The difference is a matter of how much emphasis is placed on holding activities and the amount of time for which goods are stored.

2. A holding warehouse implies that much of the warehouse space is devoted to semi-permanent or long-term storage.
3. A distribution warehouse has most of its space allocated to temporary storage and more attention is given to speed and ease of product flow.
4. Many warehouses operate in both capacities and the difference is a matter of degree.

They are illustrated in Figures 5.7 and 5.8.

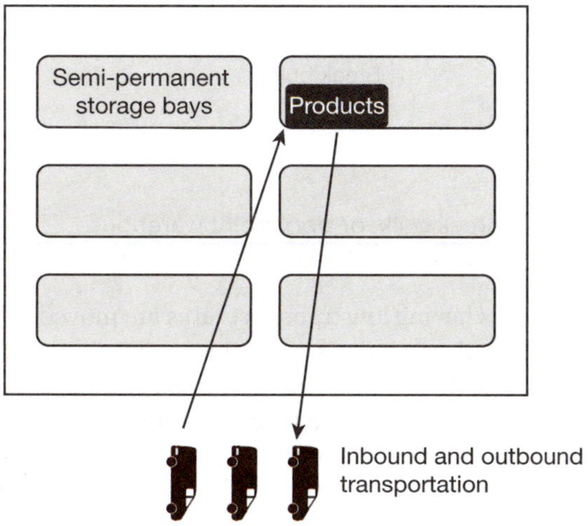

FIGURE 5.7 Low throughput, holding warehouse (warehouse with emphasis on long-term storage).

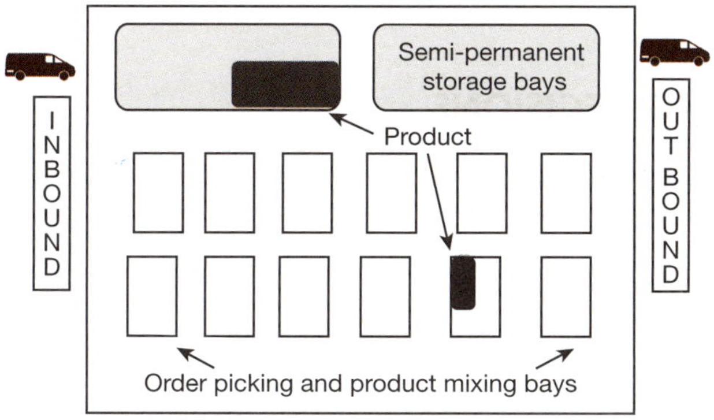

FIGURE 5.8 High throughput, distribution warehouse (warehouse with emphasis on short-term storage, mixing, and materials flow)

But, at the limit, a warehouse may focus only on receiving and shipping activities eliminating storage and order-picking activities. Such warehouses are referred to as "cross docks" or "pool points." Goods are transferred directly from inbound to outbound docks with little or no storage. The transfer is typically completed in less than a few hours.

5.2.5 Break Bulk

Break bulk uses storage facilities to break the bulk (or trans load), which is the opposite of using them to consolidate shipments as shown in Figure 5.9.

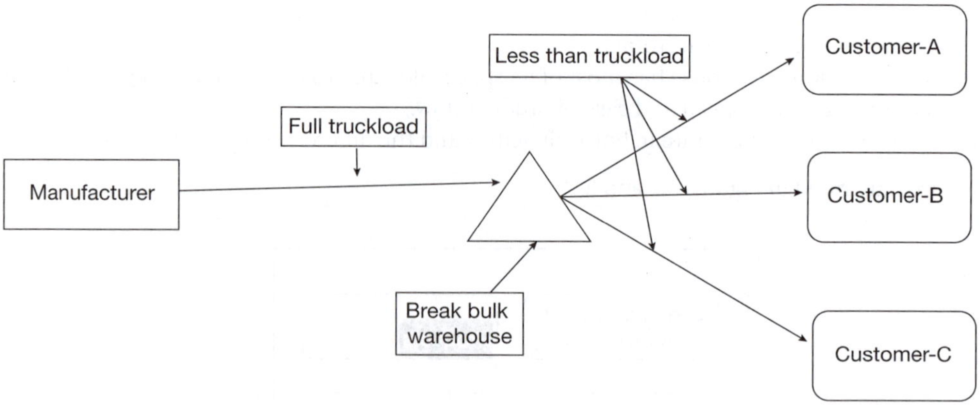

FIGURE 5.9 Distribution, break bulk, or pool point warehouse.

In break bulk, volume shipments having low transport rates are moved to the warehouse and then reshipped in smaller quantities. Break bulk is common in distribution or terminal warehouses, especially when inbound transportation rates per unit are less than the outbound rates per unit, or when customer orders are less than vehicle load quantities and the distance between manufacturer and customers is large. While transportation rate differentials tend to favor a distribution warehouse location near customers for break bulk operations, the opposite is true for freight consolidation.

5.2.6 Mixing

Firms that purchase from a number of manufacturers to fill a portion of their product line at a number of plants may find a warehouse as a product mixing point offering transportation economies.

5.3 | HANDLING DECISIONS

The strategic intent of warehouses is fast changing these days, such that they have become value-adding points in the supply chain. Various trade-off decisions in cost and value propositions lead to deciding the role of a warehouse to be a consolidation warehouse or a break bulk warehouse, etc. Scientific analysis of the cost drivers and some mathematical analysis would be useful in such decisions.

Controlling costs in handling material in a warehouse is of primary importance in the overall supply chain costs. Handling is typically a labor-intensive activity and the costs can be reduced by:

1. Reducing distance traveled
2. Increasing number of units handled at a time
3. Seeking multiple order picking in a single order-picking round trip
4. Increasing storage density
5. Carefully planning the physical layout of the building
6. Carefully locating the items within the order-picking area
7. Using automation and mechanical assists as labor substitutes
8. Using computer systems to help plan the flow of work through the building

Therefore, layout decisions are very important in planning warehouse operations. Facility layout methods are very popular and most discussed in operations management courses, and hence they are not discussed here. An important decision in layout in warehouse operations is the product layout decision, which focuses on which products to keep where in a warehouse. Some of the common methods by which products are grouped and stored are as follows:

1. By complementary
2. By compatibility
3. By popularity
4. By cube

The measure cube-per-order (CPO) index is very effective in the layout decision in a warehouse. The CPO index is the ratio of a product's average required cubic footage for storage to the average number of daily orders on which the item is requested. The products with the lowest index value are located nearest the outbound dock. Layout can be done:

1. By popularity
2. By cube
3. By CPO

We will illustrate this with the following example with details shown in Table 5.6.

TABLE 5.6 Product layout example

Product	(a) Item Size (cu ft)	(b) Expected Number of Orders/ Year	(c) Average Inventory Units	(d) = (b)/240 Average Number of Daily Orders[1]	(e) = (a)*(c) Required Storage Space (cu ft)	(f) = (e)/(d) Cube-per-Order (CPO) Index
A	7	7500	800	31	5600	179
B	4	16000	15000	67	60000	900
C	2	12500	23000	52	46000	883
D	6	27000	16000	113	96000	853
E	3	18000	12000	75	36000	480
F	5	4000	3800	17	19000	1140
G	12	7000	1000	29	12000	411
H	15	16000	12000	67	180000	2700

[1] Based on 240 working days in a year.

By Cube

By Popularity

By CPO

Table 5.7 gives the details of products arranged by cube, popularity, and CPO index.

TABLE 5.7 Classified by cube, popularity, and CPO index

Cube (Highest to Lowest)		Popularity (Highest to Lowest)		CPO Index (Lowest to Highest)	
Product	Item Size (cu ft)	Product	Expected Number of Orders/Year	Product	CPO Index
H	15	D	27000	A	179
G	12	E	18000	G	411
A	7	H	16000	E	480
D	6	B	16000	D	853
F	5	C	12500	C	883
B	4	A	7500	B	900
E	3	G	7000	F	1140
C	2	F	4000	H	2700

A suggested product layout based on the CPO index is shown in Figure 5.10.

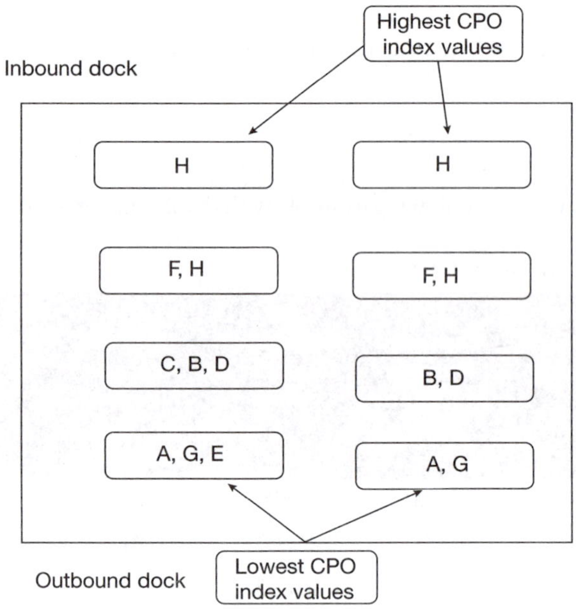

FIGURE 5.10 Product layout by CPO index.

The discussion so far focuses more on the general layout for products to be stored in a warehouse. There are specific rules and norms that are helpful in determining such layout configurations.

There are some popular layout designs practiced in operating warehouses: on-the-square layout, angular pallet placement, and V-shaped layouts. References at the end of the chapter will give more details on such layout designs. Figures 5.11, 5.12, and 5.13 give some ideas of those designs.

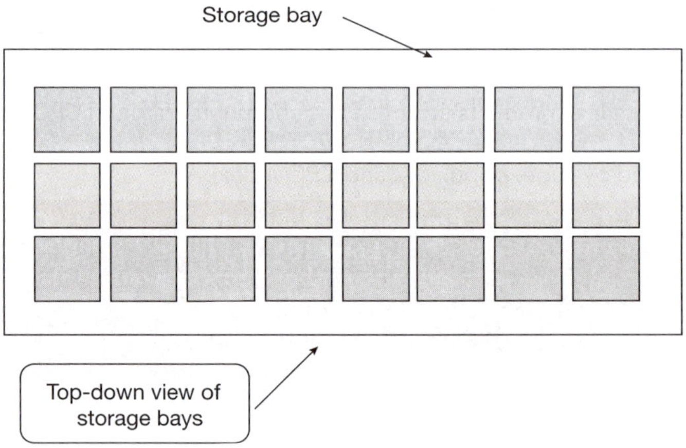

FIGURE 5.11 On-the-square pallet placement.

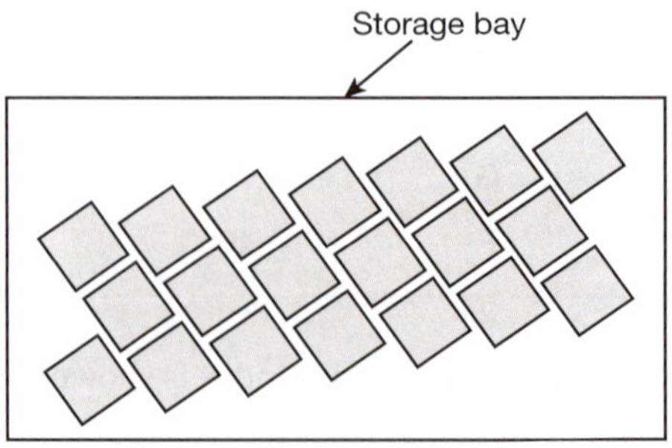

FIGURE 5.12 Angular pallet placement.

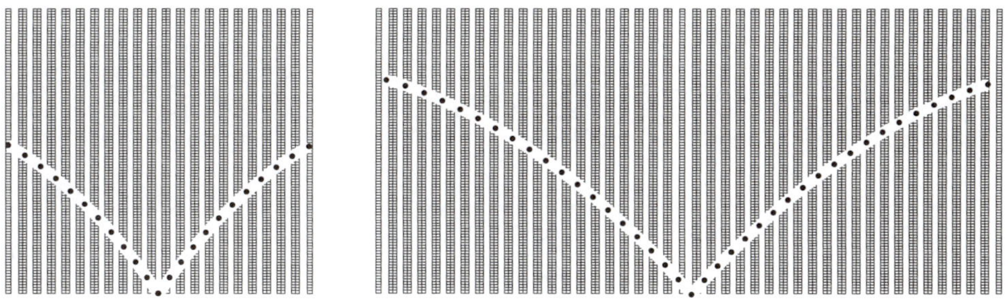

FIGURE 5.13 V-shaped designs.

In this section, we will discuss a method of allocating products to locations, which is a tactical decision to be taken in a warehouse after the design has been worked out.

5.3.1 Allocating Products to Storage Locations: Mathematical Programming Approach

As we discussed earlier, the allocation of products within the storage zone of a warehouse is based on the principle that fast-moving products must be placed closer to the entry/exit docks often referred to as in/out ports in order to minimize the overall handling time and cost.

We will discuss an illustrative way of addressing this issue through a formulation (See [6] for more details). Let

1. N be the total number of storage locations available in a storage zone.
2. n be the number of product SKUs to be allocated to these storage locations.
3. $n_j, j = 1, 2, \ldots, n$, be the number of storage locations required for product j (in a dedicated storage policy). So, this means that $\sum n_j \leq N$.
4. D be the number of entry/exit docks of the storage zone.
5. o_{jd} be the average number of handling operations on product j through entry/exit docks per time period for $j = 1, \ldots, n$ and $d = 1, \ldots, D$.
6. t_{dk} be the travel time or distance from entry/exit docks d and storage location k for $d = 1, \ldots, D$ and $k = 1, \ldots, N$.

One of the key principles in warehousing efficiency is how scientifically are they designed to enable operations within the warehouse. The cost of warehouse operations depends on the way the products are stored and retrieved. A good analysis of the history of product movements will enable such layouts for efficient handling of them to improve productivity of a warehouse.

We will assume that all storage locations available in the storage zone have the same utilization rate, and it is possible to compute the cost C_{jk} ($j = 1, \ldots, n$; $k = 1, \ldots, N$) of assigning storage location k to product j as follows:

$$C_{jk} = \sum_{d=1}^{D} \frac{o_{jd}}{n_j} t_{dk}$$

where o_{jd}/n_j represents the average number of handling operations per time period on product j between entry/exit dock d and any of the storage locations assigned to the product. Hence, the expression $\frac{o_{jd}}{n_j} t_{dk}$ represents the average travel time or distance due to storage location k if it is assigned to product j.

Let $X_{jk} = \begin{cases} 1, \text{ if storage location } k \text{ is assigned to product } j \\ 0, \text{ otherwise} \end{cases}$

for $j = 1, \ldots, n$ and $k = 1, \ldots, N$

Hence the problem of allocating products optimally to the given storage locations can be formulated as follows:

$$\text{Minimize} \sum_{j=1}^{n} \sum_{k=1}^{N} C_{jk} X_{jk}$$

Subject to

$$\sum_{k=1}^{N} X_{jk} = n_j \qquad (5.1)$$

for $j = 1, 2, \ldots, n$

$$\sum_{j=1}^{n} x_{jk} \leq 1 \qquad (5.2)$$

x_{jk} ε 0, 1 for $j = 1, \ldots, n$ and $k = 1, \ldots, N$

EXAMPLE 5.2

Company XYZ has a warehouse where there are two entry/exit docks and 40 storage locations that are arranged in some convenient number of racks. The details of the products are given in Table 5.8, and the distances between the storage locations and entry/exit docks 1 and 2 are given in Table 5.9.

TABLE 5.8 Details of products of Company XYZ

Product	Number of Storage Locations Required for Products	Daily Number of Storage and Retrieval	
		Dock 1	Dock 2
1	10	30	20
2	8	18	28
3	9	12	36
4	6	28	24
5	5	25	20

TABLE 5.9 Distances t_{dk} (in meters) between Docks 1 and 2 and the storage locations in the storage zone of the warehouse

Storage Location	Distance for Dock 1	Distance for Dock 2	Storage Location	Distance for Dock 1	Distance for Dock 2
1	3	24	13	7	16
2	5	18	14	9	18
3	6	20	15	12	16
4	9	18	16	4	24
5	11	16	17	6	22
6	4	24	18	9	23
7	6	20	19	11	19
8	8	17	20	13	18
9	9	19	21	16	12
10	12	18	22	18	9
11	3	25	23	20	7
12	5	22	24	22	5

(Continued)

TABLE 5.9 (Continued)

Storage Location	Distance for Dock 1	Distance for Dock 2	Storage Location	Distance for Dock 1	Distance for Dock 2
25	23	4	33	16	7
26	17	12	34	21	5
27	19	11	35	24	4
28	18	8	36	14	13
29	22	6	37	15	9
30	21	5	38	17	8
31	18	12	39	22	7
32	14	9	40	25	4

We will solve the formulation on Excel as follows. Table 5.10 gives the data for computing the values of o_{jd}.

TABLE 5.10 Computation of o_{jd}

	Product	Number of Storage Locations Required	Daily Number of Storage and Retrievals	
			Dock 1	Dock 2
o_{jd}	1	10	30	20
	2	8	18	28
	3	9	12	36
	4	6	28	24
	5	5	25	20
	N	**38**		

Table 5.11 shows the computation of C_{jk}, and Table 5.12 gives the data table for Solver.

TABLE 5.11 Computation of C_{jk} values

$C_{11} = (o_{11}/n_1)*t_{11}+(o_{12}/n_1)*t_{21}$
$= (30/10)*3+(20/10)*24 = 57$

Storage Locations	Products				
	1	2	3	4	5
1	57.00	90.75	100.00	110.00	111.00
2	51.00	74.25	78.67	95.33	97.00
3	58.00	83.50	88.00	108.00	110.00
4	63.00	83.25	84.00	114.00	117.00
5	65.00	80.75	78.67	115.33	119.00
6	60.00	93.00	101.33	114.67	116.00
7	58.00	83.50	88.00	108.00	110.00
8	58.00	77.50	78.67	105.33	108.00
9	65.00	86.75	88.00	118.00	121.00

(*Continued*)

TABLE 5.11 (Continued)

Storage Locations	Products				
	1	2	3	4	5
10	72.00	90.00	88.00	128.00	132.00
11	59.00	94.25	104.00	114.00	115.00
12	59.00	88.25	94.67	111.33	113.00
13	53.00	71.75	73.33	96.67	99.00
14	63.00	83.25	84.00	114.00	117.00
15	68.00	83.00	80.00	120.00	124.00
16	60.00	93.00	101.33	114.67	116.00
17	62.00	90.50	96.00	116.00	118.00
18	73.00	100.75	104.00	134.00	137.00
19	71.00	91.25	90.67	127.33	131.00
20	75.00	92.25	89.33	132.67	137.00
21	72.00	78.00	69.33	122.67	128.00
22	72.00	72.00	60.00	120.00	126.00
23	74.00	69.50	54.67	121.33	128.00
24	76.00	67.00	49.33	122.67	130.00
25	77.00	65.75	46.67	123.33	131.00
26	75.00	80.25	70.67	127.33	133.00
27	79.00	81.25	69.33	132.67	139.00
28	70.00	68.50	56.00	116.00	122.00
29	78.00	70.50	53.33	126.67	134.00
30	73.00	64.75	48.00	118.00	125.00
31	78.00	82.50	72.00	132.00	138.00
32	60.00	63.00	54.67	101.33	106.00
33	62.00	60.50	49.33	102.67	108.00
34	73.00	64.75	48.00	118.00	125.00
35	80.00	68.00	48.00	128.00	136.00
36	68.00	77.00	70.67	117.33	122.00
37	63.00	65.25	56.00	106.00	111.00
38	67.00	66.25	54.67	111.33	117.00
39	80.00	74.00	57.33	130.67	138.00
40	83.00	70.25	49.33	132.67	141.00

TABLE 5.12 Data table for Solver

Storage Locations	Products					Storage Locations	Products						
	1	2	3	4	5		1	2	3	4	5	LHS	RHS
1	57.00	90.75	100.00	110.00	111.00	**1**	0	0	0	0	0	0	1
2	51.00	74.25	78.67	95.33	97.00	**2**	0	0	0	0	0	0	1
3	58.00	83.50	88.00	108.00	110.00	**3**	0	0	0	0	0	0	1
4	63.00	83.25	84.00	114.00	117.00	**4**	0	0	0	0	0	0	1
5	65.00	80.75	78.67	115.33	119.00	**5**	0	0	0	0	0	0	1
6	60.00	93.00	101.33	114.67	116.00	**6**	0	0	0	0	0	0	1
7	58.00	83.50	88.00	108.00	110.00	**7**	0	0	0	0	0	0	1
8	58.00	77.50	78.67	105.33	108.00	**8**	0	0	0	0	0	0	1
9	65.00	86.75	88.00	118.00	121.00	**9**	0	0	0	0	0	0	1
10	72.00	90.00	88.00	128.00	132.00	**10**	0	0	0	0	0	0	1
11	59.00	94.25	104.00	114.00	115.00	**11**	0	0	0	0	0	0	1
12	59.00	88.25	94.67	111.33	113.00	**12**	0	0	0	0	0	0	1
13	53.00	71.75	73.33	96.67	99.00	**13**	0	0	0	0	0	0	1
14	63.00	83.25	84.00	114.00	117.00	**14**	0	0	0	0	0	0	1
15	68.00	83.00	80.00	120.00	124.00	**15**	0	0	0	0	0	0	1
16	60.00	93.00	101.33	114.67	116.00	**16**	0	0	0	0	0	0	1
17	62.00	90.50	96.00	116.00	118.00	**17**	0	0	0	0	0	0	1
18	73.00	100.75	104.00	134.00	137.00	**18**	0	0	0	0	0	0	1
19	71.00	91.25	90.67	127.33	131.00	**19**	0	0	0	0	0	0	1
20	75.00	92.25	89.33	132.67	137.00	**20**	0	0	0	0	0	0	1
21	72.00	78.00	69.33	122.67	128.00	**21**	0	0	0	0	0	0	1
22	72.00	72.00	60.00	120.00	126.00	**22**	0	0	0	0	0	0	1
23	74.00	69.50	54.67	121.33	128.00	**23**	0	0	0	0	0	0	1
24	76.00	67.00	49.33	122.67	130.00	**24**	0	0	0	0	0	0	1
25	77.00	65.75	46.67	123.33	131.00	**25**	0	0	0	0	0	0	1
26	75.00	80.25	70.67	127.33	133.00	**26**	0	0	0	0	0	0	1
27	79.00	81.25	69.33	132.67	139.00	**27**	0	0	0	0	0	0	1
28	70.00	68.50	56.00	116.00	122.00	**28**	0	0	0	0	0	0	1
29	78.00	70.50	53.33	126.67	134.00	**29**	0	0	0	0	0	0	1
30	73.00	64.75	48.00	118.00	125.00	**30**	0	0	0	0	0	0	1
31	78.00	82.50	72.00	132.00	138.00	**31**	0	0	0	0	0	0	1
32	60.00	63.00	54.67	101.33	106.00	**32**	0	0	0	0	0	0	1
33	62.00	60.50	49.33	102.67	108.00	**33**	0	0	0	0	0	0	1
34	73.00	64.75	48.00	118.00	125.00	**34**	0	0	0	0	0	0	1
35	80.00	68.00	48.00	128.00	136.00	**35**	0	0	0	0	0	0	1
36	68.00	77.00	70.67	117.33	122.00	**36**	0	0	0	0	0	0	1
37	63.00	65.25	56.00	106.00	111.00	**37**	0	0	0	0	0	0	1
38	67.00	66.25	54.67	111.33	117.00	**38**	0	0	0	0	0	0	1
39	80.00	74.00	57.33	130.67	138.00	**39**	0	0	0	0	0	0	1
40	83.00	70.25	49.33	132.67	141.00	**40**	0	0	0	0	0	0	1
						LHS	**0**	**0**	**0**	**0**	**0**		
						RHS	**12**	**6**	**8**	**4**	**8**		

Objective Function	0	← $\sum_{j=1}^{n}\sum_{k=1}^{N} C_{jk}X_{jk}$

Table 5.13 presents the Solver solutions.

TABLE 5.13 Solver solutions

Storage Locations	Products						
	1	2	3	4	5	LHS	RHS
1	0	0	0	0	1	1	1
2	0	0	0	0	1	1	1
3	0	0	0	0	1	1	1
4	1	0	0	0	0	1	1
5	1	0	0	0	0	1	1
6	1	0	0	0	0	1	1
7	0	0	0	0	1	1	1
8	0	0	0	0	1	1	1
9	1	0	0	0	0	1	1
10	1	0	0	0	0	1	1
11	1	0	0	0	0	1	1
12	0	0	0	0	1	1	1
13	0	0	0	0	1	1	1
14	0	0	0	0	1	1	1
15	1	0	0	0	0	1	1
16	1	0	0	0	0	1	1
17	1	0	0	0	0	1	1
18	1	0	0	0	0	1	1
19	1	0	0	0	0	1	1
20	1	0	0	0	0	1	1
21	0	1	0	0	0	1	1
22	0	1	0	0	0	1	1
23	0	1	0	0	0	1	1
24	0	0	1	0	0	1	1
25	0	0	1	0	0	1	1
26	0	1	0	0	0	1	1
27	0	0	0	0	0	0	1
28	0	1	0	0	0	1	1
29	0	0	1	0	0	1	1
30	0	0	1	0	0	1	1
31	0	0	0	0	0	0	1
32	0	0	0	1	0	1	1
33	0	0	0	1	0	1	1
34	0	0	1	0	0	1	1
35	0	0	1	0	0	1	1
36	0	0	0	1	0	1	1
37	0	0	0	1	0	1	1
38	0	1	0	0	0	1	1
39	0	0	1	0	0	1	1
40	0	0	1	0	0	1	1
LHS	**12**	**6**	**8**	**4**	**8**		
RHS	**12**	**6**	**8**	**4**	**8**		
Objective Function		**2920**					

The optimal allocation of products in the storage zone is given in Table 5.14. The total distance is minimized at a value of 2920 metres with this optimal allocation.

Mathematical programming approaches are very useful in many supply chain issues, and the example given here is one such. Allocation and assignment decisions are well done by such an approach for optimizing the given objective that is very often cost minimization in warehousing operations. Here the formulation and Solver give an interesting way to decide the allocation for products to storage locations in an optimal way.

TABLE 5.14 Optimal allocations

Storage Location	Product	Storage Location	Product
1	5	**21**	2
2	5	**22**	2
3	5	**23**	2
4	1	**24**	3
5	1	**25**	3
6	1	**26**	2
7	5	**27**	5
8	5	**28**	2
9	1	**29**	3
10	1	**30**	3
11	1	**31**	5
12	5	**32**	4
13	5	**33**	4
14	5	**34**	3
15	1	**35**	3
16	1	**36**	4
17	1	**37**	4
18	1	**38**	2
19	1	**39**	3
20	1	**40**	3

It is very interesting to analyze the scenario for single entry/exit docks where the situation can be easily solved by the following method although the same can be solved using the preceding framework using Solver.

We will first look at the Solver solution if we operate only one entry/exit dock for the preceding example for $d = 1$. The Solver table is given in Table 5.15 for this situation.

TABLE 5.15 Solver solution for the case of single entry/exit dock

Storage Location	Product					Storage Location	Product						
	1	2	3	4	5		1	2	3	4	5	LHS	RHS
1	9.00	6.75	4.00	14.00	15.00	**1**	0	0	0	0	1	1	1
2	15.00	11.25	6.67	23.33	25.00	**2**	0	0	0	1	0	1	1
3	18.00	13.50	8.00	28.00	30.00	**3**	0	0	0	1	0	1	1
4	27.00	20.25	12.00	42.00	45.00	**4**	1	0	0	0	0	1	1
5	33.00	24.75	14.67	51.33	55.00	**5**	1	0	0	0	0	1	1

(*Continued*)

TABLE 5.15 (Continued)

Storage Location	Product					Storage Location	Product						
	1	2	3	4	5		1	2	3	4	5	LHS	RHS
6	12.00	9.00	5.33	18.67	20.00	**6**	0	0	0	0	1	1	1
7	18.00	13.50	8.00	28.00	30.00	**7**	0	0	0	1	0	1	1
8	24.00	18.00	10.67	37.33	40.00	**8**	0	0	0	1	0	1	1
9	27.00	20.25	12.00	42.00	45.00	**9**	1	0	0	0	0	1	1
10	36.00	27.00	16.00	56.00	60.00	**10**	1	0	0	0	0	1	1
11	9.00	6.75	4.00	14.00	15.00	**11**	0	0	0	0	1	1	1
12	15.00	11.25	6.67	23.33	25.00	**12**	0	0	0	0	1	1	1
13	21.00	15.75	9.33	32.67	35.00	**13**	0	0	0	1	0	1	1
14	27.00	20.25	12.00	42.00	45.00	**14**	1	0	0	0	0	1	1
15	36.00	27.00	16.00	56.00	60.00	**15**	1	0	0	0	0	1	1
16	12.00	9.00	5.33	18.67	20.00	**16**	0	0	0	0	1	1	1
17	18.00	13.50	8.00	28.00	30.00	**17**	0	0	0	1	0	1	1
18	27.00	20.25	12.00	42.00	45.00	**18**	1	0	0	0	0	1	1
19	33.00	24.75	14.67	51.33	55.00	**19**	1	0	0	0	0	1	1
20	39.00	29.25	17.33	60.67	65.00	**20**	1	0	0	0	0	1	1
21	48.00	36.00	21.33	74.67	80.00	**21**	0	1	0	0	0	1	1
22	54.00	40.50	24.00	84.00	90.00	**22**	0	1	0	0	0	1	1
23	60.00	45.00	26.67	93.33	100.00	**23**	0	0	1	0	0	1	1
24	66.00	49.50	29.33	102.67	110.00	**24**	0	0	1	0	0	1	1
25	69.00	51.75	30.67	107.33	115.00	**25**	0	0	1	0	0	1	1
26	51.00	38.25	22.67	79.33	85.00	**26**	0	1	0	0	0	1	1
27	57.00	42.75	25.33	88.67	95.00	**27**	0	0	1	0	0	1	1
28	54.00	40.50	24.00	84.00	90.00	**28**	0	0	1	0	0	1	1
29	66.00	49.50	29.33	102.67	110.00	**29**	0	0	1	0	0	1	1
30	63.00	47.25	28.00	98.00	105.00	**30**	0	0	1	0	0	1	1
31	54.00	40.50	24.00	84.00	90.00	**31**	0	1	0	0	0	1	1
32	42.00	31.50	18.67	65.33	70.00	**32**	0	1	0	0	0	1	1
33	48.00	36.00	21.33	74.67	80.00	**33**	0	1	0	0	0	1	1
34	63.00	47.25	28.00	98.00	105.00	**34**	0	0	1	0	0	1	1
35	72.00	54.00	32.00	112.00	120.00	**35**	0	0	0	0	0	0	1
36	42.00	31.50	18.67	65.33	70.00	**36**	1	0	0	0	0	1	1
37	45.00	33.75	20.00	70.00	75.00	**37**	0	1	0	0	0	1	1
38	51.00	38.25	22.67	79.33	85.00	**38**	0	1	0	0	0	1	1

(*Continued*)

TABLE 5.15 (Continued)

Storage Location	Product					Storage Location	Product					LHS	RHS
	1	2	3	4	5		1	2	3	4	5		
39	66.00	49.50	29.33	102.67	110.00	**39**	0	0	1	0	0	1	1
40	75.00	56.25	33.33	116.67	125.00	**40**	0	0	0	0	0	0	1
						LHS	12	6	8	4	8		
						RHS	12	6	8	4	8		
						Objective Function			**1144.75**				

5.3.2 Procedure to Get the Allocations in Case of a Single Entry/Exit Dock

We are given the cost coefficient $C_{jk} = \frac{o_{j1}}{n_j} * t_{1k}$, which can be expressed as $\alpha_j \beta_k$ where $\alpha_j = \frac{o_{j1}}{n_j}$ and $\beta_k = t_{1k}$. As we see here, this depends only on the product j and location k.

Step 1

Construct a vector a of N components where $N = \sum_{j=1}^{n} n_j$, in which there are n_j copies of α_j (i.e., repeating α_j, n_j times) for all $j = 1$ to n. Sort these values in a non-increasing value of the components. Let these sorted values be arranged as i and $a(i)$ for $i = 1$ to N. Define $L_{a(i)} = j$ if $a(i) = \alpha_j$.

Step 2

Let d be a vector of N components of the locations 1 to k with the values of β_k, which are nothing but the values of t_{1k}. Sort these values of t_{1k} along with the location values 1 to k in a non-decreasing order. Let b be a vector of $N = \sum_{j=1}^{n} n_j$ components corresponding to the first N components of the sorted vector d. Define $L_{b(i)} = k$ if $\beta_i = b_k$ for all $i = 1$ to N.

Step 3

Define the optimal solution as $X^*_{La(i),Lb(i)} = 1$ for all $i = 1$ to N. The basic logic of this procedure is that minimizing the objective function is achieved by two vectors a and b by ordering a as non-increasing and b as non-decreasing values. This is shown in Tables 5.16, 5.17, and 5.18.

TABLE 5.16 Basic data for solving single dock

Product	Number of Storage Locations Required (n_j)	Daily Number of Storage and Retrievals	
		Dock 1	$\alpha_j = o_{j1}/n_j$
1	10	30	3.00
2	8	18	2.25
3	9	12	1.33
4	6	28	4.67
5	5	25	5.00

TABLE 5.17 Sorted *b* vector of locations and distance

b vector		b vector	
Storage Location	Distance	Storage Location	Distance
1	3	32	14
11	3	36	14
6	4	37	15
16	4	21	16
2	5	33	16
12	5	26	17
3	6	38	17
7	6	22	18
17	6	28	18
13	7	31	18
8	8	27	19
4	9	23	20
9	9	30	21
14	9	34	21
18	9	24	22
5	11	29	22
19	11	39	22
10	12	25	23
15	12	35	24
20	13	40	25

TABLE 5.18 Details of the procedure

i	a_i	$L_{a(i)}$	b_i	$L_{b(i)}$
1	5.00	5	3	1
2	5.00	5	3	11
3	5.00	5	4	6
4	5.00	5	4	16
5	5.00	5	5	2
6	4.67	4	5	12
7	4.67	4	6	3
8	4.67	4	6	7
9	4.67	4	6	17

(*Continued*)

TABLE 5.18 (Continued)

i	a_i	$L_{a(i)}$	b_i	$L_{b(i)}$
10	4.67	4	7	13
11	4.67	4	8	8
12	3	1	9	4
13	3	1	9	9
14	3	1	9	14
15	3	1	9	18
16	3	1	11	5
17	3	1	11	19
18	3	1	12	10
19	3	1	12	15
20	3	1	13	20
21	3	1	14	32
22	2.25	2	14	36
23	2.25	2	15	37
24	2.25	2	16	21
25	2.25	2	16	33
26	2.25	2	17	26
27	2.25	2	17	38
28	2.25	2	18	22
29	2.25	2	18	28
30	1.33	3	18	31
31	1.33	3	19	27
32	1.33	3	20	23
33	1.33	3	21	30
34	1.33	3	21	34
35	1.33	3	22	24
36	1.33	3	22	29
37	1.33	3	22	39
38	1.33	3	23	25
39			24	35
40			25	40

Table 5.19 presents the final allocation of storage location to products.

TABLE 5.19 Final allocation of storage location to products

Storage Location	Product	Storage Location	Product
1	5	22	2
2	5	23	3
3	4	24	3
4	1	25	3
5	1	26	2
6	5	27	3
7	4	28	2
8	4	29	3
9	1	30	3
10	1	31	3
11	5	32	1
12	4	33	2
13	4	34	3
14	1	35	
15	1	36	2
16	5	37	2
17	4	38	2
18	1	39	3
19	1	40	
20	1	**Objective Function**	**1144.75**
21	2		

As we can see, there are a few differences in the allocations; however, the total cost remains the same in both the linear programming approach and the procedure.

5.4 | LAYOUT CONFIGURATION DECISIONS

Efficiency in warehouse operations often depends on proper layout and design decisions. Various choices of layouts are available, and the optimal layout decisions relating to its height, length, and width are key dimensions of a scientific layout. A good amount of research has been done on this, and in this chapter some popular studies are presented.

We have seen how the warehouse size is a tactical decision in warehousing as well as the factors that impacted the size. We have also seen an illustration of how the size can be determined with which types of strategies. The subsequent decisions would involve how the warehouse should be configured in terms of ceiling height, length, and width; warehouses can be constructed in various shapes and sizes.

5.4.1 Ceiling Height

In the illustration on determining the size of a warehouse, we assumed a given height for stacking items in the warehouse. The decision of this height is dependent on the construction costs, material-handling requirements and costs, and stacking considerations. Changing the ceiling height of a warehouse would involve costs for added material handling and service time for stacking and picking loads at heights that are more than average. The nature and characteristics of goods that are stored also can affect the ceiling requirements in a warehouse.

The height may be constrained by stacking methods and pallet loads. Storage racks are often altered and used to increase the utilization of ceiling height and overcome product limits. Height limitations may also be imposed by local building bylaws and norms. Therefore, determining a ceiling height is a trade-off decision involving construction costs, material-handling costs, stacking and picking costs, and other related costs with all the legal constraints. In addition, a futuristic approach of keeping space for expansions and other requirements should also be kept in mind while deciding this.

5.4.2 Length and Width

The length and width or the general configuration of a warehouse often depends on various considerations like cost of material handling, picker's speed, construction cost, general norms of flow in the warehouse, de-stability of certain parameters like aisle width and pallet size and depth, etc. Hence, there are many research papers in this area that attempted to model the situations as per many assumptions and scenarios of design and considerations and came up with the optimal length, width, and layout. We will present a few simple models to illustrate the science of warehouse design and layout.

Consider the following type of storage zone of a warehouse shown in Figure 5.14.

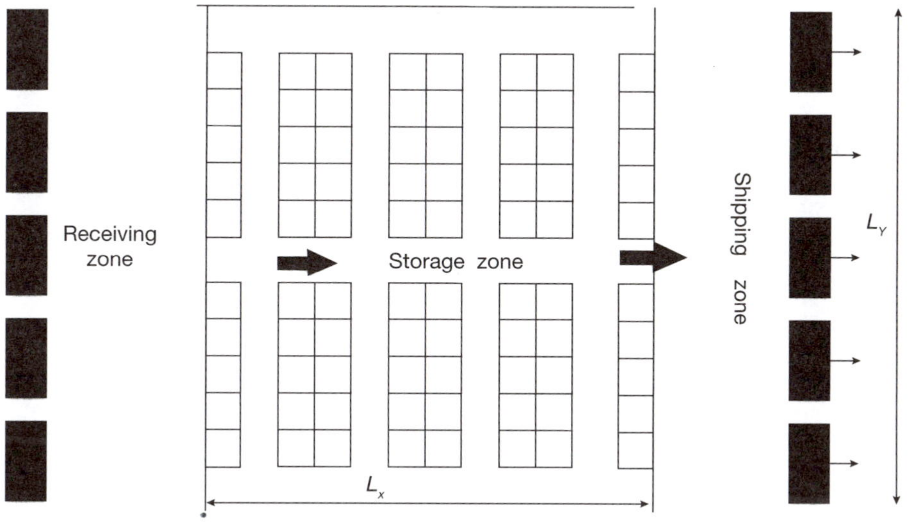

FIGURE 5.14 A storage zone of a warehouse.

Let

1. L_X and L_Y be the lengths of the storage zone along the X-direction and Y-direction, respectively.
2. s be the number of storage locations that are required for the operations.
3. O_X and O_Y be the space occupied by a unit load along the X-direction and the Y-direction of the storage zone, respectively.
4. N_X, N_Y, and N_Z be the number of storage locations along the X-, Y-, and Z-directions as followed in the system.
5. a_X and a_Y be the width of the side aisles and of the central aisle, respectively.
6. v be the average speed of a picker.

Here the problem is to determine the measurement L_X and L_Y.

It can be seen that

$$L_X = \left(O_X + \frac{a_X}{2}\right) N_X \text{ and}$$

$$L_Y = O_Y * N_Y + 3 * a_Y$$

where N_X is assumed to be an even number.

Assuming equal probability of accessing the storage locations and handling a unit load, the average distance covered by a picker is

$$L_X + \frac{L_Y}{2}$$

Therefore, the optimizing problem of sizing would become

$$\text{Minimize}\left(O_X + \frac{a_X}{2}\right)\frac{N_X}{v} + \frac{O_Y * N_Y + 3 * a_Y}{2v}$$

Subject to

$$N_X * N_Y * N_Z \geq s$$

$$N_X, N_Y \geq 0, \text{Integer}$$

$$N_X \text{ even}$$

The objective function here is the average time a picker takes, and the inequality talks about the number of locations to be at least *s*.

We can relax the inequality at the optimal stage and express

$$N_X = \frac{s}{N_Y * N_Z}$$

We can remove N_X from the formulation with this expression and the formulation becomes

$$\text{Minimize}\left(O_X + \frac{a_X}{2}\right)\frac{s}{v * N_Y * N_Z} + \frac{O_Y * N_Y + 3 * a_Y}{2v}$$

$$\text{Subject to } N_Y \geq 0$$

Since this is convex, we can find $\frac{d}{dN_Y}$ and set it to 0.

$$\frac{d}{dN_Y}\left\{\left(O_X + \frac{a_X}{2}\right)\frac{s}{v * N_Y * N_Z} + \frac{O_Y * N_Y + 3 * a_Y}{2v}\right\} = 0$$

This gives the optimal value of $N_Y^* = \sqrt{\dfrac{2 * s * \left(O_X + \dfrac{a_X}{2}\right)}{a_Y * N_Z}}$

Substituting this value in the earlier expression of N_X, we get

$$N_X^* = \sqrt{\frac{s * a_Y}{2 * N_Z\left(O_X + \dfrac{a_X}{2}\right)}}$$

Both the values of N_X^* and N_Y^* are rounded off to suitable integer numbers in such a way that the inequality $N_X * N_Y * N_Z \geq s$ is maintained and $\boldsymbol{N_X}$ is even.

EXAMPLE 5.3

XYZ Company is planning for a warehouse in Bhiwandi near Mumbai to supply its products to its sales regions in Maharashtra. An assessment was made to plan for accommodating 1200 pallets of 120 × 120 cm^2 dimension. It is also planned that conventional racks will be used to store these pallets and will be transported by pickers using reach trucks. Each rack has five shelves, each of which can store a single pallet. Each pallet occupies a 1.40 × 1.40 m^2 area. Racks will be arranged as shown in Figure 5.13 with side aisles that are 4 m wide, while the central aisle is 4.5 m wide. The average speed of a picker in the reach truck is 8 km/h.

$$N_X^* = \sqrt{\frac{sa_Y}{2N_Z\left(O_X + \frac{a_X}{2}\right)}} = \sqrt{\frac{1200*1.40}{2*5\left(1.40+\frac{4}{2}\right)}} = 7.03$$

$$N_Y^* = \sqrt{\frac{2s\left(O_X + \frac{a_X}{2}\right)}{a_Y N_Z}} = \sqrt{\frac{2*1200*\left(1.40+\frac{4}{2}\right)}{1.40*5}} = 34.14$$

By rounding the values $N_X^* = 7$ and $N_Y^* = 34$. The total number of locations comes to be 7 × 34 × 5 = 1190. So

$$L_X = \left(O_X + \frac{a_X}{2}\right)N_X = \left(1.40+\frac{4}{2}\right)7 = 23.8 \text{ m}$$

$$L_Y = O_Y N_Y + 3a_Y = 1.40*34+3*4.5 = 61.1 \text{ m}$$

5.4.3 Sizing of Receiving Zone

The sizing of receiving zone in a warehouse can be arrived at using the following steps.
Let

1. p be the average number of palletized loads that enter a warehouse in a time period (say day, week, or month).
2. t be the average time that is required to unload a vehicle.
3. C be the capacity of vehicles in terms of pallets.
4. T be the average time available in the time horizon for a vehicle's unloading operations.

Then the size of the receiving zone is computed using the number d of docking doors that can be estimated by the following relation:

$$d = \frac{pt}{CT}$$

From practical experience, the size of the receiving zone is estimated with some practical inputs on the preceding inputs. A space of about 50 m^2 for each docking door is assumed to be sufficient to facilitate easy unloading of vehicles for the movement of 50 palletized load units.

We assume that the width of a docking door is approximately 2.6 m on average, and the distance between two adjacent docking ports is about 1.5 m.

With these assumptions, L_Y and L_X become as follows:

$$L_Y = 2.6d + 1.5(d + 1) \text{ and}$$

$$L_X = 50d/L_Y$$

5.4.4 Layout of a Rectangular Warehouse Minimizing Energy Cost

In the paper "A model for storage facility design with energy costs" (2016), Ivan Derpich and Juan M. Sepúlveda [4] present a simple mathematical expression for designing a distribution center (DC). Following are the assumptions that are made in developing such expressions:

1. Goods are stored in double racks, except for the rack adjacent to the wall, which has only one side.
2. The shape of the store is rectangular (see Figure 5.15).
3. There should be wide aisles between the racks, and along the walls, the width of these aisles should be the same.
4. Goods enter through a door located in one of the walls of the store and leave through a door opposite to the front door.

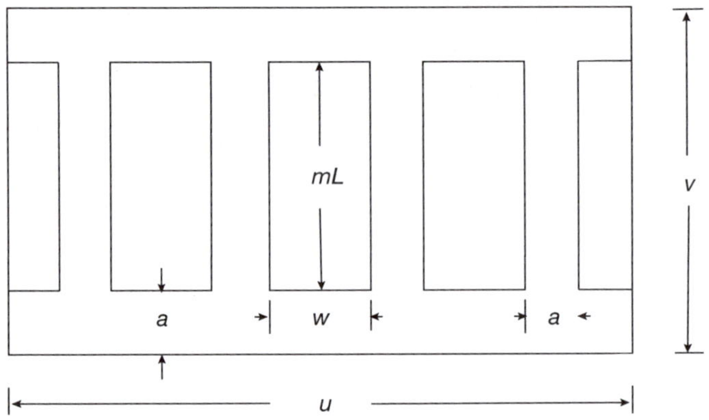

FIGURE 5.15 Layout of the rectangular warehouse.

The notations used in this study are as follows:

1. w is width of a double shelf.
2. L is length of a storage unit in the shelf.
3. m is the total number of storage spaces along a shelf.
4. h is the number of storage spaces vertically.
5. n is the number of double shelves.
6. K is the total storage capacity in storage spaces.
7. a is the width of an aisle, where it is assumed that all the aisles have the same width.
8. u is the length of the store.
9. v is the width of the store.
10. d is the annual movement (demand) of the warehouse, in storage units. It is assumed that a unit of stored article occupies a unit of space (in items/year).
11. C_h is material-handling cost of moving a unit of article per unit of length (in $/m).
12. T_v is the average travel distance on the vertical axis.
13. T_u is the average travel distance on the horizontal axis.
14. T_h is the average travel distance in height.

The objective will be to minimize the cost of moving and handling of goods inside the warehouse. Figure 5.14 is referred to for the development of the expressions for m, h, and n.

From the figure, we can determine the length and width of the warehouse as follows:

Width: $u = n(w + a)$
Length: $v = 2a + mL$

Then, the area of the distribution center whose dimensions are as follows:

$$\text{Area} = uv = n(w + a)\,(2a + mL)$$

The average travel distance of each stored unit is required to be used for cost estimation. As mentioned earlier, it is assumed that the doors are located at the centers of the walls and all goods are equally likely to be used.

To determine the cost function of the DC, the probabilities of carrying a good in the horizontal plane and in height are required. In the horizontal plane, two axes of movement, one of lateral movement (direction u) and one of movement toward the bottom of the warehouse (v direction), are defined (Figure 5.15). So, we will have T_v, T_u, and T_h representing the distances in each direction. As the probability of taking a good to the left or right from the door of the CD store is the same, the average travel distance on the horizontal axis is

$$T_u = \frac{u}{4}$$

To determine the distance in the direction v, the average travel distance would depend on the categories of products if they are A, B, or C. Let us assume that P_a, P_b, and P_c are the likelihood of the probabilities of the categories A, B, and C, respectively. We will also assume that m_a, m_b, and m_c represent the number of spaces in the direction v that are reserved for product categories A, B, and C, respectively.

Hence, the average travel distance in the direction v is given by:

$$T_v = a + P_a\left(\frac{m_a L}{2}\right) + P_b\left(m_a L + \frac{m_b L}{2}\right) + P_c\left(m_a L + m_b L + \frac{m_c L}{2}\right)$$

with $P_a + P_b + P_c = 1$

The term $P_a m_a/2$ corresponds to the average number of slots to be traveled for storing a product of type A; the term $P_b(m_a + m_b/2)$ corresponds to the average number of slots to be traveled for storing a product of type B; and the term $P_c(m_a + m_b + m_c/2)$ corresponds to the average number of slots to be traveled for storing a product of type C.

The total capacity of categories A, B, and C within the DC to store goods can be expressed as follows:

$$N_a = 2m_a nh$$

$$N_b = 2m_b nh$$

$$N_c = 2m_c nh$$

Combining these, the average travel distance in the vertical axis is

$$T_v = a + \frac{m}{K} L\left[(N_a + N_b)\left(1 - \frac{P_a}{2}\right) + (N_c + N_b)\left(\frac{P_c}{2}\right) - \frac{N_b}{2}\right]$$

The average travel distance in the height axis is given as

$$T_h = A\frac{h}{2}$$

where A is called the height loading factor, which is a factor expressing how many times more complex it is to move load in the vertical axis than in the horizontal plane.

By simplifying the expressions, the problems become

$$\text{Min } C = 4dC_h\left[a + \frac{m}{K} LCt_e + \frac{n(w+a)}{4} + A\frac{h}{2}\right]$$

Subject to $N = 2mnh$

Where $$Ct_e = \left[(N_a + N_b)\left(1 - \frac{P_a}{2}\right) + (N_c + N_b)\left(\frac{P_c}{2}\right) - \frac{N_b}{2}\right]$$

By transforming them to Lagrangian equations and solving, we get

$$m = k^3\sqrt{\frac{(w+a)A}{8L^2 cte^2}}$$

$$h = \sqrt[3]{\frac{Lcte(w+a)}{8A^2}}$$

$$n = \sqrt[3]{\frac{8ALcte}{(w+a)^2}}$$

EXAMPLE 5.4

We will assume that class A products are located closer to the door, while class B at a mid-range distance and class C at a greater distance. Once this process is completed, 20 items in class A, 30 items in class B, and 15 items in class C were found. The probabilities of belonging to each class were taken as 0.65, 0.25, and 0.1, respectively.

The total flow of the warehouse is 150,000 pallets of products per year, and the capacity of the warehouse is 8000 pallets. The capacity of the warehouse is divided into size classes 4000 (N_a), 3000 (N_b), and 1000 (N_c). With respect to the dimensions of the warehouse, there are available racks (with loading on both sides) of a total width (w) of 2.4 m, length of 1.0 m wide, and pallet height of 1 m each. The width of the aisles is 2.5 m, and the width of doors is 5 m. The cost factors considered are the cost of material handling and are obtained by adding the cost of workers using cranes and fuel and depreciation costs and the energy cost generated by the movement in 3D, whereby a cost of $\$1.25 \times 10^{-3}$ is obtained per meter transported. With this information, the summary data are as follows:

1. $w = 2.5$ m (width of double shelf)
2. $L = 1.0$ m (length of storage unit)
3. $K = 8000$ (total storage capacity)
4. $a = 2.5$ m (width of a corridor)
5. $d = 150{,}000$ (annual demand in pallets)
6. $C_h = 0.00125$ (material-handling cost, \$/mt)
7. $A = 4$ (load factor in height)
8. $N_a = 4000$ (number of pallets in category A)
9. $N_b = 3000$ (number of pallets in category B)
10. $N_c = 1000$ (number of pallets in category C)
11. $P_a = 0.65$ (probability that a product is in category A)
12. $P_b = 0.25$ (probability that a product is in category B)
13. $P_c = 0.1$ (probability that a product is in category C)

A good approximation for the load factor is to assume that $A \cong e^{\sqrt{\frac{h}{2}}}$.

We decide the value of $h = 5$ and determine the value of A as 4.14 through goal seek. The results will be

$$m = 48$$
$$h = 5$$
$$n = 17$$

and the total cost is \$40,670 as shown in the following Excel sheet.

w	2.5	w + a	5
L	1	(w + a)*A	20.68975
K	8000	8*L²*C_{te}^2	93845000
a	2.5		
d	150000		0.006041
C_h	0.00125		
A	4.14		
N_a	4000	**m**	**48**
N_b	3000	**h**	**5**
N_c	1000	**n**	**17**
P_a	0.65		
P_b	0.25		
P_c	0.1		
C_{te}	3425		
Total Cost	**40670**		

5.4.5 Rectangular Warehouse Design and Layout

Richard L. Francis (1967) [5] considered the material-handling and construction costs to explore the configuration of a warehouse theoretically. He explored the configuration of a rectangular warehouse with rectangular aisles storing n different items, having a floor space of S with two options of having the entry/exit docks of warehouse at the extreme corners of the warehouse (shown as X in Figure 5.16) and in the middle of the width of the warehouse (shown as Y in Figure 5.16).

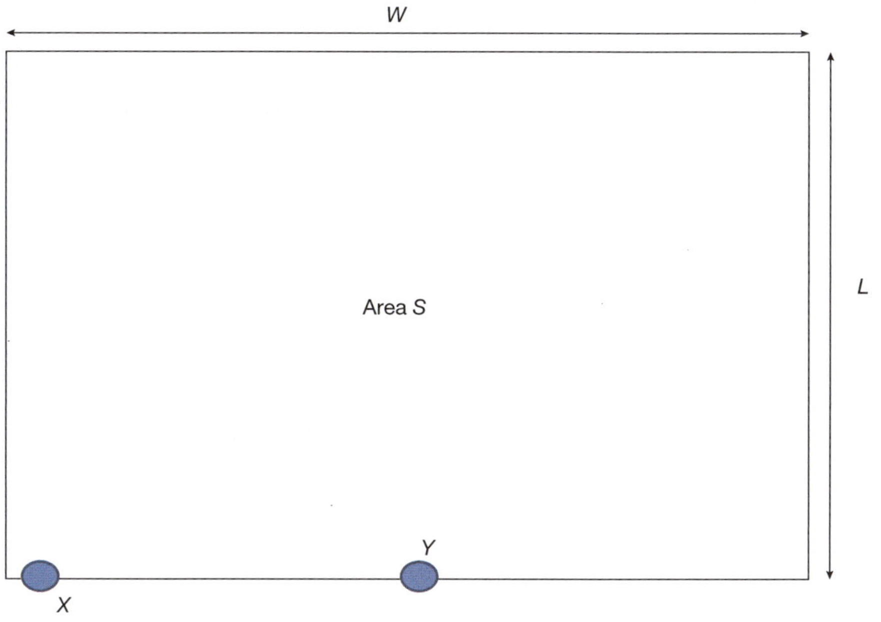

FIGURE 5.16 Configuration of a warehouse with width W and length L and possible entry/exit docks at X and Y.

The optimum length L^* and width W^* are determined by optimizing the material-handling cost and the perimeter construction cost. For the dock located at X (see Figure 5.15), the optimum width is given by

$$W^* = \sqrt{\frac{C+8k}{2C+8k}}\sqrt{S}$$

and the optimal length is given by

$$L^* = \frac{S}{W^*}$$

where

- C is the sum of total cost per foot to move an item in and out of storage multiplied by the expected number of items in and out of storage per year ($/ft).
- k is the annual perimeter cost per foot ($/ft).
- S is the required floor area of the warehouse (sq ft).

If the dock is centered at Y (see Figure 5.15), then the warehouse becomes square shaped, and hence W^* and L^* each will become $\sqrt{S}$, respectively.

The total cost of locating at dock X is given by

$$TC_X = 2\sqrt{\left[\left(\frac{1}{2}\right)C+2k\right]\left[\left(\frac{1}{4}\right)C+2k\right]}\sqrt{S}$$

and the total cost of locating at dock Y is given by

$$TC_Y = \left[\left(\frac{1}{2}\right)C + 4k\right]\sqrt{S}$$

The difference $TC_X - TC_Y$ is the premium that must be paid for locating the dock at X instead of Y.

All these expressions are in their simplistic form and discussed here to illustrate the nature of problems and assumptions behind each of the derivations. So many variations and scenarios are possible in a warehouse, and it is difficult to prescribe any one method to determine the design and the layout. References are given at the end for more in-depth understanding of these topics.

EXAMPLE 5.5

A 3PL spare parts warehouse has a monthly throughput of 200,000 cases and an average in and out material-handling cost of $0.0045 per foot per case moved. Order picking requires a round trip to the dock for each item requested. The total space required for the warehouse operation is 400,000 sq ft. Construction indicates that a 500 × 800 sq ft warehouse can be built for $80 per sq ft. The effective life of the warehouse is assumed to be 20 years. The entry/exit dock is located near a corner of the proposed building. What are the best dimensions for the building and the total relevant cost?

The approximate estimates give us the perimeter of about 2600 ft. The construction cost of an estimated 400,000 sq ft warehouse will be 400,000 × 80 = 32,000,000. Since the life span is for 20 years, the annualized cost of this will be 32,000,000/20 = 1,600,000.

Hence, the perimeter construction cost is approximately 1,600,000/2600 = 615.4/ft So, k = 615.4.

$$C = 200{,}000 \times 0.008 \times 12 = 10{,}800/\text{ft}$$

$$W^* = \sqrt{\frac{C+8k}{2C+8k}}\sqrt{S} = \sqrt{\frac{10{,}800+8\times615.4}{2\times10{,}800+8\times615.4}}\sqrt{400{,}000} = 487 \text{ ft}$$

$$L^* = \frac{S}{W^*} = 400{,}000/487 = 821 \text{ ft}$$

Total cost will be

$$TC_X = 2\sqrt{\left[\left(\frac{1}{2}\right)C+2k\right]\left[\left(\frac{1}{4}\right)C+2k\right]}\sqrt{S}$$

$$= 2\sqrt{\left[\left(\frac{1}{2}\right)10{,}800+2\times615.4\right]\left[\left(\frac{1}{4}\right)10{,}800+2\times615.4\right]}\sqrt{400{,}000}$$

$$= \$6{,}457{,}783 \text{ per year}$$

5.4.6 Internal Layout Design of Warehouse

Joseph Bassan, Yaakov Roll, and Meir J. Rosenblatt [3] explored two configurations of shelves in a homogeneous or a zoned warehouse. Optimizing the total of handling costs and other costs associated with the warehouse area, expressions are derived for the parameters for optimal design. They showed that depending on ratios between the relevant costs, some general preference rules for the two layouts examined can be laid down.

In the configurations shown in Figure 5.17, in the first layout, the shelves are perpendicular to the longitudinal wall of the warehouse building, and in the second, the shelves are arranged in parallel to the longitudinal wall. They are shown as (a) and (b) in Figure 5.17. Also, two organizational situations are considered: in one, the whole warehouse is looked upon as a single homogeneous unit, while in the other, the warehouse consists of several independent units. In each of the alternatives, the overall cost, due to the initial investment and current operations, is computed as a function of the various economic coefficients.

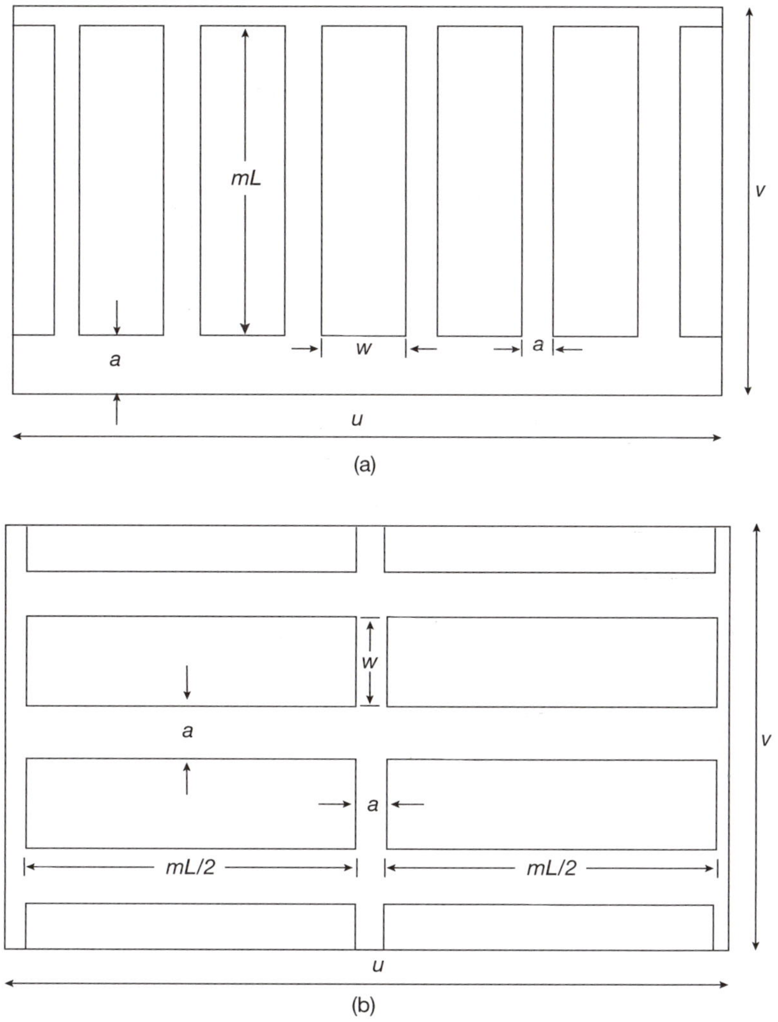

FIGURE 5.17 Two layouts for internal design in a warehouse.

5.4.7 Assumptions and Notations

The general assumptions for the design of the layouts compared here are as follows:

1. Goods are stored on shelves. The shelves are double sided, with access to both sides; except that shelves adjacent to walls are single sided, and half the width of the double ones.
2. The warehouse building is rectangular. This is considered to be the optimal geometrical shape for storing rectangular units (such as palletized goods) on shelves.
3. There should be ample passageway between the shelves and along the walls, to facilitate inspection, meet safety requirements, etc.
4. The goods are brought into the warehouse through a door (or doors) in one side of the rectangular building and taken out through the opposite side. This is equivalent to assuming a single door for incoming and outgoing traffic with a "single-command" type handling. The walls where the entrance and exit doors are located will be referred to as the longitudinal walls, and the other ones as "end" or "cross" walls. The actual dimensional proportions of the warehouse are the subject of the issuing analysis.
5. The height of the shelves and the number of levels on which goods can be stored are independent of the floor layout. Usually, storage height is predetermined by the type of goods, handling equipment, etc. Therefore, this dimension is excluded from the analysis.

The following notations will be used:

1. w is the width of a double shelf.
2. L is the length of a storage space (e.g., width of a pallet).
3. m is the number of storage spaces along a shelf.
4. h is the number of storage levels in the vertical direction.
5. n is the number of double shelves (two single ones are considered double).
6. K is the total warehouse capacity in storage spaces ($K = 2nmh$)
7. a is the width of an aisle. For simplicity sake, it is assumed that all aisles are of the same width.
8. u is the longitudinal dimension of the warehouse.
9. v is the cross dimension (width of the warehouse).
10. d is the yearly throughput (demand) of the warehouse, in storage units (e.g., pallets).

It is assumed that a storage unit occupies one space unit.

The economic comparison is based on the assumption that all costs, which are influenced by the shape and dimensions of the warehouse and its floor layout, can be grouped into the following three elements:

1. C_h is material-handling cost of moving a storage unit one length unit (rectilinear distance is assumed).
2. C_s is the annual cost per unit of warehouse area (discounted investment, maintenance costs, etc.).
3. C_p is the annual cost per unit length of the external walls.

Let the optimal parameters for m and n of the layout option (a) be referred to as m_1^*, n_1^* and layout option (b) in Figure 5.17 be referred to as m_2^*, n_2^*, respectively. For layout option (a), the optimal parameters are derived as

$$m_1^* = \frac{1}{L}\sqrt{\left[\frac{dC_h + 2aC_s + 2C_p}{2(dC_h + C_p)}\right]S}$$

and

$$n_1^* = \frac{1}{w+a}\sqrt{\left[\frac{2(dC_h + C_p)}{dC_h + 2aC_s + 2C_p}\right]S}$$

where $S = \dfrac{K(w+a)L}{2h}$

The best configuration will have a length of

$$u_1 = n_1^*(w+a)$$

and a width of

$$v_1 = 2a + m_1^* L$$

For layout option (b), the optimal parameters are derived as

$$m_2^* = \frac{1}{L}\sqrt{\left[\frac{2dC_h + 3aC_s + 2C_p}{dC_h + 2C_p}\right]S}$$

and

$$n_2^* = \frac{1}{w+a}\sqrt{\left[\frac{dC_h + 2C_p}{2dC_h + 3aC_s + 2C_p}\right]S}$$

where $S = \dfrac{K(w+a)L}{2h}$

The best configuration will have a length of

$$u_2 = 3a + m_2^* L$$

and a width of

$$v_2 = n_2^* (w+a)$$

In order to compare the two layouts from an economic point of view, the minimal costs C_1^* and C_2^* of options (a) and (b) need to be computed with the following rule.

1. If $d < C_p/C_h$, then $C_1^* < C_2^*$ and layout 1 is preferred to layout 2.
2. If $d > 2C_p/C_h$, then $C_1^* > C_2^*$ and layout 2 is preferred.
3. No such general conclusion can be drawn for the range $C_p/C_h < d < 2C_p/C_h$.

EXAMPLE 5.6

Suppose that a warehouse is to be configured according to the layouts in Figure 5.17 using the options (a) and (b). The building has to handle a throughput of 300,000 pallets per year. These require storage space of 3 × 3 × 3 ft and can be stacked five pallets high. Back-to-back pallet racks are 7 ft wide. Aisles are 9 ft wide. The material-handling cost is \$0.0015 per foot, annual space costs are \$0.06 per sq ft, and the annual cost per foot of perimeter wall is \$4. The warehouse turnover is 6 per year with a total warehouse capacity of 50,000 slots. What size building should be planned under (a) and (b) and suggest which option is better?

Using the values and substituting on the respective formula for the layouts, we get the following:

m_1	116	m_2	230
n_1	43	n_2	22
u_1	689	u_2	717
v_1	366	v_2	348

Here, $C_p/C_h = 4/0.0015 = 2666.7$ and $d = 300{,}000$.
Since $d > C_p/C_h$, layout 2 is better with length $u = 717$ ft and width $v = 348$ ft.

5.4.8 Layout of Unit-Load Area

Usually, the convenient way of describing a warehouse is using the term unit-load warehouse, which means that only a single, common "unit" of material, usually a pallet, is handled at a time. Since pallets are mostly standardized and are mostly handled one at a time in terms of both space and labor requirements, a warehouse typically charges its customers for each pallet handled (received and later shipped) and rent for space occupied.

Most 3PL warehouses charge rent from their customers based on the pallets for a period of time, say a month, year, etc. And so, this makes most of the warehouses plan for many pallet positions per unit area, which can be achieved in two ways: using vertical space properly and using deep lanes.

If vertical space is optimally used, many pallets can be stacked high, thus allowing many pallet positions per unit of floor space. If pallets are heavy or fragile or have uneven top surfaces, they cannot be stacked very high and hence this makes vertical space unusable. This underutilization of vertical space can be avoided by installing pallet racks, so that pallets may be stored independently of each other.

An important aspect of warehouse design is pallet racks and how deep they should be designed. It is interesting to study the trade-offs and some interesting formulae concerning such decisions.

How many pallet racks should be purchased and what should be stored therein is one of the critical decisions in the layout of a warehouse. This decision obviously depends on the throughput traffic of the warehouse in terms of size and movement patterns of the different SKUs. There should be an economic analysis of why a particular SKU should be stored in a pallet rack rather than in floor storage. In other words, the benefits of using a rack for an SKU should justify the cost of the rack. There are some benefits of using a pallet rack as compared to floor storage. It might reduce labor by making products easier to store and retrieve. Uneven sizes of SKUs may require additional labor involvement, which increases the cost of retrieval. It might create additional pallet positions. It is always safer using racks.

Aisles in warehouses are key to providing accessibility but not for storage and for revenue generation. However, reducing the aisle space to the necessary minimum is also important to provide adequate accessibility. If products are stored in lanes, there is an advantage of additional pallet positions sharing the same aisle space and so the cost can be amortized. How many pallets deep the lane should be is very important for effective utilization of space. A double-deep layout (lanes that are two pallet positions deep) fits approximately about 40% more pallet positions in the same floor area than a single-deep layout, as shown Figure 5.18. Deeper lanes produce more pallet storage locations, but they are of diminishing value.

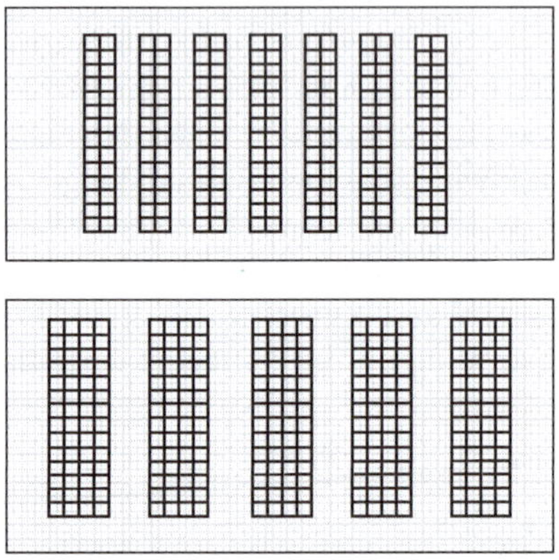

FIGURE 5.18 One-deep versus two-deep storage.

Source: Bartholdi, J. J. and S. T. Hackman. ***Warehouse & Distribution Science.***

The floor space required to hold a pallet is referred to as a pallet position. This includes not only the footprint of the pallet but also any required gap between one pallet and an adjacent one (Figure 5.19). Let the lanes be k pallet positions deep. Each lane requires aisle space at its head so that pallets can be inserted and removed. Let the aisle space in front of the pallet be of area a, measured in pallet positions. Then the total area charged for one lane is $k + (a/2)$ pallet positions. This area is the sum of space devoted to storage (k) and space that provides accessibility ($a/2$). Although it is a practice in many warehouses to use one full lane for a single SKU to avoid double handling of pallets and to save time, it costs more in space.

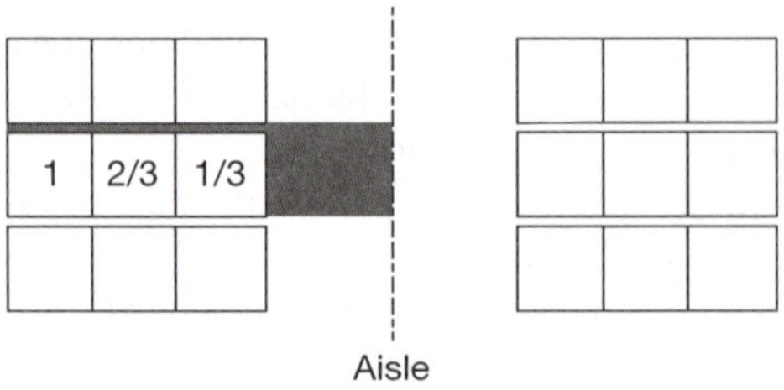

FIGURE 5.19 The floor space charged to a lane includes storage space, any gap between lanes, and one-half the aisle width in front of the lane.

Source: Bartholdi, J. J. and S. T. Hackman. ***Warehouse & Distribution Science.***

The first pallet position in a k-deep lane that holds uniformly moving products will be occupied only $1/k$ of the time, the second $2/k$ of the time, and so on (Figure 5.19). This waste is called honeycombing. Deeper lanes are more susceptible to such honeycombing, while shallow lanes use more space for accessibility. There is always a trade-off in such situations.

Figure 5.20 illustrates a typical daily snapshot of an SKU with an order size that occupies four pallet positions and is extracted at the rate of one pallet position per day. In a single-deep rack, all the unused space is the aisle space required for accessibility. Deeper aisles require less aisle space per pallet position, but the additional pallet positions are less fully occupied. Hence, if we wish to maximize the space efficiency, it is better that an SKU is stored in a lane of depth that minimizes unoccupied floor space-time. But also, such floor space-time is unavailable to other SKUs.

The optimum lane depth can be evaluated by listing all possibilities as shown in Figure 5.20. It can be seen that two-deep lanes are most space efficient when the aisle is less than four pallet positions wide; otherwise, four-deep is best.

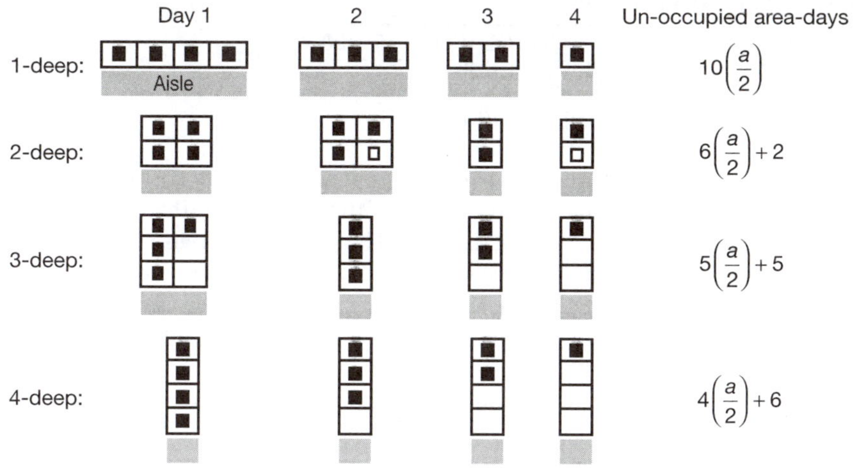

FIGURE 5.20 Four pallet positions of an SKU with constant demand are arranged in various lane depths. The area that is unoccupied but unusable by other SKUs is wasted. Area is measured in pallet positions; and **a** is the width of the aisle, measured as a fraction of the depth of a pallet position.

Source: Bartholdi, J. J. and S. T. Hackman. *Warehouse & Distribution Science.*

5.4.9 Optimal Lane Width

Suppose that SKU i has a constant demand of D_i pallets annually and that the order quantity is q_i pallets, so that a pallet departs every $1/D_i$ years and the order cycle is of duration q_i/D_i years. Assume the pallets of SKU i are stackable in columns z_i high so that a full allotment of SKU i will require (q_i/z_i) floor positions. Then the optimal lane depth, that is, the most space-efficient lane depth for SKU i with q_i pallets stackable z_i high is

$$\sqrt{\left(\frac{a}{2}\right)\left(\frac{q_i}{z_i}\right)}$$

5.4.10 Floor Storage

To minimize the average floor space consumed per pallet, floor storage should be configured with lane depth of approximately

$$\sqrt{\left(\frac{a}{2}\right)\left(\frac{1}{n}\right)\left(\sum_{i=1}^{n}\frac{q_i}{z_i}\right)}$$

In other words, the most space-efficient lane depth is of the form:

$$\sqrt{(\text{accessibility cost per lane})(\text{Average number of floor positions per SKU})}$$

EXAMPLE 5.7

Consider the following set of SKUs:

SKU	q_i	z_i
A	60	4
B	45	5
C	50	3

What is the optimal lane depth in floor storage if aisles are 18 ft across (about 4.6 m) and the pallets are 60 inches deep and 48 inches wide?

Solution

We will convert the unit of measure for aisle width to "pallet depths": 18 ft represents 18/(60/12) = 3.60 pallet positions.

$$\sqrt{\left(\frac{3.60}{2}\right)\left(\frac{1}{3}\right)\left(\frac{60}{4}+\frac{45}{5}+\frac{50}{3}\right)} = 4.94$$

So lanes should be about five pallet positions deep.

One of the important considerations in warehouse operations is the cost of labor while receiving, docking, and retrieving products into and out of the warehouse. The travel distance in such operations matters a lot while calculating the cost of labor and material-handling equipment like forklifts, stowing vehicles, etc. The decisions of these natures can be modeled using many transportation algorithms and heuristics since for modeling purposes, they are the same. Our discussions later in the Transportation Decisions module on the shortest path algorithms, scheduling algorithms using deadheading trips, etc. are quite useful in this area.

Most of the discussions on picking and retrieving depend on the warehouse configuration and layout decisions with respect to convenient storage locations and the location of the entry/exit docks. This labor cost is proportional to the distance d_i from receiving to location to shipping and hence we can represent convenience in terms of distance (see Figure 5.21). So in simple terms, in a unit-load warehouse, the cost of labor is often dependent on the distance and not so much on what is stored. If location i is visited n_i times during the year, the annual labor cost will be proportional to $\sum_i d_i n_i$. As discussed earlier, distances d_i are determined by the layout of the warehouse and are not usually fixed. But frequencies of visit n_i are determined by customer orders and by our choices of what to store where. By storing the pallets carefully, we can ensure that the most frequently visited locations are those of the greatest convenience (smallest total travel d_i), thereby minimizing $\sum_i d_i n_i$. Recall the discussion we had earlier about using the CPO index to decide which products to keep where in a warehouse.

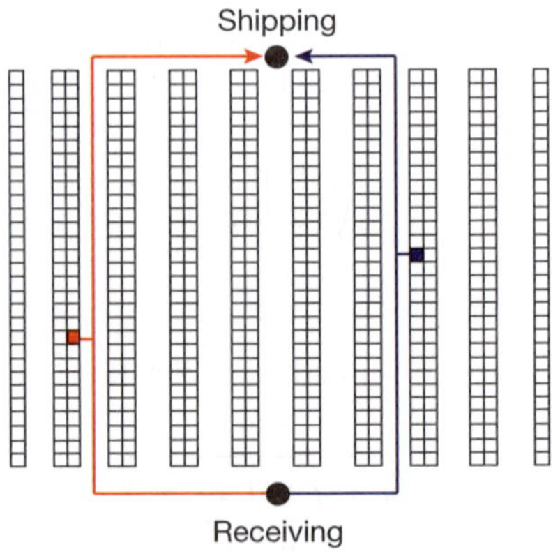

FIGURE 5.21 The blue location (right) is more convenient than the red location (left) because the total distance from receiving to the location, and from there to shipping is smaller.

Source: Bartholdi, J. J. and S. T. Hackman. *Warehouse & Distribution Science.*

The layout of the warehouse determines the cost associated with each storage location. Different choices of layouts are available, as shown in Figures 5.22 and 5.23.

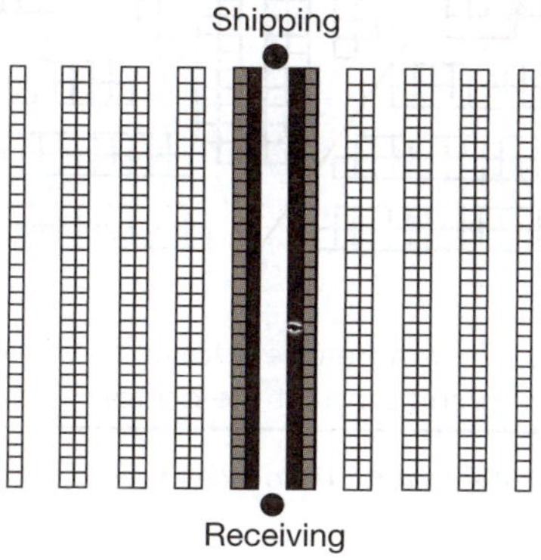

FIGURE 5.22 The darker locations are the more convenient when the receiving and shipping docks are opposite to each other.

Source: Bartholdi, J. J. and S. T. Hackman. ***Warehouse & Distribution Science.***

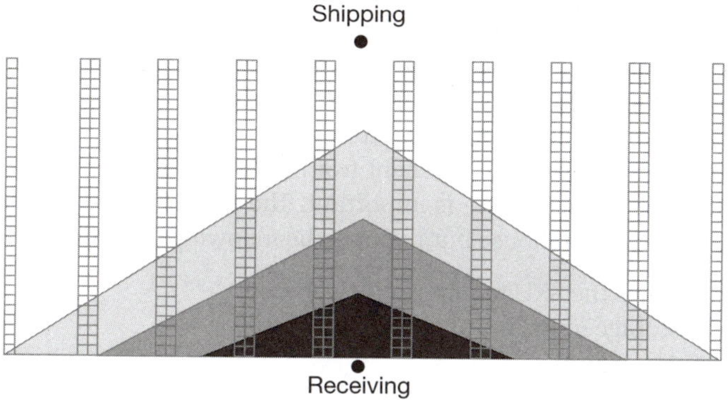

FIGURE 5.23 Darker shading indicates more convenient locations as compared to other locations when the receiving and shipping docks are the same.

Source: Bartholdi, J. J. and S. T. Hackman. ***Warehouse & Distribution Science.***

5.4.11 Aisle Configuration

It is generally preferable to configure aisles to run parallel with the direction of material flow to reduce travel between storage and receiving/shipping. Different choices like cross aisle and angled aisles are as shown in Figures 5.24 and 5.25.

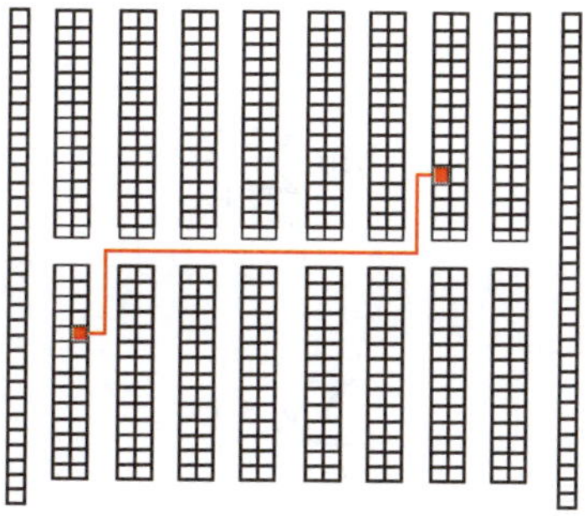

FIGURE 5.24 A cross aisle allows more direct and, therefore, shorter travel between storage locations.

Source: Bartholdi, J. J. and S. T. Hackman. ***Warehouse & Distribution Science.***

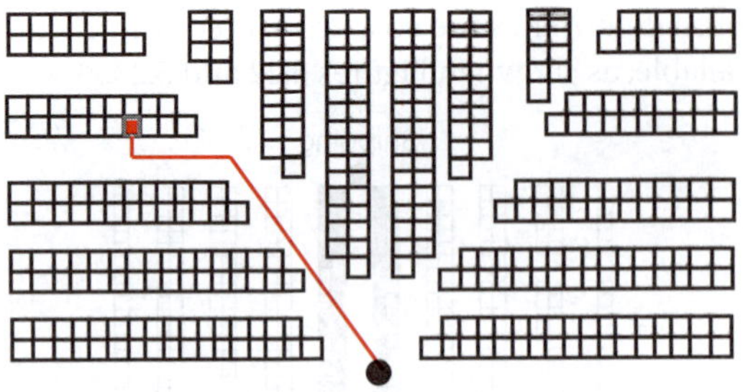

FIGURE 5.25 Angled aisles allow more direct travel between storage and a central location of receiving/shipping (at the bottom).

Source: Bartholdi, J. J. and S. T. Hackman. ***Warehouse & Distribution Science.***

5.4.12 Fast-Pick Area

An efficient way to manage a warehouse would be to consider separating the storage and picking activities. A separate picking area, also referred to as a fast-pick or forward-pick or a primary pick area, occupies a sub-space within a warehouse where the activities are mostly order picking, especially fast-moving and popular products. This arrangement facilitates increased customer responsiveness and lesser pick-up costs and time and may require frequent replenishment from bulk storage, or reserve. So the basic issues in the design of a fast-pick area are which SKUs to store in the fast-pick area and how much of each SKU to store.

Since this requires frequent replenishment from bulk storage, there is a need for restocking often and hence this cost of restocking is important. The cost of restocking an SKU depends on various other details of the warehouse but requires the following basic details:

1. The number of times the SKU requires replenishment
2. The number of storage units to be replenished
3. When the restock occurs

The number of restocks depends on the type of storage unit. If the SKUs are stored as pallets, then each pallet will require separate handling. But if the SKU is stored in smaller containers, such as cases, then the number of restocks can be determined by a fluid model.

If SKU i of volume v_i is stored in the fast-pick area and if the rate of flow of the SKU i is f_i in volume per year, then SKU i will require about $\left(\frac{f_i}{v_i}\right)$ restocks per year.

We will assume that the SKUs to be stored in the forward area have already been stored, and so the only variable cost is the labor to restock as and when necessary. We will also assume that the physical volume of available storage be normalized to 1, and f_i can be scaled accordingly. Let v_i represent the fraction of space allocated to SKU i.

The problem of allocating space among n SKUs to minimize annual restocks may be formulated as

$$\text{Min}\sum_{i=1}^{n}\frac{f_i}{v_i}$$

Subject to

$$\sum_{i=1}^{n} v_i \leq 1$$

$$v_i > 0 \text{ for } i = 1, 2, \ldots, n$$

It can be derived that to minimize total restocks over all SKUs $j = 1, \ldots, n$ in the forward-pick area, the fraction of available storage space devoted to SKU i should be

$$v_i^* = \left(\frac{\sqrt{f_i}}{\sum_{j=1}^{n} \sqrt{f_j}} \right)$$

We can also observe that under optimal allocations, each unit of storage space is restocked at the same frequency and is given by

$$\frac{f_i / v_i^*}{v_i^*} = \left(\sum_{j=1}^{n} \sqrt{f_j} \right)^2$$

EXAMPLE 5.8

Consider the following two SKU's with flows 18 and 2 units/year, respectively, which are to share 1 unit of storage. The different allocation strategies would result in the following:

	SKU A	SKU B	Total
Flow	16	4	
Equal Space Allocations	½	½	1
Restocks	32	8	40
Equal Time Allocations	16/20	4/20	1
Restocks	20	20	40
Optimum Allocations	4/6	2/6	1
Restocks	24	12	36

We observe that the optimal allocation results in 10% fewer restocks.

(The topic discussed in Section 4.8 can be seen in Bartholdi, J. J. and S. T. Hackman [2]. More details and derivation of formulae are available in the same reference for in depth reading).

SUMMARY

In this chapter, very important tools in taking tactical and operational decisions in warehouse operations are discussed. One of the important decisions is the estimation of the space that is required for storing items in the warehouse. Since the space is expensive to acquire, a good estimate for its future requirements is necessary to make the space available for the throughput of any warehouse. An illustration is given to show how such estimation can be done and how simple Excel calculations can help develop a template for such purposes. A mathematical programming approach to decide on the product allocations to the space available is shown. The major focus of the chapter is on tools that help in determining the layout design of a warehouse and approaches that help us decide on the optimal height, width, and length of the layout area. Assuming various options of layouts, such decisions are made. Towards the end of the chapter, operational decisions like width and depth of pallets and aisle widths within a warehouse for smooth operations are highlighted with examples.

Exercises

1. Century Manufacturing Company makes electronic components and plans to have a warehouse to store these items. Due to market demand fluctuations and production planning schedules, the space requirements vary considerably throughout the year. However, the space requirements are known with some uncertainty due to its usage in the market. Monthly estimated demands for a typical year are as follows:

Month	Sales (Throughput) in $
January	600000
February	700000
March	800000
April	1500000
May	1300000
June	1200000
July	350000
August	750000
September	600000
October	400000
November	700000
December	850000

Warehouse inventory turns at the rate of three times per month. A dollar's worth of merchandise occupies 0.15 cu ft of warehouse space and can be stacked 15 ft high. The product density is $7 per lb. Given aisles, administrative space, and normal operating efficiency, only 50% of the total warehouse space is actually used for storage. A private warehouse can be constructed and equipped for $40 per sq ft and can be amortized over 20 years. The cost of operation is $0.05 per dollar of throughput (lb). Annual fixed costs amount to $15 per sq ft of total space. Space may also be rented for a storage charge on inventory of $0.08 per lb per month and a handling charge of $0.06 per lb of throughput.

What size of private warehouse should be constructed, to the nearest 5000 sq ft, or what amount of public warehouse space should be rented? To what extent and when should each type of space be used? Analyze various options and prepare a report.

2. Suppose that a warehouse contains 10 storage bays. Products enter at the rear of the warehouse through a truck dock. Products are picked from the storage locations by an out-and-back selection method and shipped from a truck dock at the front of the building (see the design in Figure 5.10). Each bay can hold 3000 sq ft with product stacked 12 ft high. Fifteen products are maintained in the warehouse. The following data has been collected:

Product	Item size (cu ft)	Storage Space Required (sq ft)	Average Number of Daily Orders
A	2	500	50
B	2.5	200	65
C	4	1000	78
D	6	500	28
E	5	700	120
F	7	1200	150
G	12	800	35
H	6	400	70
I	8	300	90
J	12	2500	100
K	14	1500	60
L	16	700	30
M	6	900	70
N	5	350	40
O	9	700	90

a. Design the layout using (i) popularity method, (ii) cube method, and (iii) cube-per-order (CPO) index method.
b. Which method would you recommend?

3. Uttam Corporation is an electrotechnical company, which operates a warehouse in Jamshedpur. The warehouse has two I/O points and 32 storage locations. Tables 1 and 2 show the characteristics of the six products and the distances between the I/O points and the storage locations, respectively. Assuming that the travel time from the I/O point to storage location k ($k = 1, ..., 32$) is directly proportional to the corresponding distance, determine the optimal allocation of the products in the warehouse.

TABLE 1 Details of products of Uttam Corporation

Product	Number of Storage Locations Required for Products	Daily Number of Storage and Retrieval	
		Dock 1	Dock 2
1	8	24	18
2	6	15	28
3	4	10	35
4	6	25	28
5	5	24	18
6	3	14	24

TABLE 2 Distances (in meters) between Docks 1 and 2 and the storage locations in the storage zone of the warehouse

Storage Location	Distance for Dock 1	Distance for Dock 2
1	3	24
2	5	18
3	6	20
4	9	18
5	11	16
6	4	24
7	6	20
8	8	17
9	9	19
10	12	18
11	3	25
12	5	22
13	7	16
14	9	18
15	12	16
16	4	24
17	6	22
18	9	23
19	11	19
20	13	18
21	16	12
22	18	9
23	20	7
24	22	5
25	23	4
26	17	12
27	19	11
28	18	8
29	22	6
30	21	5
31	18	12
32	14	9

4. If only one I/O dock point is available, determine the optimal allocation of products to the storage locations. Consider each point 1 and 2 separately as available and determine the optimal allocations.
5. Uttam Corporation has a warehouse that has two receiving docks (R1 and R2) and one shipping dock (S1). The eight major products handled by the warehouse are stored in six storage bays. As seen in problem 3, different times are required to supply and distribute from a storage bay, and these service times depend on the particular product and location of the storage bay in the warehouse. Handling costs depend on the handling times for each product and storage bay.

   Handling times (hr)* per 100 units of product stored in various bays

Storage Bay→	1	2	3	4	5	6
Products↓	0.80	0.45	0.50	0.50	0.45	0.40
1	0.90	0.45	0.70	0.45	0.40	0.40
2	0.70	0.45	0.90	0.65	0.35	0.35
3	0.50	0.45	0.40	0.90	0.45	0.40
4	0.60	0.20	0.80	0.50	0.45	0.80
5	0.65	0.35	0.35	0.70	0.45	0.35
6	0.45	0.40	0.40	0.90	0.45	0.80
7	0.60	0.40	0.35	0.45	0.20	0.90
8	0.30	0.50	0.60	0.55	0.30	0.70

*For a six-month period.

Each storage bay has a certain capacity depending on the product. The following information on storage bay capacity is known:

Product	Storage Bay Capacity (units)
1	8000
2	6000
3	7000
4	9000
5	12000
6	15000
7	10000
8	9000

Uttam Corporation estimates that it needs a plan for a storage space for at least 8000 units of product 1; 9000 units of product 2; 12,000 units of product 3; 12,000 for product 4; 12,000 for product 6; 14,000 for product 7; and 10,000 for product 8 over the next six months. The decision problem is how to allocate the products to the various bays (in the proper quantities) to minimize the total handling time (cost) required for all products. Present the complete steps, formulation if any, and the solution output.

Bibliography

1. Ballou, R. H. and S. K. Srivastava (2007). *Business Logistics/Supply Chain Management*. Delhi: Pearson India.

2. Bartholdi, J. J. and S. T. Hackman (2019). *Warehouse & Distribution Science, Release 0.98.1*, The Supply Chain & Logistics Institute, H. Milton Stewart School of Industrial and Systems Engineering. Georgia Institute of Technology.
3. Bassan, Y., Y. Roll and M. J. Rosenblatt (1980). Internal layout design of a warehouse. *AIIE Transactions*, **12**(4), 317–322.
4. Derpich, I. and J. Sepulveda (2017) Lagrangian formulation for energy-efficient warehouse design. *International Journal of Computers Communications & Control*, **12**(1), 41–52.
5. Francis, R. L. (1967). On some problems of rectangular warehouse design and layout. *Journal of Industrial Engineering*, **18**, 595–604.
6. Gianpaolo Ghiani, Gilbert Laporte and Roberto Musmanno (2013). Introduction to Logistics Systems Management, Second Edition, Wiley.
7. Gray, A. E., U. S. Karmarkar, and A. Seidmann (1992). Design and operation of an order-consolidation warehouse: Models and application. *European Journal of Operational Research*, **58**, 14–36.
8. Thornton, V. D., R. L. Francis, and T. J. Lowe (1979). Rectangular layout problems with worst-case distance measures. *AIIE Transactions*, **11**(1), 2–11.
9. Vrysagotis, V. and P. A. Kontis (2011). Warehouse layout problems: Types of problems and solution algorithms. *Journal of Computations & Modelling*, **1**(1), 131–152.

SECTION

IV

Inventory Decisions

VI

CHAPTER 6

Inventory Concepts, Costs and Basic Models

LEARNING OBJECTIVES

After reading this chapter, you would be able to:

- Describe why inventory management is important in the supply chain of a firm and the reasons for and against keeping inventory.
- Understand different types of inventory and the various costs of inventory.
- Comprehend the importance and application of the ABC analysis and the Pareto principle for determining inventory policies.
- Learn various types of single period and repetitive period types of inventory models, their assumptions, and applications of their use in determining inventory levels.

6.1 | INTRODUCTION

Inventories are basically stockpiles of raw materials, supplies, components, work-in-process, and finished goods that are kept and stored at various points throughout a firm's supply chain. Inventories are usually found in warehouses, distribution centers, stock yards, shop floors, and on retail store shelves. Having inventory at any of the points in a supply chain can cost the supply chain in general and the firm in particular. Inventory accounts for nearly 40% of the current assets of a typical manufacturing company and about 50% to 60% of the current assets in wholesaling and retailing industries. Re-designing the elements of a firm's inventory management system is often the key aspect to improving a firm's working-capital position and its return on assets.

6.2 | REASONS FOR KEEPING INVENTORY

Understanding the situations and compulsions that require a firm to keep inventory is important. The following points elucidate the reasons for keeping inventory:

1. To improve product availability and thereby customer service levels by implicitly reducing stockouts.
2. To exploit scale of economies in production and to effectively plan production of multiple Stock Keeping Units (SKUs) (cycle stock).
3. To facilitate the production smoothing process so that the planned production is carried out without interruptions for want of supply (cycle stock).
4. To exploit scale of economies in purchasing to avail quantity discounts from suppliers and in transportation from transporters for bulk transportation.
5. To hedge against price fluctuations and to manage forward buying when prices fluctuate due to currency fluctuations especially in the import of materials (speculative stock).

6. To manage against the demand, supply, and lead time variabilities and their fluctuations (safety stock or buffer stock).
7. To manage seasonal variations and their variability especially in agricultural commodities (seasonal stock).
8. To accommodate the minimum order quantities that are sometimes imposed by a supplier thereby resulting in excess quantities than what is required.
9. To safeguard against a few *force majeure* situations such as natural calamities and other unforeseen situations (anticipatory stock).
10. To facilitate production setup complexities that force a large production lot size.
11. To accommodate selling compulsions from the marketing function to ensure stocks to promise to customers.
12. To comply with government norms of standards (such as Bharath IV) and the resultant obsolescence due to technological changes.

Besides the aforementioned major list of reasons, there may be specific and peculiar reasons for keeping inventories in many industries.

6.3 | REASONS AGAINST KEEPING INVENTORY

The reasons for keeping inventory may vary with types of industries and product nature. Good brainstorming will help in shortlisting key reasons for keeping inventory and for possible action plans later.

It is often said that the management's job is much easier having the security of inventories. Criticism for being overstocked is more defensible than being short of supplies. The major reasons that can be mentioned against keeping inventories are related to various associated costs.

Among the several associated costs related to managing inventory, the following major ones need to be focused on and are used to formulate inventory policy decisions:

1. Inventory-carrying cost (inventory-holding cost)
2. Acquisition cost or ordering cost or procurement cost
3. Inventory-in-transit (pipeline) (or inventory-on-wheels) carrying cost
4. Stockout cost

6.3.1 Inventory-Carrying or Holding Cost

Inventory-carrying or holding cost may include the following:

1. **Capital costs** that include interest on money tied up in inventory. This is the direct return on investment on the capital that is blocked in inventory and probably the opportunity cost of the inventory investment.
2. **Space cost** that may include property taxes, rental fees, utility and maintenance cost, equipment cost, labor cost, etc.
3. **Service cost** that may include cost of insurance on stored items, cost of Management Information System (MIS) and record keeping, stock verification, etc.
4. **Risk cost** that may include obsolescence, spoilage, deterioration, pilferage, etc.

The carrying cost, thus, may vary depending on the type of products that are stored and may vary between 12% and 30% of the cost of the item annually. The carrying cost is usually expressed as an annual cost and as a percentage of the unit cost of an item, unless expressed otherwise.

While inventories do imply inventory-carrying costs, there are circumstances that may justify the economic benefits of bulk purchases that have significant carrying costs, but the purchase costs of the material are traded off against the carrying costs. Volume purchase discounts may be substantial. Large scrap losses and multiple hours of setup expenses associated with starting-up equipment can be averaged out over large batch sizes. Expensive transportation may be cheaper than the costs of inventory tied up in the transport system.

6.3.2 Acquisition Cost (or Ordering Cost or Procurement Cost)

These costs are associated with the acquisition of goods when stocks need to be replenished and are an important factor for various inventory decisions. Costs may include the cost of setting up the production process, the cost of processing an order through the accounting and purchasing departments, the cost of transmitting the order to the supply point (usually by mail or electronic means), the cost of transporting the order when transportation charges are not included in the price of the purchased goods, and the cost of any materials handling or processing of the goods at the receiving point. Some of these procurement costs are fixed per order and do not vary with the order size. Others, such as transportation, manufacturing, and material-handling costs vary to a degree with the order size. Each requires a slightly different analytical treatment.

6.3.3 Inventory-in-Transit (Pipeline) (or Inventory-on-Wheels) Carrying Cost

These costs are incurred when a stock is moved or transported by different transportation modes from a point (which may be a plant, warehouse, or any intermediary) to customer points or intermediate points in the supply chain. When stocks are moved, they are held in inventory for the transit time of the mode and hence, there are some costs that are incurred to carry this stock. While the components are similar to carrying cost in a warehouse or a store, the space cost may not be included here as the stock is in transit. If the transit time is not significant, this cost may be ignored, but if the transit time is significant, this cost will have an impact in inventory decisions.

6.3.4 Stockout Costs

Out-of-stock costs are incurred when an order is placed but cannot be filled from the inventory to which the order is normally assigned. There are two kinds of out-of-stock costs: lost sales costs and backorder costs. A lost sales cost occurs when the customer, faced with an out-of-stock situation, chooses to withdraw his or her request for the product. The cost is the profit that would have been made on this particular sale and may also include an additional cost for the negative effect that the stockout may have on future sales. A backorder cost occurs when a customer will wait for his or her order to be filled so that the sale is not lost, only delayed. Backorders can create additional clerical and sales costs for order processing and additional transportation and handling costs when such orders are not filled through the normal distribution channel. These costs are fairly tangible, so their measurement is not too difficult. There might also be the intangible costs of lost future sales. This cost is very difficult to measure.

Products that can be differentiated in the mind of the consumer (automobiles and major appliances) are more likely to be backordered than substituted.

While inventory management decisions can often involve such trade-offs among a variety of cost drivers, the "appropriate" decision is guided by a "cost analysis" of the various trade-offs, and a total cost approach involving such trade-offs often helps in reaching better decisions and strategies.

6.4 | ABC ANALYSIS AND PARETO ANALYSIS (80–20 RULE)

Another useful way to categorize inventory is an ABC classification. This ranking system was developed in 1951 by H. Ford Dicky of General Electric (GE) and suggested that GE classify items according to relative sales volume, cash flows, lead-time, or stockout cost. Most important inventories are put in Group A, and lesser impact goods are put in Groups B and C, respectively. Each item in the inventory is classified as either an A part, a B part, or a C part, often by ranking the items based on various categories such as volume, value, annual sales, profits, revenues, and market share. Very popularly, it is done for value or for sales. Thus, A items are considered the highest valued items, while the C items are the least valued. It is not unusual for 10% of the items that are classified as A to account for 60% of the total-dollar value. The B items may account for 20% of the items while being 30% of the total-dollar value, and C items might account for 70% of the items but only 10% of the dollar value. Thus, a business would be advised to pay much more attention in terms of analysis and control to the A items than the other items. This ABC classification is sometimes referred to as Pareto analysis or the 80–20 rule. Pareto's rule (80–20 rule) is based on a 19th-century mathematician's observation that many situations were dominated by very few elements.

Clarity on understanding and estimating different types of costs is essential for understanding the trade-offs among them.

Conversely, most elements have very little influence in most situations. This rule separates the "trivial many" from the "vital few."

6.4.1 ABC Analysis (Volume)

Understanding of the "vital few and trivial many" is the basic principle of ABC and Pareto, so the efforts are concentrated on the vital few and not on every item.

For ABC analysis, we usually divide the on-hand inventory into three classes based on annual volume. Volume = Annual demand × Unit cost. We consider items in the A class as most important where approximately 15–20% of the products account for 60–80% of the value. This range is only suggestive, and the idea is that a less percentage of products accounts for more value. The B class is considered less important than A where 20–40% of the products account for 15–30% of the value, and the C class is considered the least important where 50–60% of the products account for 5–10% of the value. The following steps help in performing the ABC analysis:

1. Sort products from largest to smallest annual volume.
2. Divide into A, B, and C classes with appropriate cutoffs.

Consider Table 6.1 where there are 10 items (parts) with their respective unit costs and monthly usage.

TABLE 6.1 Details of parts and their monthly usage

Part Numbers	Unit Cost	Monthly Usage
1	60	90
2	350	40
3	30	130
4	80	60
5	30	100
6	20	180
7	10	170
8	320	50
9	510	60
10	20	120

The values and the percentage of each part's value to the total value is given in Table 6.2.

TABLE 6.2 Values and percentage of values of parts

Part Numbers	Unit Cost	Monthly Usage	Value	% of Value
1	60	90	5,400	6.32
2	350	40	14,000	16.39
3	30	130	3,900	4.57
4	80	60	4,800	5.62
5	30	100	3,000	3.51
6	20	180	3,600	4.22
7	10	170	1,700	1.99
8	320	50	16,000	18.74
9	510	60	30,600	35.83
10	20	120	2,400	2.81
		Total	**85,400**	**100**

Table 6.3 gives a suggested classification of A, B, C based on the cumulative percentage of value and corresponding cumulative percentage of usage.

TABLE 6.3 Suggested ABC classification

Part Numbers	Unit Cost	Monthly Usage	% Usage	Cumulative % Usage		Value	% of Total Value	Cumulative Value of %	A, B, C	
9	510	60	6.00%	6%		30,600	35.83%	35.83%	**A**	
8	320	50	5.00%	11%		16,000	18.74%	54.57%	**A**	
2	350	40	4.00%	15%	**15%**	14,000	16.39%	70.96%	**A**	**70.96%**
1	60	90	9.00%	24%		5,400	6.32%	77.28%	**B**	
4	80	60	6.00%	30%		4,800	5.62%	82.90%	**B**	
3	30	130	13.00%	43%	**28%**	3,900	4.57%	87.47%	**B**	**16.51%**
6	20	180	18.00%	61%		3,600	4.22%	91.69%	**C**	
5	30	100	10.00%	71%		3,000	3.51%	95.20%	**C**	
10	20	120	12.00%	83%		2,400	2.81%	98.01%	**C**	
7	10	170	17.00%	100%	**57%**	1,700	1.99%	100.00%	**C**	**12.53%**
Total		**1,000**	**100.00%**	**Total**		**85,400**	**100.00%**			

Thus, the ABC classification based on the value analysis is as follows (Table 6.4).

TABLE 6.4 Summary of the ABC analysis

Class	Parts	% of Total Value	% of Total Usage
A	9, 8, and 2	70.96%	15%
B	1, 4, and 3	16.51%	28%
C	6, 5, 10, and 7	12.53%	57%

ACTIVITY 6.1

Carry out an ABC analysis of an appropriate measure besides sales viz. profitability, market share, etc. from your own data and understand how this simple tool can help you in your focus on key items for inventory management.

6.4.2 Pareto Rule and 80–20 Curve

We will now focus on the Pareto curve and its use in inventory decisions. The 80–20 rule stipulates that 80% of sales will come from 20% of the inventory SKUs and 20% of sales will come from 80% of the inventory SKUs. The 80–20 rule has been found to explain many phenomena that interest sales and inventory managers. For example, we can observe that 80% of sales may come from 20% of customers when we analyze this principle in customer relationship management. From a revenue point of view, it may be that most of the revenue (or profit) comes from a relatively small percentage of items (products). It helps in focusing on a small number of important items where a manager can identify the important items in terms of the ABC classification and can apply the highest service level to the most important items. Some common examples of Pareto rule are as follows: 20% of the people do 80% of the work in an organization; 10% of the people cause 90% of the problems; and 15% of the items (products) create 90% of the sales.

We will apply this in an example of sales analysis and link it to inventory contexts. The steps are as follows:

1. Rank products (items) by sales ($/year).
2. a. Calculate cumulative percentage of total sales.
   b. Calculate cumulative percentage of total products (items).
3. Plot 2.a. vs. 2.b.
4. Select top items as “A,” middle as “B,” and bottom as “C.”
   a. Breakpoints are flexible and depend on data.
   b. Generally more B’s than A’s, and more C’s than B’s.

An example of sales analysis using the aforementioned ABC classification is given in Table 6.5.

TABLE 6.5 Sales data and ABC classification for Pareto 80–20 analysis

Product	Sales in $ ('000)	% of Total Sales	Cumulative % of Sales		% of Items	Cumulative % of Items		
X-74	760	38	38.0		12.5	12.5	A	
X-26	640	32	70.0	70.0	12.5	25	A	25
X-51	240	12	82.0		12.5	37.5	B	
Y-47	140	7	89.0	19.0	12.5	50	B	25
X-33	100	5	94.0		12.5	62.5	C	
Y-65	60	3	97.0		12.5	75	C	
Y-66	40	2	99.0	11.0	12.5	87.5	C	50
X-17	20	1	100.0		12.5	100	C	
	2000							

In this example, A consists of 25% of items giving 70% of sales, B consists of 25% of items giving 19% of sales, and C consists of the remaining 50% of items giving only 11% of sales. The Pareto graph is given in Figure 6.1.

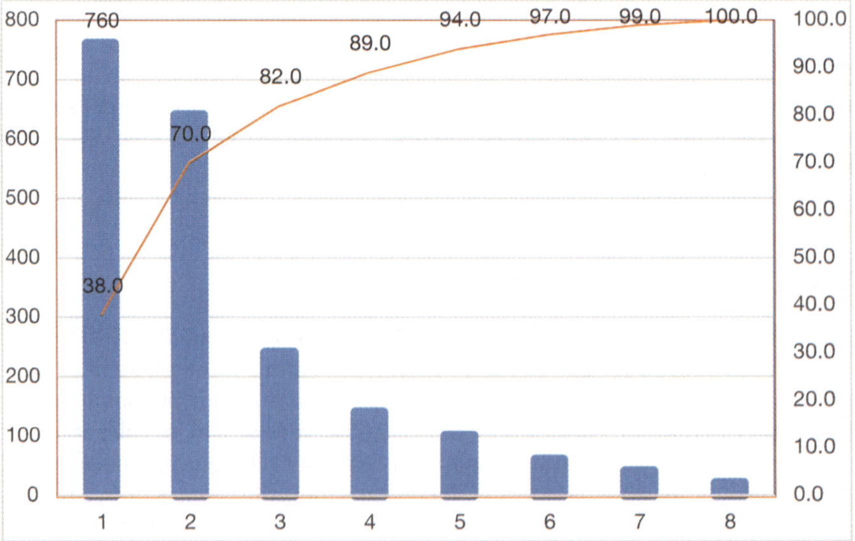

FIGURE 6.1 Pareto 80–20 graph and curve for Table 6.5.

6.4.2.1 Simple Mathematical Explanation of Pareto Curve

For practical purposes, the Pareto curve in Figure 6.1 can be modeled as follows:

$$Y = \frac{(1+A)X}{(A+X)} \tag{6.1}$$

where Y is the cumulative percentage of sales, X is the cumulative percentage of items (or products), and A is the shape constant ($A > 0$).

The following graph in Figure 6.2 shows how the curve may look depending on the shape coefficient A.

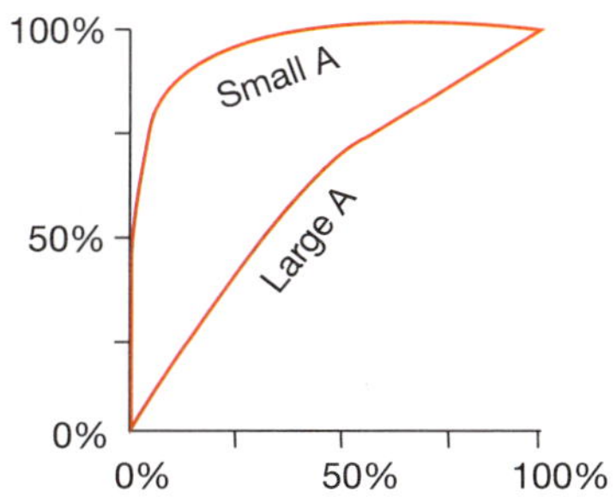

FIGURE 6.2 Pareto curve with shape coefficient *A*.

> The information about the Pareto behaviour is important for this analysis. A thorough understanding of the firm's overall functioning and its well-maintained business records are key to the determination of the constant A.

This shows that a smaller value of A determined the Pareto behavior strongly, that is, a very small percentage of items accounts for a very large percentage of sales as compared to a larger value of A where the Pareto may say that 50% of items account for 50% of sales, which is not strong Pareto behavior. Given X and Y in Equation (6.1), A can be determined as follows:

$$A = \frac{X(1-Y)}{(Y-X)} \tag{6.2}$$

In practical applications, a general Pareto behavior is seen for an organization from its business records and that is used to determine an overall A for its application to determine the inventory requirements.

EXAMPLE 6.1

Supposing that for an organization, in general, 30% of the items produce 75% of the sales as their Pareto behavior. We will look at an example where the organization wants to consider the first 20% to be A items, the next 30% to be B items, and the last 50% to be C items. The question of interest would be to determine what percentage of sales do A, B, and C items account for?

Given an X (% of items) and a corresponding Y (% of sales), we can find the shape constant A through Equation (6.2). Then for each set of items, we can use the shape constant A obtained and the percentage of items (X) to calculate the percentage of sales (Y) through Equation (6.1).

Using the mathematical model: For the given example, it is given that $X = 0.30$ and $Y = 0.75$. Putting them in Equation (6.2), we get

$$A = \frac{X(1-Y)}{(Y-X)} = \frac{0.3(1-0.75)}{0.75-0.30} = 0.1667$$

For A items, it is given that $X = 0.20$. Putting this in the equation using the value of A obtained earlier, we get

$$Y = \frac{(1+A)X}{(A+X)} = (1+0.1667)\times 0.20/(0.1667+0.20) = 0.6363$$

This means that A items would account for 63.63% of sales. It is given that the next 30% would be the B items. Hence, cumulatively A + B = 0.20 + 0.30 = 0.50 for both A + B items.

Since the Pareto curve is for cumulative values, we put $X = 0.50$ now to get the cumulative value of Y as 0.875 from Equation (6.1). So the value for B items would be 0.875 − 0.6363 = 0.2387, which means that B items would account for 23.87% of sales. Hence, the remaining 1 − 0.875 = 0.125, that is, 12.5% would be accounted for by C items. Thus, we see how a general Pareto principle gives an estimate of sales for a given set of A, B, and C items. Now we will see how this approach can help an organization determine the average inventory required for these A, B, and C items.

6.4.2.2 Pareto Analysis and Average Inventory

From financial accounting principles, it is known that the inventory turnover ratio is an important financial ratio, which reflects on the inventory and financial management of an organization. The inventory turnover ratio is the ratio of annual sales (at cost price or cost of goods sold) divided by the average inventory:

Inventory Turnover Ratio = Annual Sales (Cost of Goods Sold)/Average Inventory

This would help determine the average inventory as follows:

Average Inventory = Annual Sales/Inventory Turnover Ratio

if we are given the policy of turnover ratios of different classes of items and the sales are estimated by the Pareto curve as explained in the previous section. We will see an example to illustrate this possibility.

EXAMPLE 6.2

Suppose it is given that

1. 30% of the items produce 75% of the sales.
2. The first 25% has a 10:1 turnover ratio (A items), the next 30% has a 5:1 turnover ratio (B items), and the last 45% has a 2:1 turnover ratio (C items).
3. Total annual sales are estimated to be $5,000,000.

What is the total average value of inventory (for A, B, and C items together)?

We will calculate on similar lines as explained in the previous section. A is calculated as 0.1667.

A ite6ms: $X = 0.25$, $Y = 0.70$, 70% of sales

Hence, the sales will be estimated as 0.70 of 5,000,000 = 3,500,000, and the average inventory will be 3,500,000/10 (as 10:1 is given as the inventory turnover ratio for the A items), that is, $350,000.

Similarly,
A + B items: $X = 0.55$, $Y = 0.895$
B items alone: $Y = 0.895 - 0.7 = 0.195$, 19.5% of sales
0.195 × 5,000,000/5 = $195,000 as average inventory
C items: $Y = 1 - 0.895 = 0.105$, 10.5% of sales
0.105 × 5,000,000/2 = $262,500 as average inventory.

Hence, this scenario would result in an average inventory of 350,000+195,000+262,500 = 807,500. In other words, this would imply that 16.15% of total sales will be kept as average inventory. The scenario can be changed for various values of Pareto and ratios, and a what-if scenario can be drawn up for appropriate action by the concerned functional heads to decide on the policies.

This can be extended to various scenarios, and the following can be one such scenario to experiment.

Pareto curve analysis gives an estimate of the average inventory that can be maintained from the overall policy of the inventory turnover ratio. This is very important for a policy-level sensitivity analysis of linking inventory turnover ratio with sales and inventory.

ACTIVITY 6.2

Continue with Examples 6.1 and 6.2.
Given

1. 30% of the items produce 75% of the sales.
2. The first 25% has a 10:1 turnover ratio (A items), the next 30% has a 5:1 turnover ratio (B items), and the last 45% has a 2:1 turnover ratio (C items).
3. Total annual sales are estimated to be $5,000,000.
4. There are 260 items.

What is the average inventory value for the top 10 items? What is the average inventory value for the 11th item? What is the average inventory value for items 51–80?

6.5 MANAGING INVENTORIES AND INVENTORY-CARRYING COSTS

The important decisions in a firm's material flows from suppliers or from plants to customers are related to cycle stock and ordering issues. The purpose of any inventory policy would be to develop a management system that can improve the cost effectiveness of the investments in inventory. We will discuss those decisions in this section.

There will be multiple goals of functional areas when it comes to inventory decisions. For example, marketing functions would always want to keep stocks to service customers and to improve service levels, while finance functions would want to minimize blocked capital in inventory and have higher inventory turnover ratios. And so, supply chain management would want to look at such trade-offs while determining order policies, such as minimizing inventory costs and service levels. The interface between operations and marketing areas of a firm would result in many such trade-off decisions in deciding lot sizes for production or ordering.

The components of inventory costs have been discussed in the earlier sections; for instance, components such as space and service costs are direct costs, while capital costs are opportunity costs. While modeling inventory decisions, the basic concept of average inventory is used to determine carrying costs. Suppose an order Q is placed for an item. When it arrives (assuming a lead-time of zero), the stock level reaches Q and the item is consumed, say at a constant rate. When it reaches 0, another quantity of Q is placed, and this cycle is continued for the entire year. The situation is depicted in Figure 6.3 where the ordering cycles and the graph look like a "sawtooth."

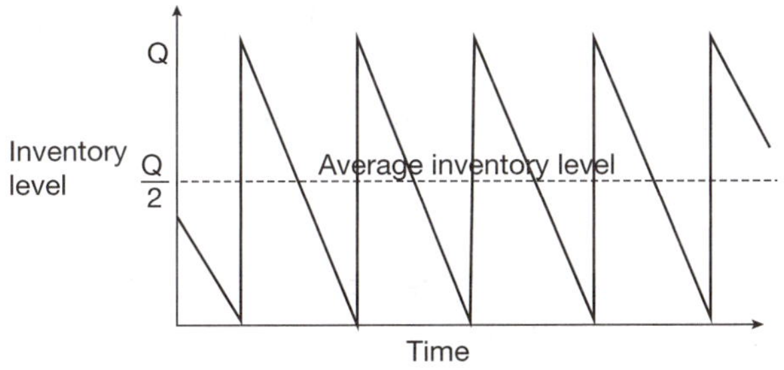

FIGURE 6.3 Sawtooth behavior of inventory model.

The inventory level starts at a maximum of Q and reaches a minimum level of 0, which makes an average inventory of Q/2 $\left(\frac{Q+0}{2}\right)$ being maintained throughout the cycle. This is often referred to as average stock or cycle stock. When calculating the inventory-carrying or holding cost, this cycle stock is taken as the average stock that is held at any point in time throughout the cycle or year. Usually, the inventory-carrying cost is given as a percentage or a fraction of the unit cost of the item in inventory. If the cost of the unit is, say, C per unit and if the carrying cost of the unit, expressed as h, is say 20% or 0.20, then the carrying cost of a unit will be hC. (If a unit cost $50 and if the inventory-carrying cost is 30%, then the inventory-carrying cost per unit is 30% of $50, i.e., $0.30 \times 50 = \$15$). This would mean the holding or the carrying cost of the average inventory would be $\frac{Q}{2}hC$. This is usually calculated on an annual basis by default. Of course, when modeling inventory-carrying costs over several years, it is better to consider the time value of money and discount future costs to present value.

EXAMPLE 6.3

Consider a firm that orders a certain part from its supplier. Suppose the part costs the firm $25 each, they are delivered in order sizes of 100, and the cost of carrying or holding the part averages 20% per year. Then the annual cost of holding the parts in the inventory can be calculated as follows:

$$\text{Annual Cost of Holding} = \frac{Q}{2}hC = \left(\frac{100}{2}\right) \times 0.20 \times 25 \ = \$250$$

EXAMPLE 6.4

Now assume that the firm orders the part in large quantities to avail volume discounts offered by its supplier. The firm requires, say, 3500 parts per year, where the carrying cost for the part is 20% annually, and the unit cost is $0.10 per part with an order quantity that is 7500. Also, after 2 years, the specifications are expected to change, and different parts will be required. Any old parts remaining in the inventory will be scrapped. Finally, assume an annual discount rate of 10%. In this case, we expect $Q/2$ to change each year. $Q/2$ represents the average inventory between the start and end of each year.

$$\text{Year 1 Cost of Holding} = \frac{Q}{2}hC = \left(\frac{7500 + (7500 - 3500)}{2}\right) \times 0.10 \times 0.20 = \$115$$

(Starting inventory is 7500, and 3500 will be used up at the end of the first year, leaving an ending inventory of $7500 - 3500 = 4000$. So average inventory will be $(7500 + 4000)/2 = 5750$.)

At the end of the first year, we expect to have 4000 parts remaining. At the end of the second year, we expect to have 500 parts left, which will be scrapped. Also, we discount the costs by 10% to bring the second-year costs to an equivalent value of first-year costs.

$$\text{Year 2 Cost of Holding} = \frac{Q}{2}hC = \left(\frac{4000 + 500}{2}\right) \times 0.10 \times \left(\frac{1}{1 + 10\%}\right) \times 0.20 = \$40.91$$

Total Costs of Carrying the Part = $115 + $40.91 = $155.91

6.6 SINGLE-PERIOD INVENTORY MODELS (NEWSVENDOR MODEL)

Inventory-holding or -carrying cost is fundamental to understand inventory policies, and hence a good way of estimating and using them is essential. Preceding examples illustrate this aspect.

A single-period inventory model is a business scenario faced by companies that order seasonal or one-time items. The objective will be to ensure an adequate supply of the item to sell to meet anticipated demand by avoiding costly “overstocking” situations as well as “understocking” situations too. Inventory control poses special challenges for companies that operate on a “single-period” inventory model, in which it gets only one chance to sell the inventory.

Suppose that a person owns a shoe store and has 10 pairs of black shoes in stock. If he or she does not sell them today, he or she can sell them the next day or in the following days. Even if styles are changing, he or she can still sell them by offering some discounts on the price of the shoes. This is the typical inventory model we usually discuss at organizational levels. Now imagine there is a newspaper vendor. If he or she orders a certain number of newspapers from a publisher, the publisher would bring them in the morning, and the newsvendor may sell them during the day. But, here, the newspapers that are not sold cannot be rolled over to the next day, like a pair of unsold shoes. At the day's end, those papers have no value. This is an example of a typical single-period inventory model.

Many small businesses encounter single-period inventory situations. For example, a clothing store may get only one chance per season to order fashions from a particular design house. On a larger scale, airlines deal with single-period inventory issues when they decide which aircraft to use on which routes, how much to charge for tickets, and whether they should overbook the flight to ensure that seats get filled even if some customers do not show up.

The aforementioned single-period models attempt to strike a balance between two types of situations: understocking and overstocking. If the vendor has only little inventory, and if any demand comes on top of his inventory, it has to be turned down and he or she loses an opportunity to make business. If the vendor, on the other hand, keeps excess inventory, he or she may not be able to sell the excess and has to carry the inventory with or without any salvage value for them. In the first case, the money he or she loses is the revenue that he or she could have otherwise earned, and in the second case, the money he or she loses is the cost he or she paid for the unsold inventory. Knowing the right amount of inventory to order comes down to his or her experience and understanding of the market.

Key factors to consider in single-period inventory situations are the average demand per period and the degree to which demand fluctuates from that average. We should also know the cost per unit of underestimating demand and overestimating demand. These are often referred to as "cost of understocking" or "underage," denoted by C_u, and "cost of overstocking" or "overage," denoted by C_o. They are interpreted as opportunity cost and inventory-carrying cost, respectively. For example, assume that a newsvendor buys newspapers for 50 cents and sells them for 75 cents. When a paper goes unsold, he or she loses 50 cents ($C_o = 0.50$), and when he or she turns away a customer because the newspapers are sold out, he or she loses the 25 cents of profit he or she would have made ($C_u = 0.25$). If he or she orders 100 newspapers, and 120 people come to buy a paper, he or she will have missed out on \$5, the cost of 20 missed sales ($20 \times 0.25 = \$5$). If he or she sells only 90 papers, he or she will have lost \$5, the cost of 10 unsold papers ($10 \times 0.50 = \$5$).

In the following section, we will determine the optimal level of inventory in such situations (often classified as newsvendor models in inventory literature).

6.7 OPTIMAL STOCK LEVEL IN NEWSVENDOR MODELS (FOR CONTINUOUS DISTRIBUTIONS)

Notation

C_o = Cost per unit of positive inventory remaining at the end of the period (known as the overage cost or cost of overstocking)

C_u = Cost per unit of unsatisfied demand. This can be thought of as a cost per unit of negative ending inventory (known as the underage cost or opportunity cost or cost of understocking)

Suppose the demand D is a continuous nonnegative random variable with density function $f(x)$ and the cumulative distribution function $F(x)$. The decision variable Q is the number of units to be purchased at the beginning of the period.

The cost function $G(Q)$ is convex:

$$G(Q) = C_o \int_0^Q (Q-x) f(x)dx + \int_Q^\infty (x-Q) f(x)dx$$

$$\frac{dG}{dQ} = 0 + C_o \int_0^Q f(x)dx + 0 + C_u \int_Q^x (-f(x))dx$$

$$= C_o \int_0^Q f(x)dx - C_u \left[1 - \int_0^Q f(x)dx\right]$$

$$= (C_o + C_u)\int_0^Q f(x)dx - C_u$$

$$= (C_o + C_u)F(Q) - C_u$$

The optimal solution equation is

$$\frac{d^2G}{dQ^2} = (C_o + C_u)f(Q) \geq 0$$

So
$$F(Q^*) = \frac{C_u}{C_o + C_u} \quad (6.3)$$

Pictorially, it can be depicted as given in Figure 6.4.

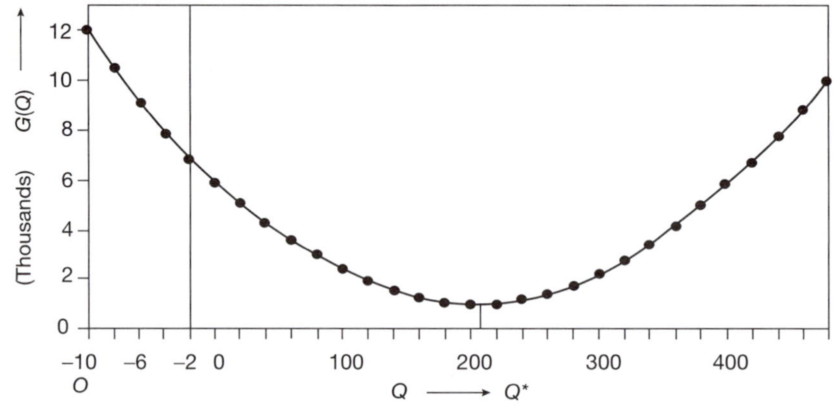

FIGURE 6.4 Determining optimal policy for newsvendor model.

6.7.1 Optimal Policy for Discrete Demand

The procedure for finding the optimal solution to the newsboy problem when the demand is assumed to be discrete is a natural generalization of the continuous case. The optimal solution procedure is to locate the critical ratio between two values of $F(Q)$ and choose the Q corresponding to the higher value. That is,

$$\sum_{x=0}^{Q^*} p(x) = F(Q^*) \geq \frac{C_u}{C_o + C_u} \quad (6.4)$$

The trade-off between the unit costs of overstocking and understocking depends on the critical ratio, which is the ratio of unit cost of understocking to the total of both over- and understocking unit costs.

EXAMPLE 6.5

A newsvendor purchases a number of copies of *The Computer Journal* (weekly). The observed demands during each of the last 52 weeks were:

15	19	9	12	9	22	4	7	8	11
14	11	6	11	9	18	10	0	14	12
8	9	5	4	4	17	18	14	15	8
6	7	12	15	15	19	9	10	9	16
8	11	11	18	15	17	19	14	14	17
13	12								

Suppose each copy is purchased for 25 cents and sold for 75 cents, and his supplier pays him 10 cents for each unsold copy. If he or she purchases a copy that he or she does not sell, then his out-of-pocket expense is 25 cents – 10 cents = 15 cents. On the other hand, if he or she is unable to meet the demand of a customer, he or she loses 75 cents - 25 cents = 50 cents profit. So, in this situation, it is clear that $C_o = 15$ and $C_u = 50$. From the given data of 52 weeks, it is easy to calculate the mean and the standard deviation, which are 11.731 and 4.74, respectively.

Assume that the demand is approximately normally distributed with mean 11.731 and standard deviation 4.74. From Equation (6.3), it is clear that the critical ratio is

$$F(Q^*) = \frac{C_u}{C_o + C_u} = \frac{50}{50+15} = 0.77$$

This implies that the decision is to purchase enough copies to satisfy all the weekly demand with probability 0.77. The optimal Q^* is the 77th percentile of the demand distribution. This is shown in Figure 6.5.

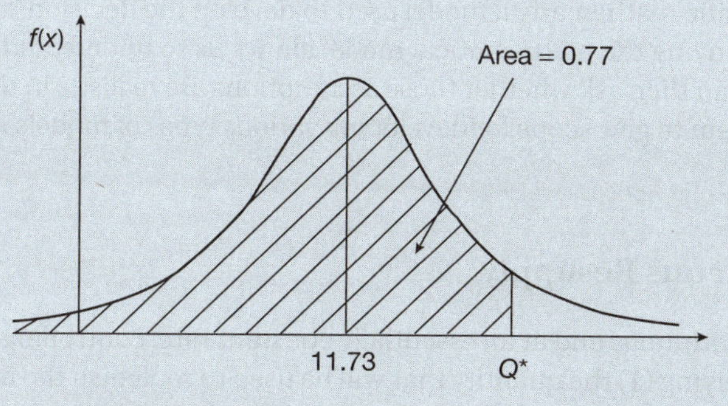

FIGURE 6.5 Critical ratio in a normal distribution.

Using normal distribution, this can be determined as

$$X = \mu + z\sigma$$

Using the data of the normal distribution, we obtain a standardized value of $z = 0.74$. The optimal Q is

$$Q^* = \mu + z\sigma = 11.73 + 0.74 \times 4.74 = 15.24 \approx 15$$

(This can be easily calculated in MS Excel by using the formula NORMINV(0.74, 11.73, 4.74) in any cell.)

Hence, he or she should purchase 15 copies every week. If we use the data as discrete data, then the frequency distribution can be seen as given in Table 6.6.

TABLE 6.6 Frequency and cumulative frequency distribution of sales

Q	f(Q)	F(Q)	Q	f(Q)	F(Q)
0	1/52	1/52(0.0192)	12	4/52	30/52(0.5769)
1	0	1/52(0.0192)	13	1/52	31/52(0.5962)
2	0	1/52(0.0192)	14	5/52	36/52(0.6923)
3	0	1/52(0.0192)	15	5/52	41/52(0.7885)
4	3/52	4/52(0.0769)	16	1/52	42/52(0.8077)
5	1/52	5/52(0.0962)	17	3/52	45/52(0.8654)
6	2/52	7/52(0.1346)	18	3/52	48/52(0.9231)
7	2/52	9/52(0.1731)	19	3/52	51/52(0.9808)
8	4/52	13/52(0.2500)	20	0	51/52(0.9808)
9	6/52	19/52(0.3654)	21	0	51/52(0.9808)
10	2/52	21/52(0.4038)	22	1/52	52/52(1.000)
11	5/52	26/52(0.5000)			

The critical ratio for this problem was 0.77, which corresponds to a value of $F(Q)$ between $Q = 14$ and $Q = 15$. Since we round up, the optimal solution is $Q = 15$. Notice that this is exactly the same order quantity obtained using the normal approximation.

6.8 | REPETITIVE ORDER QUANTITIES (PULL MODELS)

The basic EOQ model is only an illustration of how the ordering cost and the inventory-carrying cost trade off. Its use may be limited because in practice, many of the assumptions of this model may be violated. However, its simplicity is still useful in many applications in various other similar forms for many modeling purposes in supply chain decisions.

A good amount of literature is available in inventory management on models and rules for deciding how much to order (lot size) under various conditions. Given a particular situation, developing a cost model for the situation that captures the relevant characteristics of the situation shapes nearly all decision rules. In some situations, mathematical procedures such as differential calculus and other mathematical tools such as Lagrange multipliers and step-by-step algorithms are applied to obtain specific decision rules. The Economic Order Quantity (EOQ) rule presented in this section is one such rule that is popularly used in many business situations. It is important to understand the specific mathematical model used to develop the decision rules to avoid using the rules incorrectly. Studying the mathematical model allows us to understand the assumptions that are being used. We can then ask whether those assumptions are realistic in the specific situation of interest and relax them to give scope for developing various types of models in inventory decisions.

6.8.1 Instantaneous Resupply

When demand is continuous and at an essentially constant rate, controlling inventory levels is accomplished by specifying (1) the quantity that will be used to replenish the inventory on a periodic basis and (2) the frequency with which the inventory should be replenished. This is a problem of balancing conflicting cost patterns. In the simplest case, it requires balancing procurement or acquisition or ordering costs against inventory-carrying costs. Ford Harris recognized this problem as early as 1913 in his work at Westinghouse. (This is also credited to Wilson, who developed the model around 1915.) The model that he developed for finding the optimum order quantity has become known as the basic EOQ formula, and it serves as the basis for many of the pull inventory policies currently used in practice. Under the simplest assumption of level demand, the optimal rule is given by the EOQ formula, which is usually credited to Wilson because he first developed the model around 1915.

The basic EOQ formula is developed from a total cost equation involving the trade-off between ordering or procurement cost and inventory-carrying cost as it assumes a constant price for the units procured, which keeps the material cost constant irrespective of the quantity ordered. It is expressed as

Total Cost (TC) = Ordering Cost (OC) + Inventory-Carrying Cost (ICC) + Material Cost (MC)

$$TC = \frac{D}{Q} \times S + \frac{Q}{2} \times C \times h + D \times C \tag{6.5}$$

where TC is the total annual relevant inventory cost (dollars), Q is the size of each order to replenish inventory (units), D is the annual demand for the item in inventory (units), S is ordering or procurement cost (dollars/order), C is the value of the item carried in inventory (dollars/unit), and h is the carrying cost as a percent of item value (%/year or fraction, e.g., 20% or 0.20).

The term D/Q represents the number of times orders are placed to its supply source. The term $Q/2$ is the average amount of inventory on hand referred to as cycle stock.

As Q varies, the ordering cost decreases and the inventory-carrying cost increases. It can be shown mathematically that an optimal order quantity (Q^*) exists where the two costs are in balance and the minimal total cost results as shown in Figure 6.6.

To obtain the optimal Q^*, differentiate Equation (6.5) with respect to Q and equate to zero:

$$\frac{\partial TC}{\partial Q} = -\frac{D}{Q^2} \times S + \frac{1}{2} \times C \times h = 0$$

$$\frac{D}{Q^2} \times S = \frac{1}{2} \times C \times h$$

$$Q^2 = \frac{2 \times D \times S}{h \times C}$$

The formula for this EOQ is

$$Q^* = \sqrt{\frac{2DS}{hC}} \tag{6.6}$$

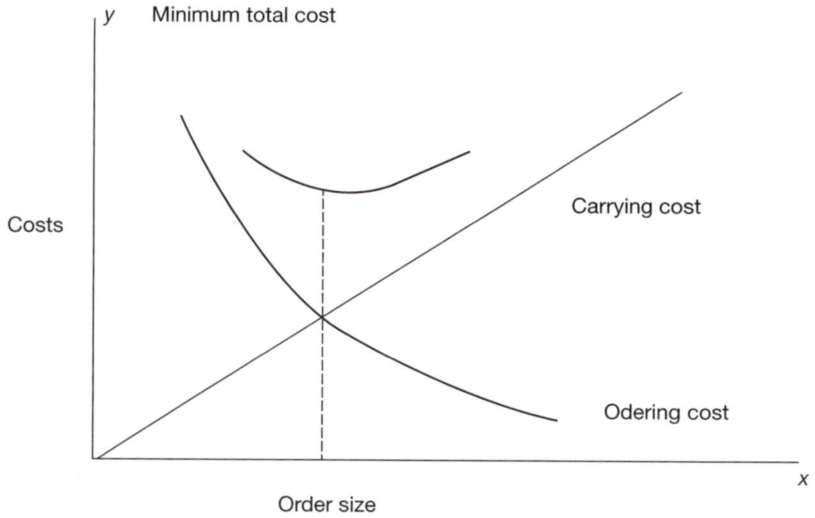

FIGURE 6.6 Cost curves of the basic EOQ model.

This formula can also be derived by observing Figure 6.6 that at optimal Q^*, both the ordering cost and the inventory-carrying cost are equal. That is,

$$\mathrm{OC} = \mathrm{ICC}$$

$$\frac{D}{Q} \times S = \frac{Q}{2} \times C \times h \tag{6.7}$$

which gives

$$Q^2 = \frac{2 \times D \times S}{h \times C} \text{ and } Q^* = \sqrt{\frac{2DS}{hC}}$$

EXAMPLE 6.6

Consider a company that sells replacement lamp bulbs. Assume that the annual demand for the bulbs is known and is constant throughout the year and has been forecast as 2000 units. The cost of preparing an order is \$14, and the unit cost of the bulbs is \$4. The inventory-holding charge is 35% per year of the unit cost. Thus, we have

$D = 2000$ (annual requirements)
$S = 14$ (cost of ordering)
$C = 4$ (cost per unit ordered)
$h = 0.35$ (annual inventory-carrying cost as a fraction of unit cost)

The optimal lot size Q^* is

$$Q^* = \sqrt{\frac{2DS}{hC}} = \sqrt{\frac{2 \times 2000 \times 14}{0.35 \times 4}} = 200$$

Thus, if this order policy is used, the average-cycle inventory level will be $Q^*/2$ or 100 units. We will place $D/Q = 2000/200 = 10$ orders per year assuming the actual demand is constant over the year (2000 units). Using Equation (6.5) and Q^*, the total annual cost will be \$8280.

6.8.2 Analysis of Assumptions

As seen in Equation (6.6), the EOQ formula is straightforward and too simplistic for practical applications. The formula should be taken as a base situation when it comes to application since some implicit assumptions are made about EOQ.

1. One key assumption is that the demand is assumed to be known and is at a constant level throughout the year. For example, if the annual demand is known to be 1200 units, it means it is 100 units per month at a constant rate and 25 units per week at a constant rate. No seasonality, trend, or lumpiness in demand is assumed. Though in real situations, demand may be uncertain and may not be at a constant rate, EOQ can still be applied for many practical situations as a lot size.
2. Another assumption we have made is that the price of the unit is constant and there are no quantity discounts. The unit cost is C dollars per unit regardless of how many we order. In practice, when quantity discounts are made for bulk volumes, this assumption may be violated. We will see later how EOQ can be fine-tuned when quantity discounts are considered.
3. Another assumption is that these models assume that the lead-time for replenishment is zero and assume instantaneous replenishment. We will see later how lead-time affects ordering policies and replacement plans. It also assumes that no backorders are allowed.

Another understanding although not explicitly stated in the formula developed for EOQ assumes that the incremental cost of placing an additional order is S. However, in many situations, the total annual costs associated with ordering are more like that shown in Figure 6.7. A slight incremental cost is associated with each order for paper, postage, phone calls, etc., but over a broad range, the costs associated with the labor of preparing and receiving a single order remain fixed.

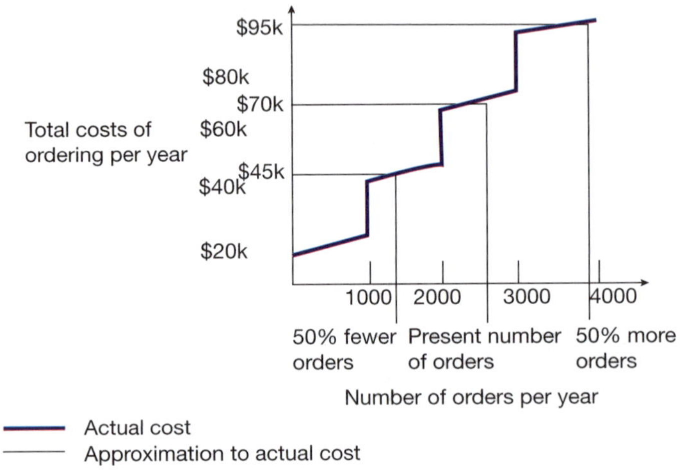

FIGURE 6.7 Ordering cost behavior.

Each of the assumptions of EOQ looks very rigid and impractical, but when each assumption was analyzed for various possible changes and violations, many popular inventory models started emerging and became applicable for many practical situations.

Despite these assumptions, the EOQ model is still popular and applied in many practical situations. Figure 6.8 shows how the ordering cycles appear. Since the cycles and ordering plans look like a sawtooth, this model is often referred to as the "sawtooth" model.

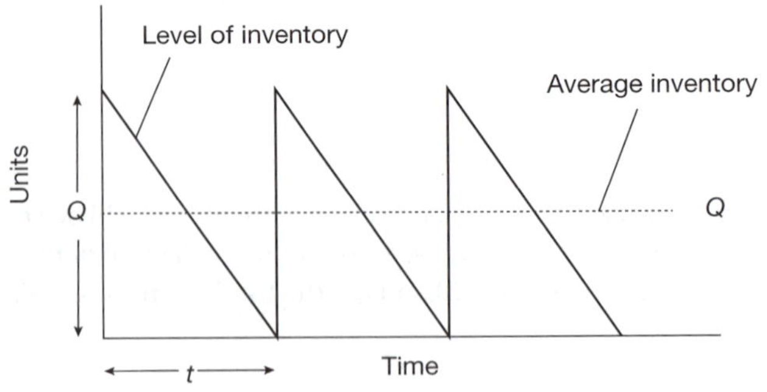

FIGURE 6.8 Order cycles of basic EOQ model.

The main reason for the popularity of EOQ models is that they are robust. That is, any small changes in the quantity of EOQ do not drastically change the total cost as the total cost curve is flatter near the optimal Q^*, as is evident from Figure 6.6. We can explain this phenomenon as follows.

Suppose that instead of ordering the optimal lot size Q^*, we fine-tune the quantity and arrive at, say, a non-optimal order quantity Q' where

$Q' = (1+f)Q^*$, and f is the fraction deviation of Q from Q^*.

The percentage error for this non-optimal order quantity is as follows:

$$\text{Deviation Error} = \frac{\text{Annual total cost or ordering } Q' - \text{Annual total cost of ordering the optimal quantity } Q^*}{\text{Annual total cost of ordering the optimal quantity } Q^*}$$

$$= \frac{\left[\frac{D}{Q'}S + \frac{Q'}{2}Ch - \frac{D}{Q^*}S - \frac{Q^*}{2}Ch\right]}{\left[\frac{D}{Q^*}S + \frac{Q^*}{2}Ch\right]} \times 100\%$$

$$= 50\left[f - 1 + \frac{1}{1+f}\right] \quad \text{as } Q' = (1+f)Q^*$$

If we assume that even $f = 0.50$, that is, 50% greater than Q^*, then

$$\text{Deviation Error} = 50\left[0.5 - 1 + \frac{1}{1+0.5}\right] = 8.33\%$$

This shows that even if Q^* is fine-tuned to the extent of 50%, the total cost is not deviating by the same amount but very marginally. This robustness makes it easier for EOQ to be used in practice as it offers flexibilities in fine-tuning the order quantity to address a few practical difficulties of lot sizing. For instance, an EOQ of, say, 87 units may not be practical for a supplier to supply because he or she supplies in multiples of 25 only. This may require the order quantity to be 100 to facilitate the lot size for the supplier. But we see that this adjustment does not change the total cost linearly and drastically. Figure 6.9 shows the percentage deviation error in total cost as a function of f. It is clear that even if we err in using a non-optimal order quantity, the error we make in terms of cost is relatively small.

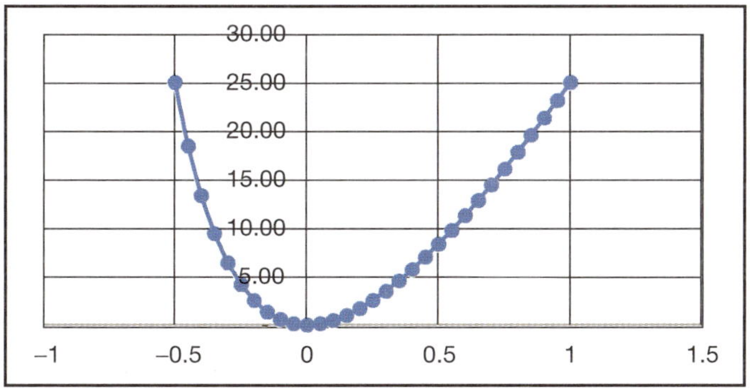

FIGURE 6.9 Percentage error in cost as a function of deviation for EOQ.

Another important aspect in inventory decisions besides how much to order is to determine when to order. In other words, it is of interest to find out the frequency of order cycles or the time t in Figure 6.8 between two successive orders. It is easier to see that T^*, the time between two successive orders, is

$$T^* = \frac{Q^*}{D} \text{year}$$

The robustness of the EOQ explained here is its major strength which made it possible to be used in practice as well by adjusting the quantity using this property in spite of rigid assumptions.

(As the number of order cycles is D/Q^*, the time between two order cycles will be the reciprocal of this!) Another important insight in this discussion would be to find out the average flow time of the units in inventory, which is the average time a unit spends in inventory. This has more practical significance as it reflects the freshness of the items in the inventory and also their obsolescence. It is quite evident from Little's formula that

$$\text{Average Flow Time} = \frac{\frac{Q}{2}}{D} = \frac{Q}{2D}\,\text{year}$$

In our example, we calculated the EOQ as 200 units. T^*, the time between two orders, will be (200/2000) year, that is, (1/10) year = 36.5 days assuming 365 days in a year. Since the number of order cycles is 10, it is obvious that the time between two orders is 36.5 days! The average flow time will be $(Q/2D)$ year, that is, 18.25 days. This indicates that the items that are ordered in each order will spend 18.25 days on an average in inventory.

6.8.3 Reorder Point (ROP)

In the assumptions section, we observed that the lead-time in the replenishment of orders in this model is zero and it assumes an instantaneous replenishment. But in practice, we are aware that there is always some lead-time in getting supply from a supplier or in dispatching orders to customers. The situation is captured in Figure 6.10 assuming a lead-time of 7 days for supply.

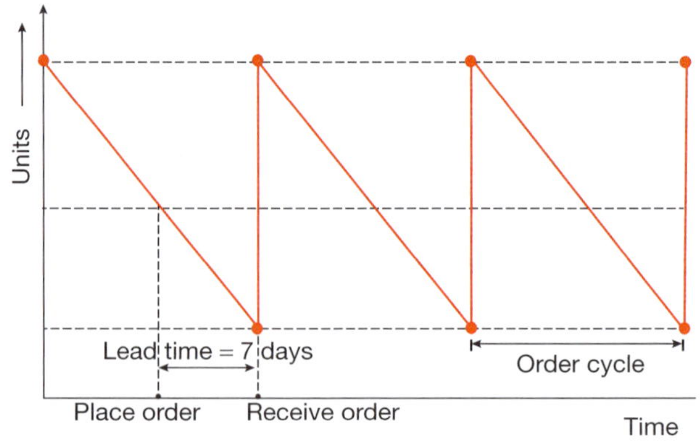

FIGURE 6.10 Lead-time in the basic EOQ model.

We observe that in such situations, when there is lead-time required, the order has to be placed in advance for it to reach when the stock level reaches zero for it to be replenished. This is the basic idea of a reorder point (ROP) or level, which is the quantity to which inventory is allowed to drop before a replacement order is placed. Because there is generally a time lapse between when the order is placed and when the items are available in inventory, the demand that occurs over this lead-time must be anticipated. The demand during this lead-time of, say, *LT* days or weeks will be the level that the stock reaches, and it is also the level at which the order has to be triggered. Hence, the ROP is

$$ROP = d \times LT \tag{6.8}$$

where ***ROP*** is the reorder point quantity (units), ***d*** is the demand rate (in time units), and ***LT*** is the average lead-time (in time units).

Note that the demand rate (*d*) and the average lead-time (*LT*) must be expressed in the same time dimension. It is also assumed here that the demand during the lead-time is still known and is at a constant rate.

We will revisit Example 6.1. Assume that the lead-time is given as 1.5 weeks. Since the lead-time is expressed in weeks, we will calculate *d*, the demand rate, also on a weekly basis as the demand rate/week assuming 52 weeks in a year. So, d = Demand rate/week = 2000/52 = 38.5 units. Since the lead-time is 1.5 weeks,

$$ROP = d \times LT = 38.5 \times 1.5 = 57.75 \approx 58$$

And so, this translates to a policy that when the stock level from the EOQ level of 200 drops to 58, a new order has to be triggered.

6.9 | PRODUCTION ORDER QUANTITIES (POQ) MODELS

The basic EOQ/ROP model discussed in the previous sections assumes that the entire lot quantity is delivered or dispatched at the end of the fixed lead-time. However, in some manufacturing situations, the end of the lead-time may signal the receipt of the first items of the production run. At a production rate, say, $p = 100$ units per day, it would take $Q/p = 1000/100 = 10$ days to produce a lot size of $Q = 1000$ units. During that time, $(Q/p)d = 10 \times 40 = 400$ units would be lost to sales assuming a daily demand of $d = 40$ units per day. Effectively, this reduces the annual carrying costs, because the 1000 units would not be held in stock, but only a maximum of 600 units, that is, $Q - (Q/p)d$. This would imply that money could be saved by increasing the lot size to reflect the fact that every unit that is received is not held and some of what is received is also passed on directly to the customer.

A good inventory policy should be able to alert a decision maker about when to replace the stock and enable smooth material flow. Reorder polices would enable the decision maker toward this.

Using the same logic that was used in the basic EOQ model, we see that the annual inventory-carrying cost is $H = \frac{1}{2}\left[Q - \left(\frac{Q}{p}\right)d\right]Ch$ and the marginal carrying cost would then be

$$\frac{dH}{dQ} = \frac{Ch}{2}\left(1 - \frac{d}{p}\right)$$

Equating the incremental carrying costs and setup costs as we did in the case of EOQ models (see Equation (6.7)),

$$\frac{DS}{Q^2} = \frac{Ch}{2}\left(1 - \frac{d}{p}\right)$$

We can, thus, derive the Economic Production Quantity (EPQ) or Production Order Quantity (POQ) as

$$\text{EPQ} = \sqrt{\frac{2DS}{hC\left(1 - \frac{d}{p}\right)}} \qquad (6.9)$$

This is illustrated in Figure 6.11.

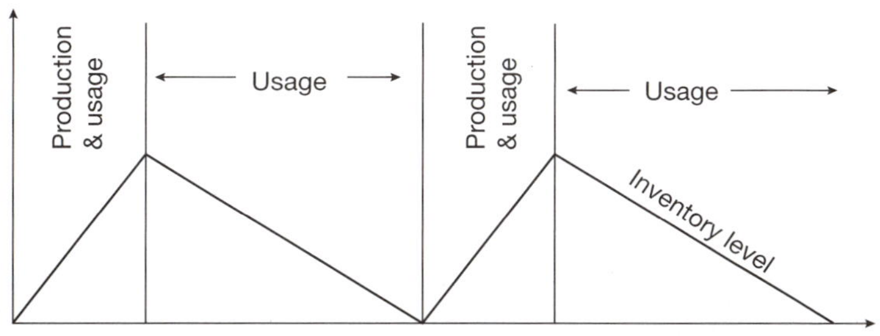

FIGURE 6.11 Production quantity model.

EXAMPLE 6.7

Suppose the annual demand for an item is 10,000 units. Assuming 250 days in a year, the daily demand rate $d = 10{,}000/250 = 40$ units per day. If the unit cost is \$10 and the carrying cost is 40% with a setup cost (S) of \$500, how much should the company produce? Assume that the production rate p is 100 units per day. It is clear that

$$\text{EPQ} = \sqrt{\frac{2DS}{hC\left(1-\frac{d}{p}\right)}} = \sqrt{\frac{2\times 10{,}000\times 500}{0.40\times 10\times\left(1-\frac{40}{100}\right)}} = 2041$$

6.10 | QUANTITY DISCOUNT EOQ MODELS

We see how the modeling approach that was used in the basic EOQ model is useful here too in determining the POQ in a similar way by exploiting the trade-off between setup cost and inventory-carrying cost.

While discussing the assumptions using the basic EOQ model, it was indicated that the EOQ model assumes that the price is constant and no quantity discounts are allowed. Whether 100 units are procured or 1000 units are procured, the price per unit is assumed to be constant. However, in practical supply chains, quantity discounts are quite common where a distributor may offer discounts to his or her wholesaler or retailer, or a supplier may offer such discounts to a buyer. Large purchases offer a benefit of reducing the procurement or material cost by availing the discount; however, they will increase the inventory-carrying cost of the stock that will have to be carried while ordering such a large quantity. There are trade-offs in evaluating quantity discounts with respect to various cost drivers such as ordering cost, inventory-carrying cost, material cost, transportation cost, warehousing cost, etc. Hence, adjusting the economic order quantity taking into account such trade-offs is essential, and so deriving a simple rule for calculating such quantities is important. In this section, we will discuss such models and see how the basic EOQ is modified while allowing quantity discounts in the model. Since the price will influence the quantity to be ordered, the material cost which was ignored in the case of total cost for the basic EOQ model will have to be considered while evaluating the trade-offs in this scenario.

Quantity discounts are basically of two types: All-Unit Discount and Marginal-Unit Discount. We will explain them with the following example.

Suppose a supplier offers the slabs of quantities with the respective prices for those slabs stated alongside (refer Table 6.7).

TABLE 6.7 Quantity slabs and prices

Quantity Slabs	Price Per Unit
Up to 500	\$100
Between 500 and 1000	\$95
1000 and more	\$90

Assume that the supplier offers the All-Unit Discount structure to a buyer, and the buyer is placing an order of 2500 units. Under this structure, the discount price of \$90, which is applicable for quantities 1000 and more, is given for all units that are ordered. Hence, the material cost or the procurement cost will be $2500 \times \$90 = \$225{,}000$.

Whereas if the supplier offers the Marginal-Unit Discount structure to a buyer who has placed an order of 2500 units, the process is applicable slab-wise incrementally. That is, for the first 500 units, the price of \$100 is applied; for the next 1000 units, the price of \$95 is applied; and for the remaining 1000 units ($2500 - 500 - 1000$), the price of \$90 is applied. In other words, the best price of \$90 for the third slab is not applicable for the entire quantity that is ordered but only incrementally or marginally. Hence, the material cost or the procurement cost in this case would be $500 \times 100 + 1000 \times 95 + 1000 \times 90 = \$235{,}000$.

We notice that the material costs in both the cases are different and it matters which discount is applied to determine the appropriate quantity that takes into account this material cost. So, in both the cases of discount structures, the total cost will be as follows:

Total Cost = Ordering Cost + Inventory Cost + Material Cost

That is,

$$TC = \frac{D}{Q} \times S + \frac{Q}{2} \times C \times h + D \times C \quad (6.10)$$

In all these quantity discount models, the pricing structure consists of specified break points q_0, q_1, ..., q_r, where $q_0 = 0$ and the prices are denoted as C_i, for $0 \le i \le r$. In the example given in Table 6.7, we see that $q_0 = 0$, $q_1 = 500$, $q_2 = 1000$ and $C_o = \$100$, $C_1 = \$95$, and $C_2 = \$90$.

6.10.1 EOQ in the All-Unit Discount Structure

Consider the discount structure given in Table 6.7. Assume that the annual demand is 1000 units, ordering cost S is \$100, and h is 20%. To determine the appropriate quantity to exploit the discount, the following steps are followed:

1. Evaluate the order quantity for each price C_i, $0 \le i \le r$

$$Q_i = \sqrt{\frac{2DS}{C_i h}}$$

2. We then select the order quantity Q_i^* for each price C_i. There are three possible scenarios:
   a. $q_i \le Q_i < q_{i+1}$
   b. $Q_i < q_i$
   c. $Q_i \ge q_{i+1}$

   Case (c) can be ignored for Q_i as it is considered for Q_{i+1}. And so, we have to consider only cases (a) and (b). For case (a), $Q_i^* = Q_i$ as this is within the range of the two limits of the slab. For case (b), $Q_i^* = q_i$, that is, adjust the quantity to q_i to qualify for the price for which the discount is eligible.

3. For each i, calculate the total cost of ordering Q_i^* units using Equation (6.10).
4. For overall i, select order quantity Q_i^* with the lowest cost TC_i.

Price Slab $i = 0$: Up to 500 with a price of \$100 per unit

We will find the EOQ for this price and check if the resulting EOQ is in the quantity range of the price that is valid.

$$Q_0 = \sqrt{\frac{2 \times 1000 \times 100}{100 \times 0.20}} = 100$$

We observe that the quantity 100 is within the range for which the price \$100 is valid. We substitute $Q_0 = 100$ in Equation (6.10).

$$\begin{aligned} TC_0 &= (1000/100) \times 100 + (100/2) \times 100 \times 0.20 + 1000 \times 100 \\ &= 1000 + 1000 + 100{,}000 \\ &= \mathbf{\$102{,}000} \end{aligned}$$

Price Slab $i = 1$: Between 500 and 1000 with a price of \$95 per unit

We will find the EOQ for this price and check if the resulting EOQ is in the quantity range of the price that is valid.

$$Q_1 = \sqrt{\frac{2 \times 1000 \times 100}{95 \times 0.20}} = 102.6$$

We observe that the quantity 102.6 is NOT within the range of 500–1000 for which the price \$95 is valid. Hence, we need to adjust Q_1 to the nearest in the range, which is a quantity of 500.

(Recall that such adjustments are based on the strength of the EOQ model being robust!) We substitute $Q_1 = 500$ in Equation (6.10).

$$\begin{aligned} TC_1 &= (1000/500) \times 100 + (500/2) \times 95 \times 0.2 + 1000 \times 95 \\ &= 200 + 4750 + 95{,}000 \\ &= \mathbf{\$99{,}950} \end{aligned}$$

Price Slab $i = 2$: 1000 and more with a price of \$90 per unit

We will find the EOQ for this price and check if the resulting EOQ is in the quantity range of the price that is valid.

$$Q_2 = \sqrt{\frac{2 \times 1000 \times 100}{90 \times 0.20}} = 105.4$$

We observe that the quantity 105.4 is NOT within the range of 1000 and more, for which the price \$90 is valid. Hence, we need to adjust Q_2 to the nearest in the range, which is a quantity of **1000**. (Again, recall that such adjustments are based on the strength of the EOQ model being robust!) We substitute $Q_2 = 1000$ in Equation (6.10).

$$\begin{aligned} TC_2 &= (1000/1000) \times 100 + (1000/2) \times 90 \times 0.20 + 1000 \times 90 \\ &= 100 + 9000 + 90{,}000 \\ &= \mathbf{\$99{,}100} \end{aligned}$$

The results can be summarized as follows:

Q	**Total costs**
<500	\$102,100
500–1000	\$99,950
≥1000	\$99,100 → Lowest

Hence, placing $\boldsymbol{Q} = \mathbf{1000}$ will be optimal to exploit the discount and also to minimize the total cost. The graph in Figure 6.12 depicts the analysis clearly.

FIGURE 6.12 Quantity discount EOQ model (All-Unit Discount structure).

6.10.2 EOQ in Marginal-Unit Discount Structure

These models are also referred to as Incremental-Unit Discount or Multi-Block Tariff structure models. As explained earlier, let the pricing schedule contain specified break points $q_0, q_1, \ldots, q_r$, where $q_0 = 0$ and the prices are denoted as C_i, for $0 \leq i \leq r$. In these models, the marginal cost of a unit decreases with the break points as compared to the average cost in the case of the All-Unit Discount structure models.

Say, an order for quantity Q is placed. Then the first $(q_i - q_0)$ units are priced at C_0, then the next $(q_2 - q_1)$ units are priced at C_1, and hence in general $(q_{i+1} - q_i)$ units are priced at C_i.

Here the objective will be to decide the optimal quantity that will minimize the total cost (annual) consisting of ordering, inventory-carrying, and material costs. Similar to the discussion we had in the previous section for the All-Unit Discount model, here too the procedure is to evaluate the optimal lot size for each marginal price C_i (which forces the lot size between q_i and q_{i+1}).

Let V_i be the material cost of placing an order of q_i units for each value of i, $0 \le i \le r$. We will also assume $V_0 = 0$. Then

$$V_i = (q_1 - q_o)C_0 + (q_2 - q_1)C_1 + \ldots + (q_i - q_{i-1})C_{i-1}$$

For each value of i, $0 \le i \le r-1$, let us assume that an order quantity of Q in the range of q_i and q_{i+1} units is placed. That is, $q_i \le Q \le q_{i+1}$. The material cost of this order quantity Q can be calculated as $V_i + (Q - q_i)C_i$. The total annual cost components shown in Equation (6.10) can be derived as follows:

$$\text{Ordering Cost} = \left(\frac{D}{Q}\right)S$$

$$\text{Inventory-Carrying Cost} = \left\lfloor V_i + (Q - q_i)C_i \right\rfloor h/2$$

(as inventory-carrying cost is actually = $(Q/2) \times \left(\left\lfloor V_i + (Q - q_i)C_i \right\rfloor / Q\right) \times h$. The weighted (average) price of each unit for the purchased quantity Q will be $\left(\left\lfloor V_i + (Q - q_i)C_i \right\rfloor / Q\right)$ and the average inventory will be valued at this price only. Q gets cancelled in the numerator and the denominator.)

$$\text{Material Cost} = D \times \left(\left\lfloor V_i + (Q - q_i)C_i \right\rfloor / Q\right)$$

So, the total annual cost will be

$$TC = \left(\frac{D}{Q}\right)S + \left\lfloor V_i + (Q - q_i)C_i \right\rfloor h/2 + D \times \left(\left\lfloor V_i + (Q - q_i)C_i \right\rfloor / Q\right) \tag{6.11}$$

The optimal lot size for price C_i is obtained by minimizing the total cost TC with respect to Q and equating to zero. The calculus gives the optimal lot size Q_i for the price C_i.

$$Q_i \text{ for the price } C_i = \sqrt{\frac{2D[S + V_i - q_i C_i]}{hC_i}} \tag{6.12}$$

This formula is quite similar to the EOQ formula, but we can observe that the fixed cost of ordering has increased from S to $S + V_i - q_i C_i$, that is, an additional cost of $V_i - q_i C_i$ due to quantity discounts.

Determining the optimal lot size Q_i^* is quite similar to the steps that are followed in the case of the All-Unit Discount structure and can be outlined as follows:

1. Evaluate the order quantity for each price C_i, $0 \le i \le r$

$$Q_i = \sqrt{\frac{2D[S + V_i - q_i C_i]}{hC_i}}$$

2. We then select the order quantity Q_i^* for each price C_i. There are three possible scenarios:
   a. If $q_i \le Q_i < q_{i+1}$, then set $Q_i^* = Q_i$.
   b. If $Q_i < q_i$, then set $Q_i^* = q_i$.
   c. If $Q_i \ge q_{i+1}$, then set $Q_i = q_{i+1}$.
3. For each i, calculate the total cost of ordering Q_i^* units using Equation (6.11) as follows:

$$TC_i = \left(\frac{D}{Q_i^*}\right)S + \left\lfloor V_i + (Q_i^* - q_i)C_i \right\rfloor h/2 + D \times \left(\left\lfloor V_i + (Q_i^* - q_i)C_i \right\rfloor / Q_i^*\right) \tag{6.13}$$

4. For overall i, select order quantity Q_i^* with the lowest cost TC_i.

In other words, the steps seek to find a local minimum for each price slab and evaluate the total cost for the same and thereby the global minimum for the total annual cost.

We will see the following in Example 6.8.

EXAMPLE 6.8

TABLE 6.8 Quantity slabs and unit prices (marginal)

Quantity Slabs	Marginal-Unit Price
First 100	$500.5
Next 100	$490.5
200 and above	$475.5

Given $D = 1200$ and $S = 25$ with $h = 0.20$. We now have the following information about the price breaks and other details:

$q_0 = 0$ $q_1 = 100$ $q_2 = 200$

$C_0 = 500.5$ $C_1 = 490.5$ $C_2 = 475.5$

$V_0 = 0$ $V_1 = (100 - 0) \times 500.5 = 50{,}050$ $V_2 = (100 - 0) \times 500.5 + (200 - 100) \times 490.5 = 50{,}050 + 49{,}050 = 99{,}100$

Using step 1, we find that

$$Q_0 = \sqrt{\frac{2D[S + V_0 - q_0C_0]}{hC_0}} = \sqrt{\frac{2 \times 1200[25]}{0.2 \times 500.5}} = 25$$

$$Q_1 = \sqrt{\frac{2D[S + V_1 - q_1C_1]}{hC_1}} = \sqrt{\frac{2 \times 1200[25 + 50050 - 49050]}{0.2 \times 490.5}} \approx 158$$

$$Q_2 = \sqrt{\frac{2D[S + V_2 - q_2C_2]}{hC_2}} = \sqrt{\frac{2 \times 1200[25 + 99100 - 95100]}{0.2 \times 475.5}} \approx 319$$

In step 2, we set $Q_0^* = 25$ because Q_0 is within the range of the first slab of the quantity discount. Similarly, $Q_1^* = 158$ as again Q_1 is within the range of the second slab of the quantity discount and $Q_2^* = 319$ as again Q_2 is in the range of the third slab.

In step 3, we find the respective TC_0, TC_1, and TC_2 for these quantities as summarized in Table 6.9.

TABLE 6.9 Summary of cost analysis for different price breaks and total costs

i	D	S	C	V_i	Q_i	Ordering Cost	Inventory-Carrying Cost	Material Cost	Total Cost
0	1,200	25	500.5	0	25	1,200	1,251.25	600,600	603,051.25
1	1,200	25	490.5	50,050	158	189.8734	7,849.9	596,195	604,234.71
2	1,200	25	475.5	99,100	319	94.04389	15,568.45	585,647	601,309.52

As seen in Table 6.9, the optimal quantity will be to place an order for 319 where the total cost is minimum. The same is depicted in Figure 6.13. We notice that the respective local minimum for each price slab occurs at 25, 158, and 319, respectively, as seen from the graph, and hence the overall minimum occurs at 319, which is the optimal lot size for placing the order.

EXAMPLE 6.8

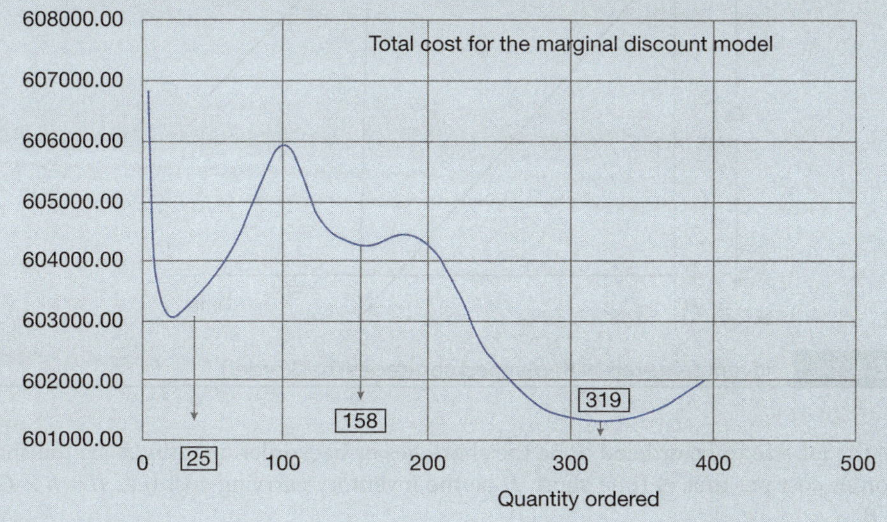

FIGURE 6.13 Total cost curve for different price breaks and optimal policies.

ACTIVITY 6.3

It will be interesting if more cost components are added to see how the EOQ gets recalculated. For example, in the analysis shown here, only three cost drivers—ordering cost, inventory-carrying cost, and material cost—are considered. It is possible to consider more cost drivers such as the cost of warehousing and leasing if the order quantity is more, cost of transportation, etc. and see how the EOQ formula can be modified and used.

6.10.3 EOQ Models with Backorders (Planned Shortages)

In the analysis of assumptions on the EOQ model, we saw that EOQ models do not assume any shortages or backorders. We saw earlier that a backorder occurs when a customer waits for his or her order to be filled so that the sale is not lost but only delayed. Backorders can create additional clerical and sales costs for order processing, and additional transportation and handling costs when such orders are not filled through the normal distribution channel.

We see that the assumption of price is constant in the basic EOQ model but if violated, the EOQ calculations are adjusted using the same modeling principle of cost trade-offs.

By assuming that planned shortages are not allowed, the basic EOQ model discussed earlier addresses the common issue to avoid shortages as much as possible. Nevertheless, unplanned shortages can still occur if the planned demand rate and deliveries do not stay on schedule. But there are situations where permitting limited planned shortages make sense from a managerial perspective. The fallout of this would be to expect customers to accept a reasonable delay in filling their orders if need be. If so, the costs of incurring shortages described, including lost future business, should not be exorbitant. If the cost of holding inventory is high relative to these shortage costs, then lowering the average inventory level by permitting occasional brief shortages may be a sound business decision. In some sense, backorders are simply negative inventory. The EOQ model with planned shortages addresses this kind of situation by replacing only an assumption of the basic EOQ model with the following new assumption. So, we replace assumption (3) of Section 6.8.2 as follows:

Planned shortages are allowed. When a shortage occurs, the affected customers will wait for the item to become available again. Their backorders are filled immediately when the order quantity arrives to replenish inventory.

Under these assumptions, the cycle pattern of the EOQ model looks like what is shown in Figure 6.14.

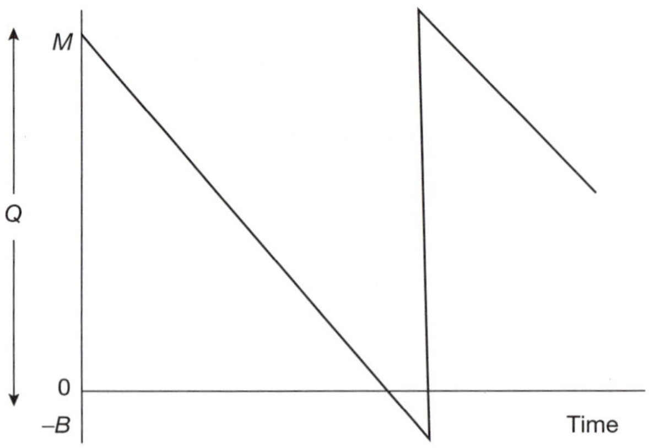

FIGURE 6.14 Inventory levels with planned shortages (backorder).

In practice, backorders are often faced due to market conditions, and if planned shortages are possible in such situations, it is worth investigating the cost benefits of such shortage planning.

Let Q be the lot size to be ordered, B be the shortages or backorder quantity, π be the shortage or backorder cost per unit of time short, H be the inventory-carrying cost (i.e., $H = h \times C$), and $M = Q - B$.

The average backorder would be $B/2$ just as the average inventory would be $M/2 = (Q - B)/2$. In each cycle, the maximum inventory would be $M = Q - B$, because the new lot is immediately depleted by the backorder quantity B from the previous cycle. So the total annual cost should now include the backorder cost, ordering (or setup) cost, and inventory-carrying cost.

Total Cost = Annual Ordering (or Setup) Cost + Inventory-Carrying Cost of Average Inventory of M + Inventory-Holding Cost of Backorder B

$$TC(Q,B) = \frac{D}{Q}S + \left(\frac{(Q-B)}{2}\right) \times H \times \left(\frac{Q-B}{Q}\right) + \left(\frac{B}{2}\right) \times \pi \times \left(\frac{B}{Q}\right) \quad (6.14)$$

Here $\left(\frac{Q-B}{Q}\right)$ refers to the proportion of the cycle time where positive inventory $M = Q - B$ exists and $\left(\frac{B}{Q}\right)$ refers to the time when the negative inventory (backorder) exists.

Differentiating the $TC(Q, B)$ with respect to B and Q, respectively, and equating them to zero, we get expressions for B and Q as follows:

$$B = Q\left(\frac{H}{H+\pi}\right) \quad (6.15)$$

$$Q = \sqrt{\frac{2DS}{H}}\sqrt{\frac{H+\pi}{\pi}} \quad (6.16)$$

The derivation is shown in Appendix 6.1.

EXAMPLE 6.9

Suppose that the annual demand $D = 10{,}000$ units, $S = \$500$, $H = \$10$, and $\pi = \$40$. We substitute them in Equations (6.15) and (6.16). We obtain Q first, and through Q we obtain the value of B.

$$Q = \sqrt{\frac{2DS}{H}}\sqrt{\frac{H+\pi}{\pi}} = \sqrt{\frac{2 \times 10{,}000 \times 500}{10}}\sqrt{\frac{10+40}{40}} = 1118$$

$$B = Q\left(\frac{H}{H+\pi}\right) = 1118 \times \left(\frac{10}{40+10}\right) = 223.6 \approx 224$$

Hence, $M = Q - B = 1118 - 224 = 894$. Substituting the values of B and M in the total cost Equation (6.14), we get

$$TC(Q,B) = \frac{10{,}000}{1118} \times 500 + \left(\frac{894}{2}\right) \times 10 \times \left(\frac{894}{1118}\right) + \left(\frac{224}{2}\right) \times 40 \times \left(\frac{224}{1118}\right)$$
$$= 4472.27 + 3574.40 + 897.60$$
$$= 8944.27$$

Let us compare the total cost if such a backorder situation does not exist and no backorders were planned. In this case, the normal EOQ "Q^*" will be obtained.

$$Q^* = \sqrt{\frac{2DS}{H}} = \sqrt{\frac{2 \times 10000 \times 500}{10}} = 1000$$

The total annual cost would have been

$$TC = \frac{D}{Q} \times S + \frac{Q}{2} \times H = \left(\frac{10{,}000}{1000}\right) \times 500 + \left(\frac{1000}{2}\right) \times 10$$
$$= 5000 + 5000 = \$10{,}000$$

We see that the planned shortage in this case has saved \$10,000 – 8944.27 = \$1055.73 even assuming a slightly higher backorder cost of \$40 as against the holding cost of \$10.

SUMMARY

This introductory chapter on inventory decisions introduced the basic notions of inventory and why organizations keep inventory and for what business reasons. It introduced in detail the types of costs that are to be dealt with while deciding the policies of inventories. The chapter discussed the idea of the ABC analysis and the 80–20 Pareto principle with practical examples and demonstrated how inventory can be estimated using the Pareto curve analysis. Then it introduced the basic single-period inventory model using the newsboy model with situations and used an example to illustrate the use of newsboy model in practice. The chapter then explained the pull model of inventory using the Economic Order Quantity (EOQ) and elaborated on the model description, basic assumptions, and usefulness in practice.

The chapter then explained how the basic EOQ model is modified and when each of the assumptions are relaxed or violated. It introduced the concept of a reorder point under certain assumptions. It then discussed production order quantities in production situations on similar lines of EOQ. The chapter then introduced the quantity discount models of EOQ when price is not constant with explanations on how the EOQ formula gets modified. Towards the end, the chapter explained the backorder case of EOQ with explanations on how the EOQ formula is modified with planned backorder as part of the inventory practices.

Case Study

It is suggested to take up the **Gentle Electric Company** Case by W. Earl Sasser Jr. (Reference No. **9-672-038** Rev. September 29, 1983) of the Harvard Business Publishing of Harvard Business School for explaining the concept of EOQ, quantity discount models discussed in this chapter. The case can be seen at https://hbsp.harvard.edu/product/672038-PDF-ENG?Ntt=gentle%20electric%20company

Appendix 6.1

Derivation of the Expression for B (Backorder) and Q (Quantity)

We can express Equation (6.14) as follows:

$$TC(Q,B)=\frac{D}{Q}S+\left(\frac{(Q-B)^2}{2Q}\right)H+\left(\frac{B^2}{2Q}\right)\pi$$

$$=\frac{D}{Q}S+\frac{(Q^2-2QB+B^2)H}{2Q}+\frac{B^2\pi}{2Q}$$

$$=\frac{DS}{Q}+\frac{QH}{2}-BH+\frac{B^2H}{2Q}+\frac{B^2\pi}{2Q}$$

$$\frac{\partial TC(Q,B)}{\partial B}=-H+\frac{BH}{Q}+\frac{B\pi}{Q}=0$$

$$\frac{B}{Q}(H+\pi)=H$$

So

$$B=Q\left(\frac{H}{H+\pi}\right) \quad (6.17)$$

Now,

$$\frac{\partial TC(Q,B)}{\partial Q}=-\frac{DS}{Q^2}+\frac{h}{2}-\frac{B^2H}{2Q^2}-\frac{B^2\pi}{2Q^2}=0$$

Multiplying throughout by $2Q^2$, we get

$$Q^2h-B^2(H+\pi)-2DS=0$$

Substituting B from Equation (i), we get

$$Q^2H-Q^2\frac{H^2}{(h+H)^2}(H+\pi)-2DS=0$$

Simplifying further, we get

$$Q^2H\left(1-\frac{H}{(H+\pi)}\right)-2DS=0$$

$$Q^2=\frac{2DS}{H}\left(\frac{H+\pi}{H}\right)$$

Hence,

$$Q=\sqrt{\frac{2DS}{H}}\sqrt{\frac{H+\pi}{\pi}} \quad (6.18)$$

Exercises

1. The following table contains various products of the business, their monthly average demand, and their sales price per unit. Perform ABC analysis for these products and explain.

Product	Average Demand in Units	Sales Price Per Unit (in $)
A	200	1500
B	250	1350
C	350	150

(Continued)

(Continued)

Product	Average Demand in Units	Sales Price Per Unit (in $)
D	400	90
E	300	80
F	500	60
G	350	20

2. An FMCG company wants to analyze its products and their sales. The goal of this analysis is to evaluate which product is of particular importance and which products are less important. The management has decided to use the annual sales value as the key figure to assess the product range. The details are given in the following table.

Product	Sales in Units	Price Per Unit ($)
1	1500	6.20
2	1750	0.25
3	10500	0.30
4	3500	0.45
5	4500	9.75
6	4750	0.35
7	4250	0.65
8	4000	0.80
9	5000	0.75
10	6000	0.05
11	2500	1.10
12	3500	4.75
13	1500	1.35
14	1400	1.45
15	900	32.00
16	5500	0.55

3. The following table gives the annual throughput of a warehouse of a company for 25 products it holds. The company normally follows the Pareto principle that 30% of its products produce 70% of sales. It wishes to maintain an inventory turnover ratio of 10:1 for its A range of products, 6:1 for its B range of products, and 2:1 for its C range of products. It is estimated that the total expected sales in the coming year is $35,000,000 ($35,000 thousands). What will be the estimate of its average inventory for the A, B, and C range of products?

Product Number	Annual Throughput (Thousands $)
1	6000
2	5000
3	3800
4	3500
5	3000
6	2500
7	1500

(Continued)

(Continued)

Product Number	Annual Throughput (Thousands $)
8	1200
9	1000
10	900
11	750
12	600
13	550
14	450
15	300
16	280
17	220
18	180
19	150
20	120
21	90
22	70
23	50
24	30
25	20
Total	**32,260**

4. Each month, the Big Market retail store sells 6000 kilos of wheat flour. Each time the parent company refills the store's stocks, it charges the station a fixed fee of $60 and an additional fee of 60 cents per gallon. Big Market's annual cost of holding a kilo of wheat flour is 20 cents. Assume that the EOQ assumptions hold, and shortages are not allowed.
   a. Determine Q^*, the Economic Order Quantity (EOQ).
   b. Determine the minimum total cost per year.
   c. Determine the optimal number of orders that should be placed per year.
   d. Using the EOQ, how much time will elapse between orders?
   e. Assuming the lead-time is 2 weeks, determine the reorder point.
   f. Assuming the lead-time is 10 weeks, determine the reorder point.
5. We will consider the following Total Cost expression for EOQ calculations:

   Total Cost (TC) = Ordering Cost (OC) + Inventory-Carrying Cost (ICC) + Material Cost (MC)

   $$TC = \frac{D}{Q} \times S + \frac{Q}{2} \times C \times h + D \times C$$

   TC = Total annual relevant inventory cost, dollars
   Q = Size of each order to replenish inventory, units
   D = Annual demand for the item in inventory, units
   S = Ordering or procurement cost, dollars/order
   C = Value of the item carried in inventory, dollars/unit
   h = Carrying cost as a percent of item value, %/year or fraction (e.g., 20% or 0.20)

   Suppose that instead of ordering Q^*, the EOQ, a quantity δQ^* is ordered. Here, δ is some constant multiplying factor. Determine an analytical expression for the extra cost incurred, that is, for the quantity $TC(\delta Q^*) - TC(Q^*)$, in terms of the constants S, D, h, and δ only. Simplify your answer as much as possible. This problem analytically examines the flatness of the total cost function $TC(Q)$, under the EOQ assumptions with no shortages.

6. Using the preceding expression, for problem 4, determine the additional cost which must be paid if Big Market, instead of ordering the EOQ,

a. Orders thrice the optimal number of kilos in each order (i.e., $Q = 2Q^*$).

b. Orders three-fourth of the optimal number of kilos in each order.

7. A retail store orders its carry baskets from its supply firm. The cost per carry basket depends on the following order size Q:

Order Size	Price Per Basket
$Q < 200$	\$0.90
$Q \geq 200$	\$0.80

The annual holding cost is 20% of the purchasing cost. Define EOQ_{90} to be the EOQ if the cost per basket is 90 cents, and EOQ_{80} to be the EOQ if the cost per basket is 80 cents.

a. Given the preceding information, which is larger: EOQ_{80} or EOQ_{90}?

b. Explain why the optimal order quantity must be either EOQ_{80} or EOQ_{90} or 200?

c. If $EOQ_{90} > 200$, then, is the optimal order quantity EOQ_{80}, EOQ_{90}, or 200, or is there not enough information to determine which is optimal?

d. If $EOQ_{90} < 200$ and $EOQ_{80} > 200$, then, is the optimal order quantity EOQ_{90}, EOQ_{80}, or 200, or is there not enough information to determine which is optimal?

e. If $EOQ_{90} < 200$ and $EOQ_{80} < 200$, then, is the optimal order quantity EOQ_{90}, EOQ_{80}, or 200, or is there not enough information to determine which is optimal?

8. Consider the EOQ problem, with all its assumptions. However, instead of a continuously depleting demand, suppose that the demand is now discrete (and periodic), with d units being demanded at times t; $2t$, $3t$, ... where $d = Dt$, so that the average slope is the same as in the EOQ case. Also, for points of time when both a demand occurs and an order arrives, assume that the demand is taken instantaneously before the order arrives. Assuming the same quantity Q is ordered at the same times in both cases, let I_d and I_c be the annual inventory costs for the discrete and continuous scenarios, respectively. Then, $(I_d - I_c)/I_c$ is the percent increase in the discrete scenario over that of the continuous scenario. Determine this value in a simple expression as simple as possible, in terms of the parameters Q, D, h, and d.

9. Every winter, Brubake Cakes sells cakes in the city of Jamshedpur. It builds inventory before the peak Christmas season starts. Due to its locational disadvantages, no replenishment is possible until autumn. Brubake's winter demand for cakes is estimated to be continuous and uniformly distributed between 600 and 800, that is,

$$f_D(d) = \int_{600}^{800} \frac{1}{200} \quad 600 \leq d \leq 800$$
$$= 0 \qquad \text{otherwise.}$$

It purchases the cakes for \$3.00 each and sells them for \$9.00 each. Unsold cakes are given away to charity at the end of the season, but it has an estimated additional penalty of \$2.00 per cake, due to handling charges.

a. Determine the number of cakes Brubake should order to maximize its profit.

b. Determine the expected number of cakes that will be sold if the optimal quantity is purchased.

c. Determine the expected number of cakes that will be given to charity if the optimal quantity is purchased.

10. Soni Fashions sells winter fashion dresses. During the next quarter for the winter season, Soni Fashions will sell a particular fashion designer dress at \$130 per dress. Any dress that remains unsold at the end of the season will be marked down to \$80 each. Soni Fashions believes that it will eventually sell all of its dresses. Soni pays its supplier \$100 for each dress piece; however, the supplier is going out of business and will accept only one more order from Soni now. The actual demand for these designer dresses during the season is unknown. However, it is known that from the past sales history of similar dresses, the demand D is given by

Number of pieces of dresses	0	10	20	30	40
Probability	0.1	0.4	0.1	0.2	0.2

a. Determine the values of C_o and C_u (the overage cost per unit of surplus and shortage (opportunity) cost per unit short, respectively).
b. If Soni orders Q pieces of dresses from its supplier, determine the total expected profit (as a function of Q). Plot the total expected profit as a function of Q.
c. Determine the number of pieces of dresses Soni should purchase from its supplier, in order to maximize its profit.
d. Is there more than one optimal solution? Discuss why this is or is not possible.

11. Suppose that the average annual demand is 900 units, the EOQ is 100 units, and the reorder point is 30 units. To achieve this, the continuous review ($s = 30$; $Q = 100$) policy is implemented. Assume that demand is continuous, that is, there are no jumps or discontinuities in the demand curve. Let X be the total demand during a lead-time. X is a random variable with probability mass function

$$P_X(x) = 1/5 \quad \text{for } x = 22, 28, 40, 50, 60$$
$$= 0 \quad \text{otherwise}$$

Define EFD to be the expected fraction of all demand that is met on time (i.e., not backordered). Thus, if the total demand is 500 units and 400 units are met on time, then EFD = 400/500 = 0.8.
a. Determine the expected demand during a lead-time.
b. Is it possible for a shortage to occur at some time other than during a lead-time? Why or why not?
c. Determine the expected number of cycles per year.
d. Determine the expected number of units of shortage (backlog) per cycle.
e. Determine the EFD.

12. Century Autos purchases 1000 parts every year for its component production in its manufacturing unit in Jamshedpur. Each time it makes a purchase, the procurement costs it a fixed cost of \$100 plus the price of the parts; the first 50 parts cost \$10 per unit. Beyond that quantity, the supplier offers a discount and charges only \$9 per unit, that is, an order of 52 parts would cost 100 + (10)(50) + (9)(2) = \$618. The monthly inventory-carrying cost is estimated to be \$2.50 per part.
a. Determine the optimum purchase quantity.
b. Determine the optimum number of purchases Century Autos should make each year.
c. Suppose another supplier provides a per order cost of \$A and a per unit cost of \$11. (There are no quantity discounts available from this second supplier.) For what values of A, if any, will Century Autos prefer to order from this second supplier?

13. Century Autos produces two items. Assume that shortages are not allowed, and the Economic Lot Scheduling Problem (**ELSP**) conditions hold. The relevant data for each item is shown as follows. Also, after finishing a production run of items of either type, it takes 3 days to set up the machine for the other item-type. Assume the machine is either idle, setting up, or processing at maximum rate.

	Item 1	**Item 2**
Annual demand	6000 items	4000 items
Maximum production rate	12,000 items/year	16,000 items/year
Production cost	\$4.00 per item	\$3.50 per item
Annual holding cost	\$3.00 per item	\$1.00 per item
Setup cost	\$35.00	\$25.00

a. Plot the optimal inventory trajectories as a function of time.
b. Determine the optimal number of production runs for Item 1 each year.
c. How many items of type 1 should be produced during each production run?
d. What is the maximum finished inventory of Item 1?
e. Determine the average fractions of time the machine will spend idle, setting up, and processing, respectively.

14. Suppose three products are being ordered. Product A has a demand of 50,000 per year, and the standard deviation of demand is 400 per week. Product B has a demand of 20,000 per year, and the standard deviation of demand is 100 per week. Product C has a constant demand of 200 per year. The purchase prices for A, B, and C are $2, $5, and $60, respectively. The in-stock probability during lead-time for A and B is 90%. The in-stock probability for C is 99%. The lead-time is 2 weeks, and the carrying cost is 30% per year. The order costs for A, B, and C are $100, $50, and $30, respectively.

a. Design a reorder point system for A and C and state the policy.
b. Design a periodic review system for B and state the policy.
c. Suppose A, B, and C can be ordered from the same supplier. In this case, the common order cost is $20, and the individual order costs for A, B, and C are $80, $30, and $20. Design a joint ordering system for A, B, and C.

15. Rudra Paperboards manufactures several types of cardboard boxes, including hat boxes. The demand for hat boxes is 3000 per month. Each box has a value of $1, the inventory-carrying charge is 20% per year, and the setup cost is $40. The production rate for hat boxes is 400 per day. (Assume 250 days per year.)

a. What is the economic production quantity?
b. How long is each production run of hat boxes?
c. What is the time between the beginning of two production runs of hat boxes?

Bibliography

1. Ballou, R. H. and S. K. Srivastava. *Business Logistics/Supply Chain Management.* Delhi: Pearson India, 2007.
2. Chopra, S., P. Meindl, and D. V. Kalra. *Supply Chain Management: Strategy, Planning and Operation.* Delhi: Pearson India, 2016.
3. Crowther, J. F. (1964) Rationale for quantity discounts. *Harvard Business Review*, 121–127.
4. Dolan, R. J. (1987). Quantity discounts: managerial issues and research opportunities. *Marketing Science*, **6**, 1–22.
5. Goyal, S. K. (1995) A simple procedure for price break models. *Production Planning & Control*, **6**, 584–585.
6. Harris, F. W. (1913) How many parts to make at once, Reprinted from *Factory, The Magazine of Management*, **10**(2), pp. 135–136, 152, in *Operations Research*, **38**(6), November-December 1990.
7. Lee, H. L. and C. Billington. (1992) Managing supply chair inventories: pitfalls and opportunities. *Sloan Management Review* (Spring 1992), 65–73.
8. Munson, C. L. and M. J. Rosenblatt. (1998) Theories and realities of quantity discounts. *Production and Operation Management*, **7**, 352–369.
9. Narasimhan, S. L., D. W. McLeavey, and P. J. Billington. *Production Planning and Inventory Control.* Delhi: Prentice-Hall India, 2000.
10. Silver, E. A., D. Pyke, and R. Petersen. *Inventory Management and Production Planning and Scheduling.* New York: Wiley, 1998.
11. Zipkin, P. H. *Foundations of Inventory Management.* Boston, MA: Irwin McGraw-Hill, 2000.

CHAPTER 7

Inventory under Uncertainty and Service Levels

LEARNING OBJECTIVES

After reading this chapter, you would be able to:

- Understand how inventory policies are formulated when faced with demand and lead time uncertainties in practice.
- Understand how to formulate the reorder and safety stock policies when faced with demand uncertainty when it is discrete and continuous.
- Understand the types of service levels—order service level and unit service level—and derive expressions for them to understand the inventory policies in depth.
- Appreciate how safety stock is determined when both demand and lead time uncertainties are faced.
- Understand various what-if scenarios in inventory situations and how the expressions derived in this chapter can help in resolving them.
- Have a deeper understanding of stock out situations under back order and lost sales situations.

7.1 | INTRODUCTION

In this chapter, we will discuss inventory decisions made when we are faced with uncertainty, especially when demand variability is observed during the lead time. In the analysis of assumptions of Economic Order Quantity (EOQ) models in the last chapter, it was mentioned that the EOQ model assumes that the demand is certain, known, and at a constant rate. While discussing the reorder point (ROP) as well, we noticed that the ROP is determined assuming that demand during the lead time is also known and is constant. However, in practice, we are aware that demand is always uncertain, and it is possible that the item in stock will be depleted even before the order arrives and is fraught with a stock-out situation. This situation is depicted in Figure 7.1.

When such a stock-out situation arises, the best way to handle it would be to keep some **safety or buffer stock** to manage that uncertainty. If lead times are longer, it is possible that demand fluctuations are also high, and with forecasting errors in predicting such fluctuations, the role of safety inventory becomes inevitable in supply chains. A manager is faced with trade-offs of keeping safety inventory besides the average (cycle) stock to handle such fluctuations for satisfying customers with a reasonable service level. We have seen in the previous chapter that there is always a trade-off between keeping inventory under control and maintaining service levels. Hence, the pertinent concern here would be to decide: how much safety inventory should be kept and what factor would determine such levels? We will discuss these concerns in the following sections.

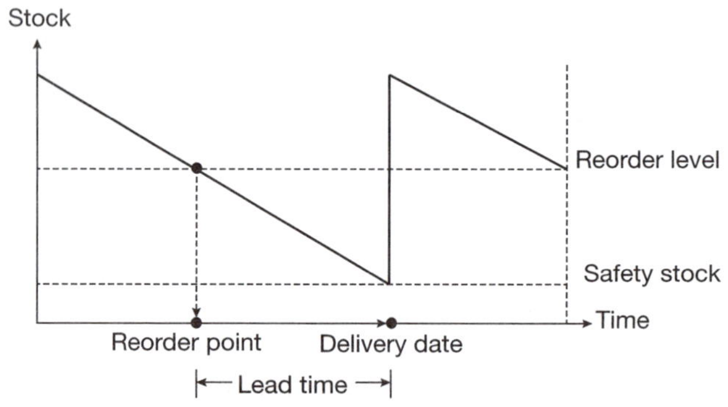

FIGURE 7.1 Inventory when demand is uncertain.

7.2 | FACTORS AFFECTING SAFETY INVENTORY

The appropriate level of safety stock is determined by the following factors:

1. Demand and supply uncertainty
2. The desired level of service in terms of product availability

The heavy fluctuation of demand or supply increases the level of safety stock. Hence, a sophisticated system of assessing the uncertainty and forecasting becomes essential for determining the safety inventory appropriately. The expectations of customers are another dimension on which the decision of safety inventory depends. The higher the expectation or the higher the level of service that has to be provided, the more the scope for higher safety stock. We will discuss them in detail in the following sections.

7.3 | UNDERSTANDING DEMAND UNCERTAINTY

We have seen that demand fluctuations are very difficult to understand, and sophisticated statistical tools are required to systematically study demand patterns and measure uncertainty. From statistical theories, we know that demand (the understanding here is that it refers to demand during the lead time to be specific) can be represented as a random variable, which may be a discrete or a continuous random variable. We will explain how the stock levels and the ROP can be determined when the demand distribution is discrete and continuous.

7.3.1 Conditions of Uncertainty: Discrete Distributions

In practice, demand is always uncertain and coupled with lead time issues, the basic EOQ model needs changes, and understanding the reason for uncertainty becomes more important. Also, it gets complicated when dealing with its nature being discrete or continuous to model it for formulating inventory policies.

We will assume the following situation of certainty initially and analyze the situation when it is uncertain.

EXAMPLE 7.1

Suppose the following information is given:

Annual Demand $D = 3600$ units, $C = \$100$, $h = 25\%$ (0.25). So, $H = h \times C = \$25$, $S = \$200$

Then, Q in this case is

$$Q^* = \sqrt{\frac{2DS}{hC}} = \sqrt{\frac{2 \times 3600 \times 200}{25}} = 240 \text{ units}$$

Hence, the number of cycles $= D/Q^* = 3600/240 = 15$

$$TC = \frac{D}{Q} \times S + \frac{Q}{2} \times C \times h = 15 \times 200 + \left(\frac{240}{2}\right) \times 25 = \$6000$$

Under the conditions of uncertainty, the fixed order quantity model is seen as given in Figure 7.2.

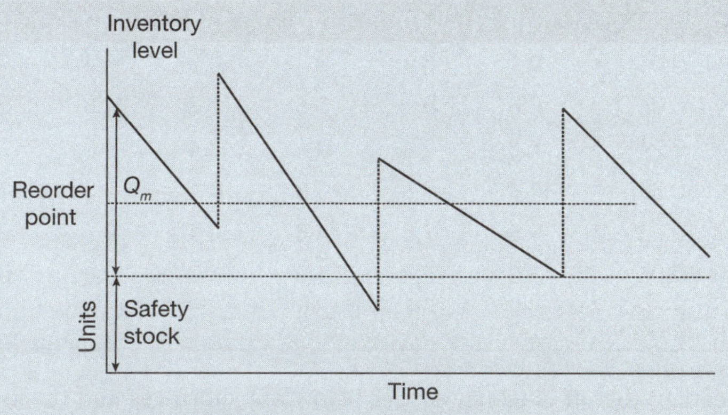

FIGURE 7.2 Fixed order quantity model under uncertainty.

Assume that the probability distribution of demand during lead time is as given in Table 7.1.

TABLE 7.1 Probability distribution of demand during the lead time

Demand	Probability
100 units	0.01
110	0.06
120	0.24
130	0.38
140	0.24
150	0.06
160	0.01

For this demand distribution, the possible units of inventory short or in excess during the lead time with various reorder points are given in Table 7.2.

TABLE 7.2 Possible units of inventory short or in excess during lead time with various reorder points

Actual Demand	Probability	Reorder Points						
		100	110	120	130	140	150	160
100	0.01	**0**	10	20	30	40	50	60
110	0.06	–10	**0**	10	20	30	40	50
120	0.24	–20	–10	**0**	10	20	30	40
130	0.38	–30	–20	–10	**0**	10	20	30
140	0.24	–40	–30	–20	–10	**0**	10	20
150	0.06	–50	–40	–30	–20	–10	**0**	10
160	0.01	–60	–50	–40	–30	–20	–10	**0**

We notice that in Table 7.2, the numbers above the diagonal elements are excess (i.e., excess inventory) and below the diagonal are shortages (opportunity losses). Recall the expected payoffs concept in decision making under uncertainty in statistics; applying the same here with the respective demand probabilities, we obtain Table 7.3 where the excesses and shortages are calculated multiplying the numbers with their respective probabilities.

TABLE 7.3 Units of excess and shortages

Actual Demand	Probability	Reorder Points						
		100	110	120	130	140	150	160
100	0.01	**0**	0.1	0.2	0.3	0.4	0.5	0.6
110	0.06	−0.6	**0**	0.6	1.2	1.8	2.4	3.0
120	0.24	−4.8	−2.4	**0**	2.4	4.8	7.2	9.6
130	0.38	−11.4	−7.6	−3.8	**0**	3.8	7.6	11.4
140	0.24	−9.6	−7.2	−4.8	−2.4	**0**	2.4	4.8
150	0.06	−3.0	−2.4	−1.8	−1.2	−0.6	**0**	0.6
160	0.01	−0.6	−0.5	−0.4	−0.3	−0.2	−0.1	**0**

As mentioned earlier, the off-diagonal entries below are shortages and those above are excesses. We summarize the total excesses and shortages and compute the respective costs associated with excesses and shortages. Excesses refer to carrying excess inventory, and we use the given inventory carrying cost $H = \$25$ for them and use the stock-out cost $\pi = \$10$ to represent shortages for Table 7.4, which gives the summary of costs for all the options of the reorder levels.

TABLE 7.4 Evaluation of the lowest cost reorder point

Demand	100	110	120	130	140	150	160
Excess (*e*)	0.0	0.1	0.8	3.9	10.8	20.1	30.0
Excess cost = 25**e*	0	\$2.50	\$20	\$97.50	\$270	\$502.50	\$750
Shortages (*g*)	30	20.1	10.8	3.9	0.8	0.1	0.0
Shortage cost per cycle $G = g\pi$	\$300	\$201	\$108	\$39	\$8	\$1	\$0
Total annual shortage cost $G(D/Q)$*	\$4500	\$3015	\$1620	\$585	\$120	\$15	\$0
Total annual cost	\$4500	\$3018	\$1640	\$682.50	**\$390**	\$517.50	\$750

- *As the number of cycles is 15 in this example
- *e*: Expected excess per cycle; *H*: Expected carrying cost @ \$25 (annual)
- g: Expected shortage per cycle; π: Stock-out cost per cycle = \$10

Notice that the minimum total cost is with a reorder level of **140 units.**

We can model this situation to determine the optimal Q^* using the following total cost expression:

Total (TC) = Ordering Cost + Inventory Carrying Cost (Cycle Stock) + Inventory Carrying Cost (Excess) + Shortage (Stock-out Cost)

$$TC = \frac{D}{Q} \times S + \frac{Q}{2} \times H + e \times H + \left(\frac{D}{Q}\right) \times g \times \pi \tag{7.1}$$

where D is the annual demand, S is the ordering cost, H is the carrying cost (i.e., $h \times C$), e is excess inventory, g is the shortage (units stock-out), and π is the shortage cost (stock-out cost per unit).

Solving this by differentiating w.r.t. to Q and equating to zero, we get

$$Q^* = \sqrt{\frac{2D[S + g\pi]}{H}} \tag{7.2}$$

In our earlier example, $D = 3600$, $S = \$200$, $H = \$25$, $\pi = \$10$, $g = 0.8$ (from Table 7.3 for reorder level 140). Hence,

$$Q^* = \sqrt{\frac{2D[S + g\pi]}{H}} = \sqrt{\frac{2 \times 3600 \times [200 + 8]}{25}} = 245$$

Substituting this Q^* in the total cost equation (7.1)

$TC = (3600/245) \times 200 + (245/2) \times 25 + 10.8 \times 25 + (3600/245) \times 8$ (as e = Excess = 10.8 from Table 7.3 for reorder level 140)

$$TC = 2938.78 + 3062.5 + 270 + 117.55 = 6388.83 \approx \$6389$$

We notice that the total has increased from \$6000 to \$6389, an increase of \$389, which is about 6.5% more. We observe the following from this discussion:

1. The following costs will rise to cover the uncertainty:
   - Stock-out costs
   - Inventory carrying costs of safety stock
2. The results may or may not be significant.
   - In the example, the total cost rose by \$389 or approximately 6.5%. The greater the dispersion of the probability distribution, the greater the cost disparity.

When dealing with the discrete nature of demand uncertainty, the basic pay-off approach that is used in decision making under uncertainty is useful to determine the reorder level and also to derive the modified EOQ formula incorporating the stock-out cost. We will see that this expression of EOQ is useful to study the inventory policies under the back order and lost sales situations.

7.3.2 Conditions of Uncertainty: Continuous Distributions

Here we assume that the demand during the lead time is a random variable that is continuous and follows a specific probability distribution with a density function. It is always challenging to fit a distribution for a given set of data. Statistical tools like frequency distribution, χ^2 goodness of fit tests, etc. can be used to ascertain the type of distribution. We will illustrate this using the following data of demand during the lead time (source: Data from the HBS Case Paper & More-Retail inventory). The data is given in Table 7.5.

TABLE 7.5 Sample demand data during the lead time

Period	Demand	Period	Demand	Period	Demand
1	37	18	43	35	42
2	37	19	50	36	27
3	75	20	41	37	63
4	73	21	53	38	51
5	53	22	47	39	5
6	47	23	57	40	83
7	44	24	15	41	11
8	41	25	45	42	50
9	37	26	66	43	20
10	35	27	33	44	15
11	25	28	58	45	27
12	15	29	76	46	48
13	12	30	31	47	3
14	43	31	35	48	53
15	72	32	26	49	2
16	29	33	71	50	9
17	40	34	41		

We attempt to fit a frequency distribution for this data. We see that the maximum value is 83 and that the minimum value is 2. While we can use Sturge's rule to determine the number of classes required, we will use the following class intervals with a width of 10 starting from 1 and obtain the following frequency distribution (Table 7.6).

TABLE 7.6 Frequency distribution for the data

Bin	Frequency
10	4
20	6
30	5
40	8
50	13
60	6
70	2
80	5
90	1

The frequency distribution (histogram for Table 7.6) along with a superimposed normal curve is shown in Figure 7.3.

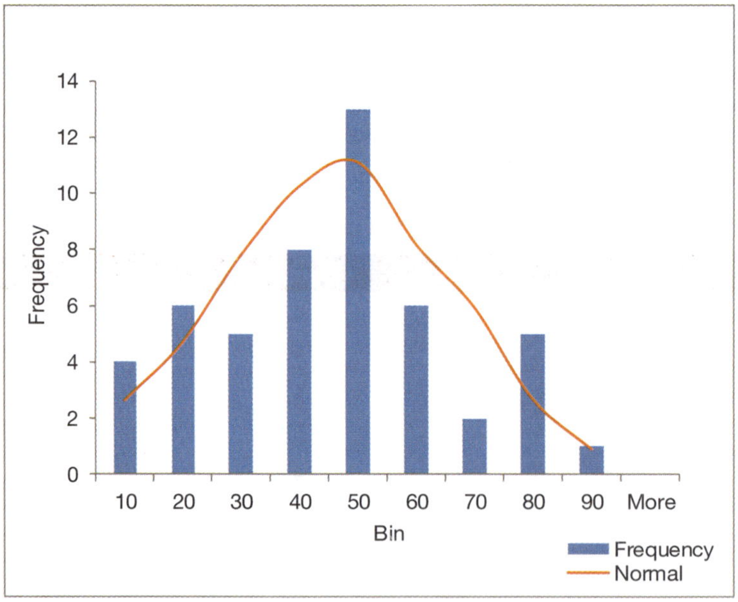

FIGURE 7.3 Histogram for Table 7.6.

It is interesting to note how the basic data can be used to fit a distribution to check the nature of demand and its distribution. It is important that these steps are clearly understood when a statement is made that states that demand follows normal distribution, what it actually means and how such statements are made based on the steps shown here. In other words, such efforts have to be made to establish the nature of demand when inventory policies are formulated. With available database on demand and ERP in place in many organizations, this should not be a problem.

In Figure 7.3, the normal curve is for assuming a mean of 40.24 and a standard deviation of 20.3546, which are computed from the data given in Table 7.5. Using statistical tests like χ^2 goodness of fit or Shapiro's test, we can check if the data fits into a normal distribution. These steps help us determine if the lead time demand data conforms to a normal distribution. Similar steps can be attempted for other distributions too.

We will discuss the determination of safety stock when faced with demand uncertainty assuming that the demand follows a normal distribution with its parameters, mean and standard deviation. Usually, the demand details are assumed to be known for a period, say weekly or monthly, which can then be extended to multiple periods of lead time, such as 3 weeks or 3 months.

Assume that the demand per period during the lead time, say, weekly demand, follows a normal distribution with the following parameters:

d = Average demand per period, say a week
s_d = Standard deviation of the demand per period, say a week

Usually, in practice, the standard deviation of demand and forecast error are interchangeably used although they are not necessarily the same. Lead time is the gap between when an order is placed and when it is received. We will denote this by *LT*. This may be some number of periods, like 3 weeks or 3 months.

If the lead time is *LT* and the demand is normally distributed with a mean of d and standard deviation of s_d in each period, then we can determine the mean and the standard deviation of the total lead time *LT* as follows:

Let the average demand during the *L* periods be d' and the standard deviation of the demand during this lead time *LT* periods be s'_d. It can be easily seen that

$$d' = d \times \text{LT} \tag{7.3}$$

$$s'_d = s_d \times \sqrt{\text{LT}} \tag{7.4}$$

(See Appendix 7.1 for derivation)

Demand in two periods is perfectly positively correlated if $\rho_{ij} = 1$, perfectly negatively correlated if $\rho_{ij} = -1$. Equations (7.3) and (7.4) are derived assuming that the demand in different periods is independent.

7.4 | SERVICE LEVELS AND PRODUCT AVAILABILITY MEASURES

When dealing with uncertainty in demand and supply, most of the inventory models we discuss will indicate or imply a stock-out risk (SOR) measured in probability values or stock-out penalty for such SOR. Then, analysis of trade-offs will be quite ubiquitous in all inventory issues and decisions. When we discussed the single-period problem (newsvendor problem) in the last chapter, we used the marginal analysis to provide an estimate of the SOR and it was evident that

$$\text{SOR} = \frac{\text{ML}}{\text{MP} + \text{ML}}$$

where ML is marginal loss and MP is marginal profit.

But in practice, it is often difficult to determine the cost of stock-outs (or marginal loss), which includes intangibles such as the loss of customer goodwill or the cost of potential delays to other parts of the system. It is also seen that on some occasions, customers may be willing to wait if the response time is as expected and is reasonable. The purpose of the safety stock is to cover these random fluctuations in demand or lead time. It is neither desirable nor possible to cover 100% of the variations during that period as it is not practical. Hence, an important consideration and desirability for covering such variations with safety stock is regarding the desired SOR or the customer service level. When the stock-out costs are not available, a common surrogate is the customer service level, which generally refers to the probability that a demand or a collection of demands is met.

Depending on the market environment and the competition, a firm may choose to keep stock-outs as small as possible to avoid losing its customers to its competitors. But this need not be the case when dealing with perishables or single-period type situations like newsvendor problems where the vendor or the firm may choose to lower the service level as the stock may not last after the season is over. So it only implies that in any case, it is important for a firm to specify the service level so that the appropriate level of safety stock can be determined and to determine the inventory investment required. A firm may decide to change the safety stock levels depending upon the demand patterns of individual items.

If adequate investments are not available, a firm could use a trade-off analysis between safety stock investment and associated service levels. Hence, a clear understanding of the concept of service levels is very important in deciding inventory policies when safety stock implications are involved. In inventory policies, service levels can be classified into two types: (1) order service level

(OSL) or cycle service level and (2) unit service level fill rate. We will explain them in detail with illustrations.

7.4.1 Order Service Level

The order service level (OSL) can be interpreted as the proportion of cycles where customer demand was satisfied. Suppose for an item, the annual demand is 12,000 and the EOQ determined is 1000. This means that there are 12,000/1000 = 12 order cycles annually where an EOQ of 1000 units is placed in each order cycle. Let us assume that we may expect some stock-outs in some specific order cycles out of the 12 cycles; however, it need not occur in all order cycles. Due to some reasons such as weather conditions like winter or monsoons seasons, terrain problems during those seasons, planned shutdowns from supply sources, etc., shortages can occur. The OSL represents the probability of not having a stock-out during the placement of an order. If there are many order cycles or orders that may exist during a year, the stock-out probability times the number of cycles provides the probability of not having stock-outs during the year. Suppose that OSL = 0.75 and the number of cycles per year is 12. Then the customer demand will be satisfied during nine (0.75 × 12 = 9) cycles on an average, whereas during the three (12 − 9 = 3 or 0.25 × 12 = 3) cycles, on average, we can expect a stock-out during the year. Hence, we also define OSOR as order stock-out risk, which is 1 − OSL, which in this case is 1 − 0.75 = 0.25.

So, Order Stock-Out Risk (OSOR) = 1 − Order Service Level (OSL)

that is,

$$\text{OSOR} = 1 - \text{OSL} \tag{7.5}$$

This will be used later in our discussions on various inventory decisions and models. Notice that the OSOR does not tell us exactly how many units were short or not filled during any cycle. It is more a macro-level measure to indicate the number of occasions or cycles where there were shortages and does not measure the intensity or the exact units that were short. We will explain this through an example later in this chapter. In many production situations, if shortages occur during any operation, the succeeding operations cannot be performed. Regardless of the quantity of items short, the remaining operations have to be curtailed during a cycle. Therefore, the impact of OSL or the OSOR is very often felt in a manufacturing environment. The other terms used for the OSL are cycle service level (CSL), in-stock probability, and Type I service level.

7.4.2 Unit Service Level

The unit service level (USL) indicates the percentage of units of demand filled during any period, whereas the unit stock-out risk (USOR) specifies the quantities of units unfilled or short during that period. The other term very often used for this is product availability. We define product availability as follows:

$$\text{Product availbility(Unit Service Level)} = 1 - \frac{\text{Expected number of units out of stock annually}}{\text{Total annual demand}} \tag{7.6}$$

Continuing from the earlier example, if the annual demand is 12,000 units and we expect shortages in three cycles out of 12 cycles as the OSL = 0.75, that is, nine cycles to have full stock and if there were 1200 units out of stock in those cycles, then from Eq. (7.6), we know that

$$\text{Product availbility(Unit Service Level)} = 1 - \frac{1200}{12{,}000} = 0.90 \text{ or } 90\%$$

The USL can provide us with exact quantities of units of customer demand that will be filled and gives an overall measure of product availability. Hence, it is a more practical and appropriate measure for many marketing applications. Suppose that USL is 0.90 as shown earlier for an item. Then 0.90 × 12,000 = 10,800 units of customer demand will be filled on average during the year. This implies that we can also expect 100 units of out of stock on an average. We assumed that 1200 units were out of stock during those three cycles. Although the stock-outs have occurred in these cycles, this implies that on an average 100 units have been out of stock in the year in those 12 cycles (1200/12 = 100). This averaging for the entire year will help us derive an expression for arriving at a formula for the calculation of unit service. We will explain later in this chapter. The other terms used for USL are fill rate, Type II service level. We can also use the term unit stock-out risk (USOR) as 1 –USL, which in this case will be $1 - 0.90 = 0.10$. So

$$USOR = 1 - USL \tag{7.7}$$

It is of interest to ask a question if both these measures are required to spell out inventory policies. An example is given here to provide some insight. Assume that in a department of an organization there are two employees, and the HR department finds that the first employee was absent on three occasions and the second employee was absent on eight occasions. The question here to ask is if the HR will be serious about the second employee who is absent on more occasions and lenient with the first employee who is absent on only three occasions. The better answers would be to ask for more details about the number of days they were absent and not just the occasions. If we know that the first employee who was absent for three occasions had a record of absenting for 10 days, 20 days, and 30 days, respectively, on these three occasions and the second employee who was absent on eight occasions was taking a casual leave of 1 day each for these eight occasions, then the HR department will have more details to study the absenteeism behavior. Here, the absenting occasions are just occasions like number of orders where there were stock-outs and the number of days of being absent is like the USL where the intensity is measured. We will revisit the example shown in Table 7.4 for explaining these two concepts.

These two service levels—order service level (or cycle service level) and unit service level—are two fundamental concepts that are key building blocks to understanding inventory policies and the examples shown here will make them very clear.

EXAMPLE 7.2

For the sample data given in Table 7.5, we will look at an Order Up To policy of keeping 45 units at the beginning of every order cycle. Here each period, that is, cycle is assumed to be 2 weeks. The vendor starts with an inventory of 45 units and meets the demand that comes to him every period. If at the end of the cycle, 5 units are left over, then he orders another 40 units (45 – 5) so that he starts the next order cycle with 45 units again. This is often referred to as Order Up To policy (fixed period policy) where the order quantity may change depending on the items left over at the end of every cycle unlike fixed order quantity models like EOQ. We will create Table 7.7 with columns to reflect the lost sales and stock-out situations if the demand shown in Table 7.5 is maintained and the Order Up To policy of keeping 45 units is followed.

TABLE 7.7 Details of lost sales and stock-out occasions for an Order Up To policy of 45 units

A	B	C	D	E	F
Period	**Demand**	**Quantity Sold**	**Quantity Left**	**Stock-out during Period (0 = N, 1 = Y)?**	**Lost Sales (units)**
1	37	37	8	0	0
2	37	37	8	0	0
3	75	45	0	1	30
4	73	45	0	1	28
5	53	45	0	1	8
6	47	45	0	1	2
7	44	44	1	0	0
8	41	41	4	0	0
9	37	37	8	0	0
10	35	35	10	0	0
11	25	25	20	0	0
12	15	15	30	0	0

(Continued)

TABLE 7.7 (Continued)

A Period	B Demand	C Quantity Sold	D Quantity Left	E Stock-out during Period (0=N, 1=Y)?	F Lost Sales (units)
13	12	12	33	0	0
14	43	43	2	0	0
15	72	45	0	1	27
16	29	29	16	0	0
17	40	40	5	0	0
18	43	43	2	0	0
19	50	45	0	1	5
20	41	41	4	0	0
21	53	45	0	1	8
22	47	45	0	1	2
23	57	45	0	1	12
24	15	15	30	0	0
25	45	45	0	1	0
26	66	45	0	1	21
27	33	33	12	0	0
28	58	45	0	1	13
29	76	45	0	1	31
30	31	31	14	0	0
31	35	35	10	0	0
32	26	26	19	0	0
33	71	45	0	1	26
34	41	41	4	0	0
35	42	42	3	0	0
36	27	27	18	0	0
37	63	45	0	1	18
38	51	45	0	1	6
39	5	5	40	0	0
40	83	45	0	1	38
41	11	11	34	0	0
42	50	45	0	1	5
43	20	20	25	0	0
44	15	15	30	0	0
45	27	27	18	0	0
46	48	45	0	1	3
47	3	3	42	0	0
48	53	45	0	1	8
49	2	2	43	0	0
50	9	9	36	0	0
Total	**2012**			**20**	**291**

For example, in Table 7.7, if the starting inventory of Period 1 is 45 units, the demand was 37 units, then the entire 37 units would have been sold leaving behind 8 units at the end of the period. Since all the units were sold, there was no stock-out situation and hence it is indicated by a NO (with 0) in column E and lost sales with 0 units in column F. But in Period 3, the demand was 75 and with a starting inventory of 45 units at the beginning of week 3, only the inventory on hand of 45 units would have been sold and the remaining 30 units (i.e., 75 – 45 = 30) would have been lost sales leading to a stock-out situation. Hence, in column E it is indicated with a YES for stock-out denoted by 1 and with 30 units in column F for lost sales.

For this policy, it can be easily seen that column E measures the OSL and column F measures the USL. We see that the total demand is 2012 units out of which 291 units are lost sales, that is, out of stock, and 20 periods out of 50 periods have stock-out situations. This means 50 – 20 = 30 periods have had full stock without any stock-out situations. Hence, for this situation,

$$\text{Order Service Level} = 30/50 = 0.60$$
$$\text{OSOR} = 1 - 0.60 = 0.40$$
$$\text{Unit Service Level} = 1 - (291/2012) = 1 - 0.1446 = 0.8554, \text{ i.e., } 85.54\%$$

We can summarize the observations thus: if we keep a policy of 45 units as the Order Up To policy, then for this demand pattern, we can expect an OSL of 60% resulting in a USL of 85.54%. We can always analyze further in this context to determine the optimal Order Up To policy for this situation. (The source of the table and the situation is from the HBS Case Paper & More: Retail Inventory).

7.4.3 Determining Reorder Point when Demand Is Uncertain

In the previous sections, we derived the expressions as shown in Eqs. (7.3) and (7.4) for lead time demand and variability when lead times are multiple periods. Using them, we derive the expressions for the reorder level when it is assumed that the demand during the lead time follows a normal distribution.

We assume that the demand during any period, for instance, a week, follows a normal distribution with parameters (d, s_d), that is, mean and standard deviation, respectively, and the lead time is denoted as LT periods or weeks.

Then it follows that the demand during the lead time LT also follows a normal distribution with parameters d' and s'_d where $d' = d \times LT$ and $s'_d = s_d \times \sqrt{LT}$ with a given OSL as shown in Figure 7.4.

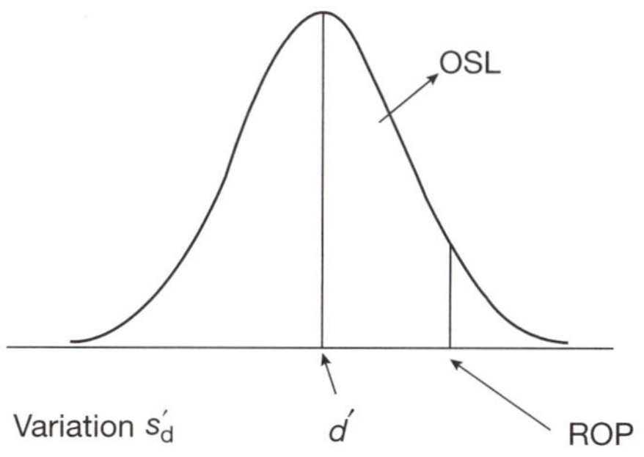

FIGURE 7.4 Reorder level assuming a normal distribution.

It is evident from Figure 7.4 that the ROP for a given OSL is

$$\text{ROP} = d' + z \times s'_d$$

This implies that

$$\text{ROP} = d \times LT + z \times s_d \times \sqrt{LT} \tag{7.8}$$

after substituting the expressions for d' and s'_d.

If we carefully examine Eq. (7.8) and compare with the expression for ROP when demand was constant (see the previous Chapter 6 in Equation 6.8), there is an additional component here with the expression $z \times s_d \times \sqrt{LT}$, which is added to account for demand variability during the lead time. Hence, it is evident that this is the extra inventory to be kept in order to handle demand fluctuations in addition to the average stock during the lead time. It can, therefore, be interpreted that this expression $z \times s_d \times \sqrt{LT}$ refers to the safety stock we have to maintain to address demand fluctuations. Hence, we have

$$\text{Safety Stock (SS)} = z \times s_d \times \sqrt{LT} \tag{7.9}$$

This simplifies Eq. (7.8) for ROP as

$$\text{ROP} = d \times \text{LT} + \text{Safety Stock (SS)} \tag{7.10}$$

ACTIVITY 7.1

It will be interesting to take a few demand datasets from your database and experiment with fitting various types of distributions of the demand and use them to determine safety stocks and reorder levels.

EXAMPLE 7.3

Consider the following details of an item:
Monthly demand, $d = 11{,}000$ units
Standard deviation of demand, $s_d = 3500$ units
Unit cost of the item, $C = \$0.15$
Lead time, $LT = 1.5$ months
Acquisition cost for processing an order, $S = \$20$
In-stock probability, $P = 0.75$, assuming a normal distribution for the demand during the lead time
Inventory carrying cost percentage, $h = 25\%$
Determine the EOQ, safety stock, and the reorder point for this item.
With the data given, we can determine the EOQ as

$$Q^* = \sqrt{\frac{2DS}{hC}}$$

Since the data given is monthly, we can determine Q^* as

$$Q^* = \sqrt{\frac{2 \times d \times S}{\left(\frac{h}{12}\right) \times C}}$$

where d is the monthly demand and so h has to be expressed on a monthly basis.

$$Q^* = \sqrt{\frac{2 \times 11{,}000 \times 20}{\frac{0.25}{12} \times 0.15}} = 11{,}866$$

Now, it is given that the lead time $LT = 1.5$ months. Hence, using Eqs. (7.3) and (7.4),

$$d' = d \times LT = 11{,}000 \times 1.5 = 16{,}500$$

$$s_d' = s_d \times \sqrt{LT} = 3500 \times \sqrt{1.5} = 4287$$

Given that $P = 0.75$, gives $z = 0.67$ from the standard normal table (We can also get this using the formula NORMINV(0.75,0,1) in any cell on an Excel sheet). Hence, safety stock using Eq. (7.9) is

$$\text{SS} = z \times s_d \times \sqrt{LT} = 0.67 \times 3500 \times \sqrt{1.5} = 0.67 \times 4287 = 2872$$

So, the reorder point for this item using Eq. (7.10) will be

$$\text{ROP} = d \times LT + \text{Safety Stock (SS)} = 11{,}000 \times 1.5 + 2872 = 16{,}500 + 2872 = 19{,}372 \text{ units}$$

Therefore, when the effective inventory level drops to 19,372 units, a reorder for 11,866 units will be placed. In practice, it is quite possible that the ROP will exceed the reorder quantity especially when lead times are long and demand is high. Hence, to make the policy work, very often the decision is made on the effective inventory level. So, when ROP > Q^*, the result of this decision will be that a second order will be placed before the first arrives.

7.5 | AVERAGE INVENTORY LEVEL

The average inventory level (AIL) is the sum of the cycle stock or the regular average stock that is carried and the safety stock that is determined. This will be the average inventory that will be carried throughout at any point in time, and the carrying cost of inventory will be calculated for this AIL.

Average inventory level (AIL) = Average regular stock (cycle stock) + Safety stock

That is,

$$\text{AIL} = \frac{Q}{2} + z \times s_d' = \frac{Q}{2} + z \times s_d \times \sqrt{LT} \tag{7.11}$$

For our example,

$$\text{AIL} = \frac{11{,}866}{2} + 2872 = 5933 + 2872 = 8805$$

So the inventory carrying cost of this AIL will be AIL × $C \times h$ = 8805 × 0.15 × 0.25 = \$330.19.

7.6 | ESTIMATION OF UNIT SERVICE LEVEL OR FILL RATE

We discussed earlier about two types of service levels: OSL and USL. While the OSL is assumed or given in a situation, the next step would be to estimate the USL. Recalling Eq. (7.6) defining USL, we know that

$$\text{Unit Service Level} = 1 - \frac{\text{Expected number of units out of stock annually}}{\text{Total annual demand}}$$

If we can estimate the expected number of units out of stock annually in the preceding expression, it is possible to derive an expression for the USL. So the motivation is to ask

"If we are given that the demand during the lead time follows a normal distribution with its parameters, as well as provided the order service level (i.e., in-stock probability), is it possible to estimate the unit service level?"

Recall our example in the beginning of Section 7.4.1 while explaining the concept of USL that if the USL is 0.90 for an item, then 0.90 × 12,000 = 10,800 units of customer demand will be filled on an average during the year given the annual demand of 12,000 units. We assumed that 1200 units were out of stock during those three cycles as the OSL was assumed to be 0.75. This implies that we can also expect 100 units out of stock on an average, although stock-outs have occurred in these three cycles only (1200/12 = 100). This averaging for the entire year will help us derive an expression for arriving at a formula for the calculation of USL.

Expected number of units out of stock annually can be averaged out for each cycle and can be expressed as (Expected number of units out of stock in each replenishment or order cycle) × (number of replenishment cycles). Recall that 1200 units out of stock can be averaged as 100 units out of stock in each order cycle × 12 cycles. That is,

$$\text{Expected number of unit out of stock annually} = \begin{pmatrix}\text{Expected number of units out of} \\ \text{stock in an order cycle}\end{pmatrix} \times (\text{Number of order cycles in a year}) \tag{7.12}$$

The basic inventory policy of an item consists of its ordering policy, reorder policy, safety inventory level, and the average inventory level. The example here is shown to make this point clear. The inventory level that should be carried throughout the year for an item can be arrived at based on these details.

But we know that the number of order cycles in a year is (D/Q). Hence, the only part that is to be estimated is the part about the expected number of units out of stock in an order cycle. So how do we estimate the expected number of units out of stock in an order cycle?

7.6.1 Estimation of Number of Units out of Stock or Shortages in an Order Cycle

Given that ROP $= d \times LT +$ Safety Stock (SS), the expected shortage or units out of stock in an order cycle can be evaluated as

$$\int_{x=\text{ROP}}^{\infty} (x - \text{ROP}) f(x) dx \tag{7.13}$$

For demand less than the reorder point, the stock-out quantity is zero. However, for demand greater than the reorder point, the stock-out quantity is the demand minus the reorder point. This is often referred to as the unit normal loss (UNL) function where $f(x)$ is a normal probability distribution function. An alternative computational formula for UNL is the following:

$$\text{Unit normal loss}(z) = E_{(z)} = f(z) - z(1 - F(z)) \tag{7.14}$$

where $f(.)$ and $F(.)$ are the probability distribution function and cumulative distribution function for standard normal distribution, respectively. Hence, $E_{(z)}$ can tabulated for given values of z and such a table is available as a UNL table like the standard normal table. (Both the standard normal and unit normal loss tables are given in Appendix 7.2).

Just as s_d' is used to calculate the safety stock by multiplying with the appropriate z value for the OSL, in a similar way, s_d' can be used to calculate the expected shortages in a cycle by multiplying it with $E_{(z)}$. See Figure 7.5. So $E_{(z)}s_d'$, in fact, gives the expected number of units out of stock in an order cycle.

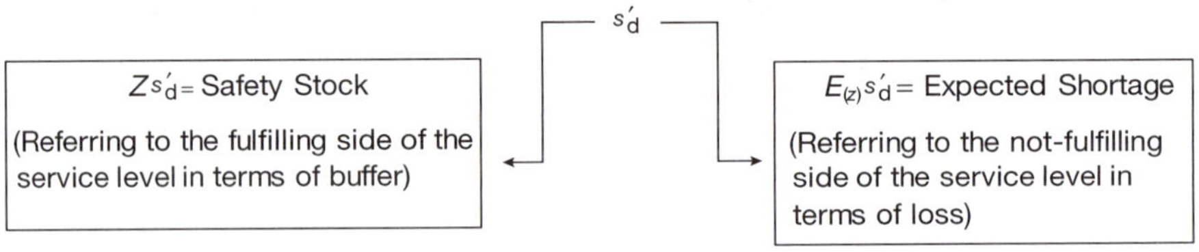

FIGURE 7.5 Explanation of z and $E_{(z)}$.

So substituting this in Eq. (7.12), we get

$$\text{Expected number of units out of stock annually} = E(z)s_d' \times \left(\frac{D}{Q}\right) \tag{7.15}$$

Now, substituting Eq. (7.15) in Eq. (7.6), we get

$$\text{Unit service level} = \text{USL} = 1 - \frac{(E(z)s_d')\left(\frac{D}{Q}\right)}{D}$$

which gets simplified as

$$\text{USL} = 1 - \frac{E(z)s_d'}{Q} \tag{7.16}$$

Equation (7.16) gives a crisp expression for calculating the USL. In other words,

$$\text{USL} = 1 - \frac{\text{Expected number of units out of stock or shortage in an order cycle}}{\text{EOQ}}$$

For our example, it was given that the in-stock probability or the OSL was 0.75 for which the z value from the normal table is 0.67. Referring to the Unit Loss Normal Table given in Appendix 7.2, we see that the value of $E_{(z)}$ is 0.15. Hence,

$$\text{USL} = 1 - \frac{E(z)s_d'}{Q} = 1 - \frac{0.15 \times 4287}{11{,}866} = 1 - 0.0542 = 0.9458, \text{ that is, } 94.58\%$$

Therefore, the USL or the fill rate is 94.58%, which means that 94.58% of the annual demand is filled while the OSL is 0.75. It also means that

Unit stock-out risk (USOR) = 0.0542, that is, 5.42%

Equation (7.16) gives an insight about how the fill rate can be improved by looking at three inputs: Q, $E_{(z)}$, and s_d'. The s_d' can be reduced by supply chain coordination efforts in terms of lag-time reduction and proper information on demand during the lead time, which can reduce the USOR considerably. Similarly, $E_{(z)}$ can be reduced by increasing the z value, which in turn means increasing the OSL values. If more cycles have no shortages, that is, the OSL is higher, the chances that the units out of stock in these cycles may be lower, which in turns makes the USOR lower. Also, increasing Q will reduce the USOR. All these efforts to reduce the USOR can make the USL higher.

The total relevant cost for an item with all these details can be calculated as follows:

Unit service level is a key performance parameter of any inventory policy of an item, which indicates the actual fill rate of an item. It is a micro-level indicator of how at the unit level, the demand of an item is fulfilled. This is often a key indicator in organizations where marketing strategies are formulated and promotions are planned. This also gives the trade-off between how much risk an organization wants to have and what service they want to provide.

Total Cost = Ordering Cost + Inventory Carrying Cost (Cycle Stock) + Inventory Carrying Cost (Safety Stock) + Stock-Out Cost + Material Cost

$$\text{TC} = \frac{D}{Q}S + \frac{Q}{2}Ch + \left(zs_d'\right)Ch + \frac{D}{Q}E_{(z)}s_d'\pi + DC \tag{7.17}$$

using the notation used earlier for various components.

For our example, the total cost will be

$$\text{TC} = \frac{11{,}000 \times 12}{11{,}866} \times 20 + \frac{11{,}866}{2} \times 0.15 \times 0.25 + 2872 \times 0.15 \times 0.25 + \frac{11{,}000 \times 12}{11{,}866} \times 0.15 \times 4287 \times 0.05 + 11{,}000 \times 12 \times 0.15$$

assuming the stock-out cost $\pi = \$0.05$

$$= 222.5 + 222.5 + 107.7 + 357.7 + 19{,}800 = \$20{,}716.4$$

It is quite useful to use Eqs. (7.6) to (7.16) to seek answers to various what-if questions in this section. We will illustrate this with a series of examples in the following sections.

7.6.2 What-If Scenarios in Inventory Decisions

EXAMPLE 7.4

Suppose for an item, the weekly demand is $d = 3000$ units and the standard deviation of the weekly demand is $s_d = 600$ units. Assume the lead time LT is given as 2 weeks. If an order of 9000 units is placed when there are 7000 units in the inventory, what will be the safety stock for this item and how much OSL is maintained for this situation? What will the USL be for this item?

Here, the weekly demand $d = 3000$, $s_d = 600$, and the lead time $LT = 2$ weeks.
Therefore, $d' = d \times LT = 3000 \times 2 = 6000$

$$s_d' = s_d \times \sqrt{\text{LT}} = 600 \times \sqrt{2} = 849$$

It is given that the ROP is 7000, so when the inventory level reaches 7000, an order of $Q = 9000$ is placed.

We know that ROP = d' + Safety stock
So 7000 = 6000 + Safety stock, and hence safety stock = 7000 − 6000 = 1000.

We know that safety stock = 1000 = $z \times s_d'$ and $s_d' = 849$.

This gives $z = 1000/849 = 1.18$. From the normal table, it is seen that the area, that is, OSL $\approx$ 88%. If $z = 1.18$, then from the normal loss table, it can be seen that $E_{(z)} = 0.058$.

$$\text{Hence USL} = 1 - \frac{E(z)s_{\text{d}}'}{Q} = 1 - \frac{0.058 \times 849}{9000} = 1 - 0.005 = 0.995, \text{ that is, } 99.5\%$$

7.6.3 Using Excel for Computing OSL, *z* Value, and USL for Various Combinations

We can use Excel for calculating OSL, *z* values, and $E_{(z)}$ values as shown in the following Excel sheet where the value of OSL is entered in Cell D4 and the subsequent *z* value and the $E_{(z)}$ values are computed in Cells D6 and D8, as shown in Figure 7.6 and Figure 7.7, respectively.

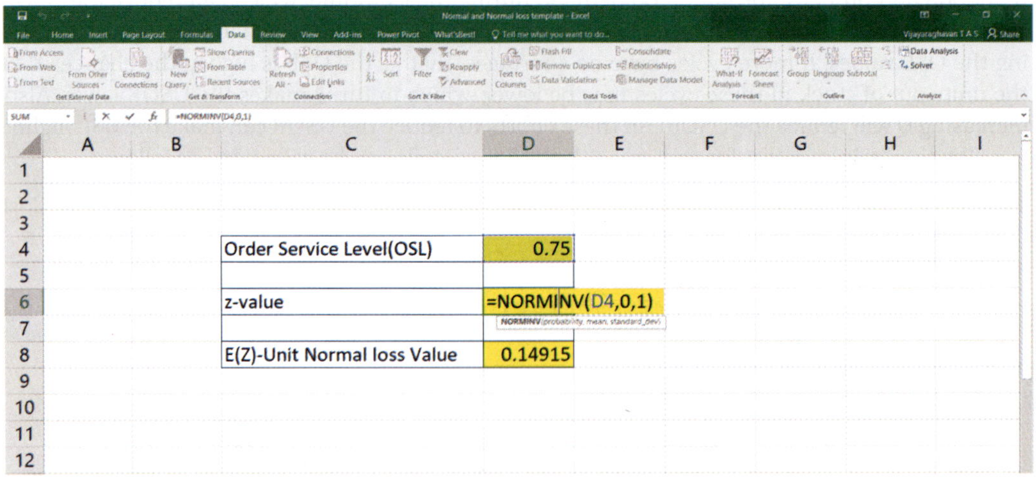

FIGURE 7.6 The *z* value for OSL shown in Cell D6.

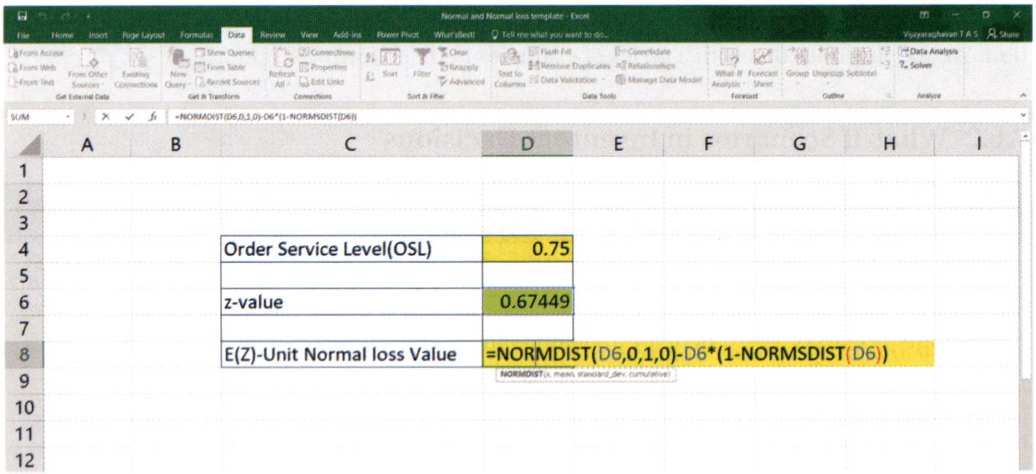

FIGURE 7.7 $E_{(z)}$ value for the *z* value is shown in Cell D8.

Note that we can use the formula in Eq. (7.14) to calculate $E_{(z)}$ in Excel, that is,

$E_{(z)}$ = NORMDIST(*z*,0,1,0) – z*(1 – NORMSDIST(*z*)) in an Excel sheet for a given value of *z*, as shown in Figure 7.7.

This can be used in various ways to answer a few questions in this context. For example, we saw that the USL is 99.5% for a given set of conditions. If we feel that this USL is on the higher side and we wish to maintain, say, 97.5% USL, and that is satisfactory for a given situation, then a few results for safety stock for this change in policy and trade-offs will be of interest to us.

This would mean that USOR $= \frac{E(z)s'_d}{Q} = 0.025$ (as USL = 0.975 means USOR = 1 − 0.975 = 0.025).

So $\frac{E(z)\times 849}{9000} = 0.025$, which implies $E_{(z)} = \frac{9000\times 0.025}{849} = 0.265$.

We will use the Excel sheet shown in Figure 7.7 and use the Goal Seek option under Data menu in Excel for a given $E_{(z)}$ value of 0.265 to calculate the OSL and the z value. This is shown in Figure 7.8.

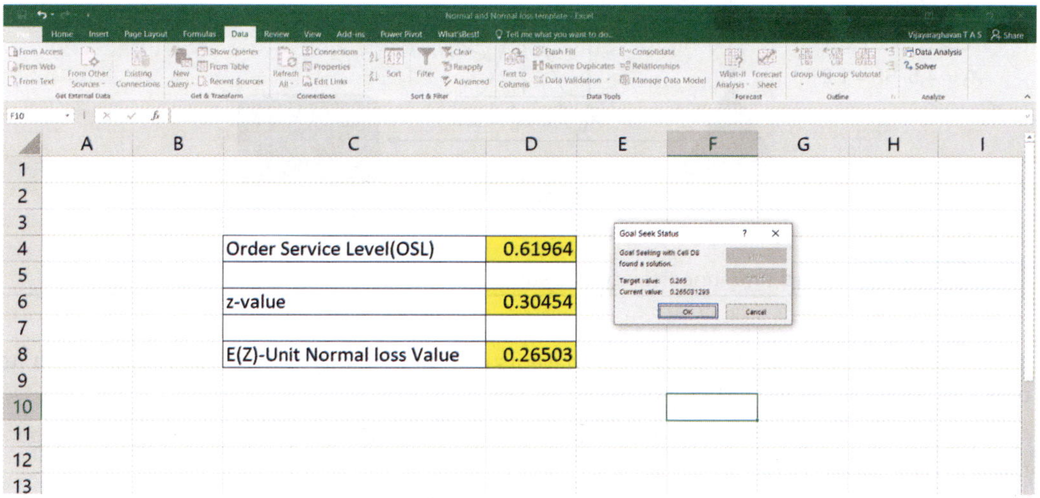

FIGURE 7.8 Goal Seek for a given $E_{(z)}$ value.

So it is seen that the z value is 0.30.

Hence Safety stock $= z \times s'_d = 0.30 \times 849 = 255$ units.

We notice that when the USL was 99.5%, the safety stock was 1000 units, while when the USL is reduced to 97.5%, the safety stock is also reduced to 255. For increasing the USL by about 2%, an additional safety stock of 1000 − 255 = 745 units is required. This is the trade-off between service and the cost of carrying such safety inventory.

It is quite possible that we will be able to generate many such scenarios looking at various options and considerations using an Excel sheet and the Goal Seek option.

7.7 IMPACT OF LEAD TIME UNCERTAINTY ON INVENTORY DECISIONS

So far we have seen how demand uncertainty is of importance during the lead time and how safety inventory is impacted by such demand uncertainty. We have all the way assumed that the lead time itself is constant and that only the demand in that lead time is uncertain. That is, if the lead time is 3 weeks and the demand is uncertain in that lead time, we only assumed that the demand is, say, normally distributed in that lead time, but the lead time per se is assumed to be constant. However, in practice, we see that even the lead time is not constant and has tremendous variations. This is shown in Figure 7.9.

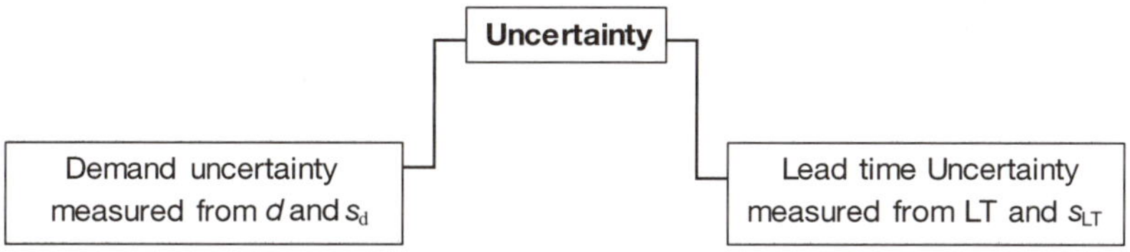

FIGURE 7.9 Demand and lead time uncertainty.

A sample scenario is shown in Figure 7.10.

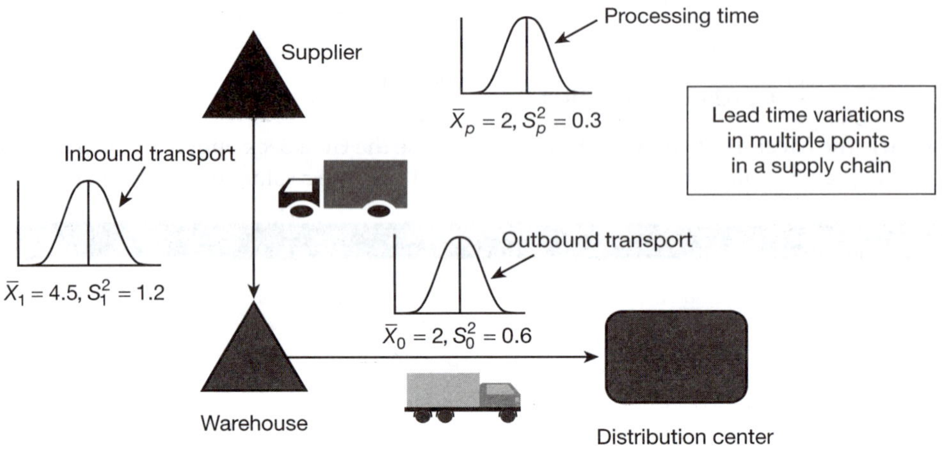

FIGURE 7.10 Lead time uncertainty in a supply channel.

It is possible that the lead time itself can have its own uncertainty with its distribution with its mean lead time as LT and a standard deviation of s_{LT}.

Under such conditions when the demand and the lead time are both uncertain, then s_d' gets modified as follows:

$$s_d' = \sqrt{LT \times s_d^2 + d^2 s_{LT}^2} \tag{7.18}$$

Hence, the safety inventory will be adjusted upward accordingly as

$$\text{Safety stock} = z \times s_d', \qquad \text{where } s_d' \text{ is as given in Eq. (7.18).}$$

EXAMPLE 7.5

Let us consider the following details:

Average demand per week, $d = 3000$
Standard deviation of demand, $s_d = 600$
Average lead time for replenishment, $LT = 2$ weeks
Standard deviation of the lead time, $s_{LT} = 0.5$ weeks

Then

$$s_d' = \sqrt{LT \times s_d^2 + d^2 s_{LT}^2} = \sqrt{2 \times 600^2 + 3000^2 \times 0.5^2} = \sqrt{720{,}000 + 2{,}250{,}000}$$
$$= \sqrt{2{,}970{,}000} = 1723$$

Recall that it was 849 when the lead time LT was not uncertain but increased to 1723 when the lead time was uncertain. So this will also impact the safety stock accordingly where both uncertainties will aggravate the need for more safety inventory to manage these uncertainties.

It is clear how more uncertainties cause deeper fluctuations that increase the safety stock levels. We see here that uncertainties due to demand and lead time aggravate the variations and thus increase the safety stock levels. It is to be observed how supply chain coordination and information sharing among partners can help reduce these uncertainties and bring about reduction in the inventory levels in the supply chain.

When we analyzed the service level in the previous sections, very often we arrived at the USL without explicitly considering the stock-out costs. This means that while determining such levels, we have assumed an implicit or imputed cost of stock-outs with the given carting costs. Can we estimate the imputed stock-out costs in such cases? We will look at such costs in both the possible scenarios of stock-out: backorder and lost sales.

7.8 | BACKORDER CASE

It is noted that increasing the safety stock level by one more unit has the same effect of increasing the ROP by an additional unit. Putting it the other way round, adding one unit in ROP is the same as adding one unit to the safety stock.

In the backorder case, the cost of increasing the ROP by one more unit will be $H(Q/D)$. (The annual cost H is proportionally charged for the cycle time Q/D for a unit.) However, if we do not add an additional unit, the backorder penalty cost of π is charged with the stock-out probability in a cycle, which is OSOR.

Therefore, the marginal cost of adding a unit in ROP = The marginal cost of not adding a unit to ROP. So

$$H(Q/D) = \pi \times \text{OSOR}$$

This gives us

$$\text{OSOR} = \frac{HQ}{\pi D} \text{ or } \pi = \frac{HQ}{\text{OSOR} \times D} \tag{7.19}$$

We will illustrate their use in determining the imputed cost of π with the following example.

Assume that $D = 15{,}000$, $S = 1000$, $H = hC = 30$, and also assume that $d' = 300$ and $s'_{\text{d}} = 50$. Let the OSL be 0.70. Then,

$$Q = \sqrt{\frac{2 \times 15000 \times 1000}{30}} = 1000$$

Therefore, $D/Q = 15{,}000/1000 = 15$ cycles. If OSL is 0.70, then OSOR = 1 − 0.70 = 0.30 and the z value of OSL is 0.52.

We can determine ROP $= d' + z\, s'_{\text{d}} = 300 + 0.52 \times 50 = 326$ and Safety Stock = 26.

$$\text{USL} = 1 - ((0.19 \times 50)/1000) = 0.9905$$

Hence USOR = 1 − 0.9905 = 0.0095.

Suppose USL = 0.99, which implies that USOR = 0.01.

$E_{(z)} = (Q \times \text{USOR})/s'_{\text{d}} = (1000 \times 0.01)/50 = 0.20$, then z value will be 0.49.

Therefore, Safety Stock = 0.49 × 50 = 25, OSL = 0.689, and OSOR = 1 − 0.689 = 0.311.

We saw that from Eq. (7.19),

$$\pi = \frac{HQ}{\text{OSOR} \times D}$$

So

$$\pi = \frac{30 \times 1000}{0.311 \times 15{,}000} = 6.43$$

If the stock-out cost is on the lower side, then we can arrive at the resulting USL by assuming a relevant cost. Let us say we fix $\pi = 10$. Then using again Eq. (7.19), we have

$$\text{OSOR} = \frac{HQ}{\pi D} = \frac{30 \times 1000}{10 \times 15000} = 0.20$$

This would mean OSL = 1 − 0.20 = 0.80 and $E_{(z)} = 0.11$ and, therefore,

USL = 1 − (0.11 × 50)/1000 = 1 − 0.0055 = 0.9945 and safety Stock = 0.84 × 50 = 42.

7.9 | LOST SALES CASE

In the case of lost sales, the stock-out cost π' will include the opportunity loss of revenue besides customer dissatisfaction. The marginal analysis also yields slightly different results because of the impact of lost sales on inventory levels. Here, adding one unit to ROP will cost $H(Q/D)$ minus OSOR × $H(Q/D)$, which is the carrying cost of the unused inventory when one unit of safety stock is being carried. And if we do not add the unit, the penalty in the event of stock-out includes π'. We will understand this through a small illustration.

Suppose that $D = 50$ and $Q = 25$. If a stock-out occurs in the first cycle, it means that 26 units have been demanded while only 25 units have been supplied. Hence, when we start the next cycle, we will have the full $Q = 25$ on hand. (Recall that in the case of a backorder, the backorder would use this one unit and would make the starting inventory come down by one unit). With $D = 50$, only 24 units are to be satisfied in the second cycle. This would make us carry one more unit additionally in the second cycle.

The marginal cost of adding one additional unit to the ROP = marginal cost of not adding (or expected savings).

$$H(Q/D) - \text{OSOR} \times H(Q/D) = \text{OSOR} \times \pi'$$

$$H(Q/D) = \text{OSOR} \times (\pi' + H(Q/D))$$

$$\text{OSOR} = \frac{H\left(Q/D\right)}{\pi' + H\left(Q/D\right)}$$

or

$$\text{OSOR} = \frac{HQ}{\pi' D + HQ} \tag{7.20}$$

Continuing with the earlier situation of assuming lost sale penalty of 10, we have

$$\text{OSOR} = \frac{30 \times 1000}{10 \times 15{,}000 + 30 \times 1000} = 0.167$$

This means OSL = 1 − 0.167 = 0.833. The z value is 0.966, and the safety stock will be 0.966 × 50 = 48.

$$\text{USL} = 1 - [(0.089 \times 50)/1000] = 1 - 0.0445 = 0.9955$$

When stock-out situations are faced, it is important to see if we are dealing with a backorder case or a lost sales case. When stock-out costs are not known explicitly, it is interesting to analyze the imputed cost of the same for evaluating various inventory policies under both these situations and use them. Examples are shown here to explain various scenarios when service levels are known or unknown.

We see that while the USL is approximately the same, the safety stock in the case of lost sales is more than the backorder case.

From the preceding discussion, it is clear that we will be able to determine various unknowns of which a few are known with respect to service level and stock-out costs. We will explore the possible two cases of this with the following common facts:

$D = 15{,}000$
$H = 30$
$Q = 1000$
$d' = 200$
$s'_d = 50$

Case 1: Stock-out cost known and service levels (both OSL and USL) unknown

Suppose the backorder cost is given as 8.
Using Eq. (7.19),

$$\text{OSOR} = \frac{HQ}{\pi D} = \frac{30 \times 1000}{8 \times 15{,}000} = 0.25$$

So OSL = 1 − 0.25 = 0.75. This gives z as 0.67.
So Safety stock = 0.67 × 50 = 34 and ROP = 200 + 34 = 234.
When $z = 0.67$, $E_{(z)} = 0.15$.
Therefore, USL = 1 − [(0.15 × 50)/1000] = 1 − 0.0075 = 0.9925.
USL = 0.9925

Case 2: Stock-out cost unknown and service levels (both OSL and USL) Known

Let us assume that OSL = 0.70.
This means that OSOR = 1 − 0.70 = 0.30.
The z value is 0.52 and the $E_{(z)}$ value is 0.19.
So the safety stock is 0.52 × 50 = 26 and ROP = 200 + 26 = 226.

So $$\pi = \frac{HQ}{\text{OSOR} \times D} = \frac{30 \times 1000}{0.30 \times 15{,}000} = 6.67$$

$\pi - 6.67$ in the case of a backorder.
In the lost sales case,

$$\text{OSOR} = \frac{HQ}{\pi' D + HQ}$$

$$0.30 = \frac{30 \times 1000}{\pi' \times 15{,}000 + 30 \times 1000}$$

So $\pi' = 4.67$ in the case of lost sales.

(Note here that we can also obtain the USL for this given OSL, which was shown in earlier examples.)

Suppose if we specify USL = 0.975,

$$\text{USOR} = 1 - 0.975 = 0.0125$$

$$E_{(z)} = (\text{Q} \times \text{USOR})/s'_{\text{d}} = [(1000 \times 0.0125)/50] = 0.25$$

Then $z = 0.35$ and OSL = 0.635 and OSOR = 0.365.

$$\pi = \frac{HQ}{\text{OSOR} \times D} = \frac{30 \times 1000}{0.365 \times 15{,}000} = 5.48$$

$\pi = 5.48$ in the case of a backorder.

In the lost sales case,

$$\text{OSOR} = \frac{HQ}{\pi' D + HQ}$$

$$0.365 = \frac{30 \times 1000}{\pi' \times 15{,}000 + 30 \times 1000}$$

So $\pi' = 3.48$ in the lost sales case.

Also Safety stock = 0.35 × 50 = 18 and ROP = 200 + 18 = 218.

In the preceding examples, if Q was 500 instead of 1000, we would have probably needed more safety stock. If Q was substituted in the expressions for OSOR, we would have different ROPs. This shows that the relationship between Q and ROP can be visualized. We will present the details for a given USL= 0.99.

Q	Safety Stock	ROP	Number of Cycles (D/Q)	Average Inventory
500	45	245	30	250
1000	25	225	15	500

In the following section, we will examine the case of jointly determining the Q and ROP when the stock-out cost π is not explicitly given.

Recall the EOQ expression we derived when the stock-out cost π is given and is given by

$$Q^* = \sqrt{\frac{2D[S + g\pi]}{H}}$$

where D is the annual demand, S is the ordering cost, H is the carrying cost (i.e., $h \times C$), g is the shortage (units stock-out), and π is the shortage cost (stock-out cost per unit).

Here $g = E_{(z)} \times s'_{\text{d}}$. So this becomes

$$Q^* = \sqrt{\frac{2D\left[S + \pi E_{(z)} s'_{\text{d}}\right]}{H}}$$

We will use this along with the following expressions we derived earlier for jointly determining Q and ROP.

$$E_{(z)} = (Q \times \text{USOR})/s'_{\text{d}}$$
$$\text{OSOR} = \frac{HQ}{\pi D} \quad \text{or} \quad \pi = \frac{HQ}{\text{OSOR} \times D}$$

and

$$\text{ROP} = d' + z \times s'_{\text{d}}$$

We will continue with the same example and consider the case for USL = 0.95.

Step 1
Calculate Q ignoring stock-outs.

$$Q = \sqrt{\frac{2 \times 15{,}000 \times 1000}{30}} = 1000$$

Step 2
Calculate $E_{(z)}$ for $Q = 1000$.

$$E_{(z)} = (Q \times \text{USOR})/s'_{\text{d}} = (1000 \times 0.01)/50 = 0.20$$

Step 3
This gives the corresponding z as 0.49 and OSL as 0.69.
Therefore, OSOR = 1 − 0.69 = 0.31.

Step 4
Calculate π using $\pi = \dfrac{HQ}{\text{OSOR} \times D}$

So $\pi = \dfrac{30 \times 1000}{0.31 \times 15{,}000} = 6.45$

Substitute this in the expression for Q.
Now

$$Q^{*} = \sqrt{\frac{2D\left[S + \pi E_{(z)} s'_{\text{d}}\right]}{H}} = \sqrt{\frac{2 \times 15{,}000 \times [1000 + 6.45 \times 0.2 \times 50]}{30}}$$

$Q^{*} = 1032$

Step 5
Now calculate $E_{(z)}$ for $Q = 1032$.

$$E_{(z)} = (Q \times \text{USOR})/s'_{\text{d}} = (1032 \times 0.01)/50 = 0.206$$

Step 6
This gives the corresponding z as 0.47 and OSL as 0.68.
Therefore, OSOR = 1 − 0.68 = 0.32.
Repeat Steps 4 and 5 until two successive values of Q (or Z) are the same.
After a few iterations, we will reach a value of Q as 1032 as the stabilized value for Q.
We can calculate similarly for USL = 0.95. We will reach $Q = 1066$ in this case.

ACTIVITY 7.2

It is worth developing an Excel-based template for trying various scenarios with key inputs that are required as shown in various examples and generate a sensitivity analysis for arriving at a proper policy for these situations.

SUMMARY

In this chapter, we discussed how the uncertainties in demand and lead times affect inventory decisions in terms of reorder and safety stock policies. Very often, an organization has a huge information on its demand and lead times. This basic data can be very useful to derive the nature of demand during the lead time and can be an important input in formulating inventory policies. The discussion about how to carry out an analysis to fit a distribution to a basic set of data of lead time demand is provided with a sample database. Derivations of reorder levels and safety inventory equations were shown in both cases when the demand distribution is discrete and continuous. How they are applied is shown with some practical examples. Service levels are an integral part of any inventory decision, and in this chapter, service level concepts are introduced with an example to illustrate the difference between order (or cycle) service level and unit service level. Expressions are also derived to estimate them when key inputs are known of an item. When uncertainties about demand and lead time uncertainties are faced, how the safety stock gets increased is shown with an example. It is also interesting to analyze the inventory situations when stock-out costs are not explicitly known, and how to explore their imputed cost is shown with many scenarios of service levels.

Case Study

It is suggested to take up the following cases for discussions that are described in this chapter:

1. **Paper and More (A)** by Noel Watson 9-606-023 Rev: January 7, 2009 of the Harvard Business Publishing of Harvard Business School for explaining the concepts of Service Levels (both Order Service Level and Unit Service Level and use of Newsvendor Model for determining inventory policies (https://hbsp.harvard.edu/product/606023-PDF-ENG).
2. **Scientific Glass Incorporated: Inventory Management (Brief Case)** by Steven C. Wheelwright, William Schmidt, 4208 Rev: January 7, 2009 of the Harvard Business Publishing of Harvard Business School No. 4208 for explaining the concept of reorder levels, safety stocks, average inventory levels and evaluating a few strategies using these concepts in an organizational context (https://hbsp.harvard.edu/product/4208-PDF-ENG).

Appendix 7.1

If the lead time is LT and the demand is normally distributed with a mean of d and standard deviation of s_d in each period, then we can determine the mean and the standard deviation of the total lead time LT as follows:

Let the average demand during the L periods be d' and the standard deviation of the demand during this lead time LT periods be s'_d. Let lead time $LT = n$.

Let the total demand in these n periods be $X = X_1 + X_2 + X_3 + \cdots + X_n$.

Then $E(X) = d' = E(X_1 + X_2 + X_3 + \cdots + X_n) = E(X_1) + E(X_2) + E(X_3) + \cdots + E(X_n)$.

That is, $d' = d + d + d + \cdots + d$ (n times) $= d \times n = d \times LT$. So

$$d' = d \times LT$$

$\text{Var}(X) = \text{Var}(X_1 + X_2 + X_3 + \cdots + X_n) = \text{Var}(X_1) + \text{Var}(X_2) + \text{Var}(X_3) + \cdots + \text{Var}(X_n)$ assuming independence of demands between periods.

That is, $s'^2_d = s^2_d + s^2_d + s^2_d + \cdots + s^2_d$ (n times) $= s^2_d \times n = s^2_d \times LT$. Therefore,

$$s'_d = s_d \times \sqrt{LT}$$

Appendix 7.2

The "z" Table

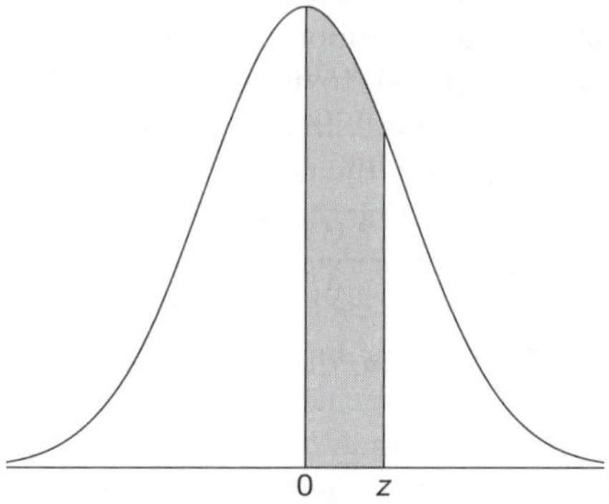

	0.00	0.01	0.02	0.03	0.04	0.05	0.06	0.07	0.08	0.09
0.0	0.0000	0.0040	0.0080	0.0120	0.0160	0.0199	0.0239	0.0279	0.0319	0.0359
0.1	0.0398	0.0438	0.0478	0.0517	0.0557	0.0596	0.0636	0.0675	0.0714	0.0753
0.2	0.0793	0.0832	0.0871	0.0910	0.0948	0.0987	0.1026	0.1064	0.1103	0.1141
0.3	0.1179	0.1217	0.1255	0.1293	0.1331	0.1368	0.1406	0.1443	0.1480	0.1517
0.4	0.1554	0.1591	0.1628	0.1664	0.1700	0.1736	0.1772	0.1808	0.1844	0.1879
0.5	0.1915	0.1950	0.1985	0.2019	0.2054	0.2088	0.2123	0.2157	0.2190	0.2224
0.6	0.2257	0.2291	0.2324	0.2357	0.2389	0.2422	0.2454	0.2486	0.2517	0.2549
0.7	0.2580	0.2611	0.2642	0.2673	0.2704	0.2734	0.2764	0.2794	0.2823	0.2852
0.8	0.2881	0.2910	0.2939	0.2967	0.2995	0.3023	0.3051	0.3078	0.3106	0.3133
0.9	0.3159	0.3186	0.3212	0.3238	0.3264	0.3289	0.3315	0.3340	0.3365	0.3389
1.0	0.3413	0.3438	0.3461	0.3485	0.3508	0.3531	0.3554	0.3577	0.3599	0.3621
1.1	0.3643	0.3665	0.3686	0.3708	0.3729	0.3749	0.3770	0.3790	0.3810	0.3830
1.2	0.3849	0.3869	0.3888	0.3907	0.3925	0.3944	0.3962	0.3980	0.3997	0.4015
1.3	0.4032	0.4049	0.4066	0.4082	0.4099	0.4115	0.4131	0.4147	0.4162	0.4177
1.4	0.4192	0.4207	0.4222	0.4236	0.4251	0.4265	0.4279	0.4292	0.4306	0.4319
1.5	0.4332	0.4345	0.4357	0.4370	0.4382	0.4394	0.4406	0.4418	0.4429	0.4441
1.6	0.4452	0.4463	0.4474	0.4484	0.4495	0.4505	0.4515	0.4525	0.4535	0.4545
1.7	0.4554	0.4564	0.4573	0.4582	0.4591	0.4599	0.4608	0.4616	0.4625	0.4633
1.8	0.4641	0.4649	0.4656	0.4664	0.4671	0.4678	0.4686	0.4693	0.4699	0.4706
1.9	0.4713	0.4719	0.4726	0.4732	0.4738	0.4744	0.4750	0.4756	0.4761	0.4767
2.0	0.4772	0.4778	0.4783	0.4788	0.4793	0.4798	0.4803	0.4808	0.4812	0.4817
2.1	0.4821	0.4826	0.4830	0.4834	0.4838	0.4842	0.4846	0.4850	0.4854	0.4857
2.2	0.4861	0.4864	0.4868	0.4871	0.4875	0.4878	0.4881	0.4884	0.4887	0.4890
2.3	0.4893	0.4896	0.4898	0.4901	0.4904	0.4906	0.4909	0.4911	0.4913	0.4916
2.4	0.4918	0.4920	0.4922	0.4925	0.4927	0.4929	0.4931	0.4932	0.4934	0.4936
2.5	0.4938	0.4940	0.4941	0.4943	0.4945	0.4946	0.4948	0.4949	0.4951	0.4952
2.6	0.4953	0.4955	0.4956	0.4957	0.4959	0.4960	0.4961	0.4962	0.4963	0.4964
2.7	0.4965	0.4966	0.4967	0.4968	0.4969	0.4970	0.4971	0.4972	0.4973	0.4974
2.8	0.4974	0.4975	0.4976	0.4977	0.4977	0.4978	0.4979	0.4979	0.4980	0.4981
2.9	0.4981	0.4982	0.4982	0.4983	0.4984	0.4984	0.4985	0.4985	0.4986	0.4986
3.0	0.4987	0.4987	0.4987	0.4988	0.4988	0.4989	0.4989	0.4989	0.4990	0.4990

The Unit Normal Loss Function Table (for a given z value)

	0.00	0.01	0.02	0.03	0.04	0.05	0.06	0.07	0.08	0.09
0.0	0.39894	0.39396	0.38902	0.38412	0.37926	0.37444	0.36966	0.36492	0.36022	0.35556
0.1	0.35094	0.34635	0.34181	0.33731	0.33285	0.32842	0.32404	0.31969	0.31539	0.31112
0.2	0.30689	0.30271	0.29856	0.29445	0.29038	0.28634	0.28235	0.27840	0.27448	0.27060
0.3	0.26676	0.26296	0.25920	0.25547	0.25178	0.24813	0.24452	0.24094	0.23740	0.23390
0.4	0.23044	0.22701	0.22362	0.22027	0.21695	0.21367	0.21042	0.20721	0.20404	0.20090
0.5	0.19780	0.19473	0.19170	0.18870	0.18573	0.18281	0.17991	0.17705	0.17422	0.17143
0.6	0.16867	0.16595	0.16325	0.16059	0.15797	0.15537	0.15281	0.15028	0.14778	0.14531
0.7	0.14288	0.14048	0.13810	0.13576	0.13345	0.13117	0.12892	0.12669	0.12450	0.12234
0.8	0.12021	0.11810	0.11603	0.11398	0.11196	0.10997	0.10801	0.10607	0.10417	0.10229
0.9	0.10043	0.09860	0.09680	0.09503	0.09328	0.09156	0.08986	0.08819	0.08654	0.08491
1.0	0.08332	0.08174	0.08019	0.07866	0.07716	0.07568	0.07422	0.07279	0.07138	0.06999
1.1	0.06862	0.06727	0.06595	0.06465	0.06336	0.06210	0.06086	0.05964	0.05844	0.05726
1.2	0.05610	0.05496	0.05384	0.05274	0.05165	0.05059	0.04954	0.04851	0.04750	0.04650
1.3	0.04553	0.04457	0.04363	0.04270	0.04179	0.04090	0.04002	0.03916	0.03831	0.03748
1.4	0.03667	0.03587	0.03508	0.03431	0.03356	0.03281	0.03208	0.03137	0.03067	0.02998
1.5	0.02931	0.02865	0.02800	0.02736	0.02674	0.02612	0.02552	0.02494	0.02436	0.02380
1.6	0.02324	0.02270	0.02217	0.02165	0.02114	0.02064	0.02015	0.01967	0.01920	0.01874
1.7	0.01829	0.01785	0.01742	0.01699	0.01658	0.01617	0.01578	0.01539	0.01501	0.01464
1.8	0.01428	0.01392	0.01357	0.01323	0.01290	0.01257	0.01226	0.01195	0.01164	0.01134
1.9	0.01105	0.01077	0.01049	0.01022	0.00996	0.00970	0.00945	0.00920	0.00896	0.00872
2.0	$8.491/10^{3}$	$8.266/10^{3}$	$8.046/10^{3}$	$7.832/10^{3}$	$7.623/10^{3}$	$7.418/10^{3}$	$7.219/10^{3}$	$7.024/10^{3}$	$6.835/10^{3}$	$6.649/10^{3}$
2.1	$6.468/10^{3}$	$6.292/10^{3}$	$6.120/10^{3}$	$5.952/10^{3}$	$5.788/10^{3}$	$5.628/10^{3}$	$5.472/10^{3}$	$5.320/10^{3}$	$5.172/10^{3}$	$5.028/10^{3}$
2.2	$4.887/10^{3}$	$4.750/10^{3}$	$4.616/10^{3}$	$4.486/10^{3}$	$4.358/10^{3}$	$4.235/10^{3}$	$4.114/10^{3}$	$3.996/10^{3}$	$3.882/10^{3}$	$3.770/10^{3}$
2.3	$3.662/10^{3}$	$3.556/10^{3}$	$3.453/10^{3}$	$3.352/10^{3}$	$3.255/10^{3}$	$3.159/10^{3}$	$3.067/10^{3}$	$2.977/10^{3}$	$2.889/10^{3}$	$2.804/10^{3}$
2.4	$2.720/10^{3}$	$2.640/10^{3}$	$2.561/10^{3}$	$2.484/10^{3}$	$2.410/10^{3}$	$2.337/10^{3}$	$2.267/10^{3}$	$2.199/10^{3}$	$2.132/10^{3}$	$2.067/10^{3}$
2.5	$2.004/10^{3}$	$1.943/10^{3}$	$1.883/10^{3}$	$1.826/10^{3}$	$1.769/10^{3}$	$1.715/10^{3}$	$1.662/10^{3}$	$1.610/10^{3}$	$1.560/10^{3}$	$1.511/10^{3}$
2.6	$1.464/10^{3}$	$1.418/10^{3}$	$1.373/10^{3}$	$1.330/10^{3}$	$1.288/10^{3}$	$1.247/10^{3}$	$1.207/10^{3}$	$1.169/10^{3}$	$1.132/10^{3}$	$1.095/10^{3}$
2.7	$1.060/10^{3}$	$1.026/10^{3}$	$9.928/10^{4}$	$9.607/10^{4}$	$9.295/10^{4}$	$8.992/10^{4}$	$8.699/10^{4}$	$8.414/10^{4}$	$8.138/10^{4}$	$7.870/10^{4}$
2.8	$7.611/10^{4}$	$7.359/10^{4}$	$7.115/10^{4}$	$6.879/10^{4}$	$6.650/10^{4}$	$6.428/10^{4}$	$6.213/10^{4}$	$6.004/10^{4}$	$5.802/10^{4}$	$5.606/10^{4}$
2.9	$5.417/10^{4}$	$5.233/10^{4}$	$5.055/10^{4}$	$4.883/10^{4}$	$4.716/10^{4}$	$4.555/10^{4}$	$4.398/10^{4}$	$4.247/10^{4}$	$4.101/10^{4}$	$3.959/10^{4}$
3.0	$3.822/10^{4}$	$3.689/10^{4}$	$3.560/10^{4}$	$3.436/10^{4}$	$3.316/10^{4}$	$3.199/10^{4}$	$3.087/10^{4}$	$2.978/10^{4}$	$2.873/10^{4}$	$2.771/10^{4}$
3.1	$2.672/10^{4}$	$2.577/10^{4}$	$2.485/10^{4}$	$2.396/10^{4}$	$2.311/10^{4}$	$2.227/10^{4}$	$2.147/10^{4}$	$2.070/10^{4}$	$1.995/10^{4}$	$1.922/10^{4}$
3.2	$1.852/10^{4}$	$1.785/10^{4}$	$1.720/10^{4}$	$1.657/10^{4}$	$1.596/10^{4}$	$1.537/10^{4}$	$1.480/10^{4}$	$1.426/10^{4}$	$1.373/10^{4}$	$1.322/10^{4}$
3.3	$1.273/10^{4}$	$1.225/10^{4}$	$1.179/10^{4}$	$1.135/10^{4}$	$1.093/10^{4}$	$1.051/10^{4}$	$1.012/10^{4}$	$9.734/10^{5}$	$9.365/10^{5}$	$9.009/10^{5}$
3.4	$8.666/10^{5}$	$8.335/10^{5}$	$8.016/10^{5}$	$7.709/10^{5}$	$7.412/10^{5}$	$7.127/10^{5}$	$6.852/10^{5}$	$6.587/10^{5}$	$6.331/10^{5}$	$6.085/10^{5}$
3.5	$5.848/10^{5}$	$5.620/10^{5}$	$5.400/10^{5}$	$5.188/10^{5}$	$4.984/10^{5}$	$4.788/10^{5}$	$4.599/10^{5}$	$4.417/10^{5}$	$4.242/10^{5}$	$4.073/10^{5}$
3.6	$3.911/10^{5}$	$3.755/10^{5}$	$3.605/10^{5}$	$3.460/10^{5}$	$3.321/10^{5}$	$3.188/10^{5}$	$3.059/10^{5}$	$2.935/10^{5}$	$2.816/10^{5}$	$2.702/10^{5}$
3.7	$2.592/10^{5}$	$2.486/10^{5}$	$2.385/10^{5}$	$2.287/10^{5}$	$2.193/10^{5}$	$2.103/10^{5}$	$2.016/10^{5}$	$1.933/10^{5}$	$1.853/10^{5}$	$1.776/10^{5}$
3.8	$1.702/10^{5}$	$1.632/10^{5}$	$1.563/10^{5}$	$1.498/10^{5}$	$1.435/10^{5}$	$1.375/10^{5}$	$1.317/10^{5}$	$1.262/10^{5}$	$1.208/10^{5}$	$1.157/10^{5}$
3.9	$1.108/10^{5}$	$1.061/10^{5}$	$1.016/10^{5}$	$9.723/10^{6}$	$9.307/10^{6}$	$8.908/10^{6}$	$8.525/10^{6}$	$8.158/10^{6}$	$7.806/10^{6}$	$7.469/10^{6}$
4.0	$7.145/10^{6}$	$6.835/10^{6}$	$6.538/10^{6}$	$6.253/10^{6}$	$5.980/10^{6}$	$5.718/10^{6}$	$5.468/10^{6}$	$5.227/10^{6}$	$4.997/10^{6}$	$4.777/10^{6}$
4.1	$4.566/10^{6}$	$4.364/10^{6}$	$4.170/10^{6}$	$3.985/10^{6}$	$3.807/10^{6}$	$3.637/10^{6}$	$3.475/10^{6}$	$3.319/10^{6}$	$3.170/10^{6}$	$3.027/10^{6}$
4.2	$2.891/10^{6}$	$2.760/10^{6}$	$2.635/10^{6}$	$2.516/10^{6}$	$2.402/10^{6}$	$2.292/10^{6}$	$2.188/10^{6}$	$2.088/10^{6}$	$1.992/10^{6}$	$1.901/10^{6}$
4.3	$1.814/10^{6}$	$1.730/10^{6}$	$1.650/10^{6}$	$1.574/10^{6}$	$1.501/10^{6}$	$1.431/10^{6}$	$1.365/10^{6}$	$1.301/10^{6}$	$1.241/10^{6}$	$1.183/10^{6}$
4.4	$1.127/10^{6}$	$1.074/10^{6}$	$1.024/10^{6}$	$9.756/10^{7}$	$9.296/10^{7}$	$8.857/10^{7}$	$8.437/10^{7}$	$8.037/10^{7}$	$7.655/10^{7}$	$7.290/10^{7}$

Important Equations and Formulae

1. $Q^* = \sqrt{\dfrac{2D[S+g\pi]}{H}}$

   where S is the ordering cost, H is the carrying cost (i.e., $h \times C$), e is the excess inventory, g is the shortage (units stock-out), and π is the shortage cost (stock-out cost per unit).
2. Reorder level (ROP) when it is assumed that the demand during the lead time follows a normal distribution.

$$\text{ROP} = d \times LT + z \times s_\text{d} \times \sqrt{LT}$$

   where d is the average demand per period (say a week), s_d is the standard deviation of the demand per period (say a week), and LT is the lead time in time periods (say weeks).
3. Safety stock (SS) is

$$\text{Safety stock (SS)} = z \times s_\text{d} \times \sqrt{LT}$$

4. Average inventory level (AIL) is

$$\text{AIL} = \frac{Q}{2} + z \times s_\text{d}' = \frac{Q}{2} + z \times s_\text{d} \times \sqrt{LT}$$

5. Unit service level (USL) is

$$\text{USL} = 1 - \frac{E(z)s_\text{d}'}{Q}$$

6. Under conditions when the demand and the lead time both are uncertain, s_d' gets modified as under.

$$s_\text{d}' = \sqrt{LT \times s_\text{d}^2 + d^2 s_\text{LT}^2}$$

   where the mean lead time is LT and its standard deviation is s_LT.
7. For imputed stock-out costs:

   Backorder case

$$H(Q/D) = \pi \times \text{OSOR}$$

   or

$$\pi = \frac{HQ}{\text{OSOR} \times D}$$

   Lost sales case

$$\text{OSOR} = \frac{HQ}{\pi' D + HQ}$$

Exercises

1. A retail store in Kolkata sells mobile phones in a city from its inventory, which it sources from a manufacturer in Mumbai who sends consignments to the retailer using airfreight services. The details are as follows:

   Average annual demand = 4500 units
   Replenishment lead time = 2 weeks
   Carrying cost = 20% per year
   Purchase price, delivered = \$275 per unit
   Procurement ordering cost = \$350 per order

   a. Establish a reorder policy for this item for the retail store.
   b. What are the annual ordering and annual carrying costs for this reorder policy?
   c. Suppose the lead time is three weeks. Is the revised ROP > Q^*? What adjustments should be suggested in this control policy?

2. Century Autos in Jamshedpur maintains the inventory for some auto parts with the following details.
Forecast of demand = 2000 boxes per week
Forecast error, standard deviation = 450 boxes per week
Lead time = 3 weeks
Carrying cost = 15% per year
Purchase price, delivered = $65 per box
Replenishment order cost = $25 per order
Stock-out cost = $12 per case
Probability of being in stock during the lead time, $P = 75\%$

a. Design a reorder point control system for this part, given the assigned *P*. How would you state the inventory control policy if ROP > Q^*?
b. Design a periodic review system for this part assuming the probability of being in stock extends to the order interval plus lead time.
c. Calculate the total cost for these two approaches in a and b.
d. What service level (fill rate) do you actually achieve with both designs?
e. Find the in-stock probability during the lead time that will optimize a reorder point system design. How does the total cost compare with that in part a?
f. Suppose the lead time is normally distributed with a standard deviation of 0.5 weeks. How do the results compare now with a and b?

3. An auto service center uses engine spare parts that it maintains in the inventory. Pertinent data about this item are as follows:

Forecasted daily usage[a]	75 units
Forecast error std. dev.[b]	12 units
Average lead time	14 days
Lead time std. dev [b]	4 days
Annual carrying cost	15%
Procurement cost per order	$60
Stock-out cost	$18 per unit
Product value	$35 per unit
In-stock probability[c]	80%

[a]365 days per year.
[b]Normally distributed.
[c]During the lead time or during the order interval plus lead time, depending on the inventory control design.

a. Design a reorder point system of control for this item.
b. Design a periodic review system of control for this item.
c. Do you think the in-stock probability is correctly specified to minimize cost? Explain in the context of the inventory policy.
d. What is the average inventory level for each of these items?
e. What is the customer (unit) service level that can be expected for these items?
f. Suppose that the lead time is set at 21 days. How will your answer to the previous questions change?

4. Bharath Computers maintains a stock of its spare parts for the entire country at one warehouse in Bangalore. Due to the restructuring of its distribution network and to provide improved customer service, the company is planning to expand the number of warehouses to 8 of equal size. The total inventory investment in the current warehouse is $8,000,000.

a. Using the square root law, estimate the amount of inventory investment that the distribution system is likely to contain with eight warehouses.
b. Suppose that 10 warehouses are operating with $1,000,000 of inventory investment in each. If the company were to consolidate the inventory into three equal-size warehouses, how much inventory would be in each of them?

5. Grand Stores uses reorder point method for all its stored inventories. But the shelf space for these items is limited. (Retail stores usually allocate a certain amount of shelf space to each item in the store.) It orders on a central distribution center for all its replenishment. A consumer item in the store has the following data.

Demand forecast, boxes/week	150
Forecast error (sd), boxes/week[a]	20
Lead time, weeks	1.5
Annual carrying cost, percent/yr	15
Item value, dollar/box	1.50
Ordering cost, dollar/order[b]	1.75
Maximum shelf space for item, boxes	300
In-stock probability	90%

[a]Normally distributed.
[b]Prorated order cost for multiple items.

What order quantity should be used so that the shelf space restriction is not exceeded?

6. Axle Motors orders in lot sizes of 200 units while facing an annual demand of 4000. Holding costs are $12 per unit per year, and the desired order service level is 90%. What is the implicit stock-out cost, assuming the backorder case? What will be the implicit stock-out cost if we assume the lost sales case?
7. Axle Motors, while planning its inventory for its spare parts, decides to order in larger lot sizes to avoid carrying safety stock. It decides to increase the order quantity from 600 units to 800 units. At the same time, a safety stock of 50 units is completely eliminated. Which order quantity yields lower annual holding costs?
8. The weekly demand for Alex Motors for a component from one of its suppliers is normally distributed, with a mean of 400 and a standard deviation of 150. The store manager continuously monitors inventory and currently orders 1000 components each time the inventory drops to 1000. Alex Motors takes two weeks to fill an order. How much safety inventory does it carry? What CSL does it achieve as a result of this policy? What fill rate does this policy achieve?
9. The weekly demand for washing powder at a Big Bazaar store is normally distributed, with a mean of 4000 and a standard deviation of 800. The store manager continuously monitors the item in the inventory and places a replenishment order for 9500 units when there are 7000 units in the inventory. The supplier takes two weeks to supply a Big Bazaar order. What CSL does the store achieve? What fill rate does the store achieve?
10. The weekly demand of electric motors at Axle Motors in its manufacturing plant is normally distributed, with a mean of 1500 and a standard deviation of 800. Motors are currently assembled in Taiwan and delivered at a cost of $200/motor. The supplier takes 6 weeks to supply an order. A local manufacturer has assured to deliver motors with a lead time of 2 weeks at a cost of $240 per motor. Axle is targeting a CSL of 99% and monitors its inventory continuously and incurs a holding cost of 25%. Should Axle accept the local supplier's offer?
11. Fashions Global sells through its online channel and also along with its retail stores, which are spread throughout the country. It needs to decide which products to carry at the retail stores and which products to carry at the central warehouse to be sold only via the online channel. Fashions Global currently has 1200 retail stores in the country. The weekly demand for large size blue jeans pants at each store is normally distributed with a mean of 900 and a standard deviation of 120. Each pair of jeans costs $40. Another product, winter woolen sweater's weekly demand at each store is normally distributed with a mean of 90 and a standard deviation of 40. Each sweater costs $120. Fashions Global maintains inventory at a holding cost of 25% and manages all inventories using a continuous review policy. The supply lead time for both the products is 3 weeks. The targeted CSL is 90%. How much reduction in holding cost per unit sold is required to make Fashions Global in moving each of the two products from the stores to the online channel? Which of the two products should it carry at the stores and which one should it carry at the central warehouse for the online channel? Why? Assume demand from one week to the next to be independent.

12. Roja Pharmacy replenishes one of its best-selling diabetes drugs using a continuous review policy. The daily demand for the drug is normally distributed, with a mean of 400 and a standard deviation of 90. The supplier for Roja Pharmacy can process a replenishment request in four days. The current replenishment policy is to order 1800 units when there are 900 units on hand.

a. What is the cycle service level that Roja Pharmacy achieves with its policy?
b. What is the fill rate that Roja Pharmacy achieves with its policy?
c. What change in fill rate would Roja Pharmacy achieve if it increased its ROP from 900 to 1100?

13. Maruti has decided to set up regional warehouses where the variants of the Swift Dzire will be customized and shipped to dealers on demand. Customizing and shipping on demand will raise production and transportation cost per car by $200. Each car costs $10,000, and Maruti has a holding cost of 20%. Cars at the dealers are owned by Maruti for the first 60 days. Thus, for all practical purposes, Maruti owns all inventory, whether at all the dealers or the regional warehouses. Consider a region with four large dealers and 20 small dealers. Maruti has partitioned the variants into two groups: popular variants and uncommon variants. The weekly demand for the two types of variants at the two types of dealers is shown in the following table. The goal is to provide a 90% cycle service level using a continuous review policy. Replenishment lead times for both dealers and regional warehouses are 3 weeks. Customization and shipping from a regional warehouse to a dealer can be done in a day, and this one can be ignored. Assume demand to be independent across all dealers.

a. How much safety inventory of a popular variant is required at a large or small dealer?
b. What is the safety inventory required if the inventory for the popular variant (for both large and small dealers) is centralized at the regional warehouse by Maruti?
c. What is the safety inventory required if the inventory for the popular variant at small dealers is centralized at the regional warehouse but for the large dealer is decentralized?
d. Given the additional customization and transportation cost, which structure do you recommend for the popular variant?
e. Repeat parts (a) to (d) for the uncommon variant.
f. How should Maruti structure inventories given its regional warehouses?

Weekly Demand at Car Dealers

	Popular Variant		Uncommon Variant	
	Mean	Standard Deviation	Mean	Standard Deviation
Large Dealer	60	18	10	5
Small Dealer	15	7	3	2

14. A manufacturer of tier belts for motors produces them in house for its own assembly of motors. The final assembly is at the rate of 150 per day for 250 working days per year. It costs $300 to start up the belt production. Production is at the rate of 300 per day when operating. The standard cost is $80, and the company's inventory carrying cost is 20% per year.

a. What should the production run quantity be?
b. How long should each production run cycle be?
c. How many times per year should the part be produced?

15. The annual demand for an item is 2000 units. The unit price is $2.50, and the annual holding cost is 35% per year. Backorder costs are $8 per unit, and setup costs are $20 per lot. Lead time is 8 days, and the standard deviation of the lead time demand is 6 units. What are the joint optimal Q and R levels?

16. The annual demand for an item is 5000 units. The unit price is $5, and the annual holding cost is 30% per year. Backorder costs are not available and difficult to estimate, although the management desires a 95% unit service level. Setup costs are $15 per lot. Lead time is 6 days, and the standard deviation of the lead time demand is 8 units. What are the joint optimal Q and R levels? What are the implicit backorder costs?

17. For a 10% order stock-out risk, what is the implied cost of a backorder for the following item? Using a combined (Q, R) model, the company faces annual sales of 1000 units. The inventory holding charge is \$20 per unit per year. The setup cost is \$25, and the standard deviation of lead time demand is 25 units.

Bibliography

1. Axsater, S. (1996). Using the deterministic EOQ formula in stochastic inventory control. *Management Science*, **42**(6), 830.
2. Ballou, R. H. and S. K. Srivastava (2007). ***Business Logistics/Supply Chain Management.*** Delhi: Pearson India.
3. Brown, R. G. (1977). ***Material Management Systems.*** New York: John Wiley & Sons.
4. Chopra, S., P. Meindl, and D. V. Kalra (2016). ***Supply Chain Management, Strategy, Planning and Operation.*** Delhi: Pearson India.
5. Narasimhan, S. L., D. W. McLeavey, and P. J. Billington (2000). ***Production Planning and Inventory Control.*** Delhi: Prentice-Hall India.
6. Zipkin, P. H. (2000). ***Foundations of Inventory Management.*** Boston, MA: Irwin McGraw-Hill.

CHAPTER 8

Joint Replenishment and Lot Sizing in Inventory Decisions

LEARNING OBJECTIVES

After reading this chapter, you would be able to:

- Understand and appreciate the inventory policies for multiple items with inventory investment limits.
- Decide lot sizing when total setup times are constrained by a maximum limit.
- Deal with various optimization scenarios in inventory situations where setup times or inventory cost or other parameters are constraints using Lagrangian multipliers.
- Understand the joint replenishment of items and devise inventory policies for complete and tailored aggregation of scenarios using various algorithms.
- Comprehend various techniques of dynamic lot sizing under time varying demand.
- Understand the implications of multi-echelon inventory decisions.

8.1 | INTRODUCTION AND INVENTORY INVESTMENT DECISIONS

In this section, we will look at inventory policy decisions when dealing with multiple items and joint replenishment ordering policies. As discussed in previous chapters, inventories imply blocked capital and investment, and hence, a careful decision involving how much money or investment needs to be blocked in such inventories becomes critical. While an inventory policy for a single item using Economic Order Quantity (EOQ) principles makes it easier to decide the inventory investment based on the average inventory $Q/2$ and C, it is not straightforward to extend the policy for multiple items. The upper limit on the total inventory investment that is blocked on all the average inventories of these items has a budgetary constraint and a limit that is strategically decided and imposed in practice. Hence, the inventory policy needs to be adjusted to meet this goal if the total average inventory investment exceeds it. We will assume that the inventory is controlled by a reorder level policy with demand and lead-time certainty. If a monetary upper limit is placed on all items that are carried in inventory, then it is clear that:

$$\sum_{i=1}^{n} \frac{Q_i}{2} C_i \leq L \tag{8.1}$$

where

- Q_i is the order quantity of item i.

- C_i is the value of the item i.
- L is the upper limit for the investment limit on all i items.

In inventory policy decisions, it is not practical to determine order quantities using EOQ as there is always a budget constraint on the money that can be blocked as capital by the finance department. Again, it is always for multiple items and not for a single item as it makes sense to decide the overall budget for multiple items. In such situations, discussions on investment limits is of great importance and the approach shown here is very useful for practicing managers.

The order quantity can be determined by the EOQ formula we used earlier. When the total average inventory value of all items exceeds the investment limit (L), the order quantities for the items need to be adjusted to decrease the average item inventory levels to meet the investment limit. A logical way to do this is to artificially inflate the carrying cost h to a value h' where $h' = h + \lambda$, which is large enough to reduce the stock levels to an appropriate quantity. This is equivalent to saying that the adjusted order quantity Q_i of the item i becomes

$$Q_i = \sqrt{\frac{2D_iS_i}{C_i(h+\lambda)}} \tag{8.2}$$

where λ is a constant to be determined. Substituting this in Eq. (8.1), we can obtain the value of $h' = h + \lambda$ as

$$h' = h + \lambda = \left(\frac{\sum_{i=1}^{n} \sqrt{2D_iS_iC_i}}{2L} \right)^2 \tag{8.3}$$

Using this h' in Eq. (8.2), we obtain the adjusted Q_i's that will meet the budgetary limit on the total investment. We will show how these equations are derived using Lagrangian multipliers later in Section 8.3.

EXAMPLE 8.1

Consider the following four items that are maintained in the inventory with all details given in Table 8.1. The management has put a limit of \$15,000 on the average investment for these items. The annual carrying cost h is given as 25%.

TABLE 8.1 Details of the four items in inventory

Item	Annual Demand D_i	Ordering Cost S_i	Cost of the Item C_i
1	15000	50	10
2	30000	60	15
3	18000	50	12
4	8000	40	10

We compute the respective Q_i's as follows:

$$Q_1 = \sqrt{\frac{2D_1S_1}{hC_1}} = \sqrt{\frac{2\times 15{,}000\times 50}{0.25\times 10}} = 774.6$$

Similarly, $Q_2 = 979.8$
$Q_3 = 774.6$
$Q_4 = 506.0$

So the total inventory investment on these items is $\sum_{i=1}^{4} \frac{Q_i}{2} C_i = 18{,}399.$

Now, since the limit on the investment is given as \$15,000, this gives us the new $h' = h + \alpha$.

$$\left(\frac{\sqrt{2\times 15{,}000\times 50\times 10} + \sqrt{2\times 30{,}000\times 60\times 15} + \sqrt{2\times 18{,}000\times 50\times 12} + \sqrt{2\times 8000\times 40\times 10}}{2\times 15{,}000} \right)^2$$

$= 0.376$

Now, we will use this h' to recalculate the Q_i as

$$\sqrt{\frac{2D_iS_i}{0.376 * C_i}}$$

The adjusted Q_i's are as follows:

$Q_1 = 631.5$
$Q_2 = 798.8$
$Q_3 = 631.5$
$Q_4 = 412.5$

We can verify that $\sum_{i=1}^{4} \frac{Q_i}{2} C_i = 15{,}000$, which was the limit that was imposed.

We can perform the same calculation on Excel using the Goal Seek option. Figure 8.1 gives the initial table with the respective order quantities Q_i's and the total investment in inventory.

	A	B	C	D	E	F	G	H
2			I	0.25				
3	Item	Annual Demand Di	Ordering Cost Si	Cost of the item Ci	Qi	Avege Invnetory	Inv.Invstment	
4								
5	1	15000	50	10	774.6	387	3873.0	
6	2	30000	60	15	979.8	490	7348.5	
7	3	18000	50	12	774.6	387	4647.6	
8	4	8000	40	10	506.0	253	2529.8	
9						Total	18398.9	
10								

FIGURE 8.1 Excel sheet showing the calculation of order quantities and the total inventory investment.

Now we can use the Goal Seek option under the Data header. Set the target cell as the Total cell and set it to 15,000 by changing the value of h as shown in Figure 8.2, which is a screenshot of the same.

Goal Seek ? ×
Set cell: $G$22
To value: 15000
By changing cell: $D$15
OK Cancel

	A	B	C	D	E	F	G
11							
12							
13							
14							
15			h	0.376			
16	Item		dering Cost Si	Cost of the item Ci	Qi	Avege Invnetory	Inv.Invstment
17							
18	1	15000	50	10	**631.5**	316	3158
19	2	30000	60	15	**798.8**	399	5991
20	3	18000	50	12	**631.5**	316	3789
21	4	8000	40	10	**412.5**	206	2062
22				Total			15000
23							
24							

FIGURE 8.2 Using the Goal Seek option to obtain the adjusted order quantities.

We can verify that the results are the same as what we obtained from Eqs. (8.2) and (8.3).

We will analyze the impact of this by comparing the order quantities before and after the adjustment keeping $h = 0.25$ in both scenarios. Figure 8.3 shows the comparisons.

Before Adjusing the Order Quantities									
		h	**0.25**						
Item	**Annual Demand Di**	**Ordering Cost Si**	**Cost of the item Ci**	Qi	**Average Inventory**	**Inv.Investment**	**Ordering Cost ((D/Q)*S)**	**Inv. Carrying Cost ((Avge.Inv)*C*h)**	**Total Cost**
1	15000	50	10	774.6	387	3873.0	968.25	968.25	1936.49
2	30000	60	15	979.8	490	7348.5	1837.12	1837.12	3674.23
3	18000	50	12	774.6	387	4647.6	1161.90	1161.90	2323.79
4	8000	40	10	506.0	253	2529.8	632.46	632.46	1264.91
					Total	**18398.9**	**4599.71**	**4599.71**	**9199.43**
After Adjusing the Order Quantities									
		h	**0.376**						
Item	**Annual Demand Di**	**Ordering Cost Si**	**Cost of the item Ci**	Qi	**Average Inventory**	**Inv.Investment**	**Ordering Cost ((D/Q)*S)**	**Inv. Carrying Cost ((Avge.Inv)*C*h)**	**Total Cost**
1	15000	50	10	**631.5**	316	3158	1187.64	789.38	1977.02
2	30000	60	15	**798.8**	399	5991	2253.39	1497.74	3751.13
3	18000	50	12	**631.5**	316	3789	1425.17	947.26	2372.43
4	8000	40	10	**412.5**	206	2062	775.76	515.62	1291.38
			Total			**15000**	**4866.20**	**3234.38**	**8100.58**

FIGURE 8.3 Comparison of order quantities before and after adjustment.

We observe that the total cost has decreased from \$ 9199.43 to \$ 8100.58. While the inventory-carrying cost has decreased from \$ 4599.71 to \$ 3234.38, the ordering cost has increased from \$ 4599.71 to \$ 4866.20. It may be an interesting question to ask at this stage if we can adjust the lot sizes further to minimize the total ordering cost but keep the inventory investment limit still at \$ 15,000. We will address this question later, after we introduce the Lagrangian multipliers in such contexts.

8.2 LOT SIZING INVENTORY MANAGEMENT INTERPOLATION TECHNIQUE

The Lot-Sizing Inventory Management Interpolation Technique (LIMIT) is another approach when dealing with the trade-offs between setup costs and inventory-carrying costs.

Using the usual notations for determining Q, referred to as trial quantity Q_T with demand D, setup cost S, and inventory-carrying percentage, referred to as trial h_T and C as the cost of the unit, we have

Although the approach shown here seeks the budget constraint and optimizes the lot sizes, it is not without any trade-off. The trade-off here is that it increases the total ordering (or total setup cost). While the overall cost is also reduced, further queries will lead us to explore more optimization in reducing the total setup cost as well. That is where the Lagrangian multipliers will be useful to us. We will see it later in this chapter.

$$Q_T = \sqrt{\frac{2DS}{h_T C}} \tag{8.4}$$

If $D = 18{,}000$, $S = 150$, $h_T = 0.25$, and $C = 15$, then

$$Q_T = \sqrt{\frac{2 \times 18{,}000 \times 150}{0.25 \times 15}} = 1200$$

This would make the number of setups 18,000/1200 = 15 setups.

If the number of setups is limited to only 9, then Q_T has to be increased to 2000. The limiting action of 10 setups may be due to the lack of adequate capacity and support or disbelief in the ratio of setup costs and the inventory-carrying cost. If Q is increased to 2000, then the implied limiting inventory-carrying percentage h_L will be 0.09.

$$Q_L = \sqrt{\frac{2 \times 18{,}000 \times 150}{0.09 \times 15}} = 2000$$

If we look at the limiting inventory-carrying percentage h_L and the trial inventory-carrying percentage h_T, we can derive a relationship between the trial quantity Q_T and the limit quantity Q_L as a function of h_L and h_T. We know that

$$Q_L = \sqrt{\frac{2DS}{h_L C}} \text{ and } Q_T = \sqrt{\frac{2DS}{h_T C}}$$

Therefore,

$$\frac{Q_L}{Q_T} = \frac{\sqrt{2DS}}{\sqrt{h_L C}} \frac{\sqrt{h_T c}}{\sqrt{2DS}} = \frac{\sqrt{h_T}}{\sqrt{h_L}}$$

So,

$$Q_L = Q_T \sqrt{\frac{h_T}{h_L}} = M * Q_T \qquad (8.5)$$

where

$$M = \sqrt{\frac{h_T}{h_L}} \qquad (8.6)$$

In our example,

$$Q_L = 1200 \times \sqrt{\frac{0.25}{0.09}} = 1200 \times \left(\frac{5}{3}\right) = 2000. \text{ Here } M = 1.67$$

If we know h_T, then Q_L will be straightforward to arrive at from Eq. (8.5). But typically, in practice, the limit-carrying percentage h_T is not known, while the trial carrying percentage h_L is known and the overall limit on the annual setup hours is imposed as a limit. And so, it is of interest to us to arrive at the limit quantities adjusting the trial quantities. How do we achieve this?

Let us assume that the overall limit on the total annual setup hours is S_L and let the overall setup hours of the trial quantities for all product SKUs be S_T. Let s_i be the setup hours required for the SKU i. Let D_i, Q_{i_T}, and Q_{i_L} be the respective annual demand, trial lot quantity, and limit quantity of the ith SKU. We also know that $Q_{i_L} = M * Q_{i_T}$ from Eq. (8.5).

Then we can express the ratio S_T/S_L as

$$\frac{S_T}{S_L} = \frac{\sum\left(\frac{D_i}{Q_{i_T}}\right)s_i}{\sum\left(\frac{D_i}{Q_{i_L}}\right)s_i} = \frac{\sum\left(\frac{D_i}{Q_{i_T}}\right)s_i}{\sum\left(\frac{D_i}{M * Q_{i_T}}\right)s_i} = \frac{\sum\left(\frac{D_i}{Q_{i_T}}\right)s_i}{\frac{1}{M}\sum\left(\frac{D_i}{Q_{i_T}}\right)s_i} = M \quad \text{using Eq. (8.5)}$$

This means

$$\frac{S_T}{S_L} = M \qquad (8.7)$$

From Eq. (8.6), we have $M = \sqrt{\frac{h_T}{h_L}}$.

So,

$$\sqrt{\frac{h_T}{h_L}} = \frac{S_T}{S_L}$$

which gives

$$h_L = h_T \left(\frac{S_L}{S_T}\right)^2 \qquad (8.8)$$

From these equations, we get the following three fundamental relationships to determine the limit quantities and the limit-carrying percentage.

$$M = \frac{S_T}{S_L} = \sqrt{\frac{h_T}{h_L}} \tag{8.9}$$

$$h_L = h_T \left(\frac{S_L}{S_T} \right)^2 \tag{8.10}$$

$$Q_{i_L} = M \times Q_{i_T} \tag{8.11}$$

We will illustrate the use of these relationships through the following example.

The LIMIT approach simplifies the effort in achieving the lot sizes to address the overall limit on the setup time and, in a way, drives the effort to achieve it by reducing the inventory cost to a desired level to achieve the lot sizes. The h_L in fact shows how the supply chain should make efforts to reach that level of h_L through various coordination and cooperation strategies so that the stipulated limit is possible to achieve.

EXAMPLE 8.2

Consider the following three items in the inventory with all the details given in Table 8.2. The setup cost per hour is $150. There is a restriction that the total setup hours cannot be increased to more than 35 hours due to resource constraints. The inventory manager suggested a lot size given in Table 8.2, which can achieve the target of 35 hours of setup. However, the suggestion is through his estimates and intuition and may not be the best lot sizes. We will analyze the suggestion and the adjusted lot size through the LIMIT approach.

TABLE 8.2 Details of three items for LIMIT analysis

Item	Annual Demand	Setup Hours per Order	Unit Cost $	Suggested Quantity by Manager	Suggested Total Setup Hours
A	24000	2	9	8800	5
B	14000	3	15	1550	27
C	12000	2	10	8500	3
				Total	35 hours

We will obtain the trial Q_T's for all the items using the information given in Table 8.2 and obtain the current total setup hours. The calculations are shown in Table 8.3.

TABLE 8.3 Trial quantities and the current total setup hours

Item	Demand D_i	Setup Hours per Setup	Unit Cost C_i	Setup Cost S_i	Trial Quantities Q_T	s_T
A	24000	2	9	300	2530	19
B	14000	3	15	450	1833	23
C	12000	2	10	300	1697	14
				Current Total Setup Hours		S_T 56
h_T	0.25		Setup Cost per Hour		150	

We use the setup cost as setup cost per hour × hours required per setup for each item. For example, for item A, the setup cost is $150 \times 2 = 300$. We use the equation $Q_L = \sqrt{\frac{2DS}{h_L C}}$ to obtain the trial quantities. For example, for item A, it will be $Q_L = \sqrt{\frac{2 \times 12000 \times 300}{0.25 \times 9}} = 2530$. Similarly, the setup hours s_i is calculated as (D/Q_T)*(setup hours per setup). For example, for item A, it will be $(12{,}000/2530) \times 2 = 19$ hours.

From Table 8.3, it is clear that the current total setup hours $S_T = 56$ hours. We are given that the limit setup hours S_L is 35 hours. Then, from Eq. (8.9), the value of M is given by

$$M = \frac{S_T}{S_L} = \frac{56}{35} = 1.6$$

Then from Eq. (8.11), we can obtain the limit quantity Q_L as

$$Q_{i_L} = M \times Q_{i_T}$$

So for item A,

$$Q_{A_L} = 1.6 \times 2530 = 4050$$

Table 8.4 gives the summary and the adjusted setup hours for each item.

TABLE 8.4 Limit quantities and the adjusted setup hours

Limit Quantities		
Item	**Limit Lot Size Q_L**	**Modified Setup Hours s_L**
Q_{AL}	4050	12
Q_{BL}	2934	14
Q_{CL}	2717	9
Total S_L		35

The limit-carrying percentage h_L is given by Eq. (8.10) and it comes to

$$h_L = h_T \left(\frac{S_L}{S_T}\right)^2 = 0.25 \times \left(\frac{35}{56}\right)^2 = 0.096$$

We can compare all the scenarios of the quantities suggested by the manager, the trial quantities and the limit quantities assuming h_L for all the scenarios. Table 8.5 gives a summary.

TABLE 8.5 Summary of all the approaches

Approach	Lot Size		Annual Setup Cost ($)	Annual Holding Cost ($)	Total Relevant Costs ($)
Suggested by Inventory Manager	QA-S	8800	818	3865	4683
	QB-S	1550	4065	1135	5199
	QC-S	8500	424	4148	4572
	Total		5306	9148	14454
Trial Quantities	QA-T	2530	2846	1111	3957
	QB-T	1833	3437	1342	4779
	QC-T	1697	2121	828	2950
	Total		8404	3281	11685
LIMIT	QA-L	4050	1778	1778	3557
	QB-L	2934	2147	2147	4295
	QC-L	2717	1325	1325	2651
	Total		5250	5250	10502
h_L		0.0976			

We observe that the total cost using the LIMIT approach is the least and the principle of EOQ is also seen where the setup costs and the carrying costs are almost equal not only for the individual items but also for the totals. It is also possible to see that if we had used the limit percentage of 0.096 instead of 0.25 in the EOQ formula, we would have got the limit lot sizes. This was not known until we obtained the value of M.

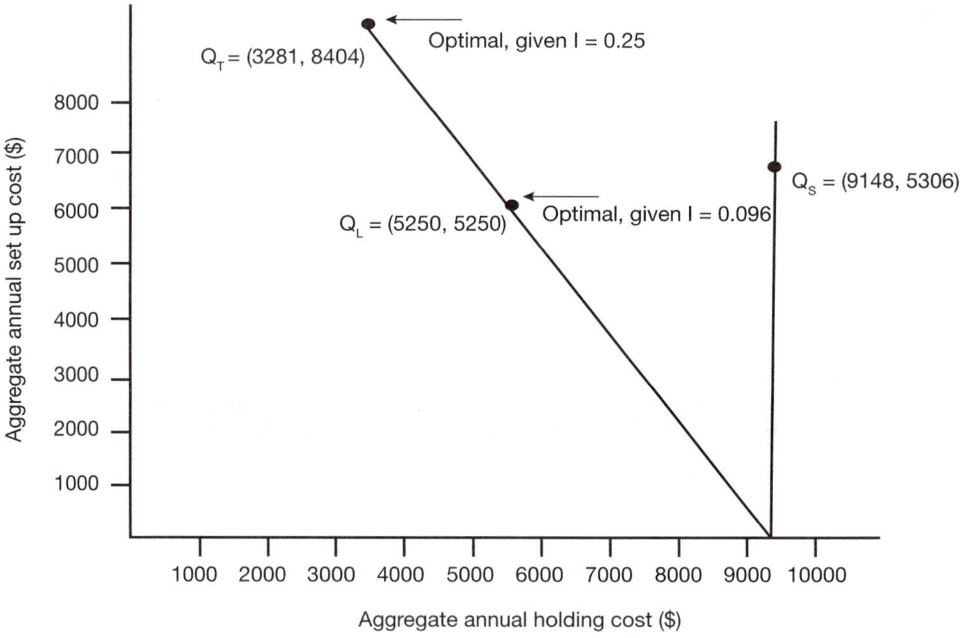

FIGURE 8.4 Holding/set up cost exchange curve.

Figure 8.4 gives a curve that provides an approximate exchange between setup and carrying costs. The suggested lot size by the inventory manager involves a very high holding cost that is much more than the total setup cost. It is of interest to explore whether the manager is still willing to incur an inventory-carrying cost of 9148 and what lot sizes would optimize the total setup cost? This question can be extended to various other options of all the scenarios for trial as well as the limit quantities. To analyze situations like this, we need to approach the problem using Lagrangian multipliers. We will introduce the concept of the Lagrangian multiplier approach and explore how this can address various inventory decisions we come across in practice.

8.3 | LAGRANGIAN MULTIPLIERS

Lagrangian multipliers are a popular method for minimizing or maximizing a function locally, subject to one or more constraints. For example, find the values of x and y that minimizes the function $x^2 + y^2$ while satisfying the constraint $xy = 1$. We will explain how to use Lagrangian multipliers and how they work with the help of this single constraint example.

We will assume a simple situation where we want to minimize a function $f(x, y)$ subject to the constraint $g(x, y) = 0$. This can be extended to functions of several variables, and such procedures are the same for maximization problems. Let us express our example as follows:

$$\text{Minimize } f(x,y) = x^2 + y^2$$

$$\text{subject to } g(x,y) = xy - 1 = 0 \text{ (because } xy - 1 = 0 \text{ is equivalent to } xy = 1)$$

To solve the problem, we create a new function $L(x,y,\lambda)$ called the Lagrangian function. It is specified as $(x,y,\lambda) = f(x,y) - \lambda g(x,y)$, where λ is a new variable called the Lagrangian multiplier. (Use of + instead of a – does not change anything except for the sign of λ and hence both are used.) Then, we take the partial derivatives of $L(x,y,\lambda)$ with respect to the original variables x and y. We set all those partials equal to zero and solve for x and y. We will have the following for this example:

$$L(x,y,\lambda) = x^2 + y^2 - \lambda(xy - 1)$$

$$\frac{\partial L}{\partial x} = 2x - \lambda y$$

$$\frac{\partial L}{\partial y} = 2y - \lambda x$$

$$\frac{\partial L}{\partial \lambda} = -(xy - 1)$$

We set all these partial derivatives to zero for solving for x and y using $xy = 1$.

$$2x - \lambda y = 0 \text{ gives } \lambda = \frac{2x}{y}$$

$$2y - \lambda x = 0 \text{ gives } \lambda = \frac{2y}{x}$$

which gives $\frac{2x}{y} = \frac{2y}{x}$, which means $\frac{x}{y} = \frac{y}{x}$ or $x^2 = y^2$.

Now, $xy = 1$ gives $x = 1/y$. Substituting this we get (x, y) as either (1, 1) or (−1, −1) and $\lambda = 2$. These points are, in fact, the local minima of $f(x, y)$ subject to the constraint that $g(x, y) = 0$. (In this case, they are also the global minima, although in general this may not be guaranteed.)

The Lagrangian multiplier technique utilizes the principle of equating the slopes of the minimizing (or maximizing) function and the constraint equations. Given an objective function $f(x, y)$ and a constraint function $g(x, y) = 0$, the technique calls for the creation of a Lagrangian function $f(x, y) - \lambda g(x, y)$. When we equate the derivatives with respect to x, y, and λ to zero, we reproduce the slope condition at the same time that we satisfy the constraint equation. (More details on this topic can be seen in references.)

We will use this approach for some of the interesting decisions in inventory management. We will revisit Table 8.5 and analyze the inventory manager's suggestion of lot sizes where he or she is willing to restrict the inventory-carrying cost at 9148 but wants to minimize the total setup cost. Let us see how the lot sizes can be changed to accommodate this objective.

One of the important uses of the Lagrangian approach is in solving nonlinear objective functions in inventory decisions with various desirable constraints depending on situations such as inventory cost limit, setup time limit, or stockout situations limit. This section shows many such situations that can be explored in inventory contexts and shows how this simple technique of Lagrangian multipliers is used in addressing such issues.

This problem can be formulated as

$$\text{Minimize } \frac{D_1}{Q_1}S_1 + \frac{D_2}{Q_2}S_2 + \frac{D_3}{Q_3}S_3$$

subject to

$$\frac{Q_1}{2}hC_1 + \frac{Q_2}{2}hC_2 + \frac{Q_3}{2}hC_3 = 9148$$

The Lagrangian function for this and their partial derivatives are as follows:

$$L(Q_1, Q_2, Q_3, \lambda) = \frac{D_1}{Q_1}S_1 + \frac{D_2}{Q_2}S_2 + \frac{D_3}{Q_3}S_3 + \lambda\left[\frac{Q_1}{2}hC_1 + \frac{Q_2}{2}hC_2 + \frac{Q_3}{2}hC_3 - 9148\right]$$

(Note that we have used + instead of − for the Lagrangian expression for $g(x, y)$. It does not alter the solution.)

$$\frac{\partial L}{\partial Q_1} = -\frac{D_1 S_1}{Q_1^2}\lambda hC_1 = 0 \quad (8.12)$$

$$\frac{\partial L}{\partial Q_2} = -\frac{D_2 S_2}{Q_2^2}\lambda hC_2 = 0 \quad (8.13)$$

$$\frac{\partial L}{\partial Q_3} = -\frac{D_3 S_3}{Q_3^2}\lambda hC_3 = 0 \quad (8.14)$$

$$\frac{\partial L}{\partial \lambda} = \frac{Q_1}{2}hC_1 + \frac{Q_2}{2}hC_2 + \frac{Q_3}{2}hC_3 = 9148 \quad (8.15)$$

Equations (8.12) to (8.14) give us

$$Q_1 = \sqrt{\frac{2D_1 S_1}{\lambda hC_1}} = \frac{1}{\sqrt{\lambda}} \times EOQ_1$$

$$Q_2 = \sqrt{\frac{2D_2S_2}{\lambda hC_2}} = \frac{1}{\sqrt{\lambda}} \times EOQ_2$$

$$Q_3 = \sqrt{\frac{2D_3S_3}{\lambda hC_3}} = \frac{1}{\sqrt{\lambda}} \times EOQ_3$$

where EOQ_i refers to the limit quantity of the ith item with $h = 0.096$, which are, respectively, 4050, 2934, and 2717 from Table 8.5. Substituting them in Eq. (8.15), we get

$$\frac{1}{\sqrt{\lambda}}\left[\frac{EOQ_1}{2}hC_1 + \frac{EOQ_2}{2}hC_2 + \frac{Q_3}{2}hC_3\right] = 9148$$

$$\frac{1}{\sqrt{\lambda}}[5250] = 9148$$

(from Table 8.5, the inventory-carrying cost under LIMIT is 5252)

Therefore,

$$\frac{1}{\sqrt{\lambda}} = \frac{9148}{5252} = 1.7425$$

$$\lambda = 0.329$$

Substituting the values of $\frac{1}{\sqrt{\lambda}} = 1.7425$ in the expressions for Q_1, Q_2, Q_3, we get

$$Q_1 = 1.742 \times 4050 = 7057$$
$$Q_2 = 1.742 \times 2934 = 5112$$
$$Q_3 = 1.742 \times 2717 = 4734$$

We can verify that with these Q_1, Q_2, and Q_3

$\frac{Q_1}{2}hC_1 + \frac{Q_2}{2}hC_2 + \frac{Q_3}{2}hC_3 = 9148$, is satisfied.

The total setup cost is

$$(24{,}000/7057) \times 300 + (14{,}000/5112) \times 450 + (12{,}000/4734) \times 300 = 3013$$

The previous setup cost based on the suggestion of the inventory manager was 5306 as seen in Table 8.5. The setup cost has been reduced to 3013 from 5306 with the revision in the lot sizes with an inventory-carrying cost of 9148.

8.3.1 Inventory Investment

Let us revisit Example 8.1 on the inventory investment. We will see how Eqs. (8.2) and (8.3) are obtained using the Lagrangian approach. Our problem can be stated, in general, as follows:

$$\text{Minimize} \sum_{i=1}^{n}\left(\frac{D_i}{Q_i}S_i + \frac{Q_I}{2}hC_i\right)$$

subject to

$$\sum_{i=1}^{n}\frac{Q_1}{2}C_1 = L$$

The Lagrangian function will be as follows:

$$L(Q_i, \lambda) = \sum_{i=1}^{n}\left(\frac{D_i}{Q_i}S_i + \frac{Q_I}{2}hC_i\right) + \lambda\left(\sum_{i=1}^{n}\frac{Q_i}{2}C_i - L\right)$$

$$\frac{\partial L}{\partial Q_i} = -\frac{D_iS_i}{Q_i^2} + \frac{1}{2}hC_i + \lambda\frac{C_i}{2} = 0$$

$$\frac{\partial L}{\partial \lambda} = \sum_{i=1}^{n} \frac{Q_i}{2} C_i - L = 0$$

So this gives us

$$\frac{C_i[h+\lambda]}{2} = \frac{D_i S_i}{Q_i^2}$$

$$Q_i = \sqrt{\frac{2D_i S_i}{C_i[h+\lambda]}} \tag{8.16}$$

Substituting them in the expression for $\frac{\partial L}{\partial \lambda}$, we get

$$\sum_{i=1}^{n} \frac{\sqrt{\frac{2D_i S_i}{C_i[h+\lambda]}}C_i}{2} = L$$

So

$$h' = h + \lambda = \left[\frac{\sum_{I=1}^{n} \sqrt{2D_I S_I C_I}}{2L}\right]^2 \tag{8.17}$$

We see that Eqs. (8.16) and (8.17) are the same as Eqs. (8.2) and (8.3). This can be operationalized on the Excel sheet as shown in Figures 8.5 and 8.6.

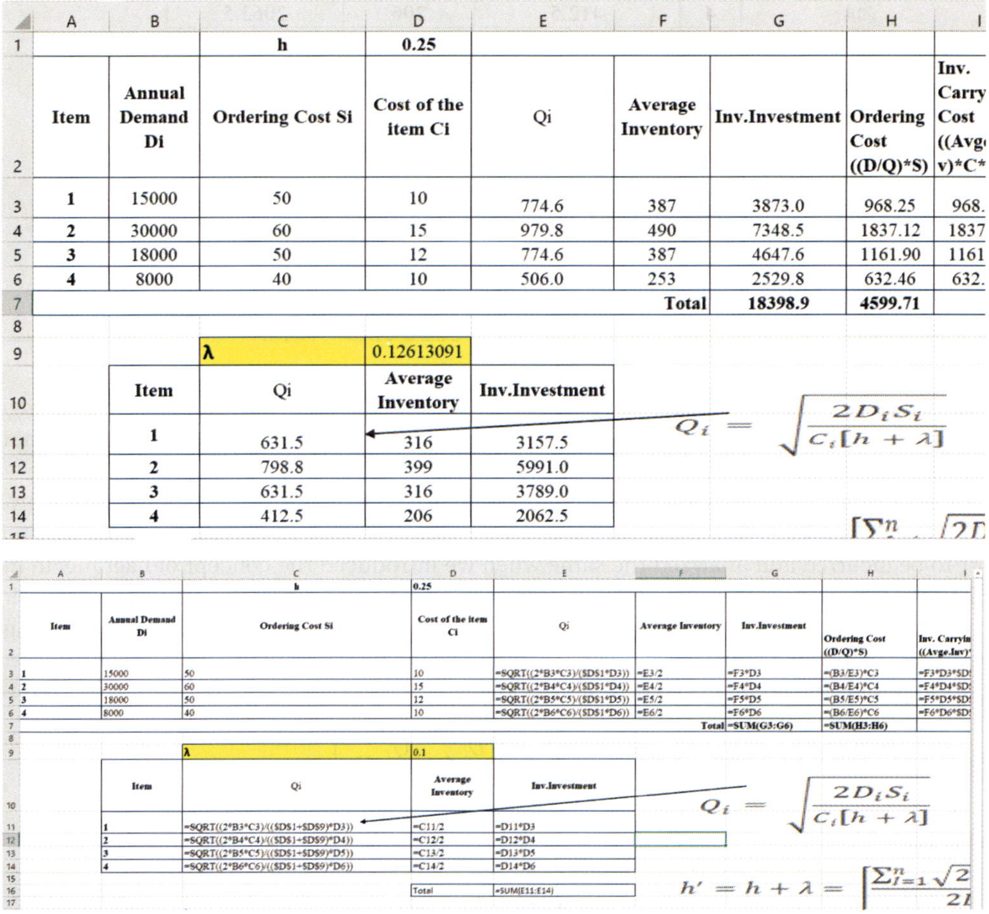

	A	B	C	D	E	F	G	H	I
1			h	0.25					
2	Item	Annual Demand Di	Ordering Cost Si	Cost of the item Ci	Qi	Average Inventory	Inv.Investment	Ordering Cost ((D/Q)*S)	Inv. Carry Cost ((Avg v)*C*
3	1	15000	50	10	774.6	387	3873.0	968.25	968.
4	2	30000	60	15	979.8	490	7348.5	1837.12	1837
5	3	18000	50	12	774.6	387	4647.6	1161.90	1161
6	4	8000	40	10	506.0	253	2529.8	632.46	632.
7						Total	18398.9	4599.71	
8									
9			λ	0.12613091					
10		Item	Qi	Average Inventory	Inv.Investment				
11		1	631.5	316	3157.5				
12		2	798.8	399	5991.0				
13		3	631.5	316	3789.0				
14		4	412.5	206	2062.5				

	A	B	C	D	E	F	G	H	I
1			h	0.25					
2	Item	Annual Demand Di	Ordering Cost Si	Cost of the item Ci	Qi	Average Inventory	Inv.Investment	Ordering Cost ((D/Q)*S)	Inv. Carryin ((Avge.Inv)*
3	1	15000	50	10	=SQRT((2*B3*C3)/($D$1*D3))	=E3/2	=F3*D3	=(B3/E3)*C3	=F3*D3*$D
4	2	30000	60	15	=SQRT((2*B4*C4)/($D$1*D4))	=E4/2	=F4*D4	=(B4/E4)*C4	=F4*D4*$D
5	3	18000	50	12	=SQRT((2*B5*C5)/($D$1*D5))	=E5/2	=F5*D5	=(B5/E5)*C5	=F5*D5*$D
6	4	8000	40	10	=SQRT((2*B6*C6)/($D$1*D6))	=E6/2	=F6*D6	=(B6/E6)*C6	=F6*D6*$D
7						Total	=SUM(G3:G6)	=SUM(H3:H6)	
8									
9			λ	0.1					
10		Item	Qi	Average Inventory	Inv.Investment				
11		1	=SQRT((2*B3*C3)/(($D$1+$D$9)*D3))	=C11/2	=D11*D3				
12		2	=SQRT((2*B4*C4)/(($D$1+$D$9)*D4))	=C12/2	=D12*D4				
13		3	=SQRT((2*B5*C5)/(($D$1+$D$9)*D5))	=C13/2	=D13*D5				
14		4	=SQRT((2*B6*C6)/(($D$1+$D$9)*D6))	=C14/2	=D14*D6				
15									
16				Total	=SUM(E11:E14)				

FIGURE 8.5 Excel sheet for setting up the Lagrangian calculations.

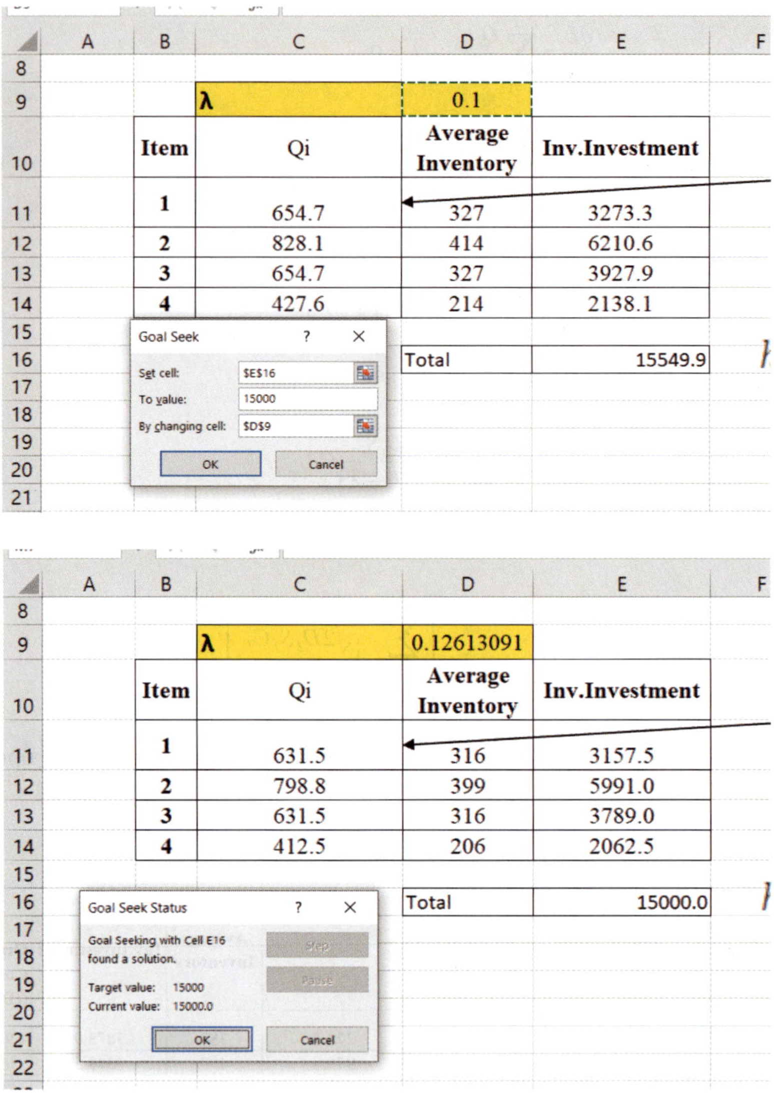

	A	B	C	D	E	F
8						
9			λ	0.1		
10		Item	Qi	Average Inventory	Inv.Investment	
11		1	654.7	327	3273.3	
12		2	828.1	414	6210.6	
13		3	654.7	327	3927.9	
14		4	427.6	214	2138.1	
16				Total	15549.9	

	A	B	C	D	E	F
8						
9			λ	0.12613091		
10		Item	Qi	Average Inventory	Inv.Investment	
11		1	631.5	316	3157.5	
12		2	798.8	399	5991.0	
13		3	631.5	316	3789.0	
14		4	412.5	206	2062.5	
16				Total	15000.0	

FIGURE 8.6 Using Goal Seek to perform the Lagrangian and obtaining the adjusted quantities.

In the preceding case, if the inventory-carrying percentage h is unknown, then the Lagrangian multiplier gives us an interesting result that is the incremental carrying percentage to arrive at the adjusted quantities.

Recall when we discussed the LIMIT approach, we ended with the question that the inventory manager wanted to minimize the total setup cost with a limit on the total inventory-carrying cost to be incurred and analyzed the same when we introduced the concept of Lagrangian multipliers. In the preceding example, we analyzed the situation to adjust the lot sizes when a limit on the inventory investment is imposed to minimize the total cost. Now, it is also interesting to analyze a situation wherein we would like to minimize the total cost with a limit on the total setup hours imposed. The problem can be stated as follows:

$$\text{Minimize} \sum_{i=1}^{n}\left(\frac{D_i}{Q_i}S_i + \frac{Q_I}{2}H_i\right)$$

subject to

$$\sum_{i=1}^{n}\left(\frac{D_i}{Q_i}\right)T_i = K$$

where

- Q_i is the production quantity or lot size of item *i*.
- S_i is the setup cost of item *i*.
- $H_i = hC_i$ is the inventory-carrying cost of item *i*.
- T_i is the setup time required ($S_i = T_i S$ where S is the setup cost per hour).
- D_i is the annual demand of item *i*.
- K is the total available setup time for all items.

The Lagrangian function for this will be as follows:

$$L(Q_i,\lambda)=\sum_{i=1}^{n}\left(\frac{D_i}{Q_i}S_i+\frac{Q_i}{2}H_i\right)+\lambda\left(\sum_{i=1}^{n}\left(\frac{D_i}{Q_i}\right)T_i-K\right)$$

So

$$\frac{\partial L}{\partial Q_i}=-\frac{D_i S_i}{Q_i^2}+\frac{1}{2}H_i-\lambda\frac{D_i T_i}{Q_i^2}=0$$

$$\frac{\partial L}{\partial \lambda}=\sum_{i=1}^{n}\left(\frac{D_i}{Q_i}\right)T_i-K=0$$

This gives us

$$Q_I^*=\sqrt{\frac{2}{H_i}(S_i+\lambda T_i)D_i}$$

Substituting this in the expression for $\frac{\partial L}{\partial \lambda}$, we get

$$\frac{\partial L}{\partial \lambda}=\sum_{i=1}^{n}\left(\frac{D_i}{Q_i^*}\right)T_i-K=0$$

That is,

$$\sum_{i=1}^{n}\frac{T_i D_i}{\sqrt{\frac{2}{H_i}(S_i+\lambda T_i)D_i}}-K=0$$

EXAMPLE 8.3

We will revisit Example 8.2 and extract the information from Tables 8.2 and 8.3. They are shown hereunder in Tables 8.6 and 8.7.

TABLE 8.6 Details of three items for LIMIT analysis

Item	Annual Demand	Setup Hours per Order	Unit Cost
A	24000	2	9
B	14000	3	15
C	12000	2	10
h	0.25	Setup cost per hour	150

We will obtain the EOQs for all the items using the information given in Table 8.2 and obtain the current total setup hours. The calculations are shown in Table 8.7.

TABLE 8.7 Trial quantities and the current total setup hours

Item	Demand D_i	Setup Hours per Setup (T_i)	Unit Cost C_i	Setup Cost S_i	EOQ_i	$H_i = hC_i$	$(D_i/Q_i)*T_i$
A	24000	2	9	300	2530	2.25	19
B	14000	3	15	450	1833	3.75	23
C	12000	2	10	300	1697	2.50	14
				Current Total Setup Hours		S_T	56
	H	0.25	Setup cost per Hour *S*		150		

Suppose we limit the total setup hours to 35 hours. That is, $K = 35$.

We will operationalize the information for the Lagrangian approach as shown in Figures 8.7 and 8.8.

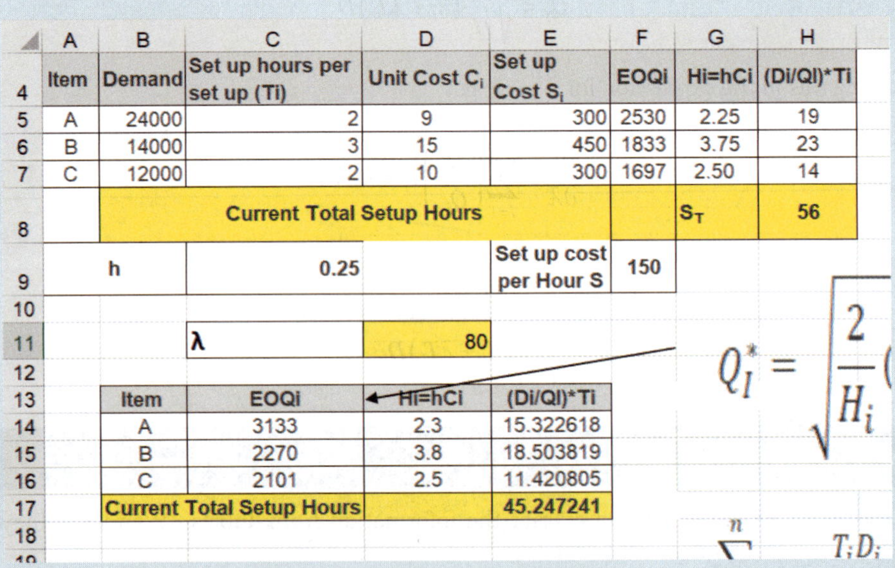

Row	A	B	C	D	E	F	G	H
4	Item	Demand	Set up hours per set up (Ti)	Unit Cost C_i	Set up Cost S_i	EOQi	Hi=hCi	(Di/QI)*Ti
5	A	24000	2	9	300	2530	2.25	19
6	B	14000	3	15	450	1833	3.75	23
7	C	12000	2	10	300	1697	2.50	14
8		Current Total Setup Hours					S_T	56
9		h	0.25		Set up cost per Hour S	150		
10								
11			λ	80				
12								
13		Item	EOQi	Hi=hCi	(Di/QI)*Ti			
14		A	3133	2.3	15.322618			
15		B	2270	3.8	18.503819			
16		C	2101	2.5	11.420805			
17		Current Total Setup Hours			45.247241			
18								

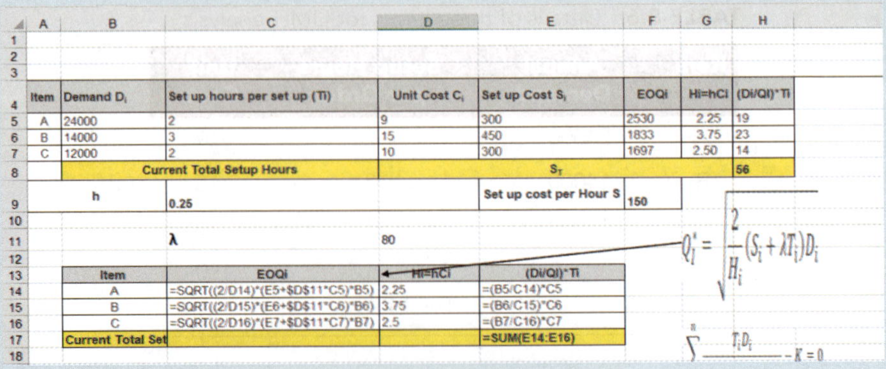

Row	A	B	C	D	E	F	G	H
1								
2								
3								
4	Item	Demand D_i	Set up hours per set up (Ti)	Unit Cost C_i	Set up Cost S_i	EOQi	Hi=hCi	(Di/QI)*Ti
5	A	24000	2	9	300	2530	2.25	19
6	B	14000	3	15	450	1833	3.75	23
7	C	12000	2	10	300	1697	2.50	14
8		Current Total Setup Hours			S_T			56
9		h	0.25		Set up cost per Hour S	150		
10								
11			λ	80				
12								
13		Item	EOQi	Hi=hCi	(Di/QI)*Ti			
14		A	=SQRT((2/D14)*(E5+$D$11*C5)*B5)	2.25	=(B5/C14)*C5			
15		B	=SQRT((2/D15)*(E6+$D$11*C6)*B6)	3.75	=(B6/C15)*C6			
16		C	=SQRT((2/D16)*(E7+$D$11*C7)*B7)	2.5	=(B7/C16)*C7			
17		Current Total Set			=SUM(E14:E16)			
18								

$$Q_i^* = \sqrt{\frac{2}{H_i}(S_i + \lambda T_i)D_i}$$

$$\sum^{n} \frac{T_i D_i}{} - K = 0$$

FIGURE 8.7 Excel sheet for setting up the Lagrangian calculations.

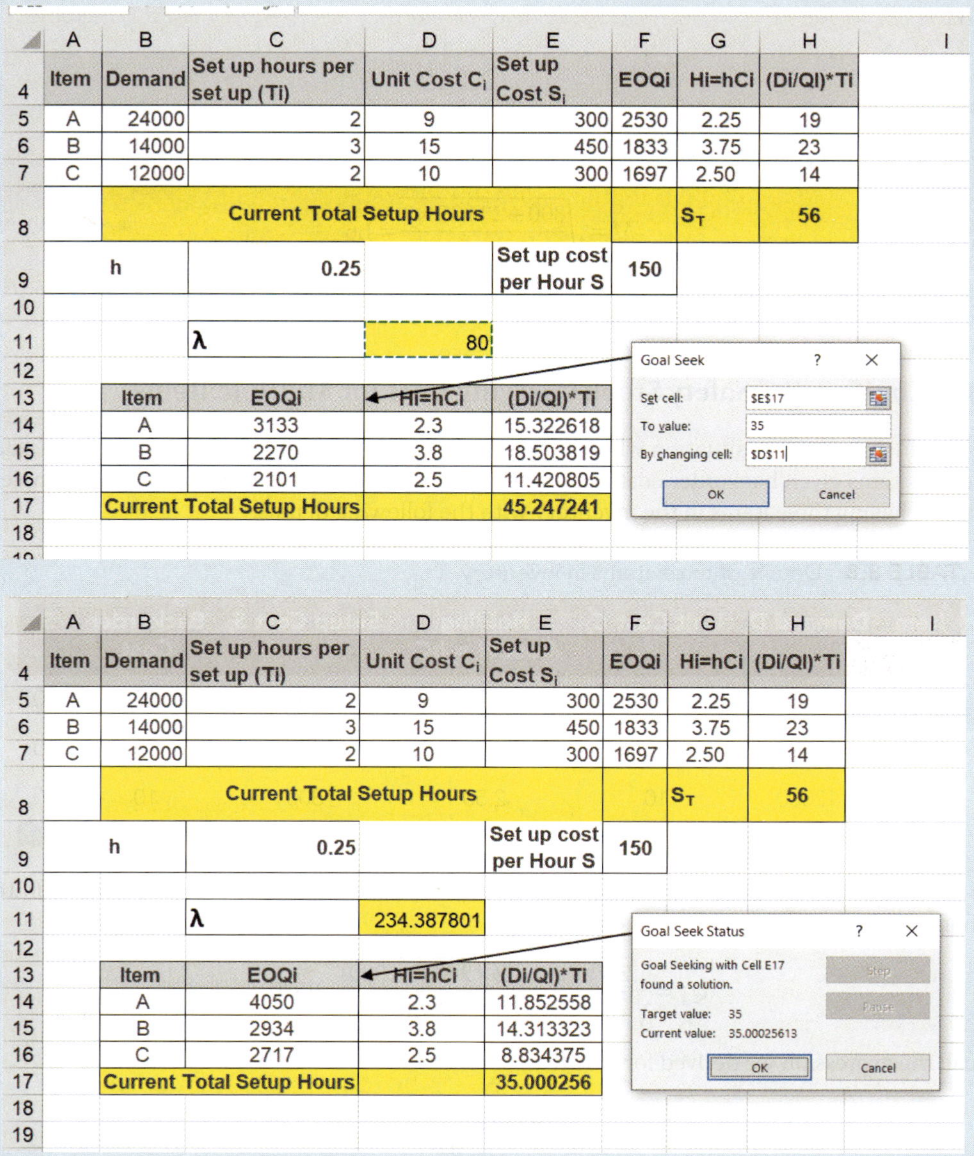

FIGURE 8.8 Using Goal Seek to perform the Lagrangian and obtaining the adjusted quantities.

It is interesting to note that these adjusted quantities are the same as what we obtained through the LIMIT approach. It is also interesting to note that the LIMIT approach was very simple to just use $M = 56/35 = 1.6$ and use it to obtain the revised lot sizes by multiplying it with the respective EOQs.

So if we attempt to find how the M of the LIMIT approach and the λ of the Lagrangian are related, we look at the ratio of adjusted Q/normal EOQ.

$$M = \frac{Q^*}{EOQ} = \frac{\sqrt{\frac{2}{H_i}(S_i + \lambda T_i)D_i}}{\sqrt{\frac{2D_iS_i}{H_i}}}$$

So

$$M = \sqrt{\frac{S_i + \lambda T_i}{S_i}}$$

We can verify this for item 1.

$$M = \sqrt{\frac{300 + 234.39 \times 2}{300}} = 1.6$$

This was the same as 56/35 = 1.60.

8.3.2 Limit on the Safety Stock Carrying Cost for Multiple Items

We will analyze another situation wherein we restrict our limit on the total carrying cost of safety stock for items given backorder costs and other details. Let us consider the following example in Table 8.8 having three items in the inventory with the following details.

TABLE 8.8 Details of three items in inventory

Item	Demand D_i	Unit Cost C_i	Holding Cost $H_i = hC_i$	Setup Cost S_i	Backorder Cost	S'_d
A	24000	9	2.25	300	10	50
B	14000	15	3.75	450	15	40
C	12000	10	2.50	300	10	50

We will show the calculation of the safety stock and the carrying cost of the safety stock for item A. For other items, it can be carried out similarly.

$$Q_A = \sqrt{\frac{2D_A S_A}{H_A}} = \sqrt{\frac{2 \times 24000 \times 300}{2.25}} = 2530$$

Recall the expression we derived for OSOR as

$$OSOR = \frac{HQ}{\pi D}$$

So

$$OSOR = \frac{2.25 \times 2530}{10 \times 24{,}000} = 0.0234$$

So OSL = 1 − 0.0234 = 0.9766. The z-value is 1.99, and so the total safety stock will be $z^* s'_d$ = $1.99 \times 50 = 99$ and the carrying cost is $99 \times 2.50 = 223$.

Similarly, we can arrive at the same for items B and C. The safety stock for B and C will be 74 and 90, respectively, and the carrying costs will be 276 and 226, respectively. So the total carrying cost of the safety stock will be 223 + 276 + 226 = 725.

We will restrict the carrying cost of the safety stock to 500 only and then see how the safety stock can be adjusted using the Lagrangian approach.

In this case, the problem can be stated as follows:

$$\text{Minimize} \sum_{i=1}^{n} \left(\frac{D_i}{Q_i}\right) s'_{d_i} E_{z_i} \pi_i$$

Subject to

$$\sum_{i=1}^{n} z_i s'_{d_i} H_i = I$$

where I is the limit on the safety inventory-carrying cost.

The Lagrangian calculations are complex due to the process of differentiating an integral function. Silver and Peterson have presented a simplified form to perform the Lagrangian calculations.

The Lagrangian for the example in Table 8.8 will be as follows:

We find

$$OSOR_i = \lambda \left[\frac{H_i Q_i}{\pi_i D_i} \right]$$

Such that

$$z_A s'_{d_A} H_A + z_B s'_{d_B} H_B + z_C s'_{d_C} H_C = 500$$

We will use Excel to set up the table for performing the Lagrangian analysis. They are shown in Figures 8.9 and 8.10.

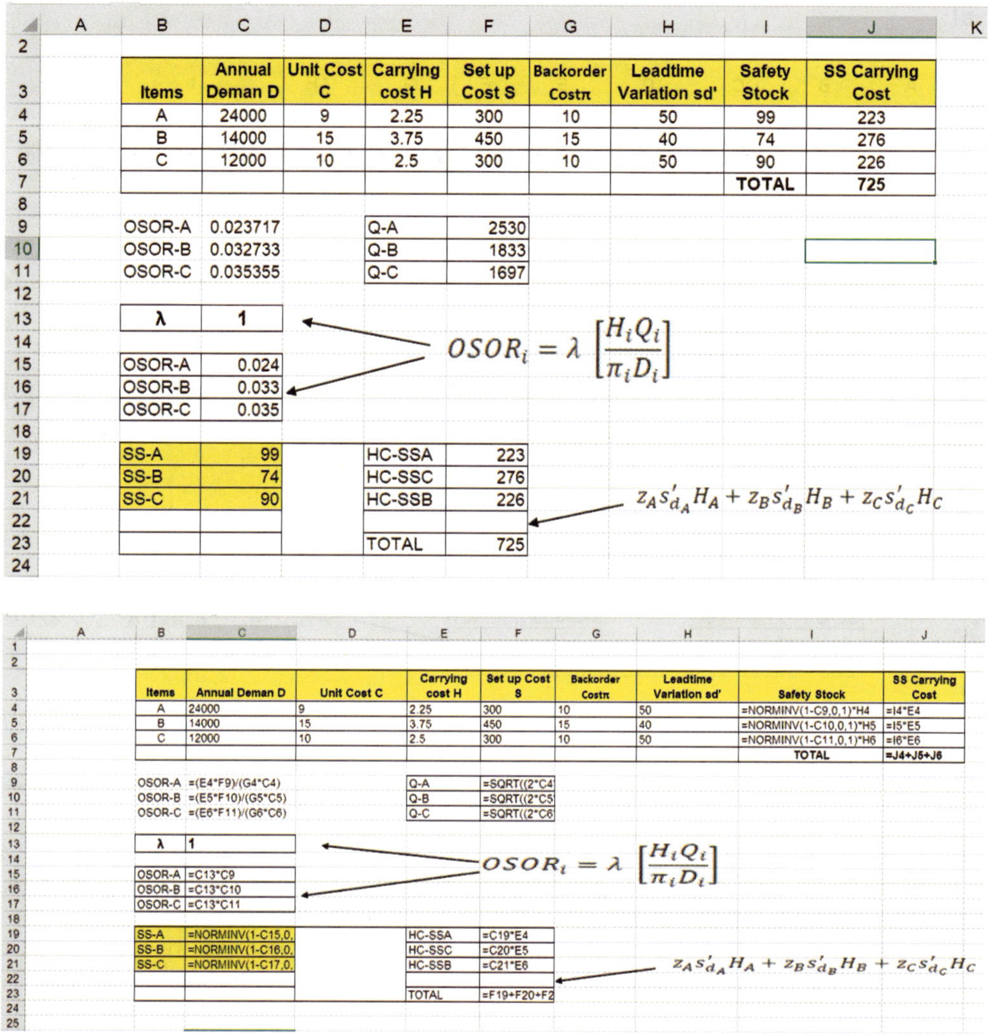

Items	Annual Deman D	Unit Cost C	Carrying cost H	Set up Cost S	Backorder Costπ	Leadtime Variation sd'	Safety Stock	SS Carrying Cost
A	24000	9	2.25	300	10	50	99	223
B	14000	15	3.75	450	15	40	74	276
C	12000	10	2.5	300	10	50	90	226
							TOTAL	725

OSOR-A	0.023717	Q-A	2530
OSOR-B	0.032733	Q-B	1833
OSOR-C	0.035355	Q-C	1697

λ	1
OSOR-A	0.024
OSOR-B	0.033
OSOR-C	0.035

$OSOR_i = \lambda \left[\frac{H_i Q_i}{\pi_i D_i} \right]$

SS-A	99	HC-SSA	223
SS-B	74	HC-SSC	276
SS-C	90	HC-SSB	226
		TOTAL	725

$z_A s'_{d_A} H_A + z_B s'_{d_B} H_B + z_C s'_{d_C} H_C$

Items	Annual Deman D	Unit Cost C	Carrying cost H	Set up Cost S	Backorder Costπ	Leadtime Variation sd'	Safety Stock	SS Carrying Cost
A	24000	9	2.25	300	10	50	=NORMINV(1-C9,0,1)*H4	=I4*E4
B	14000	15	3.75	450	15	40	=NORMINV(1-C10,0,1)*H5	=I5*E5
C	12000	10	2.5	300	10	50	=NORMINV(1-C11,0,1)*H6	=I6*E6
							TOTAL	=J4+J5+J6

OSOR-A	=(E4*F9)/(G4*C4)	Q-A	=SQRT((2*C4
OSOR-B	=(E5*F10)/(G5*C5)	Q-B	=SQRT((2*C5
OSOR-C	=(E6*F11)/(G6*C6)	Q-C	=SQRT((2*C6

λ	1
OSOR-A	=C13*C9
OSOR-B	=C13*C10
OSOR-C	=C13*C11

$OSOR_i = \lambda \left[\frac{H_i Q_i}{\pi_i D_i} \right]$

SS-A	=NORMINV(1-C15,0,	HC-SSA	=C19*E4
SS-B	=NORMINV(1-C16,0,	HC-SSC	=C20*E5
SS-C	=NORMINV(1-C17,0,	HC-SSB	=C21*E6
		TOTAL	=F19+F20+F2

$z_A s'_{d_A} H_A + z_B s'_{d_B} H_B + z_C s'_{d_C} H_C$

FIGURE 8.9 Setting up the Excel sheet for Lagrangian analysis for safety stock carrying cost.

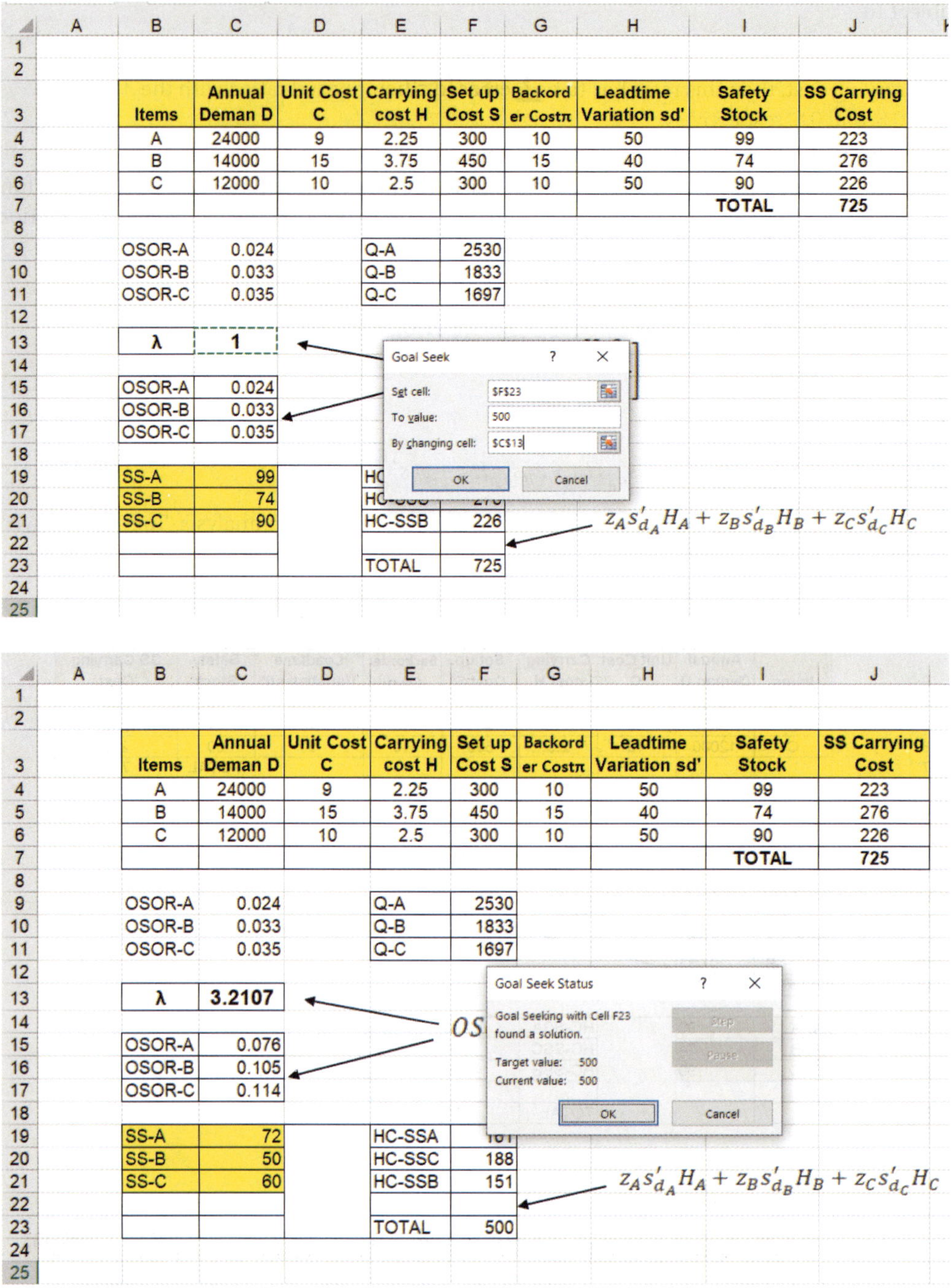

FIGURE 8.10 Lagrangian calculations for safety stock.

We see from the preceding figure that the safety stocks of items A, B, and C are adjusted to 72, 50, and 60, respectively, with the total cost of carrying them as 500 from the earlier amounts, that is, sizes of 99, 74, and 90, respectively, with the total carrying cost of 725.

Upon a close look at the Lagrangian function for solving the problem, we observe that the Lagrangian multiplier tries to adjust the ratio of carrying cost H to the stockout penalty π.

We see that

$$OSOR_i = \lambda\left[\frac{H_i Q_i}{\pi_i D_i}\right] \text{ is basically } \lambda\frac{H_i}{\pi_i}\left(\frac{Q_i}{D_i}\right)$$

The initial ratios of $\frac{H_i}{\pi_i}$ for the items were, respectively, 0.23, 0.25, and 0.25. If we need to reduce the carrying cost, then this ratio has to be increased. Their revised ratios with the λ value of 3.2 are 0.72, 0.8, and 0.8, respectively.

We also observe that if we ignore the costs here and still keep the constraint of carrying the safety stock at 500, the Lagrangian approach gives results very close to the previous one. We set up the Lagrangian as

$$OSOR_i = \lambda\left[\frac{Q_i}{D_i}\right]$$

subject to

$$z_A s'_{d_A} H_A + z_B s'_{d_B} H_B + z_C s'_{d_C} H_C = 500$$

The Excel setup and the Lagrangian calculations are shown in Figures 8.11 and 8.12.

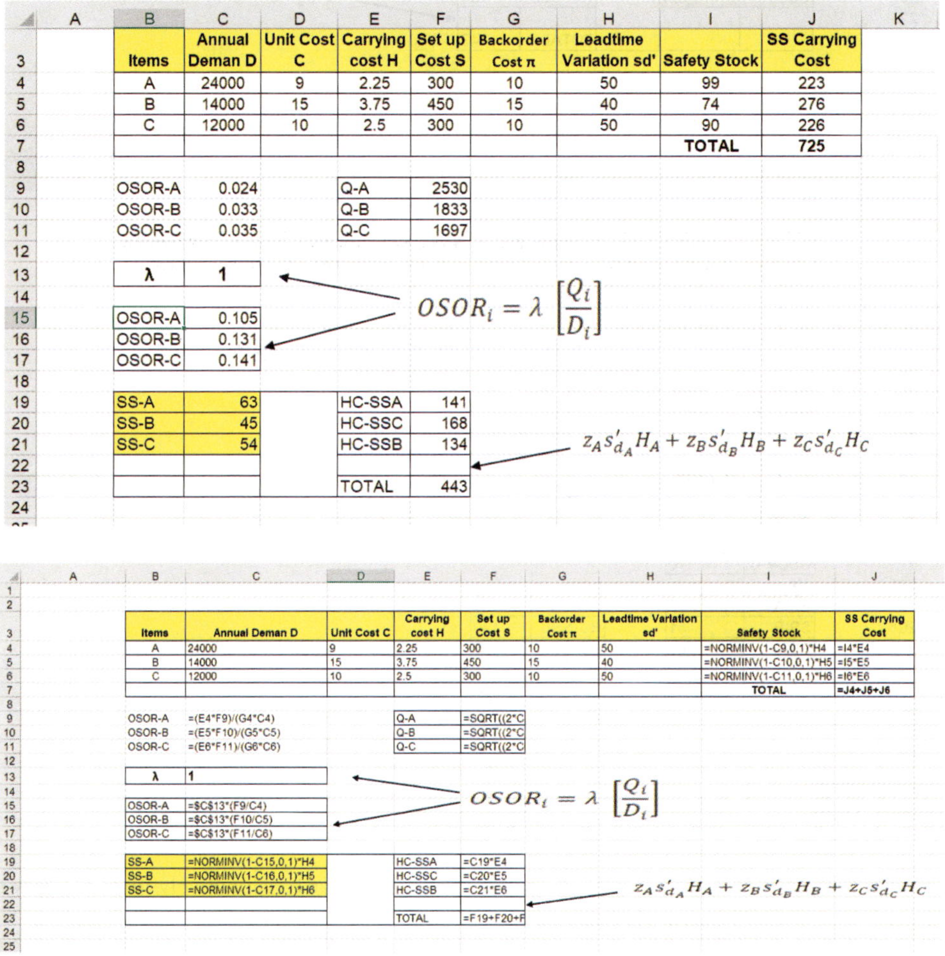

FIGURE 8.11 Setting up the Excel sheet for the safety stock carrying cost limit.

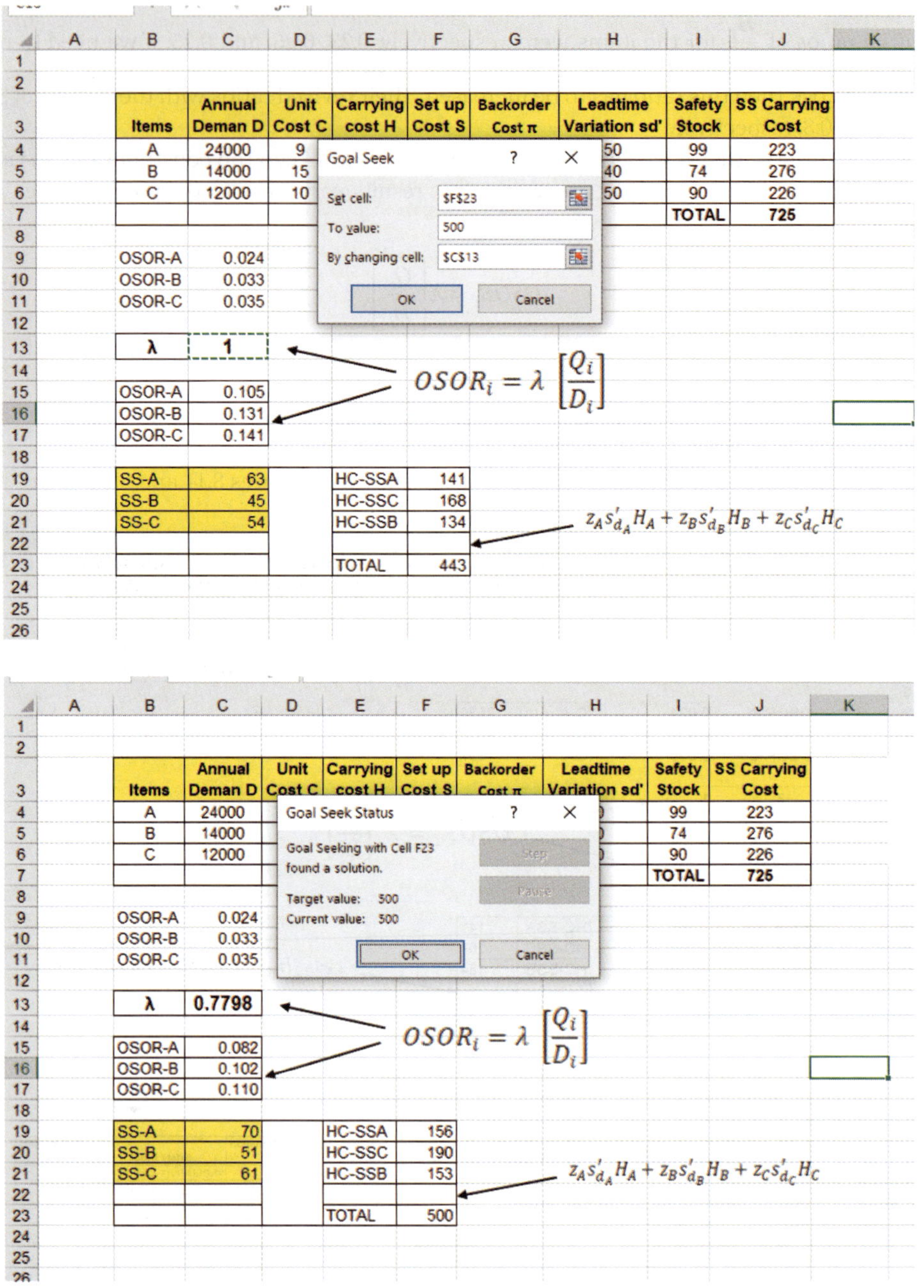

FIGURE 8.12 Lagrangian calculations for limits on the safety stock carrying cost.

We see that the safety stock values of A, B, and C are 70, 51, and 61, respectively, which is very close to the ones we obtained in the previous case.

8.3.3 Lagrangian Analysis for Stockout Situations

Stockout situations refer to the situations when stockouts occur in order cycles. As discussed earlier, this is related to the OSOR of an order cycle and is different from USOR. They refer only to occasions and not the number of units stocked out and can be expressed as:

$$\text{Number of cycles in a year} \times \text{The probability of stockout in a cycle, that is, OSOR}$$

$$(D/Q) \times \text{OSOR}$$

Let us revisit the same example which we discussed in the safety stock case. Let us assume that the safety stock value is 2901 (that is without any restriction), and now we wish to minimize the stockout situations with that level of safety stock being carried. The problem can be stated as follows in general:

$$\text{Minimize} \sum_{i=1}^{n} \frac{D_i}{Q_i} OSOR_i$$

subject to

$$\sum_{i=1}^{n} z_i s'_{d_i} C_i = K$$

where K is the total cost of the safety stocks (not the carrying cost)

The Lagrangian function will be

$$L(z_i,\lambda) = \sum_{i=1}^{n} \frac{D_i}{Q_i} OSOR_i + \lambda\left(\sum_{i=1}^{n} z_i s'_{d_i} C_i - K\right)$$

and

$$\frac{\partial L}{\partial z_i} = \frac{D_i}{Q_i} f(z_i) + \lambda(s'_{d_i} H_i) = 0$$

and

$$\frac{\partial L}{\partial z_i} = \sum_{i=1}^{n} z_i s'_{d_i} H_i - K = 0$$

where $f(z_i)$ is the density function of a unit normal distribution.

The derivations result in the following expression for $z_{i.}$

$$z_i = \sqrt{2\ln\left(\frac{D_i}{\lambda\sqrt{2\pi Q_i C_i s'_{i_d}}}\right)}$$

We will revisit the preceding example for this situation.

Figures 8.13 and 8.14 show the setting up of the Excel sheet for the Lagrangian calculations and the Lagrangian analysis.

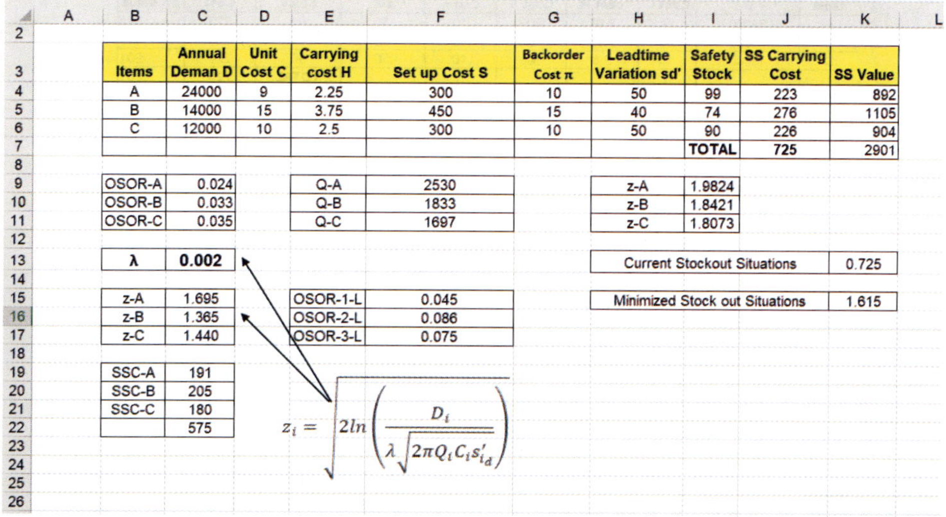

	B	C	D	E	F	G	H	I	J	K
3	Items	Annual Deman D	Unit Cost C	Carrying cost H	Set up Cost S	Backorder Cost π	Leadtime Variation sd'	Safety Stock	SS Carrying Cost	SS Value
4	A	24000	9	2.25	300	10	50	99	223	892
5	B	14000	15	3.75	450	15	40	74	276	1105
6	C	12000	10	2.5	300	10	50	90	226	904
7								TOTAL	725	2901
9	OSOR-A	0.024		Q-A	2530		z-A	1.9824		
10	OSOR-B	0.033		Q-B	1833		z-B	1.8421		
11	OSOR-C	0.035		Q-C	1697		z-C	1.8073		
13	λ	0.002					Current Stockout Situations			0.725
15	z-A	1.695		OSOR-1-L	0.045		Minimized Stock out Situations			1.615
16	z-B	1.365		OSOR-2-L	0.086					
17	z-C	1.440		OSOR-3-L	0.075					
19	SSC-A	191								
20	SSC-B	205								
21	SSC-C	180								
22		575								

$$z_i = \sqrt{2ln\left(\frac{D_i}{\lambda\sqrt{2\pi Q_i C_i s'_{i_d}}}\right)}$$

FIGURE 8.13 Setting up the Excel sheet for Lagrangian analysis of the stockout situations case.

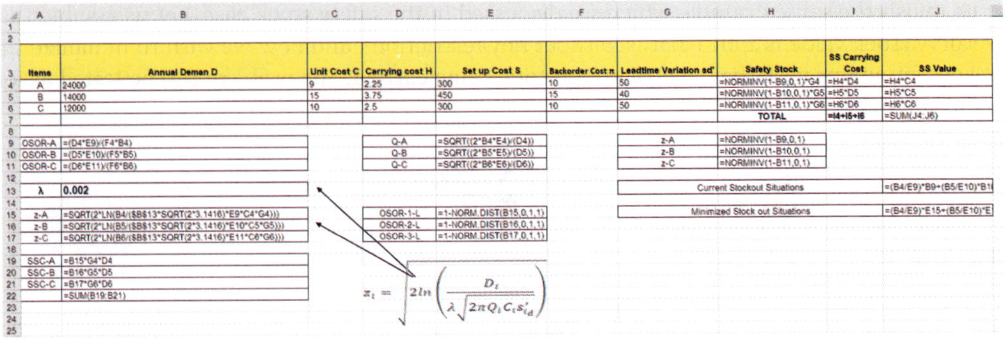

FIGURE 8.13 (Continued)

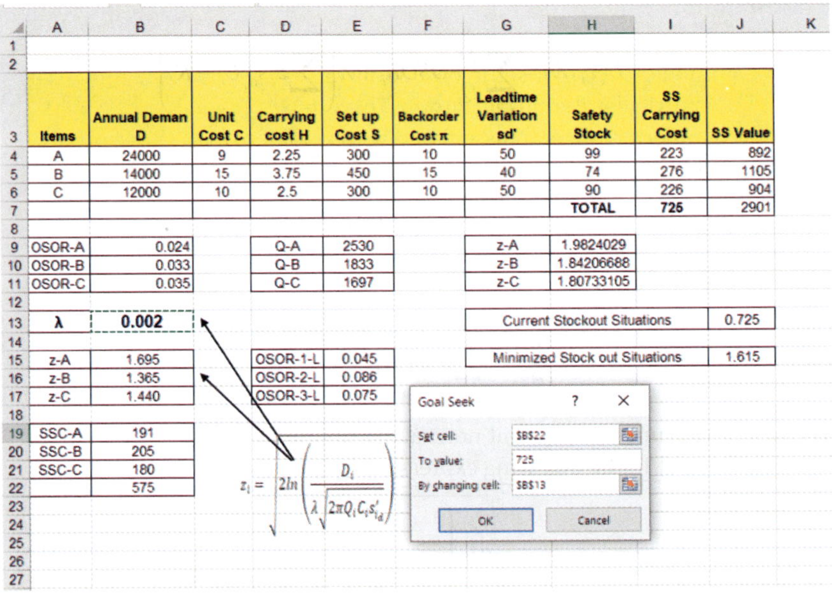

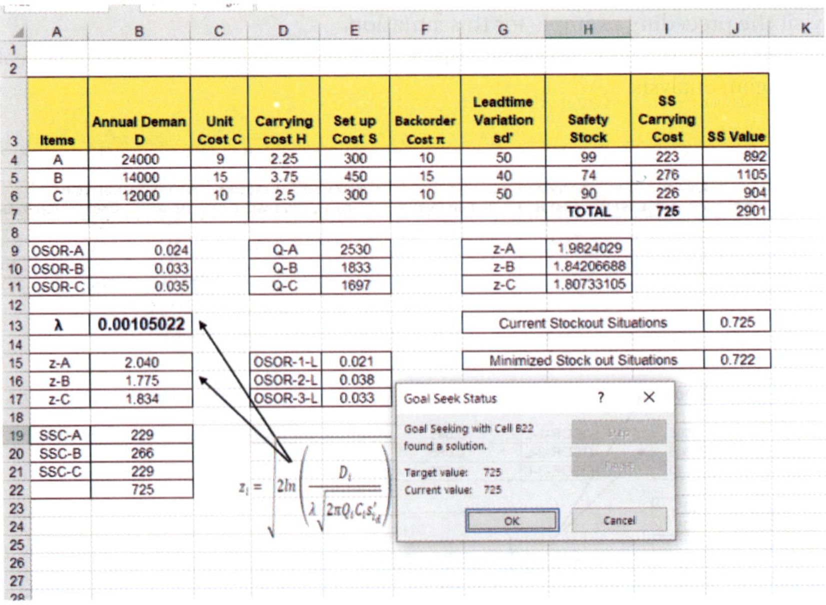

FIGURE 8.14 Using Goal Seek for Lagrangian calculations for the stockout situations case.

We see that the stockout situations have been reduced to 0.722 from 0.725. We will now look at inventory systems for multiple items in a joint replacement scenario and look at various inventory strategies for analyzing the trade-offs among various cost drivers in the following sections.

8.4 | JOINT REPLENISHMENT OF MULTIPLE ITEMS

In the previous chapter, we analyzed inventory systems dealing with a single item where the demand was assumed to be deterministic or random and presented various types of inventory models: EOQ, POQ, quantity discount scenarios in EOQs, safety stock requirements, reorder points, etc. But in practice, we come across situations where organizations deal with multiple items and very often jointly replenish items in the inventory by analyzing the trade-offs among the cost drivers: ordering costs, inventory-carrying costs, etc.

The situations shown earlier are only a few instances how the concept of Lagrangian can be used. It will be interesting to use many situations in practice to see how effective this approach could be in resolving inventory issues when dealing in practice.

Joint replenishment of items usually occurs when an organization procures items from a supplier outside or in some cases manufactures locally within the organization. There are many advantages when groups of items of a particular family of products are purchased from a supplier, which involves a common ordering or setup cost and a specific and unique minor cost of ordering, or setup cost for a particular item in the group. This enables them to combine items to share the same fixed cost of ordering or setup associated with it and involves a minor and small item-specific ordering cost or setup cost for an item in the group. For example, there are advantages if products of different sizes are manufactured together and packaged separately to save the cost of manufacturing and packaging for outbound dispatches.

In general, the fixed cost we are referring to, which is associated with the purchase of many items from a single source of supply, is independent of the quantity of the order size, that is, the number of items purchased in any given order. When we develop and discuss models in this section, the fixed cost we will be referring to refers to the major setup cost incurred in manufacturing several items with a common setup or ordering cost when placing orders for multiple items from the same supplier. Although we refer to it as setup cost while discussing the models, it equally applies to the case of ordering just as we used them in the EOQ or POQ models. In our discussion on the reasons for keeping inventory, we have listed scale of economies as one of the reasons. This scale of economy in manufacturing multiple items (or SKUs) is advantageous when the manufacturing capacities are limited. Therefore, it is of interest to determine how much of each item should be produced (purchased) during any given setup (order).

In joint replenishment inventory models, we are concerned with the following:

1. The monetary value (say dollar value) or quantity of individual items produced or ordered during each cycle.
2. The total monetary value (or dollar value) or quantities of all items produced or ordered during each cycle.
3. The frequency (or the time interval between two orders) at which these items are ordered or produced.

These models, which we are presenting in this section, address the following three important strategies for inventory aggregation.

1. Producing or ordering items individually as independent items without any aggregation.
2. Joint replenishment or ordering wherein all the items are ordered in each of the orders when placed. This is sometimes referred to as complete aggregation.
3. Improving the order frequencies by varying the replenishment cycles of individual items in the family to exploit the fixed cost of setup or ordering. In this case, every item may or may not be ordered during each order cycle. This is sometimes referred to as tailored aggregation.

The objective of all these models will be to minimize the total relevant costs for a group of items jointly ordered or produced. The total relevant cost generally includes the setup cost (ordering cost) and inventory-carrying costs in general and can include other costs wherever necessary. For discussion purposes, we will describe the context as order quantities that are placed with a supplier. However, they are equally applied for production quantities where we replace the ordering costs with setup costs.

One of the important aspects of inventory decisions in practice is about joint ordering and replacement. Most firms have common sourcing, and multiple items are sourced from a single supplier very often. It is very important how the replacement is done when trade-offs exist in ordering from a common source and its effect on the total inventory cost. This is also one of the many interesting areas for researchers to come up with methods and algorithms.

We will use the following notations:

1. n is the total number of items.
2. D_i is the annual demand of the ith item ($i = 1, 2, ..., n$).
3. S is the fixed cost for each order that is placed, independent of the items or the number of items ordered.
4. s_i is the item-specific ordering cost of the ith item (in addition to S) ($i = 1, 2, ..., n$).
5. $H_i = h^*C_i$ is the inventory-carrying cost per unit annually for the ith item ($i = 1, 2, ..., n$), where h is the inventory-carrying percentage and C_i is the unit cost of item i.
6. $T = 1/N$ is the base cycle time (time interval, in years between replenishments of the group of items and it is assumed to be continuous), where N is the total number of order cycles in a year.
7. K_i is the number of integer multiples of T that a replenishment of item i will be ordered.
8. TRC is the total relevant cost.

The ordering cost S' of all the items is placed in one order $= S + \sum_{i=1}^{n} s_i$.

If the items are independently ordered, then each item i will have an ordering cost of $S + s_i$. Let us consider the following example given in Table 8.9 for all scenarios.

EXAMPLE 8.4

TABLE 8.9 Details of items for joint replenishment

Items	D_i	C_i	D_iC_i	s_i
1	10000	5	50000	10
2	7000	8	56000	10
3	4000	10	40000	20
4	2000	8	16000	20
5	1000	10	10000	40
h	0.25			
S	150	ΣD_iC_i	172000	
$S + \Sigma s_i$	250		Σs_i	100

Strategy 1: If items are ordered independently

The calculations of the Q_i's and the costs are shown in Table 8.10.

TABLE 8.10 Calculations of Qs

Items	D_i	C_i	s_i	$S + s_i$	Q_i	Setup Cost	Inventory- Carrying Cost
1	10000	5	10	160	1600.00	1000.00	1000.00
2	7000	8	10	160	1058.30	1058.30	1058.30
3	4000	10	20	170	737.56	921.95	921.95
4	2000	8	20	170	583.10	583.10	583.10
5	1000	10	40	190	389.87	487.34	487.34
h	0.25						
S	150	Σs_i	100		Total	4050.69	4050.69
$S + \Sigma s_i$	250				Total Cost		8101.38

In this case, the total relevant cost is 8101.38.

Strategy 2: If items are jointly ordered

As mentioned earlier, in this case, the joint ordering cost is $S' = S + \sum_{i=1}^{n} s_i$ if all the items are placed in one order.

Let $D = \sum_{i=1}^{n} D_i C_i$ and let $Q = \sum_{i=1}^{n} Q_i C_i$, the monetary values of the demand and order quantities. Then it is clear that

$$N = \frac{D}{Q} = \frac{\sum_{i=1}^{n} D_i C_i}{\sum_{i=1}^{n} Q_i C_i}.$$

$$TRC = \frac{D}{Q} * S' + \frac{Q}{2} * h$$

So this gives

$$Q = \sqrt{\frac{2DS'}{h}}$$

and so,

$$N = \sqrt{\frac{Dh}{2S'}} = \sqrt{\frac{h\sum D_i C_i}{2\left[S' + \sum s_i\right]}}$$

Since $T = \frac{1}{N}$, we have

$$T = \sqrt{\frac{2\left[S' + \sum s_i\right]}{h\sum D_i C_i}}$$

This gives us each of the Q_i that can be determined by

$$Q_i = \frac{D_i}{N}$$

For the example, we have

$$N = \sqrt{\frac{h\sum D_i C_i}{2\left[S' + \sum s_i\right]}}$$

$$N = \sqrt{\frac{0.25(172000)}{2\times[150+100]}} = 9.276$$

This gives us

Item	Q_i	C_i	Q_iC_i
1	1078	5	5390
2	754.6	8	6036.8
3	431.2	10	4312
4	215.6	8	1724.8
5	107.8	10	1078
		$\sum Q_iC_i$	18541.6

The basic approach of determining lot sizes for multiple items changes from single item where the focus on optimizing them changes from determining Q first, then through that Q, the number of orders N to optimizing the number of orders N first and then through that N, the lot sizes Q of each item. This gives scope to explore a few aggregation strategies in inventory decisions as to how the items should be ordered.

Total relevant cost is 9.2764 × 250 + (18542) × 0.25 = 2319 + 2318 = 4637. To arrive at the setup cost of the individual items, we will pro-rate the major setup cost S for item i based on D_iC_i to the total D_iC_i. Here

$$\sum D_iC_i = 172{,}000$$

For example, for item 1, the major setup cost will be calculated as follows:

$$(D_1C_1)/\left(\sum D_iC_i\right) \times 150 = (50{,}000/172{,}000) \times 150 = 43.60$$

We add the item dependent setup cost 10 to this, so the calculated setup cost per setup for item 1 will be 43.60 + 10 = 53.60.

Hence, the total setup cost for item 1 will be $(D_1/Q_1) \times 53.60 = (10{,}000/1078) \times 53.60 =$ 496.28. It is calculated similarly for the other items.

The summary of the inventory-carrying cost and the setup cost summary is given in Table 8.11.

TABLE 8.11 Summary of costs

Items	D_i	s_i	C_i	D_iC_i	Q_i	Q_iC_i	Prorated Major Set Cost	Setup Cost per Setup	Setup Cost	Inventory-Carrying Cost
1	10000	10	5	50000	1078.0	5390.0	43.60	53.60	497.26	673.75
2	7000	10	8	56000	754.6	6036.8	48.84	58.84	545.80	754.60
3	4000	20	10	40000	431.2	4312.0	34.88	54.88	509.13	539.00
4	2000	20	8	16000	215.6	1724.8	13.95	33.95	314.97	215.60
5	1000	40	10	10000	107.8	1078.0	8.72	48.72	451.96	134.75
Total	24000			172000		18541.6			2319	2318
N	9.2764			T	0.1078	h	0.25	Total cost		4637

Also $T = 1/N = 1/9.2764 = 0.1078$.

We see that by jointly ordering the items, the total relevant cost has decreased from 8101.38 to 4637.

Strategy 3: Tailored aggregation of adjusting the frequencies of items

In this case, we attempt a few methods to explore the tailored aggregation of the lot sizing where we relax the policy of ordering every item in every order and arrive at optimal frequencies of the items such that the frequencies are staggered to exploit the trade-off between setup cost and the inventory-carrying cost.

For all these methods, we convert the total relevant cost equation given earlier as

$$TRC = \frac{S}{T} + \frac{1}{T}\sum_{i=1}^{n}\frac{s_i}{K_i} + \frac{T}{2}\sum_{i=1}^{n} hC_iD_iK_i$$

We will show how the earlier equation is the same as the one given earlier.

We saw that K_i refers to the number of integer multiples of T that a replenishment of item i will be ordered. This means if $K_i = 2$, for every second order that is placed, the item i will be included in that. Thus, the number of orders of the item i will be N/K_i, that is, $\frac{1}{T*K_i}$ and the average cost of including the item i will be s_i/K_i in each order. Hence, the ordering cost on an average will be $\left(S+\sum_{i=1}^{n}\frac{s_i}{K_i}\right)$; therefore, the total ordering cost will be $N\left(S+\sum_{i=1}^{n}\frac{s_i}{K_i}\right)$, which is the same as $(1/T)\left(S+\sum_{i=1}^{n}\frac{s_i}{K_i}\right)$. That is, $\frac{S}{T}+\frac{1}{T}\sum_{i=1}^{n}\frac{s_i}{K_i}$. Now the inventory-carrying cost is $\frac{Q}{2}h$.

If K_i is the frequency of item i, then it will be ordered N/K_i times in a year. So the Q_i for this item will be $(D_i/(N/K_i))$, that is, D_iK_i/N or D_iK_iT as $1/N = T$. Now

$$\frac{Q}{2}*h=\sum_{i=1}^{n}\frac{hQ_iC_i}{2}=\sum_{i=1}^{n}\frac{hD_iK_iTC_i}{2}=\frac{T}{2}\sum_{i=1}^{n}hC_iD_iK_i$$

So

$$TRC=\frac{D}{Q}*S'+\frac{Q}{2}*h$$

is the same as

$$TRC=\frac{S}{T}+\frac{1}{T}\sum_{i=1}^{n}\frac{s_i}{K_i}+\frac{T}{2}\sum_{i=1}^{n}H_iD_iK_i \tag{8.18}$$

(where $H_i = hC_i$)

We will use this expression for all the tailored aggregation methods which we will represent in the following sections.

The total relevant cost function given above has $(n + 1)$ decision variables with one variable as the continuous variable T and the other variables K_i as integers with $i = 1, 2, ..., n$. As we notice, there are many local minimum points for this total cost function, and the primary focus of the following methods will be to search for the global optimum.

We differentiate Eq. (8.18) with respect to T and that results in the optimum cycle time T^* as a function of the values of K_i's.

$$T^*=\sqrt{\frac{2\left(S+\sum_{i=1}^{n}\frac{s_i}{K_i}\right)}{\sum_{i=1}^{n}H_iD_iK_i}} \tag{8.19}$$

Substituting the value of T^* in Eq. (8.18), we get the TRC as a function of K_i's as follows:

$$TRC^*=\left[\sqrt{2\left(S+\sum_{i=1}^{n}\frac{s_i}{K_i}\right)\sum_{i=1}^{n}H_iD_iK_i}\right] \tag{8.20}$$

Now, the next step will be to find the combinations of K_i's that minimize the TRC. We will present various methods of the same. Three of them need only one iteration, while the other methods may need more iterations.

8.4.1 Brown's Algorithm

In tailored aggregation, a lot of methods have been developed and it is not very clear as to which method is the best because, for different problems, the methods give different solutions and it is difficult to establish the efficiency of methods. The bibliography gives many references where the authors report simulation results of various methods for more insight. It is always good to experiment with the methods for a given situation and use the best solution.

Brown (1967) suggested that the optimum values of K_i's can be found, which will minimize the TRC* in Eq. (8.20). Taking the derivatives with respect to K_i's, we obtain

$$K_i^2 = \frac{s_i}{\left(S + \sum_{j=1}^{n} \frac{s_j}{K_j}\right)} * \frac{\sum_{j=1}^{n} H_j D_j K_j}{H_i D_i} \tag{8.21}$$

Equation (8.21) is reduced to

$$K_i = \frac{1}{T}\sqrt{\frac{2 * s_i}{H_i D_i}} \tag{8.22}$$

after substituting the value of T from Eq. (8.19).

Brown's algorithm follows an iterative procedure. The procedure starts with $K_i = 1$ for all items and then subsequently calculates the values of multiples of K_i for each item i using Eq. (8.22). When the values of the multiples of K_i do not change significantly in two consecutive iterations, the computations are terminated. Although the calculations appear to be complicated, it is actually straightforward.

The following steps illustrate the algorithm for the example:

Step 1: Calculate the order interval T from Eq. (8.19).
$T = 0.1078$.

Step 2: Calculate the interval multiple K_i using Eq. (8.22).

$$K_i = \frac{1}{T}\sqrt{\frac{2 * s_i}{H_i D_i}}$$

The integer value of each K_i is the only integer between X and $X + 1$ where

$$X = \frac{-1 + \sqrt{\left(1 + 4K_i^2\right)}}{2}$$

Table 8.12 lists the critical values of K_i at which the actual item multiple increases to the next integer. This is actually the value that satisfies the following equations indicated by Brown.

$$n(n - 1) \le K_i^2 \le n(n + 1)$$

where n is the integer value of K_i shown in Table 8.12.

TABLE 8.12 Ranges of values for K_i

Range of K_i that Is Obtained Using Eq. (8.22)	Integer Value of K_i
0 to 1.414	1
1.414 to 2.449	2
2.449 to 3.464	3
3.464 to 4.472	4
4.472 to 5.477	5
5.477 to 6.481	6
6.481 to 7.483	7
For n >6, use the integer part of $n + 0.52$	—

For example,

$$K_1 = \frac{1}{0.1048}\sqrt{\frac{2\times 10}{1.25\times 1000}} = 0.3711 \gg K_1 = 1$$

after rounding off the value of K_i using Table 8.12.

Similarly, it is computed for all the items as shown in Table 8.13.

TABLE 8.13 K_i values

Items	D_i	s_i	C_i	H_i (h^*C_i)	K_i	Integer K_i
1	10000	10	5	1.25	0.3711	1
2	7000	10	8	2.00	0.3506	1
3	4000	20	10	2.50	0.5867	1
4	2000	20	8	2.00	0.9276	1
5	1000	40	10	2.50	1.6594	2

Step 3: Determine the revised value of T using Eq. (8.19) and the K_i's from Step 2 (refer to Table 8.13).

$$T^* = \sqrt{\frac{2\left(S + \sum_{i=1}^{n} \frac{s_i}{K_i}\right)}{\sum_{i=1}^{n} H_i D_i K_i}} = \sqrt{\frac{460}{45{,}500}} = 0.1005$$

Step 4: With the modified value of T, go to Step 2 and recompute the values of K_i's. If the values of K_i's do not change from the previous iteration, terminate the iteration. If not, use the recomputed values of K_i's in Eq. (8.19) and compute the new value of T. Repeat Steps 2 to 4 till two consecutive iterations give the same values of K_i's.

In this case, going to Step 2 gives the following values of K_i's as shown in Table 8.14.

For example,

$$K_1 = \frac{1}{0.1005}\sqrt{\frac{2\times 10}{1.25\times 10{,}000}} = 0.3978 \gg K_1 = 1$$

TABLE 8.14 New K_i values

Items	D_i	s_i	C_i	H_i	New K_i	Integer K_i
1	10000	10	5	1.25	0.3978	1
2	7000	10	8	2.00	0.3759	1
3	4000	20	10	2.50	0.6290	1
4	2000	20	8	2.00	0.9946	1
5	1000	40	10	2.50	1.7791	2

We see that the values of K_i's have not changed, and so we terminate the iterations here.

The result is that items 1 to 4 will be included in every order, while item 5 will be included in every second order. The recalculated Q_i and the total cost are shown in Table 8.15.

TABLE 8.15 Recalculated Q_i's

Items	D_i	s_i	C_i	H_i	Q_i	Inventory-Carrying Cost
1	10000	10	5	1.25	1005	628
2	7000	10	8	2.00	704	704
3	4000	20	10	2.50	402	503
4	2000	20	8	2.00	201	201
5	1000	40	10	2.50	201	251
T	0.1005	N	9.95	Setup Cost	2289	2286
S	150	h	0.25	Total Cost		4575

We see that the total cost has come down from $ 4637 to $ 4575 with the modified frequencies of the items using Brown's algorithm.

8.4.2 Silver (1976)

Silver, in 1976, proposed a simplified method improving Brown's algorithm, which does not require any iterative procedure. The steps are as follows:

1. Find $\text{Min}_i\left(\frac{s_i}{D_iC_i}\right)$
2. Define this item as *j*. Then the values of various K_i's are computed as follows:

$$K_i^* = \sqrt{\frac{s_i}{D_iC_i}} \times \sqrt{\frac{D_jC_j}{S+s_j}} \tag{8.23}$$

3. Determine $T = \sqrt{\frac{2\left(S+\sum_{i=1}^{n}\frac{s_i}{K_i}\right)}{\sum_{i=1}^{n}H_iD_iK_i}}$

The numerical operation of Eq. (8.23) can be simplified with the help of a graphical aid (Silver, 1976). For the indifference between K_i and K_i+1, the rounding rule is reduced to

$$\frac{s_i}{D_iC_i} = \sqrt{K_j + \frac{1}{2}} * \sqrt{\frac{S+s_j}{D_jC_j}}$$

which is a straight line in a plot of $\frac{s_i}{D_iC_i}$ versus $\frac{S+s_j}{D_jC_j}$. Thus, the indifference curves are a set of straight lines as shown in Figure 8.15.

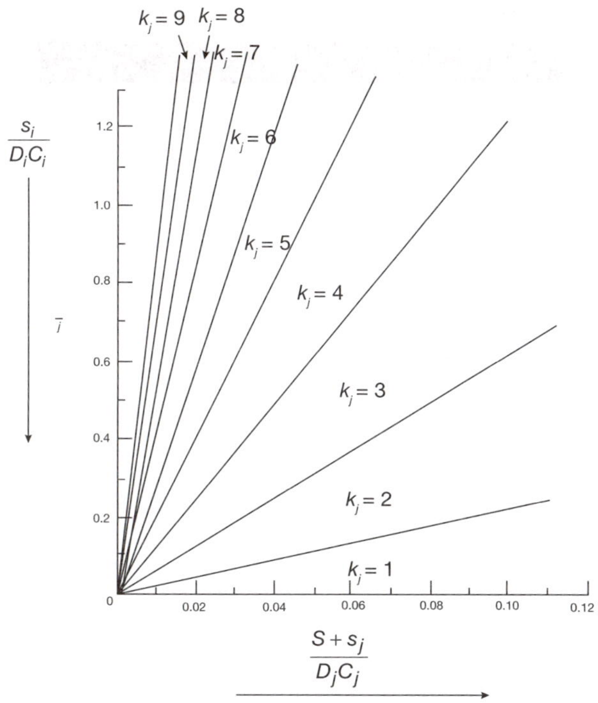

FIGURE 8.15 Indifference curves.

The multiplication of both $\frac{s_i}{D_iC_i}$ and $\frac{S+s_j}{D_jC_j}$ by the same constant will not affect the solution, which provides the flexibility in using the preceding graph especially when both the ratios are small. In such cases, we can multiply each by the same large number to ascertain the location of the new point.

We will revisit the same example for this algorithm. The calculations are shown in Figure 8.16.

E	F	G	H	I	J	K	L	M	N	O	P	Q	R	S
						Y-coordinate		X-Coordinate						
Items	Di	si	Ci	DiCi	Hi	$\frac{s_i}{D_iC_i}$	Column Kx100	$\frac{S+s_j}{D_jC_j}$	ColumnM x100	X	Y	Ki	DiHiKi	si/Ki
1	10000	10	5	50000	1.25	0.00020	0.02	0.00286	0.29	0.29	0.02	1	12500	10
2	7000	10	8	56000	2.00	0.00018	0.02	0.00286	0.29	0.29	0.02	1	14000	10
3	4000	20	10	40000	2.50	0.00050	0.05	0.00286	0.29	0.29	0.05	1	10000	20
4	2000	20	8	16000	2.00	0.00125	0.13	0.00286	0.29	0.29	0.13	1	4000	20
5	1000	40	10	10000	2.50	0.00400	0.40	0.00286	0.29	0.29	0.40	2	5000	20
N	9.95	h	0.25									Total	45500	80
T	0.1005	S	150											

FIGURE 8.16 Calculations for Silver's algorithm.

Note that the values of K_i are obtained by referring to the *X*-*Y* coordinates in the graph in Figure 8.15. The values of K_i's are the same as what we obtained in Brown's algorithm. However, this was straightforward instead of performing iterations. It can be verified that the values of K_i's will be the same even if we used the table from the values of the initial K_i's and performing them further. The quantities of the items and the total costs are calculated and shown in Table 8.16.

TABLE 8.16 Quantities under Silver's algorithm

Items	Q_i	ICC
1	1005	628
2	704	704
3	402	503
4	201	201
5	201	251
Total Inventory-Carrying Cost		2286.43
Total Setup Cost		2287.47
Total Cost		4573.90

The problem with this method is the way step 1 is computed to arrive at the item *j*. The item *j* that is arrived at like this, although will have a negligible effect in terms of ordering cost and total inventory cost, may influence the inventory ordering policy.

8.4.3 Goyal (1974)

Let N be the frequency of purchase orders and N_i be the frequency of replenishment for the *i*th item in a planning period, say 1 year. The total variable cost for all the items can then be expressed as

$$TRC = S*N + \sum_{i=1}^{n} s_j N_j + \frac{1}{2}\sum_{i=1}^{n} \frac{H_i D_i}{N_i}$$

If the *i*th item is ordered in every K_ith purchase order, then we must have $N/N_i = K_i$, and it must be a positive integer. The converse of K_i is defined as the relative ordering frequency of the *i*th item. In other words, if the relative frequency of an item is known, then its K value can be determined.

Substituting $N_i = N/N_i$ in the preceding equation for TRC, we get

$$TRC = S*N + \sum_{i=1}^{n} s_j N_j + \frac{1}{2N}\sum_{i=1}^{n} H_i D_i K_i$$

Goyal suggests the following iterative procedure to obtain the optimal solution for the frequencies $(K_1, K_2, ..., K_n)$.

The change in the K value for the *i*th item from K_l to K_{l1} is considered in order to reduce the total cost with the use of the following two expressions:

$$A_{l1} = \sum_{i=1}^{l-1} \frac{s_i}{K_i} + \sum_{i=i+1}^{n} \frac{s_i}{K_i}$$

and

$$B_{l1} = \sum_{i=1}^{l-1} H_i D_i K_i + \sum_{i=l+1}^{n} H_i D_i K_i$$

Step 1: Calculate $R_i = D_i H_i / s_i$ for each item.
Step 2: Assume initial values for the relative ordering frequencies of the items. Usually, for the first set of computations, they are assumed as 1 and this initial policy provides the combination (1, 1,..., 1) simply denoted as (K_{i0}) for all items 1 to n.

Step 3: Take the first item in the list and determine the K_{i1} value by comparing the ratio $\frac{B_{11}}{A_{11}R_1}$ with the values given in Table 8.17. The new combination is (K_{i1} 1, 1, 1,..., 1). Now move to the second item and determine K_{21} by evaluating the ratio $\frac{B_{21}}{A_{21}R_2}$ and comparing it with the values given in Table 8.17. Similarly, obtain the values K_{i1} for $i = 1, 2,..., n$. This will mark the completion of the first set of computations, and the combination of k values is given by (k_{i1}) for $i = 1, 2,..., n$.

TABLE 8.17 Upper bound and lower bound for *B/AR* for different values of *K*

	K = 1	K = 2	K = 3	K = 4	K = 5	K = 6	K = 7	K = 8
Lower Bound	0	2	6	12	20	30	42	56
Upper Bound	2	6	12	20	30	42	56	72

Step 4: Apply Step 3 to (K_{i1}) and obtain (K_{i2}) for $i = 1, 2,..., n$. The optimum policy is obtained in the ($j + 1$)th set of computations if

$$K_{i(j+1)} = (K_{ij}) \text{ for all } 1$$
$$= (K_i^*)$$

No further improvement is possible in the policy, which will be derived from (K_i^*).

Goyal suggests that convergence is usually rapid and happens in about five sets of computations.

Step 5:

a. Optimum policy arrived at is as follows:

$$N^* = \sqrt{\frac{\sum_{i=1}^{n} H_i D_i K_i^*}{2\left(S + \sum_{i=1}^{n} \frac{s_i}{K_i}\right)}}$$

b. The optimum number of replenishments for the ith item is obtained (N^*/K_i^*) for each item.

c. The optimum order quantity for the ith item is given by:

$$Q_i = D_i K_i^* / N^*$$

The first and second steps for our example are shown in Figure 8.17.

Items	Di	si	Ci	Hi	Initial-Ki	si/ki	Al_1	HiDiKi	Bl_1	Ri		New-Ki-1	si/ki	Al_2	HiDiKi	B2_1	Ri		New-Ki-2	si
1	10000	10	5	1.25	1	10.00	90	12500	30500	1250	0.27	1	10.00	53.33	12500	39500	1250	0.59	1	
2	7000	10	8	2.00	1	10.00	90	14000	29000	1400	0.23	1	10.00	53.33	14000	38000	1400	0.51	1	
3	4000	20	10	2.50	1	20.00	80	10000	33000	500	0.83	1	20.00	43.33	10000	42000	500	1.94	1	
4	2000	20	8	2.00	1	20.00	80	4000	39000	200	2.44	2	10.00	53.33	8000	44000	200	4.13	2	
5	1000	40	10	2.50	1	40.00	60	2500	40500	63	10.80	3	13.33	50.00	7500	44500	62.5	14.24	4	
h	0.25	S	150			100.00		43000					63.33		52000					

FIGURE 8.17 Calculations using Goyal's algorithm.

Further iterations are performed, and at the end of iteration 5 and iteration 6, the values do not change for *K*. Hence, we terminate here, and the frequencies are obtained as (1, 1, 2, 3, 5) for the items 1 to 5 (Iterations are not shown here). Using step 5, *N* obtained is 13.5.

The Q_i's and the cost calculations are shown in Table 8.18.

TABLE 8.18 Quantities under Goyal's algorithm

Q_i	Inventory-Carrying Cost
740.52	462.82
518.36	518.36
592.41	740.52
444.31	444.31
370.26	462.82
Total	2629
Total Setup Cost	2629
Total Cost	5258

As seen earlier, the total cost is not better than the one obtained using Brown's algorithm and Silver's algorithm. This algorithm requires many iterations, and several authors have shown that this need not guarantee the best solution although the paper claims that it gives the most optimal. A few references are given at the end of this section for understanding.

8.4.4 Goyal and Belton (1979)

Silver's algorithm considers the lowest value of $\left(\frac{s_i}{D_iC_i}\right)$ (step 1) and then determines the frequency of individual items through steps 2 and 3. Goyal and Belton suggested an improvement on Silver's method by modifying the first step of his method and claimed that this improved the solution. They suggested to denote an item with the lowest value of $\left(\frac{S+s_i}{D_iC_i}\right)$ and then proceed with steps 2 and 3 of Silver's method to determine the individual items' frequencies. We see that the solutions remain the same in our example as item 2 has the minimum ratio of $\left(\frac{S+s_i}{D_iC_i}\right)$. Steps 2 and 3 are the same as before, and hence there is no change in the solution. Counterexamples have been given that this method does not always improve the results. See the results in Figure 8.18 for results.

Items	Di	si	Ci	DiCi	Hi	si/DiCi	(S+si)/DiCi	Y	X	X	Y	Goyal Belton Ki
1	10000	10	5	50000	1.25	0.00020	0.00320	0.00	0.29	0.29	0.02	1
2	7000	10	8	56000	2.00	0.00018	0.00286	0.00	0.29	0.29	0.02	1
3	4000	20	10	40000	2.50	0.00050	0.00425	0.01	0.29	0.29	0.05	1
4	2000	20	8	16000	2.00	0.00125	0.01063	0.01	0.29	0.29	0.13	1
5	1000	40	10	10000	2.50	0.00400	0.01900	0.04	0.29	0.29	0.40	2
N	9.95	h	0.25				0.00286					
T	0.1005	S	150									

FIGURE 8.18 Results of Goyal and Belton's algorithm.

8.4.5 Kaspi and Rosenblatt (1983)

Kaspi and Rosenblatt suggested a modification of Goyal and Belton's method to further improve Silver's algorithm. The steps are as follows:

Step 1: Use the Goyal–Belton method to find the value of T.

Step 2: Find

$$K_i^2 = \frac{\left(\dfrac{2s_i}{D_i H_i}\right)}{T^2}$$

The value of K_i is found using the table that we used in Brown's algorithm.

Step 3: The new value of T is found using Eq. (8.19) with the new values of K_i's.

The calculations are shown in Figure 8.19 along with the calculations for the Goyal and Belton method as shown in Figure 8.18.

												Goyal Belton					Kaspi Rosenblatt
Items	Di	si	Ci	DiCi	Hi	si/DiCi	(S+si)/DiCi	Y	X	X	Y	Ki	DiHiKi	si/Ki	Ki^2	Ki	
1	10000	10	5	50000	1.25	0.00020	0.00320	0.00	0.29	0.29	0.02	1	12500	10	0.15826087	0.39782	1
2	7000	10	8	56000	2.00	0.00018	0.00286	0.00	0.29	0.29	0.02	1	14000	10	0.14130435	0.3759	1
3	4000	20	10	40000	2.50	0.00050	0.00425	0.01	0.29	0.29	0.05	1	10000	20	0.39565217	0.62901	1
4	2000	20	8	16000	2.00	0.00125	0.01063	0.01	0.29	0.29	0.13	1	4000	20	0.98913043	0.99455	1
5	1000	40	10	10000	2.50	0.00400	0.01900	0.04	0.29	0.29	0.40	2	5000	20	3.16521739	1.77911	2
N	9.95	h	0.25				0.00286							Total	45500	80	
T	0.1005	S	150														

FIGURE 8.19 Calculations of both Kaspi–Rosenblatt and Goyal–Belton methods.

We see that there is no change in the values of K_i's and T, other details of Q_i's, and the total cost.

8.5 | LOT-SIZING TECHNIQUES (DYNAMIC LOT SIZING)

We saw in previous chapters that inventory cost comprises of four important costs among others: purchase cost, ordering cost, inventory-carrying cost, and shortage cost. Determining the appropriate quantity to order from vendors or the lot size submitted to the firm's production units involves a search for the minimum cost resulting in a trade-off among these four costs. Often the balance between ordering cost (or setup cost) and inventory-carrying cost becomes crucial, and any imbalance may lead to stockouts, market loss, etc. Hence, an effective inventory model that will decide a lot size with minimum total inventory cost is of great importance.

We discussed in previous chapters that the analytic complexity of inventory models depends on whether the demand for an item is deterministic or probabilistic. Within either category, the demand may or may not vary with time. In practical situations, the demand pattern in an inventory model may assume one of four types:

1. Deterministic and static with time
2. Deterministic and dynamic with time
3. Probabilistic and static with time
4. Probabilistic and dynamic with time

To determine the nature of the demand, the coefficient of variation V can be used with the following guidelines:

1. If the average monthly demand is approximately constant for all months and V is reasonably small (<20%) but approximately constant, then the demand is deterministic and constant.
2. If the average monthly demand varies appreciably for different months but V is reasonably small (<20%), then the demand may be considered deterministic but variable.

3. If, in case 1, V is high (>20%) but approximately constant, then the demand is probabilistic and stationary.
4. The only remaining case is the probabilistic nonstationary demand, which occurs when the means and coefficients of variation vary appreciably over time.

We dealt with cases 1, 2, and 3 to some extent in the previous section. We will discuss a few lot-sizing techniques when the demand is time varying over a time horizon. Some of the situations where such techniques may be useful are MRP, firm orders and contracts for future periods, seasonal demand patterns, and demand with trend (increasing or decreasing over time). The lot-sizing techniques help to determine lot sizes so as to minimize the total cost by looking at the trade-off between setup cost or ordering cost and the inventory-carrying cost. They are usually referred to as dynamic lot-sizing techniques as the demand is time varying and not constant. The popular techniques are

1. Lot for lot
2. Economic order quantity (EOQ)
3. Period order quantity (POQ)
4. Part period balancing (PPB) or (least total cost (LTC))
5. Silver–Meal (SM) heuristic (least period cost)
6. Least unit cost (LUC)
7. Wagner–Whitin algorithm (using dynamic programming approach)(WW)

The methods discussed here are very useful in contexts where the demand is time varying and especially in those contexts where there are firm orders and in MRP situations. The methods are simple and amenable for computer software coding.

We will explain the techniques using the following example with details on monthly demand, which is time varying, as given in Table 8.19.

TABLE 8.19 Monthly demand for lot sizing

Month	1	2	3	4	5	6	7	8	9	10	11	12
Demand	69	29	36	61	61	26	34	67	45	67	79	56

Note: These data points are extracted from the paper of Wagner and Whitin (2004).

Let us assume that the setup cost is \$102.80 and the inventory-carrying cost per unit per month h' is \$1, where $h = 0.20$ (annual) and $C = \$60$.

8.5.1 Lot for Lot (LFL)

Here items are purchased or produced in the exact quantities required for each period. It sets planned order or production to exactly match the net requirements. And so, the exact quantity is ordered and produced with no carry forward of inventory to the next periods. The ending and beginning inventories are assumed to be zero as only the required quantity is ordered or produced. Thus, the carrying cost is zero. The only costs involved are purchase cost and ordering cost or the setup cost. However, the ordering or setup activity has to be done whenever there is demand, which results in higher ordering costs. Thus, this method is good when there is a large holding cost and when the ordering costs or setup costs are low.

Since ordering and setting up production are treated similarly in inventory models, we will use the context of setup in production for our discussion further. However, they are equally valid in the context of ordering too. The calculations are shown in Figure 8.20.

It can be seen that the total cost is \$1233.60, which is basically 12 setups for every month with each setup costing \$102.80. This is often the easiest and, so, is often referred to as the quick and dirty solution.

The total relevant cost including the purchase cost will be Purchase cost + Setup cost + Inventory-carrying cost = 630 × 60 + 1233.60 + 0 = 37,800 + 1233.60 + 0 = \$39,033.60.

Period	1	2	3	4	5	6	7	8	9	10	11	12	Totals
Beginning inventory	0	0	0	0	0	0	0	0	0	0	0	0	
Demand	69	29	36	61	61	26	34	67	45	67	79	56	630
Setup or Ordering cost/ Set up or order	$102.80	$102.80	$102.80	$102.80	$102.80	$102.80	$102.80	$102.80	$102.80	$102.80	$102.80	$102.80	
Carrying cost/unit/period	$1.00	$1.00	$1.00	$1.00	$1.00	$1.00	$1.00	$1.00	$1.00	$1.00	$1.00	$1.00	
Order quantity (lotsizes)	69	29	36	61	61	26	34	67	45	67	79	56	630
Ending inventory	0	0	0	0	0	0	0	0	0	0	0	0	
Setup or Ordering cost	$102.80	$102.80	$102.80	$102.80	$102.80	$102.80	$102.80	$102.80	$102.80	$102.80	$102.80	$102.80	$1,233.60
Carrying cost	$0.00	$0.00	$0.00	$0.00	$0.00	$0.00	$0.00	$0.00	$0.00	$0.00	$0.00	$0.00	$0.00
Total period cost	$102.80	$102.80	$102.80	$102.80	$102.80	$102.80	$102.80	$102.80	$102.80	$102.80	$102.80	$102.80	**$1,233.60**

FIGURE 8.20 Results of lot for lot method.

8.5.2 Economic Order Quantity (EOQ)

We discussed the EOQ model earlier in Chapter 6, which optimizes the total cost consisting of setup cost and inventory-carrying cost. We apply the same principles here assuming a constant demand every month by taking the average demand from the time periods given.

We see that the total demand in the given 12 months is 630, and hence the average demand d per month is 52.5. Given that the setup cost $S = 102.80$, and the inventory-carrying charge of $h' = 1$ per unit per month, the EOQ will be

$$Q = \sqrt{\frac{2 \times 52.5 \times 102.80}{1}} = 104$$

Since this is approximately two months' demand, we round Q to 105 units for completely taking care of the demand and keeping the ending inventory zero.

With $Q = 105$ now, the calculations are shown in Figure 8.21.

Period	1	2	3	4	5	6	7	8	9	10	11	12	Totals
Beginning inventory	0	36	7	76	15	59	33	104	37	97	30	56	
Demand	69	29	36	61	61	26	34	67	45	67	79	56	630
Setup or Ordering cost/ Set up or order	$102.80	$102.80	$102.80	$102.80	$102.80	$102.80	$102.80	$102.80	$102.80	$102.80	$102.80	$102.80	
Carrying cost/unit/period	$1.00	$1.00	$1.00	$1.00	$1.00	$1.00	$1.00	$1.00	$1.00	$1.00	$1.00	$1.00	
Order quantity (lotsizes)	105	0	105	0	105	0	105	0	105	0	105	0	630
Ending inventory	36	7	76	15	59	33	104	37	97	30	56	0	
Setup or Ordering cost	$102.80	$0.00	$102.80	$0.00	$102.80	$0.00	$102.80	$0.00	$102.80	$0.00	$102.80	$0.00	$616.80
Carrying cost	$36.00	$7.00	$76.00	$15.00	$59.00	$33.00	$104.00	$37.00	$97.00	$30.00	$56.00	$0.00	$550.00
Total period cost	$138.80	$7.00	$178.80	$15.00	$161.80	$33.00	$206.80	$37.00	$199.80	$30.00	$158.80	$0.00	**$1,166.80**

FIGURE 8.21 Results of EOQ lot sizing.

We see that the total cost comes to $1166.80.

For comparison purposes, we will not include the purchase cost as it will remain constant for scenarios except in the unit total cost approach.

8.5.3 Period Order Quantity (POQ)

Here, we adjust the EOQ so that the new amount could satisfy the total demand in an integer number of periods. We often see that the EOQ attempts to minimize the total cost of ordering and carrying inventory and assumes that the demand is uniform. However, often the demand is not uniform, particularly in material requirements planning, and using the EOQ does not produce a minimum cost.

The POQ lot-size method is based on similar lines of the EOQ method where the quantity is based on the economic time between orders, given as follows:

$$T_Q = \sqrt{\frac{2S}{Dh'}}$$

We round T_Q to the nearest integer greater than zero so that any replenishment of the item is made large enough to cover exactly the requirements of this integer number of periods.

In our example,

$$T_Q = \sqrt{\frac{2\times 102.80}{52.5\times 1}} = 1.97 \cong 2\,\text{months}$$

The calculations are shown in Figure 8.22.

Period	1	2	3	4	5	6	7	8	9	10	11	12	Totals
Beginning inventory	0	29	0	61	0	26	0	67	0	67	0	56	
Demand	**69**	**29**	**36**	**61**	**61**	**26**	**34**	**67**	**45**	**67**	**79**	**56**	630
Setup or Ordering cost/ Set up or order	$102.80	$102.80	$102.80	$102.80	$102.80	$102.80	$102.80	$102.80	$102.80	$102.80	$102.80	$102.80	
Carrying cost/unit/period	$1.00	$1.00	$1.00	$1.00	$1.00	$1.00	$1.00	$1.00	$1.00	$1.00	$1.00	$1.00	
Order quantity (lotsizes)	**98**	**0**	**97**	**0**	**87**	**0**	**101**	**0**	**112**	**0**	**135**	**0**	630
Ending inventory	29	0	61	0	26	0	67	0	67	0	56	0	
Setup or Ordering cost	$102.80	$0.00	$102.80	$0.00	$102.80	$0.00	$102.80	$0.00	$102.80	$0.00	$102.80	$0.00	$616.80
Carrying cost	$29.00	$0.00	$61.00	$0.00	$26.00	$0.00	$67.00	$0.00	$67.00	$0.00	$56.00	$0.00	$306.00
Total period cost	$131.80	$0.00	$163.80	$0.00	$128.80	$0.00	$169.80	$0.00	$169.80	$0.00	$158.80	$0.00	**$922.80**

FIGURE 8.22 Results of period order quantity lot sizing.

Here the total cost is $922.80, which is much less than the one we obtained in the EOQ method.

The lot sizing will be combining the demands of periods (1, 2), (3, 4), (5, 6), (7, 8), (9, 10), and (11, 12).

8.5.4 Part Period Balancing (PPB) or Least Total Cost (LTC) Method

In this PPB method, we select the number of periods covered by the replenishment such that the total inventory-carrying costs are as close as possible to the setup cost. This is implicitly using the observation we made in the EOQ model approach that at the optimal order quantity, the ordering cost or the setup cost is equal to the inventory-carrying cost. We keep tracking the setup cost and the carrying cost separately and determine the time periods to cover the total demand in those periods; this is the lot size when these two costs are close to each other. The calculations are shown in Figure 8.23.

Period	1	2	3	4	5	6	7	8	9	10	11	12	Totals
Beginning inventory	0	65	36	0	87	26	0	67	0	67	0	56	
Demand	**69**	**29**	**36**	**61**	**61**	**26**	**34**	**67**	**45**	**67**	**79**	**56**	630
Setup or Ordering cost/ Set up or order	$102.80	$102.80	$102.80	$102.80	$102.80	$102.80	$102.80	$102.80	$102.80	$102.80	$102.80	$102.80	
Carrying cost/unit/period	$1.00	$1.00	$1.00	$1.00	$1.00	$1.00	$1.00	$1.00	$1.00	$1.00	$1.00	$1.00	
Order quantity (lotsizes)	**134**	**0**	**0**	**148**	**0**	**0**	**101**	**0**	**112**	**0**	**135**	**0**	630
Ending inventory	65	36	0	87	26	0	67	0	67	0	56	0	
Setup or Ordering cost	$102.80	$0.00	$0.00	$102.80	$0.00	$0.00	$102.80	$0.00	$102.80	$0.00	$102.80	$0.00	$514.00
Carrying cost	$65.00	$36.00	$0.00	$87.00	$26.00	$0.00	$67.00	$0.00	$67.00	$0.00	$56.00	$0.00	$404.00
Total period cost	$167.80	$36.00	$0.00	$189.80	$26.00	$0.00	$169.80	$0.00	$169.80	$0.00	$158.80	$0.00	**$918.00**

FIGURE 8.23 Results of PPB lot sizing.

The total cost here comes to $918.00. The lot sizing will be combining the demands of periods (1, 2, 3), (4, 5, 6), (7, 8), (9, 10), and (11, 12).

8.5.5 Silver–Meal (SM) Heuristic or Least Period Cost (LPC)

The SM heuristic considers that if a replenishment arrives at the beginning of the first period and it covers requirements to the end of the Tth period, then the criterion function can be written as follows:

$$\frac{(\text{Set up cost} + \text{Total carrying cost to the end of period } T)}{T}$$

So the best strategy will be to replenish quantities that last for an integer number of periods. The replenishment quantity Q, associated with a particular value of T, is

$$Q = \sum_{i=1}^{T} D_i \tag{8.24}$$

where D_i is the demand of the tth time period. According to this criterion, we need to pick the value for T that minimizes the total relevant costs per unit time over the time period T.

Let the total relevant costs associated with a replenishment that lasts for T periods be denoted by TRC(T). We wish to select T to minimize the total relevant costs per unit time, TRC_UT(T), where

$$\text{TRC\_UT}(T) = \frac{\text{TRC}(T)}{T} = \frac{(\text{Set up cost } S + \text{Total carrying cost to the end of period } T)}{T}$$

If $T = 1$, then TRC_UT(1) = S only, as there are no carrying costs. If the setup cost is large, then this is unattractive when compared to including the second period's requirements in the replenishment.

When $T = 2$, the carrying cost of the second period's demand D_2 for one period is added to this total cost and, therefore,

$$\text{TRC\_UT}(2) = \frac{S + h' D_2}{2}$$

When $T = 3$, we will still carry D_2 for one period, and now we will also carry D_3 for two periods.

Thus,

$$\text{TRC\_UT}(3) = \frac{S + h' D_2 + 2hD_3}{3}$$

We see here that the setup cost is apportioned across three periods, but this may not be attractive because of the added carrying costs.

The basic idea of the heuristic is to evaluate TRC_UT(T) for increasing values of T until, for the first time,

$$\text{TRC\_UT}(T+1) > \text{TRC\_UT}(T)$$

which means, the total relevant costs per unit time start increasing. When this happens, the associated T is selected as the number of periods that the replenishment should cover, and the corresponding replenishment quantity Q is given by Eq. (8.24).

We observe that since we stop evaluating TRC_UT with the first increase in costs per unit of time, this method guarantees only a local minimum in the total relevant costs per unit time for the current replenishment. It is possible that still larger values of T would yield still lower costs per unit if we go beyond this T.

The calculations and the truncation of the time periods T are shown in Figure 8.24.

Period	**1**	**2**	**3**	**4**	**5**	**6**	**7**	**8**	**9**	**10**	**11**	**12**	**Totals**
Beginning inventory	0	29	0	61	0	26	0	67	0	67	0	56	
Demand	**69**	**29**	**36**	**61**	**61**	**26**	**34**	**67**	**45**	**67**	**79**	**56**	630
Setup or Ordering cost/ Set up or order	$102.80	$102.80	$102.80	$102.80	$102.80	$102.80	$102.80	$102.80	$102.80	$102.80	$102.80	$102.80	
Carrying cost/unit/period	$1.00	$1.00	$1.00	$1.00	$1.00	$1.00	$1.00	$1.00	$1.00	$1.00	$1.00	$1.00	
Order quantity (lotsizes)	**98**	**0**	**97**	**0**	**87**	**0**	**101**	**0**	**112**	**0**	**135**	**0**	630
Ending inventory	29	0	61	0	26	0	67	0	67	0	56	0	
Setup or Ordering cost	$102.80	$0.00	$102.80	$0.00	$102.80	$0.00	$102.80	$0.00	$102.80	$0.00	$102.80	$0.00	$616.80
Carrying cost	$29.00	$0.00	$61.00	$0.00	$26.00	$0.00	$67.00	$0.00	$67.00	$0.00	$56.00	$0.00	$306.00
Total period cost	$131.80	$0.00	$163.80	$0.00	$128.80	$0.00	$169.80	$0.00	$169.80	$0.00	$158.80	$0.00	**$922.80**

Period	**1**	**2**	**3**	**4**	**5**	**6**	**7**	**8**	**9**	**10**	**11**	**12**
	102.8	65.9	~~67.9333~~									
			102.8	81.9	~~95.2667~~							
					102.8	64.4	~~65.6~~					
							102.8	84.9	~~101.6~~			
									102.8	84.9	~~135.6~~	
											102.8	79.4

FIGURE 8.24 Results of the Silver–Meal heuristic.

We see that the total cost is \$922.80. The lot sizing will be combining the demands of periods (1, 2), (3, 4), (5, 6), (7, 8), (9, 10), and (11, 12). These are the same lot sizes we obtained using the POQ approach.

8.5.6 Least Unit Cost (LUC)

The method is identical to the SM heuristic except that it accumulates requirements until the cost per unit increases instead of cost per period. The criterion function will be

$$\text{TRC\_UT}(T) = \frac{\text{TRC}(T)}{Q} = \frac{(\text{Set up cost} + \text{Total carrying cost to the end of period } T)}{\sum_{i=1}^{T} D_i}$$

and evaluate TRC_UT(T) for increasing values of T until, for the first time,

$$\text{TRC\_UT}(T+1) > \text{TRC\_UT}(T)$$

which means that the total relevant costs per unit start increasing. When this happens, the associated T is selected as the number of periods that the replenishment should cover, and the corresponding replenishment quantity Q is given by Eq. (8.24).

The calculations and the truncation of the time periods T are shown in Figure 8.25.

Period	1	2	3	4	5	6	7	8	9	10	11	12	Totals
Beginning inventory	0	29	0	61	0	26	0	67	0	67	0	56	
Demand	**69**	**29**	**36**	**61**	**61**	**26**	**34**	**67**	**45**	**67**	**79**	**56**	630
Setup or Ordering cost/ Set up or order	\$102.80	\$102.80	\$102.80	\$102.80	\$102.80	\$102.80	\$102.80	\$102.80	\$102.80	\$102.80	\$102.80	\$102.80	
Carrying cost/unit/period	\$1.00	\$1.00	\$1.00	\$1.00	\$1.00	\$1.00	\$1.00	\$1.00	\$1.00	\$1.00	\$1.00	\$1.00	
Order quantity (lotsizes)	**98**	**0**	**97**	**0**	**87**	**0**	**101**	**0**	**112**	**0**	**135**	**0**	630
Ending inventory	29	0	61	0	26	0	67	0	67	0	56	0	
Setup or Ordering cost	\$102.80	\$0.00	\$102.80	\$0.00	\$102.80	\$0.00	\$102.80	\$0.00	\$102.80	\$0.00	\$102.80	\$0.00	\$616.80
Carrying cost	\$29.00	\$0.00	\$61.00	\$0.00	\$26.00	\$0.00	\$67.00	\$0.00	\$67.00	\$0.00	\$56.00	\$0.00	\$306.00
Total period cost	\$131.80	\$0.00	\$163.80	\$0.00	\$128.80	\$0.00	\$169.80	\$0.00	\$169.80	\$0.00	\$158.80	\$0.00	**\$922.80**

Period	1	2	3	4	5	6	7	8	9	10	11	12
	1.48986	1.3449	~~1.5209~~									
			2.85556	1.68866	~~1.80886~~							
					1.68525	1.48046	~~1.62645~~					
							3.02353	1.68119	~~2.08767~~			
									2.28444	1.51607	~~1.71623~~	
											1.30127	1.1763

FIGURE 8.25 Results of the least unit cost method.

We see that the total cost is \$922.80. The lot sizing will be combining the demands of periods (1, 2), (3, 4), (5, 6), (7, 8), (9, 10), and (11, 12). These are the same lot sizes we obtained using the POQ approach and the SM heuristic.

8.5.7 Wagner–Whitin Algorithm (WW)

Wagner and Whitin (1958) developed an algorithm that guarantees an optimal solution of replenishment quantities under one additional assumption that either the demand pattern terminates at the horizon or else the ending inventory is pre-specified. The algorithm applies the dynamic programming approach of mathematical programming, which is a procedure to solve sequential decision problems. The WW optimality properties are as follows:

1. A replenishment only takes place when the inventory level is 0.
2. There is an upper limit to how far before a period j we would include its requirements (D_j), in a replenishment quantity.

It follows from the above that

1. Under an optimal lot-sizing policy,
   a. Either the inventory carried to period t from a previous period will be zero, or
   b. The production/order quantity in period t will be zero.

2. That is, either $Q_t = 0$ or $Q_t = D_t + \cdots + D_k$ for some k.

Let us suppose that we define $F(T)$ as the total cost of the best replenishment strategy that satisfies the demand requirements in periods 1, 2, ..., T.

We will explain the procedure to find $F(T)$ with our example as follows:

1. What is the best policy for the 1-period problem?
   a. Order 69 units, which incurs setup cost of only: 102.80
   b. So, $\boldsymbol{F(1) = 102.80}$. This is the best policy for the 1-period problem.
2. What is the best policy for the 2-period problem?
   There are two options here.
   a. Setup in period 1 for total demand in periods 1 and 2.
      This involves one setup in period 1, produce the first two period's demands of $69 + 29 = 98$ units in period 1 itself and carry the inventory of 29 units for period 2.
      So the cost will be $102.80 + 29 \times 1 \times 1 = \mathbf{131.80}$.
      This is the optimal cost for the 2-period problem.
   b. The best policy of the 1-period problem, and in period 2, setup production for the production of period 2's demand of 29 units.
      So there are two setups (1 in period 1 and 1 in period 2 with no inventory being carried forward). The cost will $102.80 + 102.80 = 205.60$.
      The optimal cost in this 2-period problem is 131.80.
      So $\boldsymbol{F(2) = 131.80}$, which is the best policy for the 2-period problem.
3. What is the best policy for the 3-period problem?
   There are three options here.
   a. Setup in period 1 for total demands of periods 1, 2, and 3.
      This involves one setup in period 1 and to produce the first three period's demands of $69 + 29 + 36 = 134$ units in period 1 itself and carry the inventory of 29 units of period 2's demand in period 2 and carry 36 units of period 3's demand for two periods: periods 2 and 3.
      This will cost $102.80 + 29 \times 1 \times 1 + 36 \times 1 \times 2 = \mathbf{203.80}$.
   b. The best policy of the 2-period problem and in period 3, setup production and produce period 3's demand of 36 units.
      The cost of this will be $131.80 + 102.80 = 234.60$.
   c. The best policy of the 1-period problem and in period 2, setup production for period 2's and period 3's demands. This will involve one setup in period 1, second setup in period 2, and carrying the inventory of period 3's demand of 36 units for one period from period 2 to period 3.
      The cost will be $102.80 + 102.80 + 36 \times 1 \times 1 = 241.60$.
      So here, the best policy is option (a) with a total cost of 203.80.
      So $\boldsymbol{F(3) = 203.80}$.
4. What is the best policy for the 4-period problem?
   There are four options here.
   a. Setup in period 1 for the total demands of periods 1, 2, 3, and 4.
      This involves one setup in period 1 to produce the first four period's demands of $69 + 29 + 36 + 61 = 195$ units in period 1 itself and carry the inventory of 29 units of period 2's demand for 1 period, that is, period 2, carry 36 units of period 3's demand for two periods—periods 2 and 3—and carry 61 units of period 3's demand for three periods—periods 2, 3, and 4.
      The cost will be $102.80 + 29 \times 1 \times 1 + 36 \times 1 \times 2 + 61 \times 1 \times 3 = 386.80$.
   b. The best policy of the 3-period problem and in period 4, setup production and produce period 4's demand of 61 units.
      The cost of this will be $203.80 + 102.80 = 306.80$.
   c. The best policy of the 2-period problem and in period 3, setup production for producing period 3's demand of 36 units and period 4's demand of 61 units. This will involve one setup in period 1, a second setup in period 3, and carrying the inventory of period 4's demand of 61 units for one period from period 3 to period 4.
      The cost will be $131.80 + 102.80 + 61 \times 1 \times 1 = 295.60$.

d. The best policy of the 1-period problem and in period 2, setup production for producing period 2's demand of 29 units, period 3's demand of 36 units, and period 4's demand of 61 units in period 2 itself. This will involve a setup in period 2 and carrying the inventory of period 3's demand of 36 units for one period and period 4's demand of 61 units for two periods.
The cost will be $102.80 + 102.80 + 36 \times 1 \times 1 + 61 \times 1 \times 2 = 363.80$.
The best option is (b) here with a cost of 295.60.
So ***F*(4) = 295.60**.

Hence, for a *k*-period problem, we have *k* options:

1. Produce in 1 for all *k* periods.
2. Take the $k - 1$ period's best policy, and produce in *k* for only period *k*.
3. ...
4. Take the 2-period best policy, and produce in period 3 for periods 3, ..., *k*.
5. Take the 1-period best policy, and produce in period 2 for periods 2, ..., *k*.

From the second property given earlier,

1. If j_k^* = last period of production (order) in a *k*-period problem, then we will produce exactly $Dj_k^* + \cdots + D_k$ in period j_k^*.
2. We can then consider periods $1, ..., j_k^*-1$ as if they are an independent $j_k^* - 1$ period problem.

So, in general, if $j_k^* = T$, then the last period in which production occurs in an optimal $(T+1)$-period policy must be in the set T, $T+1$,.... For example, say, we produce in period 4 for period 4 of a 4-period problem; then we would never produce in period 3 for period 5 in a 5-period problem.

The calculations are shown in Figures 8.26 and 8.27.

Period	**1**	**2**	**3**	**4**	**5**	**6**	**7**	**8**	**9**	**10**	**11**	**12**	**Totals**
Beginning inventory	0	29	0	61	0	60	34	0	45	0	0	56	
Demand	**69**	**29**	**36**	**61**	**61**	**26**	**34**	**67**	**45**	**67**	**79**	**56**	630
Setup or Ordering cost/ Set up or order	$102.80	$102.80	$102.80	$102.80	$102.80	$102.80	$102.80	$102.80	$102.80	$102.80	$102.80	$102.80	
Carrying cost/unit/period	$1.00	$1.00	$1.00	$1.00	$1.00	$1.00	$1.00	$1.00	$1.00	$1.00	$1.00	$1.00	
Order quantity (lotsizes)	**98**	**0**	**97**	**0**	**121**	**0**	**0**	**112**	**0**	**67**	**135**	**0**	630
Ending inventory	29	0	61	0	60	34	0	45	0	0	56	0	
Setup or Ordering cost	$102.80	$0.00	$102.80	$0.00	$102.80	$0.00	$0.00	$102.80	$0.00	$102.80	$102.80	$0.00	$616.80
Carrying cost	$29.00	$0.00	$61.00	$0.00	$60.00	$34.00	$0.00	$45.00	$0.00	$0.00	$56.00	$0.00	$285.00
Total period cost	$131.80	$0.00	$163.80	$0.00	$162.80	$34.00	$0.00	$147.80	$0.00	$102.80	$158.80	$0.00	**$901.80**

FIGURE 8.26 Lot sizing using the Wagner–Whitin method.

1	**2**	**3**	**4**	**5**	**6**	**7**	**8**	**9**	**10**	**11**	**12**
69	**29**	**36**	**61**	**61**	**26**	**34**	**67**	**45**	**67**	**79**	**56**
102.8	**131.8**	**203.8**	386.8	630	760.8	964.8	1433.8	1793.8	2396.8	3186.8	3802.8
	205.6	234.6	306.8	398.4	470.5	522.4	595.2	692.2	**743**	845.8	924.8
		241.6	**295.6**	**367.6**	424.4	504.4	**589.4**	**640.2**	759.2	**822**	**901.8**
			363.8	**417.6**	**419.6**	**492.4**	688.4	679.4	774.2	917.2	934
				546.6	495.6	521.6	693.4	823.4	880.4	1011.2	
					650.6	631.6	789.6	873.4			
						820.6	966.6				
							1222.6				

FIGURE 8.27 Calculations of the Wagner–Whitin method.

We see that the total cost is **$901.80**, which is the best and the most optimal cost. The lot sizing will be combining the demands of periods (1, 2), (3, 4), (5, 6, 7), (8, 9, 10), and (11, 12).

8.6 | MULTI-ECHELON INVENTORY DECISIONS

When a firm deals with thousands of products located in many locations at the country level or at the global level, managing inventory can be very challenging. The challenges are more when the inventory decisions have to be made at different tiers or echelons in their distribution channels. Many research studies point out that the key differentiator in the inventory decisions of a firm is in their ability to increase the inventory turnover ratio, especially in retail businesses.

Broadly, there are two types of inventory systems: **single-echelon** (or single-tier) inventory system and **multi-echelon** (or multitier) inventory system. We will look at them briefly here.

8.6.1 Single-Echelon Inventory System

A single-echelon inventory system is one wherein a single location—plant, distribution center, warehouse—acts as a storing point of the inventories between the supplier and the buyer, or the firm to its customers. So if a firm sells products from a single location, then it would be categorized as a single-echelon system.

8.6.2 Multi-Echelon Inventory System

A multi-echelon inventory system is one where the system relies on tiers or levels of suppliers distributed across locations or levels of distribution centers to serve layers of customers at different locations. For example, a situation where a firm has five different plants for producing five different types of products distributed through three central distribution centers down further to 20 regional distribution centers and finally to the many retailers across geographical locations. A schematic representation of a multi-echelon is shown in Figure 8.28.

Optimizing the multi-echelon inventory system deals with right sizing regular and safety stock buffers across the entire supply chain considering the various interdependencies between levels (echelons) and all the variables that affect inventory levels: lead times, demand uncertainty, and supply volatility.

The key issues in optimizing a multi-echelon inventory system are as follows:

1. Demand variation measures for the different tiers such as regional centers, retailers, etc.
2. Demand forecasts at these different levels.
3. Desired optimal service level goals for different tiers or levels.
4. Allocating inventory up to the last levels of the echelons when there is a limited supply situation at the top echelons.

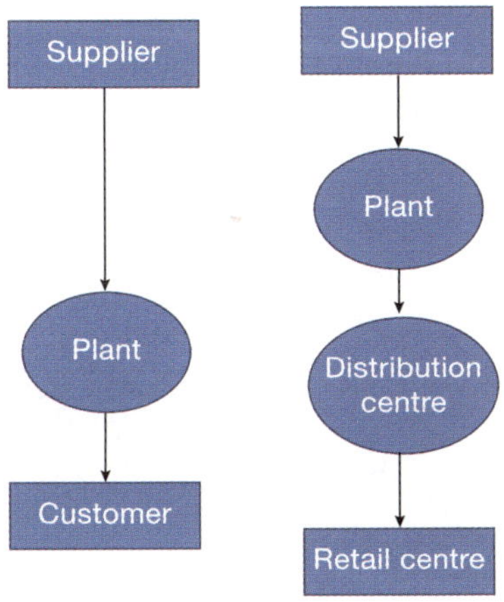

FIGURE 8.28 A schematic representation of a multi-echelon system.

In this context, the holding costs of echelon inventory are usually rated differently from the conventional holding of inventory in a single echelon.

For most of the analytical purposes, we consider the echelon inventory at a stocking point to include all the inventories that may be at the stocking point or passing through that stocking point. The inventory-carrying cost at an echelon point is determined based on the incremental cost of holding a unit at that point rather than at the preceding or succeeding point in the channel. For example, the echelon holding cost at a retailer would be the incremental cost of holding inventory at the retailer level and not at the regional warehouse. While from an accounting viewpoint, the same carrying cost will be used irrespective of whether conventional carrying cost rates are applied to conventional inventory or echelon carrying cost rates are applied to echelon inventory. EOQ calculations will be quite different though and may not apply at all to field stocks.

Consider a situation where in a serial system we have Stage 1, which is close to the end customer, and Stage 2, which services Stage 1. Suppose that there is an average of 200 units of inventory at Stage 2 and 160 units at Stage 1. Assume that the conventional carrying charge is $20 at Stage 1 and $15 at Stage 2. We will also assume that the annual demand is 5000 and at Stage 1, the setup cost is $600, and at Stage 2, it is $100.

Under both the conventional and the echelon systems, total carrying charges will be $5200, as shown in Table 8.20.

TABLE 8.20 Information regarding conventional and echelon systems

Stage	Conventional Carrying Charges	Echelon Carrying Charges	Average Inventory	Average Echelon Inventory	Conventional Carrying Charges	Echelon Carrying Charges
2	15	15	200	360	3000	5400
1	20	5	160	160	3200	800
Total					**6200**	**6200**

Standard EOQs and simple echelon EOQs are shown in Table 8.21. Note that the simple echelon EOQ uses the echelon carrying charges.

TABLE 8.21 EOQ calculations for both conventional and echelon systems

Stage	Conventional Carrying Charges	Echelon Carrying Charges	Standard EOQ	Simple Echelon EOQ
2	15	15	632	632
1	20	5	224	447

We will illustrate the complexities of multi-echelon inventory with a case of two-stage echelons assuming deterministic demand (Figure 8.29).

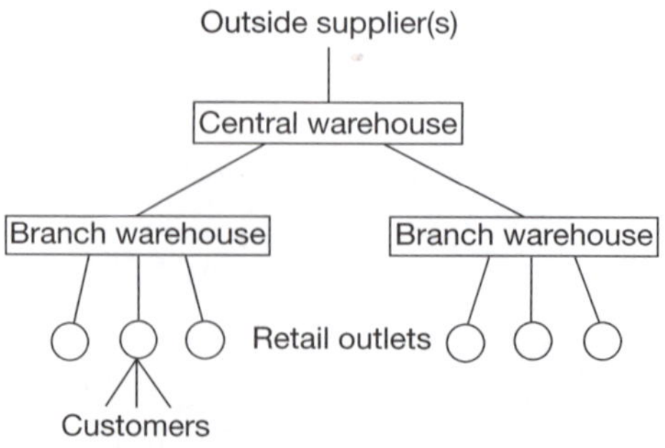

FIGURE 8.29 A two-stage multi-echelon system.

We will assume the following situations with respect to the two echelons as sequential stocking points.

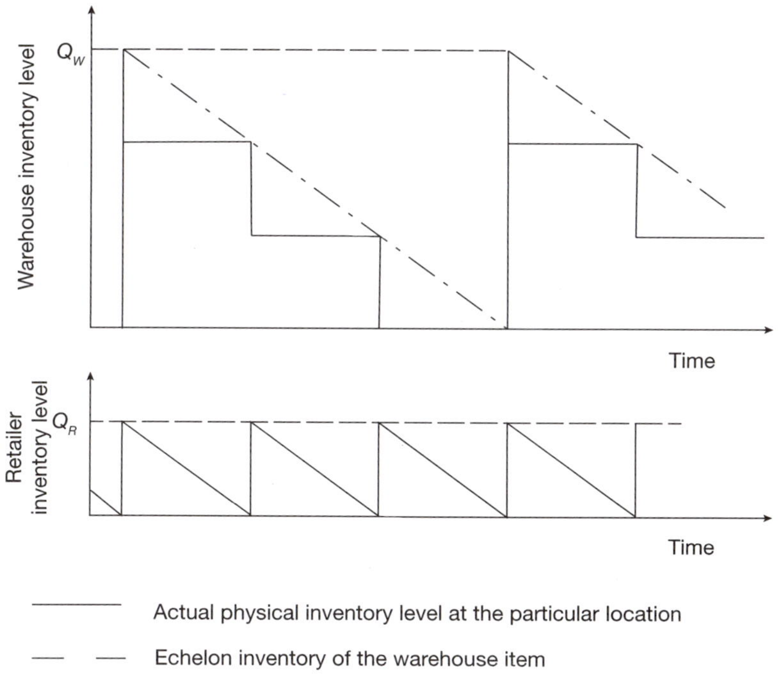

FIGURE 8.30 Two-stage multi-echelon inventory situation for a warehouse and a retailer.

Figure 8.30 shows that in the case of deterministic demand, it makes sense to assume that Q_W is an integer multiple of Q_R. Therefore, we can think of two alternative decision variables Q_R and n where

$$Q_W = n \times Q_R$$

We will develop the total cost functions for both the warehouse and the retail locations as follows.

Let

- D be total demand,
- Q_R be order quantity at the level of the retailer,
- Q_W be order quantity at the level of the warehouse,
- h be inventory-carrying percentage,
- C_R be the value of a unit at the level of the retailer,
- C_W be the value of a unit at the level of the warehouse,
- S_R be the setup cost at the retailer level, and
- S_W be the setup cost at the warehouse level.

At the first stage of the retailer level:

$$TRC_R = \frac{D}{Q_R} S_R + \frac{Q_R}{2} C_R h$$

$$TRC_W = \frac{D}{Q_W} S_W + \frac{Q_W}{2} C_W h - \frac{Q_R}{2} C_W h$$

So $$TRC(Q_W, Q_R) = TRC_R + TRC_W = \frac{D}{Q_W} S_W + \frac{Q_W}{2} C_W h + \frac{D}{Q_R} S_R + \frac{Q_R}{2}(C_R - C_W)h$$

Note that the inventory at the warehouse echelon is valued at

$$C'_W = C_W$$

while the inventory at the retail echelon is valued at

$$C'_R = C_R - C_W$$

So $TRC(Q_W, Q_R)$ needs to be optimized with respect to Q_W and Q_R.

We will substitute $Q_W = n^*Q_R$ in the $TRC(Q_W, Q_R)$ equation.

It thus becomes

$$TRC(Q_W, Q_R) = \frac{D}{n*Q_R}S_W + \frac{n*Q_R}{2}C'_W h + \frac{D}{Q_R}S_R + \frac{Q_R}{2}C'_R h$$

$$= \frac{D}{Q_R}\left(S_R + \frac{S_W}{n}\right) + \frac{Q_R}{2}h\left(nC'_W + C'_R\right)$$

The problem becomes selecting a Q_R to minimize:

$$TRC(n, Q_R) = \frac{D}{Q_R}\left(S_R + \frac{S_W}{n}\right) + \frac{Q_R}{2}h\left(nC'_W + C'_R\right)$$

$$\frac{\partial TRC}{\partial Q_R} = -\frac{D}{Q_R^2}\left(S_R + \frac{S_W}{n}\right) + \frac{h}{2}\left(nC'_W + C'_R\right) = 0$$

So,

$$Q_R^*(n) = \sqrt{\frac{2\left(S_R + \frac{S_W}{n}\right)D}{h\left(nC'_W + C'_R\right)}}$$

Substituting this in the *TRC* equation:

$$TRC^*(n) = \sqrt{2\left(S_R + \frac{S_W}{n}\right)D\left(nC'_W + C'_R\right)h}$$

It is equivalent to finding n that minimizes the following simplified expression of the preceding equation.

$$F(n) = \left(S_R + \frac{S_W}{n}\right)\left(nC'_W + C'_R\right)$$

So,

$$\frac{\partial}{\partial n}F(n) = 0$$

which gives

$$\left(nC'_W + C'_R\right)\left(-\frac{S_W}{n^2}\right) + \left(S_R + \frac{S_W}{n}\right)C'_W = 0$$

So,

$$n^* = \sqrt{\frac{S_W C'_R}{S_R C'_W}}$$

The value of n^* thus obtained need not be an integer value. And so, look at the two integers n_1 and n_2 that surround the value of n^*. (If $n^* = 1.43$, then n_1 and n_2 will be 1 and 2 that surround 1.43.)

Then evaluate the values of $F(n_1)$ and $F(n_2)$ from the preceding expression of $F(n)$. Whichever value gives the lower value of $F(n)$, that will be the appropriate n^* to choose as $F(n)$ is convex in n.

The steps can be summarized as follows:

Step 1
Compute:

$$n^* = \sqrt{\frac{S_W C'_R}{S_R C'_W}}$$

Step 2
Ascertain the two integer values n_1 and n_2 that surround n^*:

$$F(n_1) = \left(S_R + \frac{S_W}{n_1}\right)(n_1 C'_W + C'_R)$$

and

$$F(n_2) = \left(S_R + \frac{S_W}{n_2}\right)(n_2 C'_W + C'_R)f$$

Step 3
If

$$F(n_1) \le F(n_2), \text{ then } n = n_1$$

and if

$$F(n_1) > F(n_2), \text{ then } n = n_2$$

Step 4

$$Q^*_R(n) = \sqrt{\frac{2\left(S_R + \frac{S_W}{n}\right)D}{h\left(nC'_W + C'_R\right)}}$$

Step 5

$$Q_W = n^* Q_R$$

EXAMPLE 8.5

Suppose a warehouse supplies bulk liquid in a packaged and transformed form to a retailer and the demand is deterministic at the rate of 1200 liters annually. Assume that the unit value of the liquid at the bulk rate C_W or C'_W at the warehouse is \$1/liter and after its value is added with packaging and transforming, it is valued at \$4 (i.e., C'_R $(C_R - C_W)$ is \$4/liter). Assume the fixed component of the purchase charge S_W is \$12, while the setup cost for the packaging and transformation operation S_R is \$18. Finally, the estimated carrying charge is \$0.20/liter/year and is assumed to be the same for holding inventory at the warehouse and at the retailer. (Note that this charge need not be the same as what we discussed earlier.)

Step 1

$$n^* = \sqrt{\frac{S_W C'_R}{S_R C'_W}} = \sqrt{\frac{12 \times 4}{18 \times 1}} = 2.67$$

Step 2
So

$$n_1 = 2$$
$$n_2 = 3$$

Step 3

$$F(n_1)=\left(S_R+\frac{S_W}{n_1}\right)(n_1C'_W+C'_R)\text{ i.e., }F(2)=\left(18+\frac{12}{2}\right)(2\times1+4)=144$$

$$F(n_2)=\left(S_R+\frac{S_W}{n_2}\right)(n_2C'_W+C'_R)\text{ i.e., }F(3)=\left(18+\frac{12}{3}\right)(3\times1+4)=154$$

Here $F(2) < F(3)$ and so $n = n_1 = 2$.

Step 4

$$Q_R^*(n)=\sqrt{\frac{2\left(S_R+\frac{S_W}{n}\right)D}{h\left(nC'_W+C'_R\right)}}=\sqrt{\frac{2\times\left(18+\frac{12}{2}\right)\times1200}{0.2(2\times1+4)}}=219$$

Step 5

$$Q_W = n^*Q_R = 2\times219 = 438$$

In other words, the warehouse will purchase 438 liters at a time and one-half of these or 219 liters are immediately transformed, packaged, and sent to the retailer. When these 219 (finished) liters are depleted, a second package and transformed liquids are again sent to the retailer. When these are depleted, the warehouse will start a new cycle by once again purchasing 438 liters of bulk liquids.

8.7 | RISK POOLING OR CENTRALIZATION OF INVENTORIES

Multi-echelon inventory models are very tedious and complex and very difficult to implement too. A simple model is explained here, but complex models are available and can be seen in the references given in the bibliography.

In practice, we see that supply chains hold safety inventories in many locations usually served by multiple warehouses to meet customer service levels. It is good to compare key advantages and disadvantages of a centralized inventory system vis a vis the decentralized system.

We will examine the advantage of centralizing the inventory, also called risk pooling, with the example given in Table 8.22.

Table 8.22 gives the weekly demands of Market 1 and Market 2 for 10 weeks, which are, respectively, served by a decentralized system of two warehouses, 1 and 2. Also given are the ordering cost of $75 and the inventory-carrying charge of @0.40 per unit/week with a lead time of 1.5 weeks. The warehouses maintain a service level of 97.5%.

TABLE 8.22 Weekly demand of two markets

Market 1	33	45	37	38	55	30	18	58	42	35
Market 2	57	23	52	20	26	50	20	26	24	59

Summary of the data is given in Table 8.23.

TABLE 8.23 Summary of measures for Table 8.22

Decentralized	Market	Average (d)	Standard Deviation (s_d)	$s_{d'}$	Coefficient of Variation
	1	39.1	11.74	14.38	0.25
	2	35.7	16.49	20.19	0.38

If both the markets are served by a centralized warehouse, then the combined demand of markets 1 and 2 will be as shown in Table 8.24 with the summary measures.

TABLE 8.24 Results for the centralized warehouse

Centralized		90	68	89	58	81	80	38	84	66	94
Average (d)	Standard Deviation (s_d)	s'_d	Coefficient of Variation								
74.8	17.36	21.26	0.19								

The Average Inventory Level (AIL) for both the decentralized system and centralized system can be calculated as follows:

We know that $AIL = \frac{Q}{2} + \text{Safety Stock}\left(z * s'_d\right)$

$$Q_{\text{Market1}} = \sqrt{\frac{2 \times 39.1 \times 75}{0.40}} = 121.1$$

$$Q_{\text{Market2}} = \sqrt{\frac{2 \times 35.7 \times 75}{0.40}} = 115.7$$

We know that Safety Stock = $z^* s'_d$.
Here, the service level is given as 0.975 and hence the z-value is 1.96.
Safety Stock (Market 1) = 1.96 × 14.38 = 28.18
Safety Stock (Market 2) = 1.96 × 20.19 = 39.57
AIL for Market 1 = (121.1/2) + 28.18 = 88.73
AIL for Market 2 = (115.7/2) + 39.57 = 97.42

Hence, the total inventory that will be held under the decentralized system will be 88.73 + 97.42 = **186.15**.

Now we will look at the AIL for the centralized system.

$$Q_{\text{Centralized}} = \sqrt{\frac{2 \times 74.8 \times 75}{0.40}} = 168.48$$

Safety Stock (Centralized) = 1.96 × 21.26 = 41.67.

So, AIL (Centralized) = 168.5/2 + 41.67 = **125.91**.

Hence, there will be a decrease of (186.15 – 125.91) = 60.24 units of inventory if centralization of inventory is followed.

This example presents an important concept known as risk pooling or centralizing inventory in supply chain management. This is motivated by our observations that if the demands across markets are aggregated, it reduces the demand variability, as it is likely that high demand in one market is offset by low demand in another market. This reduction enables us to reduce the safety stock and, therefore, the average inventory level. We will give a mathematical explanation to this considering two locations that can be generalized.

Consider the sum of two random variables X_1 and X_2 representing the demand in two regions. Let their respective means and variances be μ_1, μ_2, σ_1^2, and σ_2^2.

We know that $E(X_1 + X_2) = E(X_1) + E(X_2) = \mu_1 + \mu_2$.

And $\text{Var}(X_1 + X_2) = \text{Var}(X_1) + \text{Var}(X_2) + 2\text{COV}(X_1, X_2)$ and if they are independent, $\text{Var}(X_1 + X_2) = \text{Var}(X_1) + \text{Var}(X_2)$.

That is, $\text{Var}(X_1 + X_2) = \sigma^2 = \sigma_1^2 + \sigma_2^2 + 2\rho\sigma_1\sigma_2$ where ρ is the correlation coefficient of X_1, X_2 and where $-1 \le \rho \le 1$. We see that $\sigma < \sqrt{\sigma_1^2 + \sigma_2^2}$ when ρ is negative. That is, when the correlation between the market demands is negative, it favors the centralization and risk pooling as most effective.

We summarize the three critical points we have made about risk pooling.

1. Centralizing inventory reduces both safety stock and average inventory in the system. In a centralized distribution system, it is possible to adjust the stock levels between markets when one market has high demand and another market has low demand, which is not possible in a decentralized distribution system where different warehouses serve different markets.
2. When the coefficient of variation is higher, it is beneficial for inventories to be centralized. We observed that the AIL has two components: one proportional to average weekly demand (Q) and the other proportional to the standard deviation of weekly demand (safety stock). When a reduction in AIL is achieved, it is mainly through a reduction in safety stock. So when the coefficient of variation is higher, the impact is on the reduction of the safety stock.
3. The benefits from risk pooling depend on the behavior of demand between markets. As explained earlier, when the correlation between the demands of the markets is negative, the standard deviation of the combined demand is much less than the square root of the individual variances of the market demands. This makes the standard deviation lower and in turn makes the safety stock lower for the centralized average inventory level as shown mathematically earlier.

SUMMARY

In this chapter, we discussed very important and advanced inventory concepts when practicing managers face various constraints in terms of overall budget limits on inventory investment, over all setup time available for production, overall limit on the safety stock to be held, overall stockout situations that can be faced, etc. The concept of Lagrangian multipliers was very useful in handling such situations, and with the help of Excel Goal Seek, it is possible to solve such problems. Inventory policy decisions dealing with multiple items and how joint ordering or replenishment helps managers trade off ordering costs with inventory-carrying costs for better lot-sizing decisions have been discussed. Various methods of aggregation strategies are discussed with examples and results to highlight the choices that are available in this area. Situations when the demand is not constant but time varying are also discussed, and how lot sizing can be decided dynamically using various dynamic lot-sizing techniques is also shown. An illustration of how complex the multi-echelon inventory is and how it can be modeled is also shown with an example. An important strategy when demand is not independent and correlated and how risk pooling can be used to manage inventories is shown at the end, which is one of the important approaches in managing inventory in practice.

Case Study

The following case studies are suggested for inventory decisions for multiple items and risk pooling:

1. Delivery Strategy by MoonChem in Supply Chain Management-Strategy, Planning and Operation by Sunil Chopra, Peter Meindl and Dharam Vir Kalra, Chapter 11.
2. Managing Inventories at ALKO Inc in Supply Chain Management-Strategy, Planning and Operation by Sunil Chopra, Peter Meindl and Dharam Vir Kalra, Chapter 12.
3. Should Packing Be Postponed to the DC (Penang Electronics) in Supply Chain Management-Strategy, Planning and Operation by Sunil Chopra, Peter Meindl and Dharam Vir Kalra, Chapter 12.

Important Equations and Formulae

1. **Inventory investment**

   Adjusted order quantity Q_i of the item i becomes

$$Q_i = \sqrt{\frac{2D_iS_i}{C_i(h+\lambda)}}$$

   where λ is a constant to be determined. We can obtain the value of $h' = h + \lambda$ as

$$h' = h + \lambda = \left(\frac{\sum_{i=1}^{n}\sqrt{2D_iS_iC_i}}{2L}\right)^2$$

2. **Lot-sizing inventory management interpolation technique (LIMIT)**

   Three fundamental relationships to determine the limit quantities and the limit-carrying percentage:

$$M = \frac{S_T}{S_L} = \sqrt{\frac{h_T}{h_L}}$$

$$h_L = h_T\left(\frac{S_L}{S_T}\right)^2$$

$$Q_{i_L} = M * Q_{i_T}$$

3. **Joint replenishment**

$$N = \sqrt{\frac{Dh}{2S'}} = \sqrt{\frac{h\sum D_iC_i}{2\left[S' + \sum s_i\right]}}$$

$$T = \sqrt{\frac{2\left[S' + \sum s_i\right]}{h\sum D_iC_i}}$$

Exercises

1. Suppose that $D = 10{,}000$, $S = \$180$, $c = \$18$. If we require any six setups in the year, what will be the implied annual holding cost percentage per unit per year?
2. Suppose that $D = 10{,}000$, $S = \$180$, $c = \$18$, and $I = 20\%$. Now we are asked to revise I to 35%. What multiplier M should be used in revising the original Q? What will the new Q be? Check this against the EOQ formula, with $I = 0.35$. What is the ratio of the number of setups under the original to the number of setups under the revised carrying percentage?
3. In a firm, the inventory manager has been managing two items in the inventory using his intuition and experience as shown in the following table:

Item	Annual Usage	Setup Hours per Order	Unit Cost	Present Quantity	Setup Cost
A	12000	3	$18	1500	$75/hour
B	6000	4	$10	1800	$75/hour

   For trial purposes, assume that $I = 0.35$ and calculate lot sizes. Within the constraint of 24 hours of setup per year, revise the lot sizes. What is the implied carrying percentage? Does the initial carrying percentage guess make any difference?

Problems 4 through 6 use the following data:

Item	Annual Demand	Cost per Unit	Holding Cost per Unit per Year	Cost per Setup	Backorder Cost	Standard Deviation of Lead-Time Demand
A	12000	18	$1	$600	$40	50
B	6000	10	$2	$300	$20	25

4. What are the optimal stockout probabilities for the two items? Assume the backorder case. What safety stocks should be set for the two items based on single-item inventory control methods?
5. With a unit stockout objective and a constraint of $180 worth of holding costs on safety stock, calculate the revised safety stocks.
6. With the same two items, A and B, determine whether a different allocation of safety stocks will minimize stockout situations subject to an inventory holding constraint of $180. What would the allocation be?
7. Consider the following problem:

Item	Annual Demand	Cost per Unit	Holding Cost per Unit/Year	Cost per Setup	Time Required per Setup (hours)	Backorder Cost	SD of Demand during Lead Time
A	8000	10	$1	$500	5	$20	40
B	8000	20	$1	$300	3	$30	30

   a. What are the optimal stockout probabilities for the two items? Assuming the backorder case, determine the safety stocks of the two items.
   b. With a unit stockout objective and a constraint of $200 worth of holding costs on safety stock, calculate the revised safety stocks.
   c. Calculate the setup hours. If the available setup hours is reduced by 25% (use rounded integer values), what will be the revised order quantities of items X and Y using the Lagrangian approach?
   d. How will you revise the safety stock levels if you wish to minimize the total stockout situations keeping the same level of safety stock before revising in (a) above.
8. The annual demand for the items produced by ABC Company, the major and minor setup costs, and other pertinent information are given as follows. Given are $S=\$180$, $I=25\%$. Based on the data, calculate the economical quantity as well as the dollar value of these individual items per cycle. What will be the quantities and costs if you apply all the tailored aggregation strategies on them? That is, apply the algorithms of
   a. Brown
   b. Silver
   c. Goyal
   d. Goyal and Belton
   e. Kaspi and Rosenblatt

   and suggest a joint replenishment scheme for these items. Summarize the results. Compare these results with the other two strategies: order them separately and complete aggregation.

Item	Annual Demand	Unit Cost ($)	Annual Demand Quantity	Minor Setup Cost ($)
1	20000	2	10000	10
2	18000	2.5	7200	10
3	16000	4	4000	20
4	10000	5	2000	20
Total	**64000**			**60**

9. A company has four items in its inventory, which are purchased from the same vendor and shipped together on the same delivery truck. The truck has a capacity of 50,000 kg. The items are purchased in a single purchase order that costs $100 to prepare. The annual carrying cost is 25% of each item's value. Other information about the items are as follows:

Item	Product Value (C_i)	Product Weight (w_i)	Weekly Demand Forecast (d_i)
1	$60/case	80 kg/case	200 cases
2	40	50	400
3	30	120	700
4	30	100	600

Due to economic considerations, the shipment size is not to exceed the truck capacity for the combined order. What size should the order quantity be for each item?

10. Suppose that a company wants to consolidate two of its warehouses into a central warehouse. Three top-selling items stocked in both warehouses are selected for evaluation. From the monthly forecasts of the demand warehouse territories, the following statistics are known:

	Warehouse 1		Warehouse 2		
Product	Monthly Demand (Units)	Monthly Standard Deviation (Units)	Monthly Demand (Units)	Monthly Standard Deviation (Units)	Product Value (Units $/Unit)
A	4000	600	6000	800	18
B	10000	350	12500	350	32
C	15000	2000	25000	2500	27

The product order quantities are determined locally at each warehouse using the EOQ formula and are ordered from separate vendors with an order processing cost of $30 per order. Replenishment lead times average three weeks, or 0.75 months. Inventory-carrying costs are 25% per year. The service level during the order cycle is set at 90%.

How much inventory can be saved through risk pooling if the inventory is consolidated into a central facility?

11. Chipcom supplies computer chips to other companies. It does not produce chips in house but opts to buy at cheaper rates from third-party vendors. It estimates that the demand for its chips for the next 12 months will be 80, 100, 125, 100, 50, 50, 100, 125, 125, 100, 50, 100.

Chipcom pays a large overhead on each order that it places, with a cost of placing an order of $500. However, holding costs are relatively small and it costs $2 for one chip in inventory for one month.

a. Determine the ordering schedule and the resulting cost if
   - Least unit cost (LUC) lot-sizing policy is implemented.
   - POQ lot-sizing policy is implemented.
   - Silver–Meal lot-sizing heuristic is implemented.

b. Which policy gives the least total cost overall?

c. Apply the other lot-sizing methods, part period balancing and EOQ, and compare the results.

d. Do you think the Wagner–Whitin algorithm gives the best result overall for this problem? Explain.

12. Axle Motors supplies compressors to other companies. It does not produce in house but opts to buy at cheaper rates from third-party vendors. It estimates that the demand for its compressors for the next 10 months will be 220, 100, 0, 340, 0, 100, 240, 100, 0, 340.

Axle incurs an order cost of $225. However, holding costs are relatively small, and it costs $0.50 for one compressor in inventory for one month. In addition, each compressor Axle purchases costs $2.00.

a. Determine the ordering schedule and the resulting cost if
   - Part period balancing (PPB) lot-sizing policy is implemented.
   - POQ lot-sizing policy is implemented.
   - Silver–Meal lot-sizing heuristic is implemented.

b. Do you think the other methods of EOQ, least unit cost (LUC), and Wagner–Whitin would yield better results?

Which policy gives the least total cost overall?

Bibliography

1. Ballou, R. H. and S. K. Srivastava. *Business Logistics/Supply Chain Management.* Delhi: Pearson India, 2007.
2. Brown, R. G. *Material Management Systems.* New York: John Wiley & Sons, 1977.
3. Chopra, S., P. Meindl, and D. V. Kalra. *Supply Chain Management, Strategy, Planning and Operation.* Delhi: Pearson India, 2016.
4. Goyal, S. K. (1973) Determination of economic packaging frequency for items jointly replenished. *Management Science,* **20**(2), 232–235.
5. Goyal, S. K. (1973) Technical note: Economic packaging frequency for items jointly replenished. *Operations Research,* **21**(2), 644–647.
6. Goyal, S. K. (1974) Determination of optimum packaging frequency of items jointly replenished. *Management Science,* **21**(4), 436–443.
7. Goyal, S. K. (1974) Optimum ordering policy for a multi item single supplier system. *Operational Research Quarterly (1970–1977),* **25**(2), 293–298.
8. Goyal, S. K. (1988) Determination of economic packaging set-up frequency of jointly replenished items: A classroom approach. *Journal of the Operational Research Society,* **39**(11), pp. 1041–1043.
9. Goyal, S. K. and A. S. Belton. (1979) Note on "a simple method of determining order quantities in joint replenishments under deterministic demand". *Management Science,* **25**(6), 604.
10. Narasimhan, S. L., D. W. McLeavey, and P. J. Billington. *Production Planning and Inventory Control.* Delhi: Prentice-Hall India, 2000.
11. Rosenblatt, M. J. and M. Kaspi. (1985) Note: A dynamic programming algorithm for joint replenishment under general order cost functions. *Management Science,* **31**(3), 369–373.
12. Silver, E. A. (1976) A simple method of determining order quantities in joint replenishments under deterministic demand. *Management Science,* **22**(12), 1351–1361.
13. Viswanathan, S. (2002) On optimal algorithms for the joint replenishment problem. *Journal of the Operational Research Society,* **53**(11), 1129–1286.
14. Zipkin, P. H. *Foundations of Inventory Management.* Boston, MA: Irwin McGraw-Hill, 2000.

SECTION

V

Transportation Decisions

CHAPTER 9

Trade-Off Decisions and Network Models in Transportation

LEARNING OBJECTIVES

After reading this chapter, you would be able to:

- Understand the basic trade-offs in transportation decisions and know the different types of trade-offs: horizontal and vertical trade-offs.
- Comprehend trade-offs in selecting transport modes and services, trade-offs in centralized inventories and transportation, and trade-offs in transportation consolidation.
- Recognize factors affecting transportation modes and various design options in the transportation network.
- Understand the basic notions of network models and minimal spanning tree algorithms: Prim's and Kruskal's algorithms.
- Learn various shortest path algorithms: labeling algorithm, Dijkstra algorithm, Bellman–Ford algorithm, Floyd–Warshall algorithm.
- Understand maximum flow models.

9.1 | INTRODUCTION

Transportation is a key decision area within the logistics mix. In the total cost of logistics, transportation cost absorbs a significant portion in general. Transport decisions at the firm level are more micro-managed, while also depending on the macro-level infrastructure in a region, the network of transportation facilities, government policies, etc. At the firm level, among other issues, a major concern is modal choices from the variety of modes available, cost and service trade-offs among them to select the best mix of modes, operational decisions of carrier routing, vehicle scheduling, and shipment consolidation.

More details of the importance of transportation in supply chain can be read from the listed references. Here, we focus more on the analytical side of transportation and present a few approaches of making cost–service trade-offs as well as some tools and techniques for making scientific transport decisions.

9.2 | BASIC TRADE-OFFS IN TRANSPORT DECISIONS

We have seen earlier that the main cost drivers in supply chain performance are purchasing costs, inventory costs, warehousing costs, and transportation costs. Among them, the most important drivers that affect transportation are warehousing, inventory, and transport costs. There are many decisions within each of the cost drivers and between or among the cost drivers.

9.2.1 Horizontal Trade-Off

The major trade-offs in transportation decisions revolve around the two trade-offs: horizontal and vertical trade-offs. Trade-offs across cost drivers or trade-offs with a cost driver give a lot of scope for many alternatives in decisions and to evaluate many options based on them. Many examples are given in this chapter to indicate such options.

The decisions that are taken after evaluating trade-offs among cost drivers for various alternatives and deciding the best alternative are referred to as horizontal trade-offs. For example, we will consider two cost drivers, say inventory cost and transportation cost, that are to be evaluated for a few transport alternatives. The trade-off between them is considered, and alternatives are evaluated based on the total cost and the best alternative is selected with the least total cost.

9.2.2 Vertical Trade-Off

The decisions that are taken after evaluating trade-offs within a cost driver under consideration are referred to as vertical trade-offs. For example, let us consider transport costs as the cost driver under evaluation. Suppose that we need to make a consolidation decision in dispatching goods from the distribution center to customers. The cost trade-off that may be considered is whether a dispatch every day is better than a dispatch every other day, or whether a dispatch every third day is more cost effective when we evaluate the cost of transportation against the penalty cost for delaying. We will present a few examples of such trade-offs while deciding transport choices for a firm.

EXAMPLE 9.1 (TRADE-OFFS IN SELECTING TRANSPORTATION MODES)

Finished goods are to be shipped from plant inventory to warehouse inventory some distance away. The expected volume to be shipped in a year is 180,000 units. The product weighs 10 tons each. The product is worth $40 per unit, and the plant and carrying costs are 25% per year. The plant keeps a safety inventory of 50% of the demand during the lead time, which includes 1 day for the processing of the order by the warehouse and the transit time of the transport mode that is used. Several options are available for transportation, which charge the firm based on the dispatch lot size they offer and charge them on a 100-ton basis. Table 9.1 shows the available options. Which option is the best to choose?

TABLE 9.1 Transport options

Transport Option	Lot Size (in Tons)	Transport Charges (in $ per 100 Tons)	Transit Time (in Days)
Rail	20000	6.00	25
Southern Roadways	10000	8.00	12
Alliance Roads*	5000–15000	8.00	12
	15000–25000	7.50	12
	25000–40000	7.00	12

* Alliance roads pricing is based on marginal pricing where the charges are on an incremental basis as per the slabs given.

This is an example of a horizontal trade-off. We see that the cost drivers include inventory costs and transportation costs. We need to evaluate the options based on the trade-offs between these two costs and see which option yields the least total cost.

We will show cost calculations for rail as the first option and another option of lot sizes in slabs for Alliance roads. Similar calculations can be carried out for the other options. We will assume that there are 365 days in a year. We will also assume that the inventory-carrying cost is the same for all types of inventory although they may not be the same for plant inventory and transit time inventory. The inventory-carrying cost for the unit will be 25% of $40, that is, $10.

Rail mode: Table 9.2 shows the calculation of different types of inventory and the cost calculations for rail.

TABLE 9.2 Calculation of different types of inventory and the cost calculations for rail

Average Inventory due to Lot Size Q (i.e., Q/2)	Safety Inventory at the Plant	Transit Inventory
Q/2 = (20000/10)/2 = 1000 units (Each unit weighs 10 tons, and hence 20,000 tons would mean 2000 units and Q/2 will be 2000/2 = 1000.)	Lead time includes 1 day of order processing and 25 days of transit (i.e., 26 days). So, 50% of the demand during the lead time will be 26/2 = 13 days of demand. So, safety inventory = (13/365) × 180000 = 6411 units	Rail takes 25 days of transit time. So, transit inventory will be (25/365) × 180000 = 12329 units.
Total inventory in units		1000 + 6411 + 12329 = 19740

Total inventory-carrying cost = 19,740 × $10 = $197,400.

Transportation cost = 180,000 × 0.60 = $108,000 (as $6.00 for 100 tons is for 10 units and per unit 6/10 = 0.6).

Total cost using the rail mode = 197,400 + 108,000 = **$305,400**

The calculations of different types of inventory and the cost calculations for Alliances Roads for a dispatch size of 20,000 tons are shown in Table 9.3.

TABLE 9.3 Calculations for Alliance Roads for a dispatch of 20,000 tons

Average Inventory due to Lot Size Q (i.e., Q/2)	Safety Inventory at the Plant	Transit Inventory
Q/2 = (20000/10)/2 = 1000 units (Each unit weighs 10 tons, and hence 20,000 tons would mean 2000 units and Q/2 will be 2000/2 = 1000.)	Lead time includes 1 day of order processing and 12 days of transit (i.e., 13 days). So, 50% of the demand during the lead time will be 13/2 = 6.5 days of demand. So, safety inventory is (6.5/365) × 180000 = 3206 units.	Rail takes 25 days of transit time. So, transit inventory will be (12/365) × 180000 = 5918.
Total inventory in units		1000 + 3206 + 5918 = 10,124

Total inventory-carrying cost = 10,124 × 10 = $101,240.

For transportation cost, we calculate the average cost per unit as it is based on marginal pricing. A dispatch size of 2000 (or 20,000 tons) falls in the second slab of 15,000–25,000 tons, and the transport charges are $6.00 for every 100 tons. However, since it is marginal, the first 15,000 tons will be charged at the first slab price of $8.00 per 100 tons and the remaining 5000 tons will be charged at the rate of $7.50 per 100 tons. We will use 0.8 and 0.75 as the transport charge per unit as 100 tons would mean 10 units. Thus

Average charge = (1500 × 0.8 + 500 × 0.75)/2000 = 1500/2000 = 0.79
Transportation cost = 180,000 × 0.79 = $142,200
Total cost for this option = $101,240 + 142,200 = **$243,440**

Table 9.4 gives a summary of the options that are considered.

TABLE 9.4 Summary of transport options and their analysis

Alternative	Dispatch Lot Size (units)	Transit Time (Days)	Average Transport Charge/ unit	Transport Cost	Cycle Inventory	Safety Inventory	Transit Inventory	Total Inventory	Inventory Cost	Total Cost
Rail	2000	25	0.6	1,08,000	1,000	6411	12,329	19,740	1,97,400	3,05,400
Southern Roadways	1000	12	0.8	1,44,000	500	3205	5,918	9,624	96,240	2,40,240
Alliance Roads	**500**	**12**	**0.8**	**1,44,000**	**250**	**3206**	**5918**	**9,374**	**93,740**	**2,37,740**
	1000	12	0.8	1,44,000	500	3206	5918	9,624	96,240	2,40,240
	1500	12	0.8	1,44,000	750	3206	5918	9,874	98,740	2,42,740
	2000	12	0.79	1,42,200	1,000	3206	5918	10,124	1,01,240	2,43,440
	2500	12	0.78	1,40,400	1,250	3206	5918	10,374	1,03,740	2,44,140
	3000	12	0.78	1,40,400	1,500	3206	5918	10,624	1,06,240	2,46,640
	3500	12	0.78	1,40,400	1,750	3206	5918	10,874	1,08,740	2,49,140
	4000	12	0.77	1,38,600	2,000	3206	5918	11,124	1,11,240	2,49,840

We see that a dispatch size of 500 units by Alliance roads is the best option to consider. We notice that for that option, the transport cost is the highest, but the inventory cost is the least and this trade-off makes that option the best. This is a typical trade-off where the transport cost is traded off against the inventory cost to achieve the best cost.

9.3 | TRANSPORT SERVICE SELECTION

While evaluating different types of transport modes, the total cost approach that considers the trade-offs among cost drivers—inventory cost, transport cost, etc.—makes more sense.

The selection of a mode of transportation or a service offering within a mode of transportation depends on a variety of service characteristics, ranging from speed to assistance in problem solving. All service characteristics are not of equal importance, and aside from cost, speed and dependability are also two important factors. Other characteristics seem less well defined in the minds of decision makers and therefore, some costs are dominant in their minds.

EXAMPLE 9.2

A manufacturer of automobile components purchases 2000 cases of some automobile metal parts from a supplier. The parts are valued at $80 per case. The supplier shall deliver the parts using rail as the mode. However, he can use truck or air for supplying parts to the manufacturer and can reduce delivery time but wants some assurance from the manufacturer. The manufacturer assures the supplier that if he can reduce the delivery time by a day, he would increase the order size by 20% for offering such premium delivery services. The details of the charges and the transit times are given in Table 9.5.

TABLE 9.5 Transport options and charges

Transport Option	Charges	Transit Time
Rail	$3.50 per case	10 days
Truck	$7.00 per case	6 days
Air	$12.50	2 days

The supplier calculates that his margin is 20% on each case before transportation charges. He is considering whether it would be worthwhile to shift from the rail mode to truck or air mode. Table 9.6 shows the calculations of such shifts and the economic benefit to the supplier.

TABLE 9.6 Summary of transport options and their analysis

Transport Option	Cases Sold	Gross Profit	Transport Cost	Net Profit
Rail	2000	32000	7000	25000
Truck	**3600[1]**	**57600**	**25200**	**32400**
Air	5200[2]	83200	65000	18200

[1] A truck takes 6 days and rail takes 10 days, and so if he shifts his delivery from rail to road, he can deliver in 6 days and get 4 days premium delivery advantage of 4 × 400 = 1600 cases additionally.
[2] Air takes 2 days and rail takes 10 days, and so if he shifts his delivery from rail to air, he can deliver in 2 days and hence get 8 days premium delivery advantage of 8 × 400 = 3200 cases additionally.

We see that the best option for the supplier is to deliver the parts by trucks where the net profit is the highest for him.

EXAMPLE 9.3

A manufacturer of electrical appliances uses an electronic part for its appliances and uses them at the rate of 10,000 motors each day. The motors are sourced from a supplier who is at a far-off place from the manufacturer. The part costs $0.80 per unit. The inventory-carrying cost of this part at the plant is 25%. The following transportation choices are available:

Train:
Lead time = 20 days
Wagon which can carry 10,000 units at $500 per wagon
Full rake of 50 wagons at $15,000 per rake

Truck:
Lead time = 6 days
Minimum cost = $30
Up to 1000 units at $0.10 per unit
Between 1000 and 2000 units at $0.8 per unit for the entire load
Between 2000 and 4000 units at $0.6 per unit for the entire load
Small TL (4000 units) for $200
Large TL (6000 units) for 300

A safety inventory of coal is kept at twice the level of consumption during the lead time of supply. What mode of transport do you recommend and why?

We evaluate the annual total cost for each of the options and select the one with the lowest cost. For the wagon option by train, the calculations are as follows:

Safety inventory held = 2(lead time)(daily consumption rate) = 2(20)(10000) = 400,000 units
Safety inventory cost per day = (400,000)(0.25)(0.80)/365 = $219.18
Cycle inventory = $Q/2$ = 10,000/2 = 5000 units
Cycle inventory cost per day = (5000)(0.25)(0.80)/365 = $2.74
Transportation cost per day = 500(10,000/10,000) = $500
Transit inventory cost per day = (10,000)(0.80)(0.25) = $5.48
Total cost per day = $724.40

Other options can be evaluated in a similar manner, and the summary is given in Table 9.7.

TABLE 9.7 Summary of modal options

Consumption Rate	10000	Units per Day			
Cost of Coal	$0.80	per unit			
Holding Cost	25%				
Mode	**Wagon**	**Full Rake**	**Truck @ 1000 units**	**Full TL@ 6000 units**	**Less TL @ 4000 units**
Shipment size	10,000	500000	1000	6000	4000
Shipment cost	$500	15000	100	300	220
Lead time	20	20	6	6	6
Safety Inventory Held	400000	400000	120000	120000	120000
Transportation cost per day of consumption	$500.00	$300.00	$1,000.00	$600.00	$660.00
Safety inventory cost per day	$219.18	$219.18	$65.75	$65.75	$65.75
Cycle inventory	$5000	$250000	$5000	$5000	$5000
Cycle inventory cost per day	$2.74	$136.99	$2.74	$2.74	$2.74
Transit inventory per day	$5.48	$13.70	$5.48	$5.48	$5.48
Total cost per day	**$727.40**	**$669.86**	**$1073.97**	**$673.97**	**$733.97**
Total cost per day without transit inventory cost	**$721.92**	**$656.16**	**$1068.49**	**$668.49**	**$728.49**

Overall, engaging a full rake is economical to minimize the total cost.

EXAMPLE 9.4 (TRADE-OFF IN CENTRALIZING INVENTORIES)

A manufacturer of automobile components is located at place M. All its products are sold throughout the country with its own sales force in bulk. The country is divided into 36 regions for the purpose of sales, and the products are stored locally but replenished from their manufacturing facility M every 4 weeks using GATI Express. The usual lead time is 1 week for such replenishments, and GATI charges them using a linear transportation charge of 0.85 + 0.55X, where X is the quantity shipped in kilograms. The products sold fall into three categories: High Quality (HQ), Medium Quality (MQ), and Average Quality (AQ). HQ products weigh 0.25 kg, MQ products weigh 0.15 kg, and AQ products weigh 0.10 kg with the respective costs as $60, $40, and $20 each. Their weekly demand is normally distributed with the following details in Table 9.8.

TABLE 9.8 Details of products with their demand parameters

Product	Mean	Standard Deviation
HQ	10	4
MQ	30	10
AQ	50	20

The manufacturer maintains safety inventories in each region to provide a service level of 0.975 for each of them with a carrying cost of 20%. In addition to the current practice, the manufacturer is considering two more options:

Option A: Keep the current structure but replenish inventory every week rather than once every 4 weeks.

Option B: Eliminate inventories in the regions, centralize all inventories in the plant warehouse at M, and replenish the warehouse once a week.

For option B, when the inventories are centralized at M, the orders will be shipped using a high-speed courier, FedEx, that charges $4.5 + 0.45$X$ per shipment where X is the quantity shipped in kilograms. As mentioned, the factory requires a 1-week lead time to replenish finished goods inventories at the M warehouse. An average customer order is for 5 units of HQ, 15 units of MQ, and 25 units of AQ. What should the manufacturer do?

Calculations for the current structure of a 4-week replenishment

Calculations for HQ

We will show how we calculate the total inventory cost for HQ.

Lot size = $Q_{HQ} = 4 \times 10 = 40$

Z value for 0.975 = 1.96

$$\text{Safety stock} = z \times s_d \times \sqrt{T+L}$$

Here $s_d = 4$ and $T = 4$ weeks and $L = 1$ week.

So,

$$\text{safety stock} = 96 \times 4 \times \sqrt{4+1} = 17.53$$

$$\text{AIL}_{HQ} = \frac{Q_{HQ}}{2} + \text{Safety Stock}$$

$$\text{AIL}_{HQ} = \frac{40}{2} + 17.53 = 37.53$$

Therefore, across all 36 regions, the total inventory = 36 × 37.53 = 1351.1

Inventory-carrying cost = 1351.1 × 60 × 0.20 = 16,213

Similar calculations are done for MQ and AQ

Inventory-carrying cost for MQ = 29,902

Inventory-carrying cost for AQ = 27,022

Therefore, the total inventory-carrying cost = 16,213 + 29,902 + 27,022 = **$73,137**

Now, we will show how to calculate the transportation cost.

Each customer requires 10, 30, and 50, respectively, for HQ, MQ, and AQ, and stocks are replenished every 4 weeks. So, this would mean dispatching 40, 120, and 200 HQ, MQ, and AQ, respectively, in one consignment.

The total weight of this will be $40 \times 0.25 + 120 \times 0.15 + 200 \times 0.10 = 10 + 18 + 20 = 48$ kg. GATI charges through the equation $0.85 + 0.55X$ where X is the total weight that is carried. So, the charges will be $5.5 + 0.55 \times 48 =$ $27.25 per consignment.

For each region, in a year of 52 weeks, there will be 13 such consignments (52/4) and such consignments have to be sent to all 36 regions. This will cost $27.25 \times 13 \times 36 =$ **$12753**.

Hence, the current structure and replenishment policy will have a total cost of $73,137 + $12,753 = **$85,890**. The complete structure is shown in Table 9.9.

TABLE 9.9 Analysis of the current structure

Product	Cost ($)	Mean	STD	z^*s_d'	z	1.96
HQ	60	10	4	17.53	T	4
MQ	40	30	10	43.83	L	1
AQ	20	50	20	87.65		

AIL	Each Region	Across All 36 Regions	Inventory-Carrying Cost
AIL-HQ	37.53	1351.1	16213
AIL-MQ	103.83	3737.8	29902
AIL-AQ	187.65	6755.5	27022
	Total inventory-carrying cost		**73137**

	Transportation cost			
	HQ	MQ	AQ	
Weight	0.25	0.15	0.1	**Total weight**
Per Region	10	18	20	48
Transportation cost per consignment per replenishment				27.25
Total cost of transportation for all 36 regions				**12753**
Total cost of current structure with 4-week replenishment policy				**85890**

Option A: Calculations for the current structure with a 1-week replenishment

Calculations for HQ

We will show how we calculate the total inventory cost for HQ.

Lot size = $Q_{HQ} = 1 \times 10 = 10$

Z value for 0.975 = 1.96

$$\text{Safety stock} = z \times s_d \times \sqrt{T+L}$$

Here $s_d = 4$ and $T = 1$ week and $L = 1$ week.

So,
$$\text{safety stock} = 1.96 \times 4 \times \sqrt{1+1} = 11.09$$

$$AIL_{HQ} = \frac{Q_{HQ}}{2} + \text{Safety Stock}$$

$$AIL_{HQ} = \frac{10}{2} + 11.09 = 16.09$$

Therefore, across all 36 regions, the total inventory = 36 × 16.09 = 579.2
Inventory-carrying cost = 579.2 × 60 × 0.20 = 6950
Similar calculations are done for MQ and AQ.
Inventory-carrying cost for MQ = 12,303
Inventory-carrying cost for AQ = 11,583
Therefore, the total inventory-carrying cost is 6950 + 12,303 + 11,583 = **$30,836**.

Now, we will show how to calculate the transportation cost. Each customer requires 10, 30, and 50, respectively, for HQ, MQ, and AQ, and stocks are replenished every week. So, this would mean dispatching 10, 30, and 50 of HQ, MQ, and AQ, respectively, in one consignment.

The total weight of this will be 10 × 0.25 + 30 × 0.15 + 50 × 0.10 = 2.5 + 4.5 + 5 = 12 kg. GATI charges through the equation 0.85 + 0.55X where X is the total weight that is carried. And so, the charges will be 5.5 + 0.55 × 12 = $7.45 per consignment.

For each region, in a year of 52 weeks, there will be 52 such consignments and such consignments have to be sent to all 36 regions. This will cost 7.45 × 52 × 36 = **$13,946**.

Hence, the current structure and replenishment policy will have a total cost of $30,836 + $13,946 = **$44,782**. The complete structure is shown in Table 9.10.

TABLE 9.10 Analysis of the option A

Product	Cost ($)	Mean	STD	$z^*s'_d$	z	1.96
HQ	60	10	4	11.09	T	1
MQ	40	30	10	27.72	L	1
AQ	20	50	20	55.44		

AIL	Each Region	Across All 36 Regions	Inventory-Carrying Cost
AIL-HQ	16.09	579.15	6950
AIL-MQ	42.7	1537.9	12303
AIL-AQ	80.4	2895.7	11583
Total inventory-carrying cost			**30836**

Transportation cost				
	HQ	MQ	AQ	
Weight	0.25	0.15	0.1	**Total weight**
Per Region	2.5	4.5	5	12.00
Transportation cost per consignment per replenishment				7.45
Total cost of transportation for all 36 regions				**13946**
Total cost of current structure with 4-week replenishment policy				**44782**

Option B: Centralizing the inventories and direct transportation to regions

In this case, the safety stocks, which are kept at the regions, will be centralized at the plant warehouse with a lead time of 1 week from the plant and with a 1-week replenishment to the customers in regions directly served by a high-speed courier.

For HQ

The safety inventory at a region is 11.09, so for 36 regions, the total safety stock is $11.09 \times 36 = 399.2$. Since this will be centralized, the total safety inventory that will be kept in the plant warehouse at M will be $399.2/\sqrt{36} = 66.5$ by applying the thumb rule, that is, the square root rule for centralizing inventories. While this is centralized, the average inventory of 5 each ($Q/2$) will be in each region, and hence in 36 regions, it will be 180. Hence, the total inventory in this case will be $66.5 + 180 = 246.5$. The inventory-carrying cost of this will be $246.5 \times 60 \times 0.20 = \$2958$.

Similar calculations are done for MQ and AQ. The total inventory of MQ will be 346.3, and the inventory-carrying cost will be 2770. The total inventory for AQ will be 512.6, and the inventory-carrying cost will be 2050.

Therefore, the total inventory-carrying cost for option B of centralizing the inventory will be $2958 + 2770 + 2051 =$ **$7779**.

Now for calculating the transportation cost, we will look at the typical order and its weight. A typical order consists of 10 HQ, 30 MQ, and 50 AQ. The total weight of this will be $10 \times 0.25 + 30 \times 0.15 + 50 \times 0.10 = 2.5 + 4.5 + 5 = 12$ kg.

FedEx will charge $4.5 + 0.45X$ where X is the total weight. So, for one consignment, 1 week's demand of a region will cost $4.5 + 0.45 \times 12 = \$9.9$.

For each region, there will be 52 consignments and to all 36 regions, it will cost $9.9 \times 52 \times 36 =$ **$18,533**.

Thus, the total cost for option B will be $7779 + $18,553 = **$26,312**. The calculations are shown in Table 9.11.

TABLE 9.11 Analysis of option B

Product	Total Safety Inventory in All 36 Regions	Centralized Inventory	Total Inventory Under Centralized Option	Inventory-Carrying Cost
HQ	399.1	66.5	246.5	2958
MQ	997.9	166.3	346.3	2770
AQ	1995.7	332.6	512.6	2051
				7779

	Transportation Cost			
	HQ	MQ	AQ	
Weight	0.25	0.15	0.1	Weight of each consignment
Typical order	10	30	50	12
Transportation cost per consignment per replenishment				9.9
Total cost of transportation for all 36 regions				**18533**
Total cost of current structure with 4-week replenishment policy				**26312**

As we see here, option B is the best wherein we centralize the inventory and replenish the stocks to the customers directly using a high-speed courier. This is often referred to as cross-docking or a rapid replenishment strategy where the total cost evaluates the trade-off between inventory aggregation and transportation. Again, another example of a horizontal trade-off.

The summary of the all the options is presented in Table 9.12.

TABLE 9.12 Summary of all options

Option	Inventory-Carrying Cost ($)	Transportation Cost ($)	Total Cost ($)
Current structure with 4-week replenishment	73137	12753	85890
Option A current structure with 1-week replenishment	30836	13946	44782
Option B: Centralizing the inventory and replenishing directly using a high-speed courier	**7779**	**18533**	**26312**

We notice that there is a reduction happening in the inventory-carrying cost as we move from the current structure to the centralized option while the transportation cost is increasing. This is the trade-off whereby increasing the transportation cost with faster movement dramatically reduces the inventory cost and the overall cost is reduced in the process.

EXAMPLE 9.5 (VERTICAL TRADE-OFF IN TRANSPORT CONSOLIDATION)

The trade-off outlined in this example is the basic principle of **cross-docking** where the inventory implications are traded off against transportation costs and the inventory is minimized at different levels in the supply chain.

A third-party service provider for a manufacturer ships its products from Ahmedabad to three cities: Mumbai, Pune, and Jaipur. The service provider can ship products every day, every other day, or every third day. There is also a penalty of $5/ton for each day delayed. We can explore consolidating shipments that allow for lower transportation costs from larger loads, but incur penalty costs due to the delay. The details are given in Table 9.13.

TABLE 9.13 Details of transportation rates for various cities

City	Demand Every Day (Tons)	Transportation Rate per Ton	
		LTL < 30 Tons	FTL 30 Tons
Mumbai	15	$20	$15
Pune	8	$30	$15
Jaipur	7	$30	$20

Shipping every day

Mumbai	LTL 15 × 20 = **$300**	FTL 30 × 15 = $450
Pune	LTL 8 × 25 = **$200**	FTL 30 × 15 = $450
Jaipur	LTL 7 × 30 = **$210**	FTL 30 × 20 = $600

Therefore, LTL is better in all the cases and the total cost per day is **$710**. There is no penalty in this case.

Shipping every other day

Mumbai	LTL 30 × 20 = $600	FTL 30 × 15 = **$450**
Pune	LTL 16 × 30 = $480	FTL 30 × 15 = **$450**
Jaipur	LTL 14 × 30 = **$420**	FTL 30 × 20 = $600

For Mumbai, FTL is preferred, and for Pune and Jaipur, LTL is preferred. So, the total cost is 450 + 450 + 420 = $1320. There is a penalty of $2 per ton for the total demand of 30 tons, thus the total cost is $1320 + $60 = $1380. And so the average cost per day is $1380/2 = **$690**.

Shipping every third day

Mumbai	LTL 45 × 20 = $900 1 LTL 15 × 20 = $300 Total **$750**	1 FTL 30 × 15 = $450
Pune	LTL 24 × 30 = $720	FTL 30 × 15 = **$450**
Jaipur	LTL 21 × 30 = $630	FTL 30 × 20 = **$600**

For Mumbai, 1 FTL and 1 LTL, and for Pune and Jaipur, 1 FTL is preferred. The total cost will be 750 + 450 + 600 = $1800. There is a penalty of delaying the first day demand of 30 tons for 2 days and the second day demand of 30 tons for a day. This cost will be $180. So, the total cost including penalty will be 1800 + 180 = 1980, making the average cost per day 1980/3 = **$660**.

Therefore, the lowest cost is to ship every third day. This illustrates a situation that consolidation in transportation can help in reducing the cost of transportation and an example of a vertical trade-off where trade-offs are evaluated within the cost driver of transportations.

9.4 | OPERATIONAL PLANNING IN TRANSPORTATION

The example discussed here is the basic principle of consolidation strategies that are found very useful in transportation decisions. Even international cargo movements are based on such consolidation strategies to minimize the total cost of transportation in the supply chain.

We observed in the last section that the modal choice in deciding the transport mode is a trade-off decision where the total cost approach is adopted by exploring the cost–service trade-offs among the cost drivers and among the alternatives of transport modes.

The characteristics of each transport mode may make that mode more or less attractive depending upon the relevant product and customer service characteristics.

A brief note comparing factors for deciding the transportation mode is given in Table 9.14.

TABLE 9.14 Factors for transportation modes

Characteristics	Air	Sea	Rail	Road
Size and weight restrictions	Little or no flexibility	Virtually unlimited	Some overhead dimensions on height and more flexibility in weight	Has both height and weight restrictions
Safety	Highly regulated	Less regulated than air	Fewer restrictions	Less than air
Fragility	Reliable product handling	Variable reliability	Can have vibration and shunting problems (packaging cost may be more)	Handling can happen often
Temperature	Temperature-controlled containers are available	Controlled	Controlled	Controlled through reefer vehicles
Cost per unit	Very high	Can be very low	Can be low	Moderate, can vary with service requirements
Transit time and reliability	Fast and reliable	Slow reliability that varies. Full container loads are more reliable.	Dedicated services are reliable, part shipments have difficulties	Versatile and usually offer good transit times; loading and unloading can slow progress. Reliability varies with the service policy of each company.

The versality and characteristics of these modes offer a variety of design options for configuring the transportation strategy for a firm.

9.4.1 Design Options for a Transportation Network

Supply chain management of a firm heavily depends on the design of a transportation network and its performance in responding to customer orders. It plays a crucial role in responsive as well as efficient supply chains. It is concerned with routing and scheduling decisions for which these design options become a basic infrastructure on which such planning is done. A well-designed transportation network allows a supply chain to achieve the desired degree of responsiveness at a low cost.

We will present a few such design options that are popularly used and are found to be effective in practice.

9.4.1.1 Direct Shipping Network

In this design option, the shipments are delivered directly to the retail stores from suppliers and is often referred to as the Direct Store Delivery (DSD) model (Figure 9.1). Here the routes are determined in advance and a decision needs to be made on the quantity to be shipped and the mode of transportation. It eliminates intermediate storage and the need for warehouses for temporary storage. It is often justified if there is an FTL requirement to justify the economies of scale of transportation to such stores.

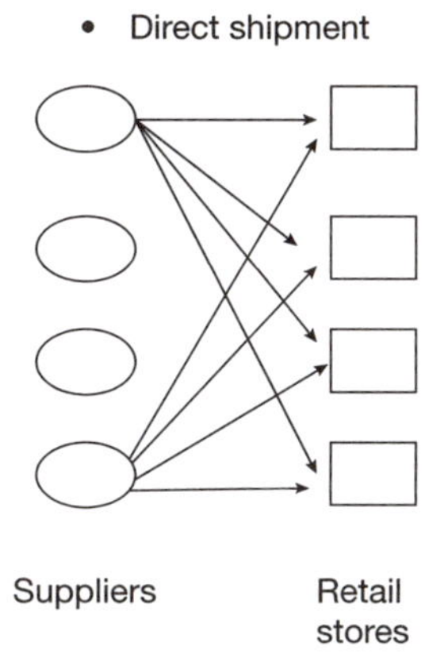

FIGURE 9.1 Direct store delivery model.

9.4.1.2 Direct Shipping with Milk Runs

Milk run is a popular practice in which a route is designed such that a vehicle either delivers products from a single supplier or depot to multiple customers or retailers or alternatively visits multiple suppliers to a single depot or a plant or a retailer (Figure 9.2). This is often referred to as the traveling salesman problem in literature, which will be discussed later in this chapter.

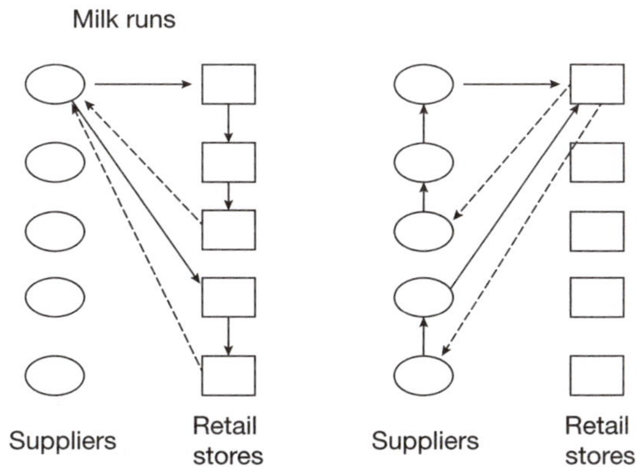

FIGURE 9.2 Milk run.

This design option provides the consolidation effect that we discussed earlier in the vertical trade-off section by consolidating shipments to multiple stores in a single vehicle. For example, Maruti Udyog uses this option for their just-in-time (JIT) production wherein a truck visits suppliers to pick up materials before the start of a production run.

9.4.1.3 All Shipments via a Central Distribution Center

In this design option, a typical hub or a distribution center is planned to serve a given region and the retail stores around them. The shipments are sent to the distribution center and from there to the retail stores (Figure 9.3).

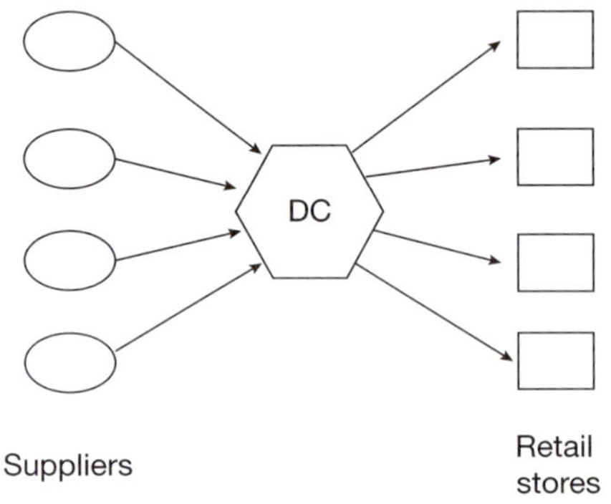

FIGURE 9.3 Shipments via a central distribution center.

The distribution center is an extra layer between suppliers and retailers and can play different roles in supply chains, achieving scale of economies in inbound and outbound transport costs and also for storing inventory.

9.4.1.4 Shipping via a Distribution Center Using Milk Runs

This design option combines the benefit of direct shipments to a distribution center and milk runs to reduce transportation costs (Figure 9.4). This is useful in implementing cross-dock strategies, which we discussed earlier.

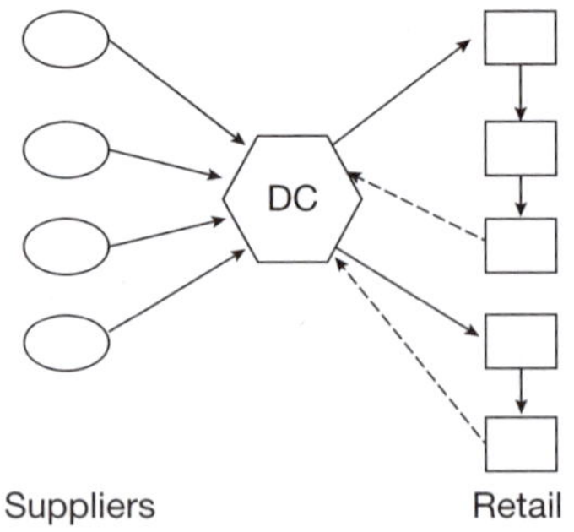

FIGURE 9.4 Direct shipments to a distribution center and milk runs.

The choice of the design depends on the supply chain network configuration of a firm. The pros and cons of these options are presented in Table 9.15.

TABLE 9.15 Pros and cons of design options

Network Design Option	Pros	Cons
Direct shipping	• No intermediate network • Simple to coordinate	• High inventories (due to large lot sizes) • Significant receiving expenses
Direct shipping with milk runs	• Lower transportation costs for small lots • Lower inventories	• Increased coordination complexity
All shipments via a central distribution center with inventory storage	• Lower inbound transportation cost through consolidation	• Increased inventory cost • Increased handling at a distribution center
All shipments via a central distribution center with cross-docking	• Very low inventory requirement • Lower transportation costs through consolidation	• Increased coordination complexity
Shipping via a distribution center using milk runs	• Lower outbound transportation costs for small lots	• Further increase in coordination complexity
Tailored network	• Transportation choice best matches the needs of individual products and customers	• Highest coordination complexity

With the characteristics of different transport modes and the availability of different design options, the following represent a typical spread from which an effective evaluation may be determined for service providers.

1. **Current performance:** Delivery accuracy and reliability
2. **Acceptance of responsibility:** Willingness to guarantee the service product offered
3. **Flexibility:** Ability to respond to emergencies
4. **Comprehensive services offer:** Range of services offered, their capacity, and the company's capabilities
5. **Information systems:** Information availability essential for control purposes
6. **Financial stability:** Necessary to ensure continuity of service and for the upgrade of equipment within the business
7. **Compatibility:** The service company's management should share the same, or similar, views on objectives and strategy for their business. They should be capable of integrating into the customer business, sharing its confidences and problems.

In the following section, we will present different aspects of network models and how they are useful in decisions of various design options and transport choices.

While modal characteristics are important for evaluating choice of transportation modes in moving goods, it is also important to see how the network is designed and combinations are made. If we compare the urban transport design in major metro cities in India, we can see how the urban form of the region enables a natural choice for the urban transport option. For example, Mumbai being in a linear urban form yields the natural choice of suburban rail system taking the major load and road system functions as feeder system to rail system where both rail and road complement. Similarly, Chennai being a semi-circle urban form yields a design to have equal role for both rail and road system as public transport. Similarly, the supply chain network configuration with its plants, warehouses, and markets yields a natural choice for a particular design outlined in this section. A careful analysis and evaluation can give a good transport option for a supply chain.

9.5 | NETWORK MODELS

Consider the following situations:

1. Consider a network for intermodal transportation. The objective is to decide which tracks (links) should be revitalized to handle intermodal traffic. All terminals are nodes and should be linked directly or indirectly such that the total length of selected tracks is minimized. That is, determining the segments that should be included in the revitalization program.
2. Determination of the shortest route joining two cities in a network of roads.
3. Determination of the maximum annual capacity in tons that can be committed of a railway

network joining various rail hubs to transport steel coils through various intermediate hubs to the desired destinations.

4. Determination of the minimum-cost flow schedule from a set of refineries and finally to a set of distribution centers. Crude oils and gasoline products can be shipped via tankers, pipelines, and/or trucks. In addition to maximum supply availability at the oil fields and minimum demand requirements at the distribution centers, restrictions on the capacity of the refineries and the modes of transportation must be taken into account.

The situations described earlier present a list of network optimization problems that can generally be modeled by one of the following network models.

1. Situation 1 describes a problem setup where the focus is to find the shortest connected set of links that can connect all the nodes and where the cost of construction is the least. The focus is not on node-to-node connectivity but to connect all of them. This is modeled as an example of the minimal spanning tree (MST) model application.
2. Situation 2 is more of finding the shortest path between any two nodes on a transportation network and is an example of the shortest path models application.
3. Situation 3 describes the problem of finding the maximum flow that can be determined from an origin terminal to a destination terminal such that the intermediate link's capacities, which can be different for different links, are not violated. This is an example of the maximum flow model application.
4. Situation 4 is an example of the minimum-cost capacitated network model application, which is solved using the typical allocation or the transportation model approach popularly used in operations research literature.

We notice that all the four situations described earlier use an underlying network with different applications. We will introduce the concept of a network and describe each of the models in detail in the following sections.

9.5.1 Network Definitions

1. A network consists of a set of nodes (which may be spatial points or centers or stations) and is connected by links or arcs or branches. Associated with each arc (we will use the word arc to refer to all related words such as link, branch, etc.) is a utility of some type such as cost, distance, time, profit, or flow. For example, in a typical transportation network, cities represent nodes and roads or highways represent arcs, with traffic representing the arc flow.
2. The standard notation to describe a network G (referring to Graph) is $G = (N, A)$ where N is the set of nodes and A is the set of arcs. Figure 9.5 gives an example of a network. We associate a utility such as cost, price, distance, time, etc. to each link in the network.

The network below is comprised of five nodes and eight arcs

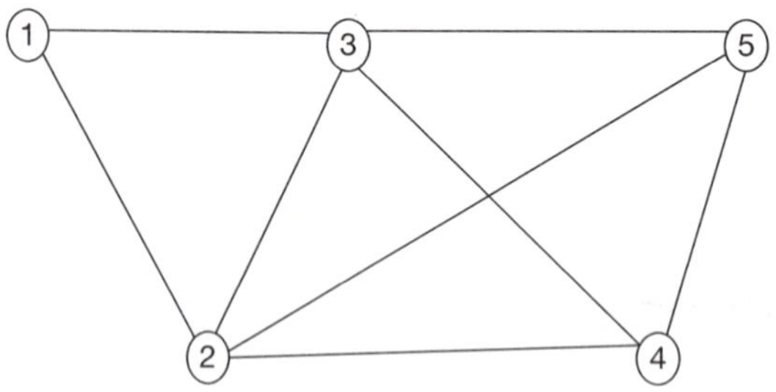

N = {1, 2, 3, 4, 5}
A = {(1, 3,), (1, 2), (2, 3), (2, 4), (2, 5), (3, 4), (3, 5), (4, 5)}

FIGURE 9.5 Example of a network.

3. An arc is said to be **directed or oriented** if it allows positive flow in one direction and zero flows in the opposite direction.
4. A **directed network** is a network in which all the arcs are directed arcs.
5. A **path** is a sequence of distinct arcs that join two nodes regardless of the orientation of the individual arcs. For example, in Figure 9.5, arcs (2, 3), (3, 4), and (4, 5) represent a path from node 2 to node 5.
6. A path will form a **loop** or **cycle** if it connects a node to itself. For example, in Figure 9.5, the arcs (1, 3), (3, 2), and (2, 1) form a loop.
7. A **directed loop (or a circuit)** is a loop in which all the arcs have the same direction or orientation.
8. A **connected network** is a network in which every two distinct nodes are linked by a path as shown in the network in Figure 9.5.
9. A **tree** is a connected network that may involve only a subset of nodes. Figure 9.6 shows a network having only four nodes.

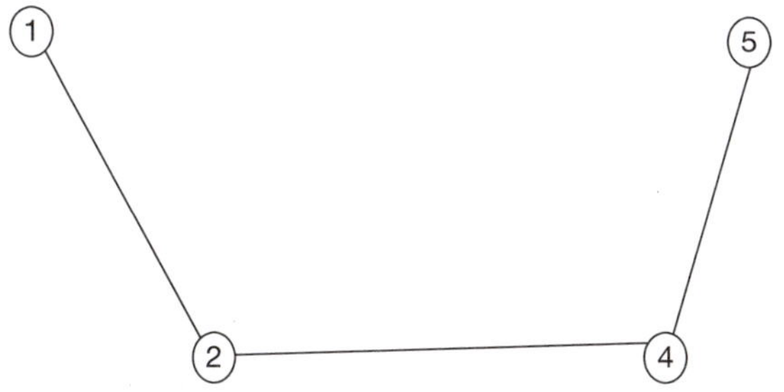

FIGURE 9.6 Example of a tree.

10. A **spanning tree** is a connected network that includes all the nodes in the network with no loops (Figure 9.7).

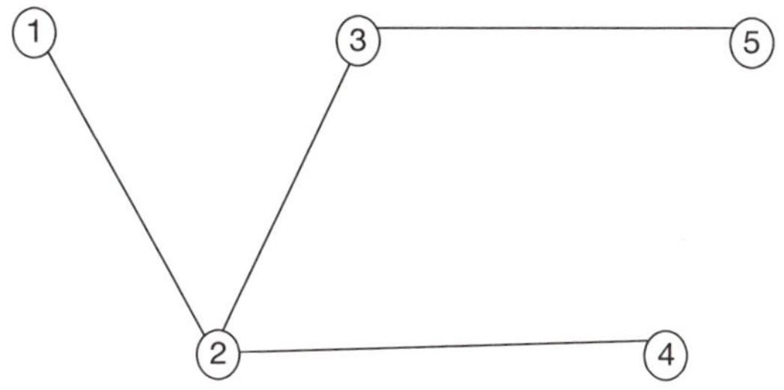

FIGURE 9.7 Example of a spanning tree.

9.6 | MINIMAL SPANNING TREE

As explained in situation 1, the minimal spanning tree (MST) deals with finding the most "efficient" connections among all the nodes in the network, which, by definition, cannot include any loops or cycles. There are two famous algorithms for finding the minimal spanning tree: Prim's algorithm and Kruskal's algorithm.

Understanding the concept of network models is essential for designing a good transport system for a supply chain and to optimize the service levels and cost. A variety of models are available in network analysis and each of them for typical applications.

9.6.1 Prim's Algorithm for MST

The MST algorithm starts with any node in the given network and joins it to the closest node in the network. The resulting two nodes then form a connected set, S, with the remaining nodes comprising the unconnected set, S'. Next, we choose a node from the unconnected set S' that is closest (has the shortest arc length) to any node in the connected set S. The chosen node is then removed from the unconnected set S' and joined to the connected set S. The process is repeated until the unconnected set becomes empty (or equivalently, until all the nodes are moved from S' to S). A tie is broken arbitrarily. Ties, however, point to the existence of alternative solutions. This can be briefly explained as follows:

Step 1: Initialization

Choose any node in the network, say i. Let $S = \{i\}$ and let S' be the set containing all the nodes other than i.

Step 2: Set *S* update

Among the arcs $\{i,j\}$ crossing from S to S', find the arcs with the smallest cost (ties broken arbitrarily), that is, find $i \in S, j \in S'$ such that

$$c_{ij^*} = \min_{i \in S,\, j \in S'} c_{ij}$$

where c_{ij} is the distance of the arc (i, j).

Bring j^* in the set S, that is, New $S = \text{Old } S \cup \{j^*\}$

Step 3: Termination test

If the set S contains all the nodes, stop; we are done. Otherwise, go to Step 2.

EXAMPLE 9.6

Consider the network in Figure 9.8 with given distances.

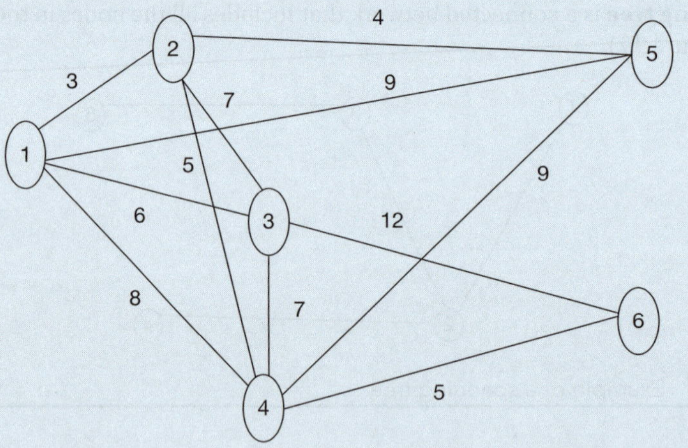

FIGURE 9.8 Network for MST.

We will start the computations with node 1. (It does not matter which node we start with.) The corresponding set of "unconnected nodes" is represented by nodes 2, 3, 4, 5, and 6. Symbolically, we write this as $S = \{1\}$, $S' = \{2, 3, 4, 5, 6\}$.

Iteration 1

Node 1 must be connected to node 2, the closest node in $S' = \{2, 3, 4, 5, 6\}$. Iteration 1 of Figure 9.9 thus shows that $S = \{1, 2\}$, $S' = \{3, 4, 5, 6\}$.

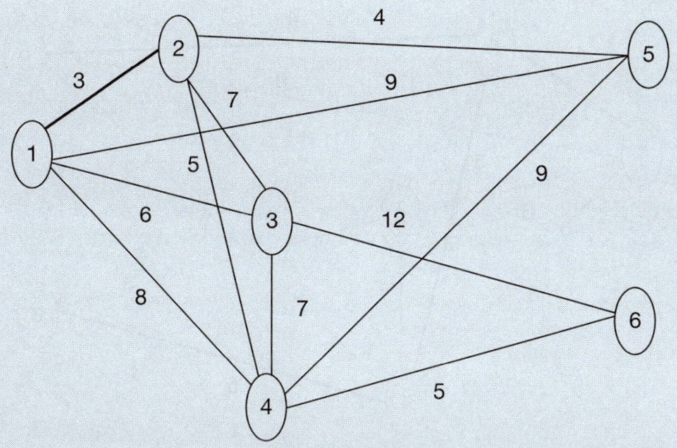

FIGURE 9.9 Iteration 1.

Figures 9.10 to 9.13 show the subsequent iterations 2 to 5 using the algorithm.

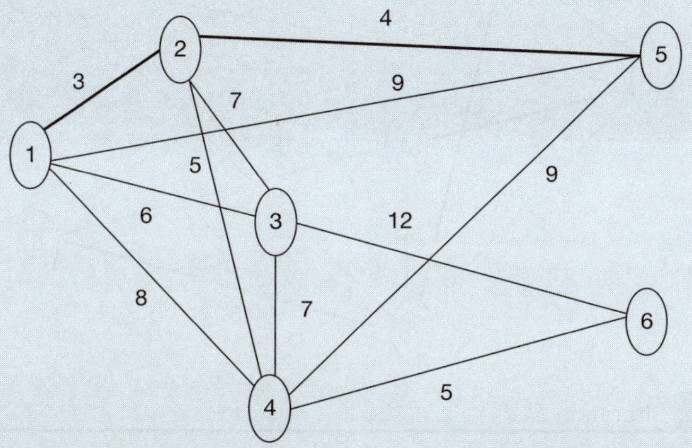

FIGURE 9.10 Iteration 2.

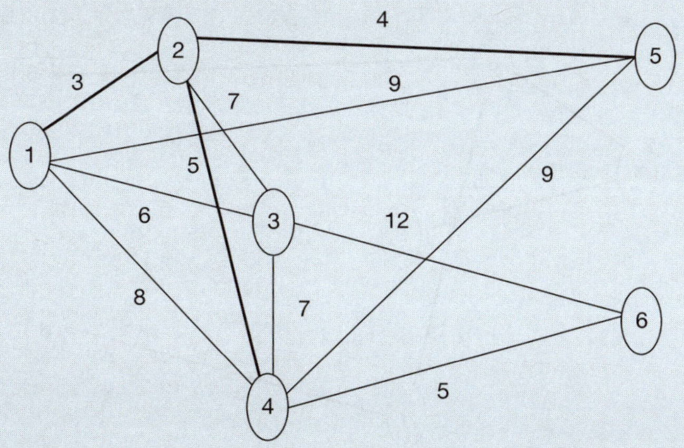

FIGURE 9.11 Iteration 3.

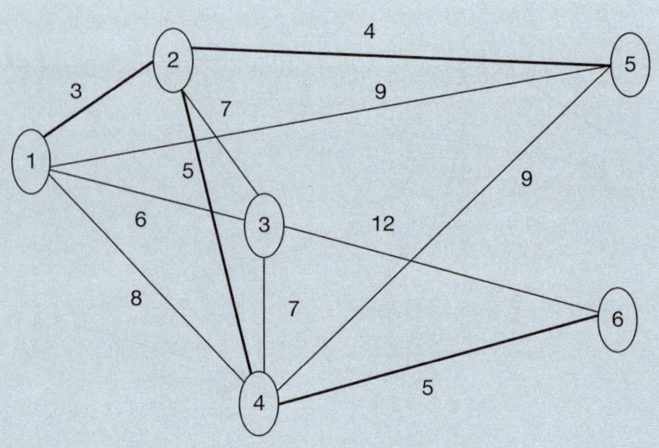

FIGURE 9.12 Iteration 4.

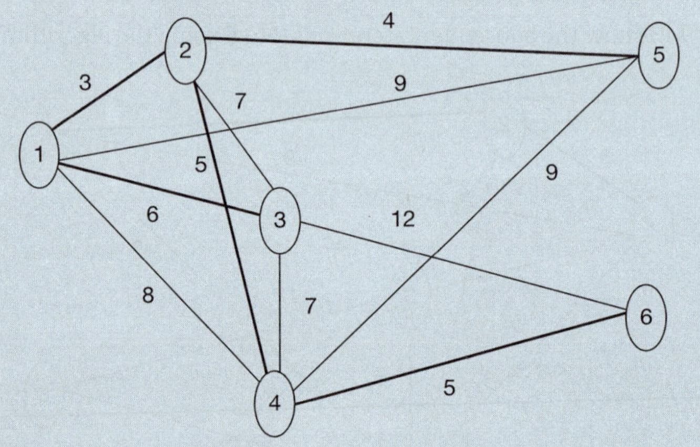

FIGURE 9.13 Iteration 5.

We see that Figure 9.13 gives the best MST with a total distance of $3+4+5+6+5=23$ km. The final tree is shown in Figure 9.14.

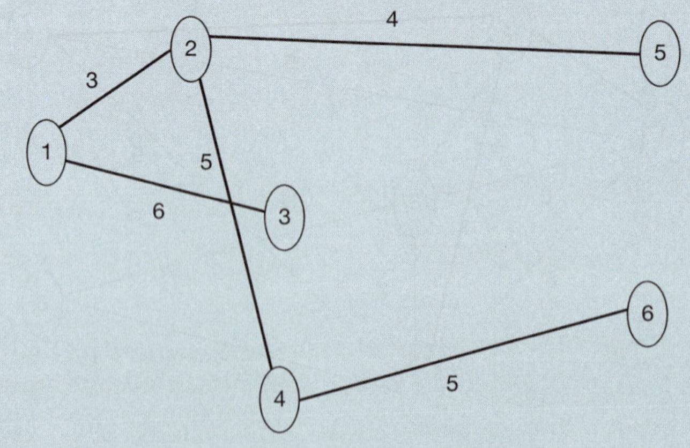

FIGURE 9.14 Final MST of Prim's algorithm.

9.6.2 Kruskal's Algorithm for MST

In Kruskal's algorithm, the spanning tree is built by adding arcs one by one into a growing spanning tree. It is a greedy algorithm with the following steps:

1. Sort the graph arcs with respect to their distances.
2. Start adding arcs to the MST from the arc with the smallest distance until the arc with the largest distance.
3. Only add arcs that do not form a cycle, arcs that connect only disconnected components.

EXAMPLE 9.7

Let us look at the example given in Figure 9.15.

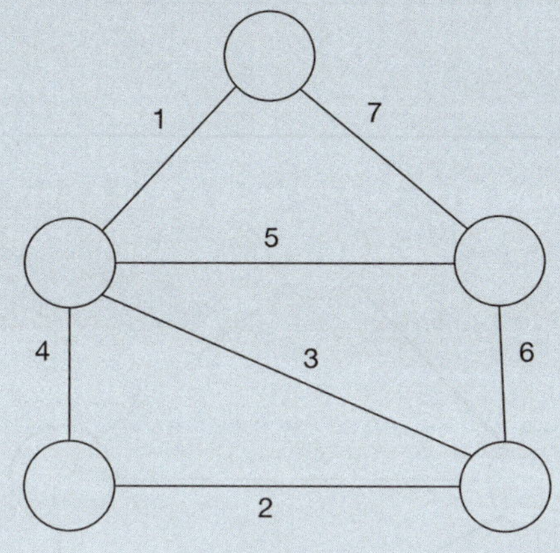

FIGURE 9.15 Example network for Kruskal's algorithm.

We will start with the lowest distance arc first, that is, the arc with distance 1. After that we will select the second lowest distance arc, that is, the arc with distance 2. But we notice that these two arcs are totally disjointed and not connected. And so, we will come back to this when we can connect this with another arc. Now, we will select the next third lowest distance arc, that is, the arc with distance 3, which connects the two disjointed pieces of the network. Now that these earlier arcs are connected with the help of the third lowest distance arc, we are not allowed to pick the arc with the next lowest distance 4, as it will create a cycle and we cannot have any cycles. So, we will select the fifth lowest distance arc, that is, the arc with distance 5. Now the other two edges will create cycles, so we will ignore them. In the end, we end up with a minimum spanning tree with total cost 11 (= 1 + 2 + 3 + 5). The steps are shown in Figures 9.16 to 9.19.

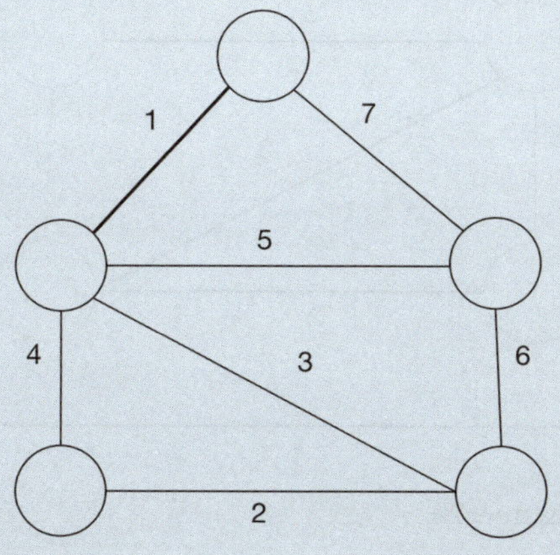

FIGURE 9.16 Step-1.

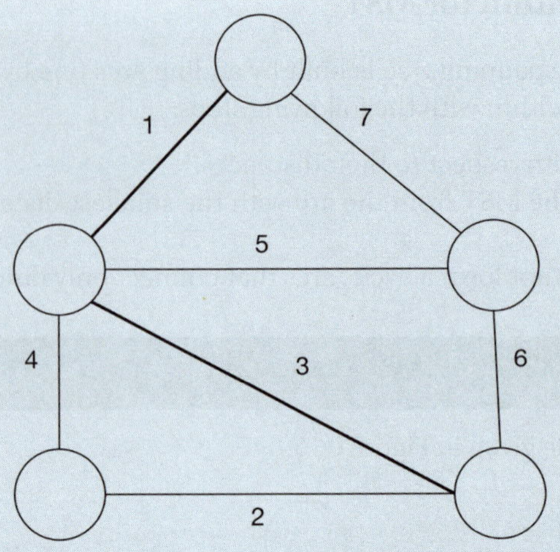

FIGURE 9.17 Step-2.

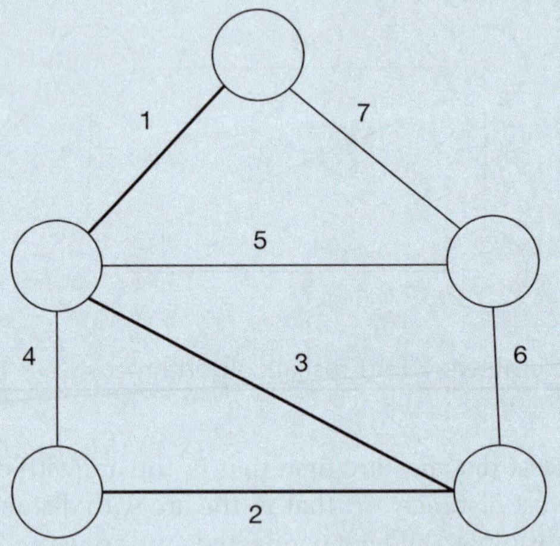

FIGURE 9.18 Step-3.

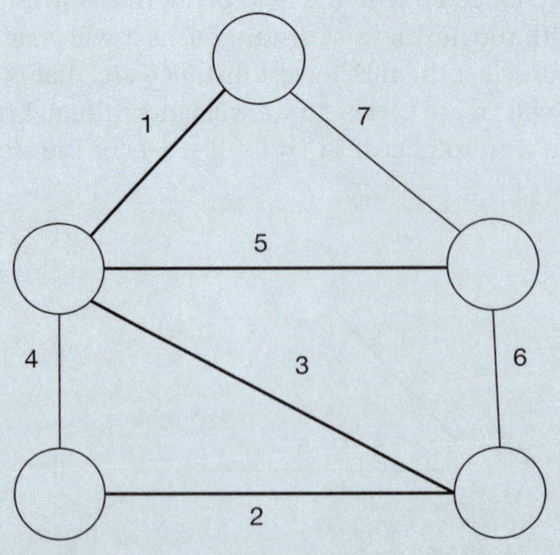

FIGURE 9.19 Step-4.

The final tree is shown in Figure 9.20.

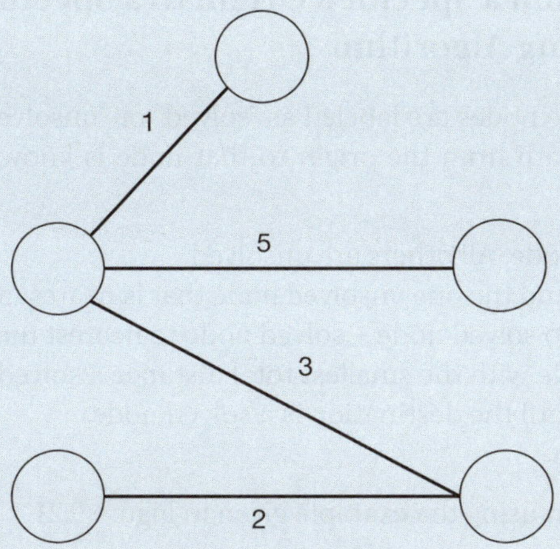

FIGURE 9.20 Final MST using Kruskal's algorithm.

The MST satisfies two important optimal properties: cut optimality and path optimality.

Cut optimality property: For every tree arc $(i, j) \in T^*$ (MST), $c_{ij} \leq c_{kl}$ for every (k, l) in the cut obtained by deleting (i, j) in the MST. Let us look at the MST obtained by Prim's algorithm (Figure 9.14).

Suppose we cut the arc (2, 5). Cut would mean cutting the tree into two separate trees or a tree with a missing arc. Then the arcs from the non-tree that can be added to make the spanning tree will be (1, 5) or (4, 5). The distances for them are 9 and 12, which are larger than the arc distance 4 of arc (2, 5). Or if you cut the arc (1, 3), then to complete the spanning tree, we have to add either arc (2, 3) or arc (4, 3) from the non-tree whose distances of 7 are more than 6 of the arc (1, 3). We notice that Prim's algorithm is the direct application of the cut optimality property.

Path optimality property: For every non-tree arc (k, l), $c_{ij} \leq c_{kl}$ for $(i, j) \in T^*$. Let us look at the same example and the MST. We pick up a non-tree arc, say (2, 3). The distance of (2, 3) is 7. Look at the arcs that are in the path (1, 2, 3) (i.e., that are in the MST). The arcs are (1, 2) and (1, 3). Their distances 3 and 6, respectively, are less than 7, which is the arc distance of (2, 3). Take another non-tree arc, say (1, 5), whose distance is 9. Look at the arcs in the path (1, 2, 5) that are in the MST. These are arcs (1, 2) and (2, 5) whose distances 3 and 4, respectively, are less than the distance of 9 of arc (1, 5). Notice that Kruskal's algorithm, in fact, is the direct application of this property.

Minimal spanning tree applications are seen in building infrastructure like pipeline constructions, laying highways, cable connectivity where the cost of infrastructure building is optimized.

9.7 | SHORTEST PATH ALGORITHMS

In these problems, we are usually given a network with node and arc specifications and the distance or travel time or cost for each arc. The objective will be to determine the shortest path from a given origin to a given destination.

There are three different variations of this problem when determining the shortest paths. The problem context may be set as one of the following:

1. Determining the shortest path from a specified origin to a specified destination. This is solved using the labeling algorithm.
2. Determining the shortest paths from a given specified origin to every other node in the network. This is solved using Dijkstra's algorithm.
3. Determining the shortest paths between a given specified pair of origins and destinations at one go although this can be solved using Dijkstra's algorithm by changing the origins.

Shortest path models are the most popular network models that are applied in logistical planning in many applications. The distribution of products through the network requires such applications to minimize the transportation cost. A good knowledge of these models is essential for a supply chain manager to manage distribution and even monitor and evaluate third-party logistic providers to enhance the effectiveness of the customer service management process in a supply chain.

9.7.1 Shortest Path from a Specified Origin to a Specified Destination Using the Labeling Algorithm

In the labeling algorithm, the nodes are labeled as "solved" or "unsolved" where the solved nodes indicate that the shortest path from the origin to that node is known. The simple steps are as follows:

1. The origin is a solved node. All others are unsolved.
2. For each solved node, find the one unsolved node that is nearest and calculate the minimum **total** distance (origin to solved node + solved node to nearest unsolved node).
3. Make the unsolved node with the smallest total distance a solved node.
4. Repeat steps 2 and 3 until the destination is a solved node.
5. Trace the shortest path.

We will explain the algorithm using the example given in Figure 9.21.

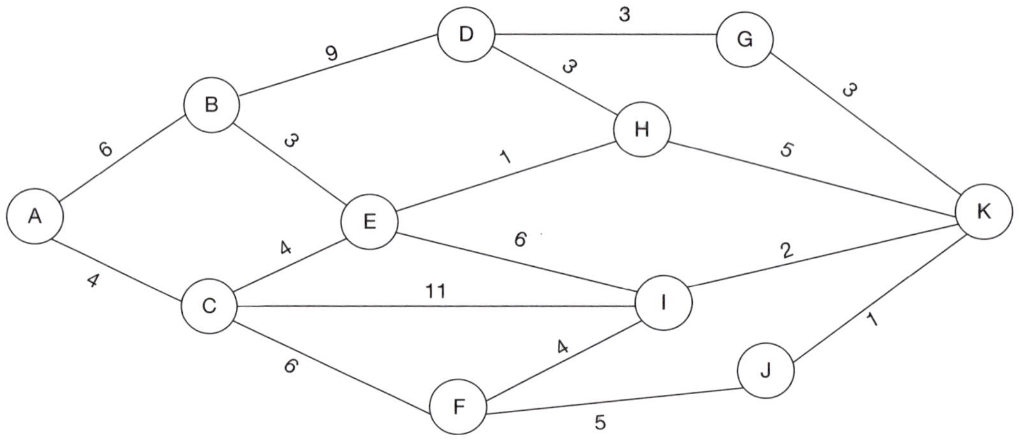

FIGURE 9.21 Example network for a shortest path model.

Iterations are shown in Figures 9.22 to 9.29.

Iteration 1

Note that node A is labeled with 0 (indicating the total distance). In each of the iterations shown here, the nodes will be labeled with the minimum distance.

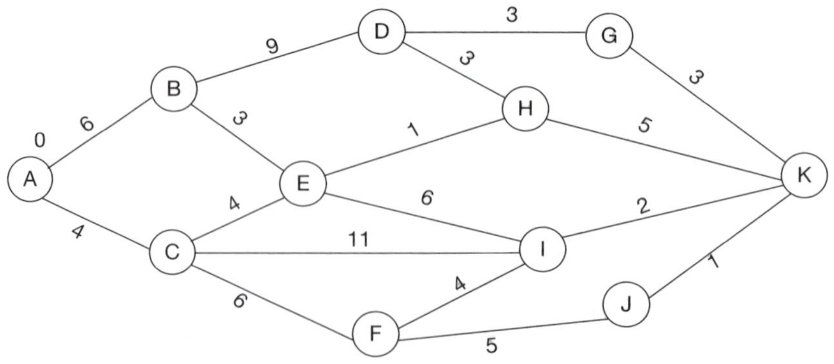

Solved	Nearest unsolved	Total distance	Nearest	Minimum distance	Path
A	C	4	C	4	A-C

FIGURE 9.22 Iteration 1.

Iteration 2

Note that nodes A and C are solved here and labeled.

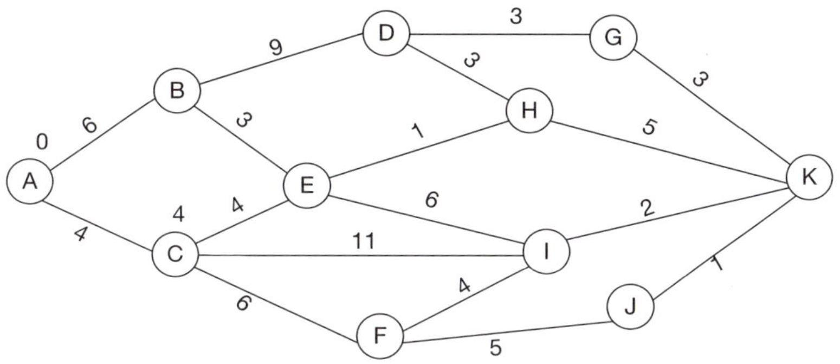

Solved	Nearest unsolved	Total distance	Nearest	Minimum distance	Path
A	C	4	C	4	A-C
A					
C					

FIGURE 9.23 Iteration 2.

Iteration 3

Note that nodes A, B, and C are solved and labeled with the minimum distances as their labels.

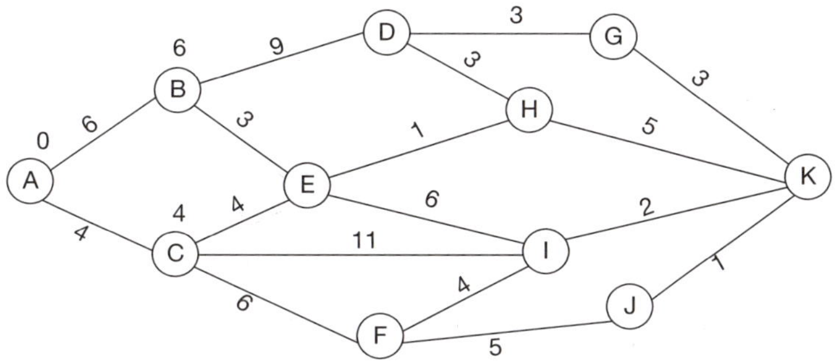

Solved	Nearest unsolved	Total distance	Nearest	Minimum distance	Path
A	C	4	C	4	A-C
A	B	6	B	6	A-B
C	E	8			
B					
C					

FIGURE 9.24 Iteration 3.

Iteration 4

Note that nodes A, B, C, and E are solved and labeled with the minimum distances as their labels. From now onwards, we can ignore node A as the immediate nodes B and C are already labeled.

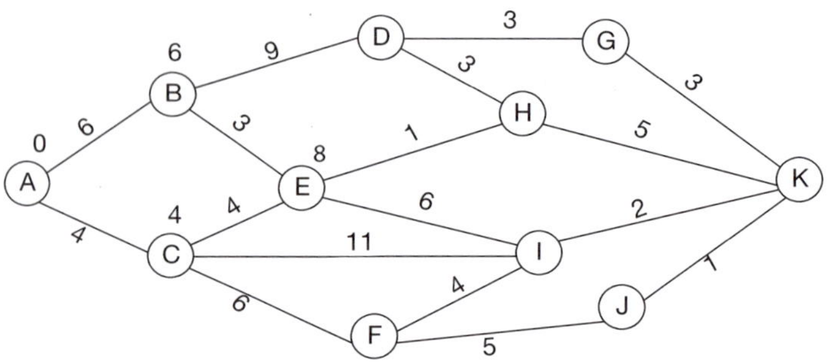

Solved	Nearest unsolved	Total distance	Nearest	Minimum distance	Path
A	C	4	C	4	A-C
A	B	6	B	6	A-B
C	E	8			
B	E	9			
C	E	8	E	8	C-E
B					
C					
E					

FIGURE 9.25 Iteration 4.

Iteration 5

Here nodes B, C, E, and H are solved and labeled.

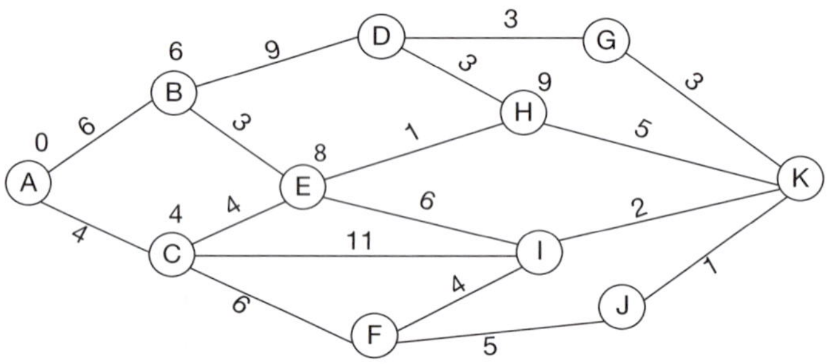

Solved	Nearest unsolved	Total distance	Nearest	Minimum distance	Path
A	C	4	C	4	A-C
A	B	6	B	6	A-B
C	E	8			
B	E	9			
C	E	8	E	8	C-E
B	D	15			
C	F	10			
E	H	9	H	9	E-H

FIGURE 9.26 Iteration 5.

Iteration 6

Note that here node F is solved and labeled.

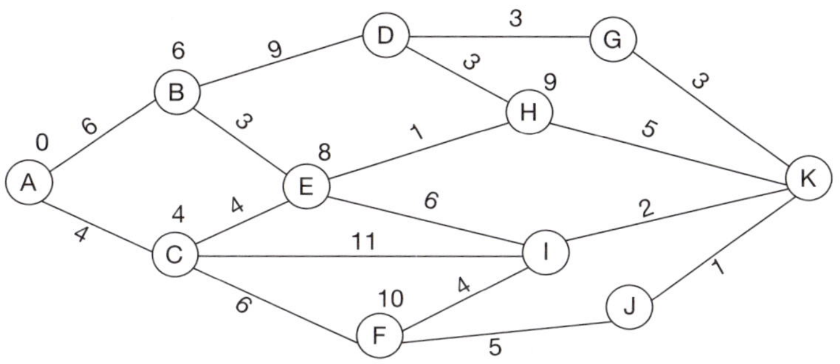

Solved	Nearest unsolved	Total distance	Nearest	Minimum distance	Path
B	D	15			
C	F	10	F	10	C-F
E	I	14			
H	D	12			

FIGURE 9.27 Iteration 6.

Iteration 7

Note here that node D is solved and labeled.

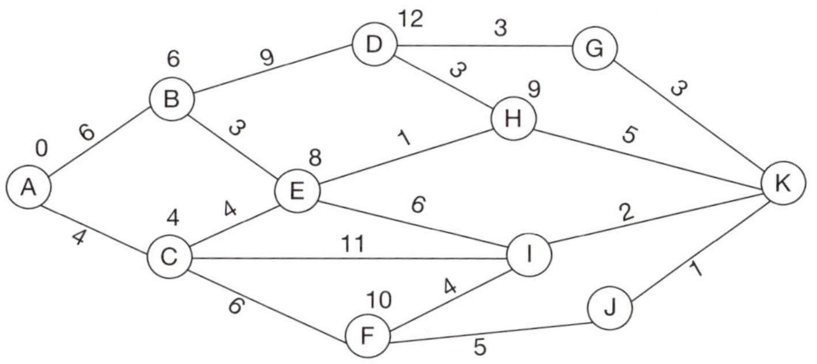

Solved	Nearest unsolved	Total distance	Nearest	Minimum distance	Path
B	D	15			
C	F	10	F	10	C-F
E	I	14			
H	D	12			
B	D	15			
C	I	15			
E	I	14			
H	D	12	D	12	H-D
F	I	14			

FIGURE 9.28 Iteration 7.

Iteration 8

Note here that the destination node K is solved and labeled. This indicates that the label value of the node K is the shortest length and is 14. We will trace the shortest path as follows from here by backtracking from K, as shown in Figures 9.30 to 9.32.

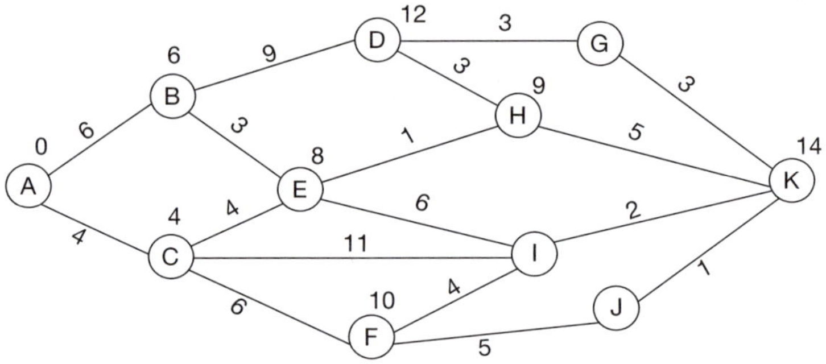

Solved	Nearest unsolved	Total distance	Nearest	Minimum distance	Path
C	I	15			
E	I	14			
H	K	14	K	14	H-K
F	I	14			
D	J	15			

Shortest length = 14

FIGURE 9.29 Iteration 8.

Trace shortest path backwards

Solved	Nearest unsolved	Total distance	Nearest	Minimum distance	Path
B	D	15			
C	F	10	F	10	C-F
E	I	14			
H	D	12			
B	D	15			
C	I	15			
E	I	14			
H	D	12	D	12	H-D
F	I	14			
C	I	15			
E	I	14			
H	K	14	K	14	H-K
F	I	14			
D	J	15			

FIGURE 9.30 Tracing shortest path.

Trace shortest path backwards

Solved	Nearest unsolved	Total distance	Nearest	Minimum distance	Path
A	C	4	C	4	A-C
A	B	6	B	6	A-B
C	E	8			
B	E	9			
C	E	8	E	8	C-E
B	D	15			
C	F	10			
E	H	9	H	9	E-H

A-C-E-H-K

FIGURE 9.31 Tracing shortest path.

Therefore, the shortest path from A to K is given by A-C-E-H-K with the total minimum distance of 14. The path is shown in Figure 9.32.

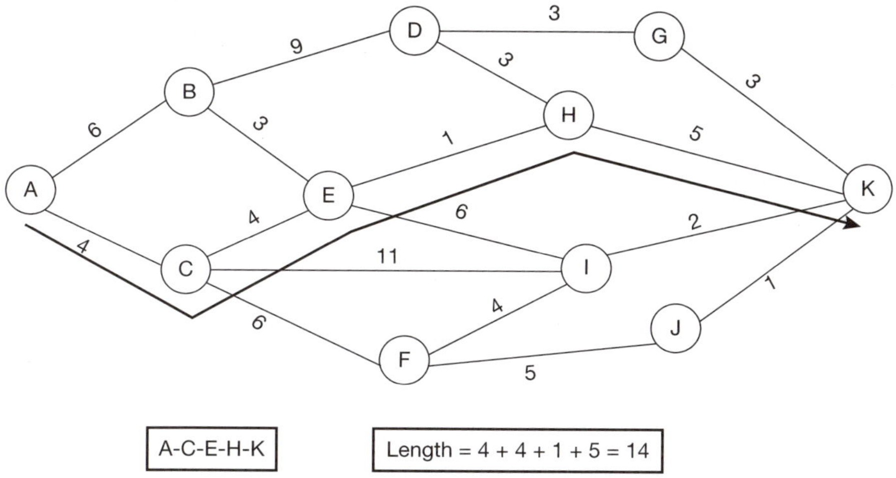

FIGURE 9.32 Shortest path from A to K.

9.7.2 Integer Programming Formulation

Interestingly, we can formulate this shortest path problem as a binary integer programming problem and solve it. We define the variable

$X_{ij} = 1$ if the arc $i - j$ is in the shortest path
$= 0$ otherwise

The objective function becomes

$$\text{Minimize} \sum_{i=A}^{K}\sum_{j=A}^{K} c_{ij} X_{ij}$$

The constraints are written as follows:

For the starting node A: $X_{AB} + X_{AC} = 1$
For the destination node K: $-X_{GK} - X_{HK} - X_{IK} - X_{JK} = -1$

For the intermediate node as node balancing constraints. For example, for node 2, the constraint will be expressed as $-X_{AB} + X_{BD} + X_{BE} = 0$ and similarly for intermediate nodes.

The formulation of this problem and the LP solution are shown in Figure 9.33.

6	4	9	3	4	6	11	3	3	1	6	4	5	3	5	2	1		
0	1	0	0	1	0	0	0	0	1	0	0	0	0	1	0	0		
X-AB	X-AC	X-BD	X-BE	X-CE	X-CF	X-CI	X-DG	X-DH	X-EH	X-EI	X-FI	X-FJ	X-GK	X-HK	X-IK	X-JK	LHS	RHS
1	1																1	1
-1		1	1														0	0
	-1			1	1	1											0	0
		-1					1	1									0	0
			-1	-1					1	1							0	0
					-1						1	1					0	0
							-1						1				0	0
								-1	-1					1			0	0
						-1				-1	-1				1		0	0
												-1				1	0	0
													-1	-1	-1	-1	-1	-1

Total Distance	14

Solution	X-AC	1
	X-CE	1
	X-EH	1
	X-HK	1

The Shortest Path	A-C-E-H-K

FIGURE 9.33 Integer programming for the shortest path problem.

9.7.3 Dijkstra's Algorithm

Dijkstra's algorithm finds the shortest paths between a given origin node to all the other nodes in a network and requires that all the arcs in the network have a non-negative value of distance or cost or time or whatever be the utility that is to be optimized. We assume that each arc in the network has a positive length for simplicity.

In order to find the shortest path from node 1 to node *j*, Dijkstra's algorithm adopts the following logic. We will denote node 1 as the starting node to begin the paths.

To start with, find the node that is closest to node 1. Then find the second closest node to node 1 (and the shortest path from node 1 to the second closest node). Then find the third closest node to node 1 (and the shortest path from node 1 to the third closest node). Continue this way, until the shortest path from node 1 to node *j* has been found.

The basic premise of Dijkstra's algorithm is the following observation: If we have found the k closest nodes to node 1 (node 1 has $k = 0$), then the shortest path from node 1 to the $(k+1)$th closest node to node 1 must consist of the shortest path from node 1 to one of the $(k+1)$ closest nodes, say m, to node 1 followed by an arc from node m to the $(k+1)$th closest node to node 1.

Let us assume $k = 2$. Let V_i $(i = 1, 2, 3)$ be the ith closest node to node 1. Then the shortest path from node 1 to node V_3 must be either

1. A single arc $(1, V_3)$, or
2. A path that passes through V_1 or V_2 and then goes to node V_3. This is because if the shortest path from node 1 to V_3 passed through another vertex, say V_4, then (because of the positivity of arc lengths) V_4 would now be closer to node 1 than V_3 is. This would contradict the fact that node V_3, is the third closest node to node 1. Thus, we see that the shortest path from node 1 to node V_3 must either be one of the following:
   a. The arc $(1, V_3)$,
   b. (The shortest path from node 1 to V_1) + (V_1, V_3).
   c. (The shortest path from node 1 to V_2) + (V_2, V_3).

We will look at the example in Figure 9.34.

Node 1 is designated as the starting node. We now want to find the shortest path from node 1 to all other nodes using Dijkstra's algorithm.

Nodes 2, 3, and 6 can be reached from the current node 1. We find the closet node connected to node 1. Nodes 2, 3, and 6 have lengths 7, 9, and 14, respectively. Hence, node 2 is the closest node to node 1. From our discussion earlier, the shortest path from node 1 to the second closest node must be one of those shown in Table 9.16.

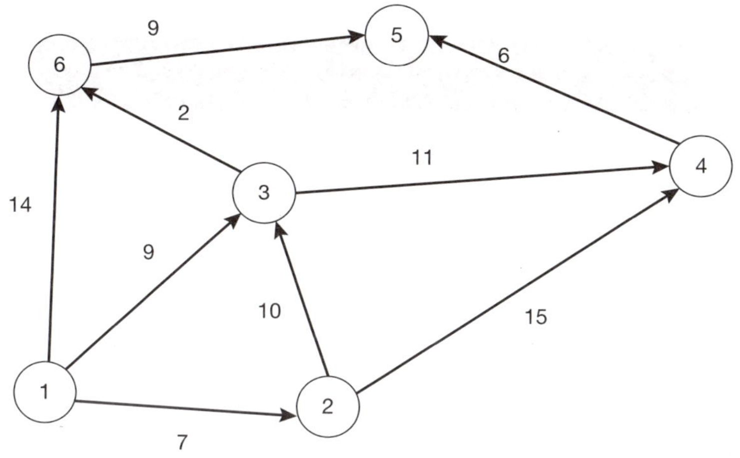

FIGURE 9.34 Example network for Dijkstra's algorithm.

TABLE 9.16 Second closes node

Path	Length of Path
Arc (1, 3)	9
Arc (1, 6)	14

So, node 3 is the second closest node to node 1. The path 1–3 is the shortest path from node 1 to node 3.

Now, the third closest node to node 1 must be one of those shown in Table 9.17.

TABLE 9.17 Third closest node

Path	Length of Path
Arc (1, 6)	14
Shortest path (1, 2) + arc (2, 4)	7 + 15 = 22
Shortest path (1, 3) + arc (3, 6)	9 + 2 = 11
Shortest path (1, 3) + arc (3, 4)	9 + 11 = 20

So, node 6 is the third closest node to node 1 and the shortest path is 1–3–6 with a total length of 11. Now, the fourth closest node to node 1 must be one of the following shown in Table 9.18.

TABLE 9.18 Fourth closest node

Path	Length
Shortest path (1, 2) + arc (2, 4)	7 + 15 = 22
Shortest path (1, 3) + arc (3, 4)	9 + 11 = 20
Shortest path (1, 6) + arc (6, 5)	11 + 9 = 20

We notice that nodes 4 and 5 both become the fourth closest node to node 1 and the shortest paths are 1–3–4 and 1–3–2–5 of length 20. A summary is presented in Table 9.19.

TABLE 9.19 Summary of the shortest paths

k	*k*th Closest Node to Node 1	Path from Node 1 to *k*th Closest Node	Length
0	1	—	—
1	2	1–2	7
2	3	1–3	9
3	6	1–3–6	11
4	4	1–3–4	20
4	5	1–3–6–6	20

9.7.4 Another Way of Dijkstra's Algorithm

We will use the same example shown in Figure 9.34. We will consider node 1 as the starting node and assign a weight with a length of 0. We will look at the direct nodes connected to node 1 and give weights to the nodes with the link length connecting to node 1. We will give the weight ∞ to those nodes that are not directly connected to node 1. This is shown in Figure 9.35.

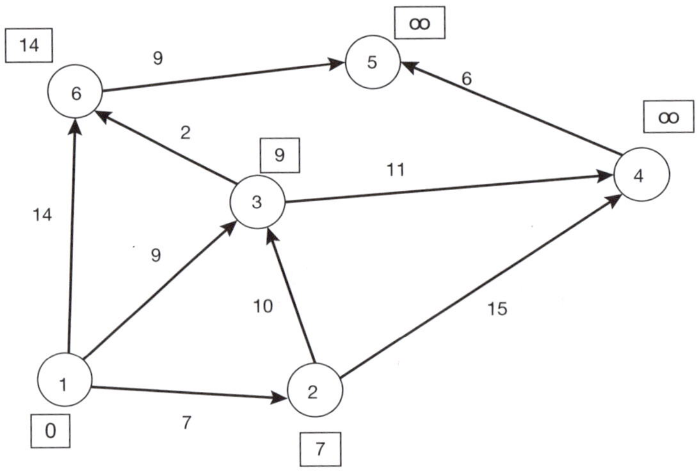

FIGURE 9.35 Starting node 1 with connecting nodes.

Here, the shortest length is to node 2 and we now select node 2 as the current node. We will update the shortest paths of other nodes connected to node 2 by updating the weights for the nodes. This is known as relaxation. We will call node 2 "*u*" and call another node other than node 1 connected to "*u*" as "*v*", the weights as $d(u)$ and $d(v)$, respectively, and the link length of "*u*" and "*v*" as $c(u, v)$. The update is done as follows:

If $d(u) + c(u, v) < d(v)$, then update $d(v) = d(u) + c(u, v)$. For example, look at node 4, which is connected to 2. The weight of $d(2)$ is 7 and $d(4)$ is currently ∞ from the previous step and $c(2, 4) = 15$. Since $7 + 15 = 22 < \infty$, the updated weight of 4 is now 22. Similarly, consider node 3 that is connected to 2. Here, $d(2) = 7$ and $d(3) = 9$ and $d(2, 3) = 10$.

Now $d(2) + d(2, 3) = 7 + 10 = 17$ while $d(3) = 7$, which is already less. So $d(3)$ remains as 7 only. Only these nodes 3 and 4 are connected to node 2, and they are now updated (or relaxed). The updated network is given in Figure 9.36.

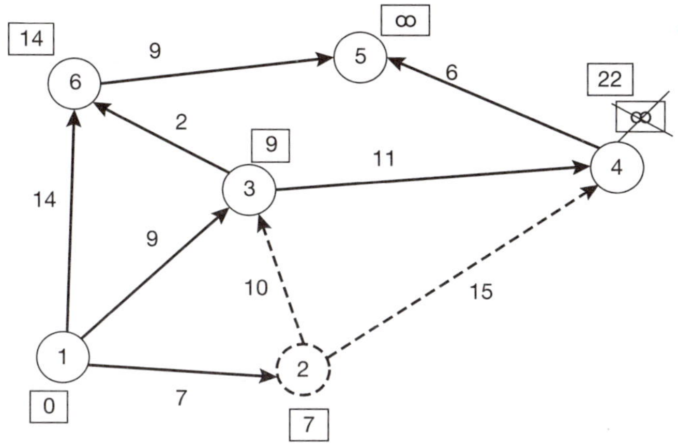

FIGURE 9.36 Updated network from the current node 2.

Here, look at the minimum weight and choose the nodes that are not chosen already. Since node 3 has the least weight of 9, now node 3 is the current node.

Nodes 4 and 6 are connected to the current node 3. The update is done as follows: $d(3) + c(3, 4) = 9 + 11 = 20$ and $d(4) = 22$ from the previous step. Now $20 < 22$ and so $d(4)$ is updated to 20.

$d(3) + c(3, 6) = 9 + 2 = 11$ and $d(6) = 14$ from the previous step. Since $11 < 14$, $d(6)$ is updated to 11. The updated network is shown in Figure 9.37.

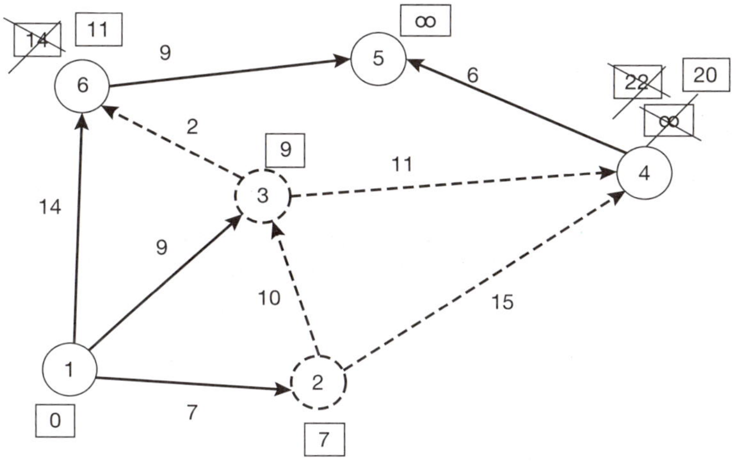

FIGURE 9.37 Updated network from the current node 3.

Here look at the minimum weight and choose the nodes that are not chosen already. Since node 6 has the least weight of 11, node 6 is now the current node.

Only node 5 is connected to the current node 6. Now, $d(6) = 11$ and $c(6, 5) = 9$ and $d(5) = \infty$. Since $11 + 9 = 20 < \infty$, $d(5)$ is updated to 20 now. The updated network is shown in Figure 9.38.

Here, look at the minimum weight and choose the nodes that are not chosen already. Since nodes 5 and 4 have the least weight of 20, we can choose either of them. We will choose node 4 as the current node since node 5 has no connected nodes to it. The only node that is connected to node 4 is node 5. The updated network is given in Figure 9.39.

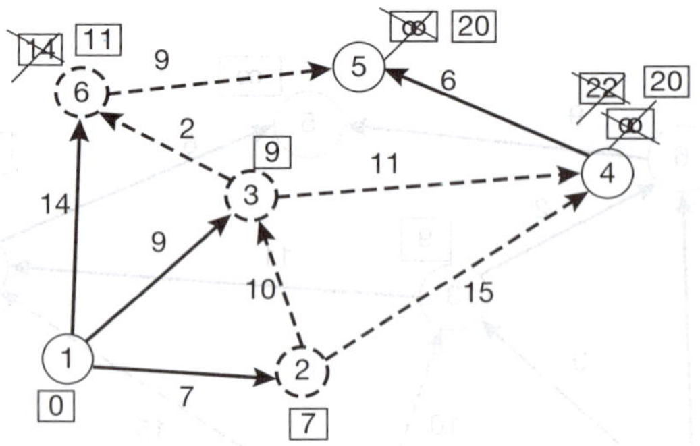

FIGURE 9.38 Updated network from the current node 6.

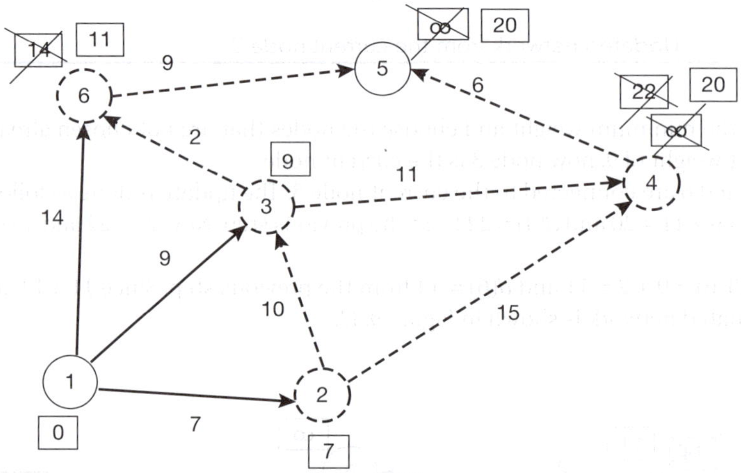

FIGURE 9.39 Updated network from the current node 4.

Hence, the summary of shortest paths and the lengths is as follows:

Node	Length	Shortest Path
1	—	—
2	7	1–2
3	9	1–3
4	20	1–3–4
5	20	1–3–6–5
6	11	1–3–6

Dijkstra's algorithm works very well for both directed and undirected networks as any undirected network can always be brought into a directed network by adding links appropriately with the same link length in opposite directions.

One of the main drawbacks of Dijkstra's algorithm is that it assumes that the link lengths are non-negative. If a link has negative length, it may find or may not find shortest paths and may give different solutions sometimes. The following two examples given in Figures 9.40 and 9.41 are worth examining for that; the first one is finding a solution with a negative length and the second one is not finding the right solution with a negative length.

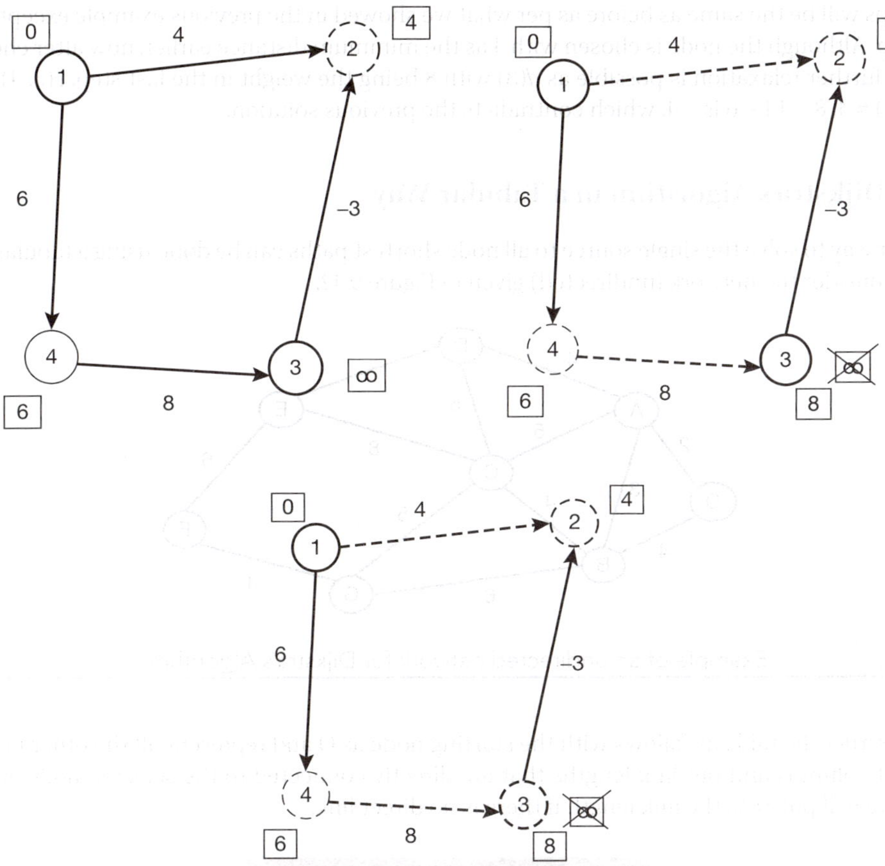

FIGURE 9.40 Finding a solution with a negative length.

Further relaxation from 3 to 2 is not required as $d(2)$ is already less as compared to $8 + (-3) = 5$. And so, in this case, Dijkstra's algorithm has worked for a negative length.

Let us change this network with a small modification for the link length of (2, 3) to −14 from its previous length of −3 now. So, the new network is given in Figure 9.41.

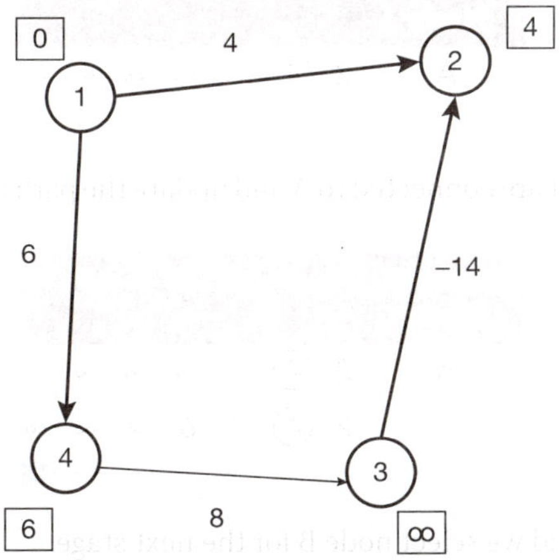

FIGURE 9.41 Not finding the right solution with a negative length.

The steps will be the same as before as per what we showed in the previous example except in the last step. Although the node is chosen with 4 as the minimum distance earlier, now after choosing node 3, further relaxation is possible as $d(3)$ with 8 being the weight in the last step, $c(3, 4)$ is –14 and $d(2) = 4$, $8 - 14 - 6$ is < 4, which contradicts the previous solution.

9.7.5 Dijkstra's Algorithm in a Tabular Way

Another way to solve the single source to all node shortest paths can be done using a tabular form. Let us consider the network (undirected) given in Figure 9.42.

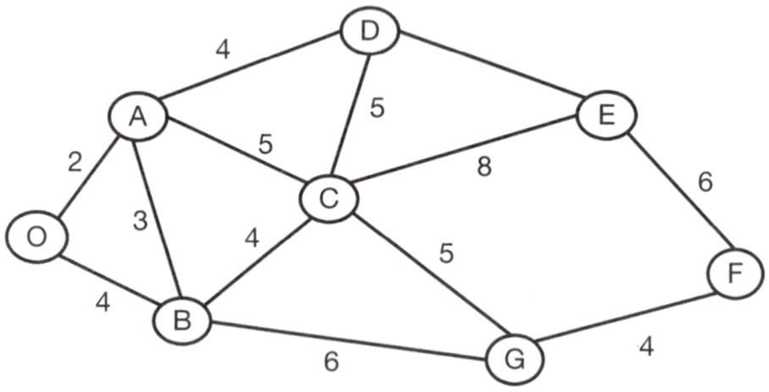

FIGURE 9.42 Example of an undirected network for Dijkstra's Algorithm.

We construct the table as follows with the starting node as O and represent all the other nodes in different columns and put link lengths that are directly connected to the selected node at every stage. We will put ∞ as the link length if there is no direct link.

Selected Node	A	B	C	D	E	F	G
	2	4	∞	∞	∞	∞	∞

The smallest is at node A and we select node A for the next stage.

Selected Node	A	B	C	D	E	F	G
A	2	(4)	∞	∞	∞	∞	∞

We look at all the nodes that are connected to A and update the paths having the shortest distance.

Selected Node	A	B	C	D	E	F	G
A	2	(4)	∞	∞	∞	∞	∞
	2	(4)	7	6	∞	∞	∞

The smallest is at node B and we select node B for the next stage.

Selected Node	A	B	C	D	E	F	G
A	2	(4)	∞	∞	∞	∞	∞
B	2	(4)	7	(6)	∞	∞	∞

We look at all the nodes that are connected to B and update the paths having the shortest distance.

Selected Node	A	B	C	D	E	F	G
A	2	4	∞	∞	∞	∞	∞
B	2	4	7	(6)	∞	(∞)	∞
	2	4	7	(6)	∞	(∞)	10

The smallest is at node D and we select node D for the next stage.

Selected Node	A	B	C	D	E	F	G
A	2	(4)	∞	∞	∞	∞	∞
B	2	(4)	7	(6)	∞	∞	∞
D	2	4	7	6	∞	∞	(10)

We look at all the nodes that are connected to B and update the paths having the shortest distance.

Selected Node	A	B	C	D	E	F	G
A	2	4	∞	∞	∞	∞	∞
B	(2)	(4)	7	6	∞	∞	∞
D	(2)	(4)	7	(6)	∞	∞	10
	(2)	(4)	(7)	6	13	∞	10

The smallest is at node C and we select node C for the next stage.

Selected Node	A	B	C	D	E	F	G
A	2	4	∞	∞	∞	∞	∞
B	(2)	(4)	7	6	∞	∞	∞
D	(2)	(4)	7	(6)	∞	∞	10
C	(2)	(4)	(7)	(6)	13	∞	10
	(2)	(4)	(7)	(6)	13	∞	(10)

We look at all the nodes that are connected to C and update the paths having the shortest distance.

Selected Node	A	B	C	D	E	F	G
A	2	4	∞	∞	∞	∞	∞
B	(2)	(4)	7	6	∞	∞	∞
D	(2)	(4)	7	(6)	∞	∞	10
C	(2)	(4)	(7)	(6)	13	∞	10
	(2)	(4)	(7)	(6)	13	∞	(10)

The smallest is at node G and we select node G for the next stage.

Selected Node	A	B	C	D	E	F	G
A	2	4	∞	∞	∞	∞	∞
B	②	④	7	6	∞	∞	∞
D	②	④	7	⑥	∞	∞	10
C	②	④	⑦	⑥	13	∞	10
G	②	④	⑦	⑥	13	∞	10

We look at all the nodes that are connected to G and update the paths having the shortest distance.

Selected Node	A	B	C	D	E	F	G
A	2	4	∞	∞	∞	∞	∞
B	②	④	7	6	∞	∞	∞
D	②	④	7	⑥	∞	∞	10
C	②	④	⑦	⑥	13	∞	10
G	②	④	⑦	⑥	13	∞	⑩
E	②	④	⑦	⑥	⑬	14	⑩

The smallest is at node E and we select node E for the next stage.

Selected Node	A	B	C	D	E	F	G
A	2	4	∞	∞	∞	∞	∞
B	②	④	7	6	∞	∞	∞
D	②	④	7	⑥	∞	∞	10
C	②	④	⑦	⑥	13	∞	10
G	②	④	⑦	⑥	13	∞	⑩
E	②	④	⑦	⑥	⑬	14	⑩
	②	④	⑦	⑥	⑬	⑭	⑩

The smallest and the final is at node F and we select node F and stop the procedure. The final table is as follows:

Selected Node	A	B	C	D	E	F	G
A	2	4	∞	∞	∞	∞	∞
B	②	④	7	6	∞	∞	∞
D	②	④	7	⑥	∞	∞	10
C	②	④	⑦	⑥	13	∞	10
G	②	④	⑦	⑥	13	∞	⑩
E	②	④	⑦	⑥	⑬	14	⑩
F	②	④	⑦	⑥	⑬	⑭	⑩

The network with the shortest distance as weights is shown in Figure 9.43.

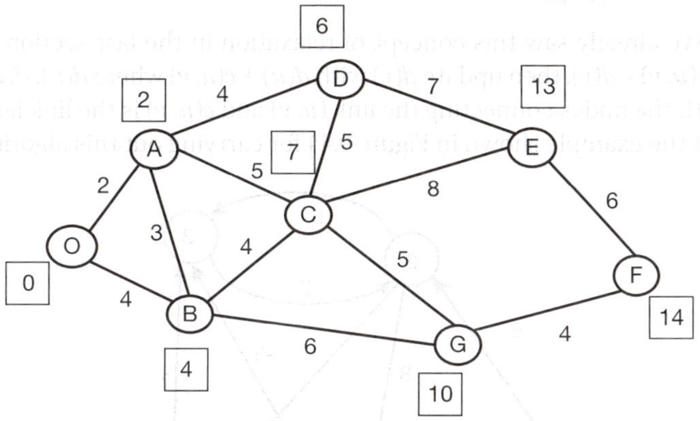

FIGURE 9.43 The network with the shortest distance as weights.

The summary of the shortest distance and the shortest paths to all nodes from the starting node O is given in Table 9.20.

TABLE 9.20 Summary of the shortest paths to all nodes from the starting node O

Node	Shortest Distance	Shortest Path
O	—	—
A	2	O–A
B	4	O–B
C	7	O–A–C
D	6	O–A–D
E	13	O–A–D–E
F	14	O–B–G–F
G	10	O–B–G

We observe that the drawback of Dijkstra's algorithm is handling networks with negative link lengths. We can handle this problem using the Bellman–Ford algorithm, which we will describe in the following section.

9.8 BELLMAN–FORD ALGORITHM (FOR NEGATIVE LINK LENGTHS)

We discussed Dijkstra's algorithm in the previous sections and calculated the shortest path from a single source to all destinations (vertices) on a graph where the link lengths are assumed to be non-negative weights since we observed that Dijkstra's algorithm fails when a graph has a negative weight cycle. In this section, we will discuss the Bellman–Ford algorithm, which handles networks having even negative link lengths.

One of the powerful algorithms in network models is Dijkstra's algorithm where shortest paths are determined from a given origin. Different ways of solving these problems have been outlined in this section, which are amenable for computer coding.

The Bellman–Ford algorithm works on the logic that if a graph has n nodes, then the shortest path never contains more than $n - 1$ links. Therefore, it is enough if we relax each edge $(v - 1)$ times to find the shortest path where v is the number of links in the graph. However, to find if there is a negative cycle, we again do one more relaxation. If we get lesser distance in the nth relaxation, we can say that there is a negative edge cycle. The reason for this is that the negative value is added and the distance is reduced. This is the drawback of the Bellman–Ford algorithm when there are negative edge cycles in the graph.

Relaxing a link: We already saw this concept of relaxation in the last section. If there is a link (u, v) and if $d(u) + c(u, v) < d(v)$, then update $d(v)$ with $d(u) + c(u, v)$ where $d(u)$, $d(v)$ are the weights that are labeled with the nodes connecting the link (u, v) and $c(u, v)$ is the link length of (u, v).

We will look at the example shown in Figure 9.44 for carrying out this algorithm.

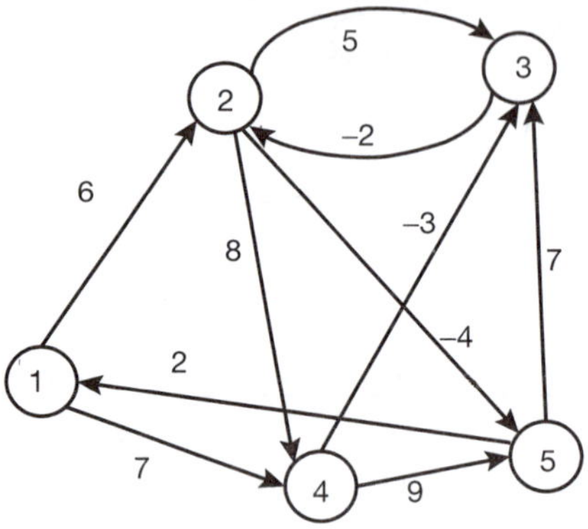

FIGURE 9.44 Example network for Bellman-Ford Algorithm.

We initialize the weights as 0 for the source node (in this case, we will take node 1 as the source node) and ∞ for all the remaining nodes. That is, $d(1) = 0$ and $d(i) = \infty$ for all $I = 2, 3, 4$, and 5. This is shown in Figure 9.45.

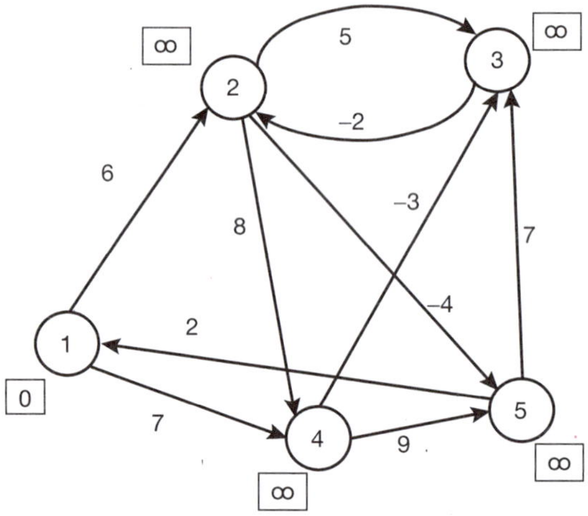

FIGURE 9.45 Initialization of the network.

We list all the links and carry out the relaxation procedure for all the links systematically so that we cover them all. The maximum number of relaxations will be $(v - 1)$ where v is the number of nodes and in this case, we carry it out four times. We can carry it out the fifth time in case there is any negative cycle to be detected. The links are (1, 3), (1, 4), (2, 3), (2, 4), (2, 5), (3, 2), (4, 3), (4, 5), (5, 1), and (5, 3).

After the first set of relaxations, the weights are shown in Figure 9.46.

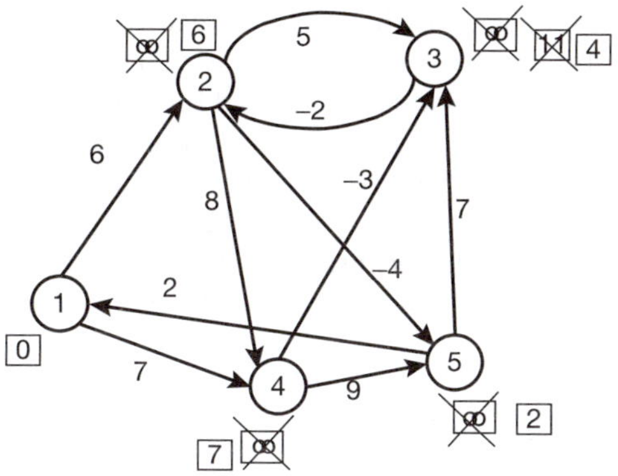

FIGURE 9.46 First set of relaxations.

After the second relaxation, the weights are shown in Figure 9.47.

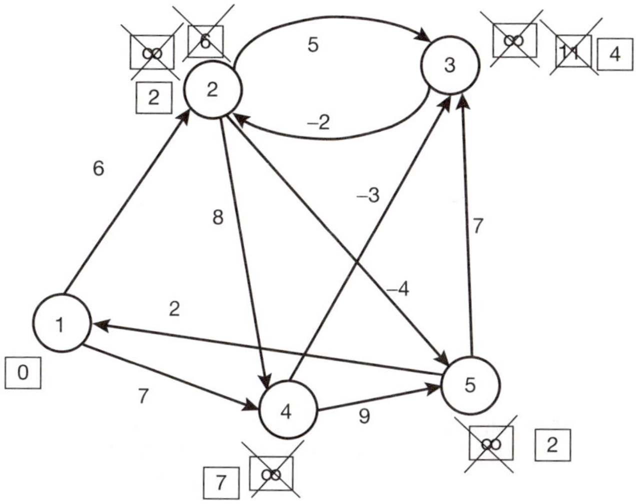

FIGURE 9.47 Second set of relaxations.

After the third relaxation, the weights are shown in Figure 9.48.

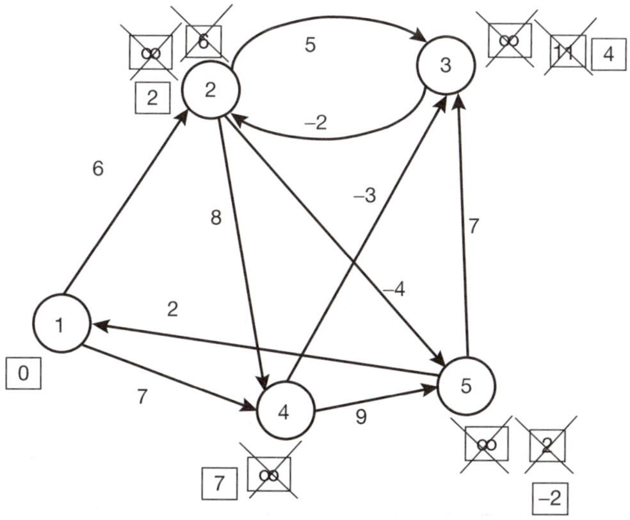

FIGURE 9.48 Third set of relaxations.

In the fourth, that is, in the last relaxation, there is no change in the weights. Therefore, we have the shortest weights and the paths for all the nodes from the source node 1.

We carried out four relaxations, that is, (5 – 1) and the shortest path is found to every node from the source node 1. Now we have to do one more iteration to find if there exists any negative edge cycle. When we do this *n*th (5th here) relaxation, if we find lesser distance to any node from any other path, we could say that there is a negative edge cycle. After carrying out the 5th relaxation, we found no edges having any lesser distance. Therefore, we can confirm that there is no negative edge cycle in this graph. The final weights are shown in Figure 9.49.

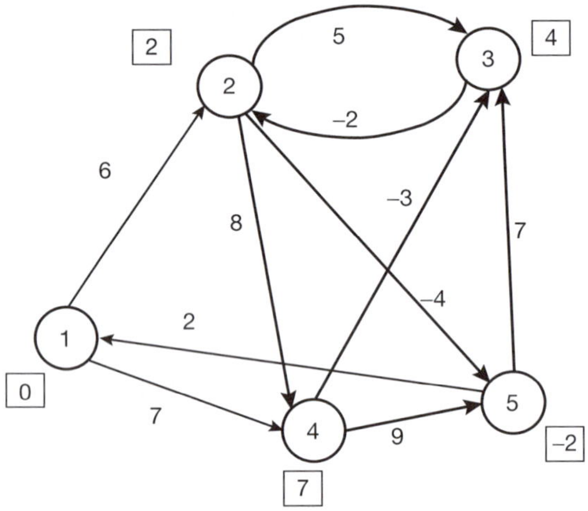

FIGURE 9.49 Final set of relaxations.

The summary of the shortest length and the shortest paths is given in Table 9.21.

TABLE 9.21 Summary of the shortest paths

Node	Shortest Length	Shortest Path
1	—	—
2	2	1–4–3–2
3	4	1–4–3
4	7	1–4
5	–2	1–4–3–2–5

We will take an example to highlight the drawback of the Bellman–Ford algorithm with a graph having negative cycles. Consider the graph given in Figure 9.50.

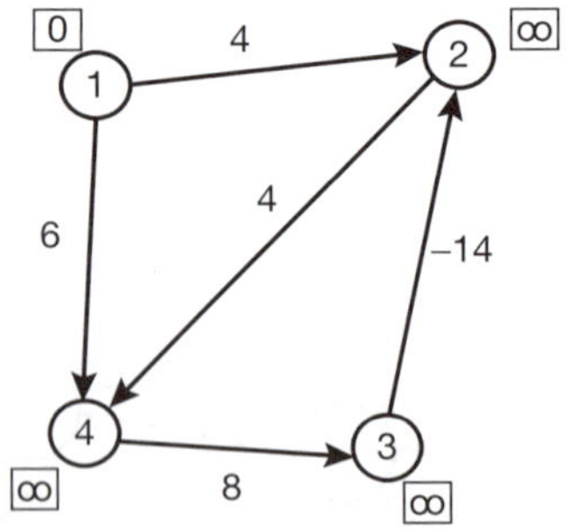

FIGURE 9.50 Example network for a negative cycle.

We notice that the cycle 2–4–3–2 has a negative total weight of −2 and we anticipate that the Bellman–Ford algorithm may have a problem here. Since there are four nodes, we should achieve the results in 4 − 1 = 3 relaxations. The successive relaxations are shown in Figure 9.51.

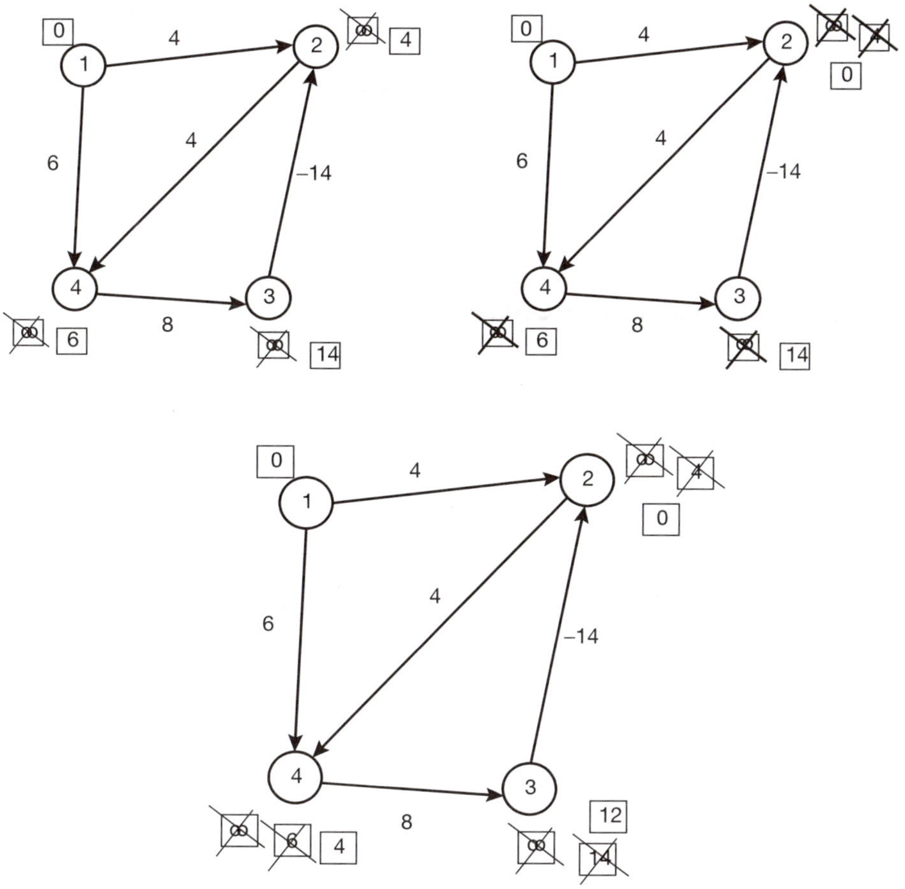

FIGURE 9.51 Successive relaxations for the network in Figure 9.50.

After carrying out 3, that is, 4 − 1 relaxations, the weights of the nodes are 0, 0, 12, and 4, respectively, for the nodes 1, 2, 3, and 4. We carry out one more relaxation to confirm if there are any negative cycles and to see if the solution is changing (see Figure 9.52).

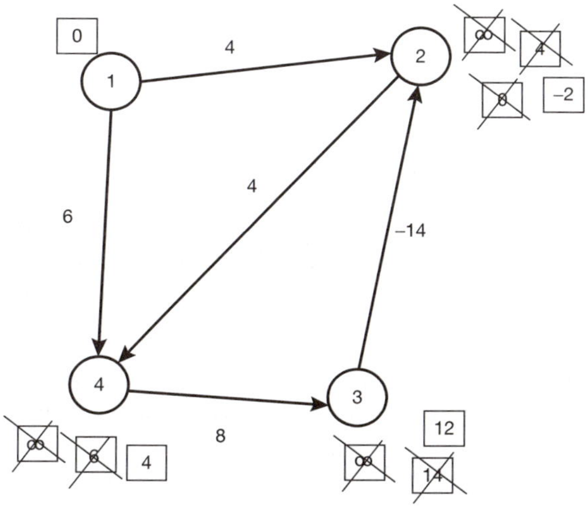

FIGURE 9.52 Final check for negative cycles.

After the allowed three relaxations, when we did the nth, that is, the 4th relaxation, we see that the solution has changed to 0, −2, 12, and 4 for the nodes 1, 2, 3, and 4, respectively. If we do one relaxation, it may change the solution further. So, the solution is not definite after the 3rd relaxation here. This is what we referred to as the drawback of the Bellman–Ford algorithm.

So far, we discussed how to determine the shortest path for a single source with all nodes covering both non-negative and negative link weights. If we require the shortest paths between any pair of nodes in the graph, it is possible to obtain them by repeating Dijkstra's algorithm or the Bellman–Ford algorithm as many times as the number of nodes by changing each one of them as the source node. But the complexity of computation will increase to $O(n^3)$ in such cases where n is the number of nodes in the graph. We can handle this by looking at the Floyd–Warshall algorithm in the following section.

9.9 | FLOYD-WARSHALL ALGORITHM

The Floyd–Warshall algorithm is very useful in determining the shortest paths at one go for all pairs of nodes although the computations are intense. It is a very useful algorithm for operational planning in determining optimal paths for physical distribution problems in supply chains.

The Floyd–Warshall algorithm is a more generalized algorithm than Dijkstra's algorithm because it determines the shortest route between any given pair of nodes in the network. The algorithm represents an n-node network as a square matrix with n rows and n columns. Entry (i, j) of the matrix gives the distance d_{ij} (here distance is taken as the context; the utility can be cost, time, etc.) from node i to node j, which is finite if i is linked directly to j, and ∞ (infinity) otherwise. The basic idea is a simple logic concerning distances.

Let us consider three nodes i, j, and k in a network as shown in Figure 9.53 (not drawn to scale). The connecting distances are shown on the three arcs in Figure 9.53.

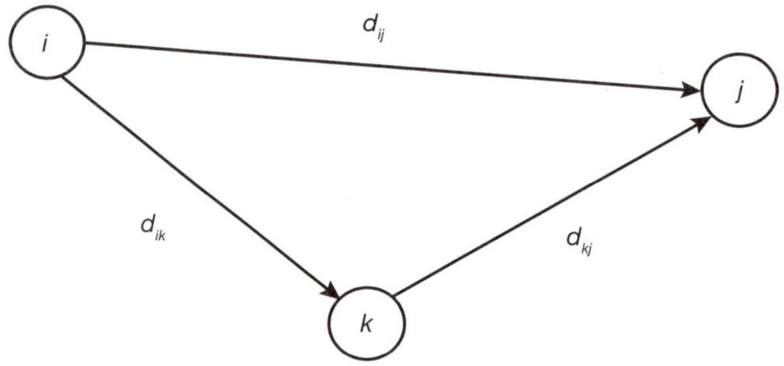

FIGURE 9.53 Representation of distances of three points i, j, and k for triple operation exchange.

We can see that it is shorter to reach j from i passing through k if

$$d_{ik} + d_{kj} < d_{ij}$$

If it is true, then it makes sense to replace the direct route from $i \rightarrow j$ with an indirect route $i \rightarrow k \rightarrow j$.

We refer to this as a "triple operation exchange," and it can be applied systematically in the network using the following steps.

Step 0: We define the starting distance matrix as D_0, which is the original distance matrix obtained from the given network and a "node sequence index matrix" I_0 as shown in Figure 9.54. The diagonal elements are marked with (−) to indicate that they are not considered blocked.

Set $k = 1$. We will explain the general step for carrying out Step k in the iterations as follows:

General step k

We define row k and column k as pivot row and pivot column. We will carry out the triple operation explained earlier to each of the elements d_{ij} in the D_{k-1} matrix for all i and j. If the condition

$$d_{ik} + d_{kj} < d_{ij} \left(i \neq k, j \neq k \text{ and } i \neq j\right)$$

is satisfied, then we will make the following changes in the matrix D_{k-1} and S_{k-1}:

1. We will construct the D_k matrix replacing d_{ij} in D_{k-1} with $d_{ik} + d_{kj}$.
2. We will construct the S_k matrix by replacing s_{ij} in the S_{k-1} matrix with k.

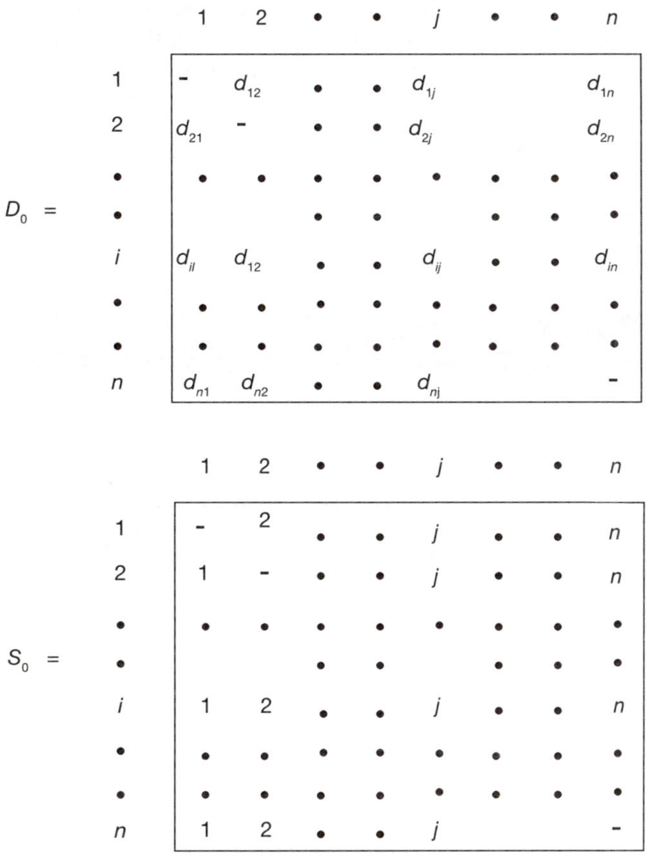

FIGURE 9.54 Starting distance and node sequence index matrices.

Once this is done, we will set $k = k+1$ and go up to $k = n$ and when $k = n + 1$, we stop there. The step k can be explained by taking the D_{k-1} matrix, as shown in Figure 9.55.

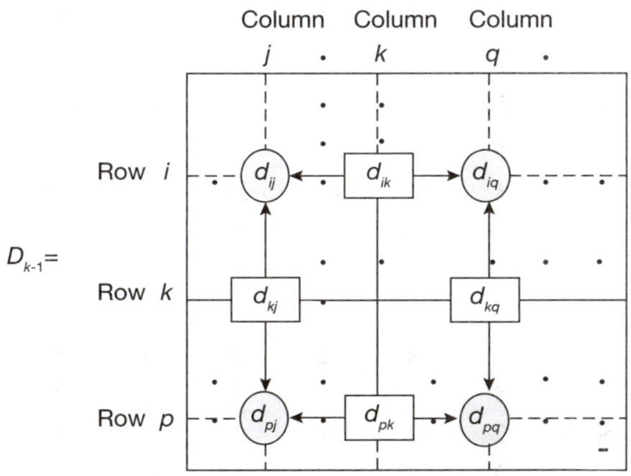

FIGURE 9.55 Pivot operation using triple operation exchange for step-k.

Here row k and column k are the current pivot row and column. Row i represents any of the rows 1 to $k - 1$ and row p represents any of the rows $k + 1, k + 2, ...,$ and n.

Similarly, column j represents columns 1 to $k-1$ and column q represents any of the columns $k+1, k+2, ...,$ and n.

The triple operations can be carried out as follows:
If the sum of the elements on the pivot row and the pivot column (indicated by squares in the figure) is smaller than the associated intersection element (shown by a circle in the figure), then it is optimal to replace the intersection distance by the sum of the pivot distances. After n steps, we can determine the shortest route between nodes i and j from the matrices D_n and S_n using the following rules:

1. From D_n, d_{ij} gives the shortest distance between nodes i and j.
2. From S_n, determine the intermediate node $k = s_{ij}$ that yields the route $i \rightarrow k \rightarrow j$. If $s_{ik} = k$ and $s_{kj} = j$, then we stop since all the intermediate nodes of the route have been found. Otherwise, repeat the procedure between nodes i and k and between nodes k and j.

EXAMPLE 9.8

Let us look at the following network with five nodes and link distances that are expressed in kilometers, as shown in Figure 9.56.

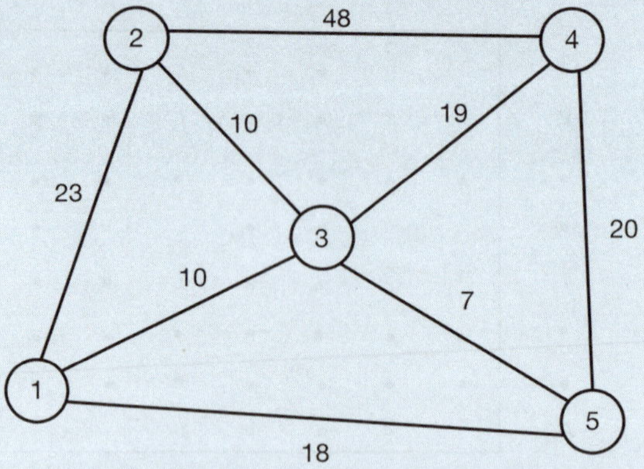

FIGURE 9.56 Example network for Floyd-Warshall Algorithm.

The distance matrix D_0 and sequence matrix S_0 are given in Figure 9.57.

$\mathbf{D_0} =$

	1	2	3	4	5
1	-	23	10	∞	18
2	23	-	10	48	∞
3	10	10	-	19	7
4	∞	48	19	-	20
5	18	∞	7	20	-

$\mathbf{S_0} =$

	1	2	3	4	5
1	-	2	3	4	5
2	1	-	3	4	5
3	1	2	-	4	5
4	1	2	3	-	5
5	1	2	3	4	-

FIGURE 9.57 Starting distance and node sequence index matrices.

Set $k = 1$. Row 1 and column 1 will be the pivot row and pivot column, and they are shown in a highlighted shade in Figure 9.58. The slightly darker cells (2, 5) and (5, 2) in D_0 are the only cells which will change due to the triple operations to 41 and 41, respectively. The reason is that the (2, 5) distance is ∞. But the link distance 2 to 1 is 23 and 1 to 5 is 18, which is the sum of the pivot row and pivot column elements of the cell (2, 5), that is,

$d(2, 1) + d(1, 5) = 23 + 18 = 41 < d(2, 5) = \infty$. So $d(2, 5)$ is updated with the value of 41. Similarly, the cell (5, 2) will also be updated with 41 with the value being symmetric.

Therefore, the shaded cells (2, 5) and (5, 2) are the ones which will change to $k = 1$, respectively. These are shown in Figure 9.58.

D_0 =

	1	2	3	4	5
1	-	23	10	∞	18
2	23	-	10	48	∞
3	10	10	-	19	7
4	∞	48	19	-	20
5	18	∞	7	20	-

S_0 =

	1	2	3	4	5
1	-	2	3	4	5
2	1	-	3	4	5
3	1	2	-	4	5
4	1	2	3	-	5
5	1	2	3	4	-

FIGURE 9.58 For Iteration-1.

The updated matrices are shown in Figure 9.59.

D_0 =

	1	2	3	4	5
1	-	23	10	∞	18
2	23	-	10	48	41
3	10	10	-	19	7
4	∞	48	19	-	20
5	18	41	7	20	-

S_0 =

	1	2	3	4	5
1	-	2	3	4	5
2	1	-	3	4	1
3	1	2	-	4	5
4	1	2	3	-	5
5	1	1	3	4	-

FIGURE 9.59 Updated matrices after Iteration-1.

Now set $k=2$. Row 2 and column 2 will be the pivot row and pivot column, and they are shown in a highlighted shade in the figure. The slightly darker cells (1, 4) and (4, 1) in D_1 are the only cells which will change due to the triple operations to 71 and 71, respectively. The reason is that the (1, 4) distance is ∞. But the link distance 1 to 2 is 23 and 2 to 4 is 48, which is the sum of the pivot row and pivot column elements of the cell (1, 4), that is,

$d(1, 2) + d(2, 4) = 23 + 48 = 71 < d(1, 4) = \infty$. So $d(1, 4)$ is updated with the value of 71.

Similarly, the cell (4, 1) will also be updated with 71 with the value being symmetric.

Therefore, the shaded cells (1, 4) and (4, 1) are the ones which will change to $k=2$, respectively. These are shown in Figure 9.60.

D_1 =

	1	2	3	4	5
1	-	23	10	∞	18
2	23	-	10	48	41
3	10	10	-	19	7
4	∞	48	19	-	20
5	18	41	7	20	-

S_1 =

	1	2	3	4	5
1	-	2	3	4	5
2	1	-	3	4	1
3	1	2	-	4	5
4	1	2	3	-	5
5	1	1	3	4	-

FIGURE 9.60 For Iteration-2.

The updated matrices are shown in Figure 9.61.

D_1 =

	1	2	3	4	5
1	-	23	10	71	18
2	23	-	10	48	41
3	10	10	-	19	7
4	71	48	19	-	20
5	18	41	7	20	-

S_1 =

	1	2	3	4	5
1	-	2	3	2	5
2	1	-	3	4	1
3	1	2	-	4	5
4	2	2	3	-	5
5	1	1	3	4	-

FIGURE 9.61 Updated matrices after Iteration-2.

Now set $k = 3$. Row 3 and column 3 will be the pivot row and pivot column, and they are shown in a highlighted shade in the figure. The slightly darker cells in D_2 are the only cells which will change due to the triple operations. Therefore, the shaded cells in S_2 are the ones which will change to $k = 2$, respectively. These are shown in Figure 9.62.

$D_2 =$

	1	2	3	4	5
1	-	23	10	71	18
2	23	-	10	48	41
3	10	10	-	19	7
4	71	48	19	-	20
5	18	41	7	20	-

$S_2 =$

	1	2	3	4	5
1	-	2	3	2	5
2	1	-	3	4	1
3	1	2	-	4	5
4	2	2	3	-	5
5	1	1	3	4	-

FIGURE 9.62 For Iteration-3.

The updated matrices are shown in Figure 9.63.

$D_2 =$

	1	2	3	4	5
1	-	20	10	29	17
2	20	-	10	29	17
3	10	10	-	19	7
4	29	29	19	-	20
5	17	17	7	20	-

$S_2 =$

	1	2	3	4	5
1	-	3	3	3	3
2	3	-	3	3	3
3	1	2	-	4	5
4	3	3	3	-	5
5	3	3	3	4	-

FIGURE 9.63 Updated matrices after Iteration-3.

Now set $k = 4$. Row 4 and column 4 will be the pivot row and pivot column, and they are shown in a highlighted shade in Figure 9.64. In this, we notice that there is no change in any values and we go to the next stage.

D₃ =

	1	2	3	4	5
1	-	20	10	29	17
2	20	-	10	29	17
3	10	10	-	19	7
4	29	29	19	-	20
5	17	17	7	20	-

S₃ =

	1	2	3	4	5
1	-	3	3	3	3
2	3	-	3	3	3
3	1	2	-	4	5
4	3	3	3	-	5
5	3	3	3	4	-

FIGURE 9.64 For Iteration-4.

Now set $k = 5$. Row 5 and column 5 will be the pivot row and pivot column, and they are shown in a highlighted shade in Figure 9.65. Here too, we find that there is no need to change any values.

D₄ =

	1	2	3	4	5
1	-	20	10	29	17
2	20	-	10	29	17
3	10	10	-	19	7
4	29	29	19	-	20
5	17	17	7	20	-

S₄ =

	1	2	3	4	5
1	-	3	3	3	3
2	3	-	3	3	3
3	1	2	-	4	5
4	3	3	3	-	5
5	3	3	3	4	-

FIGURE 9.65 Updated matrices after Iteration-4 and final matrices for the solution.

Since no further iteration is required, the matrices D_4 and S_4 contain all the information about the shortest distances and the shortest paths from any node to any other node. For example, if we need the shortest distance between, say, node 1 and node 5, then it is 17. To determine the associated route, recall that a segment (i, j) represents a direct link only if $s_{ij} = j$. Otherwise i and j are linked through at least one other intermediate node. Because $s_{15} = 3 \neq 5$, the route is $1 \rightarrow 3 \rightarrow 5$. Now, because $s_{35} = 5$, the path becomes $1 \rightarrow 3 \rightarrow 5$.

9.10 | MAXIMUM FLOW MODEL

In this model, the objective is determining the maximum amount of flow that the network would allow from source to sink. Multiple algorithms can solve the maximum flow problem. One of the popular algorithms was given by Ford and Fulkerson.

Given a network with a source S and sink T, the Ford–Fulkerson algorithm is explained as follows: An augmenting path is a simple path from source S to sink T, which does not include any cycles and passes only through positive weighted edges. A residual network graph indicates how much more flow is allowed in each edge in the network graph. If there are no augmenting paths possible from S to T, then the flow is maximum. The result, that is, the maximum flow will be the total flow out of the source node, which is also equal to the total flow into the sink node. This can be explained as follows:

Maximum flow models are useful in planning dispatches to committed orders taking into consideration the capacity constraints of intermediate nodes and planning for the right order quantities. They are useful in rail dispatching, intermodal cargo movements, etc.

1. The residual network differs from the original network only in that each directed arc $(i \rightarrow j)$ lacking a directed arc in the opposite direction $(j \rightarrow i)$ now has such an arc added with zero arc capacity.
2. Subsequently, the arc capacities in the residual network (called residual capacities) are adjusted as follows. Each time some amount of flow Δ is added to arc $i \rightarrow j$ in the original network, the residual capacity of arc $i \rightarrow j$ is decreased by Δ, but the residual capacity of arc $j \rightarrow i$ is increased by Δ.
3. Thus, the residual capacity represents the unused arc capacity in the original network or the amount of flow in the opposite direction in this network that can be canceled (or a combination of both if the original network has arcs in both directions).
4. Therefore, after assigning various flows to the original network, the residual network shows how much more can be done either by increasing flows further or by canceling previously assigned flows.
5. An **augmenting path** is a directed path from the supply node to the demand node in the residual network such that every arc on this path has strictly positive residual capacity.
6. The minimum of these residual capacities is called the residual capacity of the augmenting path because it represents the amount of flow that can be feasibly added to the entire path.
7. Therefore, each augmenting path provides an opportunity to further augment the flow through the original network.
8. The augmenting path algorithm repeatedly selects some augmenting path and adds flow equal to its residual capacity to that path in the original network.
9. This process continues until there are no more augmenting paths, so the flow from the supply node to the demand node cannot be increased further.
10. The key to ensuring that the final solution is necessarily optimal is the fact that augmenting paths can cancel some previously assigned flows in the original network, so an indiscriminate selection of paths for assigning flows cannot prevent the use of a better combination of flow assignments.

Algorithm for the Maximum Flow Problem

1. Identify an augmenting path by finding some directed path from the supply node to the demand node in the residual network such that every arc on this path has strictly positive residual capacity. (If no augmenting path exists, the net flows already assigned constitute an optimal flow pattern.)
2. Identify the residual capacity c^* of this augmenting path by finding the minimum of the residual capacities of the arcs on this path. Increase the flow in this path by c^*.
3. Decrease by c^* the residual capacity arc on this augmenting path. Increase by c^* the residual capacity of each arc in the opposite direction on this augmenting path. Return to step 1.

Consider the network with different arc capacities as shown in Figure 9.66.

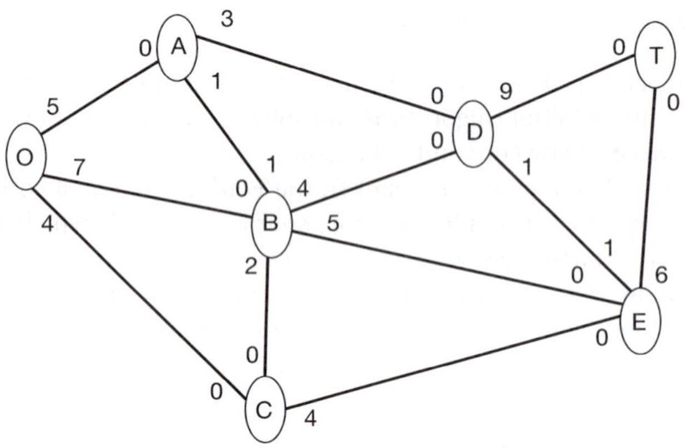

FIGURE 9.66 Example network for Maximum Flow Algorithm.

Iteration 1

Referring to Figure 9.66, one of the several augmenting paths is O → B → E → T, which has a residual capacity of min {7, 5, 6} = 5. Assigning a flow of 5 to this path, the resulting residual network is shown in Figure 9.67.

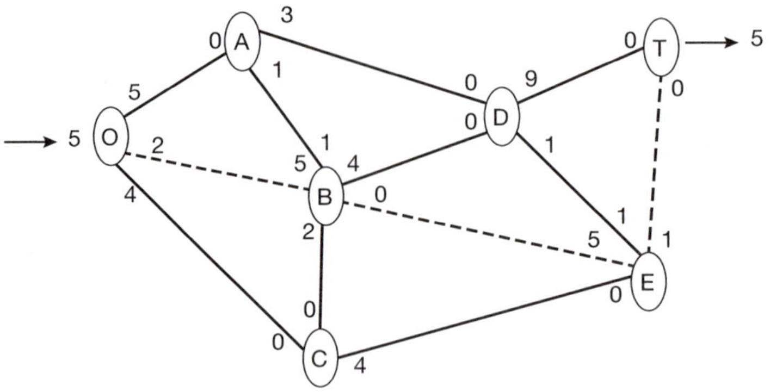

FIGURE 9.67 After Iteration-1.

Iteration 2

Assign a flow of 3 to the augmenting path O → A → D → T. The resulting residual network is shown in Figure 9.68.

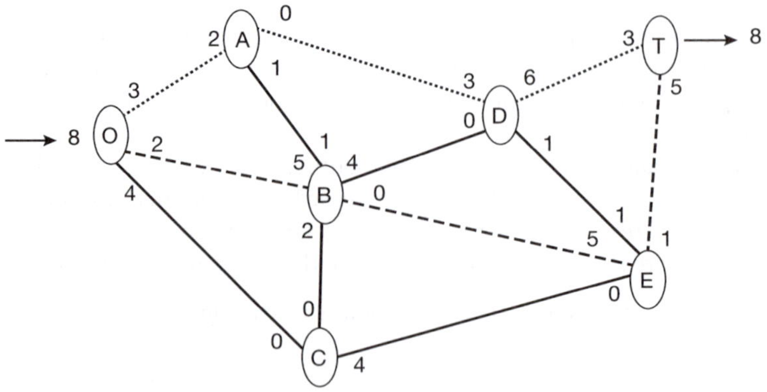

FIGURE 9.68 After Iteration-2.

Iteration 3

Assign a flow of 1 to the augmenting path O → A → B → D → T.

Iteration 4

Assign a flow of 2 to the augmenting path O → B → D → T. The resulting residual network is shown in Figure 9.69.

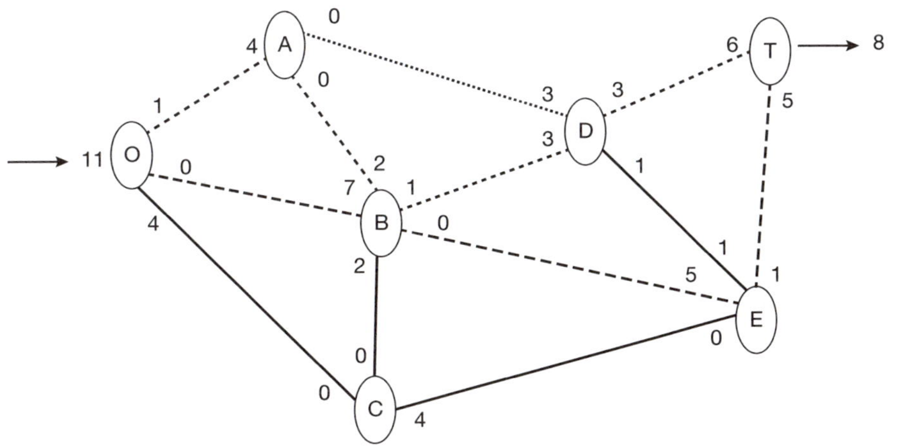

FIGURE 9.69 After Iterations 3 and 4.

Iteration 5

Assign a flow of 1 to the augmenting path O → C → E → D → T.

Iteration 6

Assign a flow of 1 to the augmenting path O → C → E → T. The resulting residual network is shown in Figure 9.70.

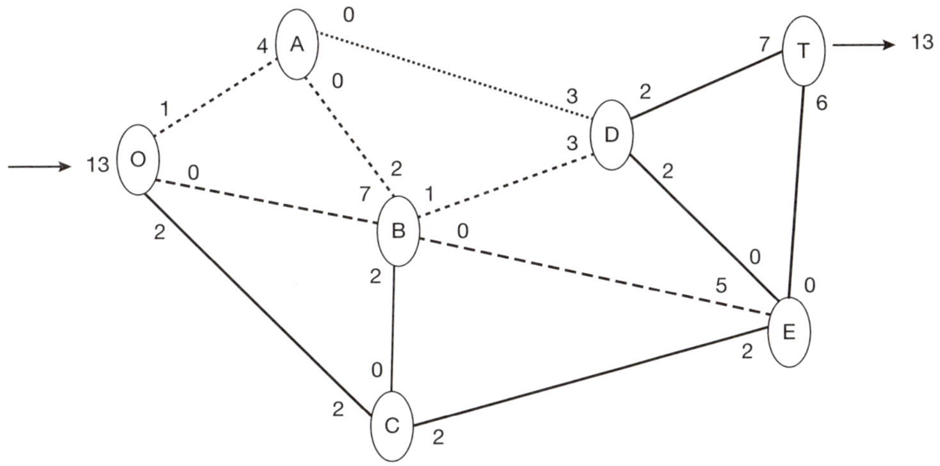

FIGURE 9.70 After Iterations 5 and 6.

Iteration 7

Assign a flow of 1 to the augmenting path O → C → E → B → D → T. The resulting residual network is shown in Figure 9.71.

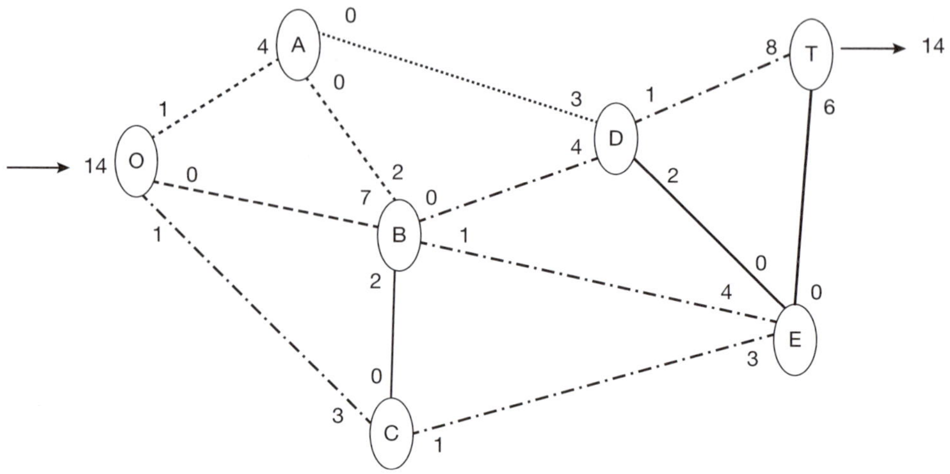

FIGURE 9.71 After Iteration-7.

Since there are no more augmenting paths available from O to T, the maximal flow from O to T is 14. Figure 9.72 shows the final flow of the network.

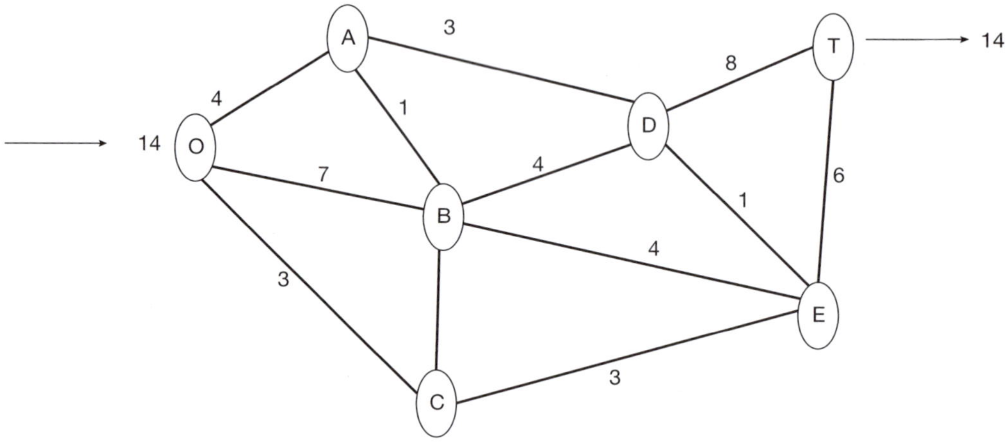

FIGURE 9.72 Final network flows.

Min-Cut

The min-cut of a weighted graph is defined as the minimum sum of weights of (at least one) edges that when removed from the graph divides the graph into two groups. The possible cuts in the network given in Figure 9.66 are arc OA–OB–OC with a total weight of 16, arc DT–ET with a total weight of 15, arc AD–BD–ED–ET with a total weight of 14, and so on. We notice that the length of the minimum cut among all the cuts is 14 given by the arc AD–BD–ED–ET.

Max-Flow Min-Cut Theorem

The max-flow min-cut theorem states that in a flow network, the **maximum** amount of flow passing from the source to the sink is equal to the total weight of the edges in a **minimum cut**, that is, the smallest total weight of the edges, which if removed would disconnect the source.

Here we notice that the minimum cut is given by the arc AD–BD–ED–ET with a total length of $3 + 4 + 1 + 6 = 14$. We also observed that the maximum flow in the network is also 14. The minimum cut is shown in Figure 9.73.

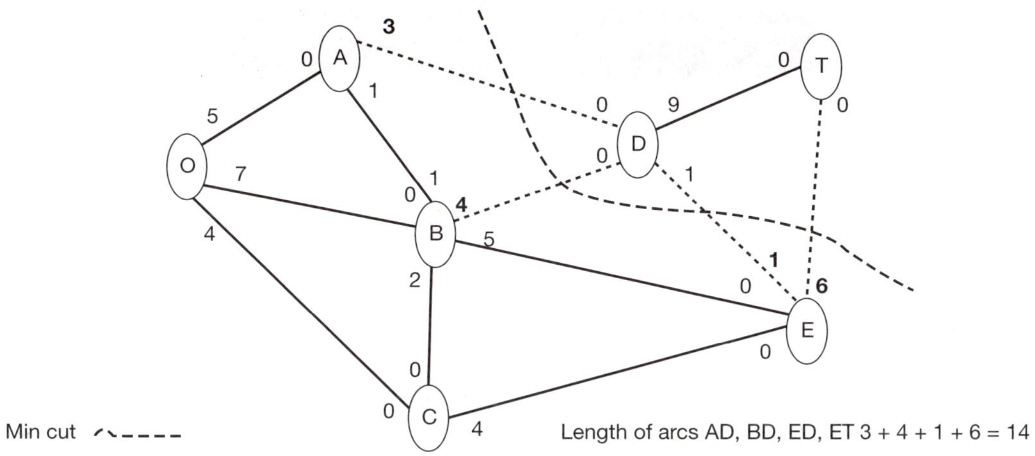

FIGURE 9.73 Max-flow and Min-cut explained.

In 1970, Y. A. Dinitz (or Dinic) developed a faster algorithm for calculating maximum flow over the networks. It includes constructing level graphs and residual graphs and finding augmenting paths along with blocking flow. Details can be seen in the original paper of Dinic provided in the references.

SUMMARY

This chapter discusses important issues in transportation decisions in supply chain management. More often, the total cost approach of supply chain management emphasizes the importance of evaluating cost and service trade-offs among the cost drivers. In the transportation side of supply chain, the decisions on choices of transport modes, service selection, and consolidation or cross-docking strategies are critical. The chapter elaborates on such horizontal and vertical trade-offs in the transport domain and presents many examples of such trade-offs. Then, the chapter focuses on the important topic of network models, which is the backbone of supply chain network and design, and presents various types of network models: minimum spanning tree, shortest paths, maximal flow models and various popular algorithms to solve such types of problems with various variants to handle many possible situations. The knowledge of such models is quite useful for a supply chain manager to plan transportation strategies in a supply chain and to use them in evaluating and managing third-party logistics providers.

Case Study

Following Case Studies are suggested.

1. Laxmi Transformers by Raghuram, G. and Mathew, Dilip, IIM Ahmedabad for modal choices in transportation and logistics planning. (http://vslir.iima.ac.in:8080/xmlui/handle/11718/6957).
2. Orion Foods Inc. in the book *Business Logistics Management* by Ronald H. Ballou and Samir K. Srivsatava, Chapter 7 for Shortest Path Model Applications.

Exercises

1. Atul Electronics supplies electric motors to Videotronics Distributors on a landed price basis. Atul Electronics provides the transportation to its distributors. The logistics manager considers four transportation service choices for delivering: rail, rail–road, air, and truck. He has compiled the following information:

Transport Mode	Transit Time, Days	Rate, $/Unit	Shipment Size, Units
Rail	15	15.00	12000
Rail–road	12	18.00	12000
Air	4	60.00	10000
Truck	9	20	15000

Videotronics purchases 60,000 units per year at a landed price of $600 per unit. The inventory-carrying cost for both companies is 20% per year. Which mode of transportation should Atul Electronics select?

2. Suppose two service providers for trucks are being considered for deliveries from a company's factory to one of its warehouses. The following information has been assembled:

Demand (known)	10,800 tons/year
Order cost	$120/order
Product price, f.o.b. source	$60/ton
Shipping quantity	As per EOQ
In-transit carrying cost	15%/year
Inventory-carrying cost	25%/year
In-stock probability during the lead time	90%
Out-of-stock costs	Unknown
Selling days	365 days/year

	Service	
	A	B
Transit time (LT)	6 days	8 days
Variability (standard deviation, s_{LT})	1.5 days	1.8 days
Rate	$15.00/ton	$12/ton

A reorder point control method of inventory control is used at the warehouse. From the point of view of the inventory in the warehouse, which truck service should be selected?

3. A manufacturer of household furniture has a factory located in Chennai and four warehouses in Tamil Nadu in Coimbatore, Madurai, Tiruchirappalli, and Tirunelveli. The warehouses collect customer orders, which are then shipped from the Chennai factory. The warehouse then distributes customer orders using small trucks after they receive the consignment from Chennai. Daily demand at each of the warehouses along with distances from Chennai are as follows:

Warehouse	Daily Demand (kg)	Distance (km)
Coimbatore	25000	520
Madurai	35000	480
Tiruchirappalli	20000	330
Tirunelveli	20000	625

All shipments are by truck. Three truck sizes are available with capacities of 40,000 (small), 60,000 (medium), and 80,000 (large). Transportation costs in dollars for the three types of trucks are as follows:

Small:	$100 + 0.15x$
Medium:	$125 + 0.20x$
Large:	$150 + 0.25x$

where x is the distance to be traveled in kilometers. For replenishment frequency varying between one and four days for each warehouse, identify the optimal transportation option and the associated costs. What other factors should be considered before deciding on the replenishment frequency?

4. The National Highways Authority of India (NHAI) is considering the following network for intermodal transportation. The objective is to decide which highway roads (links) should be strengthened and reconstructed to handle intermodal traffic. All terminals shown as nodes should be linked directly or indirectly such that the total length in miles of the selected links is minimized. Determine the segments that should be included in the program.

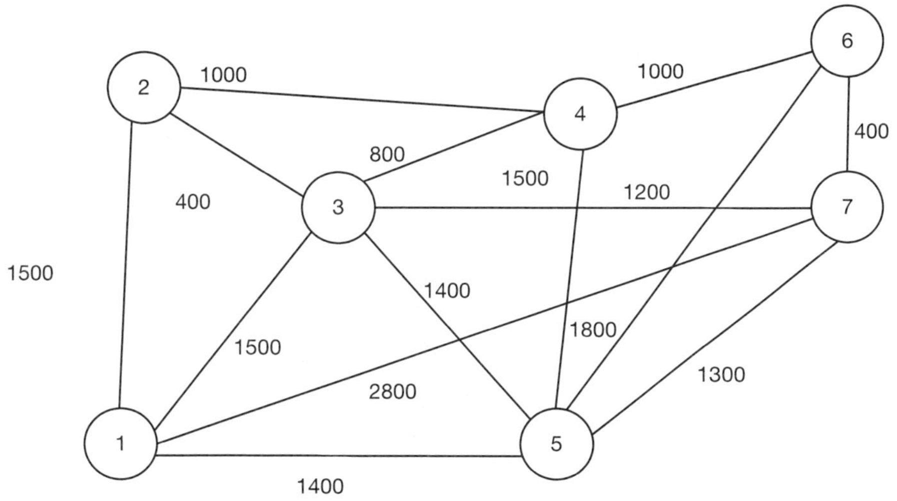

5. The following network gives the feasible links connecting nine offshore natural gas wellheads with an inshore delivery point. Location 1 is the closest to shore and to the wellhead and is equipped with sufficient pumping and storage capacity to pump the output of the remaining eight wells to the delivery point. Determine the minimum pipeline network that links the wellheads to the delivery point.

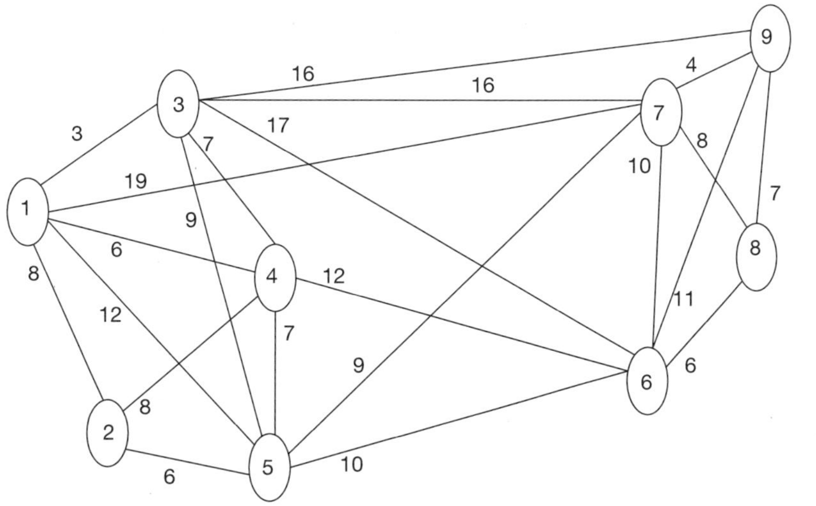

6. For the following networks in (i) and (ii), find the shortest path from A to K using the labeling algorithm.

(i)

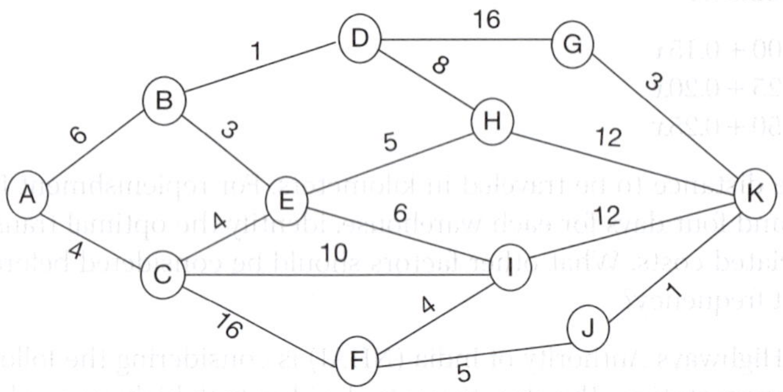

(ii)

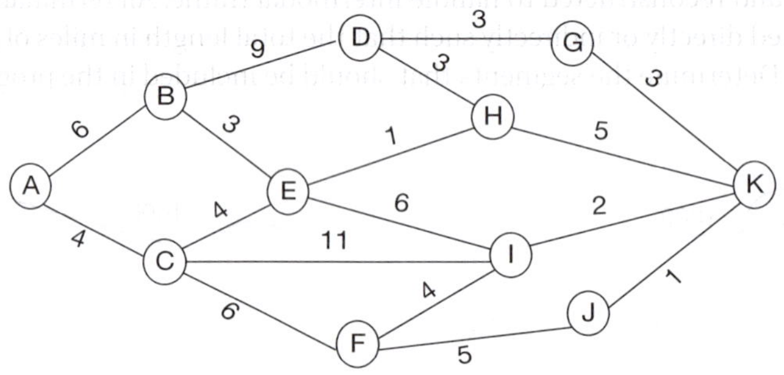

7. For the following network,

(a) Obtain the shortest paths from O to every other node using Dijkstra's algorithm.

(b) Obtain the shortest paths for all pairs of nodes using the Floyd–Warshall algorithm.

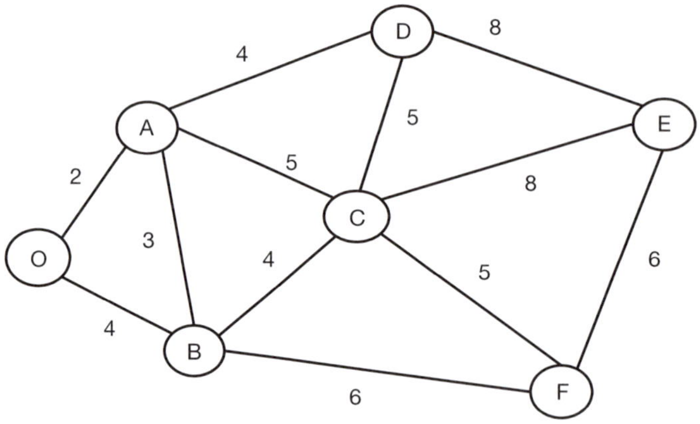

8. Determine the optimum flow and the optimal flow in each arc for the following network.

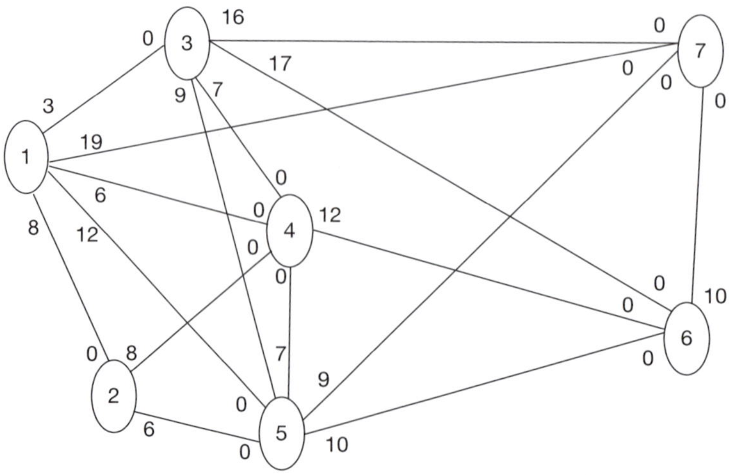

Bibliography

1. Ballou, R. H. and S. K. Srivastava (2007). *Business Logistics/Supply Chain Management.* Delhi: Pearson India.
2. Chopra, S., P. Meindl, and D. V. Kalra (2016). *Supply Chain Management: Strategy, Planning and Operation.* Delhi: Pearson India.
3. Cosares, S., D. N. Deutsch, I. Saniee, and O. J. Wasem. (1995) SONET toolkit: A decision-support system for signing robust and cost-effective fibre optic networks. *Interfaces*, **25**(1), 20–40.
4. Danzig, G. B. and M. N. Thapa (1997). *Linear Programming 1: Introduction.* New York: Springer.
5. Evers, P. F., D. V. Harper, and P. M. Needham. (1996) The determinants of shipper perceptions of modes. *Transportation Journal*, **36**(2), 13–25.
6. Hillier, F. S. and G. J. Liebermann (1969). *Introduction to Operations Research.* McGraw Hill.
7. Hillier, F. S. and M. S. Hillier (2014). *Introduction to Management Science: A Modelling and Case Studies Approach with Spreadsheets*, 5th ed. Burr Ridge, IL: McGraw-Hill/Irwin.
8. Lambert, D. M. and T. C. Harrington. (1989) Establishing customer service strategies within the marketing mix: More empirical evidence. *Journal of Business Logistics*, **10**(2), 50.
9. Lambert, D. M., M. C. Lewis, and J. R. Stock. (1993) How shippers select and evaluate general commodities LTL motor carriers. *Journal of Business Logistics*, **14**(1), 131–18.
10. Piercy, J. E. and R. H. Ballou. (1978). A performance evaluation of freight transport modes. *Logistics and Transportation Review*, **14**(2), 99–115.
11. Sierksma, G. and D. Ghosh (2009). *Networks in Action: Text and Computer* Exercises *in Network Optimization.* Springer.
12. Stock, J. R. and B. J. La Londe (1977). The transportation mode decision revisited. *Transportation Journal*, **17**(2), 51–59.
13. Taha, H. A. (2006). *Operations Research.* Delhi: Prentice Hall India.
14. Vanderbei, R. J. (2014). *Linear Programming: Foundations and Extensions*, 4th ed. New York: Springer.
15. Whittle, P. (2007). *Networks: Optimization and Evolution.* Cambridge, UK: Cambridge University Press.

CHAPTER 10

Routing Using the Traveling Salesman Problem Algorithms in Transportation

LEARNING OBJECTIVES

After reading this chapter, you would be able to:

- Understand the key issues in operational planning in transportation decisions in a supply chain and the important characteristics of routing and scheduling.
- Learn the basic ideas of tours such as the traveling salesman problem (TSP), multiple TSPs, vehicle routing problems, etc.
- Comprehend the concept of TSP and its nature.
- Learn basic definitions of Euler graphs, circuits and paths, and Fleury's algorithm to find a Euler circuit.
- Understand Hamiltonian paths and circuits.
- Formulate a TSP and solving it using Excel Solver.
- Solve a TSP using various approaches such as dynamic programming and brand and bound methods.
- Solve a TSP using a few popular heuristics to construct and improve the tour.

10.1 | INTRODUCTION

In the last chapter, we discussed the basic trade-offs in transportation decisions and some of the popular network models that are applied in transportation contexts for various decisions. In this chapter, we will discuss the more operational aspects of transportation, which deal with routing and scheduling decisions. This is an important aspect of supply chain logistics where resources such as vehicle and workforce are optimally utilized for saving capital as well as operational costs.

The objective of most of the routing and scheduling problems is to minimize the total cost of providing the service. This includes vehicle capital costs, mileage, and personnel costs. However, other aspects are also important while deciding the routing and scheduling of services depending on the context of applications. In providing public utilities like bus routing and scheduling, the focus will be on safety factors of students and minimizing student-minutes. For a company like Pizza Hut, pizzas must be delivered in a specific time window to customers. For companies like

Ola or Uber, it may be the safety of elders and the physically challenged besides normal customers. For emergency services like ambulances, fire services, police, etc., response time is critical and is of primary importance. For companies like Amazon, delivery timing is a commitment, and their fulfilment depends on such promised time windows. Therefore, it is not just the cost of operations alone that matters but also the service elements associated with that, and the "subjective" costs associated with failing to provide such a service to customers are also important.

10.2 CHARACTERISTICS OF ROUTING AND SCHEDULING PROBLEMS

Routing and scheduling problems are often presented as graphical **networks or graphs**. The advantage of this representation is that it makes it easier for decision makers to visualize a given problem, thereby enabling them to think logically about finding a solution. We saw the use of such network models in the last chapter. We will present one such context where such representation gives the advantage of solving the problem. Suppose the bottling unit of a soft drink company has to collect empty bottles from customers and distribute filled bottles to a set of customers (Figure 10.1). If all the customers are assigned to one vehicle, then we can say that 1→2→ 3→4→5→6→1 is a tour. The arcs in the network may be directed, undirected, or mixed with both depending on the context of applications. For example, if we are referring to a road network and looking at the arc as roads connecting various nodes, then the roads can allow movement on both directions, or possibly, some roads have one-way restrictions.

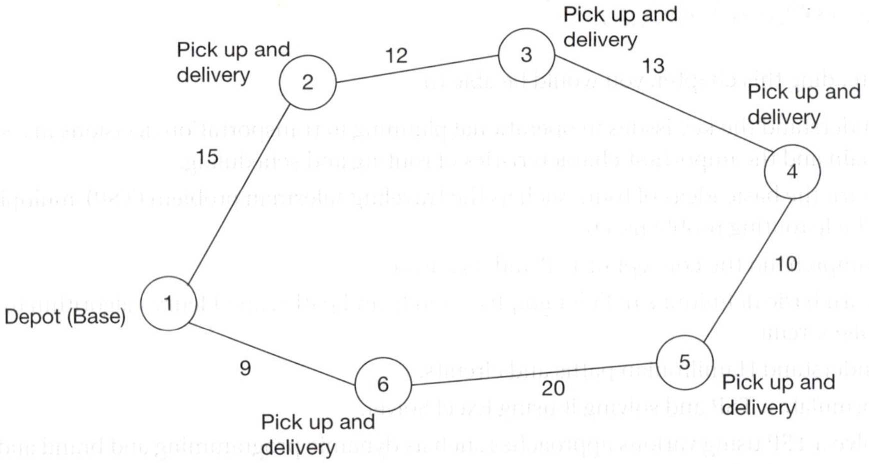

FIGURE 10.1 Example of a bottling unit's distribution.

Now, this tour may or may not be the minimum distance tour (or path) as the sequence of stoppages may be different. In Figure 10.1, only one tour is shown. If we know the distance matrix of all the distances between nodes, then it is possible to construct 6! (six factorial, i.e., $6 \times 5 \times 4 \times 3 \times 2 \times 1 = 720$) tours. For example, some sequence could be 1→3→ 2→4→6→5→1, 1→4→2→5→3→6→1, 1→6→3→5→6→4→1, and so on. One such example is given in Figure 10.2 with a network showing the connected graph of having four nodes with the depot. The minimum-cost solution, however, is subject to the tour being **feasible**. Feasibility depends on the type of problem, but, in general, implies that:

1. A tour must include all nodes.
2. A node must be visited only once.
3. A tour must begin and end at a depot.

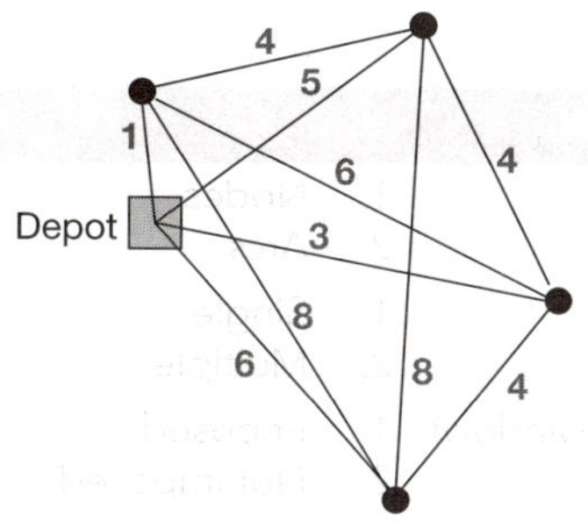

FIGURE 10.2 Example of a network with a depot and four nodes.

In other words, when we have different possibilities of sequencing, finding the minimum-cost tour is what we are looking for in such contexts as outlined in Figure 10.1. Some illustrative sequences of tours are given in Figure 10.3 for a situation with a depot having four customers to visit.

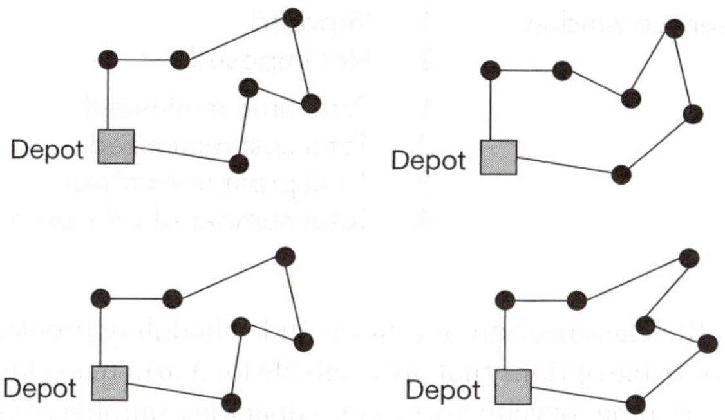

FIGURE 10.3 Different options of sequencing the customers in a tour.

Table 10.1 presents different characteristics of routing and scheduling problems and possible options. We see that the output of all routing and scheduling systems is essentially the same. That is, for each vehicle or provider, an optimal route is designed and a schedule is provided. Generally, the **route** specifies which nodes to visit and in which sequence, and a **schedule** identifies when each node is to be visited. That is, if the customers who are serviced have no time restrictions of visiting them and no precedence relationships exist, then the problem is a pure routing problem. If there is a specified time window that is imposed for the service to take place, then it is a scheduling problem. Thus, it is possible to combine both routing and scheduling problems in a context.

TABLE 10.1 Some characteristics of routing and scheduling problems

Sl. No.	Characteristic	Option
1	Number of depots	1. Single 2. Multiple
2	Number of vehicles	1. Single 2. Multiple
3	Type of vehicles	1. Homogeneous 2. Heterogeneous
4	Type of network	1. Directed 2. Undirected 3. Mixed
5	Nature of demand	1. Certain 2. Uncertain (Stochastic) 3. Mixed

(Continued)

TABLE 10.1 (Continued)

Sl. No.	Characteristic	Option
6	Demand exists at	1. Nodes 2. Arcs
7	Crew availability	1. Single 2. Multiple
8	Max route time (time window)	1. Imposed 2. Not imposed
9	Max link capacity	1. Imposed 2. Not imposed
10	Max vehicle capacity	1. Imposed 2. Not imposed
11	Type of operation	1. Pick up only 2. Drop only 3. Mixed
12	Customer service window	1. Imposed 2. Not imposed
13	Objective	1. Total time minimized 2. Total cost minimized 3. Total profit maximized 4. Total number of vehicles minimized

An important observation when we list the characteristics of routing and scheduling problems is that a supply chain can have a variety of problems depending on the operating environment and conditions it needs to address. Although the inputs and outputs appear to be similar, it is the process and the modeling assumptions that make the problems more complex and have more variety. Since each firm or a supply chain faces different conditions, it is impossible to have one method or algorithm to address the problem and find exact solutions. Hence, this is one of the areas in transportation that offers more scope for developing such heuristics and supporting software to address the issues for many firms. Hence, this area offers more opportunities for consulting and software development especially for third-party logistics providers.

As seen in Table 10.1, the classification of routing and scheduling problems depends on certain characteristics of the possible options that are available for a firm to explore, such as types of vehicles, number of depots, number of vehicles, vehicle capacities, number of crew members available, and various objectives. One of the simplest forms is when we begin with a set of nodes to be visited by a single vehicle. Suppose that the nodes may be visited in any order, and there are no precedence relationships. Also, assume that the travel costs between two nodes are the same regardless of the direction traveled and there are no delivery-time restrictions with no capacity restriction of vehicles. The output of such a simple framework for a single vehicle problem is a single route or a tour where each node is visited only once and the route begins and ends at the depot node. Figure 10.1 is one such situation. The objective here is to minimize the total tour cost or distance. This simplest case is referred to as the **traveling salesman problem** (TSP).

An extension of this to multiple tours of the TSP is referred to as the **multiple traveling salesman problem** (MTSP). The goal is to generate a set of routes, one for each vehicle in the fleet from a single depot. Here the formulation assumes that a node is assigned to only one vehicle, but a vehicle can be assigned to multiple nodes assuming no specific capacities of vehicles.

If we now impose capacity restrictions on the vehicles and have different demands for the customers at each node, then the problem is classified as a **vehicle routing problem** (VRP). This is illustrated in Figure 10.4.

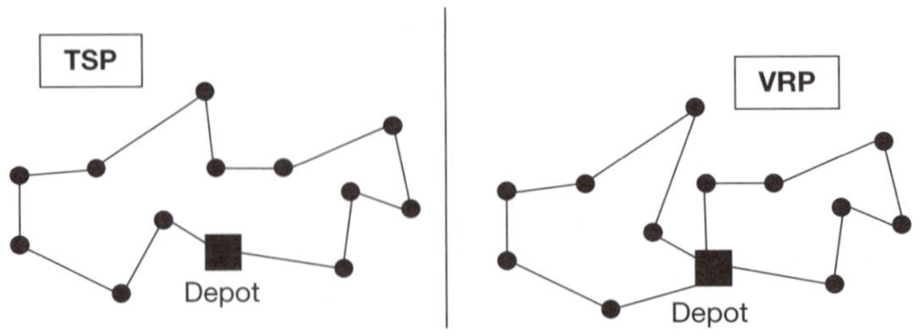

FIGURE 10.4 Difference between a TSP and a VRP.

If the demands occur on the arcs and not on the nodes, or alternatively if the demand nodes are too many to specify, then we refer to it as the **Chinese postman problem** (CRP), which is very often difficult to solve. Examples of these types of problems include garbage collection, street sweeping, snow removal, postal or paper delivery, etc.

We will present various types of routing and scheduling problems and tools and techniques to address them in the following sections.

10.3 | THE TRAVELING SALESMAN PROBLEM

The traveling salesman problem (TSP) was studied in the 18th century by a mathematician from Ireland named Sir William Rowan Hamilton and a British mathematician named Thomas Penyngton Kirkman. Detailed discussions about the work of Hamilton and Kirkman can be found in from the book titled *Graph Theory* (Biggs et al., 1976). It is believed that the general form of the TSP was first studied by Karl Menger in Vienna and at Harvard. The problem was later promoted by Hassler, Whitney, and Merrill in Princeton. A detailed description about the development of the TSP can be found in Schrijver (1960).

The basic definition of a TSP is that, given a set of cities, and the cost of travel (or distance) between each possible pair, the TSP is to find the best possible way of visiting all the cities and returning to the starting point that minimizes the travel cost (or travel distance). But the complexity of the problem is that given n as the number of cities to be visited, the total number of possible routes covering all cities can be given as a set of feasible solutions to the TSP and is $(n - 1)!/2$. The TSP can be broadly classified into the **symmetric traveling salesman problem** (sTSP), **asymmetric traveling salesman problem** (aTSP), and **multiple traveling salesman problem** (MTSP).

Let $V = \{1, 2, ..., n\}$ be a set of cities, $A = \{(i, j) : i, j \in V\}$ be the arcs set, and $d_{ij} = d_{ji}$ be a cost measure associated with the arc $(i, j) \in A$.

The **sTSP** is the problem of finding a minimal length closed tour that visits each city once. In this case, cities $i \in V$ are given by their coordinates (x_i, y_i) and d_{ij} is the Euclidean distance between i and j; then we have a **Euclidean TSP**. When it is not explicitly mentioned as the Euclidean distance and distances are given as ones that are measured practically, then it is referred to as a TSP, and by the default description, it is symmetric, unless explicitly mentioned as asymmetric. If the distances $d_{ij} \neq d_{ji}$ for at least one (i, j), then it is referred to as aTSP.

For a given set of nodes, suppose there are m salespersons located at a single depot node, and the remaining nodes (cities) that are intermediate have to be visited. Then we have the mTSP problem where the objective is to find tours for all m salespersons, who will all start and end at the depot, such that each intermediate node is visited exactly once and the total cost of visiting all nodes is minimized.

Applications of all varieties of TSPs are popular especially in the supply chain operational planning for warehousing operations and in transportation decisions such as order picking problems, vehicle routing, etc.

Consider a five-city problem where a salesperson has to visit cities 1, 2, 3, 4, and 5. Two feasible tours are shown in Figure 10.5 where the salesperson can sequence his visit. Notice that his/her visit starts at city 1 and visits all other cities exactly once only and he/she returns to city 1. That is a requirement for a TSP to satisfy.

The traveling salesman problem (TSP) is probably one of the very popular models that has good applications in practice. This is often referred to as "milk runs" by industries and is applied in most of the dispatching and distribution problems, especially for local deliveries and pick-and-drop operations.

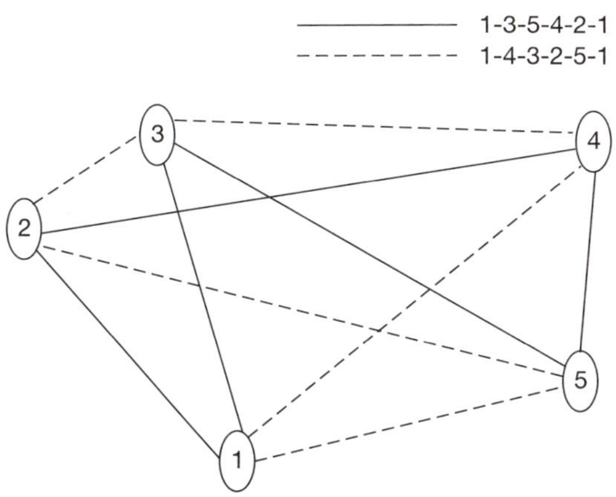

FIGURE 10.5 Feasible TSP tours for a 5-city network.

The objective of this problem is to find the best tour where the total distance traveled is minimum but satisfies the condition that he/she starts at a city and visits each other city exactly only once and returns to the starting city.

Before we describe the formulation of TSPs, we need some background of a few concepts of Euler and Hamiltonian graphs in graph theory to use some of their properties in understanding TSP.

10.3.1 Euler Graphs

We will introduce Euler path, circuit, and graphs with illustrations. Detailed discussions on them are available in the references at the end of the chapter.

A **Euler path** is a path that uses every arc or edge in a graph (network) without repeating it. Being a path, it does not have to return to the starting node or the vertex. This means that the path can use a vertex more than once but not the arc, and it need not come back to the starting node or vertex.

In the graph shown in Figure 10.6, there are several Euler paths. One such path is BACDBC. The path is shown in arrows with the order of edges numbered.

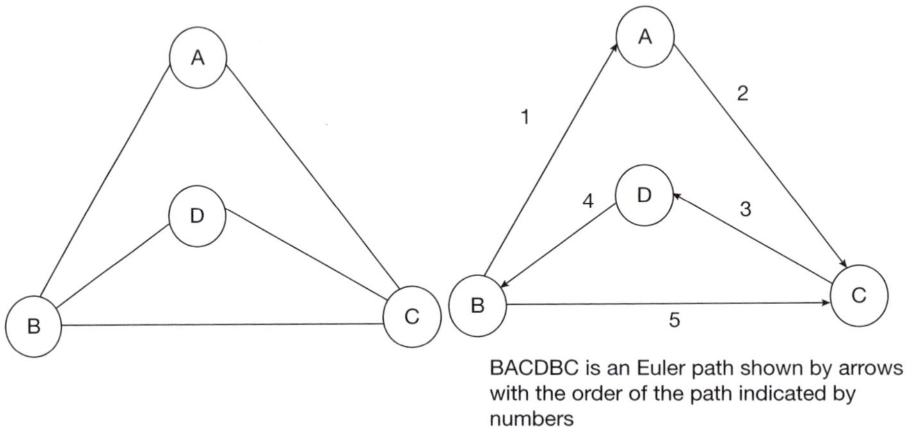

FIGURE 10.6 An example of graph and an Euler path.

A **Euler circuit** uses every arc or edge in a graph without repeating any arcs, and being a circuit, it must start and end at the same vertex or node. That is, a path where the starting vertex and the ending vertex are the same but should use every arc in the graph only once.

The graph in Figure 10.7 has several possible Euler circuits. For example, two such circuits starting and ending at vertex A are ADEACEFCBA and AECABCFEDA. The second is shown in Figure 10.7 with arrows in the order of edges numbered.

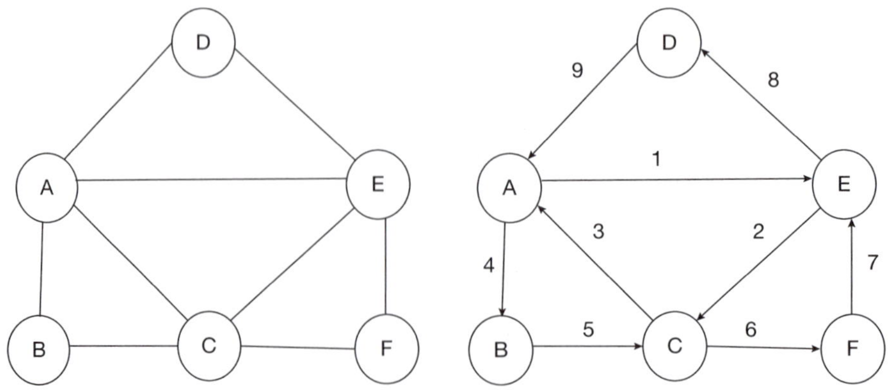

FIGURE 10.7 An example of graph and an Euler circuit.

With this understanding, we see that the graph in Figure 10.6 shown for the Euler path does not have a Euler circuit. The following will summarize two important properties about Euler paths and circuits.

1. A graph will contain a Euler path if it contains at most two vertices of odd degrees.
2. A graph will contain a Euler circuit if all vertices have even degrees.

Note that these properties do not describe how to find the paths and circuits. The degree or valence of a vertex is the number of edges or arcs meeting at that vertex. That is, it refers to the number of incidents on a vertex and the number of edges that use the vertex. The degree can also be zero.

For example, in Figure 10.7, vertex B has a degree of two with the edges labeled as 4 and 5 (read them without the direction shown by the arrows in the figure), while vertex A has four degrees with labels 9, 1, 3, and 4.

We notice that the graph in Figure 10.6 is a Euler path. In all, there are four vertices, and exactly two of them (vertex B and C) have an odd number of three degrees, indicating that this graph will have a Euler path. Also notice that in Figure 10.7, there are six vertices and two vertices have four degrees each and the remaining four vertices have two degrees each, indicating that all of them have an even number of degrees and that this graph will have Euler circuits.

While it is usually possible to find a Euler circuit just by trying on a given graph, a systematic and formal approach is applying Fleury's algorithm.

10.3.2 Fleury's Algorithm

The following are the steps in Fleury's algorithm:

1. Start at any vertex when finding a Euler circuit. When finding a Euler path, start at one of the two vertices with odd degrees.
2. Choose any edge leaving your current vertex, provided that deleting that edge will not separate the graph into two disconnected sets of edges.
3. Add that edge to your circuit and delete it from the graph.
4. Continue until you are done.

We will illustrate this with an example of a graph in Figure 10.8.

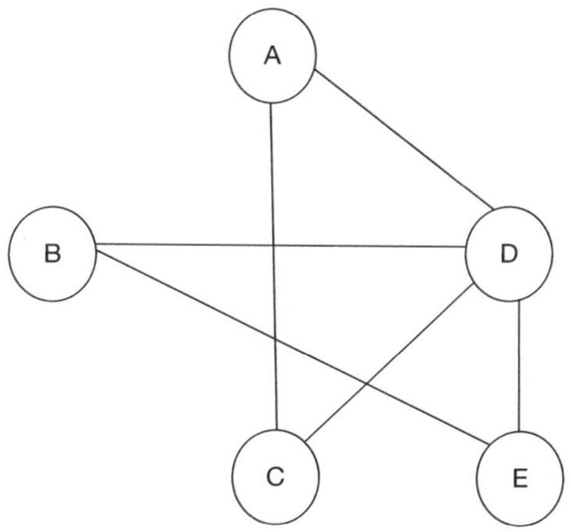

FIGURE 10.8 An example of a graph for Fleury's algorithm.

We notice that there are five vertices A, B, C, D, and E with A, B, C, and E having two degrees and D having four degrees. Since all the vertices have an even number of degrees, a Euler circuit exists for this graph.

We will now apply Fleury's algorithm on this graph. Let us start with vertex A. We can choose edge AD or AE. Let us choose edge AD. The circuit so far is AD. Now, delete edge AD. The current vertex is E. We can choose DE, DC, or DB. We cannot choose edge DC since if we delete DC, the graph will be disconnected, with AC hanging separately and BDE hanging separately. Therefore, we will choose edge DE. The circuit so far is ADE. Delete the edge DE now. The current vertex is E. We have only the option of choosing EB now; the rest is determined in similar ways. Therefore, the circuit is ADEBDCA. The steps are shown in Figures 10.9, 10.10, and 10.11.

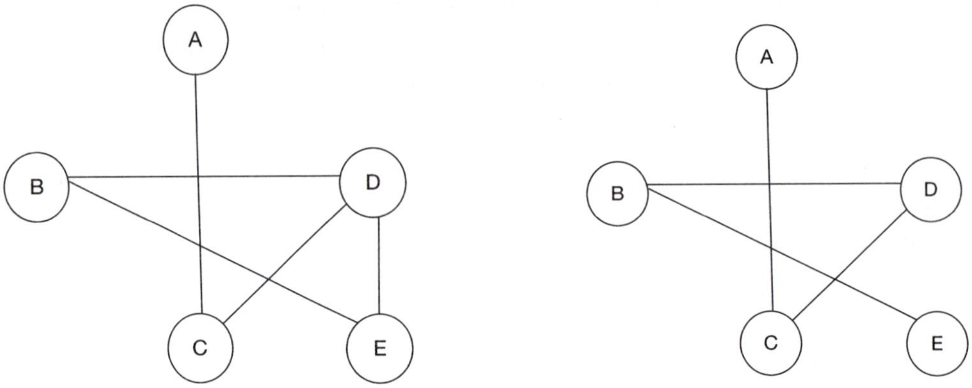

FIGURE 10.9 Steps of Fleury's algorithm for the graph in Figure 10.8.

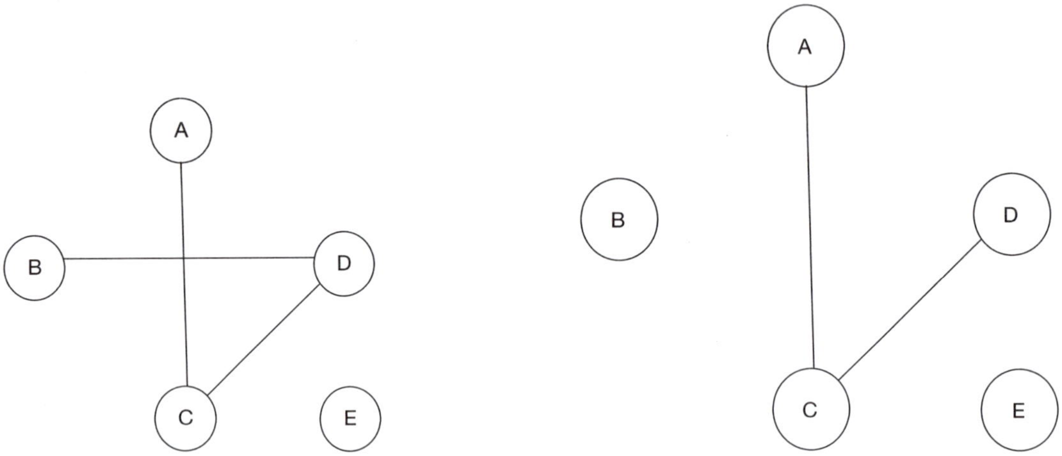

FIGURE 10.10 Further steps of Fleury's algorithm for Figure 10.9.

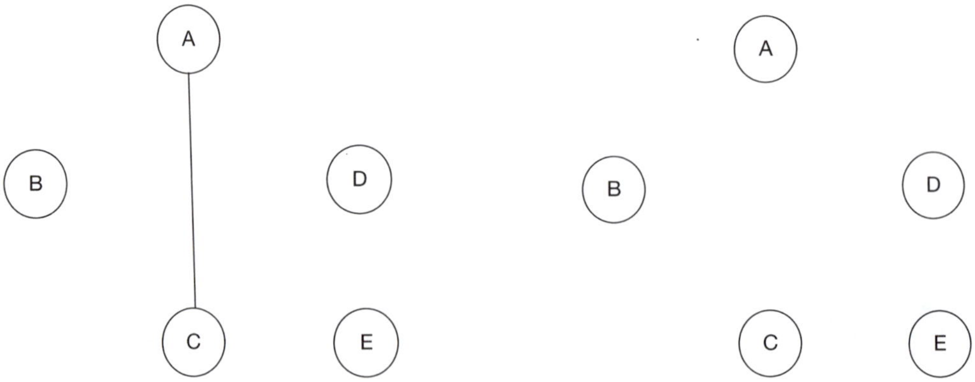

FIGURE 10.11 Final steps of Fleury's algorithm for Figure 10.10.

Eulerization is the process of adding edges to a graph to create a Euler circuit on a graph. To Eulerize a graph, edges are duplicated to connect pairs of vertices with odd degrees. Connecting two odd-degree vertices increases the degree of each, giving them both even degrees. When two odd-degree vertices are not directly connected, we can duplicate all edges in a path connecting the two. An example is shown for a graph in Figure 10.12.

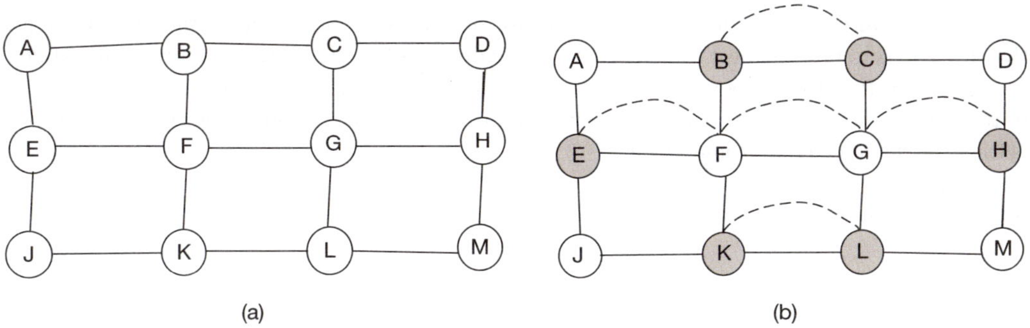

FIGURE 10.12 An example of Eulerization of a graph.

See the vertices B, C, E, H, K, and L in the preceding graph. They have three degrees for each of them, and since not all the vertices have an even number of degrees, a Eulerian path is not possible for this graph. However, Eulerization can make all the vertices have an even number of degrees. One way of Eulerization is shown here that makes all the vertices have an even number of degrees. Figure 10.12(b) shows the Eulerization with dotted lines. Note that this has made all the vertices have an even number of degrees.

Eulerization helps in solving the Chinese postman problem and also to determine the time complexities of solving TSPs.

10.3.3 Hamiltonian Paths and Circuits

A **Hamiltonian path** visits every vertex only once with no repeats but does not have to start and end at the same vertex. A **Hamiltonian circuit** is a circuit that visits every vertex only once without repeating it and starts and ends with the same vertex. That is, a circuit that visits every vertex of a graph exactly only once.

Note the difference here between the Eulerian and Hamiltonian paths and circuits. In Eulerian, the edge is visited exactly once, while in Hamiltonian, the vertex is visited exactly once. Hamiltonian circuits are named after William Rowan Hamilton who studied them in the 1800s.

We will revisit the graph shown in Figure 10.12 (a). One Hamiltonian circuit ABFGCDHMLKJEA shown as dotted lines is given in Figure 10.13. It is possible to have more Hamiltonian circuits on this graph. Note that the circuit has to visit every vertex only, and it does not need to use every edge. Notice also that the same circuit could be written in the reverse order or starting and ending at a different vertex as well.

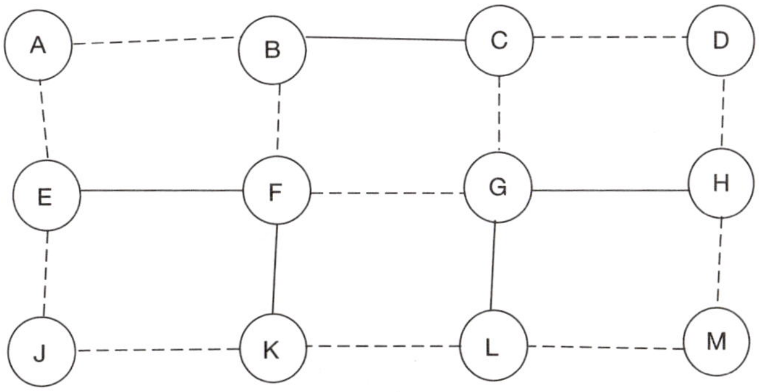

FIGURE 10.13 Hamiltonian circuit for the graph in 10.12 (a).

Unfortunately, there is no nice theorem that enables us to determine if a Hamiltonian circuit exists for all graphs like the way we observed in the Eulerian context. It is of interest to explore optimization opportunities in Hamiltonian circuits if the given graph has edges with weights. That is, can we find the optimal Hamiltonian circuit with the lowest total weight? This question is precisely a TSP, which we started at the beginning of this section.

We will continue with the discussion of the formulations of TSP. We saw earlier that the objective of a TSP is to find the best tour where the total distance traveled is the minimum but satisfies the condition that the story starts at a city and visits every other city exactly once and returns to the starting city. From the discussions on Hamiltonian circuits or tours, it is clear that the TSP is the least distance Hamiltonian tour.

While determining the tours for TSP, only a complete tour of all nodes is allowed and sub-tours are not allowed. For our example of five cities, the following sub-tour, shown in Figure 10.14, is not allowed.

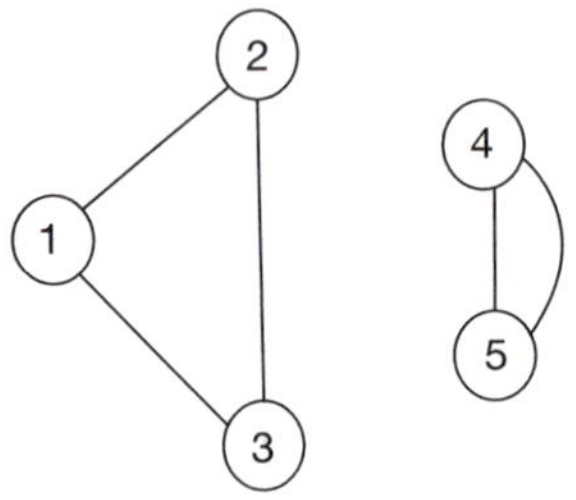

FIGURE 10.14 Sub-tours for the TSP example in Figure 10.5.

Let

$X_{ij} = 1$ if the person goes immediately from i to j

$\quad\quad 0$ otherwise

c_{ij} = distance or cost of going from i to j

Then the formulation becomes

$$\text{Minimize} \sum_{j=1}^{n}\sum_{i=1}^{n} c_{ij}X_{ij}$$

Subject to

$$\sum_{j=1}^{n} X_{ij} = 1 \forall i = 1,2,\ldots,n$$

$$\sum_{i=1}^{n} X_{ij} = 1 \forall j = 1,2,\ldots,n$$

The formulation so far resembles the formulation of an assignment problem. However, we need to also add a few more constraints that will eliminate the sub-tours for this formulation. Many types of formulations are available in the references. An interesting formulation was given by Miller in 1960 and is as follows:

Find variables X_{ij} and U_i for $i, j = 1, 2,\ldots, n$ that minimize

$$Z = \sum_{j=1}^{n}\sum_{i=1}^{n} c_{ij}X_{ij}$$

$$\sum_{j=1}^{n} X_{ij} = 1 \forall i = 1,2,\ldots,n$$

$$\sum_{i=1}^{n} X_{ij} = 1 \forall j = 1,2,\ldots,n$$

$$U_i - U_j + nX_{ij} \leq n - 1 \forall i, j = 1,2,\ldots,n; i \neq j$$

This is a mixed integer programming formulation with n^2 zero-one variables and $(n - 1)$ continuous variables. In spite of the compactness of this formulation, it has not been used in any computational algorithms to solve a TSP. This formulation is also limited to the TSP only. More interesting formulations can be seen in the Bibliography.

Now we will look at some of the solutions approached in solving a TSP. Before we look at formal approaches, we will see how Excel can help us get a solution for a TSP. We will consider the example given in Table 10.2 for obtaining an optimal tour for a TSP.

Euler circuits and Hamiltonian circuits are fundamental concepts in understanding TSP and various heuristics that are developed. Although the formulation of a TSP looks simple, solution approaches are more complex, and it is difficult to find exact solutions that are usually found for a typical LP formulation.

TABLE 10.2 Example of TSP

	1	2	3	4	5
1	0	8	4	9	9
2	8	0	6	7	10
3	4	6	0	5	6
4	9	7	5	0	4
5	9	10	6	4	0
1	**2**	**3**	**4**	**5**	**1**
	8	6	5	4	9
Total Distance		32			

We will start with an arbitrary tour starting from 1, visiting 2, 3, 4, and 5 and returning to 1, that is, 1→2→3→4→5→1. The total distance traveled is 32. We will now use Excel Solver to obtain an optimal tour using the Evolutionary Method by the INDEX function of Excel. The screenshots of the steps are shown in Figures 10.15, 10.16, and 10.17.

	B	C	D	E	F	G
3		1	2	3	4	5
4	1	0	8	4	9	9
5	2	8	0	6	7	10
6	3	4	6	0	5	6
7	4	9	7	5	0	4
8	5	9	10	6	4	0
9						
10	1	2	3	4	5	=B10
11		=INDEX($C$4:$G$8,B10,C10)	=INDEX($C$4:$G$8,C10,D10)	=INDEX($C$4:$G$8,D10,E10)	=INDEX($C$4:$G$8,E10,F10)	=INDEX($C$4:$G$8,F10,G10)
12		Total Distance	=SUM(C11:G11)			

FIGURE 10.15 Use of Excel for the TSP example.

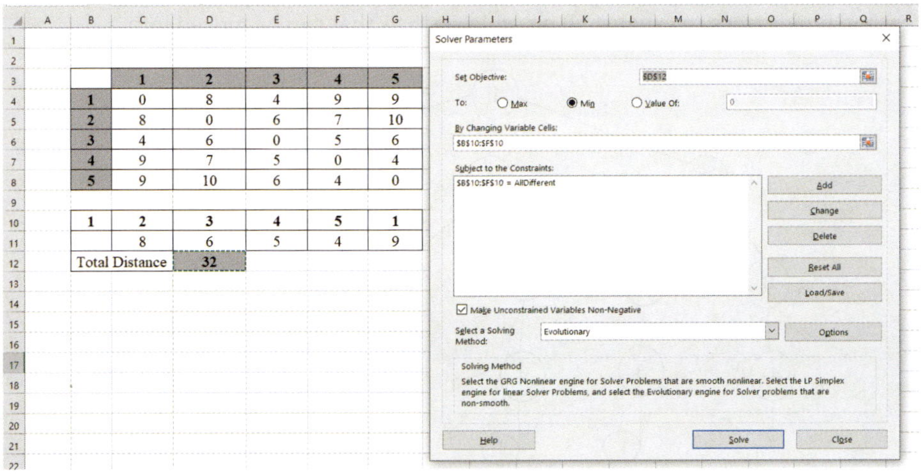

FIGURE 10.16 Setting Solver for solving the TSP.

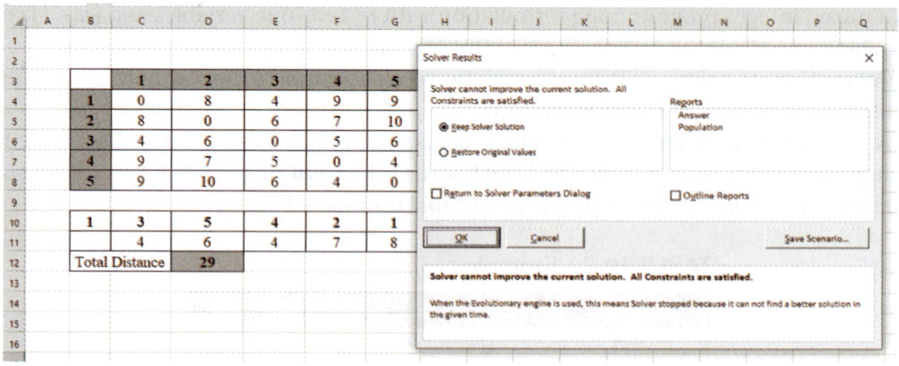

FIGURE 10.17 Solver output for the TSP.

We see that the optimal tour is 1⟶3⟶5⟶4⟶2⟶1 with a total distance of 29 km.

10.3.4 Solving TSP Using Dynamic Programming

Many approaches for solving a TSP are presented in this chapter. Exact methods using the dynamic programming approach, and branch and bound methods and many heuristics giving good solutions are presented. These methods are amenable for software coding and are very useful for many practical applications when a dispatching plan needs to be implemented.

We will describe how a dynamic programming approach can give an exact optimum solution for a TSP with the help of the example shown in Table 10.3.

TABLE 10.3 Example of a TSP for dynamic programming.

	1	2	3	4
1	0	2	9	10
2	1	0	6	4
3	15	7	0	8
4	6	3	12	0

Note that the distance matrix is not symmetric as the distance between 1 and 2 is 2, while the distance between 2 and 1 is 1 and so on for the other vertices.

We will present the possible options of tours if we take the starting vertex as 1. They are given in Figure 10.18. This is also referred to as the state space tree as it explores all possible states (i.e., vertices) and builds trees to exhaust all possible vertices that can be moved into.

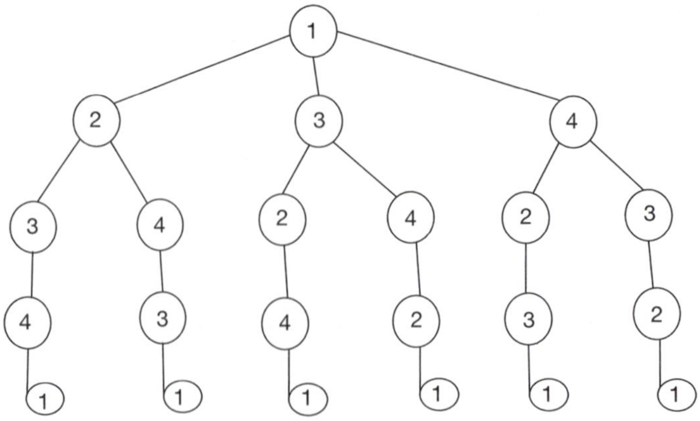

FIGURE 10.18 Possible tours for the example in Table 10.3.

As we see in Figure 10.18, the last vertex is the starting vertex 1 so that each option of tours is a compete tour. We can use backtracking and evaluate all possible tours and determine the optimal one. (This is a small problem where we can still get the solution using this!) But this approach will take more computational time. We will approach determining the optimal path using the dynamic programming approach where we track backwards and reach the starting vertex at the end. The last vertex is where we will be before we complete the tour at 1. If we look from left to right in Figure 10.18, the last vertices are 4, 3, 4, 2, 3, and 2, respectively. Take the left most vertex 4. If we are in vertex 4 at that stage, then we will reach vertex 1 with a distance of 6 (Table 10.3). Similarly, if we are at vertex 3, then we will reach vertex 1 with a distance of 15. We complete this stage for all of them, as shown in Figure 10.19 where the distances are shown adjacent to the vertex number and vertices are shown in shaded circles.

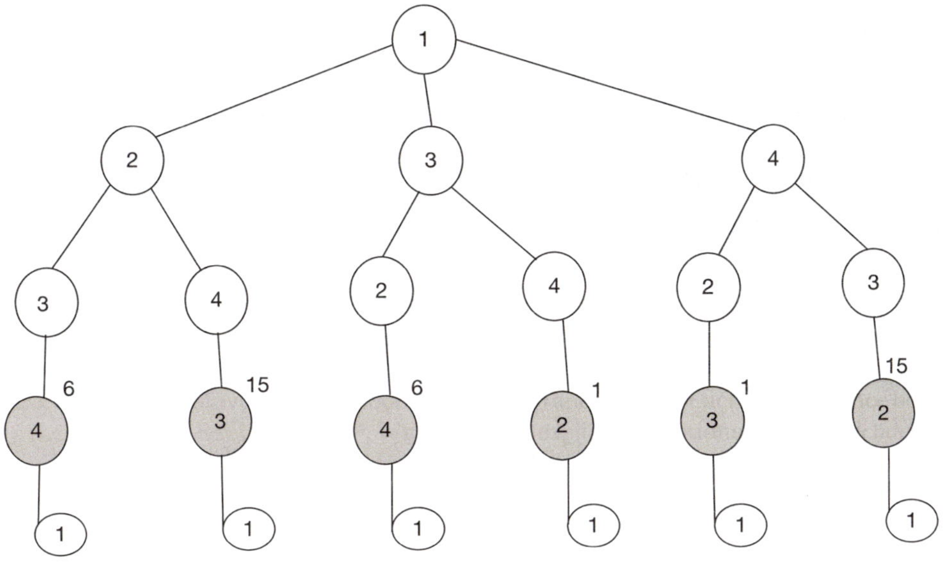

FIGURE 10.19 Evaluations of the last but one stage before reaching the starting vertex 1.

Now we will go one stage earlier than that shown in Figure 10.19. See the figure again and look from left to right. One stage before the stage shown in shaded circles, we will be in vertices 3, 4, 2, 4, 2, and 3. We will see the first one on the left. If we are at vertex 3 at this stage, then we will visit vertex 4 with a distance of 8 (Table 10.2) and from the previous stage, we know that the distance is 6 to reach from vertex 4 to 1. Therefore, the total distance will be $8 + 6 = 14$. If we are at vertex 4 now at this stage, we will move to vertex 3 with a distance of 12 and we know that the distance is 15 to move from 3 to 1 from the previous stage. Therefore, the total distance is $12 + 15 = 27$ at this stage. We complete this stage for all of them, as shown in Figure 10.20 where the distances are shown adjacent to the vertex number and vertices are shown in shaded circles.

Now we will go one stage earlier than that shown in Figure 10.20. See the figure again and look from left to right. One stage before the stage shown in shaded circles, we will be in vertices 2, 3, and 4. We will see the first one on the left. If we are at vertex 2 at this stage, then we have two options to go to either vertex 3 or vertex 4. Let us move to vertex 3. The distance from vertex 2 to 3 is 6 (Table 10.3), and from vertex 3, the best distance from the previous stage is 14 from Figure 10.20. Therefore, this option of visiting vertex 3 and moving further results in a distance of $6 + 14 = 20$. If we move to vertex 4 from vertex 2 (which is the other option), the distance will be 4 (Table 10.3) and the best distance from vertex 4 is 27 from the previous stage from Figure 10.20. Thus, this option of moving to vertex 4 from vertex 2 will be $4 + 27 = 31$. Therefore, at vertex 2, going to 3 and further gives a distance of 20 and going to 4 and further gives a distance of 31. We will take the minimum of these two, that is, moving to vertex 3 with a total distance of 20. We will evaluate the same for the other vertices 3 and 4. The complete evaluation is shown in Figure 10.21 where the distances are shown adjacent to the vertex number and vertices are shown in shaded circles.

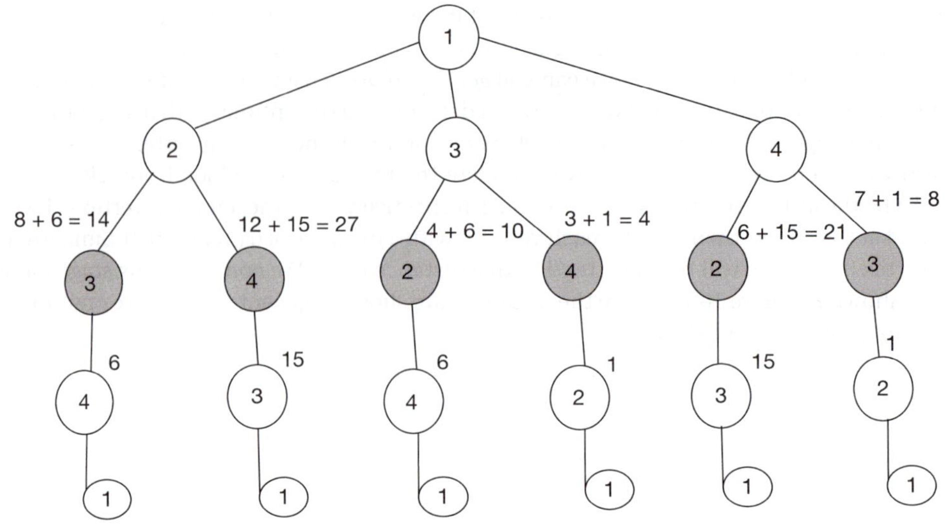

FIGURE 10.20 Evaluations of the last but second stage before reaching the starting vertex 1.

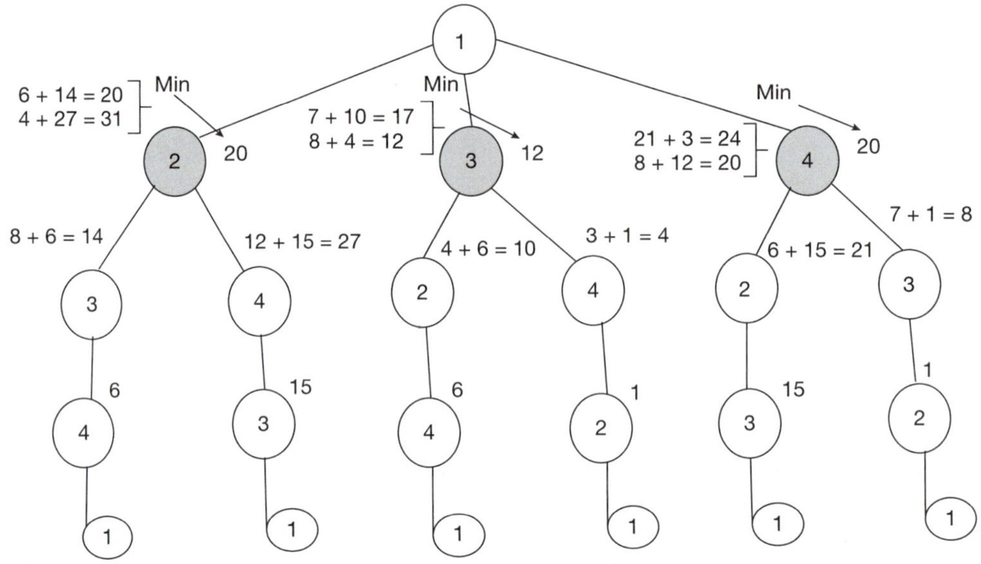

FIGURE 10.21 Evaluations of the last but third stage before reaching the starting vertex 1.

Now we will go one stage earlier than that shown in Figure 10.21. See the figure again and notice that we are at vertex 1 now, which was our starting vertex. From this vertex 1, we can move to vertex 2 or vertex 3 or vertex 4. If we move to vertex 2, the distance is 2 (Table 10.3) and the best distance from vertex 2 further (from Figure 10.21) is 20. So, the total distance will now be 2 + 20 = 22. If we move to vertex 3, the distance will be 9 (Table 10.3), and the best distance from vertex 3 further (from Figure 10.21) is 12. Therefore, the total distance is 9 + 12 = 21. Finally, if we move to vertex 4, the distance will be 10 (Table 10.3), and the best distance from vertex 4 further (from Figure 10.21) is 20. Therefore, the total distance is 10 + 20 = 30. We take the minimum distance here, that is, min (22, 21, 30) = 21. This is the optimal distance of the TSP.

The complete evaluation is shown in Figure 10.22 where the distances are shown adjacent to vertex 1 and is shown in shaded circles.

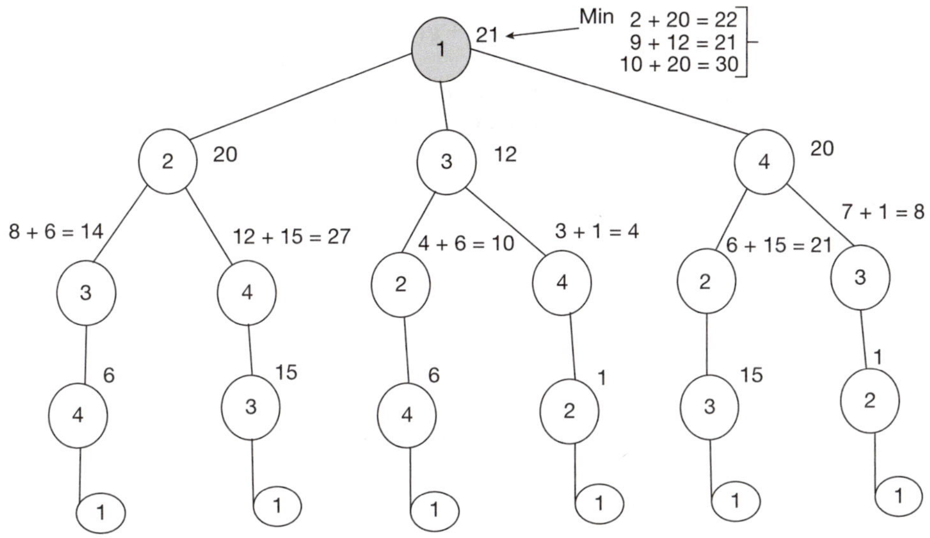

FIGURE 10.22 Evaluations of the last but fourth stage (final step) before reaching the starting vertex 1.

At this stage, we have solved the TSP and the shortest distance from the starting vertex is 21. We will now trace the optimal tour, which is 1→3→4→2→1, and the same is shown in Figure 10.23 where the optimal tour is shown in double-dotted thick lines from vertex 1 with the chosen vertices in shaded circles and the edge distances shown within thin boxes along the edges.

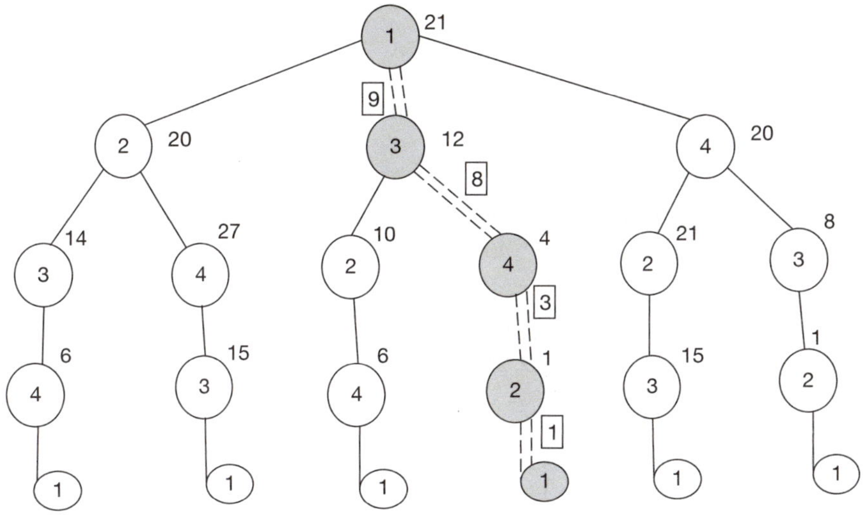

FIGURE 10.23 Optimal TSP tour using dynamic programming approach.

The recursive expression for the steps can be given as follows for this problem.

$$g(1,\{2,3,4\}) = \min_{k \in \{2,3,4\}} \{c_{ik} + g(k,\{2,3,4\} - \{k\})\}$$

where $g(\ldots)$ is the evaluation of the total distance from a given node to other nodes in the set $\{\ldots\}$ and c_{ik} is the length of the edge of (i, k).

If we take the set of vertices as S and a starting vertex of i, then the general recursive expression can be given as

$$g(i,S)=\min_{k\in S}\{c_{ik}+g(k,S-\{k\})\}$$

and $p(i, S)$ = value of j that gave the minimum (successor of vertex i in set S)

We will explain the steps using the recursive equations for this example. Refer to Table 10.3 for the example.

$g(2, \varphi) = c21 = 1$
$g(3, \varphi /) = c31 = 15$
$g(4, \varphi /) = c41 = 6$

Here φ refers to vertex 1 as the connecting set is null.

k = 1, consider sets of one element:

Set {2}:
$g(3, \{2\}) = c32 + g(2, \varphi) = c32 + c21 = 7 + 1 = 8$. The successor node is referred to by $p(...)$. $p(3, \{2\}) = 2$
$g(4, \{2\}) = c42 + g(2, \varphi) = c42 + c21 = 3 + 1 = 4$. So $p(4, \{2\}) = 2$

Set {3}:
$g(2, \{3\}) = c23 + g(3, \varphi) = c23 + c31 = 6 + 15 = 21$ $\quad p(2, \{3\}) = 3$
$g(4, \{3\}) = c43 + g(3, \varphi) = c43 + c31 = 12 + 15 = 27$ $\quad p(4, \{3\}) = 3$

Set {4}:
$g(2, \{4\}) = c24 + g(4, \varphi) = c24 + c41 = 4 + 6 = 10$ $\quad p(2, \{4\}) = 4$
$g(3, \{4\}) = c34 + g(4, \varphi) = c34 + c41 = 8 + 6 = 14$ $\quad p(3, \{4\}) = 4$

k = 2, consider sets of two elements:

Set {2, 3}:
$g(4, \{2, 3\}) = \min \{c42 + g(2, \{3\}), c43 + g(3, \{2\})\} = \min \{3 + 21, 12 + 8\} = \min \{24, 20\} = 20$
$p(4, \{2, 3\}) = 3$

Set {2, 4}:
$g(3, \{2, 4\}) = \min \{c32 + g(2, \{4\}), c34 + g(4, \{2\})\} = \min \{7 + 10, 8 + 4\} = \min \{17, 12\} = 12$
$p(3, \{2, 4\}) = 4$

Set {3, 4}:
$g(2, \{3, 4\}) = \min \{c23 + g(3, \{4\}), c24 + g(4, \{3\})\} = \min \{6 + 14, 4 + 27\} = \min \{20, 31\} = 20$
$p(2, \{3, 4\}) = 3$

Length of an optimal tour:
$f = g(1, \{2, 3, 4\}) = \min \{c12 + g(2, \{3, 4\}), c13 + g(3, \{2, 4\}), c14 + g(4, \{2, 3\})\}$
$= \min \{2 + 20, 9 + 12, 10 + 20\} = \min \{22, 21, 30\} = 21$
Successor of node 1: $p(1, \{2, 3, 4\}) = 3$
Successor of node 3: $p(3, \{2, 4\}) = 4$
Successor of node 4: $p(4, \{2\}) = 2$
Optimal TSP tour: $1 \rightarrow 3 \rightarrow 4 \rightarrow 2 \rightarrow 1$

The complexity of this approach is the number of operations: $T(n) = O(n^2 2^n)$.

10.3.5 Branch and Bound Method 1

In this section, we will explore a few methods of determining the optimal tours of a TSP using the branch and bound method. The reference can be seen for more detailed descriptions of the branch and bound method, which is one of the approaches in solving an integer programming problem. Similar explorations through various branches in the state space tree are attempted to determine the optimal tour. We will explain the methods using the example in Table 10.2 (which is reproduced here again as Table 10.4) for which we already saw the Excel Solver solution.

TABLE 10.4 Same example as shown in Table 10.2.

	1	2	3	4	5
1	0	8	4	9	9
2	8	0	6	7	10
3	4	6	0	5	6
4	9	7	5	0	4
5	9	10	6	4	0

Usually, most TSPs are assumed to be a square and symmetric distance matrix (although they need not be always symmetric) and satisfy the triangular property of vertices. That is, if *i*, *j*, and *k* are the vertices, then $d_{ij} + d_{jk} \geq d_{ik}$.

We determine the lower bound (LB) for the starting vertex by finding the minimum of each row (or column as both will be the same since the matrix is symmetric). The sum of the row minima is the LB as it is the least distance that will be incurred when moving from one vertex to another vertex, and the optimal tour that satisfies the TSP conditions may be equal to or more than this LB. This is shown in Table 10.5.

TABLE 10.5 Determining the lower bound.

	1	2	3	4	5	Row Minimum
1	999	8	4	9	9	**4**
2	8	999	6	7	10	**6**
3	4	6	999	5	6	**4**
4	9	7	5	999	4	**4**
5	9	10	6	4	999	**4**
					Total	**22**

We start at vertex 1, and the LB for vertex 1 to start the branch and bound is 22. This gives options to move to vertex 2 or 3 or 4 or 5 in the next step. We will show how we determine the value of the total distance if we branch off to vertex 2 from 1. Since the path (1, 2) is already decided as a result of this branching, we block row 1 and column 2 in Table 10.5. We will also block cell (2, 1). This is because going from vertex 2 to 1 is not allowed as it will form a sub-tour and that violates the TSP conditions. We will find the total as before by taking the row minima of each row and add the distance of the edge (1, 2) to that total. We will refer to it as *Z* for that node at this branch. This is shown in Table 10.6.

TABLE 10.6 Lower bound for vertex 2 after branch (1, 2) is chosen.

	LB for Vertex 2 after Branch (1, 2) is Chosen						
	1	2	3	4	5	Row Minimum	
1	999	999	999	999	999	—	
2	999	999	6	7	10	**6**	
3	4	999	999	5	6	**4**	
4	9	999	5	999	4	**4**	
5	9	999	6	4	999	**4**	
Total						**18**	**Z**
Distance of edge (1, 2)						**8**	**26**

Note that row 1 and column 2 corresponding to the branch (1, 2) are blocked as well as cell (2, 1) with a high number 999. The *Z* for this vertex is 26. Similar steps can be carried out for vertices 3, 4, and 5 to obtain the *Z* values for them. Table 10.7 shows similar steps for vertex 3.

TABLE 10.7 Lower bound for vertex 3 after branch (1, 3) is chosen.

LB for Vertex 3 after Branch (1, 3) is Chosen							
	1	2	3	4	5	Row Minimum	
1	999	999	999	999	999	**0**	
2	8	999	999	7	10	**7**	
3	999	6	999	5	6	**5**	
4	9	7	999	999	4	**4**	
5	9	10	999	4	999	**4**	
Total						**20**	**Z**
Distance of edge (1, 3)						**4**	**24**

The *Z* values for vertices 4 and 5 will be 29 and 28, respectively. The results are shown in Figure 10.24.

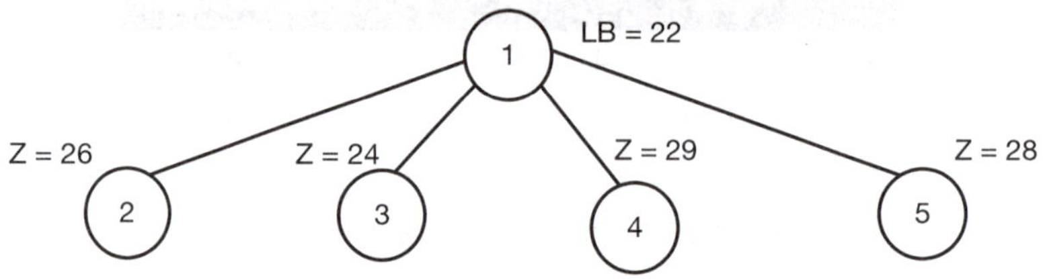

FIGURE 10.24 Results of lower bounds for the vertices 2, 3, 4, and 5.

We notice that among the branches, it is worth branching off from vertex 3 as it has the lowest value of $Z = 24$ and so we shift the LB now to vertex 3. We can branch off to vertices 2, 4, or 5 from this vertex, as shown in Figure 10.25.

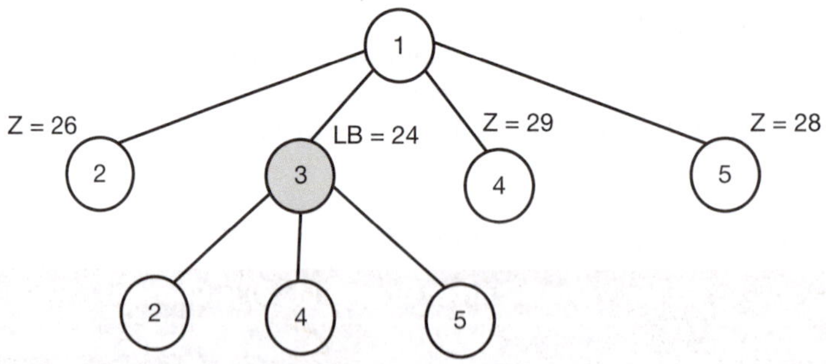

FIGURE 10.25 Branching on vertex 3.

For all the evaluation of branches from vertex 3, we will use Table 10.6 as the relevant table as it has evaluated the branch (1, 3) already. Now we will explain how we calculate *Z* for the branch (3, 2). This would mean that we block row 3 and column 2 of Table 10.6 and also cell (2, 3) since going from vertex 3 to 2 is not allowed. Then obtain the row minimum as before and add the edge distances of (1, 3) and (3, 2), which are already included in the path. This is shown in Table 10.8. The *Z* value at this stage is 25.

TABLE 10.8 Calculating Z for the branch (3, 2)

	1	2	3	4	5	Row Minimum	
1	999	999	999	999	999	**0**	
2	8	999	999	7	10	**7**	
3	999	999	999	999	999	**0**	
4	9	999	999	999	4	**4**	
5	9	999	999	4	999	**4**	**Z**
		Edge (1, 3) = 4			**Edge (3, 2) = 6**	**15**	**25**

In a similar way, we can obtain the *Z* values for vertices 4 and 5, that is, branching off from vertex 3 as seen in Figure 10.25. The values for vertices 4 and 5 are 30 and 28, respectively. The summary is shown in Figure 10.26.

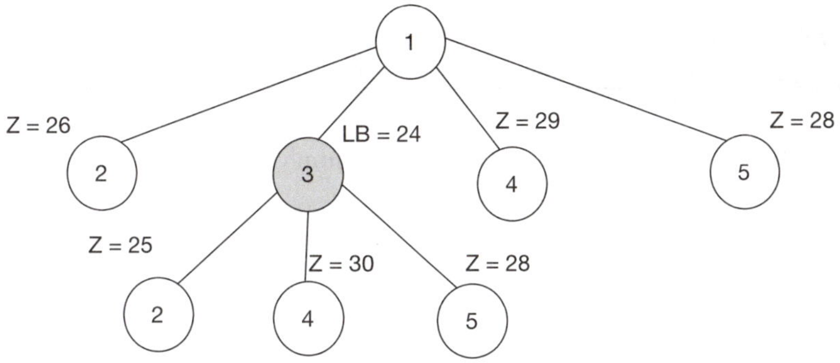

FIGURE 10.26 Results of branching on vertex 3.

We see that among the vertices of vertex 3, vertex 2 has the minimum value of *Z* and we will explore branching off from this vertex now.

The procedure is similar to what we explained earlier about how to obtain the *Z* value for each of the options. We block the relevant row and column of the branch we are considering in the relevant reduced matrix of the vertex we are branching off. For example, for the case now, we will consider the distant matrix given in Table 10.7. The results are shown in Figure 10.27.

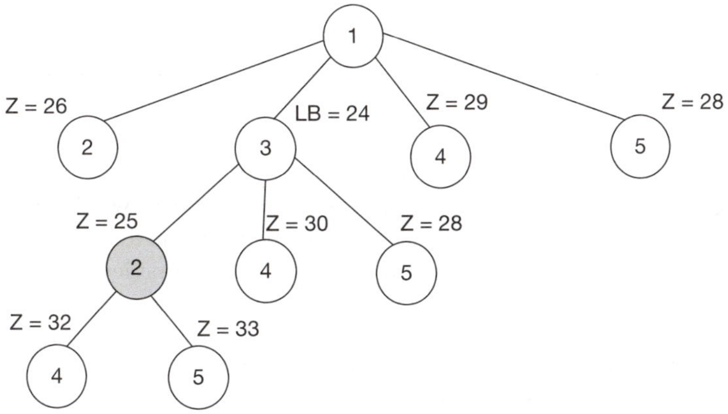

FIGURE 10.27 Branching on vertex 2 along vertex 3.

We notice that the Z values of this branching off are 32 and 33, respectively, for vertices 3 and 4. These values are more than the first-level *Z* values for vertices 2, 4, and 5 as shown in Figure 10.24. So, we will not explore further from here as any branching further would have the *Z* value to be the same or more than these values. So, we will temporarily fathom these vertices, and they are shown with a notation of cross lines X. Refer to Figure 10.24. We will now explore branching off from vertex 2 as it has the lowest value of 26. The evaluations are shown in Figure 10.28.

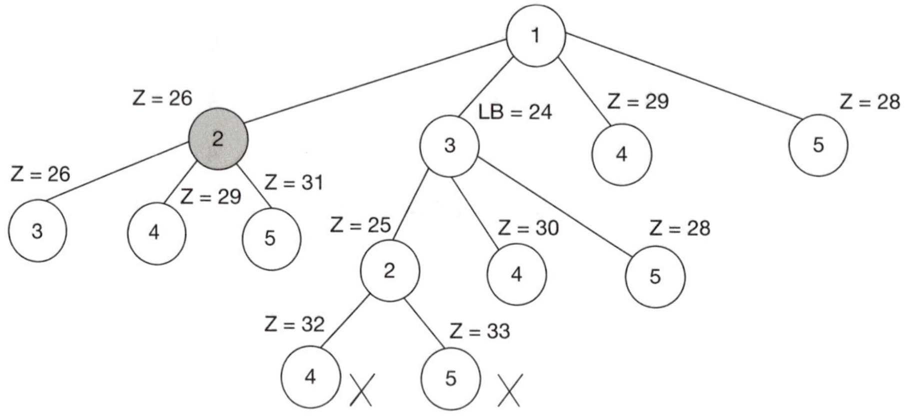

FIGURE 10.28 Fathoming vertices 4 and 5 at the third level under vertex 2 along vertex 3 and branching along vertex 2 at the fist level.

From Figure 10.28, it is clear that vertex 3 has the minimum value of *Z*. We decide to branch off on vertex 3. The evaluations are shown in Figure 10.29.

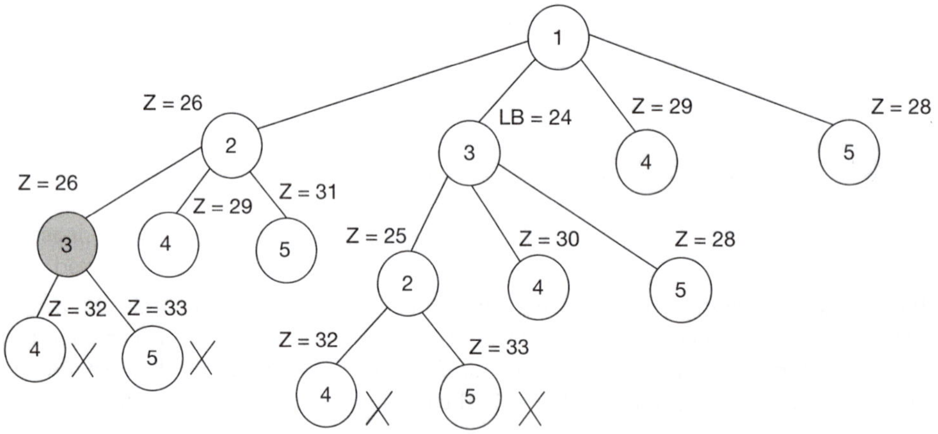

FIGURE 10.29 Evaluations by choosing vertex 2 in the first level and branching on vertex 3 and fathoming vertices 4 and 5.

It can be seen that the *Z* values are 32 and 33, respectively, for vertices 4 and 5. But we see that vertex 5 at the first level and at the second level as a branch of 3 of the first level have a value of $Z = 28$, which is smaller than these values. Although both have $Z = 28$, we choose the second level as a branch of vertex 3 since the scope for it to have a better value for *Z* is more. Therefore, we chose vertex 5 at the second level of branching of vertex 3 at the first level. So, from vertex 5, the possible options are to branch off to vertex 2 or 4. The evaluations are shown in Figure 10.30.

Now the only option further from vertex 4 at the last level in Figure 30 is to move to vertex 2 and finally to vertex 1 to complete the tour. The entire path is shown with shaded circles in Figure 10.31 with the edge lengths on their sides.

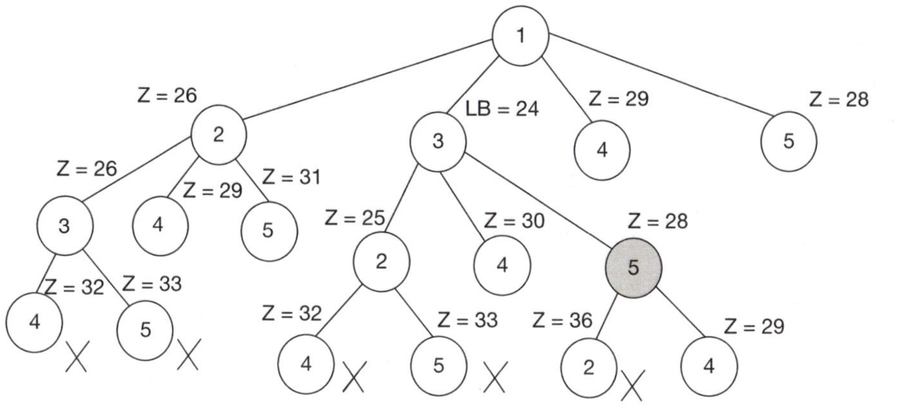

FIGURE 10.30 Evaluations of branching on vertex 5 in the second level along vertex 3 in the first level and fathoming vertex 2 in the third level.

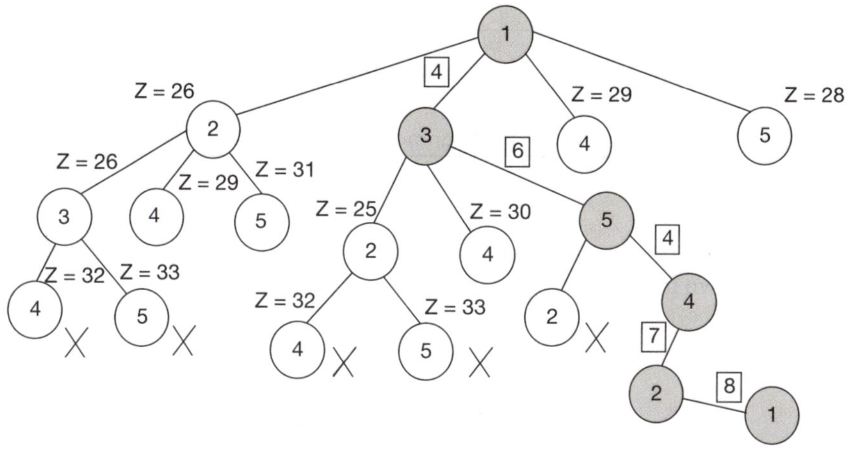

FIGURE 10.31 The optimal path for the TSP.

We see that the optimal tour is 1 ⟶3⟶5⟶4⟶2⟶1 with a total distance of 29 km.

10.3.6 Branch and Bound Method 2

Consider the example as given in Table 10.2 (and Table 10.4). We will show it on Table 10.9.

TABLE 10.9 TSP example (same as Tables 10.2 and 10.4)

	1	2	3	4	5
1	0	8	4	9	9
2	8	0	6	7	10
3	4	6	0	5	6
4	9	7	5	0	4
5	9	10	6	4	0

We will solve this as an assignment problem initially. If we find a feasible solution to this assignment problem, then it is optimal to the TSP. By a feasible solution, we reiterate that the solution to this assignment problem should not have any sub-tours, which violates the TSP conditions. We will use Solver instead of using the manual method of the Hungarian algorithm so that the computations are easier for the branch and bound method. The Excel Solver steps are shown in Figure 10.32.

	1	2	3	4	5
1	999	8	4	9	9
2	8	999	6	7	10
3	4	6	999	5	6
4	9	7	5	999	4
5	9	10	6	4	999

	1	2	3	4	5	LHS	RHS
1	0	0	1	0	0	1	1
2	1	0	0	0	0	1	1
3	0	1	0	0	0	1	1
4	0	0	0	0	1	1	1
5	0	0	0	1	0	1	1
LHS	1	1	1	1	1		
RHS	1	1	1	1	1		

Z	26

FIGURE 10.32 Solver solution using Assignment Method for the TSP.

The solution is $X_{13}=X_{21}=X_{32}=X_{45}=X_{54}=1$ with $Z=26$. We see that this solution has two sub-tours 4→5→4 and 1→3→2→1. Since there are sub-tours, this solution is a feasible solution to the original TSP. They are shown in Figure 10.33.

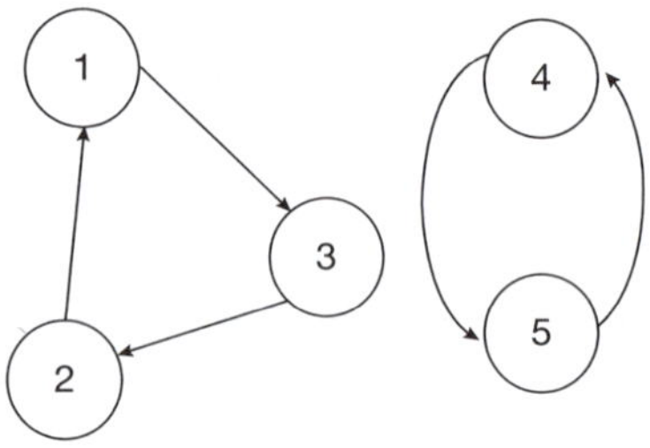

FIGURE 10.33 Sub tours resulting from the Solver solution.

Therefore, we have to break one of the sub-tours to make it feasible and that is carried out using the branch and bound method. The Z value of 26 becomes the lower bound (LB). We usually take one of the sub-tours, which is smaller in case the sub-tours are of different length, and any sub-tour if that is not the case. In this case, we will consider the sub-tour 4→5→4. Since we have to break the sub-tour, we create two branches—one with $X_{45}=0$ or $X_{45}=1$—as shown in Figure 10.34. Here we will evaluate the branch for which we will assume $X_{45}=0$.

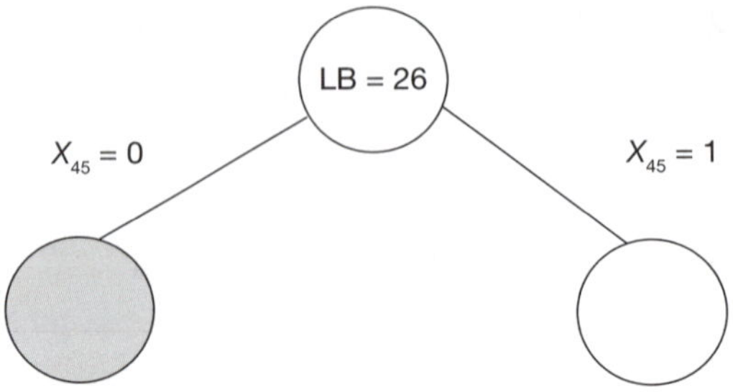

FIGURE 10.34 Branching on the sub-tour 4-5.

Since $X_{45} = 0$ here, this would mean that the cell (4, 5) in Table 10.9 will not be in solution. So, we will block the cell with a distance of a high number of 999 as shown in Table 10.10 in a light green color and solve the resulting distance matrix by the assignment method.

TABLE 10.10 Modified assignment table after blocking cell (4,5)

	1	2	3	4	5
1	999	8	4	9	9
2	8	999	6	7	10
3	4	6	999	5	6
4	9	7	5	999	999
5	9	10	6	4	999

If this modified assignment problem has a feasible solution, then it is optimal to the original TSP. The steps of the assignment method are shown in Figures 10.35 and 10.36.

	1	2	3	4	5
1	999	8	4	9	9
2	8	999	6	7	10
3	4	6	999	5	6
4	9	7	5	999	999
5	9	10	6	4	999

	1	2	3	4	5
1	0	0	1	0	0
2	1	0	0	0	0
3	0	0	0	0	1
4	0	1	0	0	0
5	0	0	0	1	0

LHS	1	1	1	1	1
RHS	1	1	1	1	1

Z	29

FIGURE 10.35 Solver solution for Table 10.10.

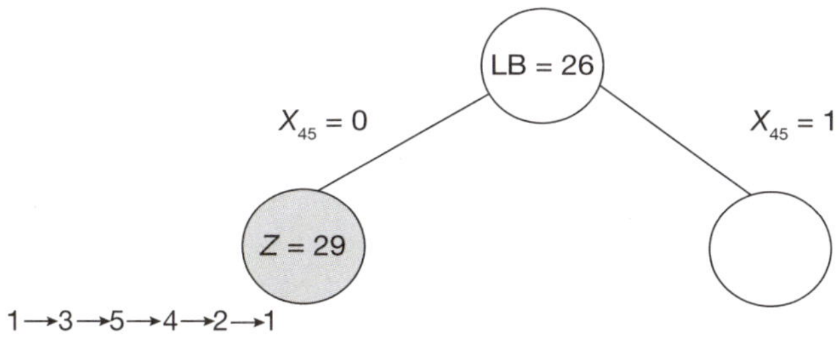

FIGURE 10.36 Branching on $X_{45} = 0$ resulting in optimal TSP tour.

We see the solution to the branch $X_{45} = 0$ is $X_{13} = X_{21} = X_{35} = X_{42} = X_{54} = 1$ with $Z = 29$. We also notice that there are no sub-tours in this solution and the tour is 1→3→5→4→2→1 with a total distance of 29. This is a feasible solution to the problem and hence an optimal solution to the original TSP.

Let us see what would have happened if we had branched off on the branch where we assumed $X_{45} = 1$. In this case, row 4 and column 5 will be blocked and the remaining matrix is used for solving the problem using the assignment method. The solution is shown in Figure 10.37.

	1	2	3	4
1	999	8	4	9
2	8	999	6	7
3	4	6	999	5
5	9	10	6	999

	1	2	3	4
1	0	0	1	0
2	0	0	0	1
3	1	0	0	0
5	0	1	0	0

LHS	RHS
1	1
1	1
1	1
1	1

LHS	1	1	1	1
RHS	1	1	1	1

Total	25	C_{45}	4
Z	**29**		

FIGURE 10.37 Solver solution for the branch $X_{45} = 1$.

We see that besides $X_{45} = 1$, $X_{13} = X_{24} = X_{31} = X_{52} = 1$, with $Z = 29$. We still see a sub-tour with 1⟶3⟶1 and another 2⟶4⟶5⟶2. We will take the smaller sub-tour 1⟶3⟶1 and branch off with $X_{13} = 0$ and $X_{13} = 1$, as shown in Figure 10.38.

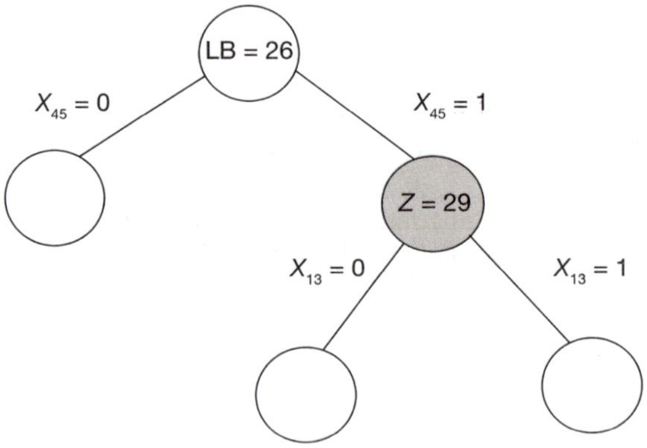

FIGURE 10.38 Branching on $X_{45} = 1$ resulting in subtour branches $X_{13} = 0$ and $X_{13} = 1$.

We will block cell (1, 3) with a high value of 999 and solve the modified matrix using the assignment method. The solution is shown in Figures 10.39 and 10.40.

	1	2	3	4
1	999	8	999	9
2	8	999	6	7
3	4	6	999	5
5	9	10	6	999

	1	2	3	4
1	0	1	0	0
2	0	0	0	1
3	1	0	0	0
5	0	0	1	0

LHS	RHS
1	1
1	1
1	1
1	1

LHS	1	1	1	1
RHS	1	1	1	1

Total	25	C_{45}	4
Z	**29**		

FIGURE 10.39 Solver solution for $X_{13} = 0$.

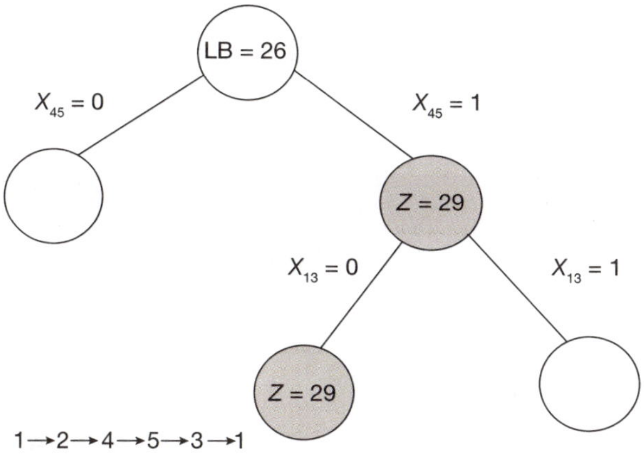

FIGURE 10.40 Branching on $X_{13} = 0$ resulting in optimal TSP.

We see that besides $X_{45} = 1, X_{12} = X_{24} = X_{31} = X_{53} = 1$ with $Z = 29$. We notice that there are no sub-tours and the tour is 1→2→4→5→3→1. Since this is a feasible solution to the problem, it is optimal for the original TSP. We also notice that the tour we obtained in the earlier branch of $X_{45} = 0$ and this tour are the same but in the reverse order. There is no need to evaluate the other branches and the solution will be the same.

10.3.7 Branch and Bound Method 3

In this method, we proceed quite similarly to the earlier method and obtain the reduced matrix after row minimum subtraction for each row and column minimum subtraction for all columns. The steps are shown in Tables 10.11, 10.12, and 10.13 for the same example.

TABLE 10.11 Establishing row minimum for Table 10.9

	1	2	3	4	5	Row Minimum
1	—	8	4	9	9	**4**
2	8	—	6	7	10	**6**
3	4	6	—	5	6	**4**
4	9	7	5	—	4	**4**
5	9	10	6	4	—	**4**
					Total	**22**

The reduced matrix after subtracting the row minimum for every row is given as follows.

TABLE 10.12 Reduced matrix after subtracting row minimum from each row

	1	2	3	4	5
1	—	4	0	5	5
2	2	—	0	1	4
3	0	2	—	1	2
4	5	3	1	—	0
5	5	6	2	0	—

Column 2 does not have a zero, and we carry out the column minimum subtraction for column 2. The reduced matrix is given as follows.

TABLE 10.13 Reduced matrix after subtracting column minimum from each column

	1	2	3	4	5
1	—	2	0	5	5
2	2	—	0	1	4
3	0	0	—	1	2
4	5	1	1	—	0
5	5	4	2	0	—

Therefore, the total of row and column minimums is 22 + 2 = 24. Therefore, we start the branch and bound with a lower bound of 22. Now the following procedure is followed to determine the branching strategy. We scan the rows and columns and identify the assignable zeros for this strategy. There should always be assignable zeros in the rows and column. In Table 10.13, the cells (1, 3), (2, 3), (3, 1), (3, 2), (4, 5), and (5, 4) have assignable zeros by the row and column minimum reduction method. This is already taken care of in the first step here, but in the subsequent steps, it has to always be ensured. We use the concept of opportunity cost for all the cells in Table 10.13, which have assignable zeros and assign a penalty for not making any assignment for the cell. This penalty is the sum of the row minimum and the column minimum of the assignable zero. For example, let us look at the assignable zero in cell (1, 3) in Table 10.13. The row minimum for the cell is 2, and the column minimum is 0. Therefore, the total penalty for this is 2 + 0 = 2. We interpret this as the penalty of the distance by this much if we do not make any assignment in this cell. In a similar way, we compute the penalties for all the assignable cells in Table 10.13. The same is shown in Table 10.14 where the penalties are shown in brackets in shaded cells.

TABLE 10.14 Penalty calculations for assignable zeroes

	1	2	3	4	5
1		2	0 (2)	5	5
2	2		0 (1)	1	4
3	0 (2)	0 (1)		1	2
4	5	1	1		0 (3)
5	5	4	2	0(3)	

It is obvious that we wish to always minimize the opportunity cost, and hence we choose the cell which has the maximum penalty such that by choosing that cell, we try and minimize the opportunity cost. In the case of a tie, we can choose any one of them arbitrarily. Here we notice that both cells (4, 5) and (5, 4) have the maximum penalty. We will choose, say, cell (4, 5). This would mean that we would branch off on this with two options $X_{45} = 0$ and $X_{45} = 1$ as the two possibilities. Since the opportunity cost is 3 already if we do not assign in cell (4, 5), the lower bound becomes 24 + 3 for this branch $X_{45} = 0$. Then we evaluate the other branch $X_{45} = 1$ by removing row 4 and column 5 from Table 10.13 as this will be in the solution. The same is shown in Figure 10.41.

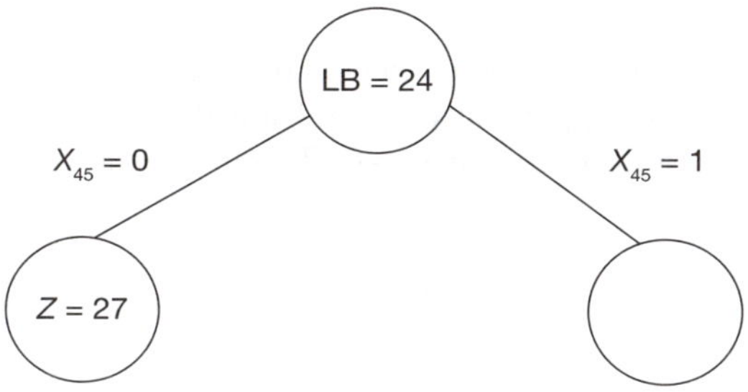

FIGURE 10.41 Branching off on $X_{45} = 0$ and $X_{45} = 1$.

We remove row 4 and column 5 from Table 10.13 and also make the cell (5, 4) not assignable as an inclusion of it will make a sub-tour of (4, 5) and (5, 4). We will put a "–" for this cell. The matrix is given in Table 10.15.

TABLE 10.15 Modified matrix after removing (4,5)

	1	2	3	4
1	—	2	0	5
2	2	—	0	1
3	0	0	—	1
5	5	4	2	—

Now we will ensure that all rows and columns have assignable zeros for computing the penalties. We notice that row 5 and column 4 do not have zeros. We will proceed with the same procedure and reduce the fifth row by the row minimum of 2 and reduce column 4 by the column minimum of 1. So, there is a reduction of 2 + 1 in this process, and that will make the lower bound increase by 3 to 27 for further branching. This is shown in Table 10.16 where the assignable zeros are shown in the shaded cells.

TABLE 10.16 Assignable zeroes identification

	1	2	3	4
1	—	2	0	4
2	2	—	0	0
3	0	0	—	0
5	3	2	0	—

We will compute the penalties as before after the reduction for all the assignable zeros, and they are shown in Table 10.17 with penalties shown in brackets.

TABLE 10.17 Penalty calculations

	1	2	3	4
1	—	2	0 (2)	4
2	2	—	0 (0)	0 (0)
3	0(2)	0(2)	—	0(0)
5	3	2	0(2)	—

Here we notice that cells (3, 1), (3, 2), and (5, 3) have a maximum penalty of 2. We will choose, say, cell (5, 3). This would mean that we would branch off on this with two options $X_{53} = 0$ and $X_{53} = 1$ as the two possibilities. Since the opportunity cost is 2 already, if we do not assign in cell (5, 3), the lower bound becomes 27 + 2 for this branch $X_{53} = 0$. The same is shown in Figure 10.42.

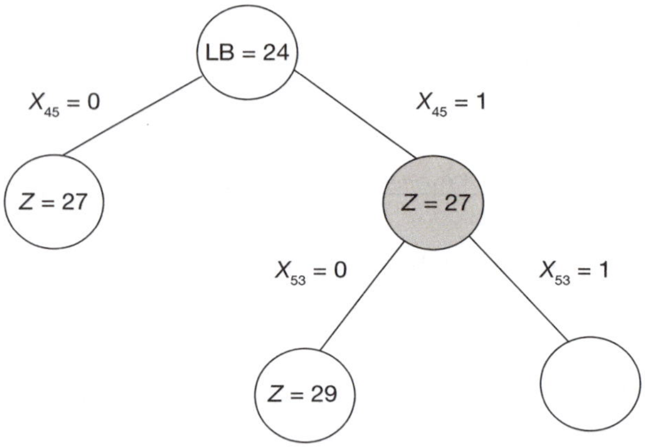

FIGURE 10.42 Evaluation of $X_{45} = 1$ and branching off on $X_{53} = 0$ and $X_{53} = 1$.

We remove row 5 and column 3 from Table 10.15. Since the cell (3, 5) is not there to be kept out, we need not bother about sub-tours at this stage. The matrix is given in Table 10.18.

TABLE 10.18 After removing cell (5,3)

	1	2	4
1	—	2	4
2	2	—	0
3	0	0	0

Now we will ensure that all rows and columns in Table 10.18 have assignable zeros for computing penalties. We notice that row 1 has no assignable zero. We will proceed with the same procedure and reduce row 1 by the row minimum of 2. So, there is a reduction of 2 in this process, and that will make the lower bound increase by 2 to 29 for further branching. This is shown in Table 10.19 where the assignable zeros are shown in the shaded cells.

TABLE 10.19 Assignable zeroes identification

	1	2	4
1	—	0	2
2	2	—	0
3	0	0	0

We will compute the penalties as before after the reduction for all the assignable zeros, and they are shown in Table 10.20 with penalties shown in brackets.

TABLE 10.20 Penalty calculations

	1	2	4
1	—	0 (2)	2
2	2	—	0(2)
3	0(2)	0(0)	0(0)

Here we notice that cells (2, 4) and (3, 1) have the maximum penalty of 2. We will choose, say, cell (2, 4). This would mean that we would branch off on this with the two options $X_{24} = 0$ and $X_{24} = 1$ as the two possibilities. Since the opportunity cost is 2 already, if we do not assign in cell (2, 4), the lower bound becomes $29 + 2 = 31$ for this branch $X_{24} = 0$. The same is shown in Figure 10.43.

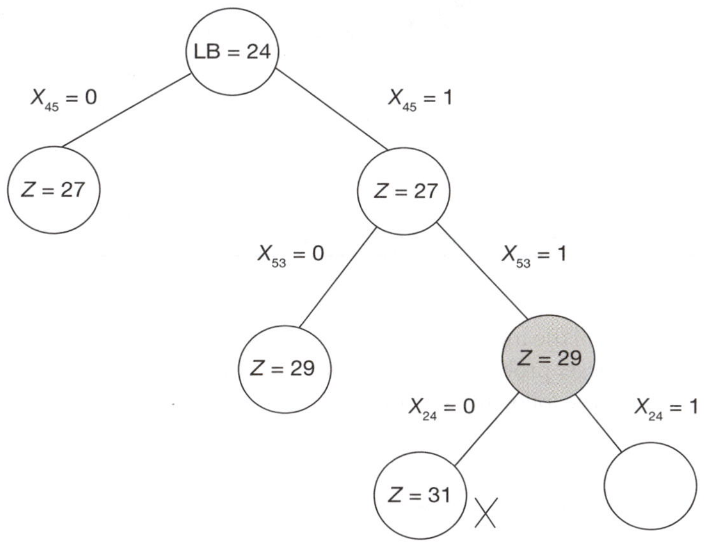

FIGURE 10.43 Evaluations of $X_{53} = 1$ and further branching off on $X_{24} = 0$ and $X_{24} = 1$ with fathoming $X_{24} = 0$.

We remove row 2 and column 4 from Table 10.19. Since cell (4, 2) is not there to be kept out, we need not bother about a sub-tour at this stage. The matrix is given in Table 10.21.

TABLE 10.21 Final stage after removing row 2 and column 4

	1	2
1	—	0
3	0	0

Since there is already a reduced matrix available here, we assign 1 to 2 and 3 to 1. This makes $X_{12} = 1$ and $X_{31} = 1$. From Figure 10.43 and Table 10.20, we have $X_{45} = X_{53} = X_{24} = X_{12} = X_{31} = 1$ with $Z = 29$. This is a feasible solution and optimal to the TSP. From Figure 10.43, we see that since we have a feasible solution with $Z = 29$, further branches need not be evaluated from the branch $X_{24} = 0$ as it is more than this lower band and is hence indicated by the cross lines X. We could also go on branching from the branches of $X_{53} = 0$, but since the value is equal to the current lower bound, we fathom that also. We can explore the branch $X_{45} = 0$ further, and you will notice that the solution will be the same, but the tour may be in a different order. Hence, the current tour 4→5→3→1→2→4 is optimal with a total distance of 29. Notice that this is the same tour except that it starts at 4. Figure 10.44 gives the complete summary of the tour.

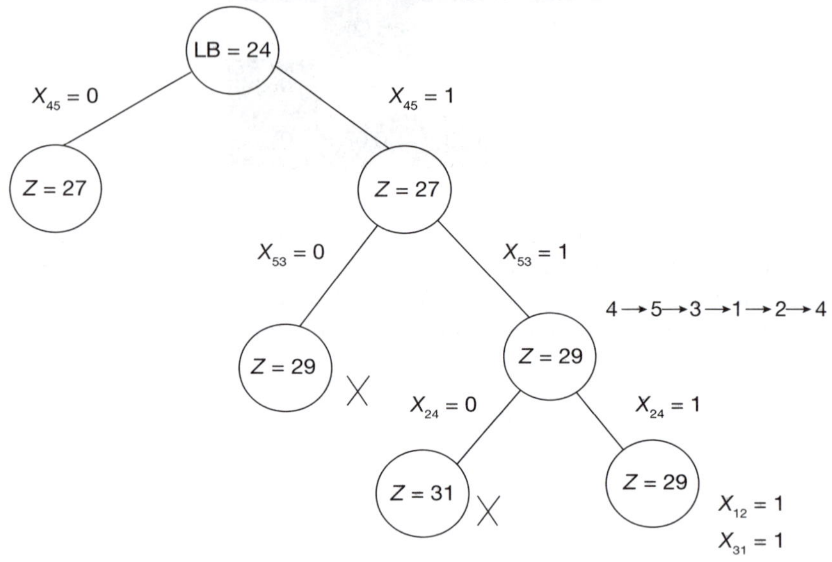

FIGURE 10.44 Evaluations of branching on $X_{53} = 0$.

So far, we have seen some of the methods that give us exact solutions. These methods are complex especially when solving larger problems. There are a few popular heuristics available to solve a TSP. We will describe them in the following sections.

10.4 | HEURISTICS FOR SOLVING A TSP

The branch and bound method using this approach is more logical using the opportunity cost principle and offers solutions based on that. However, the computation complexity still exists like other exact methods outlined here.

Most of the heuristic methods we will describe in this section are developed for solving symmetric cases although they can be modified to handle asymmetric cases too. We will use the following notations for discussion:

1. L_a is the length of the tour given by an algorithm.
2. L_{opt} is the length of the optimal tour.

We will also assume the following:

1. The distances are nonnegative and symmetric.
2. They satisfy the triangular property.

These are assumed for establishing the bound for the objective function. While specifying the tour, the direction is irrelevant, and it is possible to start at any vertex and complete the tour to return to that vertex. We will discuss them in two parts: construction heuristics and improvement heuristics.

10.5 | CONSTRUCTION HEURISTICS

Most of the heuristics methods for a TSP are addressed in two stages: first to construct a tour and second to improve it further by swapping a few links in the tour. Most of the construction methods need not be good solutions as the logic is to systematically develop a tour first and try some swapping options to exchange links to improve the tour further.

In construction methods, the tour is built by adding a new vertex to an existing tour systematically by a heuristic method. To increase reliability, the procedure can be repeated from several (or all) vertices in turn. The computation time multiplies correspondingly.

We will use the same example in Table 10.22 that we used in the last section for all these methods.

TABLE 10.22 Example of a TSP (same as earlier Tables 10.2, 10.4, and 10.9)

	1	2	3	4	5
1	—	8	4	9	9
2	8	—	6	7	10
3	4	6	—	5	6
4	9	7	5	—	4
5	9	10	6	4	—

10.5.1 Nearest Neighbor Method

1. Choose an arbitrary starting node for the tour. This is the initial path of one node.
2. Find an unconnected node that is closest to the last node of the path. Join this node to the last node.
3. Repeat step (2) until all nodes are joined to the path without forming any sub-tours. Then, join the last node to the first one.

Let us start with vertex 1. The next closest vertex is 3. From 3, the closest vertex is vertex 4 as vertex 1 cannot be connected to avoid a sub-tour. From 4, the closest vertex is 5, and from 5, the closest is 2, and from 2, we will complete the tour to return to 1. So, the tour suggested by this method is **1→3→4→5→2→1 with $L_a = 31$**. This is shown in Table 10.23 and Figure 10.45.

TABLE 10.23 Steps of Nearest Neighbor Method

	1	2	3	4	5
1	—	8	4	9	9
2	8	—	6	7	10
3	4	6	—	5	6
4	9	7	5	—	4
5	9	10	6	4	—

1→3→4→5→2→1 $L_a = 31$

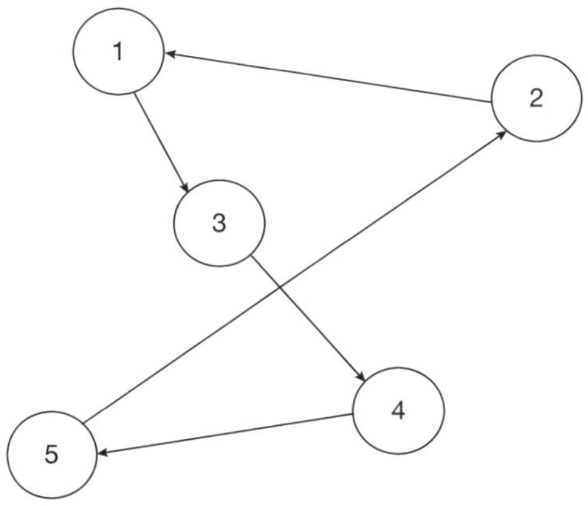

FIGURE 10.45 TSP tour using Nearest Neighbor Method.

Had we started with vertex 2, then the solution would have been **2→3→1→4→5→2 with L_a = 33**. Therefore, different solutions can result from different starting vertices.

10.5.2 Insertion Methods

In insertion methods, the tour is constructed systematically by inserting new nodes into sub-tours, that is, partial tours are constructed. We will use the following notations while describing these methods:

1. T is the sub-tour or partial tour.
2. L is the tour length (i.e., total distance).
3. $\Delta L = c_{ik} + c_{kj} - c_{ij}$ is the increase in tour length L, when node k is inserted between vertices i and j.
4. Distance from node k to sub-tour T is $d(k,T) = \min_{j \in T} c_{kj}$.

10.5.2.1 Nearest Insertion Method

1. We choose any arbitrary vertex, say, i as the starting vertex.
2. Find a vertex j closest to i and form a sub-tour $T = i \to j \to i$.
3. Find a vertex k not in the sub-tour that is closest to any of the sub-tour nodes (that is, for which the minimum distance to the sub-tour vertices is the smallest):

$$d(k,T) = \min_{i \notin T} d(i,T)$$

4. Find an edge i-j of the sub-tour to insert k, such that the increase of length $\Delta L = c_{ik} + c_{kj} - c_{ij}$ is minimized Then modify the sub-tour by inserting k between i and j.
5. Go to step 3 until a Hamiltonian cycle is formed.

We will revisit the example again. Let us assume that the starting vertex is i = 1. The closest vertex is 3. Therefore, j = 3 and T = 1→3→1. Next, we will explore the closest node to the sub-tour: Vertex 3 is the closest and so T = 1→3→4→1.

Then, for vertex 4, the closest vertex is 5 and so T = 1→3→4→5→1. These are the best possible insertions so far. Then the vertex is left out, and we have to see in which sub-tour vertex 2 can be inserted. There are four possibilities.

The increase in length ΔL can be evaluated as follows:

Insertion to
1-3: $\Delta L = c_{12} + c_{23} - c_{13} = 8 + 6 - 4 = 10$
3-4: $\Delta L = c_{32} + c_{24} - c_{34} = 6 + 7 - 5 = \mathbf{8}$ **← smallest**
4-5: $\Delta L = c_{42} + c_{25} - c_{45} = 7 + 10 - 4 = 13$
5-1: $\Delta L = c_{52} + c_{21} - c_{51} = 1 + 8 - 9 = 9$

So, it is better to insert vertex 2 in between 3 and 4.

Therefore, **T = 1→3→2→4→5→1 with L_a = 30.**
Figures 10.46 and 10.47 show the steps.

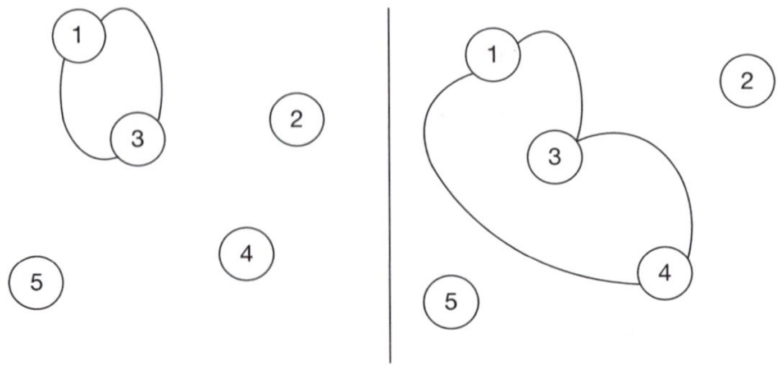

FIGURE 10.46 Steps of Nearest Insertion Method.

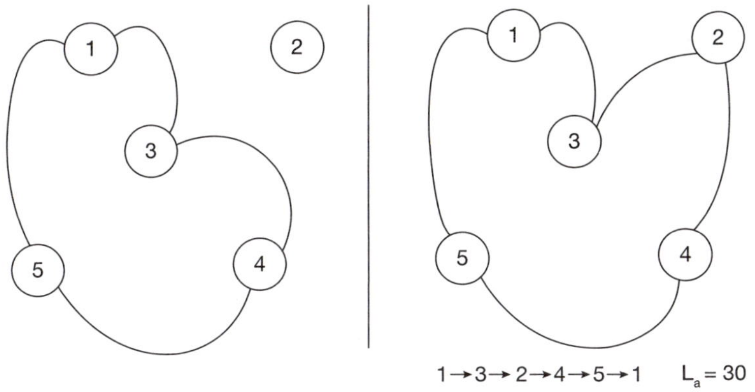

FIGURE 10.47 Steps of Nearest Insertion Method.

10.5.2.2 Cheapest Insertion Method

1. We choose any arbitrary vertex, say, i as a starting vertex.
2. Find a vertex j closest to i and form a sub-tour $T = i \to j \to i$.
3. Find an edge i-j of the sub-tour and a node k not in the sub-tour, such that the increase of length $\Delta L = c_{ik} + c_{kj} - c_{ij}$ is minimized.
4. Modify the sub-tour by inserting k between i and j.
5. Go to step 3 until a Hamiltonian cycle is formed.

We will use the same example.

1. Let us assume that the starting vertex i = 1. The closest vertex is 3. Therefore, j = 3 and $T = 1 \to 3 \to 1$.
2. Now for edge 1-3 (or 3-1),
   Inserting vertex 2 will have $\Delta L = c_{12} + c_{23} - c_{13} = 8 + 6 - 4 = \mathbf{10}$ **←smallest**
   Inserting vertex 4 will have $\Delta L = c_{14} + c_{43} - c_{13} = 9 + 5 - 3 = 11$
   Inserting vertex 5 will have $\Delta L = c_{15} + c_{53} - c_{13} = 9 + 6 - 3 = 12$
   Here, the smallest increase is by inserting vertex 2 and so $T = 1 \to 2 \to 3 \to 1$.
3. In the next step we have three edges in T and two unattached vertices 4 and 5. Therefore, we have to evaluate six possibilities:

   Edge 1-2, insert vertex 4: $\Delta L = c_{14} + c_{42} - c_{12} = 9 + 7 - 8 = 8$
   Edge 1-2, insert vertex 5: $\Delta L = c_{15} + c_{52} - c_{12} = 9 + 10 - 8 = 11$
   Edge 2-3, insert vertex 4: $\Delta L = c_{24} + c_{43} - c_{23} = 7 + 5 - 6 = \mathbf{6}$ **← smallest**
   Edge 2-3, insert vertex 5: $\Delta L = c_{25} + c_{53} - c_{23} = 10 + 6 - 6 = 10$
   Edge 3-1, insert vertex 4: $\Delta L = c_{34} + c_{41} - c_{31} = 5 + 9 - 4 = 10$
   Edge 3-1, insert vertex 5: $\Delta L = c_{35} + c_{51} - c_{31} = 6 + 9 - 4 = 11$

   Here, the smallest increase is by inserting vertex 4 between vertex 2 and vertex 3. So $T = 1 \to 2 \to 4 \to 3 \to 1$.
4. Now, we have only vertex 5 unattached. We evaluate all possible insertions: inserting 5 between 1 and 2, 2 and 4, 4 and 3, and finally 3 and 1 in the same as explained earlier. We find that the best insertion is between 4 and 3. So, $\boldsymbol{T = 1 \to 2 \to 4 \to 5 \to 3 \to 1}$ **with** $\boldsymbol{L_a = 29}$. Note that this is also the optimal tour, which we saw in the earlier sections.

Figures 10.48 and 10.49 show the steps.

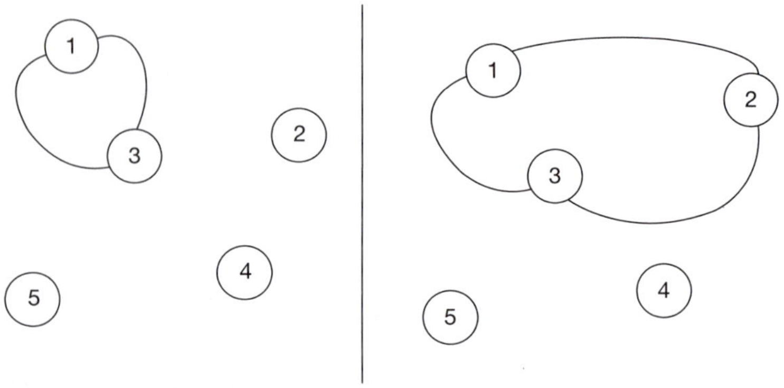

FIGURE 10.48 Steps of Cheapest Insertion Method.

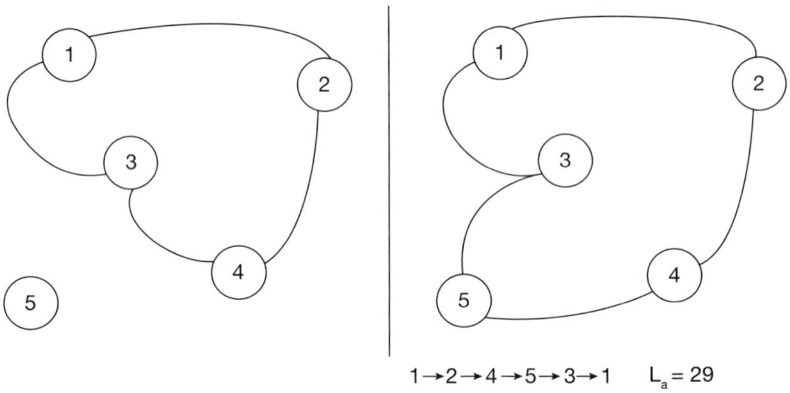

FIGURE 10.49 Steps of Cheapest Insertion Method.

10.5.2.3 Farthest Insertion Method

1. We choose any arbitrary vertex, say, i as a starting vertex.
2. Find a vertex j that is farthest to i, that is, for which distance c_{ij} is the longest, and form a sub-tour $T = i \to j \to i$.
3. Find a vertex k not in the sub-tour that is farthest from the sub-tour.
   Remember that the distance from vertex i to sub-tour T was defined as

$$d(i,T) = \min_{j \in T} c_{ij}$$

4. Find an edge i-j of the sub-tour to which the insertion of k gives the smallest increase in length, that is, for which $\Delta L = c_{ik} + c_{kj} - c_{ij}$ is the smallest (as in the nearest insertion method).
5. Go to step 3 until a Hamiltonian cycle is formed.

We will look at the same example.

1. We will assume that the starting vertex node i = 1. Now the farthest vertex j = 4. So, $T = 1 \to 4 \to 1$.
2. Distance to T from vertex
   2: $d(2, T) = c_{24} = 7 \leftarrow$ largest
   3: $d(3, T) = c_{31} = 4$
   5: $d(5, T) = c_{54} = 4$
   Since the largest is with vertex 2, we insert 2 in the tour and so $T = 1 \to 2 \to 4 \to 1$.

3. Now in the next step, we have two unattached vertices 3 and 5. We evaluate the ΔL for all combinations of inserting 3 and 5 in T. We see that inserting 3 between 4 and 1 has the smallest increase of 4 as per step 3. Now $T = 1 \rightarrow 2 \rightarrow 4 \rightarrow 3 \rightarrow 1$.
4. Now the last vertex is 5. We evaluate the options of inserting 5 between 1 and 2, 2 and 4, 4 and 3, and 3 and 1. We see that the small increase of 5 comes by inserting vertex 5 between 4 and 3. Therefore, $T = 1 \rightarrow 2 \rightarrow 4 \rightarrow 5 \rightarrow 3 \rightarrow 1$ with $L_a = 29$. Note that this is also the optimal tour, which we saw in the earlier sections. Figures 10.50 and 10.51 show the steps.

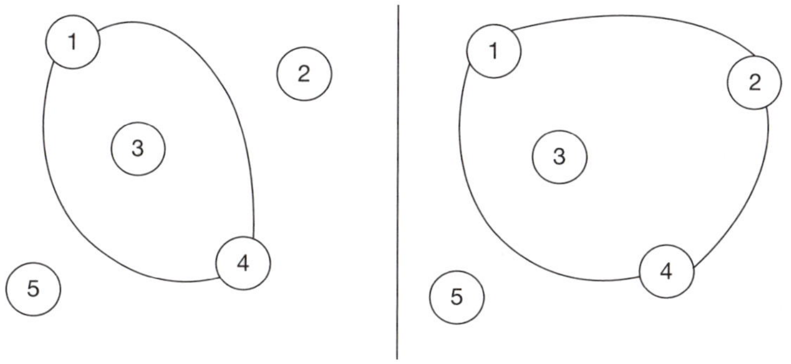

FIGURE 10.50 Steps of Farthest Insertion Method.

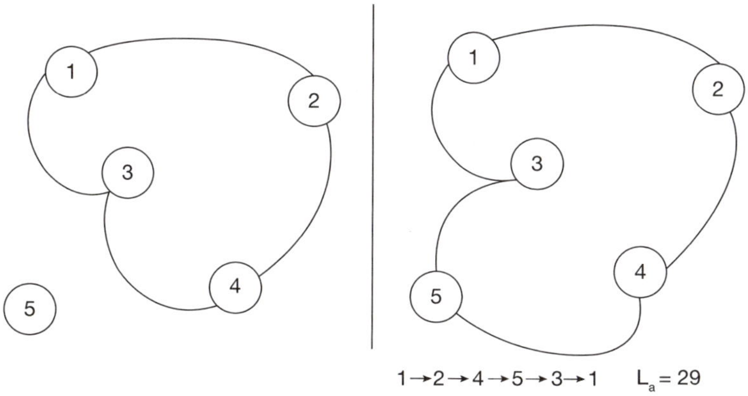

FIGURE 10.51 Steps of Farthest Insertion Method.

10.5.3 Minimal Spanning Tree Method

In this algorithm, a Eulerian cycle (actually circuit) is formed where the edges of a minimum spanning tree are doubled during the algorithm.

1. Use any of the minimum spanning tree algorithms (Prim's or Kruskal's) for the given weighted graph G.
2. Choose a leaf vertex i_0 (i.e., node of degree 1). Set $i = i_0$.
3. If an untraversed edge i-j incident to i exists, go from i to j (edge i-j is added to the path). Now set $i = j$ and repeat step 3. If all edges from i are traversed, return to the first predecessor of i. Let it be the vertex k. If $k = i_0$ (the starting node), a Eulerian cycle is formed: Go to step 4 or else, set $i = k$ and repeat step 3.
4. Form a Hamiltonian cycle using shortcuts, that is, traverse the Eulerian cycle by skipping every node already visited.

The minimal spanning tree for our example is given in Figure 10.52.

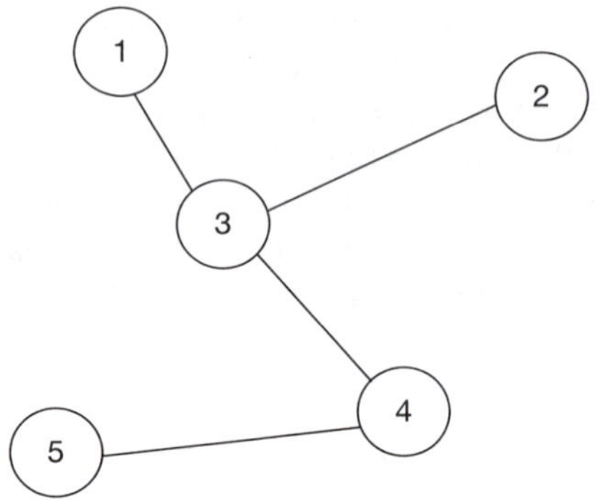

FIGURE 10.52 TSP tour using Minimal Spanning Tree Method.

The following steps describe the construction of the Eulerian cycle:

1. Let us choose $i_o = 1$.
2. Join 1-3. So now $i = 3$.
3. Join 3-2. So now $i = 2$.
4. Return to $k = 3$ using 2-3 and so now $i = 3$.
5. Join 3-4 and so now $i = 4$.
6. Join 4-5 and so $i = 5$.
7. Return to $k = 4$ using 5-4 and so $i = 4$.
8. Return to $k = 3$ using 4-3 and so $i = 3$.
9. Return to $k = 1$ using 3-1 and so $i = 1 = i_o$.
10. Therefore, the Eulerian cycle is 1-3-2-3-4-5-4-3-1.

These are shown with arrow marks in Figure 10.53.

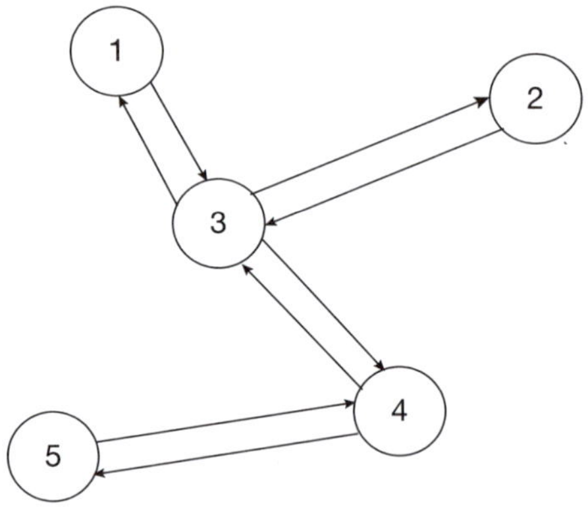

FIGURE 10.53 Construction Eulerian cycle for Figure 10.52.

Now on this Eulerian cycle, we apply step 4. So, the solution to the TSP is **1→3→2→4→5→1 with $L_a = 30$**. This is the same as the one we got using the nearest insertion method and is shown in Figure 10.47.

10.5.5 Christofides Method

The steps are quite similar to the minimal spanning tree method:

1. First, construct the minimum spanning tree T for the given weighted graph G.
2. Identify the vertices with odd degrees and list all the perfect matches from these vertices. Identify the minimum weight perfect matches from these and append the edges of the matches to the minimum spanning tree. Now every vertex will have an even degree.

3. Generate a Eulerian cycle as explained in the previous method for this graph.
4. Form a Hamiltonian cycle using shortcuts as in the previous method.

Revisit Figure 10.52, which has the minimal spanning tree for our example. The vertices with odd degrees are 1, 2, 3, and 5. From this set of vertices {1, 2, 3, 5}, the following are possible matches with their respective weights:

(1, 2), (3, 5) with weight of 14 ← Minimum
(1, 3), (2, 5) with weight of 14 ← Minimum
(2, 3), (1, 5) with weight of 15

We will choose, say, the first one (1, 2) and (3, 5) and append these edges to the minimal spanning tree given in Figure 10.52. We get the following as given in Figure 10.54.

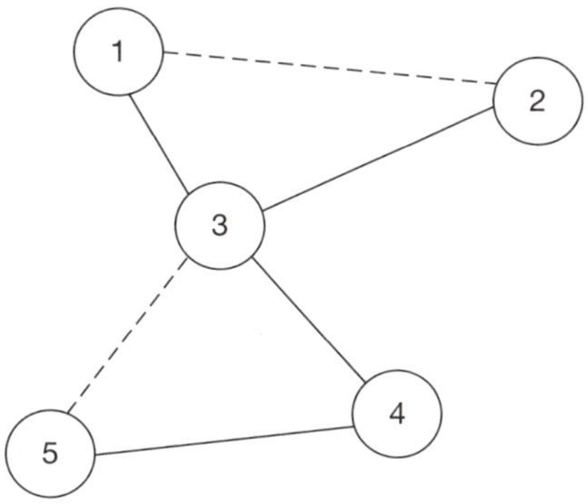

FIGURE 10.54 Appending (1, 2) and (3, 5) to the MST in Figure 10.52.

From Figure 10.54, we see that the Eulerian cycle is 1-2-3-4-5-3-1. So, the last step of obtaining a Hamiltonian cycle will be **1→2→3→4-→5→1**. Therefore, this will be the solution to the TSP **with $L_a = 32$.**

There is also another method to construct a TSP using the Clarke–Wright savings method. We will explain the method when we elaborate on the vehicle routing problems later in this chapter.

We described some of the popular heuristics of constructing a tour for a TSP. In the following section, we will present the k-opt improvement method.

10.6 | k-OPT TOUR IMPROVEMENT METHOD

The following definitions are useful while discussing the k-opt algorithm:

1. When we perform a ***k-change*** on the given solution to a TSP, it means deleting k edges from a tour and replacing them with k edges such that the result is a Hamiltonian cycle.
2. A ***k-neighborhood*** of a TSP solution (Hamiltonian cycle) X is the set of Hamiltonian cycles that result from X with a k-change.
3. A TSP tour (Hamiltonian cycle) is ***k-optimal*** if it cannot be improved with any k-change. Then we can say that any k-optimal solution is a locally optimal solution of the TSP with respect to the k-neighborhood.

See the example given in Figure 10.55. The edges with dotted lines are the ones to be exchanged.

The general steps of the k-opt algorithm for a typical local search for a TSP can be as follows:

1. Construct a Hamiltonian cycle X using any of the tour construction methods outlined in the previous sections or using any random choice.
2. Execute a k-change, resulting in a cycle Y.
3. If $f(Y) < f(X)$, set $X = Y$.
4. Go to step 2 until a local optimum is obtained.

We will examine for $k = 2$, that is, 2-opt exchange for the same example.

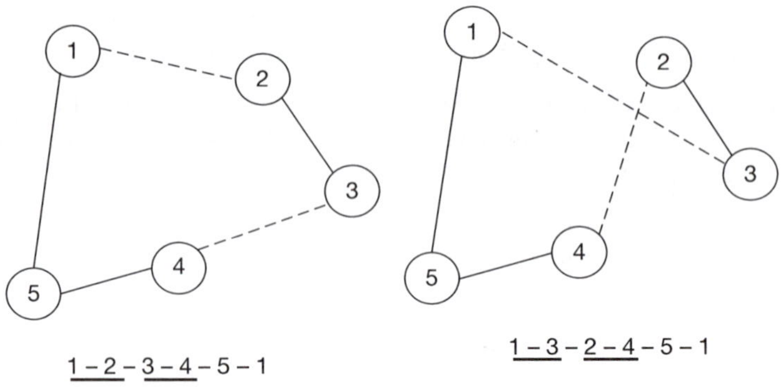

FIGURE 10.55 Example of 2-opt Exchanges.

We will start with the tour construction we used in the Christofides method and use the tour given in Figure 10.56.

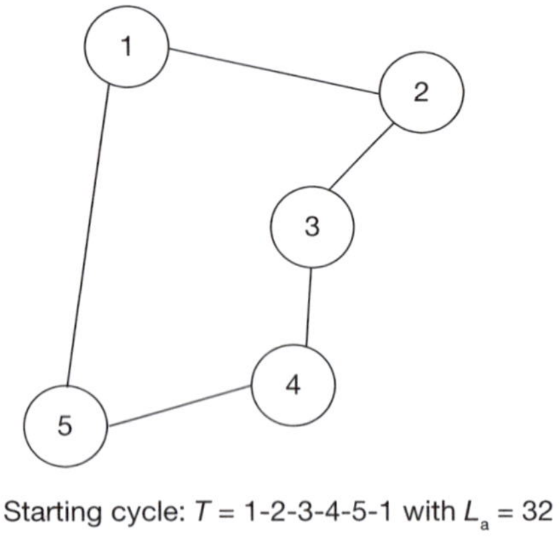

FIGURE 10.56 TSP tour using Christofides Method.

We will list all the possibilities for a 2-change: All possible 2-exchange edges to be changed will be as follows with their corresponding values of L_a.

1-2, 3-4 resulting in the tour T = 1-3-2-4-5-1 with $L_a = 30 < 32$ ← Best
1-2, 4-5 resulting in the tour T = 1-4-3-2-5-1 with $L_a = 39 > 32$
2-3, 4-5 resulting in the tour T = 1-2-4-3-5-1 with $L_a = 35 > 32$
2-3, 5-1 resulting in the tour T = 1-2-5-4-3-1 with $L_a = 31 < 32$
3-4, 5-1 resulting in the tour T = 1-2-3-5-4-1 with $L_a = 33 > 32$

Therefore, the first round of 2-opt exchanges improves the solution with a distance 30 from 32 with the tour T = 1-3-2-4-5-1, as shown in Figure 10.57.

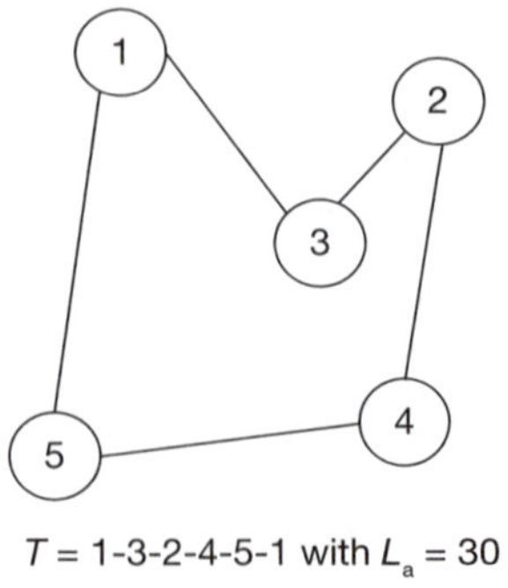

FIGURE 10.57 Result of 2-opt exchanges on Figure 10.56.

Now we will take this tour and carry out one more set of 2-exchanges. The following gives the summary.

Edges to be changed	Resulting Tour	L_a
1-3, 2-4	1-2-3-4-5-1	32
1-3, 4-5	1-4-2-3-5-1	37
3-2, 4-5	1-3-4-2-5-1	35
3-2, 5-1	**1-3-5-4-2-1**	**29 < 30 Best and improvement!**
2-4, 5-1	1-3-2-5-4-1	33

So, the tour T = 1-3-5-4-2-1 has improved the distance from 30 to 29 by exchanging 3-2 and 5-1, as shown in Figure 10.58.

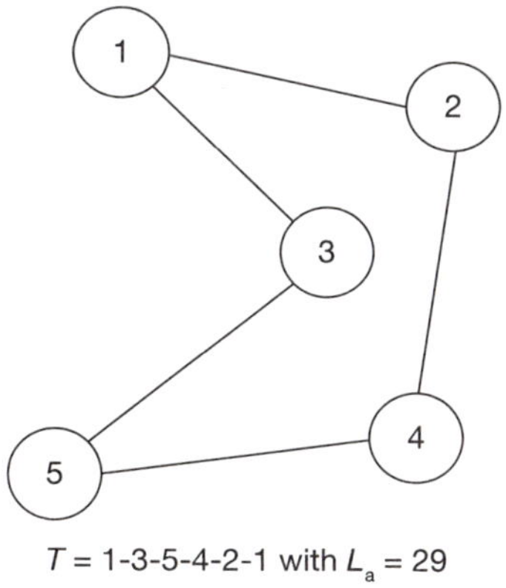

FIGURE 10.58 Result of second round of 2-opt exchanges on Figure 10.57.

Now at this stage, if we check all 2-exchanges, we will observe that there is no improvement from the current distance of 29. Hence, the tour $T = 1 \to 3 \to 5 \to 4 \to 2 \to 1$ **with** $L_a = 29$ is the optimal tour for the TSP, as seen in Figure 10.58.

While performing k-opt exchanges, k values are taken as 2 or 3 as it is relatively less cumbersome to perform the computations and also because the neighborhoods are small. The 3-opt procedure is the same as the 2-opt procedure we explained earlier but takes a little longer to perform the iterations. These procedures can be repeated for different randomly selected solutions to improve the solution further. In practice, it is seen that when k is more than 3, there is not much advantage in the quality of solutions. However, it is possible to get better solutions when k is changed dynamically. We can also use a composite k-opt heuristic. The steps are as follows:

1. Construct a Hamiltonian cycle, say, X.
2. Then apply 2-opt algorithm to X, resulting a tour Y.
3. Then apply 3-opt algorithm to Y.
4. Keep repeating steps 2 and 3 to find an improved solution.

We repeat the construction step 1 for several starting vertices and several construction methods to apply steps 2 and 3 to improve the solutions.

There are some advanced methods like the Kernighan–Lin heuristic, which use partitioning techniques to exchange edges in a graph. There are also a few more methods using simulated annealing, Tabu search, and genetic algorithms to obtain solutions to a TSP. A few references are given at the end of chapter for further reading on such techniques.

SUMMARY

In this chapter, one of the operational concerns dealing with dispatching is addressed. Routing is an important area in transportation where costs can be optimized by properly constructing the routes. TSP is one of the popular approaches found useful in practical applications. Fundamental concepts such as Euler and Hamiltonian circuits have been introduced and some exact and heuristic methods have been discussed in detail which are amenable to develop computer codes for software development.

Exercises

1. Find a Eulerian path for the following graph *G*.

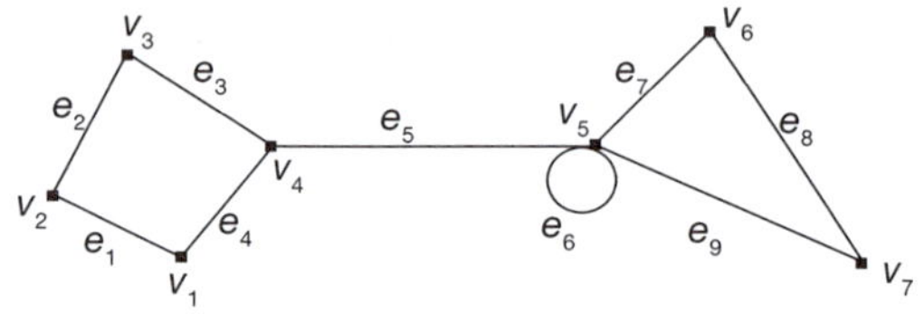

2. Apply Fleury's algorithm on the following graph and obtain Euler's path.

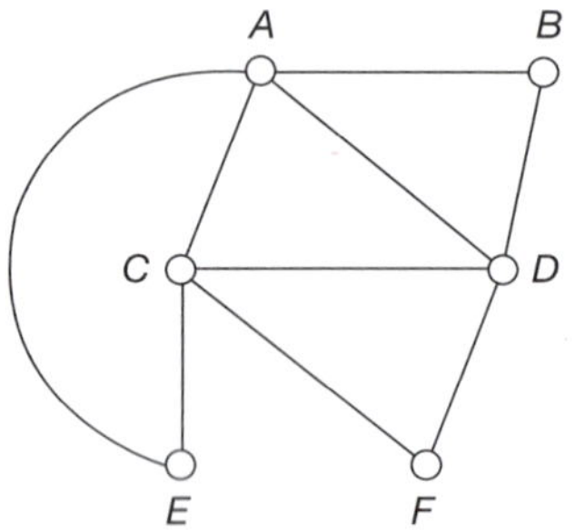

3. Apply Fleury's algorithm on the following graph to obtain Euler's path.

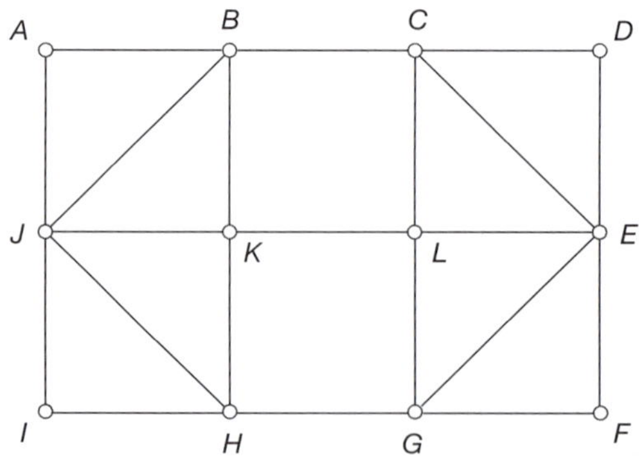

4. Consider the following graph:

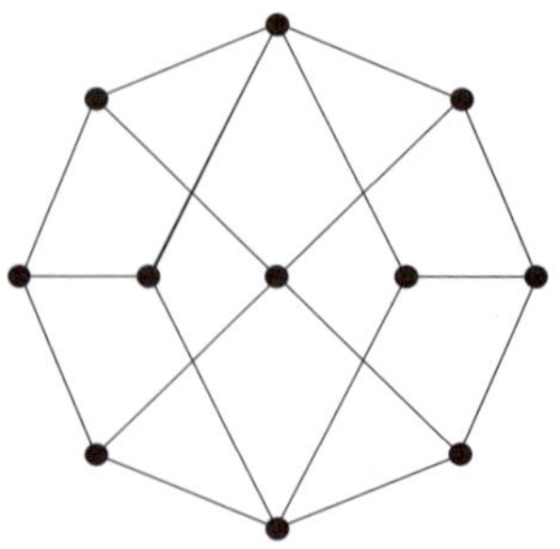

Find a Hamiltonian path. Can your path be extended to a Hamiltonian cycle?

5. Does the following **Petersen** graph have a Hamiltonian cycle? Justify your answer. Does it have a Hamiltonian path? Justify your answer.

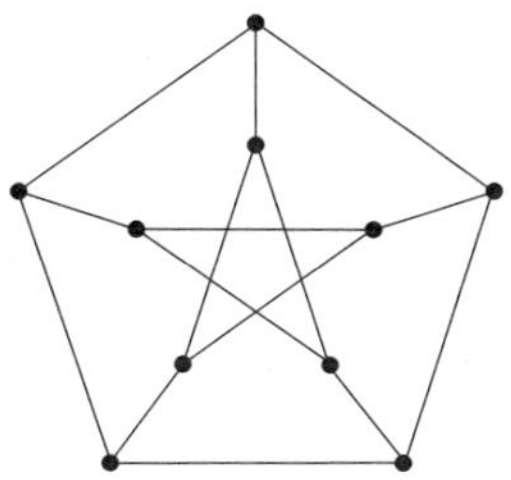

6. Does the following graph have a Hamiltonian path and a Hamiltonian Cycle? Explain.

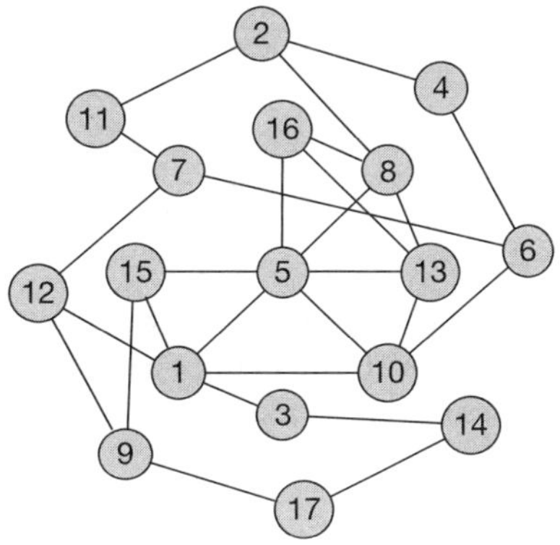

7. Consider the following network:

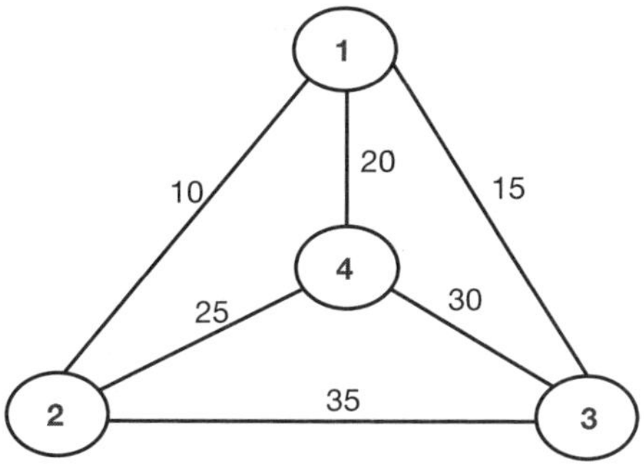

Obtain the optimal tour for a TSP tour using

a. Excel Solver,
b. Dynamic Programming Approach,
c. Using Branch and Bound Methods discussed in this chapter.

8. Consider the following network with five vertices:

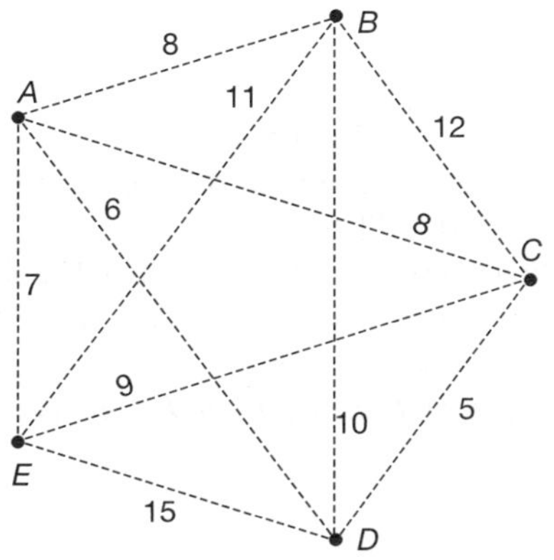

Obtain the TSP tour using the following construction heuristics:

a. Nearest neighbor method
b. Nearest insertion method
c. Cheapest insertion method
d. Farthest insertion method
e. Minimal spanning tree
f. Christofides method

9. Do you think you can improve the TSP tour using k-opt tour improvement methods on the network in problem 8?
10. Consider the following set of cities:

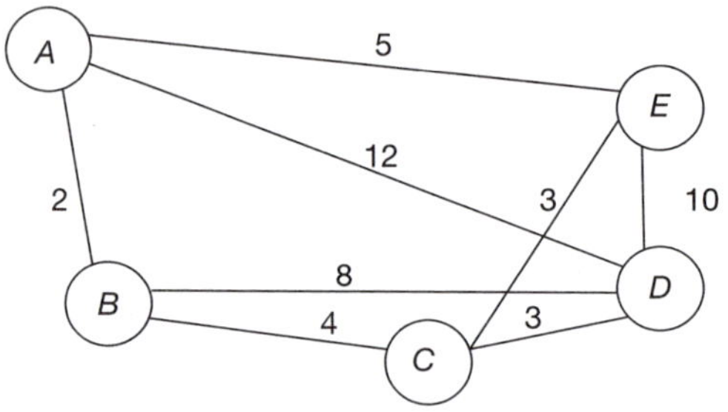

Use the branch and bound method of John, Murty, Sweeney, and Karel to obtain the optimal TSP tour. Compare this solution with the heuristic solution obtained through the minimal spanning tree method for the same network.

Bibliography

1. Achuthan, N. R., L. Caccetta, and S. P. Hill (1996). A new sub-tour elimination constraint for the vehicle routing problem. *European Journal of Operational Research*, **91**, 573–586.
2. Ballou, R. H. and S. K. Srivastava (2007). *Business Logistics/Supply Chain Management.* Delhi: Pearson India.
3. Biggs, N. L., Lloyd E. Keith, and Wilson Robin J. (1986) *Graph Theory 1736–1936.* Oxford: Clarendon Press, ISBN 978-0-19-853916-2.
4. Bollobás, B. (1979) *Graph Theory: An Introductory Course.* New York: Springer-Verlag.
5. Chopra, S., P. Meindl, and D. V. Kalra. (2016) *Supply Chain Management, Strategy, Planning and Operation.* Delhi: Pearson India.
6. Gavish, B. and S. C. Graves. (1978) The travelling salesman problem and related problems, *Working Paper.* Operations Research Center, Massachusetts Institute of Technology.
7. Gersting, J. L. (2007) *Mathematical Structures for Computer Science.* W. H. Freeman and Company.
8. Hillier, F. S. and G. J. Liebermann. (1969) *Introduction to Operations Research.* McGraw Hill.
9. Hillier, F. S. and M. S. Hillier. (2014) *Introduction to Management Science: A Modelling and Case Studies Approach with Spreadsheets*, 5th ed. Burr Ridge, IL: McGraw-Hill/Irwin.
10. Little, J. D. C., K. G. Murty, D. W. Sweeney, and C. Karel. (1963) An algorithm for the traveling salesman problem. *Operations Research*, **11**(6), 972–989.
11. Matai, R., S. P. Singh, and M. L. Mittal. (2010) Traveling salesman problem: An overview of applications, formulations and solution approaches. In *Traveling Salesman Problem: Theory and Applications*, D. Davendra (Ed.). IntechOpen.
12. Schrijver, A. (1960) On the history of combinatorial optimization. In *Handbooks in OR & MS, Vol. 12, 2005*, K. Aardal et al. (Eds.), Elsevier.
13. Taha, H. A. (2006) *Operations Research.* Delhi: Prentice Hall India.
14. Thomas, C. H., L. E. Charles, R. L. Ronald, and S. Clifford. (1989) *Introduction to Algorithms*, 2nd ed. McGraw Hill Book Company.
15. Whittle, P. (2007) *Networks: Optimization and Evolution.* Cambridge, UK: Cambridge University Press.

CHAPTER 11

Routing and Scheduling Problems and Methods

LEARNING OBJECTIVES

After reading this chapter, you would be able to:

- Understand the complexities and types of Vehicle Routing Problems (VRPs) and solution approaches.
- Comprehend integer programming formulations using Solver to solve VRPs.
- Understand branch and bound approaches to solve VRPs.
- Learn heuristics such as the Clarke and Wright savings method and the sweeping method.
- Solve VRPs using Fisher and Jayakumar's method.
- Understand the nature of scheduling problems and a few simple approaches to solve them.
- Comprehend scientific approaches to solve vehicle scheduling problems using the deficit function approach.

11.1 | INTRODUCTION

We saw several approaches to solving the famous Traveling Salesman Problem, both exact and heuristic algorithms. In this chapter, we will present a few popular methods to solve vehicle routing and vehicle scheduling problems. As mentioned in Table 10.1 of Chapter 10, many characteristic type of problems are dealt with in Vehicle Routing Problems (VRPs), and the literature is vast in this area. However, we will present only a few popular types of problems and the solution approaches for them.

11.2 | VEHICLE ROUTING PROBLEMS

As seen in Table 10.1, the basic objective of any VRP is to find the best set of vehicle route(s) or tours to serve a set of demand points or customers or cities or any other relevant vertices that are labeled. The objective may be to minimize the total cost, minimize the total distance, minimize the total travel time or any other appropriate utility.

These problems can be formulated imposing vehicle capacities or without imposing capacities. The demand can be of different types: delivery from depot to customer, pickup at customer and return to depot, pickup at one place and deliver to another place, etc.

A variety of problems can be formulated with only pickup operations or drop operations or both, or can even be formulated separately. The options listed in Table 10.1 give an idea of the variety of problems that can be faced by any firm, and this necessitates a solution approach for them, as any one method will not solve all varieties. As mentioned earlier, although the inputs and outputs are seemingly similar, the process, which is different for various situations faced by firms, makes it difficult to develop methods for such problems. If we list, say, 10 characteristics like the preceding list and if each of them has a minimum number of options of two each, then there are 2^{10}, that is, 1024 possible types of problems that can be generated and it is highly doubtful that we have a method for every type of problem in the list of 1024 combinations! (For example, capacity can be a characteristic and it being imposed or not imposed could lead to various options.) For some, there are hardly any exact algorithms to solve them. The entire field of routing and scheduling has tremendous scope for developing heuristics. In the following sections, we will present some of the popular types of problems that can be solved using either exact or heuristic approaches.

11.2.1 Vehicle Routing Problems without Capacity Restrictions

To start with, let us consider the simple example of the problem given in Table 11.1 where we have five customer demand points shown as vertices 1 to 5 with their demand alongside and the distances from the depot with respect to vertex 0.

TABLE 11.1 Example of a 5-customer problem

d_{ij}	0	1	2	3	4	5	Customer	Demand
0	—	4	3	5	2	3	1	8
1		—	2	7	3	1	2	8
2			—	7	3	8	3	6
3				—	3	5	4	6
4					—	4	5	8

We will assume that the distances d_{ij} are symmetric and that this satisfies the triangular property. We will also assume that no vehicle capacities are imposed. In this problem, we can deal with the following two options:

1. Given a set of vehicles, find out the best routes that they should follow to minimize the total distance that is traveled by those vehicles.
2. The best option for routes based on the requirement itself. That is, it may or may not use all the vehicles.

VRP is an interesting but complicated problem to address in terms of computational efforts. Varieties of problems are encountered in VRPs with various characteristics like vehicle capacity, route distance, link capacities, types of operations, etc., which make them unviable for any specific method of solving them. Hence, this gives more scope for many heuristics to be developed and applied for various applications. Here we show some simple illustrations of them using Excel Solver.

To explain this, let us assume that two vehicles can be used. Option 1 indicates that both will hold true, that is, the vehicles will be used and we need to determine the best routes for them with the minimum total distance. Option 2 indicates that we need to determine the routes that may or may not use both the vehicles. A possible solution for option 1 can be D-1-4-D-2-3-5-D, which means that the first route will be starting from depot (D) and visit customers at vertices 1 and 4 and will return to depot and the second route will start from the depot and visit customers at vertices 2, 3, and 5 and then return to the depot. The total distance covered by these routes will be 9 + 18 = 27. This may not be the best, albeit, a feasible route. A possible solution for option 2 can be D-1-3-4-5-2-D-D, that is, only one route or vehicle is used to cover all the customers and the second route is not required. The total distance in this case will be 29. This may also be the best route to cover all of them. (Note that this option is more of a TSP!)

We will present the different approaches in the following sections. We will consider the following:

1. We are given two vehicles, and **both have to be used**.
2. No capacity restrictions on the vehicles.
3. Vehicles to start and end at depot 0.

We will transform the given distance matrix of the vertices (leaving the first row, which gives the distances of the customer locations from the depot) and consider the two vehicles as vertices 6 and 7. When we start the method, they will be at the depot only and hence their distances from the customers will be two identical columns and rows of the first-row values of Table 11.1. In order to use both the vehicles, we restrict the distances between them, i.e., between 6 and 7, as infinite. Table 11.2 provides the setup distance matrix after these transformations.

TABLE 11.2 Setting up of distance matrix with 2 vehicles as vertices

		Customer					Vehicle	
		1	2	3	4	5	6	7
Customer	**1**	0	2	7	3	1	4	4
	2	2	0	7	3	8	3	3
	3	7	7	0	3	5	5	5
	4	3	3	3	0	4	2	2
	5	1	8	5	4	0	3	3
Vehicle	**6**	4	3	5	2	3	0	999
	7	4	3	5	2	3	999	0

Note that this transformation is made to use the solution approaches of solving it as a TSP, which was discussed in Chapter 10, and interpret vertices 6 and 7 as depot D in the output.

We will initially solve this using Excel Solver. This was explained in Chapter 10, and hence we will skip the steps and present the results only. The solution is presented in Table 11.3.

TABLE 11.3 Solution of the example in Table 11.2 using Solver

		Customer					Vehicle	
		1	2	3	4	5	6	7
Customer	**1**	0	2	7	3	1	4	4
	2	2	0	7	3	8	3	3
	3	7	7	0	3	5	5	5
	4	3	3	3	0	4	2	2
	5	1	8	5	4	0	3	3
Vehicle	**6**	4	3	5	2	3	0	999
	7	4	3	5	2	3	999	0
Tour	6	5	1	2	7	4	3	6
Edge distance	3	1	2	3	2	3	5	
Total distance	**19**							

The optimal tour is 6→5→1→2→7→4→3→6. As mentioned earlier, we will interpret the vertices as depot D and translate this as D→5→1→2→D→4→3→D. This means that route 1 will start from the depot and visit customers at 5, 1, and 2 and return to the depot, and the second route will start from the depot and visit customers at 4 and 3 and return to the depot. The distance of the first route is 3 + 1 + 2 + 3 = 9; the distance of the second route is 2 + 3 + 5 = 10, and hence the total distance is 9 + 10 = 19. We will consider the following:

1. We are given two vehicles, but **we need not use both of them**.
2. No capacity restrictions on the vehicles.
3. Vehicles to start and end at depot 0.

In this case, Table 11.3 is modified with the distance of 0 for vertices 6 and 7 so that D→D coming continuously in the tour is possible. Table 11.4 gives the modified matrix, and Table 11.5 gives the output using Excel Solver.

TABLE 11.4 Modified Table 11.2 with vertices 6 and 7 having distance 0

		Customer					Vehicle	
		1	2	3	4	5	6	7
Customer	**1**	0	2	7	3	1	4	4
	2	2	0	7	3	8	3	3
	3	7	7	0	3	5	5	5
	4	3	3	3	0	4	2	2
	5	1	8	5	4	0	3	3
Vehicle	**6**	4	3	5	2	3	0	0
	7	4	3	5	2	3	0	0

TABLE 11.5 Solution of Table 11.4 using Solver

		Customer					Vehicle	
		1	2	3	4	5	6	7
Customer	**1**	0	2	7	3	1	4	4
	2	2	0	7	3	8	3	3
	3	7	7	0	3	5	5	5
	4	3	3	3	0	4	2	2
	5	1	8	5	4	0	3	3
Vehicle	**6**	4	3	5	2	3	0	0
	7	4	3	5	2	3	0	0
Tour	5	3	4	6	7	2	1	5
Edge distance	5	3	2	0	3	2	1	
Total distance	**16**							

The optimal tour is 5→3→4→6→7→2→1→5. As mentioned earlier, we will interpret the vertices as depot D and translate this as 5→3→4→D→D→2→1→5. This can be read as D→2→1→5→3→4→D. This means that we need only one route that will start from the depot and visit customers at 2, 1, 5, 3, and 4 and return to the depot. The second vehicle or route is not required. (This is indicated by a continuous D→D sequence without any customer vertices in between them.) The distance of this single route, which is a TSP tour, is 3 + 2 + 1 + 5 + 3 + 2 = 16.

Now, all these scenarios can be easily carried out if we formulate this as an integer programming (binary) problem. A nice formulation is given by Kulkarani and Bhave (1985) with an improved version by Achuthan and Caccetta (1991) to explore the VRP to handle a few scenarios such as number of vehicles, number of maximum customers to be handled by a tour, maximum distance or time allowed for each tour, etc. The formulation is explained in the following section.

11.2.2 Integer Programming Formulation for VRP

A set of $N-1$ customers is given with their locations and requirements for a product or commodity. They are supplied from a single depot, the location of which is the depot denoted by N, using a set of delivery vehicles each with a prescribed capacity.

The problem is to determine the delivery routes, one for each vehicle, that minimize the total distance traveled by all the vehicles and that address the following restrictions:

1. All customer requirements are met. Moreover, each customer appears on exactly one route.
2. The maximum number of customers serviced by a vehicle is L.
3. The total requirement of customers appearing in each vehicle route cannot exceed the capacity W.
4. The total distance traveled by each vehicle cannot exceed T.

Let
Q_j = Demand of customers at location j,
V = Number of delivery vehicles,
c_{ij} = Distance traveled from location i to location j,
X_{ij} = 1 if a vehicle travels from i to j,
0 otherwise.

In this model, the formulation is transformed from a problem of finding a vehicle route (cycle) into a path problem. Consider the depot N as an origin location with demand $Q_N = 0$. A vehicle route is a sequence of locations $R = (i_1 = N, i_2, i_3, \ldots, i_k = N)$ beginning and ending at N and all intermediate locations are distinct.

Here, the origin N is duplicated and denoted by N'. Interpret N' as a destination depot (location with demand $Q_{N'} = 0$). Travel is allowed from N to any location i where $1 \le i \le N-1$; location i to any location j, $1 \le i \ne j \le N-1$; and any location j to N', $1 \le j \le N-1$. Also note that traveling to N and out of N' is prohibited. Let $c_{iN'} = c_{Ni}$ for $1 \le i \le N-1$.

A vehicle path is a sequence of distinct locations $P = (N = i_1, i_2, i_3, \ldots, i_k = N')$, beginning at N, ending at N' with at least one intermediate location. Note that a vehicle path (N, i, N') is allowed. The length $l(P)$ of P is defined as

$$l(P) = \sum_{t=1}^{k-1} c_{i_t i_{t+1}}$$

Define $\mathcal{A} = \{(N,i),(i,j),(i,N'): 1 \le i \ne j \le N-1\}$

Note that $\mathcal{A}$ defines all the arcs in the network model $G = (\mathcal{N}, \mathcal{A})$

where $\mathcal{N} = \{1,2,\ldots,N-1\} \cup \{N,N'\}$

With these notations and explanations, the general formulation is as follows:

$$\text{Minimize} \sum_{(i,j)\in\mathcal{A}} c_{ij} X_{ij} \tag{11.1}$$

Subject to

$$\sum_{i=1 i\ne j}^{N} X_{ij} = 1 \text{ for } j = 1,2,\ldots,N-1 \tag{11.2}$$

$$\sum_{j=1 j\ne i}^{N-1} X_{ij} + X_{iN'} = 1 \text{ for } i = 1,2,\ldots,N'-1 \tag{11.3}$$

$$\sum_{j=1}^{N-1} X_{Nj} = V \tag{11.4}$$

$$\sum_{i=1}^{N-1} X_{iN'} = V \tag{11.5}$$

$$X_{ij} = 0, 1 \text{ for all } (i, j) \in \mathcal{A} \tag{11.6}$$

$$y_i - y_j + (L+1)X_{ij} \le L \text{ for all } (i, j) \in \mathcal{A} \tag{11.7}$$

$$y_{N'} - y_N \le L+1 \tag{11.8}$$

Note that Eqs. (11.6) and (11.7) are introduced to eliminate subtours. In Excel, we make Eq. (11.6) as

$$2(L+1)\left(X_{ij} + X_{ji}\right) \le 2L \text{ for all } i = 1 \text{ to } N-1 \text{ and } j \in N-1\ i \ne j$$

$$u_i - u_j + WX_{ij} \le W - Q_j \text{ for all } (i, j) \in \mathcal{A} \tag{11.9}$$

$$u_{N'} - u_N = W \tag{11.10}$$

$$\vartheta_i - \vartheta_j + \left(c_{ij} + T\right)X_{ij} \le T \text{ for all } (i, j) \in \mathcal{A} \tag{11.11}$$

$$\vartheta_{N'} - \vartheta_N = T \tag{11.12}$$

where y_i, u_i, and v_i are arbitrary real numbers.

Note that constraints shown in Eqs. (11.2) to (11.6) will ensure that each customer is served at most once and that all vehicles are used. Further, constraints in Eqs. (11.4) and (11.5) ensure that a feasible solution to these constraints forms a set of vehicle paths. The customers not served by the vehicles will form some cycles free of depots (subtours). So, constraints shown in Eqs. (11.7) and (11.8) will eliminate these subtours (i.e., cycles) and ensure that no vehicle serves more than L customers. Thus, every customer appears on exactly one of the V vehicle paths. These are quite similar to the one we showed earlier in the formulation of TSP to eliminate subtours in Chapter 10. Constraints shown in Eqs. (11.9) and (11.10) will ensure that the load in every vehicle path is at most equal to the vehicle capacity W. Finally, constraints shown in Eqs. (11.11) and (11.12) will bound the length of each vehicle path to T.

We can use Excel for solving these for each type of problem discussed earlier. We will show some examples of the formulation initially focusing on the set of constraints from Eqs. (11.2) to (11.6) only for a single vehicle, two vehicles, and three vehicles without any vehicle capacity restrictions. This part was shown earlier without this formulation.

For the case $V = 1$ (this becomes a typical TSP to be determined)

Figure 11.1 shows the scenarios. Here we do not include the cell for depot to depot while forming Solver equations.

Note that for subtour elimination, we have used $2(L+1)(X_{ij} + X_{ji}) \le 2L$ for the i's and j's. We see that the optimal route is D→2→1→5→3→4→D with a total distance of 16. We obtained this same solution in Table 11.5.

	1	2	3	4	5	Depot
1	999	2	7	3	1	4
2	2	999	7	3	8	3
3	7	7	999	3	5	5
4	3	3	3	999	4	2
5	1	8	5	4	999	3
Depot	4	3	5	2	3	

V	1
L	5
L+1	6

	1	2	3	4	5	Depot	LHS	RHS
1	0	0	0	0	1	0	1	1
2	1	0	0	0	0	0	1	1
3	0	0	0	1	0	0	1	1
4	0	0	0	0	0	1	1	1
5	0	0	1	0	0	0	1	1
Depot	0	1	0	0	0	0	1	1
LHS	1	1	1	1	1	1		
RHS	1	1	1	1	1	1		

Total Distance	16

Sub-tour Elimination	
LHS	RHS
6	10
0	10
0	10
6	10
0	10
0	10
0	10
6	10
6	10
0	10

FIGURE 11.1 Integer programming solution to VRP for $V = 1$.

For the case $V = 2$ (without capacity restriction)

Figure 11.2 shows the scenarios. Here too we do not include the cell for depot to depot while forming Solver equations.

	1	2	3	4	5	Depot
1	999	2	7	3	1	4
2	2	999	7	3	8	3
3	7	7	999	3	5	5
4	3	3	3	999	4	2
5	1	8	5	4	999	3
Depot	4	3	5	2	3	

V	2
L	5
L+1	6

	1	2	3	4	5	Depot	LHS	RHS
1	0	1	0	0	0	0	1	1
2	0	0	0	0	0	1	1	1
3	0	0	0	0	0	1	1	1
4	0	0	1	0	0	0	1	1
5	1	0	0	0	0	0	1	1
Depot	0	0	0	1	1	0	2	2
LHS	1	1	1	1	1	2		
RHS	1	1	1	1	1	2		

Total Distance	19

Sub-tour Elimination	
LHS	RHS
6	10
0	10
0	10
6	10
0	10
0	10
0	10
6	10
0	10
0	10

FIGURE 11.2 Integer programming solution to VRP for $V = 2$.

We see that the optimal route is D→5→1→2→D and D→4→3→D with a total distance of 19. We obtained this same solution in Table 11.3.

For the case $V = 3$ (without capacity restriction)

Figure 11.3 shows the scenario.

	1	2	3	4	5	Depot
1	999	2	7	3	1	4
2	2	999	7	3	8	3
3	7	7	999	3	5	5
4	3	3	3	999	4	2
5	1	8	5	4	999	3
Depot	4	3	5	2	3	

V	3
L	5
L+1	6

	1	2	3	4	5	Depot	LHS	RHS
1	0	0	0	0	1	0	1	1
2	1	0	0	0	0	0	1	1
3	0	0	0	0	0	1	1	1
4	0	0	0	0	0	1	1	1
5	0	0	0	0	0	1	1	1
Depot	0	1	1	1	0	0	3	3
LHS	1	1	1	1	1	3		
RHS	1	1	1	1	1	3		

Total Distance	23

Sub-tour Elimination

LHS	RHS
6	10
0	10
0	10
6	10
0	10
0	10
0	10
0	10
0	10
0	10

FIGURE 11.3 Integer programming solution to VRP for $V = 3$.

We see that the optimal route is D→2→1→5→D and D→3→D and D→4→D with a total distance of 23. Note that the distance increases as we increase the number of vehicles.

We will now look at a few scenarios where we impose vehicle capacities on the vehicles. We will look at the case with $V = 2$, and let us assume that the vehicle capacity W of each vehicle is 20.

The additional constraints from Eqs. (11.9) to (11.12) can also be handled in a similar way and can be solved using Excel Solver.

Excel Solver is powerful enough to handle a few VRP formulations as shown here. Most of the formulations assume a few relaxations and are good for small-scale problems.

Now we will present another VRP formulation as a flow problem and its mixed integer programming formulation. Let

n = Number of points (let 1 denote the depot and 2 to n denote the customer points),
d_{ij} = Distance between points i and j,
D_i = Demand of the customer i,
C = Capacity of the vehicle.

Let

X_{ij} = 1 if a vehicle goes from point i to point j,
f_{ij} = Number of units in a while going from point i to point j.

Then the problem becomes

$$\text{Minimize} \sum_{i=0}^{n}\sum_{j=1}^{n} d_{ij}X_{ij}$$

Subject to

$$\sum_{j=1}^{n} X_{ij} = 1 \forall i = 2,\ldots,n$$

$$\sum_{j=1}^{n} X_{ji} = 1 \forall i = 2,\ldots,n$$

$$\sum_{j=1}^{n} f_{ji} - \sum_{j=1}^{n} f_{ij} = D_i \forall i = 2,\ldots,n$$

$$f_{ij} \le CX_{ij} \forall i, j = 1,2,\ldots,n$$

$$X_{ij} \in \{0,1\} \forall i, j = 1,2,\ldots,n$$

Figures 11.4 and 11.5 present the Excel implementation of the same.

Xij	0	1	2	3	4	5	Out
0	0	0	1	0	0	1	2
1	1	0	0	0	0	0	1
2	0	1	0	0	0	0	1
3	0	0	0	0	1	0	1
4	1	0	0	0	0	0	1
5	0	0	0	1	0	0	1
Incoming	2	1	1	1	1	1	

Capacity C	20

fij	0	1	2	3	4	5	Outflow	Inflow	Balance	Demand
0	0	0	20	0	0	20	40	4	-36	
1	4	0	0	0	0	0	4	12	8	8
2	0	12	0	0	0	0	12	20	8	8
3	0	0	0	0	6	0	6	12	6	6
4	0	0	0	0	0	0	0	6	6	6
5	0	0	0	12	0	0	12	20	8	8
Incoming	4	12	20	12	6	20				

FIGURE 11.4 Integer programming formulation and solution of VRP as a flow problem-screen 1.

Linking	0	1	2	3	4	5
0	0	0	0	0	0	0
1	-16	0	0	0	0	0
2	0	-8	0	0	0	0
3	0	0	0	0	-14	0
4	-20	0	0	0	0	0
5	0	0	0	-8	0	0

dij	0	1	2	3	4	5
0	0	4	3	5	2	3
1	4	0	2	7	3	1
2	3	2	0	7	3	8
3	5	7	7	0	3	5
4	2	3	3	3	0	4
5	3	1	8	5	4	0

Total Distance	22

FIGURE 11.5 Integer programming formulation and solution of VRP as a flow problem-screen 2.

We see from Figure 11.4 that the routes are given by 0→2→1→0 and 0→5→3→4→0 with a total distance of 22.

As we see here, the problem size may be very large if we deal with more points. Here itself, the number of variables is $6^2 + 6^2 = 72$ for X_{ij} and f_{ij} for six points. Imagine if we dealt with a problem of 40 points. This will then be in the range of more than 3000 variables. The usual Solver function in Excel may not handle this. And so, in such large problems, Open Solver (which is available free on the site www.opensolver.org) can be quite useful.

11.3 BRANCH AND BOUND METHOD FOR SOLVING ROUTING PROBLEMS

We will revisit Table 11.2 and use it as Table 11.6 with a "—" for all the diagonal elements for the customer points and for all the blocks of cells for vertices 6 and 7 for the penalty method of the branch and bound approach.

TABLE 11.6 Example for using branch and bound method for VRP

		Customer					Vehicle	
		1	2	3	4	5	6	7
Customer	1	—	2	7	3	1	4	4
	2	2	—	7	3	8	3	3
	3	7	7	—	3	5	5	5
	4	3	3	3	—	4	2	2
	5	1	8	5	4	—	3	3
Vehicle	6	4	3	5	2	3	—	—
	7	4	3	5	2	3	—	—

We will establish the lower bound for the branch and bound method by looking at the sum of row minimums and column minimums. The reduced matrices are given in Tables 11.7 and 11.8. The labels are removed for easy reading.

TABLE 11.7 Reduced matrix of Table 11.6 after subtracting row minima

	Reduced Matrix after Subtracting Row Minimum							
	1	2	3	4	5	6	7	Row Minimum
1	—	1	6	2	0	3	3	1
2	0	—	5	1	6	1	1	2
3	4	4	—	0	2	2	2	3
4	1	1	1	—	2	0	0	2
5	0	7	4	3	—	2	2	1
6	2	1	3	0	1	—	—	2
7	2	1	3	0	1	—	—	2

The total sum of the row minimum is 13.

TABLE 11.8 Reduced matrix of Table 11.7 after subtracting column minima

	Reduced Matrix after Subtracting Column Minimum						
	1	2	3	4	5	6	7
1	—	0	5	2	0	3	3
2	0	—	4	1	6	1	1
3	4	3	—	0	2	2	2
4	1	0	0	—	2	0	0
5	0	6	3	3	—	2	2
6	2	0	2	0	1	—	—
7	2	0	2	0	1	—	—
Column Minimum	—	1	1	—	—	—	—

The total sum of the column minimum is 2. Hence, the lower bound (LB) is 13 + 2 = 15. Penalties for assignable zeros are shown in shaded colors within brackets in Table 11.9.

TABLE 11.9 Penalties for assignable zeroes

	1	2	3	4	5	6	7
1	—	0 (0)	5	2	0(1)	3	3
2	0(1)	—	4	1	6	1	1
3	4	3	—	0(2)	2	2	2
4	1	0(0)	0(2)	—	2	0(1)	0(1)
5	0(2)	6	3	3	—	2	2
6	2	0(0)	2	0(0)	1	—	—
7	2	0(0)	2	0(0)	1	—	—

Maximum penalties are seen in cells (3, 4) and (5, 1). We can choose either of them. We will choose, say, cell (5, 1) and branch off on two branches $X_{51} = 0$ and $X_{51} = 1$. If we branch off on X51 = 0, the lower bound will increase by 2 more, which is the maximum penalty for (5, 1). If we branch off on X51 = 1, then we will block row 5 and column 1 and also cell (1, 5) with a "—" to avoid a subtour and proceed as before for penalties for further branches. The branches are shown in Figure 11.6.

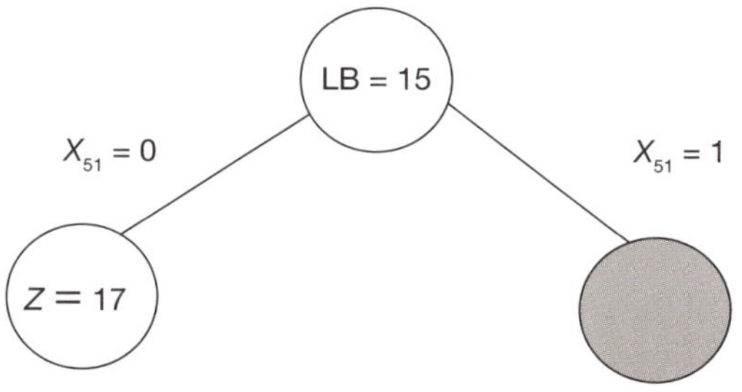

FIGURE 11.6 Branching with $X_{51} = 0$ and $X_{51} = 1$ with a LB of 15.

The modified reduced matrix is given in Table 11.10.

TABLE 11.10 Modified reduced matrix of Table 11.9

	2	3	4	5	6	7
1	0	5	2	—	3	3
2	—	4	1	6	1	1
3	3	—	0	2	2	2
4	0	0	—	2	0	0
6	0	2	0	1	—	—
7	0	2	0	1	—	—

We check if all the rows and columns have assignable zeros. The row for vertex 2 does not have assignable zeros, and so we subtract the row minimum of 1 from all the elements and the resultant matrix is given in Table 11.11.

TABLE 11.11 Establishing assignable zeroes through row minima

	2	3	4	5	6	7
1	0	5	2	—	3	3
2	—	3	0	5	0	0
3	3	—	0	2	2	2
4	0	0	—	2	0	0
6	0	2	0	1	—	—
7	0	2	0	1	—	—

We check the columns for assignable zeros and notice that the column for vertex 5 does not have it. We subtract the column minimum of 1 from this column, and the resultant matrix is given in Table 11.12.

TABLE 11.12 Establishing assignable zeroes through column minima

	2	3	4	5	6	7
1	0	5	2	—	3	3
2	—	3	0	4	0	0
3	3	—	0	1	2	2
4	0	0	—	1	0	0
6	0	2	0	0	—	—
7	0	2	0	0	—	—

Therefore, the total sum 2 of the row and column minimums will be added to the current lower bound and will increase to 15 + 2 = 17 for the shaded circle of Figure 11.1. We decide to branch off from this vertex because usually we branch off on the branch where the decision variables are assumed to be 1 in this method as a convenient approach. We calculate the penalties and decide the branches. Penalties for assignable zeros are shown in shaded colors within brackets in Table 11.13 for Table 11.12.

TABLE 11.13 Penalties for the Table 11.12

	2	3	4	5	6	7
1	0(2)	5	2	—	3	3
2	—	3	0(0)	4	0(0)	0(0)
3	3	—	0(1)	1	2	2
4	0(0)	0(2)	—	1	0(0)	0(0)
6	0(0)	2	0(0)	0(0)	—	—
7	0(0)	2	0(0)	0(0)	—	—

Since most of the VRPs are solved using integer programming formulations, the branch and bound method is a popular approach to solve such problems. But the main drawback of such an approach is the computational complexities for large-scale routing problems. Although they may yield exact solutions, for large-scale problems, very often heuristics are found useful and give workable solutions.

Maximum penalties are seen in cells (1, 3) and (4, 3). We can choose either of them. We will choose, say, cell (1, 2) and branch off on two branches $X_{12} = 0$ and $X_{21} = 1$. If we branch off on $X_{12} = 0$, the lower bound will increase by 2 more, which is the maximum penalty for (1, 2). If we branch off on $X_{12} = 1$, then we will block row 1 and column 2 and also the cell (2, 1) with a "—" to avoid a subtour. But cell (2, 1) is not here, and so we ignore it. We proceed as before for the penalties for further branches. The branches are shown in Figure 11.7.

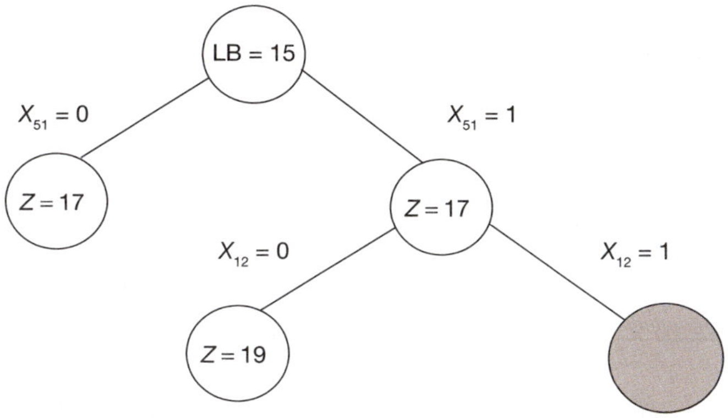

FIGURE 11.7 Branching off from $X_{51} = 1$ with $X_{12} = 0$ and $X_{12} = 1$ with a LB of 17.

The procedure is repeated until we see that a feasible solution is obtained, and other branches are fathomed. We skip those steps and leave it to the reader to complete this. At the end, we will have the complete evaluation as shown in Figure 11.8.

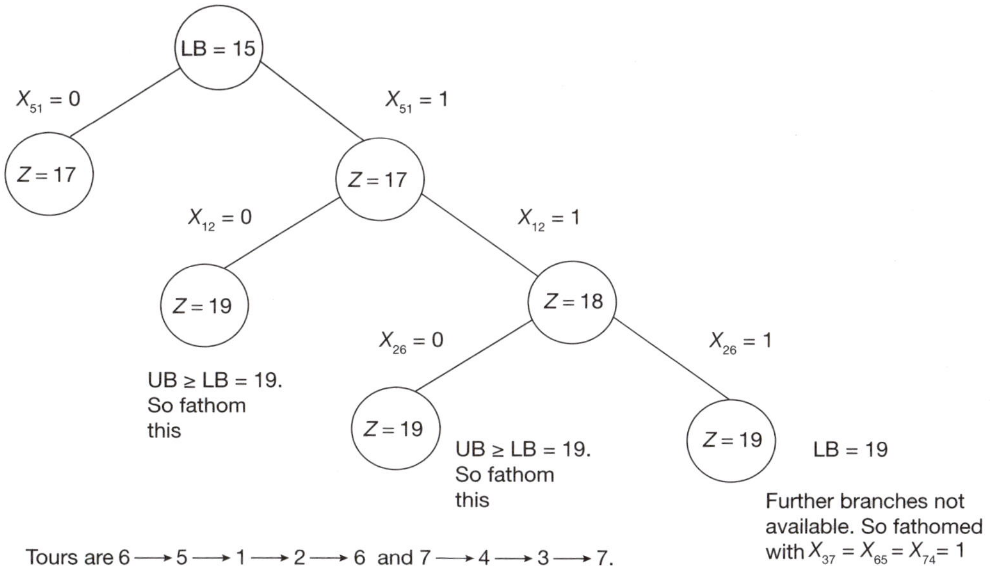

FIGURE 11.8 Final branches and bounds to establish the tours for the VRP.

We see the that tours are 6→5→1→2 → 6 and 7→4→3→7. We will replace vertices 6 and 7 with depot D, and so the tours become D→5→1→2 →D and D→4→3→D, which is similar to what we obtained by using Excel Solver with a total distance of 19.

Now we will see what happens to the routes if we impose the vehicle capacities stated in Table 11.1 along with the given customer demands at vertices 1 to 5. Suppose we have two vehicles with a capacity of 20 each. We, therefore, have a total demand of 36 and a total capacity of 40. We will present a popular heuristic known as the Clarke–Wright savings algorithm for solving a typical problem described here.

11.4 CLARKE–WRIGHT SAVINGS ALGORITHM FOR SOLVING ROUTING PROBLEMS

Assume that the depot is D and is so denoted (usually as vertex 0). Consider any pair of customers at vertices i and j with the respective distances $d_{\mathrm{D}i}$ and $d_{\mathrm{D}j}$ from depot 0 and the distance d_{ij} between them, as shown in Figure 11.9.

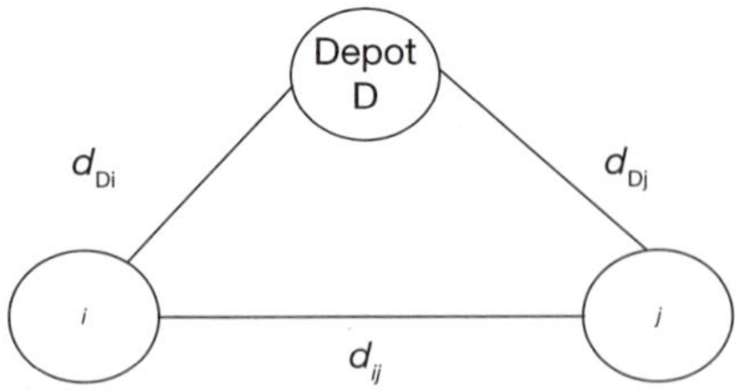

FIGURE 11.9 Representation of depot and two customers with their respective distances between them.

In the worst case, the route will cover each customer separately for all the customer vertices. So, in this case, the total distance that will be required to serve customers at *i* and *j* will be $2d_{Di} + 2d_{Dj}$. However, if the route can include both *i* and *j* from depot D, the distance will be $d_{Di} + d_{ij} + d_{Dj}$. So, the saving from combining *i* and *j* in the route will be $(2d_{Di} + 2d_{Dj}) - (d_{Di} + d_{ij} + d_{Dj})$, which is referred to as s_{ij}. Therefore,

$$s_{ij} = d_{Di} + d_{Dj} - d_{ij}$$

Sample Savings Calculation for Table 11.1 for a pair of customers at 1 and 2

The distance from depot 0 to the customer at 1 is 4, the distance from depot D (i.e., vertex 0) to the customer at 2 is 3, and that between 1 and 2 is 2. The total distance that will be traveled if the vehicle had served 1 and 2 separately is 8 + 6 = 14 km. If 1 and 2 are combined, the total distance to be traveled is 4 + 2 + 3 = 9 km only. Hence, the total saving is (14 – 9) = 5 km. In other words, $S_{12} = d_{01} + d_{02} - d_{12} = 4 + 3 - 2 = 5$ km.

11.4.1 Algorithm

The Clarke and Wright savings algorithm is probably the most popular heuristic to solve a VRP and is practical to apply in real-life applications. Most of the routing decisions in practice adopt this method and use it for the Milk-run deliveries for distribution problems. It is possible to implement this in a computer and generate what-if scenarios for it.

Step 1: Calculate the savings $s(i, j) = d(D, i) + d(D, j) - d(i, j)$ for every pair (i, j) of customer demand points.

Step 2: Rank the savings $s(i, j)$ and create a savings list, which lists them in descending order, that is, from the highest to the lowest in magnitude. Process the savings list beginning with the topmost entry on the list (the largest $s(i, j)$).

Step 3: For the savings $s(i, j)$ under consideration, include link (i, j) in a route if no route constraints are violated through the inclusion of (i, j) in a route, and if

a. *Either*, neither *i* nor *j* have already been assigned to a route, in which case a new route is initiated, including both *i* and *j*.
b. *Or*, exactly *one* of the two points (*i* or *j*) has already been included in an existing route and that point is not interior to that route (a point is interior to a route if it is not adjacent to the depot D in the order of traversal of points), in which case the link (i, j) is added to that same route.
c. *Or, both i* and *j* have already been included in two different existing routes and neither point is interior to its route, in which case the two routes are merged.

Step 4: If the savings list $s(i, j)$ has not been exhausted, return to Step 3, processing the next entry in the list; otherwise, ***stop***. The solution to the VRP consists of the routes created during Step 3.

Any customer points that have not been assigned to a route during Step 3 must be served by a vehicle route that begins at depot D, visits the unassigned point, and returns to D.

We will revisit Table 11.1 and apply this Clarke–Wright algorithm. We can compute the savings for all the pairs of customers at 1 to 5 as follows.

$s_{12} = 4 + 3 - 2 = 5$
$s_{13} = 4 + 5 - 7 = 2$
$s_{14} = 4 + 2 - 3 = 3$
$s_{15} = 4 + 3 - 1 = 6$
$s_{23} = 3 + 5 - 7 = 1$

$s_{24} = 3 + 2 - 3 = 2$
$s_{25} = 3 + 3 - 8 = -2$
$s_{34} = 5 + 2 - 3 = 4$
$s_{35} = 5 + 3 - 5 = 3$
$s_{45} = 2 + 3 - 4 = 1$

Savings in order:

$s_{15} = 6$
$s_{12} = 5$
$s_{34} = 4$
$s_{14}, s_{35} = 3$
$s_{13}, s_{24} = 2$
$s_{45} = 1$
$s_{25} = -2$

We are given the customer demands at 1 to 5 as 8, 8, 6, 6, and 8, respectively, and the two vehicles with 20 as capacities.

s_{15} 0→1→5→0 total demand = 16
s_{12} If we add 2 to this route, then the demand would exceed 20 and so we cannot add this. Hence 0→1→5→0 will be one tour as of now. Since we have frozen 1 and 5 now, the second saving $s_{12} = 5$ will be of no use to consider and we move to the next savings s_{34}.
s_{34} This is possible as the total demand is only 12 and capacity is 20; this is a feasible tour as 0→3→4→0 with $d = 12$.
s_{14} If we add 4, whose demand is 6, to the first tour 0→1→5→0, it will exceed the capacity and, hence, is not useful. We cannot add to the tour of 0→3→4→0 as 1 is already added to the first tour.
s_{35} Since both 3 and 5 are already part of the tour earlier, 4 and 5 cannot be added. s_{13} is not useful as they are already added to the previous tours.
s_{24} Is possible as adding 2 to the tour 0→3→4→0 will exactly equal the capacity of 20. So, 0→2→4→3→0 is a tour with $d = 20$.

Hence, there are two tours 0→1→5→0 with a demand of 16 and 0→2→4→3→0 with a demand of 20. The total savings will be 6 + 6 = 12.

We observe that while merging the tours, we ignored quite a few savings while picking up, and to this effect, this algorithm is more of a greedy algorithm and has its limitations, although it is efficient. This algorithm usually gives a good solution. Another heuristic by Holmes and Parker gives an improved solution in many cases. It tries to explore more options, which may, in some cases, or may not improve the solution given by the Clarke–Wright algorithm. We will explain this with our example here. In our steps of picking trips, we started with the best savings of 6 given by the edge 1-5. We try to start saying that we will not consider this edge and try to start with the second best edge 1-2 with a saving of 5. Then the steps go like this:

s_{15} We will not consider this.
s_{12} This is feasible as the demand is 16 and less than the capacity of 20. Hence 0→1→2→0 will be one tour as of now.
s_{34} This is possible as the total demand is only 12 and capacity is 20; this is a feasible tour as 0→3→4→0 with $d = 12$.
s_{14} If we add 4, whose demand is 6, to the first tour 0→1→2→0, it will exceed the capacity and hence is not useful. Cannot add to the tour of 0→3→4→0 as 1 is already added to the first tour.
s_{35} Feasible, since adding 5 to the tour 0→3→4→0 exactly equals the capacity. Hence, the tour is 0→5→3→4→0.
s_{24} Not required as 2 and 5 are already in two different tours.

Hence, there are two tours 0→1→2→0 with a demand of 16 and 0→5→3→4→0 with a demand of 20. The total savings will be 5 + 7 = 12. So, we got two tours that have the same total distance of 22 and a saving of 12. In some cases, this approach may give some better solutions as well. This is shown as a branching strategy in Figure 11.10.

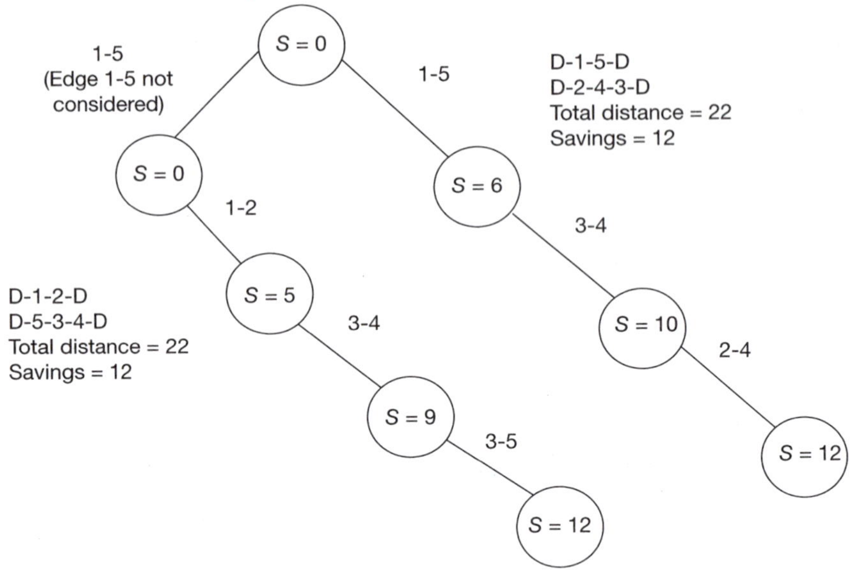

FIGURE 11.10 Branching strategy using Holmes and Parker's heuristic.

We can explore further too. We can now say we will not consider the second best 1-2 and check for any other possibility. If we do that, then the options will be D→1→3→4→D and D→2→5→D, but this is not a good solution as the saving will be 7 + (−2) = 5. If we explore further, we may get solutions that are inferior to this. The scope for such exploration is good in bigger problems where the savings list is fairly good and larger.

11.4.2 Clarke–Wright Savings Method for TSP

We mentioned earlier that the Clarke–Wright savings algorithm can also be a good heuristic for solving a TSP. We will describe the same for the example we took for TSP in Chapter 10 in Table 10.1 (reproduced in Table 11.14).

TABLE 11.14 Example for TSP using Clarke and Wright Savings Method

	1	2	3	4	5
1	0	8	4	9	9
2	8	0	6	7	10
3	4	6	0	5	6
4	9	7	5	0	4
5	9	10	6	4	0

Let us assume that the center is vertex 3. The savings can be computed with the center as 3 for all the other vertices. The savings are given in descending order.

$s_{45} = 7$
$s_{24} = 4$
$s_{12} = 2$
$s_{25} = 2$
$s_{15} = 1$
$s_{14} = 0$

So, the sequence will be 3→5→4→3, then 3→5→4→2→3, then 3→5→4→2→1→3, which completes the Hamiltonian cycle with a total distance of 29. This is also the optimal solution for the TSP.

11.4.3 Clarke–Wright Savings Algorithm Using XY Coordinates

We will explain the Clarke–Wright savings algorithm with another example where the depot and customer locations are available as XY coordinates.

The manager of a grocery chain, also selling online, has 12 orders that are to be delivered to customers. The location and order size for each customer is shown in Table 11.15.

TABLE 11.15 Example of a grocery store for Clarke-Wright savings method

Customer/DC	X-Coordinate	Y-Coordinate	Order Size
DC	0	0	
1	–12	0	74
2	–5	6	55
3	–15	7	68
4	–12	9	109
5	–3	15	81
6	0	20	41
7	2	17	74
8	4	7	52
9	6	1	80
10	6	15	69
11	7	20	103
12	9	7	75

The store has five trucks capable of carrying up to 225 units each. The distance matrix and the savings matrix for this data are given in Tables 11.16 and 11.17.

TABLE 11.16 Distance matrix

	DC	1	2	3	4	5	6	7	8	9	10	11	12
DC	0.00	12.00	7.81	16.55	15.00	15.30	20.00	17.12	8.06	6.08	16.16	21.19	11.40
1	12.00	0.00	9.22	7.62	9.00	17.49	23.32	22.02	17.46	18.03	23.43	27.59	22.14
2	7.81	9.22	0.00	10.05	7.62	9.22	14.87	13.04	9.06	12.08	14.21	18.44	14.04
3	16.55	7.62	10.05	0.00	3.61	14.42	19.85	19.72	19.00	21.84	22.47	25.55	24.00
4	15.00	9.00	7.62	3.61	0.00	10.82	16.28	16.12	16.12	19.70	18.97	21.95	21.10
5	15.30	17.49	9.22	14.42	10.82	0.00	5.83	5.39	10.63	16.64	9.00	11.18	14.42
6	20.00	23.32	14.87	19.85	16.28	5.83	0.00	3.61	13.60	19.92	7.81	7.00	15.81
7	17.12	22.02	13.04	19.72	16.12	5.39	3.61	0.00	10.20	16.49	4.47	5.83	12.21
8	8.06	17.46	9.06	19.00	16.12	10.63	13.60	10.20	0.00	6.32	8.25	13.34	5.00
9	6.08	18.03	12.08	21.84	19.70	16.64	19.92	16.49	6.32	0.00	14.00	19.03	6.71
10	16.16	23.43	14.21	22.47	18.97	9.00	7.81	4.47	8.25	14.00	0.00	5.10	8.54
11	21.19	27.59	18.44	25.55	21.95	11.18	7.00	5.83	13.34	19.03	5.10	0.00	13.15
12	11.40	22.14	14.04	24.00	21.10	14.42	15.81	12.21	5.00	6.71	8.54	13.15	0.00

TABLE 11.17 Savings matrix

	2	3	4	5	6	7	8	9	10	11	12
1	10.59	20.94	18.00	9.80	8.68	7.09	2.60	0.06	4.72	5.60	1.27
2		14.31	15.19	13.89	12.94	11.89	6.82	1.81	9.75	10.56	5.18
3			27.95	17.43	16.70	13.95	5.62	0.80	10.24	12.19	3.95
4				19.48	18.72	15.99	6.94	1.39	12.18	14.24	5.31
5					29.47	27.03	12.73	4.74	22.45	25.31	12.28
6						33.51	14.46	6.16	28.35	34.19	15.59
7							14.98	6.71	28.80	32.48	16.31
8								7.82	15.97	15.91	14.46
9									8.24	8.25	10.78
10										32.25	19.01
11											19.44

The savings along with links are presented in Table 11.18.

TABLE 11.18 Savings along with respective Links

Link	Saving	Link	Saving	Link	Saving
1 2	10.59	3 5	17.43	5 12	12.28
1 3	20.94	3 6	16.70	6 7	33.51
1 4	18.00	3 7	13.95	6 8	14.46
1 5	9.80	3 8	5.62	6 9	6.16
1 6	8.68	3 9	0.80	6 10	28.35
1 7	7.09	3 10	10.24	6 11	34.19
1 8	2.60	3 11	12.19	6 12	15.59
1 9	0.06	3 12	3.95	7 8	14.98
1 10	4.72	4 5	19.48	7 9	6.71
1 11	5.60	4 6	18.72	7 10	28.80
1 12	1.27	4 7	15.99	7 11	32.48
2 3	14.31	4 8	6.94	7 12	16.31
2 4	15.19	4 9	1.39	8 9	7.82
2 5	13.89	4 10	12.18	8 10	15.97
2 6	12.94	4 11	14.24	8 11	15.91
2 7	11.89	4 12	5.31	8 12	14.46
2 8	6.82	5 6	29.47	9 10	8.24
2 9	1.81	5 7	27.03	9 11	8.25
2 10	9.75	5 8	12.73	9 12	10.78
2 11	10.56	5 9	4.74	10 11	32.25
2 12	5.18	5 10	22.45	10 12	19.01
3 4	27.95	5 11	25.31	11 12	19.44

The analysis and the determination of the routes is presented in Table 11.19.

TABLE 11.19 Determining routes based on savings

Link	Saving	Observation		Load	Links Added	Route	Distance
6 11	34.19	144	Feasible		6 11		
6 7	33.51	74	Can add customer 7	218	7 6 11	**DC-7-6-11-DC**	48.92
7 11	32.48	Not feasible					
10 11	32.25	Not feasible					
5 6	29.47	Not feasible					
7 10	28.80	Not feasible					
6 10	28.35	Not feasible					
3 4	27.95	177	Feasible	177	3 4	**DC-3-4-DC**	35.16
5 7	27.03	Not feasible					
5 11	25.31	Not feasible					
5 10	22.45	150	Feasible				
1 3	20.94	Not feasible					
4 5	19.48	Not feasible					
11 12	19.44	Not feasible					
10 12	19.01	75	Can add customer 12	225	5, 10, 12	**DC-5-10-12-DC**	44.24
4 6	18.72	Not feasible					
1 4	18.00	Not feasible					
3 5	17.43	Not feasible					
3 6	16.70	Not feasible					
7 12	16.31	Not feasible					
4 7	15.99	Not feasible					
8 10	15.97	Not feasible					
8 11	15.91	Not feasible					
6 12	15.59	Not feasible					
2 4	15.19	Not feasible					
7 8	14.98	Not feasible					
8 12	14.46	Not feasible					
6 8	14.46	Not feasible					
2 3	14.31	Not feasible					
4 11	14.24	Not feasible					
3 7	13.95	Not feasible					
2 5	13.89	Not feasible					
2 6	12.94	Not feasible					
5 8	12.73	Not feasible					

(*Continued*)

TABLE 11.19 (Continued)

Link	Saving	Observation	Load	Links Added	Route	Distance
5 12	12.28	Not feasible				
3 11	12.19	Not feasible				
4 10	12.18	Not feasible				
2 7	11.89	Not feasible				
9 12	10.78	Not feasible				
1 2	10.59	129 Feasible				
2 11	10.56	Not feasible				
3 10	10.24	Not feasible				
1 5	9.80	Not feasible				
2 10	9.75	Not feasible				
1 6	8.68	Not feasible				
9 11	8.25	Not feasible				
9 10	8.24	Not feasible				
8 9	7.82	Not feasible				
1 7	7.09	Not feasible				
4 8	6.94	Not feasible				
2 8	6.82	52 Can add customer 8	181	1 2 8	**DC-1-2-8-DC**	38.34
7 9	6.71	Not feasible				
6 9	6.16	Not feasible				
3 8	5.62	Not feasible				
1 11	5.60	Not feasible				
4 12	5.31	Not feasible				
2 12	5.18	Not feasible				
5 9	4.74	Not feasible				
1 10	4.72	Not feasible				
3 12	3.95	Not feasible				
1 8	2.60	Not feasible				
2 9	1.81	Not feasible				
4 9	1.39	Not feasible				
1 12	1.27	Not feasible				
3 9	0.80	Not feasible				
1 9	0.06	Not feasible				
9	Separate route		80		**DC-9-DC**	12.16
					Total distance	**178.82**

If we apply Holmes and Parker's improvement heuristic, we get a solution of a total distance of 179.52, which is marginally higher than the one we got through Clarke–Wright savings. The steps are shown in Table 11.20.

TABLE 11.20 Steps of Holmes and Parker's heuristic

Holmes and Parker's Improvement							
Link	**Saving**	**Observation**		**Load**	**Links Added**	**Route**	**Distance**
6 11	34.19	**Feasible but decide not to consider**					
6 7	33.51	115			6 7		
7 11	32.48	Can add 11	103	218	6 7 11	**DC-6-7-11-DC**	50.63
10 11	32.25	x					
5 6	29.47	x					
7 10	28.80	x					
6 10	28.35	x					
3 4	27.95	177		177	3 4	**DC-3-4-DC**	35.16
5 7	27.03	x					
5 11	25.31	x					
5 10	22.45	150			5 10		
1 3	20.94	x					
4 5	19.48	x					
11 12	19.44	x					
10 12	19.01	Can add 12	75	225	5 10 12	**DC-5-10-12-DC**	44.24
4 6	18.72	x					
1 4	18.00	x					
3 5	17.43	x					
3 6	16.70	x					
7 12	16.31	x					
4 7	15.99	x					
8 10	15.97	x					
8 11	15.91	x					
6 12	15.59	x					
2 4	15.19	x					
7 8	14.98	x					
8 12	14.46	x					
6 8	14.46	x					
2 3	14.31	x					
4 11	14.24	x					
3 7	13.95	x					
2 5	13.89	x					

(*Continued*)

TABLE 11.20 (Continued)

Holmes and Parker's Improvement						
Link	Saving	Observation	Load	Links Added	Route	Distance
2 6	12.94	x				
5 8	12.73	x				
5 12	12.28	x				
3 11	12.19	x				
4 10	12.18	x				
2 7	11.89	x				
9 12	10.78	x				
1 2	10.59	129	129	1 2	**DC-1-2-DC**	29.03
2 11	10.56	x				
3 10	10.24	x				
1 5	9.80	x				
2 10	9.75	x				
1 6	8.68	x				
9 11	8.25	x				
9 10	8.24	x				
8 9	7.82	132	132	8 9	**DC-8-9-DC**	20.46
1 7	7.09	x				
4 8	6.94	x				
2 8	6.82	x				
7 9	6.71	x				
6 9	6.16	x				
3 8	5.62	x				
1 11	5.60	x				
4 12	5.31	x				
2 12	5.18	x				
5 9	4.74	x				
1 10	4.72	x				
3 12	3.95	x				
1 8	2.60	x				
2 9	1.81	x				
4 9	1.39	x				
1 12	1.27	x				
3 9	0.80	x				
1 9	0.06	x				
					Total distance	**179.52**

We can keep exploring further possibilities though they may or may not have improvements. For example, if we ignore the first two links that are maximum and further explore the solution, we get a total distance of 179.55, which is again very close to what we got earlier. We can ignore the first three and explore further.

11.5 | SWEEP HEURISTIC FOR SOLVING VRPS

While discussing VRPs, we observed that capacitated VRPs (CVRPs) with additional constraints like time windows would be too cumbersome to solve, and hence there are many heuristics that are popular. We discussed a few exact approaches and a heuristic method using the Clarke–Wright savings method. We will now describe the sweep algorithm, which often uses commonsense and makes it convenient to construct routes based on capacities. This method is very convenient if we use the coordinates of the points in an XY graph.

The sweep Method is a very simple logical heuristic where a VRP can be solved. It gives a sensible clustering of routes for implementing schedules and offers very practical solutions although it may not give optimal routes.

11.5.1 The Sweep (SW) Algorithm

The Sweep algorithm is the least complex grouping strategy for CVRPs. Cluster formation begins from 0° and, therefore, propels toward 360° to allot every customer under various vehicles while keeping up the capacity of a vehicle. This kind of sweeping is named forward sweep. The clustering direction is clockwise, which means that the grouping begins at 0° in the backward sweep, and at that point it progresses calculation from 360° to 0°. The common recipe for computing the polar angle of customers with respect to a warehouse is

$$\theta = \tan^{-1}\left(\frac{y}{x}\right) \tag{11.13}$$

where θ is depot/customer, that is, angle of a node; x, y are coordinates of customers. Algorithm 1 shows the steps of SW.

Algorithm 1: Sweep

Initialization

1. Calculate the polar angle of each customer using Eq. (11.13).
2. Sort customers according to their increasing order of polar angles.

Clustering

1. Set $C = 1$.
2. Begin sweeping customers by expanding polar angles and allocating customers to the present cluster.
3. Stop the sweep when including the following client would violate the vehicle capacity limit.
4. Set $C = C + 1$.
5. Repeat steps 2–4 until each customer has been allotted.

11.5.2 The Sweep Nearest Algorithm

The Sweep Nearest (SN) algorithm combines the nearest neighbor algorithm with the classical SW. SW groups the customers exclusively by the polar angle. There are chances that the customers are generally isolated but yet have less precise distinctions, and they might be assembled in a similar group. This diminishes the optimality of the solution cluster. To determine this issue, SN initially appoints to a vehicle the customer with the smallest polar angle among the rest of the customers and afterward finds the closest stop to those officially relegated and then embeds that customer. Figure 11.11 shows a graphical representation of the clustering with SW and SN for a sample scenario of CVRP customer points. In SW (Figure 11.11a), points with relatively large distances are inserted into the same cluster due to a closer polar angle. On the other hand, the nearest customers have a place with a similar group in SN as shown in Figure 11.11b. For such cases, SN will give a better CVRP solution than SW.

Algorithm 2: SN

Initialization

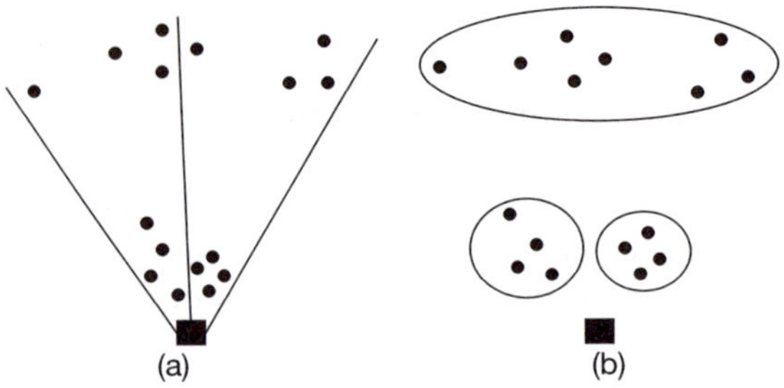

FIGURE 11.11 Graphical representation of the clustering with SW and SN for a sample scenario of CVRP customer points.

As of sweep algorithm, that is, Algorithm 1.

Clustering

1. Set $C = 1$.
2. Select the smallest angle customer and assign to a cluster.
3. Select a customer who is nearest to the already inserted customers and insert into the cluster. Continue clustering until vehicle capacity is not violated.
4. Set $C = C + 1$.
5. Repeat steps 2–4 until each customer has been allotted.

11.5.3 Distance-based Sweep Nearest Algorithm

This section describes the proposed Distance-Based Sweep Nearest (DSN) clustering method and mentions its differences from SW and SN. SW starts clustering with the customer having the smallest polar angle. SN also starts clustering with the smallest angle customer but grows a cluster selecting its nearest ones. In both SW and SN, the distant customers from the origin may be inserted later. In such a case, a cluster (i.e., new route) with the remaining one or few far distance customer(s) incurs a relatively large CVRP cost. On the one hand, cluster formation starting from far distance customers is the alternative and the better option. In such cases, the customer closer to the depot may remain for new clusters. A new cluster with closer customers is cost effective. Moreover, the remaining closer customers may be inserted into the existing clusters without increasing costs. On these motivations, the proposed DSN starts cluster formation with the farthest customer from the depot and completes it like the nearest neighbor approach. When a cluster finishes, the next cluster starts with the farthest among the remaining ones. DSN does not consider the polar angles of customers at all; it is only concerned with the Euclidean distance of the customers. Algorithm 3 shows the steps of DSN.

Algorithm 3: DSN

Initialization

1. Compute the Euclidean distance of each customer from the depot.
2. Sort the customers according to the descending order of their distances.

Clustering

1. Set $C = 1$.
2. Start a formation for the cluster assigning the farthest customer from the depot.
3. Select a customer nearest to the already inserted customers and insert them into the cluster. Continue clustering until vehicle capacity is not violated.

4. Set $C = C + 1$.
5. Repeat Steps 2–4 until all customers have been assigned.

We will revisit the example in Table 11.15. We will use the three types of sweep algorithms to construct the routes.

11.5.4 Sweep Algorithm (Algorithm 1)

We compute the polar angles as shown in Table 11.21 and arrange the customers from the largest polar angle to the smallest and sweep clockwise from the largest positive polar angle, as shown in Figure 11.12.

TABLE 11.21 Computation of polar sngles and listing in the descending order

Customer/DC	X-Coordinate	Y-Coordinate	Order Size	$\theta = \tan^{-1}(y/x)$
DC	0	0		—
1	–12	0	74	0.00
2	–5	6	55	–0.88
3	–15	7	68	–0.44
4	–12	9	109	–0.64
5	–3	15	81	–1.37
6	0.001	20	41	1.57
7	2	17	74	1.45
8	4	7	52	1.05
9	6	1	80	0.17
10	6	15	69	1.19
11	7	20	103	1.23
12	9	7	75	0.66

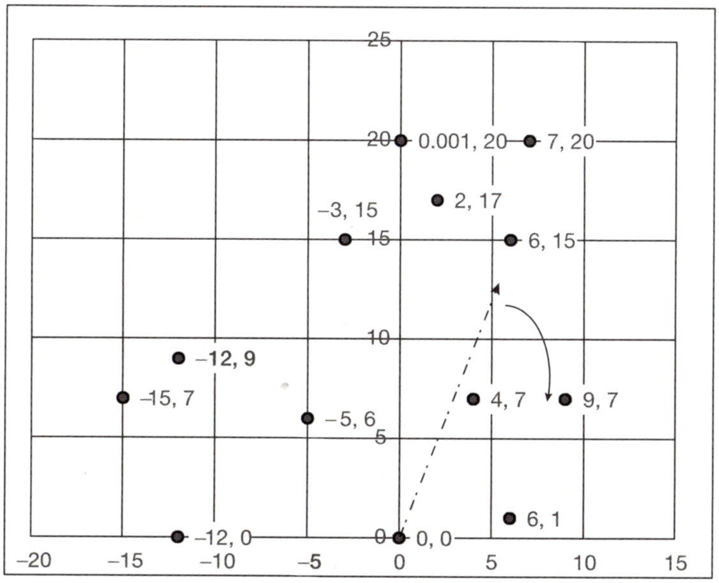

FIGURE 11.12 Graphical representation of the polar angles.

We carry out steps 1 to 5 of Algorithm 1, and the results are shown in Figure 11.13.

Customer/DC	X coordinate	Y coordinate	Order size	θ =tan-1(y/x)	Cumulative Loads	Clusters	Customers in the Sweep and each Cluster
6	0.001	20	41	1.57	41	C=1	6.7.11
7	2	17	74	1.45	115		
11	7	20	103	1.23	218		
10	6	15	69	1.19	69	C=2	10,8,12,
8	4	7	52	1.05	121		
12	9	7	75	0.66	196		
9	6	1	80	0.17	80	C=3	9,1,3
DC	**0**	**0**					
1	-12	0	74	0.00	74		
3	-15	7	68	-0.44	142		
4	-12	9	109	-0.64	109	C=4	4,2
2	-5	6	55	-0.88	164		
5	-3	15	81	-1.37	81	C=5	5

FIGURE 11.13 Computations using Sweep Algorithm-1.

We see that for each cluster, we can determine a TSP tour to get the best sequence, and the same is done for Figure 11.13. The routes and the respective distances are calculated using the depot and the customer coordinates and are shown in Table 11.22 and Figure 11.14.

TABLE 11.22 Routes using Sweep Algorthm-1.

Cluster	Customer in Sweep and Each Cluster	Route	Route Distance
C = 1	**6, 7, 11**	**DC-7-6-11-DC**	**48.92**
C = 2	**10, 8, 12**	**DC-10-8-12-DC**	**36.25**
C = 3	**9, 1, 3**	**DC-9-13-DC**	**47.54**
C = 4	**4, 2**	**DC-4-2-DC**	**30.43**
C = 5	**5**	**DC-5-DC**	**30.6**
Total			**193.74**

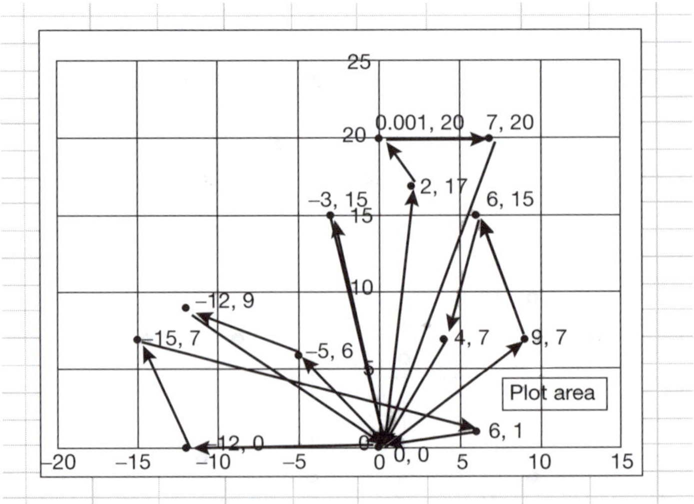

FIGURE 11.14 Routes using Sweep Algorithm-1.

11.5.5 The Sweep Nearest (SN) Algorithm

We apply steps 1 to 5 of the SN Algorithm and group the clusters as shown in Figure 11.15, and the results are shown in Figure 11.16.

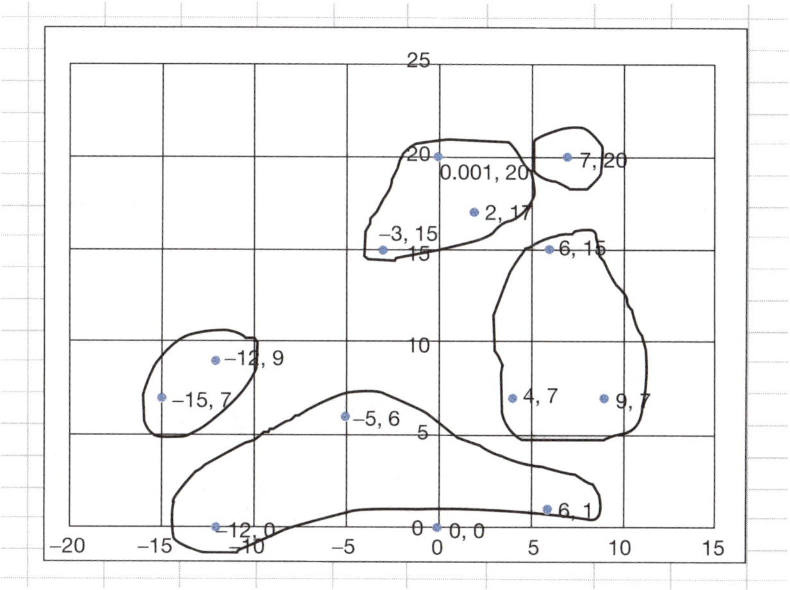

FIGURE 11.15 Clustering using SN Algorithm.

Customer/DC	X coordinate	Y coordinate	Order size	θ =tan-1(y/x)	Clusters	Customers in the Sweep and in each Cluster	Load on each Cluster
DC	0	0					
5	-3	15	81	-1.37			
6	0.001	20	41	1.57	C=1	5,6,7	196
7	2	17	74	1.45			
2	-5	6	55	-0.88			
9	6	1	80	0.17	C=2	2,9,1	209
1	-12	0	74	0.00			
4	-12	9	109	-0.64	C=3	4,3	177
3	-15	7	68	-0.44			
12	9	7	75	0.66			
8	4	7	52	1.05	C=4	12,8,10	196
10	6	15	69	1.19			
11	7	20	103	1.23	C-5	11	103

FIGURE 11.16 Results of SN Algorithm.

As we did earlier, for each cluster, we can determine a TSP tour to get the best sequence, and the same is done for Figure 11.16. The routes and respective distances are calculated using the depot and the customer coordinates and are shown in Table 11.23 and Figure 11.17.

TABLE 11.23 Routes using SN Algorithm

Cluster	Customer in Sweep and in Each Cluster	Route	Distance
C = 1	5, 6, 7	DC-5-6-7-DC	41.86
C = 2	2, 9, 1	DC-1-2-9-DC	39.38
C = 3	4, 3	DC-3-4-DC	35.16
C = 4	12, 8, 10	DC-12-8-10-DC	36.25
C = 5	11	DC-11-DC	42.38
Total			**195.03**

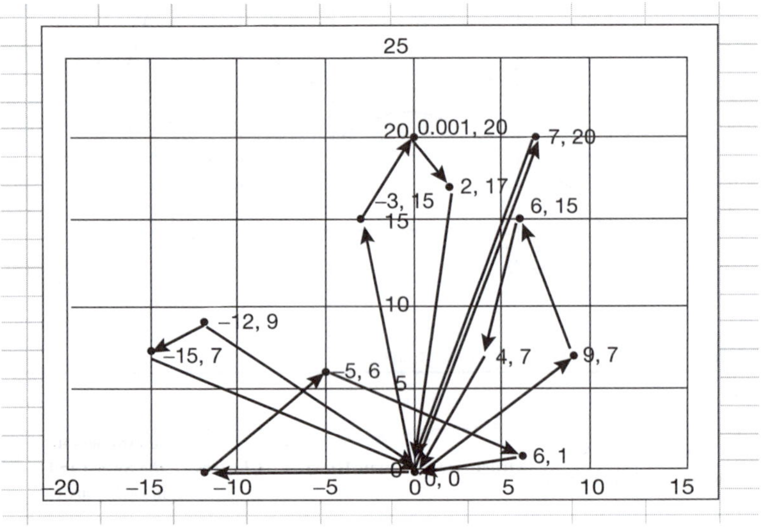

FIGURE 11.17 Routes using SN Algorithm.

11.5.6 Algorithm 3: Distance-based Sweep Nearest

We perform the computations of the Euclidean distances of the customers from the depot and carry out steps 1 to 5. They are shown in Figures 11.18 and 11.19.

DC	0	0	0				
Customer/DC	**X coordinate**	**Y coordinate**	**Order Size**	**Euclidean Distance from the Depot**	**Cumulative Load**	**Clusters**	**Customers in the Sweep and in each Cluster**
11	7	20	103	**21.19**	103	C=1	11,6,7
6	0	20	41	**20.00**	144		
7	2	17	74	**17.12**	**218**		
3	-15	7	68	**16.55**	68	C=2	3,10,5
10	6	15	69	**16.16**	137		
5	-3	15	81	**15.30**	**218**		
4	-12	9	109	**15.00**	109	C=3	4,1
1	-12	0	74	**12.00**	**183**		
12	9	7	75	**11.40**	75	C=4	2,12,8
8	4	7	52	**8.06**	127		
2	-5	6	55	**7.81**	**182**		
9	6	1	80	**6.08**	**80**	C=5	9

FIGURE 11.18 Clustering using Sweep Algorithm-3.

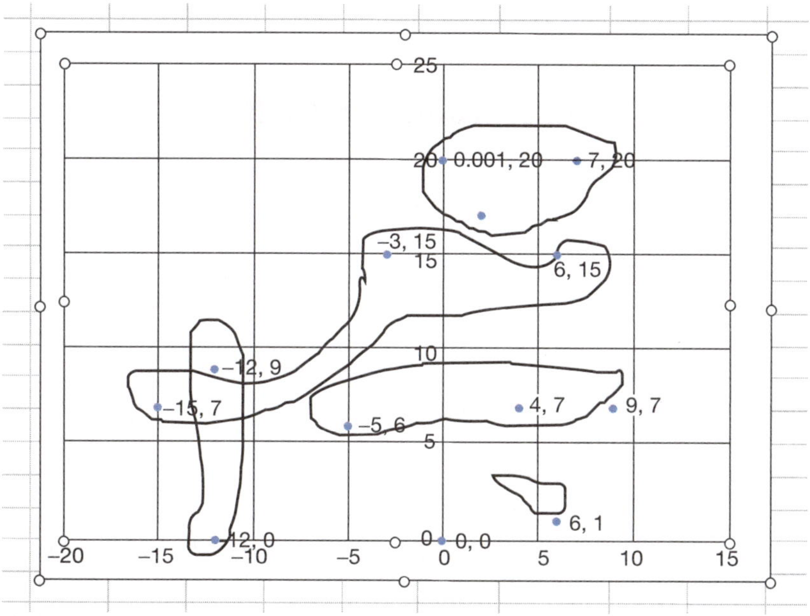

FIGURE 11.19 Clustering using Sweep Algorithm-3.

As we did earlier, for each cluster, we can determine a TSP tour to get the best sequence, and the same is done for Figure 11.19. The routes and the respective distances are calculated using the depot and the customer coordinates and are shown in Table 11.24 and Figure 11.20.

TABLE 11.24 Routes using Sweep Algorithm-3

Cluster	Customer in Sweep and in Each Cluster	Route	Distances
C = 1	11, 6, 7	DC-7-6-11-DC	48.92
C = 2	3, 10, 5	DC-3-5-10-DC	56.13
C = 3	4, 1	DC-1-4-DC	36.00
C = 4	2, 12, 8	DC-12-8-2-DC	33.36
C = 5	9	DC-9-DC	12.16
Total			**186.57**

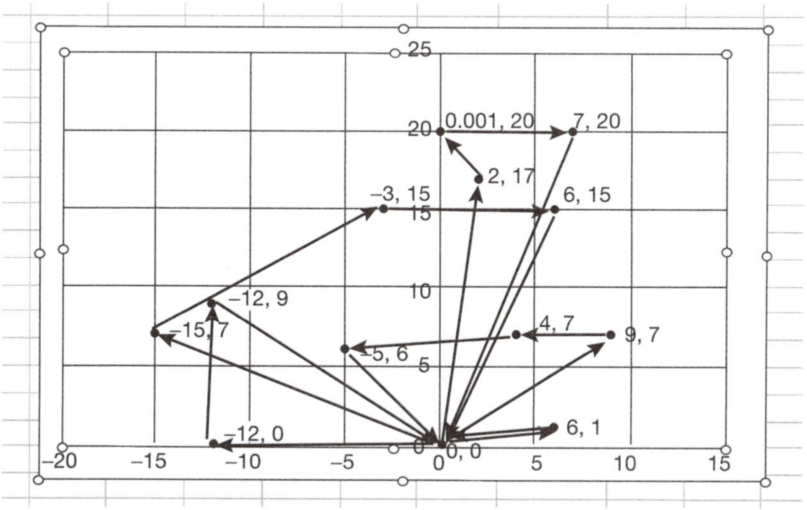

FIGURE 11.20 Routes using Sweep Algorithm-3.

We observe that the total distance is the least in the DSN method with a total distance of 186.48.

11.6 | GENERALIZED ASSIGNMENT METHOD

The generalized assignment method proposed by Fisher and Jayakumar is more sophisticated than the Clarke–Wright savings method and usually results in better solutions in most cases, although not necessarily in all cases. The method is based on determining cones using seed points for each vehicle (route) for assigning customers, evaluating the cost of inserting each customer in each cone, and using mixed integer programming to obtain the best assignment. The steps are as follows:

1. Assign seed points for each route.
2. Evaluate insertion cost for each customer.
3. Assign customers to routes.
4. Sequence customers within routes.

The first three steps assign customers to vehicles, while the fourth step involves a TSP solution for each route for optimal sequencing so that the total distance traveled is minimized.

We will describe the steps using the example in Table 11.15, which we used for the Clarke–Wright savings method and for the sweep algorithms. The main step in this method is determining the seed points that correspond to the center of the trip taken by each vehicle. We will use the following procedure:

1. Divide the total demand to be shipped to all customers by the number of trucks available to obtain the average load that will be allocated to each seed point. Each vehicle corresponds to one seed point. Let us call it AL.
2. Starting at any customer, use a ray starting at the DC to sweep clockwise as we used in the sweep algorithm to obtain cones assigned to each seed point. Each cone is assigned a load of AL.
3. Within each cone, we locate the seed point in the middle (in terms of polar angle) at a distance equal to that of the customer with a partial or complete load allocated to the cone farthest from the DC.

We will use these steps for our example to generate the cones and the corresponding seed points. In our example, the total demand of the given 12 customers is 881, and with five vehicles for delivering the products, the average load AL will be 881/5 = 176.2. We need the polar angular positions of the 12 customers for this purpose. The method is already discussed in the sweep algorithm 1. We use Table 11.21 and Figure 11.12, which lists them in descending order for this purpose. The sequence we will follow that sweeps customers using the ray will be 6, 7, 11, 10, 8, 12, 9, 1, 3, 4, 2, and 5. Starting with customer 6, we need to form five cones for the seed points to be determined. The average load AL is 176.2. Customers 6 and 7 will require 115. Customer 11 requires 103, and we cannot satisfy the complete load. We will partially satisfy that to the extent of (176.2 – 115 =) 61.2 of customer 11's demand so that the remaining demand of (103 – 61.2 =) 41.8 will be included in the second cone. Therefore, cone 1 extends from customer 6 up to a point that is 61.2 of 103 of customer 11 between customers 7 and 11. Customer 7 has an angular position of 1.45, and customer 11 has an angular position of 1.23 and contains an angle of 1.45 – 1.23 = 0.22. Therefore, the first cone will extend up to 1.45 – (61.2/103) × 0.22 = 1.32. Hence, the first cone will start at 1.57 and extends up to 1.32. The seed point is at an angular position in the middle of these two, that is, $\alpha_1 = (1.57+1.32)/2 = 1.445$. The farthest customer in the first cone among 6, 7, and 11 is 6 with a distance of 20. (Although the farthest, customer 11 is not considered as it satisfies, as of now, only a partial load.) Given this distance $d_1 = 20$, the coordinates (X_1, Y_1) of the seed point 1 are given by

$X_1 = d_1 \cos(\alpha_1) = 20 \cos(1.445) = 2.51$ and
$Y_1 = d_1 \sin(\alpha_1) = 20 \sin(1.445) = 19.84$.

That is, the **seed point S_1** is **(2.51, 19.84)**. Now the second cone starts from the angular position of 1.32. We will include the balance 41.8 of customer 11's demand in this cone. We see that customers 10 and 8 can be fully covered, and 13.4 of customer 12 can be accommodated with the balance (75 – 13.4 =) 61.6 of customer 12 in the third cone. Now, between customers 8 and 12, it covers an angular position of (1.05 – 0.66 =) 0.39. Hence, the second cone will start from 1.32 and will extend up to 1.05 – (13.4/75) × 0.39 = 0.98. The seed point 2 will be at an angular position in the middle of these two, that is, $\alpha_2 = (1.32 + 0.98)/2 = 1.15$. The farthest is customer 11 as it satisfies the complete load now with a distance of 21.2. Given this distance $d_2 = 20$, the coordinates (X_2, Y_2) of seed point 2 are given by

$X_2 = d_2 \cos(\alpha_2) = 21.2 \cos(1.15) = 8.66$ and
$Y_2 = d_2 \sin(\alpha_2) = 21.2 \sin(1.15) = 19.35$.

So, the **seed point S_2** is **(8.66, 19.35)**. Now the third cone starts from 0.98 and will include the balance 61.6 of customer 12 in that. Along with customer 12, customer 9 with a demand of 80 and 34.6 of customer 1 will be part of this cone to satisfy the average load AL of 176.2. So, the cone will have an angular position between customers 9 and 1, which covers an angle of 0.17 – 0.00 = 0.17. Hence, it will extend up to 0.17 – (34.6/74) × 0.17 = 0.09. The seed point 3 will be at an angular position in the middle of these two, that is, $\alpha_3 = (0.98 + 0.09)/2 = 0.535$. The farthest is customer 12 as it satisfies the complete load now with a distance of 11.4. Given this distance $d_3 = 11.4$, the coordinates (X_3, Y_3) of the seed point 3 are given by

$X_3 = d_3 \cos(\alpha_3) = 11.4 \cos(0.535) = 9.81$ and
$Y_2 = d_3 \sin(\alpha_3) = 11.4 \sin(0.535) = 5.81$

So, the **seed point S_3** is **(9.81, 5.81)**. Cone 4, now, will start from 0.09 with the balance load of 39.4 of customer 1 and will include customer 3 and a partial load of 68.8 of 109 of customer 4 in this cone. An angle of 0.22 (i.e., –0.44 and –0.64) is covered between customers 3 and 4. So the cone will extend up to 0.44 – (68.8/109) × 0.22 = –0.58. The seed point 4 will be at an angular position in the middle of these two, that is, $\alpha_4 = (0.09 + (-0.58))/2 = -0.245$. The farthest is customer 3 with a distance of 17.5. Given this distance $d_4 = 17.5$, the coordinates (X_4, Y_4) of seed point 4 are given by

$X_4 = d_4 \cos(\alpha_4) = 17.5 \cos(-0.245) = 16.98$ and
$Y_4 = d_4 \sin(\alpha_4) = 17.5 \sin(-0.245) = -4.24$

So, the **seed point S_4** is **(16.98, –4.24)**. Cone 5, now, will start from –0.58 and will include the balance 40.2 of customer 4 and the demands of customers 2 and 5 fully. The cone will extend up to the last angle, that is, –1.37. Therefore, the seed point 5 will be at an angular position in the middle of these two. So $\alpha_5 = (-0.58 + (-1.37))/2 = -0.975$. The farthest is customer 5 with a distance of 15.3. Given this distance $d_5 = 15.3$, the coordinates (X_5, Y_5) of seed point 5 are given by

$X_5 = d_5 \cos(\alpha_5) = 15.3 \cos(-0.975) = 8.59$ and
$Y_5 = d_5 \sin(\alpha_5) = 15.3 \sin(-0.975) = -12.66$

So, the **seed point S_5** is **(8.59, –12.66)**.

The summary of the five seed points is given in Table 11.25.

TABLE 11.25 Summary of seed points

Seed Point	X-Coordinate	Y-Coordinate
S_1	2.51	19.84
S_2	8.66	19.35
S_3	9.81	5.81
S_4	16.98	–4.24
S_5	8.59	–12.66

Fisher and Jayakumar's method usually gives better solutions in most cases when compared to the Clarke–Wright method, although an example here is shown wherein it does not give better solutions than the Clarke–Wright method. It has a very strong logic of generating seed points and penalties of opportunity costs for not including customer points in any seed point that should logically give better routes.

11.6.1 Evaluating the Insertion Cost for Each Customer

For each seed point S_k and customer i, the insertion cost C_{ik} is the extra distance that would be incurred if the customer is inserted into a trip from the DC to the seed point and back and is given by

$$C_{ik} = \text{Dist (DC}, i) + \text{Dist} (i, S_k) - \text{Dist (DC}, S_k)$$

where distance is evaluated through the normal Euclidean distance. For example, for customer 1, the cost will be $C_{11} = \text{Dist (DC}, 1) + \text{Dist} (1, S_1) - \text{Dist (DC}, S_1) = 12 + 24.58 - 20 = 16.58$. The insertion cost is given in Table 11.26.

TABLE 11.26 Evaluation of insertion costs

	S_1	S_2	S_3	S_4	S_5
1	16.58	19.11	23.17	23.79	20.87
2	3.56	5.71	11.22	14.56	15.60
3	18.27	22.04	29.99	32.95	31.96
4	13.11	16.91	25.64	29.36	29.59
5	2.63	6.54	19.66	25.53	29.99
6	2.52	7.48	25.85	32.09	38.47
7	0.00	2.98	19.36	25.61	32.20
8	0.99	0.06	2.59	7.73	12.95
9	5.25	3.43	0.82	0.75	4.69
10	2.12	0.05	14.70	20.81	28.64
11	5.68	1.77	24.25	29.90	38.59
12	5.79	2.56	1.44	7.69	15.77

Now we will see how we can assign customers to the seed points. We will formulate this as a binary integer programming problem.

Let $X_{ik} = 1$ if customer i is assigned to seed point k
0 otherwise
C_{ik} = Insertion cost of customer i to seed point k
d_i = Demand or the order size of customer i for $i = 1, 2, ..., n$
C_k = Capacity of vehicle k for $k = 1, 2, ..., K$
The formulation is as follows:

$$\text{Minimize} \sum_{k=1}^{K}\sum_{i=1}^{n} C_{ik} X_{ik}$$

Subject to

$$\sum_{k=1}^{K} X_{ik} = 1 \text{ for all } i = 1,2,\ldots,n$$

$$\sum_{i=1}^{n} d_i X_{ik} \le C_k \text{ for all } k = 1,2,\ldots,K$$

$$X_{ik} = 0 \text{ or } 1 \text{ for all } i \text{ and } K$$

The formulation is applied on Table 11.26, and the solutions are obtained through Solver. They are shown in Table 11.27.

TABLE 11.27 Binary integer programming formulation table and Solver solution

Customer	Seed Point					
	S_1	S_2	S_3	S_4	S_5	Order Size
1	16.58	19.11	23.17	23.79	20.87	74
2	3.56	5.71	11.22	14.56	15.60	55
3	18.27	22.04	29.99	32.95	31.96	68
4	13.11	16.91	25.64	29.36	29.59	109
5	2.63	6.54	19.66	25.53	29.99	81
6	2.52	7.48	25.85	32.09	38.47	41
7	0.00	2.98	19.36	25.61	32.20	74
8	0.99	0.06	2.59	7.73	12.95	52
9	5.25	3.43	0.82	0.75	4.69	80
10	2.12	0.05	14.70	20.81	28.64	69
11	5.68	1.77	24.25	29.90	38.59	103
12	5.79	2.56	1.44	7.69	15.77	75

	S_1	S_2	S_3	S_4	S_5	LHS	RHS
1	0.00	0.00	0.00	0.00	**1.00**	1.00	1
2	0.00	0.00	**1.00**	0.00	0.00	1.00	1
3	**1.00**	0.00	0.00	0.00	0.00	1.00	1
4	0.00	0.00	0.00	**1.00**	0.00	1.00	1
5	**1.00**	0.00	0.00	0.00	0.00	1.00	1
6	0.00	**1.00**	0.00	0.00	0.00	1.00	1
7	**1.00**	0.00	0.00	0.00	0.00	1.00	1
8	0.00	0.00	**1.00**	0.00	0.00	1.00	1
9	0.00	0.00	0.00	**1.00**	0.00	1.00	1
10	0.00	**1.00**	0.00	0.00	0.00	1.00	1
11	0.00	**1.00**	0.00	0.00	0.00	1.00	1
12	0.00	0.00	**1.00**	0.00	0.00	1.00	1
LHS	223	213	182	189	74		
RHS	225	225	225	225	225		
Total Insertion cost	**96.45**						

This gives us the routes DC-3-5-7-DC, DC-10-11-6-DC, DC-12-8-2-DC, DC-4-9-DC, and DC-1-DC with the total distance of 189.17 after applying a TSP routine for every seed point. The solution is no better than the Clarke–Wright savings method for this example. However, this method in many cases yields better solutions when compared to other methods. We can always perform k-opt improvement heuristics on all these routes to get an improved solution. There are many methods available for VRPs, but we presented a few that are popular and implementable. In the next section, we will present a few methods of vehicle scheduling, which is also an important area in the operational side of transportation.

11.7 | VEHICLE SCHEDULING METHODS

Vehicle scheduling is one area where many firms have not reaped the best benefits as this area gets outsourced to third-party logistics providers, most of whom are not familiar with optimization methods in vehicle scheduling. This is one area where the capital cost of resources like vehicles, be it trucks or airplanes, can be saved for better utilization.

Scheduling problems are usually characterized by time windows and delivery-time restrictions. The starting and ending times for a service will usually be specified in advance. Flight schedules, fast food delivery schedules, etc. fall into this category where the arrival times at each specified destination or stops are known in advance and the flight or the delivery vehicle must meet the schedule. Time windows may be one-side open or tight on both sides depending on the type of services. The general input for a scheduling problem consists of a set of tasks or trips, each with a starting and ending time, and a set of directed arcs, each with a starting and ending location. The delivery vehicles may be housed at one or more depots.

Consider the example in Table 11.28. It shows that there are five tasks indicated as five nodes that are associated with a single depot with a start and end time for each task.

TABLE 11.28 Example of tasks for a depot

	Node 1	Node 2	Node 3	Node 4	Node 5
Depot	S 8.00	S 8.30	S 9.30	S 10.15	S 10.45
	E 8.45	E 9.25	E 9.50	E 11.25	E 11.20

The scheduling is done by partitioning the nodes into a set of paths, and a vehicle is assigned to each path. So, the objective will be to see if we can identify the minimum number of paths, so that we can minimize the number of vehicles required and, hence, the vehicle capital costs. We can also assign a weight to each arc that is proportional or equal to the travel time for each arc and minimize personnel and vehicle operating costs as well as time. The directed arcs indicate that the two tasks are assigned to the same vehicle. The dashed arcs show other feasible connections that were not used in the schedule. It is commonsense that an arc may join node *i* to node *j* if the start time of task *j* is greater than the end time of task *i*. An additional restriction is that the start time of task *j* must include a user-specified period longer than the end time of task *i*. This may be referred to as layover time or buffer time, which can be utilized for various administrative purposes. For example, if a flight reached node *j*, it may need some layover time for boarding and/or alighting, maintenance, crew takeover, etc. This is also referred to as **deadhead time** and is the nonproductive time required for the vehicle to travel from one task location to another or return to the depot empty. We will assume 45 minutes for this example. In some scheduling algorithms, the dead heading trips are introduced to schedule vehicles and to save the number of vehicles required. We will discuss them later in this chapter. Also, the paths are not restricted in length. Finally, each vehicle must start and end at the depot. The scheduling for the example in Table 11.28 is shown in Figure 11.21.

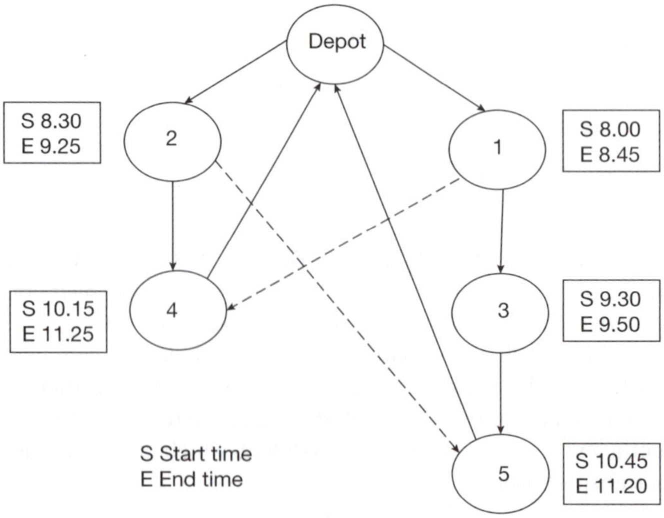

FIGURE 11.21 Scheduling of tasks in Table 11.28.

Here we require a minimum of two vehicles as we have two minimum partitions as shown earlier. Hence, we can have a few possibilities of the schedule as Depot-1-3-5-Depot and Depot-2-4-Depot for these two vehicles and also Depot-1-4-Depot and Depot-2-5-Depot and Depot-3-Depot with three vehicles. We need an objective function to choose the best schedule, which may be based on distance or operating cost or time or number of vehicles depending on the type of applications.

11.7.1 Concurrent Scheduler Approach or Link-Diagram Approach

This problem may be formulated as a special type of network problem called a **minimal-cost-flow problem**. Alternatively, a heuristic approach may be used. This is a popular method referred to as the link-diagram approach that is practiced in most of the transport undertakings (known as state transport undertakings (STUs) like the Maharashtra State Road Transport corporation, Gujarat SRTC, etc.) for their vehicle scheduling. This approach is used with the origin and destination along with the start and end times so that comprehensive vehicle schedules are prepared. We will give an example of this later in this chapter. The general procedure is as follows:

1. Order all tasks by starting times. Assign the first task to vehicle 1.
2. For the remaining number of tasks, do the following. If it is feasible to assign the next task to an existing vehicle, assign it to the vehicle that has the minimum deadhead time to that task. Otherwise, create a new vehicle and assign the task to the new vehicle.

Table 11.29 presents start and end times for 12 tasks. The deadhead time or the layover time is 15 minutes. The problem is solved using the concurrent scheduler approach.

TABLE 11.29 Example of tasks for concurrent scheduling approach

Task	Start Time	End Time
1	8.15 am	9.30 am
2	8.15 am	9.15 am
3	9.30 am	10.45 am
4	9.45 am	10.45 am
5	10.00 am	11.30 am
6	11 am	11.45 am
7	1.00 pm	1.45 pm
8	1.15 pm	2.45 pm
9	1.45 pm	3.00 pm
10	2.00 pm	2.45 pm
11	3.00 pm	3.45 pm
12	3.30 pm	4.00 pm

Table 11.29 is also represented as a link diagram in Figure 11.22 where each task is represented by a thick line bar with their start and end times.

Initially, vehicle 1 is assigned to task 1. Because task 2 begins before vehicle 1 is available, a second vehicle is assigned to this task. Vehicle 2 finishes task 2 in time to take care of task 3 as well. In the meantime, vehicle 1 completes task 1 and is available for task 4. A third vehicle is not required until task 5, when vehicles 1 and 2 are busy with tasks 4 and 3, respectively. So, this gives us 1-4, 2-3-6, and 5 for three vehicles. We also notice that there is a gap after task 6. Here we can combine 7-10-12, 8-11, and 8 separately and add these links to the previous links. This can give all the possible nine combinations of linking as follows:

Most of the expert schedulers in many transport organizations use this link diagram to schedule vehicles with ease. But scientific approaches can help them do it more effectively and the use of computers can make the task much easier. Many theoretical algorithms can be used here, which is beyond the scope of this book.

1. 1-4-7-10-12,
2. 1-4-8-11,
3. 1-4-9,

4. 2-3-6-7-10-12,
5. 2-3-6-8-11,
6. 2-3-6-9,
7. 5-7-10-12,
8. 5-8-11, and
9. 5-9.

As mentioned earlier, the best combination depends on which objective we wish to optimize.

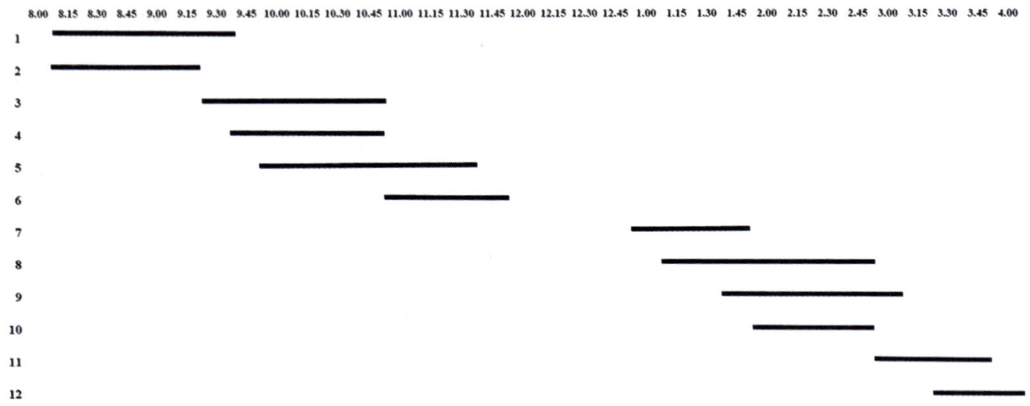

FIGURE 11.22 Link diagram for tasks in Table 11.29.

11.7.2 Assignment Method Approach of Scheduling

In this approach, we consider the given scheduling problem as an assignment problem and use standard procedure to solve an assignment problem in linear programming using either the Hungarian algorithm or Excel Solver. We illustrate this using the following flight scheduling problem, which is a very popular textbook example.

EXAMPLE 11.1

Consider Table 11.30 giving details of trips to be made by flights from the given origin to destinations at the given timings.

TABLE 11.30 Details of trips of flights

Trip No.	From	Departure Time	To	Arrival Time
1	Chennai	9 am	Kolkata	12 noon
2	Chennai	10 am	Kolkata	1 pm
3	Chennai	3 pm	Kolkata	6 pm
4	Chennai	8 pm	Mumbai	12 midnight
5	Chennai	10 pm	Mumbai	2 am
6	Kolkata	4 am	Chennai	7 am
7	Kolkata	11 am	Chennai	2 pm
8	Kolkata	3 pm	Chennai	6 pm
9	Mumbai	7 am	Chennai	11 am
10	Mumbai	3 pm	Chennai	7 pm

The following conditions have to be considered while scheduling these flights:

1. A plane cannot make more than two trips in any schedule cycle.
2. A plane flying from a particular city must be back within 24 hours for the next scheduled trip from the city. This means that the scheduling horizon is 24 hours as a cycle.

When a plane reaches a destination or when starting from an origin, there is layover time (also referred to as deadhead time) for various activities such as alighting, boarding of passengers, maintenance crew change over, refueling, etc. Usually, this time is very expensive as the airport has to use its resources and charges the airlines. The airlines try to minimize this layover time as much as possible in order to save costs. Let us assume that the layover cost is the square of the layover time, which is a unit that is converted into monetary value. For example, if a flight starting from Chennai and heading to Mumbai spends 2 hours as layover time before it starts another trip, then the layover cost is 2^2 units. This may mean 4 units (say \$400 or \$4000 or whatever). The objective here is to minimize the overall total layover cost while scheduling these trips. In other words, what will be the optimal scheduling of these trips that will be attached to each plane such that it will minimize the overall layover cost.

If we carefully look at the trips in Table 11.30, we notice that trips were made between Chennai and Kolkata and Chennai and Mumbai, as shown in Figure 11.23.

This is an illustration to indicate how practical problems in scheduling can be brought to familiar formats for applying known methods in linear programming like assignment models. Not every problem is amenable for such formulation!

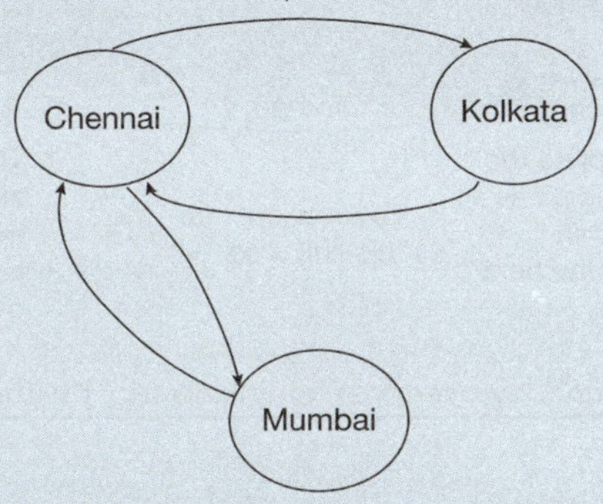

FIGURE 11.23 Schematic representation of trips in Table 11.30.

We see that trips 1, 2, and 3 are made from Chennai to Kolkata and trips 6, 7, and 8 are made from Kolkata to Chennai. This means that these trips, if feasible in meeting the conditions that are to be considered, can be chained together as a schedule and can be given to flights. Similarly, trips 4 and 5 are made between Chennai and Mumbai and trips 9 and 20 are made from Mumbai to Chennai. So, these trips, if feasible, can be chained and given to flights. Since a plane cannot make more than two trips and 10 trips are to be scheduled here, it is obvious that we need five planes, out of which 3 are required for the Chennai–Kolkata sector and two are required for the Chennai–Mumbai sector.

We will evaluate the layover cost of the Chennai–Mumbai sector for trips 1, 2, and 3 with trips 6, 7, and 8. There are $3 \times 3 = 9$ possible links that can be evaluated: 1-6, 1-7, 1-8, 2-6, 2-7, 2-8, 3-6, 3-7, and 3-8. We will look at the first link, trip 1 with trip 6, which is linked if it is feasible and if feasible, the layover time and cost. This is schematically shown in Figure 11.24.

This link of trip 1 with trip 6 is feasible as it returns within 24 hours for the next schedule cycle to start. The evaluation is shown in Figure 11.24 with the layover times at both the cities and the total layover cost. Therefore, if we link these trips, it will cost 260.

Now we will evaluate the linking feasibility of trip 1 with trip 7. This is shown in Figure 11.25.

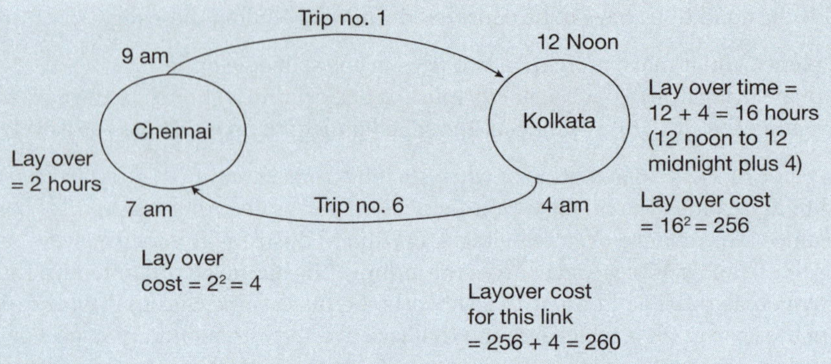

FIGURE 11.24 Evaluating lay over cost for linking trip-1 with trip-6.

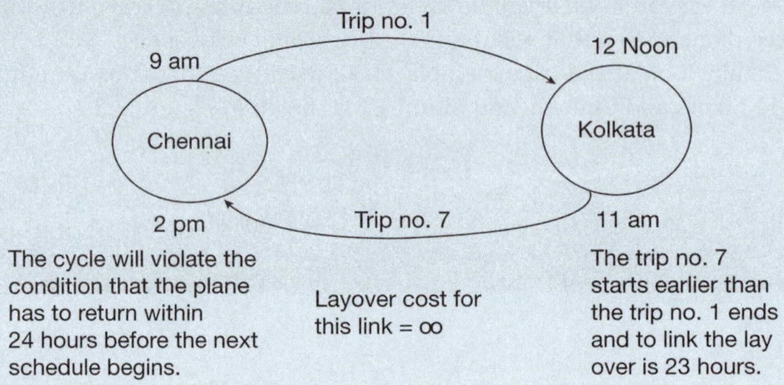

FIGURE 11.25 Evaluating lay over cost for linking trip-1 with trip-7.

We observe that this link of combining trip 1 with trip 7 is infeasible, as the plane cannot return within 24 hours for the next schedule to begin. Hence, the layover cost is assumed to be ∞ to indicate that this is not possible to link.

We carry out the evaluations in a similar way and obtain the following cost matrix given in Table 11.31 of linking trips 1, 2, and 3 with trips 6, 7, and 8.

TABLE 11.31 Layover cost matrix for linking trips Chennai to Kolkata

	6	7	8
1	260	∞	234
2	234	∞	260
3	164	290	∞

Using Excel Solver, the following solutions shown in Table 11.32 are obtained and complete Solver solutions are shown in Table 11.33.

TABLE 11.32 Solutions to the Chennai–Kolkata Links

	6	7	8
1	0	0	1
2	1	0	0
3	0	1	0

TABLE 11.33 Solver solutions to Chennai-Kolkatta links

	6	7	8	LHS	RHS
1	0	0	1	1	1
2	1	0	0	1	1
3	0	1	0	1	1
LHS	1	1	1		
RHS	1	1	1		
Total Layover Cost 758					

The solution is to link trips 1 and 8, trips 2 and 6, and trips 3 and 7. The total layover cost is 758. A similar analysis is done for the Chennai–Mumbai sector, and Tables 11.34 and 11.35 show the steps and solutions.

TABLE 11.34 Layover costs of Chennai-Mumbai links

	9	10
4	130	226
5	146	178

TABLE 11.35 Solver solutions to Chennai-Mumbai links

	9	10	LHS	RHS
4	1	0	1	1
5	0	1	1	1
LHS	1	1		
RHS	1	1		
Total Layover Cost		308		

The solution is to link trips 4 and 9 and trips 5 and 10. The total layover cost is 308. The optimal trip links are as follows:

1-8
2-6
3-7
4-9
5-10

with a total layover cost of 758 + 308 = 1066. Here the problem was brought to the known format of an assignment model and was solved using known methods.

In fact, this provides a direction in supply chain analytics. If we can formulate and bring a problem to a known format such as linear programming, a transportation problem, or an assignment problem, then it is possible to use the exact known methods to solve them. Only when we are unable to bring them to known formats do we resort to developing procedures and heuristics to solve them.

11.8 | DEFICIT FUNCTION APPROACH TO VEHICLE SCHEDULING

In this section, a scientific method of preparing vehicle schedules is outlined using the concept of the deficit function and linking algorithm for trips. It is assumed throughout that the scheduling process starts with the given timetable of trips to be operated from multi-terminals for a given schedule horizon. The given timetable would specify the trip number, originating terminal, departure time, arriving terminal, and arrival time for each trip.

11.8.1 Deficit Function and Related Concepts

The concept of a "deficit function" was initially introduced by I. Gertsbach and Y. Gurevich. Consider a set of terminals T where vehicles may originate and terminate their trips. Given a set of trips S (a schedule) to be serviced, a function can be constructed for each terminal, say $i \in T$. Such a function, for terminal i, will take on a value at time t, the total number of departures from i less the total number of arrivals at i up to and including time t. Gertsbakh and Gurevich called this function the "Deficit Function" as it represents the deficit number of vehicles at a particular terminal needed to meet the required schedule.

For a trip, say r from terminal A, referred to as A^r and arriving at terminal B, referred to as B^r, let t_s^r and t_e^r represent the start and end times, respectively. Let us denote the schedule horizon as $[T_1, T_2]$ where $T_1 \le t_s^r < t_e^r \le T_2$. Let $S = \{A^r, t_s^r, B^r, t_e^r / r = 1, 2, \ldots, n\}$ represent a fixed multi-terminal trip schedule with n trips for a given schedule horizon.

For each terminal i, let $s(i, t, S)$ denote the cumulative number of trips from S starting at i from the beginning of the schedule horizon up to and including time t. Similarly, let $e(i, t, S)$ be the cumulative number of trips from S ending at terminal i up to and including time t.

Let $d(i, t, S)$ denote the deficit function for terminal i at time t for the schedule S. That is,

$$d(i, t, S) = s(i, t, S) - e(i, t, S) \text{ where } t \in [T_1, T_2]$$

Let the maximal value of this deficit function $d(i, t, S)$ be denoted by $D(i, S)$. Also define $D(S)$ as the sum of the deficits across all terminals $i \in T$. That is,

$$D(S) = \sum_{i=1}^{T} D(i,S)$$

Let $g(t,S) = \sum_{i=1}^{T} g(i,t,S)$ represent an overall deficit function. This function represents the number of trips in simultaneous operations at time t for the schedule S. Let the maximal value of this function over $[T_1, T_2]$ be denoted by $G(S)$.

11.8.2 Fleet Size Theorem

The well-known fleet size theorem was first derived by Bartlett in 1957 and subsequently derived by Gertsbakh and Gurevich as well as Salzborn using the concept of the deficit function. The theorem states that the minimum number of vehicles required to service a multi-terminal fixed schedule of trips is equal to the total deficit at all terminals. The theorem is stated as follows without proof. Complete details of the proof can be seen in the references at the end of the chapter.

Minimum Fleet Size Theorem

Given a set of terminals T and a schedule of trips S such that all trips start and end within the schedule horizon, let $N(S)$ be the minimal number of vehicles required to service all trips in S. Then,

$$N(S) = \sum_{i=1}^{T} D(i,S) = \sum_{i \in T} \text{Max}\, d(i,t,S) = D(S)$$

11.8.3 Maximum Possible Reduction Proposition

For a given fixed schedule of trips, the maximum possible number of vehicles that can be saved through insertions of dead trips (non-revenue earning trips between terminals) is

$$N(S) - G(S) \geq 0$$

($G(S)$, as defined earlier, refers to the overall deficit function.)

This difference $N(S) - G(S)$ indicates the scope for improvement in fleet savings and also gives the lower bound beyond which no saving is possible unless the trip timings are perturbed.

We will illustrate the approach and the propositions with the following timetable of trips that are operated between three terminals A, B, and C with their departure times and arrival times at terminals given in Table 11.36.

The deficit function approach is probably one of the best methods to estimate the minimum fleet requirements for a given schedule and is useful in looking for a scope for improvement in scheduling with a few strategies like deadhead trips for better vehicle utilization and for reducing the capital cost of such vehicles.

TABLE 11.36 Sample timetable trips between three terminals A, B, and C

Trip No.	Originating Terminal (Origin)	Departure Time	Ending Terminal (Destination)	Arrival Time
1	B	6.00	A	6.50
2	B	10.30	C	11.20
3	C	11.30	B	12.20
4	A	6.00	B	6.50
5	B	8.00	C	8.50
6	C	9.00	B	9.50
7	A	10.00	B	10.50
8	B	6.10	C	7.00
9	C	13.20	A	14.10
10	B	7.00	A	7.50
11	A	8.00	B	8.50
12	B	9.00	C	9.50
13	C	10.00	A	10.50
14	A	11.00	B	11.50

Since there are 14 trips, the worst-case solution is to have 14 vehicles to serve trips separately. That is the upper bound. However, our aim is to determine the minimum number of vehicles that are required to meet this schedule of 14 trips. The deficit function approach can help us determine this. The steps are as follows:

1. We calculate the deficit function for each terminal in the set of terminals. In our example, we calculate for A, B, and C separately.
2. We list the trips with the departure times that depart from terminal *i* and arrival times of the trips that arrive at terminal *i* in the increasing order of time. That is 8.00 will be after 6.15, etc. For terminal A, the same is shown in Table 11.37.

TABLE 11.37 Listing of departures and arrivals at Terminal A

Trip No.	Departures at Time	Trip No.	Arrivals at Time
4	6.00	1	6.50
11	8.00	10	7.50
7	10.00	13	10.50
14	11.00	9	14.10

3. Choose time intervals, say 5 minutes or 10 minutes, depending on the given schedule of the timetable. Construct the deficit function starting from the earliest time 6.00 until the latest time 14.10, as seen in Table 11.37. We can construct it for every time interval, but we notice

that the deficit values will change with every departure and every arrival at the times shown in Table 11.37. However, constructing continuously for the timeline has its advantages in looking for a scope for improvement for introducing dead trips. The deficit function of terminal A is shown in Table 11.38.

TABLE 11.38 Calculations of deficit function values for Terminal A

Timeline t	Cumulative Number of Departures up to and Including Time t (Referred to as D)	Cumulative Number of Arrivals up to and Including Time t (Referred to as A)	Deficit ($D - A$)
6.00	1	0	0
6.50	1	1	1
7.50	1	2	−1
8.00	2	2	0
10.00	3	2	1
10.50	3	3	0
11.00	4	3	1
14.10	4	4	0

* Note that the deficit calculations are shown only at time t where there is a change in the status of departure or arrival. However, a deficit function is constructed for the entire timeline from 6.00 to 14.10 in this case.

4. Maximum value is taken in this deficit function. That maximum is the minimum number of vehicles required for terminal i. Here we observe that the maximum deficit is 1, as seen in Table 11.38. In other words, $D(A, S) = 1$.

We carry out steps 1 to 4 for all the terminals $i \in T$. We add the maximum deficit value of each terminal, that is, $\sum_{i=1}^{T} D(i,S)$. This total of maximum deficit at each terminal is the minimum number of fleets that are required to service the schedule as per the fleet size theorem. Similar calculations for terminals B and C in our example give us the values of maximum deficit as 3 and 0, respectively. So, the total sum of the deficit ($1+3+0=4$ vehicles) will be the minimum number of vehicles that are required to service the schedule given in Table 11.36. The graphical representation of the deficit functions of terminals A, B, and C is given in Figure 11.26.

11.8.4 Linking Algorithm for Vehicle Scheduling

After determining the minimum number of vehicles that are required for servicing a given timetable, the next step is to assign trips to each vehicle called a vehicle schedule. This involves a linking procedure, which was proposed by J. L. Saha. The procedure is as follows:

1. Let the trips be serially numbered as 1, 2, ..., n.
2. Group the serial numbers with common destinations (destination terminals). Then arrange the serial numbers (i.e., trip numbers) in each group in the increasing order of ending time. This was shown in our earlier stage for each terminal. These would form the **rows** of the linking array.
3. Arrange the serial numbers in the order of starting points (departure terminals) such that the first departure terminal corresponds to the first ending point in (2), the second to the second ending point in (2), and so on. Trips having the same starting points are then arranged in the increasing order of starting time. These would form the **column** of the array. Note that this arrangement will take care of the linking condition that the ending terminal is the same as the starting terminal.
4. A cell (i, j) is an admissible cell if the ith trip and the jth trip are such that (1) starting point of $j =$ ending point of i, and (2) starting time of $j \geq$ ending time of i. Circle all the admissible cells in the array.

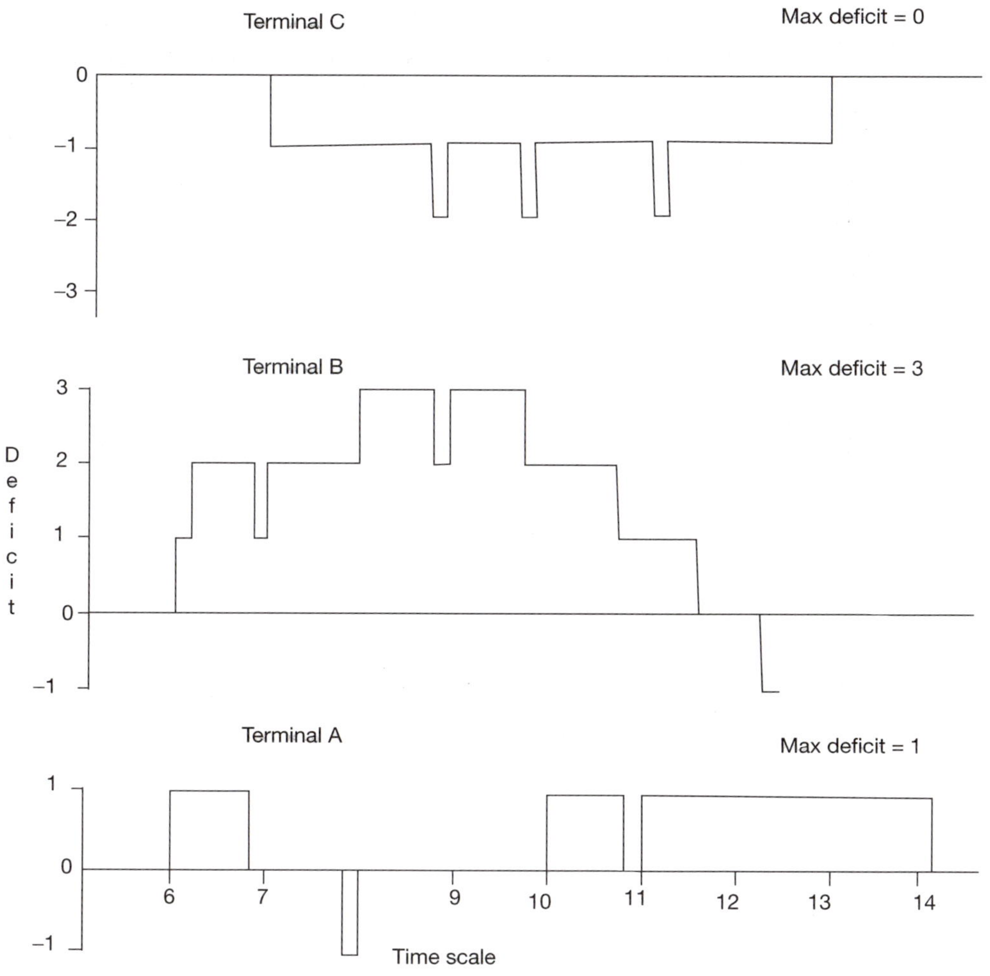

FIGURE 11.26 Graphical representation of deficit function values at terminals A, B, and C.

5. Place "1's" in the admissible cells as follows: Scan the first row. Put 1 in the first admissible cell. Delete the row and column in which the admissible cell lies and repeat the process in the reduced array. Continue till all the rows are scanned.
6. Form the chains (or links or schedules) as follows: If a column contains a 1 in it, it is the starting trip of a chain. If the row with the same column number contains no 1, it will be a single element chain or schedule. If this row contains a 1, then the trip corresponding to the column number where 1 lies will be the next element in the chain or schedule and so on.
7. Each completed chain corresponds to vehicle schedules where a vehicle is assigned with the duty of servicing the trip numbers in the chain.

We have seen that for the timetable, we require four vehicles to service all the 14 trips. Now, we shall apply Saha's algorithm to obtain the chains as shown in the array in Figure 11.27.

We see that the trip chains are {1, 11, 12, 3}, {8, 6, 2, 9}, {5, 13, 14}, and {4, 10, 7} and respectively assigned to each of the four vehicles. The solution of four vehicles could have been directly arrived from here too, but the deficit function has its advantages of analyzing further for any scope for fleet reduction. We saw that the scope for fleet size reduction is possible if the overall deficit function $G(S)$ shows a lesser value than that of the $N(S)$ value. That is, if the $N(S)$, which is the sum of the maximum deficit of all terminals, is say 5 and if the overall deficit $G(S)$ is 4, then 5 – 4 is the scope for reduction. This reduction is achieved by inserting dead trips in the schedule if those dead trips are feasible. We will illustrate this with an example from the original paper of Gertsbakh and Gurevich. Consider the following timetable given in Table 11.39.

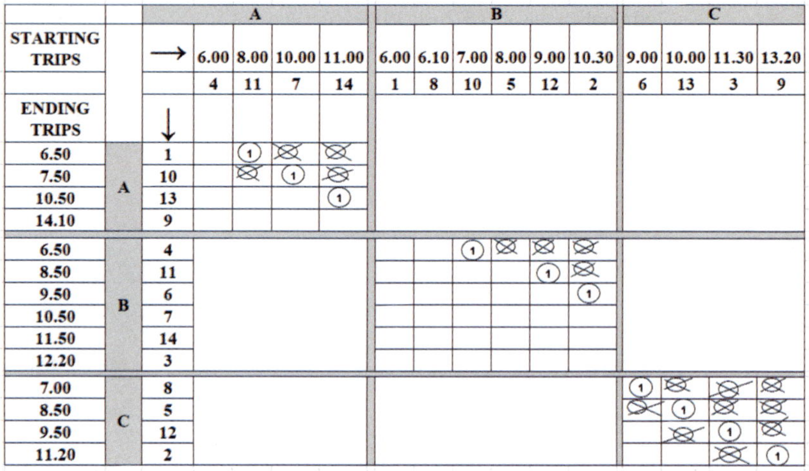

FIGURE 11.27 Linking of trips using Saha's Algorithm.

TABLE 11.39 Time table for dead-heading trips

Trip No.	Originating Terminal	Destination Terminal	Departure Time (in hours)	Arrival Time (in hours)
1	A	C	0	2
2	A	B	3	7
3	C	A	0	4
4	A	C	7	11
5	B	A	2	6
6	A	B	9	13
7	C	B	8	12
8	B	C	4	8
9	C	A	8	12

This schedule will require $N(S) = 5$ vehicles by applying the deficit function approach. The trip chains are [1-7], [2], [3-4], [5-6], and [8-9]. If we construct the overall deficit function for this timetable given in Table 11.39, we will notice that the maximum value of this overall deficit $G(S)$ is 4, as shown in Figure 11.28.

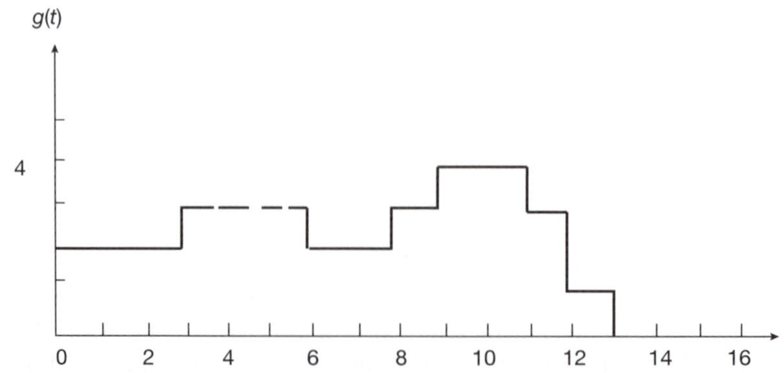

FIGURE 11.28 Determining overall deficit G(S) for all terminals.

So, $N(S) - G(S) = 5 - 4 = 1$ will be a possible reduction in the fleet requirement. Suppose the following feasible dead trips are introduced in the timetable in Table 11.40.

TABLE 11.40 Modified time table with insertion of Dead-Heading trips

Trip	Originating Terminal	Destination Terminal	Departure Time (in hours)	Arrival Time (in hours)
DH-1	C	B	2	4
DH-2	A	C	4	6
DH-3	B	A	7	9

Their introduction is shown in Figure 11.29.

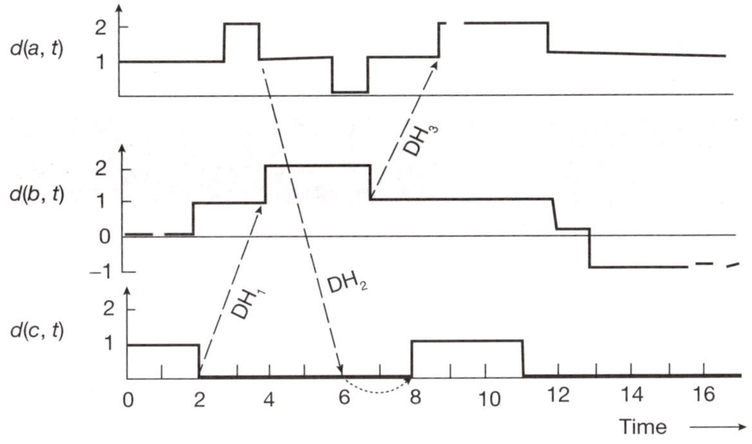

FIGURE 11.29 Insertion of Dead-Heading trips in the schedule.

We can see that the fleet can be reduced by 1 and we need only four vehicles. This can be verified by adding these trips in the schedule as three additional trips and recalculating the deficit values. The trip chains are 4 now and will be [1-DH1-8-9], [2-DH2-6], [3-DH3-7], and [5-4]. More details on this method can be seen in the references given at the end of the chapter.

We have shown how the scheduling of vehicles can be carried out efficiently using these approaches. In all these methods, the scheduling is done without changing the timings of the trips in the schedule, that is, without changing the start or end time of the different trips. However, if the trip timings can be perturbed, then the scope for even further fleet reduction is possible. More details are available in the bibliography section.

SUMMARY

One of the important concerns related to operational decisions in transportation is regarding routing and scheduling, where routing focuses on which nodes to visit in the supply chain network while scheduling focuses on when to visit the nodes. They are low hanging fruits in resource utilization and investments, which very often get neglected in supply chains due to the lack of application of scientific approaches. Moreover, these areas are often outsourced to third-party logistics providers who may not be equipped with such knowledge to optimize these decisions. This chapter provided a few popular methods in routing and scheduling, which can be applied in such areas and are amenable for developing computer-based software. The chapter discussed a few methods of finding exact solutions for solving routing problems using the branch and bound methods that are popular and presented a few heuristics such as the Clarke–Wright savings method, the sweep method, and Fisher and Jayakumar's method. Scheduling methods using link diagrams, assignment methods, and deficit function approaches are also presented towards the end. These methods are explained with the help of a few examples.

Case Study

Following case studies are suggested:

1. **Fowler Distributing Company** in the Book by Business Logistics Management by Ronald H. Ballou and Samir K. Srivsatava, Chapter 7 for Routing Problems.
2. **R&T Wholesalers** in the in the Book by Business Logistics Management by Ronald H. Ballou and Samir K. Srivsatava, Chapter 7 for Scheduling applications.

Exercises

1. Given the distance matrix shown in the following table.
   a. Construct VRP tours for two vehicles using Solver.

	Distance to Node (in km)							
From Node	**1**	**2**	**3**	**4**	**5**	**6**	**7**	**8**
1	—	2.2	6.0	4.5	5.6	8.5	3.8	4.6
2	2.2	—	4.5	5.6	5.8	10.4	5.8	6.8
3	6.0	4.5	—	5.2	6.1	6.9	6.7	10.2
4	4.5	5.6	5.2		3.5	6.9	3.9	6
5	5.6	5.8	6.1	3.5		3.6	2	6
6	8.5	10.4	6.9	6.9	3.6		3.6	8.5
7	3.8	5.8	6.7	3.9	2	3.6	—	4
8	4.6	4.6	10.2	7	6	8.5	4	—

   b. Formulate this as an integer programming problem and obtain the solution.
   c. Use the branch and bound method to obtain the solution and show the steps.
2. Using the Clark–Wright savings heuristic, construct a tour for the data given in problem 1. Assume node 1 is the depot node.
3. Consider the distance matrix given in the following table. You have to route two vehicles. Node 1 is the depot node; nodes 2 through 5 have been assigned to vehicle 1 and nodes 6 through 10 to vehicle 2.
   a. Construct the two tours using the nearest neighbor procedure and state the total distance of the tour.
   b. Construct the two tours using the Clark–Wright savings heuristic and state the total cost of the tour.

	Distance to Node (in km)									
From Node	**1**	**2**	**3**	**4**	**5**	**6**	**7**	**8**	**9**	**10**
1	—	12	25	39	22	20	25	56	55	45
2	12	—	30	25	34	38	47	75	65	35
3	25	30	—	20	46	31	45	47	70	39
4	39	25	20	—	65	55	70	85	83	63
5	22	34	46	65	—	30	20	35	50	55
6	20	38	31	55	30	—	40	50	40	29

From Node	Distance to Node (in km)									
	1	2	3	4	5	6	7	8	9	10
7	25	47	45	70	20	45	—	20	42	71
8	56	75	47	85	35	50	20	—	32	71
9	55	65	70	83	50	40	42	32	—	45
10	45	35	39	63	55	29	71	71	45	

4. Referring to problem 3, assume that each vehicle has a capacity of 100. The number of passengers to be picked up at each node is given in the following table.

Node	Number of Passengers
2	20
3	25
4	10
5	15
6	10
7	25
8	25
9	20
10	30

Construct routes using the Clarke–Wright method and improve the routes using k-opt methods.

5. The manager of a grocery chain, also selling online, has 12 orders that are to be delivered to customers. The location and order size for each customer are given in the following table.

Customer/DC	X-Coordinate	Y-Coordinate	Order Size
DC	0	0	
1	–15	2	74
2	–8	6	55
3	–12	8	68
4	–15	10	109
5	–3	15	81
6	0	15	41
7	3	18	74
8	6	7	52
9	7	2	80
10	12	15	69
11	7	20	103
12	9	7	75

The store has five trucks capable of carrying up to 225 units each. Use the following methods to generate routes:

1. Clarke–Wright method
2. Sweep method
3. Fisher and Jayakumar's method

Compare the results and comment.

6. For the following demand, apply the deficit function approach to determine the minimum number of vehicles and obtain the number of fleets that can be saved. Also obtain the scheduling of vehicles using Saha's link algorithm.

Trip No.	Originating Terminal	Departure Time	Ending Terminal (Destination)	Arrival Time
1	B	6.00	A	7.30
2	B	10.40	C	11.40
3	C	11.20	B	12.20
4	A	6.10	B	6.50
5	B	8.10	C	9.10
6	C	9.10	B	10.10
7	A	10.30	B	11.10
8	B	7.10	C	8.10
9	C	13.10	A	14.20
10	B	7.20	A	8.50
11	A	8.30	B	9.10

Bibliography

1. Achuthan, N. R. and L. Caccetta (1991). Integer linear programming formulation for a vehicle routing problem. *European Journal of Operational Research*, **52**, 86–89.
2. Achuthan, N. R., L. Caccetta, and S. P. Hill (1996). A new sub tour elimination constraint for the vehicle routing problem. *European Journal of Operational Research*, **91**, 573–586.
3. Ankelekar, S. R. and N. R. Patel (1980). *Optimization of Vehicle Schedule for a Road Transport Corporation*, WP No. 333, Indian Institute of Management, Ahmedabad.
4. Bach, L. (2014). *Routing and Scheduling Problems: Optimization using Exact and Heuristic Methods*, PhD Thesis, 2014, Department of Economics and Business Aarhus University, Denmark.
5. Ballou, R. H. and S. K. Srivastava (2007). *Business Logistics/Supply Chain Management*. Delhi: Pearson India.
6. Bellman, R. (1958). On a routing problem. *Quarterly of Applied Mathematics*, **16**(1), 87–90.
7. Ceder, A. and H. I. Stern (1981). Deficit function bus scheduling with deadheading trip insertions for fleet size reduction. *Transportation Science*, **15**(4), 338–363.
8. Chopra, S., P. Meindl, and D. V. Kalra (2016). *Supply Chain Management: Strategy, Planning and Operation*. Delhi: Pearson India.
9. Clarke, G. and J. W. Wright (1964). Scheduling of vehicles from a central depot to a number of delivery points. *Operations Research*, **12**(4), 568–581.
10. Dantzig, G. B. (1960). On the shortest route through a network. *Management Science*, **6**(2), 187–190.

11. Desrochers, M., J. K. Lenstra, and M. W. P. Savelsbergh (1988). *A Classification Scheme for Vehicle Routing and Scheduling Problems. Designing Decision Support Systems Notes*, vol. 8801. Technische Universiteit Eindhoven.

12. Gertsbach, I. and Y. Gurevich (1977). Constructing an optimal fleet for a transportation schedule. *Transportation Science*, **11**(1), 20–36.

13. Hillier, F. S. and G. J. Liebermann (1969). *Introduction to Operations Research*. McGraw Hill.

14. J. L. Saha (1970). "An Algorithm for Bus Scheduling Problems," Operational Research Quarterly, 21, 463-474.

15. Peya, Z. J., M. A. H. Akhand, T. Sultana, and M. M. H. Rahman (2019). Distance based sweep nearest algorithm to solve capacitated vehicle routing problem. *International Journal of Advanced Computer Science and Applications*, **10**(10), 259–264.

16. Taha, H. A. (2006). *Operations Research*. Delhi: Prentice Hall India.

17. Toth, P. and D. Vigo (2002). *The Vehicle Routing Problem*. Philadelphia: Society for Industrial and Applied Mathematics.

SECTION

VI

Multicriteria Decision Making

CHAPTER 12

Multi-Criteria Decision Making

LEARNING OBJECTIVES

After reading this chapter, you would be able to:

- Understand what Multi-Criteria Decision Making (MCDM) and Multi-Attribute Decision Making (MADM) are and their uses and popularity.
- Learn the basics of Multi-Attribute Utility Theory (MAUT) and its simple applications.
- Understand various terminologies used in MCDM.
- Comprehend the basic ideas of Analytic Hierarchy Process (AHP) and its applications.
- Understand the basic ideas of TOPSIS and its applications.
- Learn the basic notions of fuzzy numbers and logic.
- Understand how fuzzy logic is used in AHP and TOPSIS.

12.1 | INTRODUCTION

Multiple-criteria decision making (MCDM) has grown as a powerful approach for developing computational and mathematical tools for evaluating performance criteria by decision makers. The application of these tools is applied in many fields such as material management, supply chain management, quality management, energy, environment and sustainability, construction and project management, production and tourism management, soft computing, safety and risk management, and manufacturing management, to name a few.

MCDM methods have been developed to arrive at a better or preferred alternative from a set of alternatives in a small number of categories, and/or rank alternatives in a subjective preference order. MCDM is a generic term for all such methods that have been developed to support the decision-making process and to make decisions according to their preferences, especially when there is more than one conflicting criterion. MCDM is, in a way, breaking a complex problem into small components, taking judgments about such small components and then reassembling the components to get the decisions for the overall problem.

Most MCDM methods deal with situations where there are discrete alternatives that are described by a set of criteria. This information on the values of these criteria is arrived at as cardinal or ordinal information that could be determined exactly or also could be fuzzy, and thus, determined in intervals. There is always a problem of aggregation in most of these MCDM procedures. MCDM methods are broadly classified into two groups: discrete MCDM or discrete Multi-Attribute Decision Making (MADM) and continuous Multi-Objective Decision Making (MODM) methods. The details of all these methods can be found in "Multiple criteria decision-making techniques and their applications" by Abbas Mardani et al. (2015). Some of the popular methods are as follows:

1. Multi-Attribute Utility Theory (MAUT)
2. Analytic Hierarchy Process (AHP)

3. Fuzzy AHP
4. Technique for Order of Preference by Similarity to Ideal Solution (TOPSIS)
5. Fuzzy TOPSIS
6. Analytic Network Process (ANP)
7. ELimination Et Choix Traduisant la REalité (ELECTRE)
8. Multi-Objective Optimization by Ratio Analysis (MOORA)
9. Multiple-Objective Optimization on the Basis of Ratio Analysis Plus Full Multiplicative Form (MULTIMOORA)
10. Decision-Making Trial and Evaluation Laboratory (DEMATEL)
11. Preference Ranking Organization Method for Enrichment Evaluations (PROMETHEE),
12. VlseKriterijumska Optimizcija I Kaompromisno Resenje in Serbian (VIKOR)
13. TODIM

In this chapter, we will present a few of these popular methods of MCDM with examples.

12.2 | MULTIPLE-ATTRIBUTE UTILITY THEORY

The developments in the area of MCDM are very rapid, and many methods have been developed in a short span of time. With a variety of applications and contexts, the methods vary, but the basic theme remains that multiple criteria are evaluated in deciding the best course of action while situations still can use judgments of the decision makers.

The Multiple-Attribute Utility Theory (MAUT) uses an expected utility theory to arrive at the best course of action in a problem context. It assigns a utility to every possible consequence and calculates the best possible utility. Such a utility approach is the major advantage of MAUT as it takes uncertainty into account, which is not normally used in other MCDM approaches. It is very comprehensive in that it accounts for and incorporates the preferences of each of the consequences at every step of the method. Hence, it is more accurate but has a few disadvantages too. The amount of inputs and data is intensive as it calculates the utility for every consequence to account for the preferences of the decision makers. In practice, such details may not be available to the extent that is required at every step of the method. Moreover, the preferences of the decision makers have to be precisely stated and specific weights have to be given for each of the consequences, which may need stronger assumptions. Therefore, as a method, MAUT can be difficult to use and apply in practice as these preferences and weights may be subjective. Despite these limitations, MAUT has the major strength of taking uncertainty into account, which makes it applicable in areas such as actuary, energy and water resource management, agriculture, etc.

12.2.1 Steps of MAUT

The steps of MAUT are as follows:

Step 1: Use utility functions to convert numerical attribute scales into a utility unit scale.

Step 2: Assign weights to the attributes and then calculate the weighted average of each result set as an overall utility score.

Step 3: Compare utilities using the overall utility score. The utility quantifies the degree of fulfilment of an outcome, and for n possible outcomes $X_1, X_2, X_3, \ldots, X_n$, the expected utility (EU) is

$$EU = \sum_{i=1}^{n} p(X_i)U(X_i)$$

where $p(X_i)$ is the probability of the outcome X_i and $U(X_i)$ is the utility value of the outcome X_i.

Now the probabilities are replaced by the weights of importance involving the criteria. The expression for the expected utility given earlier is used, and utility functions are used to express the desirability of the attributes. The overall utility of an alternative with a number of criteria is defined by the following additive function:

$$U(X) = \sum_{i=1}^{n} w_i u_i(X_i)$$

where

$$\sum_{i=1}^{n} w_i = 1$$

The MAUT method is suitable when the decision maker has to consider several requirements. It is a normative method because it notifies what we should do. Here the probabilities ($p(X)$) are judged by the decision maker based on his/her own experience. As mentioned earlier, the method permits a hierarchical tree structure of criteria, which enables the users to focus on specific criteria when allocating weights. We will illustrate this method with a simple example.

EXAMPLE 12.1

Suppose Dento Design Company plans to decide which of the three suppliers A, B, or C will develop its new toothbrushes. The following three factors are critical for them. They are given with their respective weightages.

1. Cost (25%)
2. Quality broken down to the following subcomponents (55%):
   a. PPM performance (parts per million (PPM) specification in the last 3 months)(40%)
   b. QR performance (quality rejects in the last 3 months) (35%)
   c. Quality system status (through ISO/Qs, etc., current or OLD, third party, self-evaluated, etc.) (25%)
3. Delivery broken down to the following subcomponents (20%):
   a. Supplier communication system (30%)
   b. Up to schedule shipping (50%)
   c. Over-shipment (20%)

The tree structure of the criteria and subcomponents is given in Figure 12.1.

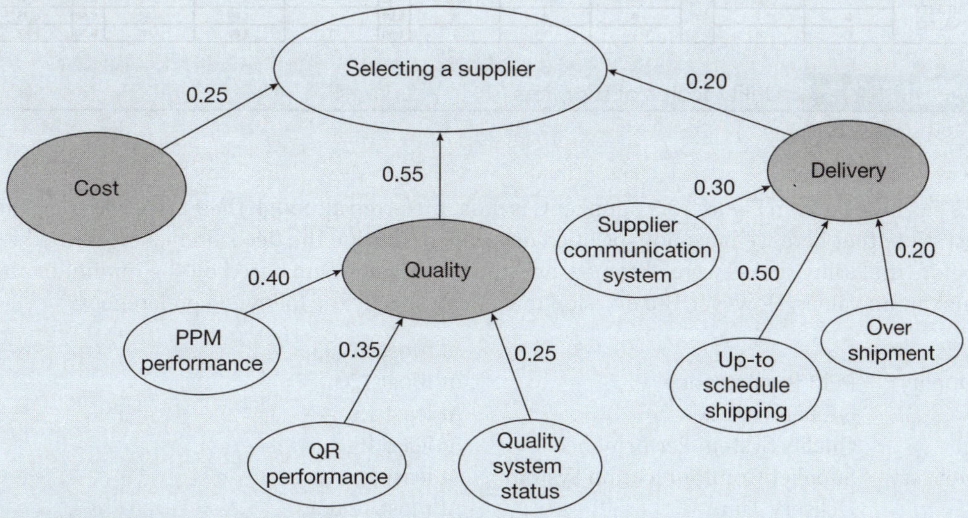

FIGURE 12.1 Structure of selecting a supplier.

The data on these three criteria and sub-criteria for the three suppliers A, B, and C are collected and expressed in Figure 12.2.

WEIGHTS	0.25	0.55			0.2		
	COST	QUALITY			DELIVERY		
CRITERIA		PPM Performance	QR Performance (0 to 25)	Quality System Performance (0 to 20)	Supplier Communication system (0 to 10)	Delivery Time (in days)	Overshipment (0 to 10)
SUPPLIERS	$ PER UNIT	0.4	0.35	0.25	0.3	0.5	0.2
A	100	200	15	15	7	11	3
B	90	700	10	10	6	8	6
C	140	80	25	25	10	15	2

FIGURE 12.2 Data on suppliers.

For the cost and the PPM performance sub-criterion, we will use the following utility function and assign the utility scores:

$$\frac{(X_U - X)}{(X_U - X_L)}$$

For other sub-criteria, we will use the following utility function and assign utility scores:

$$\frac{(X - X_L)}{(X_U - X_L)}$$

The calculation of the utility scores for each of them and the final scores is given in Figure 12.3.

WEIGHTS		0.25	0.55				0.2				
		COST	QUALITY				DELIVERY				
CRITERIA			PPM Performance	QR Performance (0 to 25)	Quality System Performance (0 to 20)		Supplier Communication System (0 to 10)	Delivery Time (in days)	Overshipment (0 to 10)		Overall Utility Score
SUPPLIERS		$ PER UNIT	0.4	0.35	0.25		0.3	0.5	0.2		
A		100	200	15	15		7	11	3		
B		90	700	10	10		6	8	6		
C		140	80	25	25		10	15	2		
UTILITY VALUES	A	0.8	0.81	0.33	0.33	0.52	0.25	0.57	0.75	0.51	0.59
	B	1	0	0	0	0.00	0	1.00	0.00	0.50	0.35
	C	0	1	1	1	1.00	1	0.00	1.00	0.50	0.65

FIGURE 12.3 Utility scores of suppliers.

MAUT is a very simple and common-sensical method to evaluate the best alternative. It is quite logical and, of course, needs a good sense of judgment to arrive at the decision. It is based on utility scores obtained out of utility functions that can be defined for the context.

As can be seen from Figure 12.3, supplier C is most preferred although their price was the highest. Note that here we have not specified any preferred value the decision makers wished for before the utility scores were obtained, and the utility values are based on the minimum and maximum values. However, the decision maker can specify the following preferences:

Cost		At most $100
Quality	PPM Performance	At most 120
	QR Performance	At least 15
	Quality System Performance	At least 15
Delivery	Supplier Communication System	At least 6
	Delivery Time	At most 12 days
	Over-shipment	At most 4

The utility scores are obtained based on the preceding cut-off values. For example, for suppliers A and B, the score will be 1. Since the price of supplier A is very far from this cut-off, the score will be 0.

For those sub-criteria where the values are close to the cut-off, we can assign an absolute value so as not to completely reject the value. That is, we can assign a fuzzy score (we will introduce this later). For example, for the QR performance, supplier B has 10. This does not meet the cut-off value of 15 but is short by 5. However, we will not completely reject this and see how much the deviation is proportionally. We use the following utility function where X is the excess of the cut-off and take the absolute value:

$$\frac{(X - X_L)}{(X_U - X_L)}$$

So it will be the absolute value of (5 – 10)/(25 – 10) = (5/15) = 0.333. Similarly, the utility values are assigned scores using this approach. Figure 12.4 summarizes the results.

			QUALITY			DELIVERY			
		COST	PPM Performance	QR Performance (0 to 25)	Quality System Performance (0 to 20)	Supplier Communication System (0 to 10)	Delivery Time (in days)	Overshipment (0 to 10)	Overall Utility Score
		<=$100	<=120	=>15	=>15	=>6	<= 12	<=4	
	SUPPLIERS								
UTILITY VALUES	A	1.00	0.00	1.00	1.00	1.00	1.00	1.00	
	B	1.00	0.00	0.33	0.33	1.00	1.00	0.50	
	C	0.00	1.00	1.00	1.00	1.00	0.43	1.00	
		1.00		0.60			1.00		0.78
		1.00		0.20			0.90		0.54
		0.00		1.00			0.71		0.69

FIGURE 12.4 Summary of scores.

Here we find that supplier A is the most preferred supplier as the cut-off values are in favor of this supplier.

12.3 | TERMINOLOGIES IN MADM OR MCDM METHODS

We will use the following terminologies for most of the MADM methods:

Alternatives: Alternatives are basically different choices of actions available to a decision maker. Usually, the set of alternatives is assumed to be finite, ranging from several to hundreds. The alternatives are usually screened, prioritized, and eventually ranked.

Multiple attributes: Attributes are different dimensions from which the alternatives can be viewed in a decision environment. They are also referred to as "goals" or "decision criteria." They are basically finite and in situations where the number of attributes is large (say more than 50), they may be arranged in a hierarchical manner. That is, some attributes may be major attributes. Each major attribute may be associated with several sub-attributes. Similarly, each sub-attribute may be associated with several sub-sub-attributes and so on (in the previous MAUT method for quality and delivery, we had such sub-attributes). However, most MADM methods assume a single level of attributes (e.g., no hierarchical structure).

Conflict among attributes: While listing the attributes, it is assumed that they are the desirable set of attributes a decision maker wished to explore and analyze. Hence, it is possible that they will conflict with each other. For instance, cost may conflict with profit, etc.

Incommensurable units: Since we may have different attributes to consider in a decision environment, they may be measured by different units of measurement. For example, price as an attribute may be measured in dollars, while delivery may be measured in number of days, which are not commensurable. This aspect of being incommensurable makes the MADM a bit more complex and difficult to solve.

Decision weights: Since the methods deal with attributes and not all attributes are of the same importance, these methods require some weights for the attributes that are either given explicitly or arrived at. The weights are always normalized to add up to one.

Decision matrix: A decision matrix is used to represent the alternatives and decision criteria. Let **A** be an $m \times n$ matrix in which element x_{ij} indicates the performance of alternative A_i when it is evaluated in terms of decision criterion C_j (for $i = 1, 2, 3, ..., m$ and $j = 1, 2, 3, ..., n$). It is also assumed that the decision maker has determined the weights of relative performance of the decision criteria (denoted as w_j, for $j = 1, 2, 3, ..., n$). This is represented in Figure 12.5.

$$
\begin{array}{c}
 \\ \\
A_1 \\ A_2 \\ A_3 \\ \cdots \\ \cdots \\ A_m
\end{array}
\begin{array}{cccccc}
C_1 & C_2 & C_3 & \cdots & \cdots\cdots & C_n \\
w_1 & w_2 & w_3 & \cdots & \cdots\cdots & w_n \\
\end{array}
$$

$$
\begin{array}{c}
A_1 \\ A_2 \\ A_3 \\ \cdots \\ \cdots \\ A_m
\end{array}
\begin{pmatrix}
x_{11} & x_{12} & x_{13} & \cdots & \cdots & x_{1n} \\
x_{21} & x_{22} & x_{23} & \cdots & \cdots & x_{2n} \\
x_{31} & x_{32} & x_{33} & \cdots & \cdots & x_{3n} \\
\cdots & \cdots & \cdots & \cdots & \cdots & \cdots \\
\cdots & \cdots & \cdots & \cdots & \cdots & \cdots \\
x_{m1} & x_{m2} & x_{m3} & \cdots & \cdots & x_{mn}
\end{pmatrix}
$$

FIGURE 12.5 Decision matrix representation.

12.4 | ANALYTIC HIERARCHY PROCESS

The terminologies that are given here are the popular terms used in most of the MCDM methods and familiarity with them will be useful to study more advanced tools in MCDM.

The Analytic Hierarchy Process (AHP) (Saaty, 1980, 1983, 1990, and 1994) deals with complex problems by decomposing an MCDM problem into a system of hierarchies. The final step in the AHP deals with the structure of an $m \times n$ matrix (where m is the number of alternatives and n is the number of criteria). This matrix is constructed by using the relative importance of the alternatives in terms of each criterion. The vector $(a_{i1}, a_{i2}, a_{i3}, \ldots, a_{in})$ for each i is the principal eigenvector of an $n \times n$ reciprocal matrix, which is determined by pairwise comparisons of the impact of the m alternatives on the ith criterion. The entry a_{ij} in the $m \times n$ matrix represents the relative value of the alternative A_i when it is considered in terms of criterion C_j. In the original AHP, $\sum_{i=1}^{m} a_{ij}$ is equal to 1. According to AHP, the best alternative (in the maximization case) is indicated by the following relationship:

$$A^*_{\text{AHP}} = \max_i \sum_{j=1}^{n} a_{ij} w_j \text{ for } i = 1, 2, 3, \ldots, m$$

where A^*_{AHP} is the AHP score of the best alternative, n is the number of decision criteria, a_{ij} is the actual value of the ith alternative in terms of the jth criterion, and w_j is the weight of importance of the jth criterion.

For applying AHP, one of the most important steps is data collection and acquisition and data accuracy. Since most of the situations will use qualitative data, it is often challenging to quantify such data and express it properly. This is often a problem with linguistics expressions for a few opinions and cannot be backed up with quantitative support. There are methods that attempt to determine the relative importance, or weight, of the alternatives in terms of each criterion involved in a given decision-making problem. Saaty (1980 and 1983) suggested an approach based on pairwise comparisons, which has long attracted the interest of many researchers. It is argued that ranking is easier to give preferences if a pair of alternatives is given instead of a long list. For example, if we are asked to rank 15 items, it is easy to rank a few initially but the later ones become tougher and may be arbitrary also. But if we are given a pair from the list to express the preference, it is comprehensible and possible to express the preferences. So pairwise comparisons are used to determine the relative importance of each alternative in terms of each criterion. Hence, in this approach, a decision maker has to express his/her opinion about the value of one single pairwise comparison at a time. Usually, the decision maker has to choose among several discrete choices. Each choice is a linguistic phrase. Some examples of such linguistic phrases are "*A is more important than B*," or "*A is of the same importance as B*," or "*A is a little more important than B*," and so on. The focus here is not on the wording of these linguistic statements, but on the numerical values that should be associated with such statements.

Although it is easy to express a comparison in linguistic terms as explained earlier, the problem with such comparisons is still **how to quantify it**. These problems appear not only with AHP, but even for many MADM methods.

The values of the pairwise comparisons are determined according to the scale introduced by Saaty (1980). According to this scale (which we call Scale 1), the available values for the pairwise comparisons are members of the set {9, 8, 7, 6, 5, 4, 3, 2, 1, 1/2, 1/3, 1/4, 1/5, 1/6, 1/7, 1/8, 1/9}. The preceding numbers illustrate that the values for the pairwise comparisons can be grouped into the two intervals [9, 1] and [1, 1/9]. As can be observed, the values in the interval [9, 1] are **evenly distributed**, while the values in the interval [1, 1/9] are **skewed** to the right end of this interval. An alternative has been proposed by Ma and Zheng (1991).

12.4.1 Steps for AHP

Step 1: List the overall goal, criteria, and decision alternatives.

Step 2: Develop a pairwise comparison matrix.

Rate the relative importance between each pair of decision alternatives. The matrix lists the alternatives horizontally and vertically and has the numerical ratings comparing the horizontal (first) alternative with the vertical (second) alternative.

Ratings are given in Table 12.1:

Among all the MCDM methods, AHP is the most popular and often-applied tool in most decision-making areas. Although it is based on pairwise ranking and judgments, a good database of records and transactions can help a decision maker make appropriate judgments based on them and can lead to good-quality decisions. The consistency steps help a decision maker also check his/her judgments to take any corrective actions.

TABLE 12.1 Ratings for using AHP

Compared to the Second Alternative, the First Alternative is	Numerical Rating
Extremely preferred	9
Very strongly preferred	7
Strongly preferred	5
Moderately preferred	3
Equally preferred	1

Intermediate numeric ratings of 8, 6, 4, 2 can be assigned. A reciprocal rating (i.e., 1/9, 1/8, etc.) is assigned when the second alternative is preferred to the first. The value of 1 is always assigned when comparing an alternative with itself.

Step 3: Develop a normalized matrix.

Divide each number in a column of the pairwise comparison matrix by its column sum.

Step 4: Develop the priority vector.

Average each row of the normalized matrix. These row averages form the priority vector of alternative preferences with respect to the particular criterion. The values in this vector sum to 1.

Step 5: Calculate a consistency ratio (CR).

The consistency of the subjective input in the pairwise comparison matrix can be measured by calculating a consistency ratio. A consistency ratio less than 0.1 is good. For ratios greater than 0.1, the subjective input should be re-evaluated.

Step 6: Develop a priority matrix.

After steps 2 through 5 have been performed for all criteria, the results of step 4 are summarized in a priority matrix by listing the decision alternatives horizontally and the criteria vertically. The column entries are the priority vectors for each criterion.

Step 7: Develop a pairwise development matrix for the criteria.

Steps 1 to 6 are done for each criterion for the alternatives, while this step is done for the criteria themselves in the same manner as that used to construct alternative pairwise comparison matrices by using subjective ratings (step 2). Similarly, normalize the matrix (step 3) and develop a criteria priority vector (step 4).

Step 8: Develop an overall priority vector.

Multiply the criteria priority vector (from step 7) by the priority matrix (from step 6).

12.4.2 Determining the Consistency Ratio

Step 1: For each row of the pairwise comparison matrix, determine a weighted sum by summing the multiples of the entries by the priority of its corresponding (column) alternative.

Step 2: For each row, divide its weighted sum by the priority of its corresponding (row) alternative.

Step 3: Determine the average λ_{max} of the results of step 2.

Step 4: Compute the consistency index, CI, of the n alternatives by CI = $(\lambda_{max} - n)/(n - 1)$.

Step 5: Determine the random index, RI, as follows (Table 12.2):

TABLE 12.2 Random index (RI) table

Number of Alternative (n)	Random Index (RI)	Number of Alternative (n)	Random Index (RI)
3	0.58	6	1.24
4	0.90	7	1.32
5	1.12	8	1.41

Step 6: Compute the consistency ratio CR = CR/RI. If the consistency ratio, CR, is less than 0.10, this is well within the acceptable range for consistency.

EXAMPLE 12.2

Atul Auto Pvt Ltd plans to introduce a new design of seat cushions for its client and must decide which of the three suppliers will develop the new cushions. Three factors seem important to the company: (1) cost, (2) quality of the product, and (3) delivery time. The three suppliers are Century Industries, Republic Cushions, and National Auto. The situation is shown in Figure 12.6.

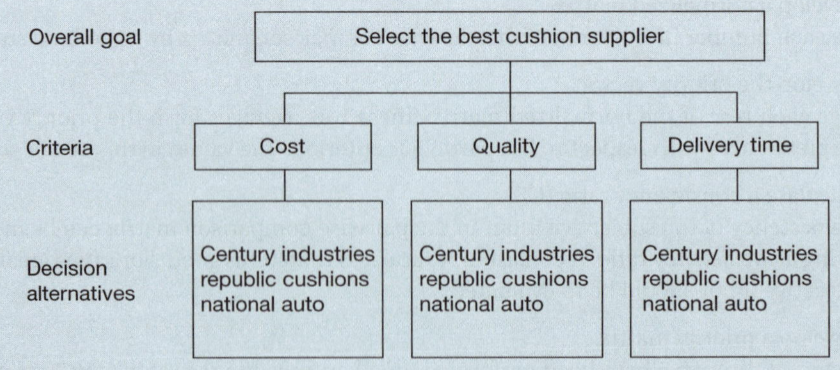

FIGURE 12.6 Hierarchy for the supplier selection problem.

Steps 1 and 2: Forming the pairwise comparison matrix for cost

Century Industries will sell the cushions to Atul Auto for \$120 per seat, Republic will sell for \$100 per seat, and National Auto will sell for \$160 per seat. Atul has decided that in terms of price, Republic is moderately preferred to Century and very strongly preferred to National Auto. Atul also decided that Century is strongly to very strongly preferred to National Auto. We will translate them into pairwise scores and construct the pairwise comparison matrix.

1. Since Republic Cushions is moderately preferred to Century Industries, Century's entry in the Republic Row is 3 and Republic's entry in the Century row is 1/3.
2. Since Republic is very strongly preferred to National Auto, National's entry in the Republic row is 7 and Republic's entry in the National row is 1/7.
3. Since Century is strongly to very strongly preferred to National, National's entry in the Century row is 6 and Century's entry in the National row is 1/6.

The pairwise comparison matrix for cost is as follows:

	Century	Republic	National
Century	1	1/3	6
Republic	3	1	7
National	1/6	1/7	1

Step 3: Normalized matrix for cost

Divide each entry in the pairwise comparison matrix by its corresponding column sum. For example, for Century, the column sum is $1+3+1/6=25/6$. This gives:

	Century	Republic	National
Century	6/25	7/31	6/14
Republic	18/25	21/31	7/14
National	1/25	3/31	1/14

Step 4: Priority vector for cost

The priority vector is determined by averaging the row entries in the normalized matrix. Converting to decimals, we get:

	Century	Republic	National	Priority Vector
Century	6/25	7/31	6/14	**0.298**
Republic	18/25	21/31	7/14	**0.632**
National	1/25	3/31	1/14	**0.069**

Step 5: Checking consistency

1. Multiply each column of the pairwise comparison matrix by its priority:

$$0.298\times\begin{pmatrix}1\\3\\1/6\end{pmatrix}+0.632\times\begin{pmatrix}1/3\\1\\1/7\end{pmatrix}+0.069\times\begin{pmatrix}6\\7\\1\end{pmatrix}=\begin{matrix}0.925\\2.013\\0.209\end{matrix}$$

2. Divide these numbers by their priorities to get:

$$0.923/0.298 = 3.104$$
$$2.009/0.632 = 3.182$$
$$0.209/0.069 = 3.018$$

3. Average the preceding results to get λ_{max}.

$$\lambda_{max} = (3.097 + 3.179 + 3.029)/3 = 3.101$$

4. Compute the consistency index, CI, for two terms by:

$$CI = (\lambda_{max} - n)/(n - 1) = (3.102 - 3)/2 = 0.051$$

5. Compute the consistency ratio, CR, by CI/RI, where RI = 0.58 for three factors:

$$CR = CI/RI = 0.051/0.58 = 0.087$$

Since the consistency ratio, CR, is less than 0.10, this is well within the acceptable range for consistency.

Forming the Pairwise Comparison Matrix for Quality

Atul Auto, from its past records, determined that for quality, Century is strongly preferable to Republic. It also determined that National is very strongly preferable to Republic and moderately preferable to Century. Based on this, the pairwise comparison matrix for quality is as follows:

	Century	Republic	National
Century	1	6	1/4
Republic	1/6	1	1/8
National	4	8	1

Normalized Matrix for Quality

Divide each entry in the pairwise comparison matrix by its corresponding column sum. For example, for Century, the column sum is $1 + 1/6 + 4 = 31/6$. This gives:

	Century	Republic	National
Century	6/31	6/15	8/44
Republic	1/31	1/15	4/44
National	24/31	8/15	32/44

Priority Vector for Quality

The priority vector is determined by averaging the row entries in the normalized matrix. Converting to decimals, we get:

Century: $(6/31 + 6/15 + 8/44)/3 = $ **0.259**
Republic: $(1/31 + 1/15 + 4/44)/3 = $ **0.063**
National: $(24/31 + 8/15 + 32/44)/3 = $ **0.678**

Checking Consistency

Atul's responses to quality could be checked for consistency in the same manner as was done for cost.

Forming the Pairwise Comparison Matrix for Delivery Time

Atul determined from the delivery history of these suppliers that for delivery time, Century is equally preferable to National. Both Century and National are very strongly preferable to Republic. Based on this, the pairwise comparison matrix for quality is as follows:

	Century	Republic	National
Century	1	6	1
Republic	1/6	1	1/6
National	1	6	1

Normalized Matrix for Delivery Time

Divide each entry in the pairwise comparison matrix by its corresponding column sum. For example, for Century, the column sum is 1 + 1/6 + 1 = 13/6. This gives:

	Century	Republic	National
Century	6/13	6/13	6/13
Republic	1/13	1/13	1/13
National	6/13	6/13	6/13

Priority Vector for Delivery Time

The priority vector is determined by averaging the row entries in the normalized matrix. Converting to decimals, we get:

$$\begin{array}{l} \text{Century: } (6/13+6/13+6/13)/3 = \\ \text{Republic: } (1/31+1/15+4/44)/3 = \\ \text{National: } (6/13+6/13+6/13)/3 = \end{array} \begin{pmatrix} \mathbf{0.4615} \\ \mathbf{0.077} \\ \mathbf{0.4615} \end{pmatrix}$$

Checking Consistency

Atul's responses to delivery time could be checked for consistency in the same manner as was done for cost.

Now the next step is also to look at the criteria cost, quality, and delivery time and construct the priority vector for them.

The supply chain team determined that in terms of criteria, quality is very strongly preferable to cost and moderately preferable to delivery time, and cost is moderately preferable to delivery time, from its experience. Based on this, the pairwise comparison matrix for criteria is as follows:

	Cost	Quality	Delivery Time
Cost	1	1/8	4
Quality	8	1	4
Delivery Time	1/4	1/4	1

Normalized Matrix for Criteria

Divide each entry in the pairwise comparison matrix by its corresponding column sum. For example, for Cost, the column sum is $1 + 8 + 1/4 = 37/4$. This gives:

	Cost	Quality	Delivery Time
Cost	4/37	4/44	4/9
Quality	32/37	32/44	4/9
Delivery Time	1/37	8/44	1/9

Priority Vector for Criteria

The priority vector is determined by averaging the row entries in the normalized matrix. Converting to decimals, we get:

$$\begin{aligned}
&\text{Cost:} && (4/37 + 4/44 + 4/9)/3 &&= \mathbf{0.214} \\
&\text{Quality:} && (32/37 + 32/44 + 4/9)/3 &&= \mathbf{0.679} \\
&\text{Delivery time:} && (1/37 + 8/44 + 1/9)/3 &&= \mathbf{0.107}
\end{aligned}$$

The responses to criteria could be checked for consistency in the same manner as was done for cost. This priority vector gives more weight to quality, then cost, and after that, the delivery time. This vector forms the weightage vector for the respective suppliers for the priority vector that we obtained for cost, quality, and delivery time.

Overall Priority Vector

The overall priorities are determined by multiplying the priority vector of the criteria by the priorities for each decision alternative for each objective:

Priority Vector for Criteria →	0.214	0.679	0.107
	Cost	Quality	Delivery Time
Century Industries	0.298	0.259	0.4615
Republic Cushions	0.632	0.063	0.077
National Auto	0.069	0.678	0.4615

Thus, the overall priority vector is:

$$\begin{aligned}
&\text{Century Industries:} && (0.214)(0.298) + (0.679)(0.259) + (0.107)(0.4615) &&= \mathbf{0.289} \\
&\text{Republic Cushions:} && (0.214)(0.632) + (0.679)(0.063) + (0.107)(0.077) &&= \mathbf{0.186} \\
&\text{National Auto:} && (0.214)(0.069) + (0.679)(0.678) + (0.107)(0.4615) &&= \mathbf{0.525}
\end{aligned}$$

Therefore, National Auto will be the overall recommendation to be selected as the supplier followed by Century Industries.

12.5 TECHNIQUE FOR ORDER OF PREFERENCE BY SIMILARITY TO IDEAL SOLUTION (TOPSIS)

TOPSIS as a tool was originally proposed and developed by Hwang and Yoon in 1981. It is based on the simple idea that the optimal solution or criteria should be chosen in such a way that it is farthest from the anti-ideal solution and closest to the ideal solution.

A typical MCDM problem is one where there are m alternatives ($A_1, A_2, A_3, \ldots, A_m$) and n criteria ($C_1, C_2, C_3, \ldots, C_n$). A decision maker has to evaluate the alternatives on the basis of these n criteria. This can be expressed in the form of the following matrix D and W.

$$
\begin{array}{cc}
 & \begin{array}{ccccccc} C_1 & C_2 & C_3 & \ldots & \ldots\ldots & C_n \\ w_1 & w_2 & w_3 & \ldots & \ldots\ldots & w_n \end{array} \\
D = \begin{array}{c} A_1 \\ A_2 \\ A_3 \\ \ldots \\ \ldots \\ A_m \end{array} & \begin{pmatrix} x_{11} & x_{12} & x_{13} & \ldots & \ldots & x_{1n} \\ x_{21} & x_{22} & x_{23} & \ldots & \ldots & x_{2n} \\ x_{31} & x_{32} & x_{33} & \ldots & \ldots & x_{3n} \\ \ldots & \ldots & \ldots & \ldots & \ldots & \ldots \\ \ldots & \ldots & \ldots & \ldots & \ldots & \ldots \\ x_{m1} & x_{m2} & x_{m3} & \ldots & \ldots & x_{mn} \end{pmatrix}
\end{array}
$$

$$W = [\, w_1 \quad w_2 \ldots \quad w_n \,]$$

In matrix D, x_{ij} represents the rating of the alternative A_i with respect to the criteria C_j, and w_j in the weight matrix W is the weight of the criteria C_j.

12.5.1 Process and Algorithm of TOPSIS

In the MCDM methods, TOPSIS made way for using judgments in a logical manner and comparing with ideal and anti-ideal solutions so that the decision is more balanced. Although it is also based on ratings or judgments, the followed steps try to bring more consistency and lead to a proper conclusion.

Step 1: Calculate the normalized ratings (r_{ij}) by using the vector normalization procedure.

1. If the attribute is positive (for example, a type of benefit), $r_{ij} = \dfrac{x_{ij}}{\sqrt{\sum_{i=1}^{m} x_{ij}^2}}$

2. If the attribute is negative (for example, a type of cost), $r_{ij} = 1 - \dfrac{x_{ij}}{\sqrt{\sum_{i=1}^{m} x_{ij}^2}}$

Calculate the normalized ratings (r_{ij}) by using the linear normalization procedure.

1. If the attribute is positive, $r_{ij} = \dfrac{x_{ij} - \text{Min}\, x_{ij}}{\text{Max}\, x_{ij} - \text{Min}\, x_{ij}}$ over all i

2. If the attribute is negative, $r_{ij} = \dfrac{\text{Max}\, x_{ij} - x_{ij}}{\text{Max}\, x_{ij} - \text{Min}\, x_{ij}}$ over all i

Step 2: Calculate the weighted normalized rating value by

$$v_{ij} = w_j{}^* r_{ij}, \text{ where } i = 1, 2, \ldots, m; j = 1, 2, \ldots, n$$

Step 3: Identify the positive ideal solution (PIS), A^*, and negative ideal solution (NIS), A- for each criterion.

Here $A^* = (v_1^*, v_2^*, \ldots, v_n^*)$ and v_j^* is the best possible value of the jth criterion with respect to all the other available alternatives.

$A- = (v_{1-}, v_{2-}, \ldots, v_{n-})$ and v_{j-} is the worst possible value of the jth criterion with respect to all the other available alternatives.

Step 4: Calculate the separation of each alternative from the ideal solution and anti-ideal solution.

1. Distance from ideal solution, $D^+ = \sqrt{\sum_{j=1}^{m} \left(x_{ij} - \text{PIS}\right)^2}$

2. Distance from anti-ideal solution, $D^- = \sqrt{\sum_{j=1}^{m} \left(x_{ij} - \text{NIS}\right)^2}$

Step 5: Calculate the similarity rating or similarity score from the ideal solution (relative closeness to the ideal solution) by

$$C_i = \left(\frac{D^-}{D^+ + D^-} \right)$$

Step 6: Rank the preference order according to the value of C_i.

EXAMPLE 12.3

We will look at an example of a person selecting a brand of car. She has come up with the following brands of cars, and a set of criteria to select the brand as well as the weights she wants to assign to each criterion. They are presented in Table 12.3.

TABLE 12.3 Example of selection of a car with attributes and criteria

Attributes	Life of Car (C1)	Cost of Car (C2)	Fuel Economy (per Liter of Petrol) (C3)	Elegance (A4)
Attribute Weights	**0.3**	**0.25**	**0.35**	**0.1**
Brands (Alternatives)				
Swift Dzire (A1)	12 years	$12500	15 km	Decent
Ertiga (A2)	10 years	$11000	18 km	Good
Toyota Innova (A3)	12 years	$20500	13 km	Very elegant
Xcent Prime (A4)	12 years	$11000	15 km	Good

Based on the data collected, she has assigned scores for each brand on each criterion as shown in Table 12.4 with a score of 1 to 10 where 1 is very poor and 10 is excellent.

TABLE 12.4 Assigning scores to attributes

	Attributes	Life of Car (C1)	Cost of Car (C2)	Fuel Economy (per Liter of Petrol) (C3)	Elegance (A4)
Alternatives	**Attribute Weights**	**0.3**	**0.25**	**0.35**	**0.1**
	Swift Dzire (A1)	8	7	7	7
	Ertiga (A2)	7	8	8	6
	Toyota Innova (A3)	8	4	5	8
	Xcent Prime (A4)	8	8	7	6

We will use the TOPSIS method to select the brand of car (alternative). The steps are presented in the following tables using the vector normalization method as mentioned in the steps.

Step 1: Calculate the normalized ratings (Table 12.5).

TABLE 12.5 Calculation of normalized ratings

	Attribute			
	Life of Car (C1)	Cost of Car (C2)*	Fuel Economy (C3)	Elegance (A4)
Attribute Weights	**0.3**	**0.25**	**0.35**	**0.1**
Swift Dzire (A1)	8	7	7	7
Ertiga (A2)	7	8	8	6
Toyota Innova (A3)	8	4	5	8
Xcent Prime (A4)	8	8	7	6
Norm (*j*)	**15.524**	**13.892**	**13.675**	**13.601**
	Life of Car (C1)	Cost of Car (C2)*	Fuel Economy (C3)	Elegance (A4)
Attribute Weights	**0.3**	**0.25**	**0.35**	**0.1**
Swift Dzire (A1)	0.5153	0.4961	0.5119	0.5147
Ertiga (A2)	0.4509	0.4241	0.5850	0.4411
Toyota Innova (A3)	0.5153	0.7121	0.3656	0.5882
Xcent Prime (A4)	0.5153	0.4241	0.5119	0.4411

* Cost as an attribute is taken as negative, and so the normalization is done accordingly.

Step 2: Calculate the weighted normalized rating values using the weights that are assigned for the attributes, as shown in Table 12.6.

TABLE 12.6 Calculation of weighted normalized ratings

	Weighted Normalized Rating Values			
	Attribute			
	Life of Car (C1)	Cost of Car (C2)	Fuel Economy (C3)	Elegance (A4)
Attribute Weights	**0.3**	**0.25**	**0.35**	**0.1**
Swift Dzire (A1)	0.1546	0.1240	0.1792	0.0515
Ertiga (A2)	0.1353	0.1060	0.2048	0.0441
Toyota Innova (A3)	0.1546	0.1780	0.1280	0.0588
Xcent Prime (A4)	0.1546	0.1060	0.1792	0.0441

Step 3: Identify the PIS and NIS for each of the attributes among the alternatives as shown in Table 12.7.

TABLE 12.7 Identification of PIS and NIS

Ideal PIS and NIS				
Ideal Solution	**Life of Car (C1)**	**Cost of Car (C2)**	**Fuel Economy (C3)**	**Elegance (A4)**
PIS (+)	0.1546	0.1780	0.2048	0.0588
NIS (–)	0.1353	0.1060	0.1280	0.0441

Steps 4–6: Calculate the separation of each alternative from the ideal solution and anti-ideal solution. Calculate the similarity rating or similarity score from the ideal solution (relative closeness to the ideal solution C_i), and rank the preference order according to the value of C_i. They are shown in Tables 12.8 and 12.9.

TABLE 12.8 Separation of each alternative from the PIS and NIS

PIS(+)	NIS(-)	Swift Desire (A1)	(xij-PIS) sqr	(xij-NIS) sqr	Ertiga (A2)	(xij-PIS) sqr	(xij-NIS) sqr	Toyota Innova (A3)	(xij-PIS) sqr	(xij-NIS) sqr	Xcent Prime (A4)	(xij-PIS) sqr	(xij-NIS) sqr
0.1546	0.1353	0.1546	0.0000	0.0004	0.1353	0.0004	0.0000	0.1546	0.0000	0.0004	0.1546	0.0000	0.0004
0.1780	0.1060	0.1240	0.0029	0.0003	0.1060	0.0052	0.0000	0.1780	0.0000	0.0052	0.1060	0.0052	0.0000
0.2048	0.1280	0.1792	0.0007	0.0026	0.2048	0.0000	0.0059	0.1280	0.0059	0.0000	0.1792	0.0007	0.0026
0.0588	0.0441	0.0515	0.0001	0.0001	0.0441	0.0002	0.0000	0.0588	0.0000	0.0002	0.0441	0.0002	0.0000
			0.0036	0.0034		0.0058	0.0059		0.0059	0.0058		0.0061	0.0030
			0.0602	0.0581		0.0760	0.0768		0.0768	0.0760		0.0778	0.0547

TABLE 12.9 Similarity score from ideal solution and preference rank

	Swift Dzire (A1)	Ertiga (A2)	Toyota Innova (A3)	Xcent Prime (A4)
D+	0.0602	0.0760	0.0768	0.0778
D–	0.0581	0.0768	0.0760	0.0547
C*	**0.4910**	**0.5027**	**0.4973**	**0.4129**
Rank	**3rd**	**1st**	**2nd**	**4th**

As can be seen, Ertiga is preferred first followed by Innova and the others after that. Innova is preferred to Swift Dzire due to the weights, with a weight of only 0.25 given to the cost and more weights to the other attributes.

If we had used the linear normalization method, then the table would have changed as follows from step 1 onwards. Tables 12.10 to 12.15 show the steps using linear normalization method.

TABLE 12.10 Assigning scores to attributes using linear normalization method

	Attribute			
	Life of Car (C1)	Cost of Car (C2)	Fuel Economy (C3)	Elegance (A4)
Attribute Weights	**0.3**	**0.25**	**0.35**	**0.1**
Swift Dzire (A1)	8	7	7	7
Ertiga (A2)	7	8	8	6
Toyota Innova (A3)	8	4	5	8
Xcent Prime (A4)	8	8	7	6
Max	**8.00**	**8.00**	**8.00**	**8.00**
Min	**7**	**4**	**5**	**6**
Range	**1.00**	**4.00**	**3.00**	**2.00**
	Life of Car (C1)	**Cost of Car (C2)**	**Fuel Economy (C3)**	**Elegance (A4)**
Attribute Weights	**0.3**	**0.25**	**0.35**	**0.1**
Swift Dzire (A1)	0.0000	0.2500	0.6667	0.5000
Ertiga (A2)	1.0000	0.0000	1.0000	0.0000
Toyota Innova (A3)	0.0000	1.0000	0.0000	1.0000
Xcent Prime (A4)	0.0000	0.0000	0.6667	0.0000

TABLE 12.11 Scores using linear normalization method

	Attribute			
	Life of Car (C1)	Cost of Car (C2)	Fuel Economy (C3)	Elegance (A4)
Attribute Weights	**0.3**	**0.25**	**0.35**	**0.1**
Swift Dzire (A1)	0.0000	0.0625	0.2333	0.0500
Ertiga (A2)	0.3000	0.0000	0.3500	0.0000
Toyota Innova (A3)	0.0000	0.2500	0.0000	0.1000
Xcent Prime (A4)	0.0000	0.0000	0.2333	0.0000

TABLE 12.12 Identification of PIS and NIS

Ideal Solution	Life of Car (C1)	Cost of Car (C2)	Fuel Economy (C3)	Elegance (A4)
PIS(+)	0.3000	0.2500	0.3500	0.1000
NIS(–)	0.0000	0.0000	0.0000	0.0000

TABLE 12.13 Separation of each alternative from the PIS and NIS

PIS(+)	NIS(-)	Swift Desire (A1)	(xij-PIS) sqr	(xij-NIS) sqr	Ertiga (A2)	(xij-PIS) sqr	(xij-NIS) sqr	Toyota Innova (A3)	(xij-PIS) sqr	(xij-NIS) sqr	Xcent Prime (A4)	(xij-PIS) sqr	(xij-NIS) sqr
0.3	0	0.0000	0.0900	0.0000	0.3000	0.0000	0.0900	0.0000	0.0900	0.0000	0.0000	0.0900	0.0000
0.25	0	0.0625	0.0352	0.0039	0.0000	0.0625	0.0000	0.2500	0.0000	0.0625	0.0000	0.0625	0.0000
0.35	0	0.2333	0.0136	0.0544	0.3500	0.0000	0.1225	0.0000	0.1225	0.0000	0.2333	0.0136	0.0544
0.1	0	0.0500	0.0025	0.0025	0.0000	0.0100	0.0000	0.1000	0.0000	0.0100	0.0000	0.0100	0.0000
			0.1413	0.0609		0.0725	0.2125		0.2125	0.0725		0.1761	0.0544
			0.3759	0.2467		0.2693	0.4610		0.4610	0.2693		0.4197	0.2333

TABLE 12.14 Similarity score from ideal solution and preference rank

Separation and Closeness	Swift Dzire (A1)	Ertiga (A2)	Toyota Innova (A3)	Xcent Prime (A4)
D+	0.3759	0.2693	0.4610	0.4197
D–	0.2467	0.4610	0.2693	0.2333
C*	**0.3962**	**0.6313**	**0.3687**	**0.3573**
Rank	**2nd**	**1st**	**3rd**	**4th**

We see that there is a change in preference using the linear normalization method. Although Ertiga is preferred the most, it is followed by Swift Dzire, Innova, and then Xcent.

12.6 | BASICS OF FUZZY LOGIC

The concept of fuzzy sets and logic was developed by Zadeh in the 1960's. Fuzzy logic is used to model problems involving imprecise data and for problems where the boundaries between categories are not precise. Fuzzy logic takes the position that everything that we measure is vague and imprecise. For example, let us consider the heights of a sample of people. What would one call a person who is 5′7″ tall? Would he or she be called tall or short? In practice, we use linguistic terms to judge a person's decision. However, they do not have very precise boundaries. Hence, the use of fuzzy logic is appropriate to model such real-world problems using linguistic variables and quantifiers.

12.6.1 Definition of Fuzzy Set

A fuzzy set $\tilde{A}$ in a universe X can be characterized by a membership function $\mu_{\tilde{A}}(x)$, which has an association with every element x in X, a real number in the interval [0, 1]. The value of the function $\mu_{\tilde{A}}(x)$ is called the grade of the membership function of x in $\mu_{\tilde{A}}(x)$. The degree of membership of an individual in a fuzzy set expresses the degree of compatibility of the individual with the concept represented by the fuzzy set. Each fuzzy set A is defined in terms of a relevant universal set X by a function called its membership function that assigns to each element x of X a number $A(x)$ in the closed unit interval [0, 1]. This function characterizes the degree of membership of x in A, that is, $A: X \rightarrow [0,1]$. This is shown in Figure 12.7.

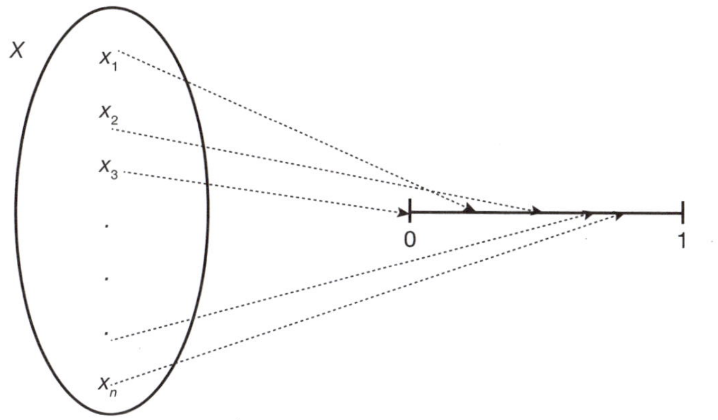

FIGURE 12.7 Representation of fuzzy membership function.

Let us take an example of graphically representing the education level of a person with the following details for different membership functions where the education level of a person with a bachelor's degree is "highly educated" with the degree of 0.8 and "very highly educated" with the degree of 0.5. Table 12.15 presents details of education levels and numerical code used.

TABLE 12.15 Details of education levels

Level No.	Education Level Attained
0	No education
1	Elementary school
2	High school
3	Two-year college degree
4	Bachelor's degree
5	Master's degree
6	Doctoral degree

This is shown in Figure 12.8.

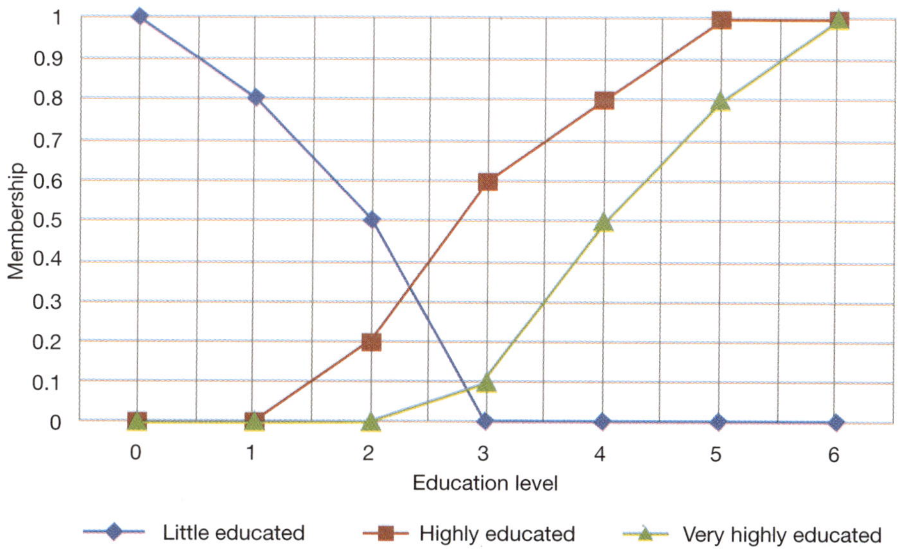

FIGURE 12.8 Membership functions for educational level.

Different types of membership functions (MFs) are used in fuzzy logic and some of them are as follows:

1. Triangular MF
2. Trapezoidal MF
3. Gaussian MF
4. Generalized bell MF

These are illustrated in Figure 12.9.

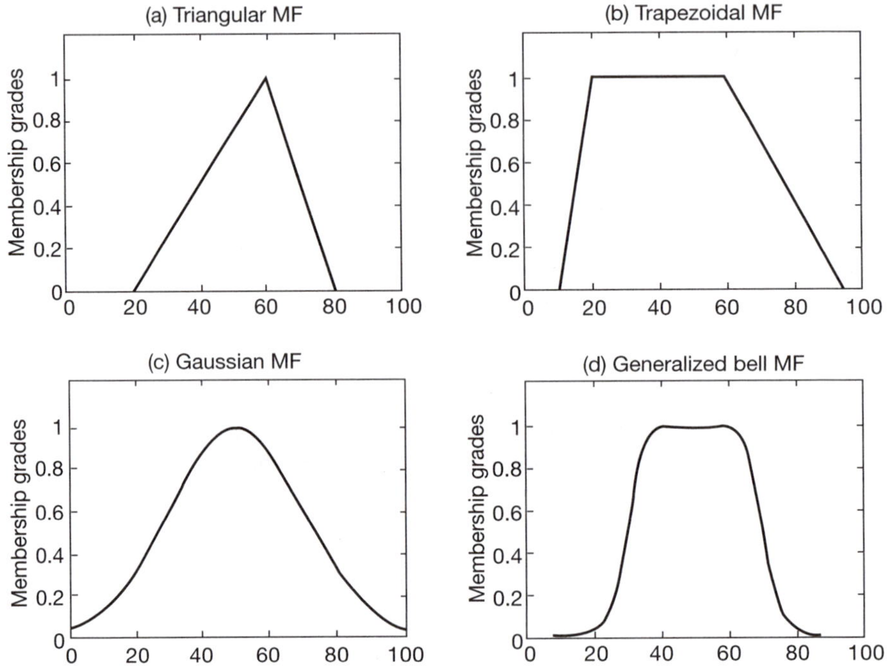

FIGURE 12.9 Types of membership functions.

For example, we will explain how the triangular membership function is formed and used. A triangular fuzzy number $\tilde{U}$ can be defined by a triplet (l, m, u), where the membership function $\mu_{\tilde{U}}(x)$ can be defined by

$$\mu_{\tilde{U}}(x) = \begin{cases} (x-l)/(m-l), l \leq x \leq m \\ (x-u)/(m-u), m \leq x \leq u \\ 0, \text{otherwise} \end{cases}$$

The membership function is shown in Figure 12.10.

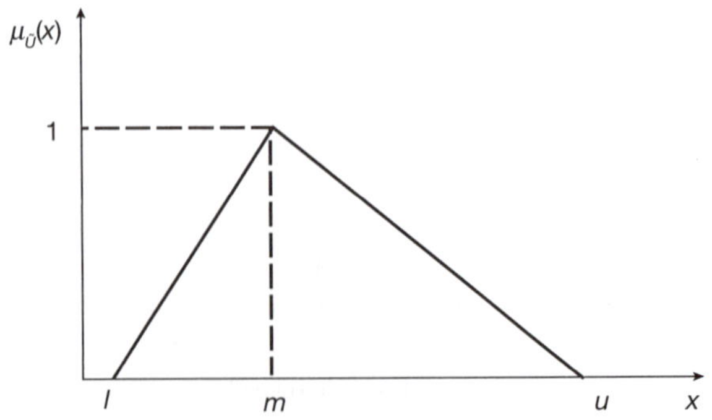

FIGURE 12.10 Triangular membership function.

12.6.2 Some Basic Definitions on Fuzzy Numbers

1. **Equality of two fuzzy numbers:** Let $\tilde{O} = (o_1, o_2, o_3)$ and $\tilde{U} = (u_1, u_2, u_3)$ be two triangular fuzzy numbers. If $\tilde{O} = \tilde{U}$, then $o_1 = u_1$, $o_2 = u_2$, and $o_3 = u_3$.
2. **Definition of fuzzy matrix:** $\tilde{O}$ is called a fuzzy matrix if at least an entry in $\tilde{O}$ is a fuzzy number.
3. **Distance between two fuzzy numbers:** Let $\tilde{O} = (o_1, o_2, o_3)$ and $\tilde{U} = (u_1, u_2, u_3)$ be two triangular fuzzy numbers. Then the distance $(d(\tilde{O}, \tilde{U}))$ between them is calculated by

$$d(\tilde{O}, \tilde{U}) = \sqrt{1/3[(o_1 - u_1)^2 + (o_2 - u_2)^2 + (o_3 - u_3)^2}$$

4. **Equality of fuzzy numbers from distance property:** Two triangular fuzzy numbers $\tilde{O}$ and $\tilde{U}$ are identical if and only if $d(\tilde{O}, \tilde{U}) = 0$.
5. **Closeness of fuzzy numbers:** Let $\tilde{O}$ and $\tilde{U}$ be two triangular fuzzy numbers. The fuzzy number $\tilde{O}$ is closer to the fuzzy number $\tilde{U}$ as $d(\tilde{O}, \tilde{U})$ approaches 0.
6. Let $\tilde{A}$, $\tilde{O}$, and $\tilde{U}$ be three triangular fuzzy numbers. The fuzzy number $\tilde{O}$ is closer to the fuzzy number $\tilde{A}$ than the other fuzzy number $\tilde{U}$ if and only if $d(\tilde{A}, \tilde{O}) < d(\tilde{A}, \tilde{U})$.
7. Let $\tilde{n} = (0, 0, 0)$ be the origin. If $d(\tilde{O}, \tilde{n}) < d(\tilde{U}, \tilde{n})$, then the fuzzy number $\tilde{O}$ is closer to the origin than the other fuzzy number $\tilde{U}$.

We will see how fuzzy numbers are used in MADM in the following section.

12.6.3 Fuzzy MADM

MADM problems often consider subjective views of human beings in the decision-making process. Therefore, fuzzy logic is found to be more appropriate for handling MADM problems to include the ambiguities and vagueness in human judgments in linguistic terms. A collection of expert opinions is followed by fuzzification, that is, the generation of fuzzy numbers (triangular, etc.) to include the vagueness in priorities and then defuzzification is done using the center of area or center of gravity method to get crisp numbers for the criteria and alternatives. A fuzzy logic system (FLS) can be defined as the nonlinear mapping of an input dataset to a scalar output data. An FLS consists of the following three main parts:

1. **Fuzzifier (Fuzzification):** A crisp set of input data are gathered and converted to a fuzzy set.
2. **Inference engine with rules:** An inference is made based on a set of rules.
3. **Defuzzifier (defuzzification):** The fuzzy output is mapped to a crisp output using the membership functions.

This is shown in Figure 12.11.

One of the mathematical developments in modern science is the concept of fuzzy developed by Zadeh. It is so practical that it makes sense to apply them in real-life problems where most of the contexts, phenomena, etc. are imprecise and nebulous. Most of the terms we use in normal life such as feeling good, tall, intelligent, handsome, beautiful, etc. are fuzzy in nature. Fuzzy numbers and logic make it more usable to apply them in practice to arrive at decisions. In MCDM, most of the methods use fuzzy logic to fine-tune the steps we carry out in deciding the best course of action through fuzzy logic. Here we present two methods: fuzzy AHP and fuzzy TOPSIS.

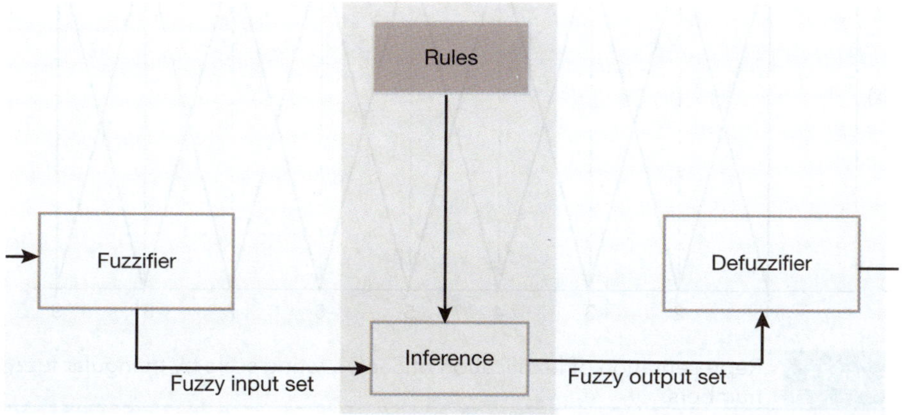

FIGURE 12.11 Mapping of fuzzy numbers.

Now we will see how fuzzy logic can be used in AHP and TOPSIS for the same examples we took in their respective discussions.

12.7 | FUZZY ANALYTIC HIERARCHY PROCESS

12.7.1 Steps for FAHP

We carry out the following steps in fuzzy AHP.

Step 1: Use triangular fuzzy numbers (TFNs) to include the vagueness in the priorities, that is, fuzzification of crisp numbers for preference (Saaty's rating scale) as shown in Table 12.16.

TABLE 12.16 Fuzzification of crisp numbers for preference (Saaty's rating scale)

Linguistic Expression	Equivalent Fuzzy Number	Triangular Fuzzy Numbers	Reciprocal of Equivalent Fuzzy Numbers	Triangular Fuzzy Numbers for Reciprocals
Equally preferred (EP)	1	(1, 1, 2)	1	(1/2, 1, 1)
Equally preferred to moderately preferred (MP)	2	(1, 2, 3)	1/2	(1/3, 1/2, 1)
Moderately preferred (MP)	3	(2, 3, 4)	1/3	(1/4, 1/3, 1/2)
Moderately preferred to strongly preferred (SP)	4	(3, 4, 5)	1/4	(1/5, 1/4, 1/3)
Strongly preferred (SP)	5	(4, 5, 6)	1/5	(1/4, 1/5, 1/6)
Strongly preferred to very strongly preferred (VSP)	6	(5, 6, 7)	1/6	(1/5, 1/6, 1/7)
Very strongly preferred (VSP)	7	(6, 7, 8)	1/7	(1/8, 1/7, 1/6)
Very strongly preferred to extremely preferred (ExP)	8	(7, 8, 9)	1/8	(1/9, 1/8, 1/7)
Extremely preferred (ExP)	9	(8, 9, 9)	1/9	(1/9, 1/9, 1/8)

This can be graphically represented in Figure 12.12.

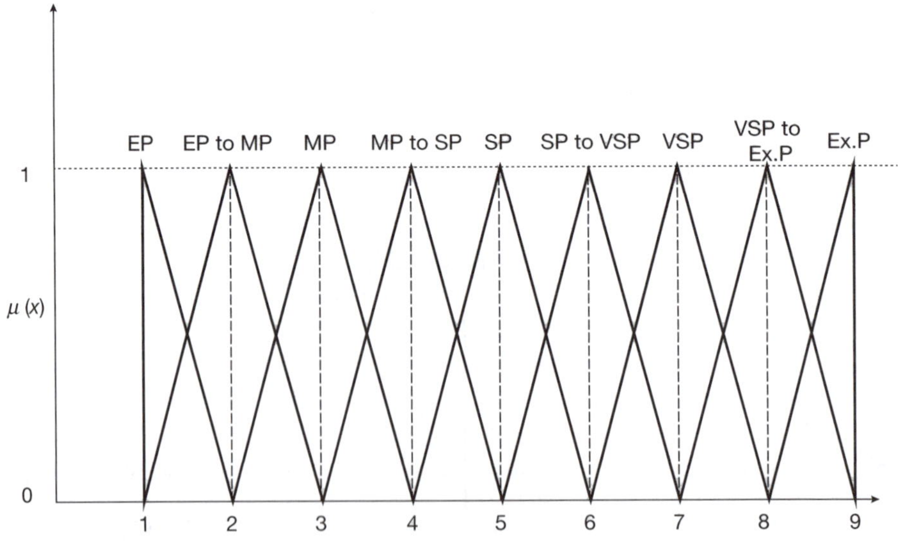

FIGURE 12.12 Representation of fuzzification of Saaty's rating scale by triangular fuzzy numbers.

We will revisit Example 12.2 of Atul Auto Pvt Ltd, which was planning for a new design of seat cushions and exploring the choice of three suppliers namely Century Industries, Republic Cushions, and National Auto with respect to three factors: cost, quality, and delivery time. The pairwise comparison matrix for cost is given on the following table.

Pairwise Comparison Matrix (Fuzzy) for Cost (Original)			
	Century	Republic	National
Century	1	1/3	6
Republic	3	1	7
National	1/6	1/7	1

Now the equivalent triangular fuzzy numbers for the same are given in the following table:

Equivalent TFNs for Cost			
	Century	Republic	National
Century	(1, 1, 1)	(1/4, 1/3, 1/2)	(5, 6, 7)
Republic	(2, 3, 4)	(1, 1, 1)	(6, 7, 8)
National	(1/7, 1/6, 1/5)	(1/8, 1/7, 1/6)	(1, 1, 1)

Step 2: Apply any of the algorithms proposed to get the priority vectors in all the cases. Some of the popular methods are

1. Van Laarhoven and Pedrycz's approach (1983)
2. Buckley's (1985) fuzzy AHP algorithm
3. Chang's (1996) extent analysis approach
4. Cheng's (1996) entropy-based approach

We will use Buckley's algorithm for fuzzification and defuzzification for all the alternatives and criteria.

Buckley's Fuzzy AHP Algorithm

1. **Fuzzification of the preference**
   a. Find the geometric mean (GM) of all l, m, and u of the TFN in each row.
   b. Take column sum of the GMs of l, m, and u.
   c. Take the reciprocal of the column sum.
   d. Arrange the reciprocal in ascending order.
   e. Multiply the reciprocal arranged in ascending order with the GM of l, m, and u, respectively (lowest one with l in all cases and so on) to get the fuzzy weight in the form of (l, m, u).
2. **Defuzzification of the fuzzy weight**
   a. Use the center of area method, that is, the arithmetic mean of l, m, and u.
   b. Normalize the defuzzified weights.
   c. The normalized defuzzified weights are priority vectors.

Step 3: Develop a priority matrix. After Buckley's algorithm has been performed for all criteria, the results are summarized in a priority matrix by listing the decision alternatives horizontally and the criteria vertically. The column entries are the priority vectors for each criterion.

Step 4: Develop a criteria pairwise development matrix in the same manner using Buckley's algorithm.

Step 5: Develop an overall priority vector. Multiply the criteria priority vector by the priority matrix.

We will complete steps 2 and 3 for the alternatives for each criterion and for the criteria also. They are presented in the following tables.

Pairwise Comparison Matrix (Fuzzy) for Cost (Original)

	Century	Republic	National
Century	1.000	0.333	6.000
Republic	3.000	1.000	7.000
National	0.167	0.143	1.000

Step 1: Development of TFN (*l*, *m*, *u*) for fuzzy numbers

Step 2a: Fuzzification using Buckley's algorithm

	Century			Republic			National			GM for *l*	GM for *m*	GM for *u*
	l	*m*	*u*	*l*	*M*	*u*	*l*	*m*	*u*			
Century	1.000	1.000	1.000	0.250	0.333	0.500	5.000	6.000	7.000	**1.077**	**1.260**	**1.518**
Republic	2.000	3.000	4.000	1.000	1.000	1.000	6.000	7.000	8.000	**2.289**	**2.759**	**3.175**
National	0.143	0.167	0.200	0.125	0.143	0.167	1.000	1.000	1.000	**0.261**	**0.288**	**0.322**
								Total		**3.628**	**4.307**	**5.015**
								Reciprocal		**0.276**	**0.232**	**0.199**
								Ascending Order		**0.199**	**0.232**	**0.276**

Step 2b: Defuzzification using Buckley's algorithm

Criteria	Fuzzified Weight			Defuzzified Weights	Normalized Weights (Priority Vector)
	l	*m*	*u*		
Century	0.215	0.293	0.418	0.309	**0.298**
Republic	0.457	0.641	0.875	0.657	**0.635**
National	0.052	0.067	0.089	0.069	**0.067**
			Total	**1.035**	

Pairwise Comparison Matrix (Fuzzy) for Quality (Original)

	Century	Republic	National
Century	1.00	6.00	0.25
Republic	0.17	1.00	0.13
National	4.00	8.00	1.00

Step 1: Development of TFN (*l*, *m*, *u*) for fuzzy numbers

Step 2a: Fuzzification using Buckley's algorithm

	Century			Republic			National			GM for *l*	GM for *m*	GM for *u*
	l	*m*	*u*	*l*	*m*	*u*	*l*	*m*	*u*			
Century	1.000	1.000	1.000	5.000	6.000	7.000	0.200	0.250	0.333	**1.000**	**1.145**	**1.326**
Republic	0.143	0.167	0.200	1.000	1.000	1.000	0.111	0.125	0.143	**0.251**	**0.275**	**0.306**
National	3.000	4.000	5.000	7.000	8.000	9.000	1.000	1.000	1.000	**2.759**	**3.175**	**3.557**
								Total		**4.010**	**4.595**	**5.189**
								Reciprocal		**0.249**	**0.218**	**0.193**
								Ascending Order		**0.193**	**0.218**	**0.249**

Step 2b: Defuzzification using Buckley's algorithm

Criteria	Fuzzified Weight			Defuzzified Weights	Normalized Weights (PV)
	l	*m*	*u*		
Century	0.193	0.249	0.331	0.258	**0.252**
Republic	0.048	0.060	0.076	0.062	**0.060**
National	0.532	0.691	0.887	0.703	**0.688**
			Total	**1.022**	

Pairwise Comparison Matrix (Fuzzy) for Delivery Time (Original)

	Century	Republic	National
Century	1.000	6.000	1.000
Republic	0.167	1.000	0.167
National	1.000	6.000	1.000

Step 1: Development of TFN (*l*, *m*, *u*) for fuzzy numbers

Step 2a: Fuzzification using Buckley's algorithm

	Century			Republic			National			GM for *l*	GM for *m*	GM for *u*
	l	*m*	*u*	*l*	*m*	*u*	*l*	*m*	*u*			
Century	1.000	1.000	1.000	5.000	6.000	7.000	1.000	1.000	1.000	**1.710**	**1.817**	**1.913**
Republic	0.143	0.167	0.200	1.000	1.000	1.000	0.143	0.167	0.200	**0.273**	**0.303**	**0.342**
National	1.000	1.000	1.000	5.000	6.000	7.000	1.000	1.000	1.000	**1.710**	**1.817**	**1.913**
								Total		**3.693**	**3.937**	**4.168**
								Reciprocal		**0.271**	**0.254**	**0.240**
								Ascending Order		**0.240**	**0.254**	**0.271**

Step 2b: Defuzzification using Buckley's algorithm

Criteria	Fuzzified Weight			Defuzzified Weights	Normalized Weights (PV)
	l	*m*	*u*		
Century	0.410	0.462	0.518	0.463	**0.461**
Republic	0.066	0.077	0.093	0.078	**0.078**
National	0.410	0.462	0.518	0.463	**0.461**
			Total	**1.005**	

Pairwise Comparison Matrix (Fuzzy) for Criteria (Original)

	Cost	Quality	Delivery Time
Cost	1.000	0.125	4.000
Quality	8.000	1.000	4.000
Delivery Time	0.250	0.250	1.000

Step 1: Development of TFN (*l*, *m*, *u*) for fuzzy numbers

Step 2a: Fuzzification using Buckley's algorithm

	Cost			Quality			Delivery Time			GM for *l*	GM for *m*	GM for *u*
	l	*m*	*u*	*l*	*m*	*u*	*l*	*m*	*u*			
Cost	1.000	1.000	1.000	0.111	0.125	0.143	3.000	4.000	5.000	**0.693**	**0.794**	**0.894**
Quality	7.000	8.000	9.000	1.000	1.000	1.000	3.000	4.000	5.000	**2.759**	**3.175**	**3.557**
Delivery Time	0.200	0.250	0.333	0.200	0.250	0.333	1.000	1.000	1.000	**0.342**	**0.397**	**0.481**
								Total		**3.794**	**4.365**	**4.932**
								Reciprocal		**0.264**	**0.229**	**0.203**
								Ascending Order		**0.203**	**0.229**	**0.264**

Step 2b: Defuzzification using Buckley's algorithm

Criteria	Fuzzified Weight			Defuzzified Weights	Normalized Weights (PV)
	l	*m*	*u*		
Cost	0.141	0.182	0.236	0.186	**0.182**
Quality	0.559	0.727	0.937	0.741	**0.725**
Delivery Time	0.069	0.091	0.127	0.096	**0.093**
			Total	**1.023**	

Overall Priority Calculations

Step 6: Priority matrix

	Cost	Quality	Delivery Time
Century	0.298	0.252	0.461
Republic	0.635	0.060	0.078
National	0.067	0.688	0.461

Step 7: Criteria pairwise development matrix

	Priority Vector
Cost	0.182
Quality	0.725
Delivery Time	0.093

Step 8: Overall priority vector

	OPV
Century	0.280
Republic	0.166
National	0.554

Therefore, National Auto will be the overall recommended supplier followed by Century Industries.

12.8 | FUZZY TOPSIS

We will use the concept of group MCDM in fuzzy TOPSIS for evaluating fuzzy weights from different experts' opinions. We will explain this later using the same example we discussed under TOPSIS in this chapter. If more than one expert gives their preferences on a scale of 1 to 10 with 1 being very low and 10 being very high on a criterion C1, then we use the judgments as shown in the following example.

Criteria	Expert 1	Expert 2	Expert 3	Expert 4	Final	Method Used
C1 (Fuzzy)	3	3	5	3	3.5	AM of all scores
Option 1 C1 (TFN)	(2, 3, 4)	(2, 3, 4)	(4, 5, 6)	(2, 3, 4)	2.5, 3.5, 4.5	(AM of *l*), (AM of *m*), (AM of *u*)
Option 2 C1 (TFN)	(2, 3, 4)	(2, 3, 4)	(4, 5, 6)	(2, 3, 4)	2, 3.4, 6	(min of *l*), (GM of *m*), (max of *u*)

Step 1:

1. Collect fuzzy inputs from experts for criteria and develop TFN.
2. The fuzzy criteria weights can be evaluated using GM or AM (group MCDM methods) and the corresponding matrix $\acute{W}$ can be expressed as

$$\acute{W} = [\tilde{\omega}_1 \quad \tilde{\omega}_2 \ldots\ldots\ldots\ldots \quad \tilde{\omega}_n]$$

3. Similarly, the importance of each criterion corresponding to each alternative solution can be evaluated if different expert's linguistic opinions are taken.
4. Develop the fuzzy decision matrix. This can be expressed in the form of the following matrix $\check{D}$:

$$\check{D} = \begin{bmatrix} \tilde{\iota}_{11} & \cdots & \tilde{\iota}_{1n} \\ \vdots & \ddots & \vdots \\ \tilde{\iota}_{m1} & \cdots & \tilde{\iota}_{mn} \end{bmatrix}$$

We will revisit Example 12.3 about the selection of the best car.

Attributes	Life of Car (C1)	Cost of Car (C2)	Fuel Economy (per Liter of Petrol) (C3)	Elegance (A4)
Brands (Alternatives)				
Swift Dzire (A1)	12 years	$12500	15 km	Decent
Ertiga (A2)	10 years	$11000	18 km	Good
Toyota Innova (A3)	12 years	$20500	13 km	Very elegant
Xcent Prime (A4)	12 years	$11000	15 km	Good

We will use the method (min of l), (GM of m), (max of u) for evaluating fuzzy weights for the above seeking expert judgments. Also, we will use the same method to evaluate the importance of each criterion corresponding to each alternative solution from different experts' linguistic opinions, and from that the fuzzy decision matrix $\check{D}$ and $\acute{W}$ can be developed.

Step 2: Normalization and weighted normalized fuzzy decision matrix

1. For benefit type criterion, the normalized fuzzy ratings are found by

$$\check{r}_{ij} = \left(\frac{a_{ij}}{c_j^*}, \frac{b_{ij}}{c_j^*}, \frac{c_{ij}}{c_j^*} \right) \text{where } c_j^* \text{ is Max } (c_{ij})$$

2. For cost type criterion, the normalized fuzzy ratings are found by

$$\check{r}_{ij} = \left(\frac{a_j^*}{c_{ij}}, \frac{a_j^*}{b_{ij}}, \frac{a_j^*}{a_{ij}} \right) \text{where } a_j^* \text{ is Min}(a_{ij})$$

3. Then the weighted normalized fuzzy decision matrix can be obtained using fuzzy product of criteria weights and normalized fuzzy weights.

Step 3: Identification of fuzzy PIS and fuzzy NIS

1. $\text{FPIS} = (\tilde{v}_1^*, \tilde{v}_2^*, \tilde{v}_3^*, \ldots\ldots)$ where, $\tilde{v}_j^* = \text{Max}(\tilde{v}_{ij})$

2. $\text{FNIS} = (\tilde{v}_1^-, \tilde{v}_2^-, \tilde{v}_3^-, \ldots\ldots)$ where, $\tilde{v}_j^- = \text{Min}(\tilde{v}_{ij})$

Step 4: Sum of the distances between each alternative and ideal solution (FPIS and FNIS)

1. $D^+ = \sum_{j=1}^{n} d\left(\tilde{v}_{ij}, \tilde{v}_{ij}^*\right)$

2. $D^- = \sum_{j=1}^{n} d\left(\tilde{v}_{ij}, \tilde{v}_{ij}^-\right)$

3. d can be calculated by the formula

$$d(\tilde{O}, \tilde{U}) = \sqrt{1/3[(o_1 - u_1)^2 + (o_2 - u_2)^2 + (o_3 - u_3)^2}$$

Step 5: Calculation of closeness coefficient (CC_i) for each alternative and ranking of the alternative accordingly

$$CC_i = \left(\frac{D^-}{D^+ + D^-} \right) \text{Higher the preferable alternative}$$

We will carry out the steps for the example as shown in the following tables. It can be seen that the experts' judgments recommend that Toyota Innova be preferred to Swift Dzire, followed by Ertiga and Xcent. This is quite different from the analysis we did while using TOPSIS without experts' judgments but based on predefined weights for the criteria.

Step 1a: Attributes/criteria fuzzy weights determination

	Expert 1			Expert 2			Expert 3			Expert 4			Fuzzy Weights		
	l	*m*	*u*	*l*	*m*	*u*	*l*	*m*	*u*	*l*	*m*	*u*	*l*	*m*	*u*
Life of Car (C1)	3	4	5	4	5	6	1	2	3	5	6	7	**1**	**3.94**	**7**
Cost of Car (C2)	5	6	7	6	7	8	7	8	9	4	5	6	**4**	**6.40**	**9**
Fuel Economy (C3)	4	5	6	4	5	6	5	6	7	3	4	5	**3**	**4.95**	**7**
Elegance (C4)	3	4	5	2	3	4	4	5	6	5	6	7	**2**	**4.36**	**7**

Step 1b: Fuzzy decision matrix development with aggregate ratings

For life of car

	Expert 1			Expert 2			Expert 3			Expert 4			Fuzzy Weights		
	l	*m*	*u*	*l*	*m*	*u*	*l*	*m*	*u*	*l*	*m*	*u*	*l*	*m*	*u*
Swift Dzire (A1)	5	6	7	6	7	8	6	7	8	7	8	9	**5**	**6.96**	**9**
Ertiga (A2)	4	5	6	5	6	7	5	6	7	5	6	7	**4**	**5.73**	**7**
Toyota Innova (A3)	5	6	7	6	7	8	7	8	9	6	7	8	**5**	**6.96**	**9**
Xcent Prime (A4)	3	4	5	4	5	6	4	5	6	5	6	7	**3**	**4.95**	**7**

For cost of car

	Expert 1			Expert 2			Expert 3			Expert 4			Fuzzy Weights		
	l	*m*	*u*	*l*	*m*	*u*	*l*	*m*	*u*	*l*	*m*	*u*	*l*	*m*	*u*
Swift Dzire (A1)	6	7	8	7	8	9	5	6	7	5	6	7	**5**	**6.70**	**9**
Ertiga (A2)	5	6	7	7	8	9	7	8	9	6	7	8	**5**	**7.20**	**9**
Toyota Innova (A3)	2	3	4	5	6	7	2	3	4	3	4	5	**2**	**3.83**	**7**
Xcent Prime (A4)	5	6	7	4	5	6	6	7	8	5	6	7	**4**	**5.96**	**8**

For fuel economy

	Expert 1			Expert 2			Expert 3			Expert 4			Fuzzy Weights		
	l	*m*	*u*	*l*	*m*	*u*	*l*	*m*	*u*	*l*	*m*	*u*	*l*	*m*	*u*
Swift Dzire (A1)	6	7	8	5	6	7	6	7	8	6	7	8	**5**	**6.74**	**8**
Ertiga (A2)	7	8	9	6	7	8	7	8	9	7	8	9	**6**	**7.74**	**9**
Toyota Innova (A3)	4	5	6	3	4	5	4	5	6	3	4	5	**3**	**4.47**	**6**
Xcent Prime (A4)	6	7	8	5	6	7	6	7	8	5	6	7	**5**	**6.48**	**8**

For elegance

	Expert 1			Expert 2			Expert 3			Expert 4			Fuzzy Weights		
	l	*m*	*u*	*l*	*m*	*u*	*l*	*m*	*u*	*l*	*m*	*u*	*l*	*m*	*u*
Swift Dzire (A1)	5	6	7	5	6	7	4	5	6	4	5	6	**4**	**5.48**	**7**
Ertiga (A2)	5	6	7	5	6	7	2	3	4	4	5	6	**2**	**4.82**	**7**
Toyota Innova (A3)	6	7	8	7	8	9	8	9	10	7	8	9	**6**	**7.97**	**10**
Xcent Prime (A4)	3	4	5	2	3	4	2	3	4	2	3	4	**2**	**3.22**	**5**

Fuzzy decision matrix with aggregated ratings

		Criteria											
		Life of Car (C1)			Cost of Car (C2)			Fuel Economy (C3)			Elegance (C4)		
		l	*m*	*u*	*l*	*m*	*u*	*l*	*m*	*u*	*l*	*m*	*u*
	Criteria Fuzzy Weights	1	3.94	7	4	6.40	9	3	4.95	7	2	4.36	7
Alternatives	**Swift Dzire (A1)**	5	6.96	9	5	6.70	9	5	6.74	8	4	5.48	7
	Ertiga (A2)	4	5.73	7	5	7.20	9	6	7.74	9	2	4.82	7
	Toyota Innova (A3)	5	6.96	9	2	3.83	7	3	4.47	6	6	7.97	10
	Xcent Prime (A4)	3	4.95	7	4	5.96	8	5	6.48	8	2	3.22	5

Step 2a: Normalized fuzzy decision matrix

		Benefit Type Criterion			Cost Type Criterion			Benefit Type Criterion					
		Life of Car (C1)			Cost of Car (C2)			Fuel Economy (C3)			Elegance (C4)		
		l	*m*	*u*	*l*	*m*	*u*	*l*	*m*	*u*	*l*	*m*	*u*
	Criteria Fuzzy Weights	1	3.94	7	4	6.40	9	3	4.95	7	2	4.36	7
Alternatives	Swift Dzire (A1)	0.56	0.77	1.00	0.22	0.30	0.40	0.56	0.75	0.89	0.40	0.55	0.70
	Ertiga (A2)	0.44	0.64	0.78	0.22	0.28	0.40	0.67	0.86	1.00	0.20	0.48	0.70
	Toyota Innova (A3)	0.56	0.77	1.00	0.29	0.52	1.00	0.33	0.50	0.67	0.60	0.80	1.00
	Xcent Prime (A4)	0.33	0.55	0.78	0.25	0.34	0.50	0.56	0.72	0.89	0.20	0.32	0.50

Step 2b: Normalized weighted fuzzy decision matrix

		Benefit Type Criterion			Cost Type Criterion			Benefit Type Criterion					
		Life of Car (C1)			Cost of Car (C2)			Fuel Economy (C3)			Elegance (C4)		
		l	*m*	*u*	*l*	*m*	*u*	*l*	*m*	*u*	*l*	*m*	*u*
Alternatives	Swift Dzire (A1)	0.56	3.05	7.00	0.89	1.91	3.60	1.67	3.70	6.22	0.80	2.39	4.90
	Ertiga (A2)	0.44	2.51	5.44	0.89	1.78	3.60	2.00	4.25	7.00	0.40	2.10	4.90
	Toyota Innova (A3)	0.56	3.05	7.00	1.14	3.34	9.00	1.00	2.46	4.67	1.20	3.47	7.00
	Xcent Prime (A4)	0.33	2.16	5.44	1.00	2.15	4.50	1.67	3.56	6.22	0.40	1.40	3.50

Step 3: Identify PIS and NIS

	Life of Car (C1)			Cost of Car (C2)			Fuel Economy (C3)			Elegance (C4)		
	l	*m*	*u*	*l*	*m*	*u*	*l*	*m*	*u*	*l*	*m*	*u*
PIS (+)	7.00	7.00	7.00	9.00	9.00	9.00	7.00	7.00	7.00	7.00	7.00	7.00
NIS (–)	0.33	0.33	0.33	0.89	0.89	0.89	1.00	1.00	1.00	0.40	0.40	0.40

Step 4: Calculate distances of alternatives from FPIS and FNIS

	Life of Car (C1)	Cost of Car (C2)	Fuel Economy (C3)	Elegance (C4)	Total Distance (D)
FPIS (A1)	4.365	6.957	3.648	4.624	19.594
FNIS (A1)	4.157	1.673	3.417	2.849	12.096
FPIS (A2)	4.676	7.002	3.293	4.898	19.870
NPIS (A2)	3.207	1.647	3.983	2.777	11.615
FPIS (A3)	4.365	5.591	4.548	3.920	18.424
NPIS (A3)	4.157	4.894	2.278	4.228	15.558
FPIS (A4)	4.839	6.613	3.690	5.389	20.531
NPIS (A4)	3.135	2.209	3.381	1.881	10.606

Step 5: Calculate the Closeness Coefficient for each alternative and rank the alternatives

Separation and Closeness	Swift Dzire (A1)	Ertiga (A2)	Toyota Innova (A3)	Xcent Prime (A4)
D+	19.5939	19.8696	18.4242	20.5310
D–	12.0963	11.6150	15.5582	10.6058
CC	**0.382**	**0.369**	**0.458**	**0.341**
Rank	**2nd**	**3rd**	**1st**	**4th**

SUMMARY

In this chapter, we introduced the multi-criteria decision-making methods and outlined their basic ideas and applications. Some of the MCDM methods are listed, however, only five methods—Multi-Attribute Utility Theory (MAUT), AHP, TOPSIS, Fuzzy AHP, and Fuzzy TOPSIS—are presented in the chapter with practical examples illustrating the various steps and how they are computed. The basic differences and commonalities are highlighted while describing the methods.

Exercises

1. The Vice President of Hunting Head Pvt Ltd needs to select a new director of marketing. The two probable candidates are Jacob and Paul, and the criteria thought to be most relevant in the selection are leadership ability (L), personal skills (P), and administrative skills (A). The following pairwise comparison matrices were obtained.

Criterion			
	L	P	A
L	1	⅓	¼
P	3	1	2
A	4	½	1

Leadership		
	Jacob	Paul
Jacob	1	4
Paul	¼	1

Personal		
	Jacob	Paul
Jacob	1	⅓
Paul	3	1

Administrative		
	Jacob	Paul
Jacob	1	2
Paul	½	1

   a. Compute the priorities for each pairwise comparison matrix.
   b. Carry out the consistency check and irrespective of the outcome, determine an overall priority for each candidate. Which candidate is preferred?
   c. Apply Fuzzy AHP and see the results. Does the decision change?

2. (*Problem Courtesy: Aditya Kashyap, RDC Santhosh, Jayanth Jain BMD 2019–21, XLRI*). The city council of Mahishur is debating how to use its budget surplus for the present year. The surplus is the tax money left after regular and non-discretionary expenses like utilities, law and order, transportation infrastructure, etc., which are the statutory obligations of the city administration. Five different proposals have been put up for consideration, and there is money for only one of the proposals:
   a. Hold a town fair (A1)
   b. Build a public swimming pool (A2)
   c. Add greenery to roadsides (A3)
   d. Set up a vocational training center (A4)
   e. Build a commercial complex (A5)

   The city council has come up with a list of decision criteria. These criteria are used to make decisions on spending the budgetary surplus:

   a. Raises employment (C1)
   b. Preserves cultural heritage (C2)
   c. Reduces carbon footprint (C3)
   d. Modernizes public spaces (C4)
   e. Improves leisure and recreation (C5)

   The relevant details of pairwise comparisons for criteria and for alternatives under each criterion are as follows:

Criteria Weight Calculation

	Pairwise Comparison Matrix				
	C1	C2	C3	C4	C5
C1	1	5	3	1/5	1/3
C2	1/5	1	1/3	1/9	1/7
C3	1/3	3	1	1/7	1/5
C4	5	9	7	1	3
C5	1/3	7	5	1/3	1

Alternative comparison under C1

	Pairwise Comparison Matrix				
	A1	A2	A3	A4	A5
A1	1	3	5	1/5	1/3
A2	1/3	1	3	1/7	1/5
A3	1/5	1/3	1	1/9	1/7
A4	5	7	9	1	3
A5	1/3	5	7	1/3	1

Alternative comparison under C2

	Pairwise Comparison Matrix				
	A1	A2	A3	A4	A5
A1	1	7	3	5	9
A2	1/7	1	1/5	1/3	3
A3	1/3	5	1	3	7
A4	1/5	3	1/3	1	5
A5	1/9	1/3	1/7	1/5	1

Alternative comparison under C3

	Pairwise Comparison Matrix				
	A1	A2	A3	A4	A5
A1	1	7	3	5	9
A2	1/7	1	1/5	1/3	3
A3	1/3	5	1	3	7
A4	1/5	3	1/3	1	5
A5	1/9	1/3	1/7	1/5	1

Alternative comparison under C4

Pairwise Comparison Matrix	A1	A2	A3	A4	A5
A1	1	1/5	1/3	1/7	1/9
A2	5	1	3	1/3	1/5
A3	3	1/3	1	1/5	1/7
A4	7	3	5	1	1/3
A5	9	5	7	3	1

Alternative comparison under C5

Pairwise Comparison Matrix	A1	A2	A3	A4	A5
A1	1	1/5	3	5	1/3
A2	5	1	7	9	3
A3	1/3	1/7	1	3	1/5
A4	1/5	1/9	1/3	1	1/7
A5	3	1/3	5	7	1

a. Use the AHP method and arrive at the best alternative.
b. If fuzzy AHP is used, how do the results change? Explain.

3. Consider Problem 2. The TOPSIS method will be used to decide the best alternative. The details of the information required are as follows:

Weights	0.2	0.1	0.15	0.3	0.25
Criteria	**C1**	**C2**	**C3**	**C4**	**C5**
Alternatives					
A1	4	8	1	2	3
A2	3	2	1	4	8
A3	1	4	8	3	2
A4	8	3	2	4	1
A5	4	1	1	8	4

Follow the steps of TOPSIS and decide the best alternative.

4. For the same problem, two decision makers are involved in the decision-making process and their judgments are given as follows.

TOPSIS Score Matrix Decision Maker 1					
Criteria	**C1**	**C2**	**C3**	**C4**	**C5**
Alternatives					
A1	Good	Excellent	Dismal	Poor	Average
A2	Average	Poor	Dismal	Good	Excellent
A3	Dismal	Good	Excellent	Average	Poor
A4	Excellent	Average	Poor	Good	Dismal
A5	Good	Dismal	Dismal	Excellent	Good

TOPSIS Score Matrix Decision Maker 2					
Criteria	C1	C2	C3	C4	C5
Alternatives					
A1	Average	Excellent	Poor	Dismal	Good
A2	Average	Poor	Dismal	Excellent	Good
A3	Dismal	Average	Good	Excellent	Poor
A4	Excellent	Poor	Average	Good	Dismal
A5	Good	Dismal	Poor	Excellent	Average
Criteria Weights	Significant	Minute	Marginal	Crucial	Important

	l	*m*	*u*
Dismal	1	1	3
Poor	1	3	5
Average	3	5	7
Good	5	7	9
Excellent	7	9	9
Minute	1	1	3
Marginal	1	3	5
Significant	3	5	7
Important	5	7	9
Crucial	7	9	9

Convert the judgments into a fuzzy score and obtain the best decision using the fuzzy TOPSIS method.

Bibliography

1. Belton, V. and T. J. Stewart (2002). *Multiple Criteria Decision Analysis: An Integrated Approach.* Dordrecht: Kluwer Academic Publishers.
2. Chen, S. J. and C. L. Hwang (1992). *Fuzzy Multiple Attribute Decision Making: Methods and Applications, Lecture Notes in Economics and Mathematical Systems*, No. 375, Berlin, Germany: Springer-Verlag.
3. Hwang, C. L. and K. Yoon (1981). *Multiple Attribute Decision Making: Methods and Applications.* New York: Springer-Verlag.
4. Kazimieras, E., Z. J. Antucheviciene, and P. Chatterjee (2019). *Multiple-Criteria Decision-Making (MCDM) Techniques for Business Processes Information Management.* Switzerland: MDPI.
5. Keeney, R. and H. Raiffa (1976). *Decisions with Multiple Objectives: Preferences and Value Tradeoffs.* New York: Wiley.
6. Ma, D. and X. Zheng. (1991) 9/9-9/1 scale method of the AHP. *Proceedings of the 2nd International Symposium on the AHP*, **1**, Pittsburgh, PA, 197–202.
7. Mardani, A., A. Jusoh, K. MD Nor, Z. Khalifah, N. Zakwan, and A. Valipour (2015). Multiple criteria decision-making techniques and their applications: a review of the literature from 2000 to 2014. *Economic Research-Ekonomska Istraživanja*, **28**(1), 516–571.
8. Masuda, T. (1990). Hierarchical sensitivity analysis of the priorities used in the analytic hierarchy process. *Systems Science*, **21**(2), 415–427.
9. Saaty, T. L. (1977). A scaling method for priorities in hierarchical structures. *Journal of Mathematical Psychology*, **15**, 57–68.

10. Saaty, T. L. (1980). *The Analytic Hierarchy Process.* New York: McGraw-Hill International.
11. Saaty, T. L. (1994). *Fundamentals of Decision Making and Priority Theory with the AHP.* Pittsburgh, PA: RWS Publications.
12. Shanmuganathan, M., K. Kajendran, A. N. Sasikumar, and M. Mahendran (2018). Multi-attribute utility theory: an overview. *International Journal of Scientific & Engineering Research*, **9**(3), 698–706.
13. Triantaphyllou, E., B. Shu, S. Nieto Sanchez, and T. Ray (1998). *Multi-Criteria Decision Making: An Operations Research Approach.* New York: John Wiley & Sons.
14. Triantaphyllou, E., F. A. Lootsma, P. M. Pardalos, and S. H. Mann (1994). On the evaluation and application of different scales for quantifying pairwise comparisons in fuzzy sets. *Multi-Criteria Decision Analysis*, **3**, 1–23.
15. Velasquez, M. and P. T. Hester (2013). An analysis of multi-criteria decision-making methods. *International Journal of Operations Research*, **10**(2), 56–66.
16. Zimmermann, H.-J. (1991). *Fuzzy Set Theory and Its Applications*, 2nd Edition. Boston, MA: Kluwer Academic Publishers.

Index

T